THE ENCYCLOPAEDIA OF ISLAM
ENCYCLOPÉDIE DE L'ISLAM

INDEX OF SUBJECTS/INDEX DES MATIÈRES

THE ENCYCLOPAEDIA OF ISLAM

NEW EDITION

ENCYCLOPÉDIE DE L'ISLAM

NOUVELLE ÉDITION

INDEX OF SUBJECTS
INDEX DES MATIÈRES

to Volumes / des Tomes
I-IX
and to the Supplement, Fascicules / et du Supplément,
Livraisons
1-6

COMPILED BY/ÉTABLI PAR

P.J. BEARMAN

BRILL
LEIDEN · BOSTON · KÖLN
1998

The paper in this book meets the guidelines for permanence and durability of the Committee on Production Guidelines for Book Longevity of the Council on Library Resources.

Library of Congress Cataloging-in-Publication Data

Bearman, P.J.
The Encyclopaedia of Islam, new edition. Index of Subjects = Encyclopédie de l'islam, nouvelle édition. Index des matières / compiled by P.J. Bearman.
p. cm.
English and French.
ISBN 9004097392 (alk. paper)
1. Encyclopaedia of Islam—Indexes. 2. Islam—Indexes. 3. Islamic countries—Indexes. I. Title. II. Title: Encyclopédie de l'islam, nouvelle édition. Index des matières.
DS35.53.E533B4 1992
909'.097671—dc20 92-31738
CIP
Rev.

ISBN 90 04 11080 1

PRINTED IN THE NETHERLANDS

TABLE OF CONTENTS/TABLE DES MATIÈRES

ENGLISH SECTION

Preface vii
List of Entries 1
Index of Subjects 19

SECTION FRANÇAISE

Préface 149
Liste des Entrées 151
Index des Matières 169

PREFACE TO THE FOURTH EDITION

This edition of the Index of Subjects indexes Volumes I through IX, the latest published volume of the *Encyclopaedia of Islam* which appeared in November 1997.

A List of Entries precedes the actual subject index. The List of Entries refers the reader to single articles in the *Encyclopaedia of Islam*. For an overview of what the *Encyclopaedia* offers on a larger subject, however, the reader should consult the Index of Subjects proper. Thus, in order to find the entry on chess in the *Encyclopaedia*, one would look in the List of Entries, which refers one to Shaṭrandj, while reference to this article in its larger context can be found in the Index of Subjects under the heading RECREATION.GAMES.

Comments and suggestions for improvement of this Index are welcome.

May 1998

Peri Bearman

LIST OF ENTRIES

References are given either to the main article in the *Encyclopaedia* or to the Index of Subjects proper, which groups all articles concerned with the subject under one heading. An arrow refers the reader to the entry in the Index of Subjects, which follows the List of Entries on p.19. Countries and names of dynasties or caliphates, which are included *in extenso* in the Index of Subjects, are not given in the following list.

A

Abbreviations [in Suppl.] Abbreviations
Ablution → ABLUTION
Abridgement Mukhtaṣar
Abstinence Istibrā᾿
Academy Madjma῾ ῾Ilmī
Accident ῾Araḍ
Accounting → ACCOUNTING
Acquisition Kasb
Acrobat Djānbāz
Act ῾Amal; Fi῾l
Addax Mahāt
Administration → ADMINISTRATION
Admiral Ḳapudan Pasha
Adoption → ADOPTION
Adultery → ADULTERY
Aesthetics ῾Ilm al-Djamāl
Agriculture → AGRICULTURE
Album Muraḳḳa῾
Alchemy → ALCHEMY
Alfa-grass Ḥalfā᾿
Algebra → MATHEMATICS
Alms → ALMS
Aloe Ṣabr
Alphabet → ALPHABET
Amber Kahrubā
Ambergris ῾Anbar
Americas → NEW WORLD
Analogy Ḳiyās
Anatomy → ANATOMY
Anecdote Nādira
Anemone Shaḳīḳat al-Nu῾mān
Angel → ANGELOLOGY
Animal → ANIMALS
Ant Naml
Antelope → ANIMALS
Anthology Mukhtārāt
Anthropomorphism → ANTHROPOMORPHISM
Antinomianism Ibaḥa (II)
Apostasy → APOSTASY
Appeal Isti᾿nāf
Apricot Mishmish
Aqueduct → ARCHITECTURE.MONUMENTS
Arabic → LANGUAGES.AFRO-ASIATIC; LINGUISTICS
Arachnoids → ANIMALS
Arbitrator Ḥakam
Archaeology → ARCHAEOLOGY
Architecture → ARCHITECTURE
Archives → ADMINISTRATION
Arithmetic → MATHEMATICS
Army → MILITARY
Arsenal Dār al-Ṣinā῾a
Art → ART

Artemisia Shīḥ
Article Maḳāla
Artisans → PROFESSIONS.CRAFTSMEN AND TRADESMEN
Ascensions al-Maṭāliʿ
Asceticism → ASCETICISM
Assignation Ḥawāla
Association Andjuman; Djamʿiyya
Associationism Shirk
Astrolabe Asṭurlāb
Astrology → ASTROLOGY
Astronomy → ASTRONOMY
Atomism Djuzʾ
Avarice Bukhl

B

Bābism → SECTS
Bacchism → WINE.BACCHIC POETRY
Backgammon Nard
Bahais → BAHAIS
Balance al-Mīzān
Banking → BANKING
Barber [in Suppl.] Ḥallāḳ
Bargaining Sawm
Barley Shaʿīr
Barter Muʿāwaḍa
Basques → BASQUES
Bath → ARCHITECTURE.MONUMENTS
Beauty ʿIlm al-Djamāl
Bedding Mafrūshāt; Mifrash
Bedouin → BEDOUINS
Bee Naḥl
Beggar Sāsān
Belomancy Istiḳsām
Ben-nut Bān
Berbers → BERBERS
Betrothal Khiṭba
Bible → BIBLE
Bibliography → BIBLIOGRAPHY
Bier Djanāza
Biography → LITERATURE.BIOGRAPHICAL
Bird → ANIMALS
Bitumen Mūmiyāʾ
Blacksmith Ḳayn
Blessing Baraka
Blood [in Suppl.] Dam
Blood-letter [in Suppl.] Faṣṣād
Blood-vengeance Ḳiṣāṣ
Boar, wild Khinzīr
Boat Safīna
Body Djism
Book Kitāb
Bookbinding → WRITING
Booty → MILITARY
Botany → BOTANY
Bow Ḳaws
Bowing → PRAYER
Bread Khubz
Bribery → PAYMENTS
Brick Labin
Bridge → ARCHITECTURE.MONUMENTS
Brigand Ṣuʿlūk
Broadcasting Idhāʿa
Broker Dallāl
Buddhism Budd; Sumaniyya
Buffalo [in Suppl.] Djāmūs
Building Bināʾ
Butcher [in Suppl.] Djazzār
Butter al-Samn
Byzantines → BYZANTINE EMPIRE

C

Calendar → Time
Caliph Khalīfa
Caliphate → Caliphate
Call to prayer Adhān
Calligraphy → Art
Camel → Animals
Camel-driver [in Suppl.] Djammāl
Camomile [in Suppl.] Bābūnadj
Camphor Kāfūr
Canal Ḳanāt
Candle Shamʿa
Candle-maker Shammāʿ
Capitulations Imtiyāzāt
Caravan → Transport
Carmathians → Shiites.branches
Carpet → Art.tapestry
Cart ʿAdjala; Araba
Cartography → Cartography
Cattle Baḳar
Cause ʿIlla
Cedar-oil Ḳaṭrān
Cemetery Maḳbara
Ceramics → Art.pottery
Cession Ḥawāla
Chair Kursī
Chamber, underground Sardāb
Chamberlain Ḥādjib
Chameleon Ḥirbāʾ
Chancellery → Documents
Charity → Alms
Charms → Charms
Cheetah Fahd
Chess Shaṭrandj
Chest → Anatomy
Child → Life Stages
Childbirth → Life Stages
Childhood → Life Stages
Chintz Ḳalamkārī
Chirognomy al-Kaff
Christianity → Christianity
Church Kanīsa
Cinema Cinema
Cinnamon [in Suppl.] Dār Ṣīnī
Circumcision → Circumcision
Cistern Ḥawḍ
Citizen Muwāṭin
Citrus fruits Nārandj
Civilisation Medeniyyet
Clan Āl
Clime Iḳlīm
Cloak Khirḳa
Clock Sāʿa
Clothing → Clothing
Clove Ḳaranful
Cock Dīk
Codes → Cryptography
Coffee Ḳahwa
Coinage → Numismatics
Coitus Bāh
Coitus interruptus ʿAzl
Colour → Colour
Column ʿAmūd
Comedians → Humour
Commentary Sharḥ; *and* → Koran
Commerce → Commerce
Communications → Communications
Communism → Communism
Companions (of the Prophet) → Muḥammad, the Prophet
Compass Maghnāṭīs.2
Concubinage → Women
Conference Muʾtamar
Congress Muʾtamar
Conjunction Ḳirān
Constellation → Astronomy
Constitution Dustūr
Consul Consul

Consultation   S̲h̲ūrā
Contract   → LAW.LAW OF OBLIGA-
    TIONS
Cooking   → CUISINE
Copper   Nuḥās; *and see* Malachite
Copts   → CHRISTIANITY.DENOMINA-
    TIONS
Coral   Mard̲j̲ān
Cornelian   ʿAḳīḳ
Corpse   D̲j̲anāza
Corpse-washer   [in Suppl.] G̲h̲assāl
Cosmetics   → COSMETICS
Cosmography   → COSMOGRAPHY
Cotton   Ḳuṭn
Court (of law)   Maḥkama
Court Ceremony   → COURT CER-
    EMONY
Courtier   Nadīm
Couscous   Kuskusū
Craftsmanship   → PROFESSIONS

Creation   → CREATION
Creditor   G̲h̲ārim
Creed   ʿAḳīda
Crescent   Hilāl
Criticism, literary   → LITERATURE
Cross   al-Ṣalīb
Crow   G̲h̲urāb
Crucifixion   Ṣalb
Crusades   → CRUSADE(R)S
Crustaceans   → ANIMALS
Cryptography   → CRYPTOGRAPHY
Crystal   *see* Rock-crystal
Cubit   D̲h̲irāʿ
Cuisine   → CUISINE
Cumin   Kammūn
Cupper   [in Suppl.] Faṣṣād
Custody   Ḥaḍāna
Custom   → CUSTOM
Customary law   → LAW
Cymbal   Ṣand̲j̲

D

Dactylonomy   Ḥisāb al-ʿAḳd
Dam   → ARCHITECTURE.MONUMENTS
Dance   Raḳṣ
Date   Nak̲h̲l
Day   → TIME
Death   → DEATH
Debt   [in Suppl.] Dayn
Debtor   G̲h̲ārim
Declension   Iʿrāb
Declination   al-Mayl
Decoration   → ARCHITECTURE;
    ART.DECORATIVE; MILITARY
Decree, divine   al-Ḳaḍāʾ wa ʾl-Ḳadar
Deer   Ayyil
Demography   [in Suppl.] Demogra-
    phy
Demon   D̲j̲inn
Dentistry   → MEDICINE

Dervish   → MYSTICISM
Desert   → DESERTS
Devil   Iblīs; S̲h̲ayṭān
Dialect   → LANGUAGES.AFRO-
    ASIATIC.ARABIC; LINGUISTICS.
    PHONETICS
Diamond   Almās
Dictionary   → DICTIONARY
Dill   S̲h̲ibit̲h̲t̲h̲
Diplomacy   → DIPLOMACY
Disease   → DISEASE
Disputation   → THEOLOGY
Dissolution   Fask̲h̲
Ditch   K̲h̲andaḳ
Divination   → DIVINATION
Divorce   → DIVORCE
Documents   → DOCUMENTS
Dog   Kalb

Donkey Ḥimār
Doubt S͟hakk
Dove Ḥamām
Dowry → MARRIAGE
Drama → LITERATURE
Drawing → ART
Dreams → DREAMS
Dress → CLOTHING
Dressmaker K͟hayyāṭ
Drinks → CUISINE
Dromedary → ANIMALS.CAMEL
Drugs → DRUGS
Druggist al-ʿAṭṭār
Drum Darabukka
Druze → DRUZES
Dulcimer Sanṭūr
Duress [in Suppl.] Ikrāh
Dwelling Bayt; Dār
Dye → DYEING
Dyer → DYEING
Dynasty → DYNASTIES

E

Earthquakes → EARTHQUAKES
Ebony Abanūs
Eclipse Kusūf
Ecliptic Minṭaḳat al-Burūd͟j
Economics → ECONOMICS
Edict Farmān
Education → EDUCATION
Elegy Mart͟hiya
Elephant Fīl
Elixir al-Iksīr
Eloquence Balāg͟ha; Bayān; Faṣāḥa
Emancipation → EMANCIPATION
Embalming Ḥināṭa
Emigration → EMIGRATION
Encyclopaedia Mawsūʿa
Endive [in Suppl.] Hindibāʾ
Epic Ḥamāsa
Epigraphy → EPIGRAPHY
Epistolography → LITERATURE. EPISTOLARY
Epithet → ONOMASTICS
Equator Istiwāʾ
Equines → ANIMALS
Error K͟haṭaʾ
Eschatology → ESCHATOLOGY
Espionage *see* Spy
Estate Ḍayʿa
Eternity Abad; Ḳidam
Ethics → ETHICS
Ethnicity → ETHNICITY
Etiquette → ETIQUETTE
Etymology Is͟htiḳāḳ
Eulogy Madīḥ
Eunuch → EUNUCH
Evidence Bayyina
Ewer [in Suppl.] Ibrīḳ
Exception Istit͟hnāʾ
Expedition → MILITARY
Expiation Kaffāra
Eye → ANATOMY; EVIL EYE

F

Faculty Kulliyya
Faïence Kās͟hī
Faith → FAITH
Faith, profession of *see* Profession of faith
Falconry → FALCONRY

Family ʿĀʾila
Fan Mirwaḥa
Farming → AGRICULTURE
Fasting → FASTING
Fate → PREDESTINATION
Fauna → ANIMALS
Felines → ANIMALS
Felt Lubūd
Female circumcision Khafḍ
Fennec-fox Fanak
Fennel [in Suppl.] Basbās
Festival → FESTIVAL
Fief Iḳṭāʿ
Film Cinema
Finance → ADMINISTRATION
Fine Djurm
Fire Nār
Fiscal system → TAXATION
Fish → ANIMALS
Fishing Samak.3
Five Khamsa
Flag ʿAlam; Sandjaḳ
Flamingo Nuḥām
Flax Kattān
Flora → FLORA
Flowers → FLORA
Fly Dhubāb
Food → CUISINE
Forest Ghāba
Foreword Muḳaddima
Formulas → ISLAM
Fortress → ARCHITECTURE.MONUMENTS.STRONGHOLDS
Foundling Laḳīṭ
Fountain Shadirwān
Fowl Dadjādja
Fox Fanak
Fraction Kasr
Frankincense Lubān
Free Will → PREDESTINATION
Freedom Ḥurriyya; [in Suppl.] Āzādī
Freemasonry [in Suppl.] Farāmūsh-khāna; Farmāsūniyya
Fruit *see* Citrus fruits
Fundamentalism → REFORM.POLITICO-RELIGIOUS.MILITANT
Funeral Djanāza
Fur Farw
Furnishings → FURNISHINGS
Furniture [in Suppl.] Athāth

G

Gain Kasb
Gambling → GAMBLING
Games → RECREATION
Garden → ARCHITECTURE.MONUMENTS.GARDENS
Gate → ARCHITECTURE.MONUMENTS
Gazehound Salūḳī
Gazelle Ghazāl
Gemstones → JEWELRY
Gender studies → WOMEN
Genealogy → GENEALOGY
Geography → GEOGRAPHY
Geometry → MATHEMATICS
Gesture Ishāra
Gift → GIFTS
Girdle Shadd
Glass → ART
Gloss Ḥāshiya
Goats [in Suppl.] Ghanam
God Allāh; Ilāh
Gods, pre-Islamic → PRE-ISLAM
Gold Dhahab
Goldsmith Ṣāʾigh
Gospels Indjīl
Government Ḥukūma
Grammar → LINGUISTICS

Gratitude Shukr
Greyhound *see* Gazehound
Grocer Baḳḳāl
Guild → GUILDS
Gum resins Ṣamgh
Gunpowder Bārūd
Gynaecology → LIFE STAGES
Gypsies → GYPSIES

H

Hagiography → HAGIOGRAPHY
Hair → ANATOMY
Hairdresser [in Suppl.] Ḥallāḳ
Hamito-Semitic Ḥām
Handicrafts → ART
Handkerchief Mandīl
Harbour Mīnā᾽
Hare [in Suppl.] Arnab
Headware → CLOTHING
Health → MEDICINE
Heart Ḳalb
Heaven Samā᾽
Hedgehog Ḳunfudh
Hell → HELL
Hemerology Ikhtiyārāt
Hemp Ḥashīsh
Hempseed Shahdānadj
Henbane Bandj
Henna Ḥinnā᾽
Heraldry → HERALDRY
Hereafter → ESCHATOLOGY
Heresy → HERESY
Hippopotamus [in Suppl.] Faras al-Mā᾽
Hire, contract of → LAW
Historiography → LITERATURE. HISTORICAL
Holiness Ḳadāsa
Holy War Djihād
Homicide Ḳatl
Homonym Aḍdād
Homosexuality Liwāṭ
Honour ʿIrḍ
Hoopoe Hudhud
Horn Būḳ
Horse Faras
Horseback rider Fāris
Horseback riding Furūsiyya
Horticulture → ARCHITECTURE. MONUMENTS.GARDENS; FLORA
Hostelry → HOSTELRY
Houris Ḥūr
House *see* Dwelling
Humour → HUMOUR
Hunting → HUNTING
Hydrology → HYDROLOGY
Hydromancy Istinzāl
Hyena [in Suppl.] Ḍabuʿ
Hymn Nashīd
Hyperbole Mubālagha
Hypnotism Sīmiya᾽.1
Hypocrisy Riyā᾽

I

Iconography → ART
Idol → IDOLS
Illness → ILLNESS
Image Ṣūra
Incubation Istikhāra
Independence Istiḳlāl

Indigo   Nīl
Individual   S̲h̲akhṣ
Industry   → INDUSTRY
Infidel   Kāfir
Inflection   Imāla
Inheritance   → INHERITANCE
Inimitability (of Ḳurʾān)   Iʿd̲j̲āz
Ink   Midād
Ink-holder   [in Suppl.] Dawāt
Innovation   Bidʿa
Inscriptions   → EPIGRAPHY
Insects   → ANIMALS
Insignia   → MILITARY.DECORATIONS;
    MONARCHY.ROYAL INSIGNIA
Inspection (of troops)   Istiʿrāḍ
Instrument   Āla
Instrument, musical   → MUSIC

Insulting verse   Hid̲j̲āʾ
Intellect   ʿAḳl
Intercession   S̲h̲afāʿa
Intercourse, sexual   Bāh
Interdiction   Ḥad̲j̲r
Interest   Ribā
Interrogation   Istifhām
Introduction   Ibtidāʾ; Muḳaddima
Inventions   → INVENTIONS
Invocation   Duʿāʾ
Ipseity   Huwiyya
Iris   Sūsan
Iron   al-Ḥadīd
Irrigation   → IRRIGATION
Islam   → ISLAM
Ivory   ʿĀd̲j̲

J

Jackal   Ibn Āwā
Javelin   D̲j̲erīd
Jewelry   → JEWELRY
Journalism   → PRESS
Judaism   → JUDAISM

Judge   Ḳāḍī
Jurisconsult   → LAW.JURIST
Jurisprudence   → LAW
Jurist   → LAW
Justice   ʿAdl

K

King   Malik; S̲h̲āh
Kingdom   Mamlaka
Kinship   Ḳarāba
Kitchen   Maṭba<u>kh</u>

Knowledge   ʿIlm; Maʿrifa
Kohl   al-Kuḥl
Koran   → KORAN
Kurdish   → KURDS

L

Labour   *see* Trade union
Labourers   → PROFESSIONS.CRAFTS-
    MEN AND TRADESMEN
Lakes   → GEOGRAPHY.PHYSICAL

    GEOGRAPHY.WATERS
Lamentation   → LAMENTATION
Lamp   Sirād̲j̲
Land   → LAND

Language → LANGUAGES
Law → LAW
Leasing Kirā'
Leather Djild
Legend → LEGENDS
Lemon Nārandj
Leprosy [in Suppl.] Djudhām
Lesbianism Siḥāḳ
Letter(s) Ḥarf; Ḥurūf al-Hidjā'
Lexicography → LEXICOGRAPHY
Library → EDUCATION.LIBRARIES
Lice Ḳaml
Licorice Sūs
Life → LIFE STAGES
Light Nūr
Lighthouse → ARCHITECTURE.MONUMENTS
Lily Sūsan
Linen Kattān; Khaysh
Linguistics → LINGUISTICS
Lion al-Asad
Literature → LITERATURE
Lithography → PRINTING
Liver Kabid
Lizard Ḍabb
Locust Djarād
Logic → PHILOSOPHY
Longevity Muʿammar
Louse *see* Lice
Love → LOVE
Lute Sāz
Lyre Ḳithāra

M

Mace Dūrbāsh
Madman Madjnūn
Magic → MAGIC
Magnet Maghnāṭīs.1
Malachite al-Dahnadj
Malaria Malāryā
Man Insān
Mandrake Sirādj al-Ḳuṭrub
Manuscript Nuskha
Map Kharīṭa
Market Sūḳ
Marriage → MARRIAGE
Martyr Shahīd
Martyrdom → MARTYRDOM
Marxism Mārk(i)siyya
Masonry Binā'
Mathematics → MATHEMATICS
Matter Hayūlā
Mausoleum → ARCHITECTURE.MONUMENTS.TOMBS
Mayor Ra'īs
Measurements → WEIGHTS AND MEASUREMENTS
Mechanics → MECHANICS
Mediation Shafāʿa
Medicine → MEDICINE
Melilot [in Suppl.] Iklīl al-Malik
Menstruation Ḥayḍ
Merchants → PROFESSIONS.CRAFTSMEN AND TRADESMEN
Messenger Rasūl
Messiah al-Masīḥ
Metallurgy → METALLURGY
Metalware → ART
Metamorphosis → ANIMALS.TRANSFORMATION INTO
Metaphor Istiʿāra
Metaphysics → METAPHYSICS
Meteorology → METEOROLOGY
Metonymy Kināya
Metrics → METRICS
Migration → EMIGRATION

Militancy → REFORM.POLITICO-RELIGIOUS.MILITANT
Military → MILITARY
Milky Way al-Madjarra
Millet [in Suppl.] Djāwars
Minaret Manāra
Mineralogy → MINERALOGY
Miniatures → ART.PAINTING
Mint [in Suppl.] Fūdhandj
Mint (money) Dār al-Ḍarb
Miracle → MIRACLES
Mirage Sarāb
Mirror Mirʾāt
Misfortune Shaḳāwa
Modernism → REFORM
Modes, musical Maḳām
Molluscs → ANIMALS
Monarchy → MONARCHY
Monastery → CHRISTIANITY
Monasticism Rahbāniyya
Money → NUMISMATICS
Mongols → MONGOLIA
Mongoose Nims
Monk Rāhib
Monkey Ḳird
Months → TIME
Moon Hilāl; al-Ḳamar
Morphology Ṣarf
Mosaics → ART
Mosque → ARCHITECTURE.MONUMENTS
Mountain → MOUNTAINS
Mountain Goat Ayyil
Mule Baghl
Municipality Baladiyya
Murder Ḳatl
Music → MUSIC
Musk Misk
Mussel Ṣadaf
Myrobalanus [in Suppl.] Halīladj
Myrtle [in Suppl.] Ās
Mystic → MYSTICISM
Mysticism → MYSTICISM
Myths → LEGENDS

N

Name Ism
Narcissus Nardjis
Narcotics → DRUGS
Nationalism → NATIONALISM
Natron [in Suppl.] Bawraḳ
Natural science → NATURAL SCIENCE
Nature → LITERATURE.POETRY.NATURE
Navigation → NAVIGATION
Navy → MILITARY
New World → NEW WORLD
Newspaper Djarīda
Nickname Laḳab
Night Layl and Nahār
Night watch ʿAsas
Nightingale Bulbul
Nilometer Miḳyās
Nomadism → NOMADISM
Noun Ism
Novel Ḳiṣṣa
Nullity Fāsid wa Bāṭil
Number → NUMBER
Numerals → NUMBER
Numismatics → NUMISMATICS

O

Oak ʿAfṣ
Oath Ḳasam
Obelisk → ARCHITECTURE.MONUMENTS
Oboe G͟hayṭa
Obscenity → OBSCENITY
Observatory → ASTRONOMY
Obstetrics → MEDICINE
Ocean → OCEANS AND SEAS
Octagon Mut͟hamman
Oil → OIL
Omen Faʾl
Oneiromancy → DREAMS
Onomastics → ONOMASTICS
Onomatomancy Ḥurūf, ʿIlm al-
Ophthalmology → MEDICINE
Opium Afyūn
Opposites Aḍdād; Ḍidd
Optics → OPTICS
Orange Nārand͟j
Orchestra Mehter
Order, mystical → MYSTICISM
Organs (body) → ANATOMY
Orientalism Mustas͟hriḳūn
Ornithomancy ʿIyāfa
Orthodoxy Sunna
Oryx Lamṭ; Mahāt
Ostentation Riyāʾ
Ostrich Naʿām
Ottoman Empire → OTTOMAN EMPIRE
Ownership Milk

P

Paediatrics → LIFE STAGES
Paganism → PRE-ISLAM
Painting → ART
Palace → ARCHITECTURE. MONUMENTS
Palaeography → EPIGRAPHY; WRITING
Palanquin Maḥmal
Paleography *see* Palaeography
Palm Nak͟hl
Palmoscopy Ik͟htilād͟j
Panarabism → PANARABISM
Panegyric Madīḥ
Panislamism → PANISLAMISM
Pantheism → RELIGION
Panther Namir
Panturkism → PANTURKISM
Paper Kāg͟had
Papyrology → PAPYROLOGY
Papyrus Papyrus
Paradise → PARADISE
Parakeet Babbag͟hāʾ
Parasol Miẓalla
Parchment Raḳḳ
Parliament Mad͟jlis
Paronomasia Muzāwad͟ja
Parrot Babbag͟hāʾ
Partnership S͟harika
Party, political → POLITICS
Past Māḍī
Pastimes → RECREATION
Pasture Marʿā
Patronymic Kunya
Pauper Faḳīr; Miskīn
Pavilion → ARCHITECTURE.MONUMENTS
Pay → PAYMENTS
Peace Ṣulḥ
Pearl al-Durr; Luʾluʾ
Pediatrics *see* Paediatrics

Pen Ḳalam
Penal law → LAW
People Ḳawm; Shaʿb
Performers → PROFESSIONS.CRAFTSMEN AND TRADESMEN
Perfume → PERFUME
Periodicals → PRESS
Persian → LANGUAGES.INDO-EUROPEAN.IRANIAN; LINGUISTICS
Person Shakhṣ
Petroleum → OIL
Pharmacology → PHARMACOLOGY
Philately → PHILATELY
Philology → LINGUISTICS
Philosophy → PHILOSOPHY
Phlebotomist [in Suppl.] Faṣṣād
Phonetics → LINGUISTICS
Physician → MEDICINE
Physiognomancy Ḳiyāfa
Physiognomy → PHYSIOGNOMY
Pig Khinzīr
Pigeon Ḥamām
Pilgrimage → PILGRIMAGE
Pillar Rukn
Piracy → PIRACY
Pirate → PIRACY
Plague → PLAGUE
Planet → ASTRONOMY
Plants → FLORA
Plaster Djiṣṣ
Pleasure-garden → ARCHITECTURE.MONUMENTS.GARDENS
Pledge Rahn
Plough Miḥrāth
Plural Djamʿ
Poem → LITERATURE.GENRES.POETRY
Poet Shāʿir
Poetry → LITERATURE
Poison Summ
Pole al-Ḳuṭb
Police → MILITARY
Politics → POLITICS
Poll-tax Djizya
Polytheism Shirk
Pomegranate blossom [in Suppl.] Djullanār
Porcupine Ḳunfudh
Port Mīnāʾ
Porter Ḥammāl
Postal history → PHILATELY
Postal service → TRANSPORT
Potash al-Ḳily
Pottery → ART
Prayer → PRAYER
Prayer direction Ḳibla
Prayer niche Miḥrāb
Pre-emption Shufʿa
Pre-Islam → PRE-ISLAM
Precious stones → JEWELRY
Predestination → PREDESTINATION
Preface Muḳaddima
Pregnancy → LIFE STAGES
Press → PRESS
Primary school Kuttāb
Printing Maṭbaʿa
Prison Sidjn
Prisoner → MILITARY
Procedure, legal → LAW
Processions Mawākib
Profession of faith Shahāda
Professions → PROFESSIONS
Profit Kasb
Prologue Ibtidāʾ
Property → PROPERTY
Prophecy → PROPHETHOOD
Prophet → MUḤAMMAD, THE PROPHET; PROPHETHOOD
Prophethood → PROPHETHOOD
Prose → LITERATURE
Prosody → LITERATURE.POETRY; METRICS; RHYME
Prostitution [in Suppl.] Bighāʾ
Protection Ḥimāya; Idjāra

Proverb → LITERATURE; PROVERBS
Pulpit Minbar
Punishment → (DIVINE) PUNISHMENT; LAW.PENAL LAW
Pyramid Haram

Q

Qat Ḳāt
Quadrant Rubʿ
Quail Salwā
Quiddity Māhiyya
Qurʾān → KORAN

R

Rabies *see* Dog
Raid → RAIDS
Railway → TRANSPORT
Rain prayer Istisḳāʾ
Rainbow Ḳaws Ḳuzaḥ
Ransoming [in Suppl.] Fidāʾ
Reading (Koranic) → KORAN
Recitation → KORAN.READING
Records → ADMINISTRATION
Recreation → RECREATION
Reed Ḳaṣab
Reed-pen Ḳalam
Reed-pipe Ghayṭa; Mizmār
Reflection Fikr
Reform → REFORM
Register → ADMINISTRATION.RECORDS
Religion → RELIGION
Reptiles → ANIMALS
Republic Djumhūriyya
Resemblance Shubha
Resurrection Ḳiyāma
Retaliation Ḳiṣāṣ
Retreat Khalwa
Revelation Ilhām
Rhapsodomancy Ḳurʿa
Rhetoric → RHETORIC
Rhinoceros Karkaddan
Rhyme → RHYME
Rice al-Ruzz
Riddle Lughz
Ritual → RITUALS
River → RIVERS
Road Shāriʿ
Robbery, highway Sariḳa
Robe of honour Khilʿa
Rock-crystal Billawr
Rod ʿAṣā; Ḳaḍīb
Rodents → ANIMALS
Rooster *see* Cock
Rosary Subḥa
Rose Gul
Rug → ART.TAPESTRY

S

Saddle, horse Sardj
Saint → SAINTHOOD
Salamander Samandal
Sale, contract of → LAW

Salt Milḥ
Sand Raml
Sandalwood Ṣandal
Sandgrouse Ḳaṭā
Sappan wood Baḳḳam
Satire Hidjā᾽
Scapulomancy Katif
School, primary Kuttāb
Science → Science
Scorpion ʿAḳrab
Scribe Kātib; [in Suppl.] Dabīr
Sea → Oceans and Seas
Seafaring → Navigation
Seal Khātam; Muhr
Secretary Kātib; [in Suppl.] Dabīr
Semitic languages Sām.2
Sense Ḥiss; Maḥsūsāt
Sermon Khuṭba
Sermoniser Ḳāṣṣ
Servant Khādim
Sesame Simsim
Seven Sabʿ
Seveners → Shiites.branches
Sex Djins
Sexuality → Sexuality
Shadow play Ḳaragöz; Khayāl al-Ẓill
Sheep [in Suppl.] Ghanam
Sheep-herder Shāwiya
Shiism → Shiites
Ship → Navigation
Siege warfare Ḥiṣār
Siegecraft Ḥiṣār; Mandjanīḳ
Silk Ḥarīr
Silver Fiḍḍa
Sin Khaṭī᾽a
Singer → Music
Singing → Music.song
Skin blemish Shāma
Slander Ḳadhf
Slaughterer [in Suppl.] Djazzār
Slave ʿAbd
Slavery → Slavery
Snail Ṣadaf
Snake Ḥayya
Snake-charmer Ḥāwī
Snipe Shunḳub
Soap Ṣābūn
Socialism Ishtirākiyya
Society Djamʿiyya
Soda al-Ḳily; *and see* Natron
Sodium Naṭrūn; *and see* Natron
Sodomy Liwāṭ
Son Ibn
Song → Music
Sorcery → Magic
Soul Nafs
Sphere Falak; al-Kura
Spices → Cuisine
Spider ʿAnkabūt
Sport → Animals.sport; Recreation
Springs → Geography.physical geography
Spy Djāsūs
Stable Iṣṭabl
Stamps → Philately
Standard Sandjaḳ; Sandjaḳ-i Sherīf
Star → Astronomy
Statecraft Siyāsa
Stone Ḥadjar
Stool Kursī
Story Ḥikāya
Storyteller Ḳāṣṣ; Maddāḥ
Straits → Geography.physical geography.waters
Street Shāriʿ
Stronghold → Architecture.monuments
Substance Djawhar
Suckling → Life Stages
Sufism → Mysticism
Sugar Sukkar
Sugar-cane Ḳaṣab al-Sukkar

Suicide Intiḥār
Sulphur al-Kibrīt
Sultan-fowl [in Suppl.] Abū Barāḳish.2
Sun Shams
Sundial Mizwala
Sunshade Miẓalla
Superstition → SUPERSTITION
Surety-bond Kafāla
Surgeon Djarrāḥ
Swahili → KENYA
Sweeper Kannās
Symbolism Ramz.3

T

Tablet Lawḥ
Tailor Khayyāṭ
Talisman → CHARMS
Tambourine Duff
Tanner [in Suppl.] Dabbāgh
Tapestry → ART
Tar Mūmiyā'
Taxation → TAXATION
Tea Čay
Tea-house [in Suppl.] Čāy-khāna
Teak Sādj
Teeth → MEDICINE.DENTISTRY
Tent Khayma
Textiles → ART; CLOTHING.MATERIALS
Thankfulness Shukr
Theatre → LITERATURE.DRAMA
Theft Sariḳa
Theology → THEOLOGY
Theophany Maẓhar
Thief Liṣṣ
Thistle Shukā'ā
Thought Fikr
Tide al-Madd wa 'l-Djazr
Tiles → ART
Tiller Miḥrāth
Time → TIME
Timekeeping → TIME
Tithe → TAXATION
Titulature → ONOMASTICS.TITLES
Tobacco → DRUGS
Tomb → ARCHITECTURE.MONUMENTS
Toothbrush Miswāk
Tooth-pick Miswāk
Tower Burdj
Town Ḳarya; Ḳaṣaba
Toys → RECREATION.GAMES
Trade → COMMERCE; INDUSTRY; NAVIGATION
Trade union Niḳāba
Tradition → LITERATURE.TRADITION-LITERATURE
Translation → LITERATURE
Transport → TRANSPORT
Travel → TRAVEL
Treasury → TREASURY
Treaty → TREATIES
Trees → FLORA
Triangle Muthallath
Tribal chief Sayyid
Tribe → TRIBES
Tribute → TREATIES
Trope Madjāz
Trousers Sirwāl
Trumpet Būḳ
Turkic languages → LANGUAGES
Turquoise Fīrūzadj
Turtle Sulaḥfā
Twelvers → SHIITES.BRANCHES
Twilight al-Shafaḳ

U

Uncle Khāl
Underground chamber Sardāb
University Djāmiʿa
Urbanism → ARCHITECTURE; GEOGRAPHY
Usurpation Ghaṣb
Usury Ribā

V

Vehicle → TRANSPORT.WHEELED VEHICLES
Veil → CLOTHING.HEADWARE
Ventilation → ARCHITECTURE.URBAN
Verb Fiʿl
Verse Āya
Veterinary science → MEDICINE
Vices → VIRTUES
Vikings al-Madjūs
Village Ḳarya
Vine Karm
Viol Rabāb
Viper Afʿā
Volcanoes → GEOGRAPHY.PHYSICAL GEOGRAPHY
Vow Nadhr
Voyage → TRAVEL
Vulture Humā; Nasr

W

Wagon *see* Cart
Walnut [in Suppl.] Djawz
War Ḥarb
Wardrobe → CLOTHING
Washer [in Suppl.] Ghassāl
Washing → ABLUTION
Washing (of the dead) Ghusl
Water Māʾ
Water-carrier Saḳḳāʾ
Waterhouse → ARCHITECTURE. MONUMENTS
Waterways → GEOGRAPHY.PHYSICAL GEOGRAPHY
Waterwheel Nāʿūra
Weapon → MILITARY
Weasel Ibn ʿIrs
Weather → METEOROLOGY
Weaver al-Nassādj; [in Suppl.] Ḥāʾik
Weaver-bird [in Suppl.] Abū Barāḳish.1
Weaving → ART.TEXTILES
Week → TIME
Weights → WEIGHTS AND MEASUREMENTS
Welfare Maṣlaḥa
Well → ARCHITECTURE.MONUMENTS
Werewolf Ḳuṭrub
Wheat Ḳamḥ
Wind → METEOROLOGY
Wine → WINE
Wisdom Ḥikma
Witness Shāhid
Wolf Dhiʾb
Women → WOMEN
Wood Khashab
Wool Ṣūf

World ʿĀlam
Wormwood Afsantīn
Wrestling Pahlawān
Writing → WRITING

Y

Young Turks → TURKEY.OTTOMAN PERIOD

Z

Zaydis → SHIITES
Zero al-Ṣifr
Zodiac Minṭaḳat al-Burūdj
Zoology → ZOOLOGY
Zoroastrianism → ZOROASTRIANS

INDEX OF SUBJECTS

The Muslim world in the Index of Subjects is the world of today. What once was the greater realm of Persia is given here under Central Asia, Caucasus and Afghanistan, just as part of the region once governed by the Ottoman Empire is covered by individual countries in Eastern Europe and in the Near East. Modern countries, such as Jordan and Lebanon, are given right of place. Countries with a long history of Islam, e.g. Egypt and Syria, have a subsection 'modern period', where *Encyclopaedia* articles covering the 19th and 20th centuries have been brought together. When an individual is listed as '15th-century', the dating refers to his/her year of death C.E.

References in regular typeface are to *Encyclopaedia* articles; those printed in boldface type indicate the main article. Entries in capitals and following an arrow refer to lemmata in the Index of Subjects itself. Thus, in the case of

BEDOUINS **Badw**; Biʾr; Dawār; Ghanīma; Ghazw; al-Hidjar
see also Liṣṣ; *and* → NOMADISM; SAUDI ARABIA; TRIBES.ARABIAN PENINSULA

Badw; Biʾr; Dawār; Ghanīma; Ghazw; al-Hidjar refer to articles in the *Encyclopaedia* that deal primarily with Bedouins, Badw being the article on Bedouins; Liṣṣ refers to an article in the *Encyclopaedia* that contains information of interest relating to Bedouins; and NOMADISM; SAUDI ARABIA; TRIBES.ARABIAN PENINSULA refer the reader to analogous lemmata in the Index of Subjects.

A

ʿABBĀSIDS → CALIPHATE

ABLUTION **Ghusl**; Istindjāʾ; Istinshāḳ; al-Masḥ ʿalā ʾl-Khuffayn
see also Djanāba; Ḥadath; Ḥammām; Ḥawḍ; Ḥayḍ

ABYSSINIA → ETHIOPIA

ACCOUNTING Muḥāsaba.2; Mustawfī
see also Daftar; *and* → ADMINISTRATION.FINANCIAL

ADMINISTRATION Barīd; Bayt al-Māl; Daftar; Diplomatic; **Dīwān**; Djizya; Kātib; [in Suppl.] Demography.I
see also al-Ḳalḳashandī.1; al-Ṣūlī

for specific caliphates or dynasties → Caliphate; Dynasties; Ottoman Empire
diplomatic → Diplomacy
financial ʿAṭāʾ; Bayt al-Māl; Daftar; Dār al-Ḍarb; Ḳānūn.ii and iii; Kasb; Khāzin; Khaznadār; Makhzan; Muṣādara.2; Mustawfī; Rūznāma; Siyāḳat
see also Dhahab; Fiḍḍa; Ḥisba; *and* → Numismatics; Ottoman Empire.administration
fiscal → Taxation
functionaries ʿĀmil; Amīn; Amīr; Amīr al-Ḥādjdj; ʿArīf; Dawādār; Djahbadh; Ḥisba; Īshīk-āḳāsī; Kalāntar; Kātib; Khāzin; Mushīr; Mushrif; Mustakhridj; Mustawfī; Parwānačī; Raʾīs; Ṣāḥib al-Madīna; [in Suppl.] Dabīr
see also Barīd; Consul; Fatwā; Fuyūdj; Kōtwāl; Malik al-Tudjdjār; Mawlā; Muwāḍaʿa.2; *and* → Law.offices; Military.offices; Ottoman Empire
geography → Geography.administrative
legal → Law
military → Military
Ottoman → Ottoman Empire
records **Daftar**.I; Ḳānūn.iii
and → Documents; Ottoman Empire.administration
archives Dār al-Maḥfūẓāt al-ʿUmūmiyya; Geniza
and → Ottoman Empire.administration

Adoption [in Suppl.] ʿĀr
see also ʿĀda.iii

Adultery Ḳadhf; Liʿān
see also al-Marʾa.2
punishment of Ḥadd

Afghanistan Afghān; **Afghānistān**
architecture → Architecture.regions
dynasties Aḥmad Shāh Durrānī; Ghaznawids; Ghūrids; Kart
and → Dynasties.afghanistan and india
historians of Sayfī Harawī
language → Languages.indo-iranian.iranian
modern period Djāmiʿa; Dustūr.v; Khaybar; Madjlis.4.B; Maṭbaʿa.5
see also Muhādjir.3
statesmen ʿAbd al-Raḥmān Khān; Ayyūb Khān; Dūst Muḥammad; Ḥabīb Allāh Khān; Muḥammad Dāwūd Khān; Shīr ʿAlī; [in Suppl.] Amān Allāh
see also [in Suppl.] Faḳīr of Ipi
physical geography Afghānistān.i

mountains Hindū Kush; Kūh-i Bābā; Safīd Kūh
see also Afghānistān.i
waters Dehās; Hāmūn; Harī Rūd; Kābul.1; Ḳunduz.1; Kurram; Murghāb; Pandjhīr; [in Suppl.] Gūmāl
see also Afghānistān.i
population Abdālī; Čahār Aymak; Durrānī; Ghalča; Ghalzay; Moghols; Mohmand; [in Suppl.] Demography.III; Hazāras
see also Afghān.i; Afghānistān.ii; Khaladj; Özbeg.1.d; [in Suppl.] Djirga
toponyms
ancient Būshandj; Bust; Dihistān; Djuwayn.3; Farmūl; Fīrūzkūh.1; Khōst; Khudjistān; Marw al-Rūdh; al-Rukhkhadj
present-day
districts Andarāb.1; Bādghīs; Farwān; Ḳūhistān.3; Lamghānāt
regions Badakhshān; Dardistān; Djūzdjān; Ghardjistān; Ghūr; Kāfiristān; Khōst; Nangrahār; Sīstān; [in Suppl.] Hazāradjāt
see also Pandjhīr
towns Andkhūy; Balkh; Bāmiyān; Djām; Farāh; Faryāb.1; Gardīz; Ghazna; Girishk; Harāt; Kābul.2; Ḳandahār; Karūkh; Khulm; Ḳunduz.2; Maymana; Mazār-i Sharīf; Rūdhbār.1; Sabzawār.2; Sar-i Pul; Shibarghān; [in Suppl.] Djalālābād

AFRICA Lamlam
Central Africa Cameroons; Congo; Gabon; [in Suppl.] Čad
see also Hausa; Muḥammad Bello; al-Murdjibī; [in Suppl.] Demography.V
for individual countries → CHAD; CONGO; NIGER; NIGERIA; ZAIRE
literature Hausa.iii; Kano; Shāʿir.5 and 6; Shiʿr.7
physical geography
deserts Sāḥil.2
population Kanuri; Kotoko; Shuwa
East Africa Djibūtī; Eritrea; Ḥabesh; Ḳumr; Madagascar; Mafia; Somali; Sūdān
see also Emīn Pasha; Muṣāḥib; Nikāḥ.II.5; al-Nudjūm; Shīrāzī; [in Suppl.] Djarīda.viii
for individual countries → ETHIOPIA; KENYA; MADAGASCAR; MALAWI; SOMALIA; SUDAN; TANZANIA; ZANZIBAR
architecture Manāra.3; Masdjid.VI; Mbweni; Minbar.4
see also Shungwaya
festivals Mawlid.2; Nawrūz.2
languages Eritrea.iv; Ḥabash.iv; Kūsh; Nūba.3; Somali.5; Sūdān.2; Swahili
see also Ḳumr; Madagascar
literature Miʿrādj.3; Somali.6
see also Kitābāt.6; *and* → KENYA.SWAHILI LITERATURE

physical geography

waters Atbara; Baḥr al-Ghazāl.1; Shebelle

see also Baḥr al-Hind; Baḥr al-Zandj

population ʿAbābda; ʿĀmir; Antemuru; Bedja; Beleyn; Bishārīn; Dankalī; Djaʿaliyyūn; Galla; Māryā; Mazrūʿī; Oromo; Somali.1; [in Suppl.] Demography.V

see also Diglal; Lamlam; al-Manāṣir

North Africa Algeria; Atlas; Ifrīḳiya; Lībiyā; Maghāriba; al-Maghrib (2x); Mashāriḳa

see also al-ʿArab.v; ʿArabiyya.A.iii.3; Badw.II.d; Djaysh.iii; Ghuzz.ii; Ḥawz; Kharbga; Kitābāt.4; Lamṭ; Leo Africanus; Libās.ii; Maḥalla; Mānū; Ṣaff.3; Sipāhī.2; [in Suppl.] ʿĀr; *and* → DYNASTIES.SPAIN AND NORTH AFRICA

for individual countries → ALGERIA; LIBYA; MOROCCO; TUNISIA

architecture → ARCHITECTURE.REGIONS

modern period Baladiyya.3; Djamāʿa.ii; Djarīda.B; Hilāl; Ḳawmiyya.ii

and → ALGERIA; LIBYA; MOROCCO; TUNISIA

mysticism → MYSTICISM

physical geography Reg; Rīf; Sabkha; al-Ṣaḥrāʾ; Shaṭṭ

and → *the section Physical Geography under individual countries*

population Ahaggar; Berbers; Dukkāla; Khulṭ; al-Maʿḳil; Shāwiya.1; [in Suppl.] Demography.IV

see also Khumayr; Kūmiya; al-Manāṣir; Mandīl; Moors; *and* → BERBERS

Southern Africa Mozambique; South Africa

see also [in Suppl.] Djarīda.ix

for individual countries → MOZAMBIQUE

West Africa Côte d'Ivoire; Dahomey; Gambia; Ghana; Guinea; Liberia; Mali; Mūrītāniyā; Niger; Nigeria; Senegal; Sierra Leone

see also Kitābāt.5; Ḳunbi Ṣāliḥ; al-Maghīlī; Malam; Murīdiyya; Sūdān (Bilād al-).2; Sulṭān.3

for individual countries → BENIN; GUINEA; IVORY COAST; MALI; MAURITANIA; NIGER; NIGERIA; SENEGAL; TOGO

architecture Ḳunbi Ṣāliḥ; Masdjid.VII

empires Mande; Oyo; Songhay.3

see also Muḥammad b. Abī Bakr; Samori Ture

languages Hausa.ii; Nūba.3; Shuwa.2; Songhay.1; Sūdān (Bilād al-).3

see also Fulbe; Kanuri; Senegal.1; *and* → LANGUAGES.AFRO-ASIATIC.ARABIC

literature → AFRICA.CENTRAL AFRICA

physical geography

deserts Sāḥil.2

mountains Fūta Djallon
waters Niger
population Fulbe; Ḥarṭānī; Ifoghas; Kunta; Songhay.2; [in Suppl.] Demography.V
see also Lamlam; Mande

AGRICULTURE **Filāḥa**; Marʿā; Raʿiyya
see also Mazraʿa; Mugharasa; Musāḳāt; Muzāraʿa; [in Suppl.] Akkār; *and* → BOTANY; FLORA; IRRIGATION
products Ḳahwa; Ḳamḥ; Karm; Ḳaṣab al-Sukkar; Khamr.2; Ḳuṭn; [in Suppl.] Djāwars; Hindibāʾ
see also Ḥarīr; *and* → CUISINE
terms Āgdāl; Baʿl.2.b; Čiftlik; Ghūṭa; Maṭmūra
tools Miḥrāth
treatises on Abu ʾl-Khayr al Ishbīlī; Ibn Wāfid; Ibn Waḥshiyya

ALBANIA **Arnawutluḳ**; Iskender Beg; Ḳarā Maḥmūd Pasha
see also Muslimūn.1.B.4; Sāmī; *and* → OTTOMAN EMPIRE
toponyms Aḳ Ḥiṣār.4; Awlonya; Delvina; Drač; Elbasan; Ergiri; Korča; Krujë; Lesh

ALCHEMY Dhahab; Fiḍḍa; al-Iksīr; al-Kibrīt; **al-Kīmiyāʾ**
see also Ḳārūn; Maʿdin; al-Nūshādir; *and* → METALLURGY; MINERALOGY
alchemists Djābir b. Ḥayyān; Ibn Umayl; Ibn Waḥshiyya; al-Rāzī, Abū Bakr; [in Suppl.] Abu ʾl-Ḥasan al-Anṣārī; al-Djildakī
see also Hirmis; Khālid b. Yazīd b. Muʿāwiya; [in Suppl.] al-Djawbarī, ʿAbd al-Raḥīm; Findiriskī; Ibn Daḳīḳ al-ʿĪd
equipment al-Anbīḳ
terms Rukn.2

ALGERIA **Algeria**
see also ʿArabiyya.A.iii.3; ʿArsh; Ḥalḳa; *and* → BERBERS; DYNASTIES.SPAIN AND NORTH AFRICA
architecture → ARCHITECTURE.REGIONS.NORTH AFRICA
dynasties ʿAbd al-Wādids; Fāṭimids; Ḥammādids; Rustamids
and → DYNASTIES.SPAIN AND NORTH AFRICA
literature Ḥawfī
modern period Djāmiʿa; Djarīda.i.B; Ḥizb.i; Ḥukūma.iv; Maʿārif.2.B; Madjlis. 4.A.xx
reform Ibn Bādīs; (al-)Ibrāhīmī; Salafiyya.1(b)
see also Fallāḳ
Ottoman period (1518-1830) ʿAbd al-Ḳādir b. Muḥyī al-Dīn; Algeria.ii.(2);

- ʿArūdj; Ḥasan Agha; Ḥasan Baba; Ḥasan Pasha; al-Ḥusayn; Ḥusayn Pasha, Mezzomorto; Khayr al-Dīn Pasha

physical geography Algeria.i
- *mountains* ʿAmūr; Atlas; Awrās; Bībān; Djurdjura; Kabylia

population Ahaggar; Algeria.iii; Berbers
- *see also* Kabylia; *and* → BERBERS

religion Algeria.iii; Shāwiya.1
- *mystical orders* ʿAmmāriyya; Raḥmāniyya
  - *see also* Darḳāwa; *and* → MYSTICISM

toponyms
- *ancient* Arshgūl; Ashīr; al-Manṣūra; Sadrāta; [in Suppl.] Hunayn
- *present day*
  - *oases* Biskra; Ḳanṭara.1; al-Ḳulayʿa.2.1; Laghouat; Sūf; [in Suppl.] Gourara
  - *regions* Ḥuḍna; Mzāb; Sāḥil.1.b
  - *towns* Adrar.1; al-ʿAnnāba; Ārzāw; ʿAyn Temushent; Bidjāya; Biskra; Bulayda; Colomb-Béchar; al-Djazāʾir; Djidjelli; Ghardāya; Ḳalʿat Banī ʿAbbās; Ḳalʿat Huwwāra; al-Ḳulayʿa.2.2; Ḳusṭanṭīna; Laghouat; al-Madiyya; Masīla; Milyāna; al-Muʿaskar; Mustaghānim; Nadrūma; Saʿīda; Sharshal; Sīdī Bu ʾl-ʿAbbās

ALMS Khayr; **Ṣadaḳa**

ALPHABET **Abdjad**; Ḥarf; Ḥisāb; **Ḥurūf al-Hidjāʾ**
- *see also* Djafr; Khaṭṭ; [in Suppl.] Budūḥ; *and* → WRITING.SCRIPTS
- *for the letters of the Arabic and Persian alphabets, see* Ḍād; Dāl; Dhāl; Djīm; Fāʾ; Ghayn; Hāʾ; Ḥāʾ; Hamza; Kāf; Ḳāf; Khāʾ; Lām; Mīm; Nūn; Pāʾ; Rāʾ; Ṣād; Sīn and Shīn

secret → CRYPTOGRAPHY

ANATOMY Djism; Katif; [in Suppl.] Aflīmūn
- *see also* Ishāra; Khiḍāb; Ḳiyāfa; Shāma; [in Suppl.] Dam

chest **Ṣadr**

eye **ʿAyn**; al-Kuḥl; Manāẓir; Ramad
- *and* → MEDICINE.OPHTHALMOLOGISTS; OPTICS

hair ʿAfṣ; Afsantīn; Ḥinnāʾ; Liḥya-yi Sherīf; **Shaʿr**
- *see also* [in Suppl.] Ḥallāḳ

organs Kabid; Ḳalb

teeth → MEDICINE.DENTISTRY

treatises on
- *Turkish* Shānī-zāde
  - *and* → MEDICINE.MEDICAL HANDBOOKS/ENCYCLOPAEDIAS

ANDALUSIA **al-Andalus**; Gharb al-Andalus; Moriscos; Mozarab; Mudéjar; Shark al-Andalus
see also Kitābāt.3; Libās.ii; Mā'.7; al-Madjūs; Moors; Muwallad.1; Safīr.2.b; Ṣā'ifa.2; *and* → DYNASTIES.SPAIN AND NORTH AFRICA; SPAIN
administration Dīwān.iii; Ḳūmis; Ṣāḥib al-Madīna
see also Fatā
architecture → ARCHITECTURE.REGIONS
dynasties al-Murābiṭūn.4; al-Muwaḥḥidūn; [in Suppl.] ʿAzafī
see also al-Andalus.vi; (Banū) Ḳasī; *and* → DYNASTIES.SPAIN AND NORTH AFRICA
reyes de taifas period (11th century) ʿAbbādids; Afṭasids; ʿĀmirids; Dhu 'l-Nūnids; Djahwarids; Ḥammūdids; Hūdids; **Mulūk al-Ṭawā'if**.2; Razīn, Banū
see also Balansiya; Dāniya; Gharnāṭa; Ibn Ghalbūn; Ibn Rashīḳ, Abū Muḥammad; Ishbīliya; Ḳurṭuba; Mudjāhid, al-Muwaffaḳ; Parias; al-Sīd
governors until Umayyad conquest ʿAbd al-Malik b. Ḳaṭan; ʿAbd al-Raḥmān al-Ghāfiḳī; Abu 'l-Khaṭṭār; al-Ḥurr b. ʿAbd al-Raḥmān al-Thaḳafī; al-Ḥusām b. Ḍirār
see also Kalb b. Wabara; Mūsā b. Nuṣayr; al-Ṣumayl
grammarians Abū Ḥayyān al-Gharnāṭī; al-Baṭalyawsī; Djūdī al-Mawrūrī; Ibn al-ʿArīf, al-Ḥusayn; Ibn ʿĀṣim; Ibn al-Iflīlī; Ibn Khātima; Ibn al-Ḳūṭiyya; Ibn Maḍā'; Ibn Mālik; Ibn Sīda; al-Rabaḥī; al-Shalawbīn; al-Shantamarī; al-Sharīf al-Gharnatī; al-Sharīshī; [in Suppl.] Ibn Hishām al-Lakhmī
see also al-Shāṭibī, Abū Isḥāḳ
historians of al-Ḍabbī, Abū Djaʿfar; Ibn al-Abbār, Abu ʿAbd Allāh; Ibn ʿAbd al-Malik al-Marrākushī; Ibn Bashkuwāl; Ibn Burd.I; Ibn al-Faraḍī; Ibn Ghālib; Ibn Ḥayyān; Ibn ʿIdhārī; Ibn al-Khaṭīb; Ibn al-Ḳūṭiyya; Ibn Saʿīd al-Maghribī; al-Maḳḳarī; al-Rushāṭī
see also al-Shaḳundī; *and* → DYNASTIES.SPAIN AND NORTH AFRICA
jurists al-Bādjī; al-Dānī; al-Ḥumaydī; Ibn Abī Zamanayn; Ibn ʿĀṣim; Ibn al-Faraḍī; Ibn Ḥabīb, Abū Marwān; Ibn Ḥazm, Abū Muḥammad; Ibn Maḍā'; Ibn Rushayd; ʿĪsā b. Dīnār; ʿIyāḍ b. Mūsā; al-Ḳalaṣādī; al-Ḳurṭubī, Abū ʿAbd Allāh; al-Ḳurṭubī, Yaḥyā; (al-)Mundhir b. Saʿīd; Shabṭūn; [in Suppl.] Ibn Rushd
see also al-Khushanī; Mālikiyya; Ṣāʿid al-Andalusī; Shūrā.2; Shurṭa.2; [in Suppl.] Ibn al-Rūmiyya
literature Aljamía; ʿArabiyya.B.Appendix; Fahrasa
and → ANDALUSIA.HISTORIANS OF; LITERATURE.POETRY
mysticism → MYSTICISM.MYSTICS
physical geography → SPAIN
toponyms → SPAIN

ANGELOLOGY **Malāʾika**
see also ʿAdhāb al-Ḳabr; Dīk; Iblīs; Ḳarīn; Rūḥāniyya; Siḥr
angels ʿAzāzīl; Djabrāʾīl; Hārūt wa-Mārūt; Isrāfīl; ʿIzrāʿīl; Mīkāl; Munkar wa-Nakīr; Riḍwān

ANIMALS Dābba; **Ḥayawān**
see also Badw; (Djazīrat) al-ʿArab.v; Farw; Hind.i.l; Khāṣī; Marbaṭ; [in Suppl.] Djazzār; *and* → ZOOLOGY
and art al-Asad; Fahd; Fīl; Ḥayawān.6; Karkaddan; Maʿdin; Namir and Nimr; [in Suppl.] Arnab
and proverbs Ḥayawān.2; Mathal
and see articles on individual animals, in particular Afʿā; Dhiʾb; Fahd; Ghurāb; Ḳaṭā; Khinzīr; Ḳird; Lamṭ; Naml
aquatic animals
crustaceans **Saraṭān**
fish **Samak**
molluscs **Ṣadaf**
land animals
antelopes Ghazāl; Lamṭ; Mahāt
arachnoids ʿAḳrab; ʿAnkabūt
birds Babbaghāʾ; Dadjādja; Dīk; Ghurāb; Ḥamām; Hudhud; Humā; Ḳaṭā; Naʿām; Nasr; Nuḥām; al-Rukhkh; Salwā; Shunḳub; [in Suppl.] Abū Barāḳish
see also Bayzara; Bulbul; ʿIyāfa; al-Ramādī; Sonḳor
camels **Ibil**
see also (Djazīrat) al-ʿArab.v; Badw.II.c and d; Kārwān; Raḥīl; [in Suppl.] Djammāl; *and* → TRANSPORT.CARAVANS
canines Dhiʾb; Fanak; Ibn Āwā; Kalb; Salūḳī; [in Suppl.] Ḍabuʿ
domesticated Baḳar; Fīl; Ibil; Kalb; Khinzīr; Nims; [in Suppl.] Djāmūs; Ghanam
see also Shāwiya.2; *and* → ANIMALS.EQUINES
equines Badw.II; Baghl; **Faras**; Ḥimār; **Khayl**
see also Fāris; Furūsiyya; Ḥazīn; Ibn Hudhayl; Ibn al-Mundhir; Iṣṭabl; Marbaṭ; Maydān; Mīr-Ākhūr; Sardj
felines ʿAnāḳ; al-Asad; Fahd; Namir and Nimr; Sinnawr
insects Dhubāb; Djarād; Ḳaml; Naḥl; Naml; Nāmūs.2
reptiles Afʿā; Ḍabb; Ḥayya; Ḥirbāʾ; Samandal; Sulaḥfā
see also Ādam; Almās
rodents [in Suppl.] Faʾr
sport Bayzara; Fahd; Furūsiyya; Ḥamām; Khinzīr; Mahāt; [in Suppl.] Ḍabuʿ
see also Čakïrdjï-bashï; Doghandjï; Kurds.iv.C.5; *and* → HUNTING
transformation into Ḥayawān.3; Ḳird; **Maskh**

wild *in addition to the above, see also* Ayyil; Fanak; Fīl; Ibn 'Irs; Karkaddan; Ḳird; Ḳunfudẖ; [in Suppl.] Arnab; Faras al-Māʾ
and → HUNTING

ANTHROPOMORPHISM Ḥashwiyya; Karrāmiyya
see also Bayān b. Samʿān al-Tamīmī; Ḏjism; Hishām b. al-Ḥakam; Ḥulmāniyya

APOSTASY Mulḥid; Murtadd
see also Ḳatl; *and* → HERESY

ARCHAEOLOGY
and → ARCHITECTURE.REGIONS; EPIGRAPHY; *and the section Toponyms under individual countries*
Turkish archaeologists 'Othmān Ḥamdī

ARCHITECTURE **Architecture**; Bināʾ
see also Kitābāt; *and* → MILITARY
architects Ḳāsim Agẖa; Ḵẖayr al-Dīn; Sinān
decoration Fusayfisāʾ; Kāshī; Ḵẖaṭṭ; Parčīn-kārī
materials Ḏjiṣṣ; Labin
see also Bināʾ
monuments
aqueducts Ḳanṭara.5 and 6
see also Faḳīr; Sinān
baths **Ḥammām**; Ḥammām al-Ṣarakẖ
bridges **Ḏjisr**; Ḏjisr Banāt Yaʿḳūb; Ḏjisr al-Ḥadīd; Ḏjisr al-Shugẖr
see also Dizfūl; Ḳanṭara; Sayḥān
churches → CHRISTIANITY
dams **Band**
see also Dizfūl; Sāwa.2.i; Shushtar; [in Suppl.] Abū Sinbil; *and* → HYDROLOGY
gardens **Būstān**; Ḥāʾir
see also Bostāndjĭ; Gẖarnāṭa.B; Ḥawḍ; Māʾ.12; Srīnagar.2; *and* → FLORA; LITERATURE.POETRY.NATURE
gates **Bāb**; Bāb-i Humāyūn; Ḥarrān.ii.d
lighthouses **Manār**; al-Nāẓūr
mausolea → ARCHITECTURE.MONUMENTS.TOMBS
monasteries → CHRISTIANITY
mosques Ḥawḍ; Külliyye; Manāra; **Masd̲j̲id**; Miḥrāb; Minbar
see also 'Anaza; Bāb.i; Bahw; Balāṭ; Dikka; Ḵẖaṭīb; Muṣallā.2
individual mosques Aya Sofya; al-Azhar; Ḥarrān.ii.(b); Ḥusaynī Dālān; Kaʿba; al-Ḳarawiyyīn; Ḳubbat al-Ṣakẖra; Ḳuṭb Mīnār; al-

Masdjid al-Aḳṣā; al-Masdjid al-Ḥarām
see also Anḳara; Architecture; Bahmanīs; Dhār.2; Djām; Edirne; Ḥamāt; Ḥimṣ; Kāẓimayn; Ḳazwīn; Maʿarrat al-Nuʿmān; Makka.4; Sinān

obelisks **Misalla**

palaces **Sarāy**
see also Balāṭ
individual palaces Čirāghān; Ḳaṣr al-Ḥayr al-Gharbī; Ḳaṣr al-Ḥayr al-Sharḳī; Kayḳubādiyya; Khirbat al-Mafdjar; Khirbat al-Minya; Ḳubādābād; Maḥall; al-Mushattā; [in Suppl.] Djabal Says
see also Gharnāṭa.B; Khirbat al-Bayḍāʾ; Ḳubbat al-Hawāʾ; Lashkar-i Bāzār

pavilions Köshk

strongholds Burdj; Ḥiṣār; **Ḥiṣn**; Ḳaṣaba; Sūr
see also Bāb.ii; al-Ḳalʿa; Ribāṭ
individual strongholds Abū Safyān; Āgra; Alamūt.i.; Alindjaḳ; ʿAmādiya; Anadolu Ḥiṣārî; Anamur; Anapa; Asīrgarh; Atak; al-ʿAwāṣim; Bāb al-Abwāb; Bālā Ḥiṣār; Balāṭunus; Barzūya; Baynūn; Bhakkar; Čandērī; Čirmen; al-Dārūm; Djaʿbar; al-Djarbāʾ; Gaban; Gāwilgaṙh; Ghumdān; Gök Tepe; Golkonḋā; Ḥadjar al-Nasr; Hānsī; Ḥarrān.ii.(a); Ḥiṣn al-Akrād; Ḥiṣn Kayfā; Iṣṭakhr; Kakhtā; Ḳalʿat Nadjm; Ḳalʿat al-Shaḳīf; Ḳalāwdhiya; Ḳalʿe-i Sefīd; Ḳandahār; Kanizsa; al-Karak; Kawkab al-Hawāʾ; Kharāna; Khartpert; Khērla; Khotin; Khunāṣira; Kilāt-i Nādirī; Ḳoron; Ḳoyul Ḥiṣār; Lanbasar; Lüleburgaz; Mānḋū; Manōhar; al-Marḳab; Muḋgal; Narnālā; Parendā; al-Rāwandān; Rōhtās; Rūm Ḳalʿesi; Rūmeli Ḥiṣārî; Ṣahyūn; Shalbaṭarra; Softa; al-Ṣubayba; [in Suppl.] Bādiya; Bubashtru; al-Dīkdān; Firrīm
see also Ashīr; Bahmanīs; Bīdar; Dawlatābād; Diyār Bakr; Ḥimṣ; Kawkabān.2; Khursābād; Maḥall; Māhūr

tombs **Ḳabr**; **Ḳubba**; **Maḳbara**; Mashhad
see also Muthamman
individual buildings Baḳīʿ al-Gharḳad; Golkonḋā; Ḥarrān.ii.(c); Maklī; Nafīsa; Rādkān; Sahsarām
see also Abarḳūh; Abū Ayyūb al-Anṣārī; Abū Madyan; Āgra; Aḥmad al-Badawī; Aḥmad Yasawī; Bahmanīs; Barīd Shāhīs.II; Djahāngīr; Ghāzī Miyān; Gunbadh-i Ḳābūs; Ḥimṣ; Imāmzāda; Karak Nūḥ; Ḳarbalāʾ; Ḳazwīn; al-Khalīl; Ḳubbat al-Hawāʾ; Maʿarrat al-Nuʿmān; al-Madīna; Sulṭāniyya.2

water-houses **Sabīl**.2
fountains Shadirwān

wells Bā'olī; **Bi'r**; Bi'r Maymūn
see also Ḥawḍ

regions

Afghanistan and Indian subcontinent Āgra; Bahmanīs; Barīd Shāhīs.II; Bharōč; Bīdar; Bīdjāpūr; Bihār; Čāmpānēr; Dawlatābād; Dihlī.2; Djūnāgaṙh; Ghaznawids; Ghūrids; Golkonḍā; Hampī; Hānsī; Ḥaydarābād; Hind.vii; Ḥusaynī Dālān; Ḳuṭb Mīnār; Lahore; Lakhnaw; Maḥall; Mahisur; Māndū.2; Mughals.7; Multān.2; Nāgawr; Sind.4; Srīnagar.2
see also Burdj.iii; Bustān.ii; Imām-bārā; Lashkar-i Bāzār; Mā'.12; Maḳbara.5; Maklī; Manāra.2; Masdjid.II; Miḥrāb; Minbar.3; Miẓalla.5; Muthamman; Parčīn-kārī; Pīshṭāḳ

Africa → AFRICA; *for North African architecture, see below*

Andalusia al-Andalus.ix; Burdj.II; Gharnāṭa; Ishbīliya; Ḳurṭuba; Naṣrids.2
see also al-Nāẓūr

Arabian peninsula al-Ḥidjr; Ka'ba; al-Masdjid al-Ḥarām
see also Makka.4; Ṣan'ā'

Central Asia Bukhārā; Ḥiṣn.iii; Īlkhāns; Samarḳand.2
see also Miḥrāb

Egypt Abu 'l-Hawl; al-Azhar; Haram; al-Ḳāhira; Mashrabiyya.1; Nafīsa
see also Miḥrāb; Misalla; Miṣr; Sa'īd al-Su'adā'; [in Suppl.] Abū Sinbil

Fertile Crescent Baghdād; Dimashḳ; Ḥarrān.ii; Ḥimṣ; 'Irāḳ.vii; Ḳubbat al-Ṣakhra; al-Ḳuds; Ma'arrat al-Nu'mān; al-Marḳab.3; al-Masdjid al-Aḳṣā; al-Raḳḳa; [in Suppl.] Bādiya; Dār al-Ḥadīth.I
see also Ḳaṣr al-Ḥayr al-Gharbī; Ḳaṣr al-Ḥayr al-Sharḳī; Khirbat al-Mafdjar; Miḥrāb; al-Rāwandān

Iran Ḥiṣn.ii; Iṣfahān.2; Iṣṭakhr; Ḳazwīn; Khursābād; Mashrabiyya.2; Rādkān; al-Rayy.2; Ṣafawids.V; Saldjūḳids.VI; Sāmānids.2(b); Sulṭāniyya.2
see also Ḳaṣr-i Shīrīn; Miḥrāb; Ribāṭ-i Sharaf

North Africa Fās; Fāṭimid Art; Ḥiṣn.i; Ḳal'at Banī Ḥammād; al-Ḳarawiyyīn
see also 'Anaza; Bidjāya; Miḥrāb

Southeast Asia Ḥiṣn.iv; Indonesia.v; Masdjid.III-V

Turkey Adana; Anḳara; Aya Sofya; Diwrigī; Diyār Bakr; Edirne; Ḥarrān.ii; Ḥiṣn Kayfā; Istanbul; Konya.2; Lāranda; 'Othmānli̊.V
see also Ḳapli̊dja; Ḳāsim Agha; Khayr al-Dīn; Köshk; Miḥrāb; Rūm Ḳal'esi; Sinān

terms 'Amūd; 'Anaza; Bahw; Balāṭ; Īwān; Muḳarbaṣ; Muḳarnas; Muthamman; Pīshṭāḳ; Riwāḳ; Sarāy; Sardāb; Shadirwān

urban Dār; Funduḳ; Ḥammām; Īwān; Ḳaysāriyya; Khān.II; Madrasa.III; Masdjid; Muṣallā.2; Rab'; Selāmli̊ḳ; Shāri'; Sūḳ; Sūr
see also Kanīsa; Sarāy; *and* → SEDENTARISM

ventilation Mirwaḥa; [in Suppl.] Bādgīr
see also Khaysh; Sardāb; Sind.4

ARMENIA   **Armīniya**; Rewān; S̲h̲ims̲h̲āṭ
  and → CAUCASUS

ART   Arabesque; Fann; Fusayfisāʾ; Kās̲h̲ī; K̲h̲aṭṭ; K̲h̲azaf; Kitābāt; Lawn;
  Maʿdin.4; Parčīn-kārī; Rasm
  see also Architecture; Billawr; D̲h̲ahab; Fiḍḍa; ʿIlm al-D̲j̲amāl; K̲h̲ātam; Muhr;
  Ṣūra; *and* → ANIMALS.AND ART; ARCHITECTURE
calligraphy   **K̲h̲aṭṭ**
    see also ʿAlī; Īnal; Ḳum(m)ī; Murakka̲ʿ; Nus̲h̲a; *and* → WRITING
    calligraphers   ʿAlī Riḍā-i ʿAbbāsī; Ḥamza al-Ḥarrānī; Ibn al-Bawwāb; Ibn
        Muḳla; Muḥammad Ḥusayn Tabrīzī; Müstaḳīm-zāde
ceramics   → ART.POTTERY
decorative   ʿĀd̲j̲; al-Asad; D̲j̲iṣṣ; Fahd; Ḥayawān.6; Hilāl.ii; Īlk̲h̲āns; al-Ḳamar.II;
  Mas̲h̲rabiyya; Parčīn-kārī; S̲h̲ams.3
  see also Kās̲h̲ī; Maʿdin.4
drawing   **Rasm**
glass   al-Ḳily; ʿOt̲h̲mānlî.VII.d; Sāmānids.2(a)
handicrafts   Ḳalamkārī; [in Suppl.] Bisāṭ; Dawāt
  see also Ḥalfāʾ
metalware   Bīdar; Īlk̲h̲āns; Maʿdin.4; ʿOt̲h̲mānlî.VII.b; Sāmānids.2(a); [in Suppl.]
  Ibrīḳ
mosaics   **Fusayfisāʾ**; Kās̲h̲ī
painting
  miniatures   Īlk̲h̲āns; Mug̲h̲als.9; Naḳḳās̲h̲-k̲h̲āna; ʿOt̲h̲mānlî.VIII
    see also Fīl; Kalīla wa-Dimna.16; Māndū.3; Miʿrād̲j̲.5; al-Mīzān.3;
    Murakka̲ʿ; Rustam.2; Sāḳī.3; [in Suppl.] D̲j̲awhar; *and* → ANIMALS.AND
    ART; ART.DRAWING
    miniaturists   Bihzād; Manṣūr; Maṭrāḳčî; Naḳḳās̲h̲ Ḥasan (Pas̲h̲a); Riḍā
      ʿAbbāsī; Riḍāʾī; Siyāh-ḳalem
      see also ʿAlī; Luḳmān b. Sayyid Ḥusayn
  modern painting   D̲j̲abrān K̲h̲alīl D̲j̲abrān; ʿOt̲h̲mān Ḥamdī; Sipihrī; [in
    Suppl.] Dinet; Eyyūbog̲h̲lu, Bedrī
    and → ART.DRAWING
pottery   Anadolu.iii.6; al-Andalus.ix; **Fak̲h̲k̲h̲ār**; Īlk̲h̲āns; Iznīḳ; Ḳallala;
  K̲h̲azaf; Mināʾī; ʿOt̲h̲mānlî.VII.a; Sāmānids.2(a); Ṣīnī
regional and period   al-Andalus.ix; Berbers.VI; Fāṭimid Art; Īlk̲h̲āns; ʿIrāḳ.vii;
  Mug̲h̲als.8 and 9; ʿOt̲h̲mānlî.VII; Saldjūḳids.VI; Sāmānids.2(a)
silhouette-cutting   Fak̲h̲rī
tapestry   ʿOt̲h̲mānlî.VI; Sad̲j̲d̲j̲āda.2; [in Suppl.] **Bisāṭ**
  see also Karkaddan; Mafrūs̲h̲āt; Mifras̲h̲; Mīlās.2
textiles   Anadolu.iii.6; al-Andalus.ix; al-Bahnasā; Bursa; Dabīḳ; Ḥarīr; Īlk̲h̲āns;

Ḳumā<u>sh</u>; Mu<u>gh</u>als.8; ʿO<u>th</u>mānli̊.VI; al-Rayy.2; Sāmānids.2(a); [in Suppl.] Ḥāʾik
see also Ḳalamkārī; Ḳaṣab; Kattān; Ḳurḳūb; Mandīl; al-Nassā<u>dj</u>; *and* → Clothing

tiles **Kā<u>sh</u>ī**

Asceticism Bakkāʾ; Malāmatiyya
see also <u>Kh</u>alwa; Manāḳib; [in Suppl.] Asad b. Mūsā b. Ibrāhīm
for ascetics → Mysticism.mystics; Sainthood

Asia Almali̊<u>gh</u>; Baikal
see also Baraba; Mo<u>gh</u>olistān

Central → Central Asia

East Čam; <u>Dj</u>āwī; Indochina; Indonesia; Ḳimār; Malay Peninsula; Malaysia; Patani; Philippines; al-<u>Sh</u>īlā; al-Ṣin; Singapore; [in Suppl.] Brunei
see also Kitābāt.8; Ṣanf; <u>Sh</u>āh Bandar.2; [in Suppl.] Demography.VIII; *and* → Architecture.regions.southeast asia; Law.in southeast asia; Onomastics.titles
for individual countries → China; Indonesia; Malaysia; Mongolia; Thailand

Eurasia → Europe

South Burma; Ceylon; Hind; Laccadives; Maldives; Mauritius; Minicoy; Nepal; Nicobars; Seychelles
see also Ruhmī
for individual countries → Bangladesh; Burma; India; Nepal; Pakistan; Sri Lanka

Assyria <u>Kh</u>ursābād; Nimrūd; Nīnawā.1; [in Suppl.] A<u>th</u>ūr

Astrology I<u>kh</u>tiyārāt; Ḳaws Ḳuzaḥ; al-Kayd; Ḳirān; Minṭaḳat al-Burū<u>dj</u>; Muna<u>djdj</u>im; **Nu<u>dj</u>ūm (Aḥkām al-)**
see also <u>Kh</u>aṭṭ

astrologers Abū Maʿ<u>sh</u>ar al-Bal<u>kh</u>ī; al-Bīrūnī; Ibn Abi ʾl-Ri<u>dj</u>āl, Abu ʾl-Ḥasan; Ibn al-<u>Kh</u>aṣīb, Abū Bakr; al-Ḳabīṣī; al-<u>Kh</u>ayyāṭ, Abū ʿAlī; Mā<u>sh</u>āʾ Allāh
see also Baṭlamiyūs; *and* → Astronomy; Divination

terms al-<u>Dj</u>awzahar; Ḥadd; Ḳaṭʿ; Mu<u>th</u>alla<u>th</u>; Saʿd wa-Naḥs (*and* al-Saʿdāni; <u>Sh</u>aḳāwa); al-Sahm.1.b

Astronomy Anwāʾ; Asṭurlāb; Falak; Hayʾa; **ʿIlm al-Hayʾa**; al-Ḳamar.I; al-Kayd; Kusūf; al-Ḳuṭb; al-Madd wa ʾl-<u>Dj</u>azr; al-Ma<u>dj</u>arra; al-Manāzil; Minṭaḳat al-Burū<u>dj</u>; al-Nu<u>dj</u>ūm

see also Djughrāfiyā; Ḳibla.ii; al-Ḳubba; al-Kura; Makka.4; Mīḳāt.2; Mizwala
astronomers ʿAbd al-Raḥmān al-Ṣūfī; Abu ʾl-Ṣalt Umayya; ʿAlī al-Ḳūshdjī; al-Badīʿ al-Asṭurlābī; al-Battānī; al-Bīrūnī; al-Biṭrūdjī; Djābir b. Aflaḥ; al-Djaghmīnī; al-Farghānī; Ḥabash al-Ḥāsib al-Marwazī; Ibn Amādjūr; Ibn al-Bannāʾ al-Marrākushī; Ibn ʿIrāḳ; Ibn al-Ṣaffār; Ibn al-Samḥ; Ibn Yūnus; al-Kāshī; al-Khwārazmī, Abū Djaʿfar; al-Khāzin; al-Khazīnī; al-Khudjandī; Kushiyār b. Labān; Ḳuṭb al-Dīn Shīrāzī; al-Madjrīṭī; al-Mārdīnī; al-Marrākushī; Muḥammad b. ʿĪsā al-Māhānī; Muḥammad b. ʿUmar; al-Nayrīzī; al-Shayzarī; [in Suppl.] ʿAbd al-Salām b. Muḥammad
see also Baṭlamiyūs; al-Falakī; Falakī Shirwānī; Ibn al-Haytham; Ḳusṭā b. Lūḳā; Sindhind; [in Suppl.] Ibn al-Adjdābī; *and* → Astrology
celestial objects
comets **al-Nudjūm**.III.b
planets al-Ḳamar.I; al-Mirrīkh; al-Mushtarī; **al-Nudjūm**.II
see also Minṭaḳat al-Burūdj; Ruʾyat al-Hilāl; al-Saʿdānī
stars and constellations ʿAḳrab; ʿAnāḳ; al-Asad; Dadjādja; Fard; Kalb; Ḳird; Mahāt; Minṭaḳat al-Burūdj; Muthallath; Naʿām; Nasr; **al-Nudjūm**; Radīf.1; al-Sahm.1.c; Samak.9; Saraṭān.6; Shams.2; al-Shiʿrā; [in Suppl.] Arnab; Ghanam
see also al-Kayd; Saʿd wa-Naḥs (*and* al-Saʿdānī; Shaḳāwa); al-Sāḳ; Sulaḥfā
observatory Marṣad
terms al-Djawzahar; Istiḳbāl; al-Maṭāliʿ; al-Maṭlaʿ; al-Mayl; Muḳābala.1; Muḳanṭarāt; Niṣf al-Nahār; Radīf.1; Rubʿ; Ruʾyat al-Hilāl; al-Sāḳ; al-Samt; Shakkāziyya

Austria Beč; **Nemče**
see also Muslimūn.2.ii

B

Bābism → Sects

Bahais Bāb; Bābīs; Bahāʾ Allāh; **Bahāʾīs**; Mashriḳ al-Adhkār; Naḳḍ al-Mīthāḳ; Shawḳī Efendi Rabbānī
see also Lawḥ; Maẓhar; [in Suppl.] Anṣārī

Bahrain **al-Baḥrayn**; āl-Khalīfa; Madjlis.4.A.x; Maḥkama.4.ix
see also Ḳarmaṭī
toponyms al-Manāma; al-Muḥarraḳ
see also al-Mushaḳḳar

BALKANS **Balkan**; **Rūmeli**; al-Ṣaḳāliba
and → EUROPE

BANGLADESH **Bangāla**; Madjlis.4.C
see also Bengali; Nadhr al-Islām; Satya Pīr; [in Suppl.] Djarīda.vii
literature → LITERATURE.IN OTHER LANGUAGES
toponyms Bāḳargandj; Bangāla; Bōgrā; Chittagong; Ḍhākā; Dīnādjpur; Djassawr; Farīdpur; Sātgā'on; Silhet; Sundarban
see also Ruhmī; Sonārgā'on

BANKING Muḍāraba; Ribā.5; Suftadja
see also Djahbadh; Sharika

BASQUES **al-Bashkunish**
see also Ibn Gharsiya

BEDOUINS **Badw**; Bi'r; Dawār; Ghanīma; Ghazw; al-Hidjar
see also Liṣṣ; *and* → NOMADISM; SAUDI ARABIA; TRIBES.ARABIAN PENINSULA
writings on Rzewuski

BENIN Kandi; Kotonou; Kouandé

BERBERS **Berbers**; Judaeo-Berber
see also Ḥimāya.ii.II; Imẓad; al-Irdjānī; Ḳallala; Ḳiṣṣa.8; Leff; Libas.ii; Lithām; Mafākhir al-Barbar; Ṣaff.3; Shawiya.1; Ṣufriyya.2; *and* → ALGERIA
customary law 'Āda.ii; Ḳānūn.iv
dynasties 'Abd al-Wādids; 'Ammār; Marīnids; Midrār; al-Murābiṭūn; al-Muwaḥḥidūn; Razīn, Banū
language → LANGUAGES.AFRO-ASIATIC
religion al-Badjalī; Berbers.III; Ḥā-Mīm; Ṣāliḥ b. Ṭarīf
resistance Berbers.I.c; al-Kāhina; Kusayla; Maysara
tribes al-Barānis; Barghawāṭa; Birzāl; al-Butr; Djazūla; Ghāniya; Ghubrīnī; Ghumāra; Glāwā; Gudāla; Ḥāḥā; Hargha; Hawwāra; Hintāta; Ifoghas; Īfran; Iraten; Kutāma; Lamṭa; Lamtūna; Lawāta; Maghīla; Maghrāwa; Malzūza; Maṣmūda; Māssa; Maṭghara; Maṭmāṭa; Mazāta; Midyūna; Misrāta; al-Nafūsa; Nafza; Nafzāwa; Ṣanhādja; [in Suppl.] Awraba

BIBLE **Indjīl**
and → CHRISTIANITY; JUDAISM
biblical personages Ādam; 'Amālīḳ; Ayyūb; Āzar; 'Azāzīl; Bal'am; Bilḳīs; Binyāmīn; Bukht-naṣ(ṣ)ar; Dāniyāl; Dāwūd; Djabrā'īl; Djālūt; Fir'awn; Ḥābīl wa-Ḳābīl; Ḥām; Hāmān; Hārūn b. 'Imrān; Hārūt wa-Mārūt; Ḥawwā';

Ḥizḳīl; Ilyās; ʿImrān; Irmiyā; ʿĪsā; Isḥāḳ; Ismāʿīl; Kanʿān; Ḳārūn; Ḳiṭfīr; Kūsh; Lamak; Lazarus; Lūṭ; Maryam; al-Masīḥ; Namrūd; Nūḥ; Rāḥīl; Sām.1; al-Sāmirī; Sāra; Shamsūn; Shamwīl; Shaʿyā; Shīth; Sulaymān b. Dāwūd
see also Dhu 'l-Kifl; al-Fayyūm; Hūd; Idrīs
biblical toponyms Ṣihyawn
see also Djūdī
translations
into Arabic Fāris al-Shidyāḳ; Saʿadyā Ben Yōsēf; [in Suppl.] al-Bustānī.2
see also ʿArabiyya.A.ii.1; Judaeo-Arabic.iii.B
into Persian Abu 'l-Faḍl ʿAllāmī
see also Judaeo-Persian.i.2

BIBLIOGRAPHY **Bibliography**; Fahrasa

BOTANY Adwiya; al-ʿAshshāb; Nabāt
and → AGRICULTURE; FLORA; MEDICINE; PHARMACOLOGY
botanists Abū ʿUbayd al-Bakrī; al-Dīnawarī, Abū Ḥanīfa; Ibn al-Bayṭār; [in Suppl.] al-Ghāfiḳī; Ibn al-Rūmiyya
see also Abu 'l-Khayr al-Ishbīlī; Filāḥa; Nīḳūlāʾūs; al-Suwaydī

BULGARIA **Bulgaria**; Pomaks
see also Küčük Ḳaynardja; Muhādjir.2; Muslimūn.1.B.5
rivers Merič
toponyms Burgas; Deli-Orman; Dobrudja; Filibe; Hezārghrad; Küstendil; Newrokop; Nīkbūlī; ʿOthmān Pazar; Plewna; Rusčuk; Selwi; Shumnu; Ṣofya

BURMA Arakan; **Burma**; Mergui; Rangoon

BYZANTINE EMPIRE Biṭrīḳ; Ḳayṣar; **Rūm**
see also Anadolu.iii.1 and 2; Hiba.i; Iznīḳ; Ḳalāwdhiya; Ḳubrus; (al-) Ḳusṭanṭīniyya; al-Maṣṣīṣa; Muʾta; Nauplion.1; Saracens; *and* → PALESTINE; SYRIA; TURKEY
allies Djarādjima; Djarrāḥids; Ghassān; al-Ḥārith b. Djabala; Kinda.1; Salīḥ; [in Suppl.] Djabala b. al-Ḥārith
and → TRIBES
military Alay; Lamas-ṣū; Malāzgird.2; Naft.2; [in Suppl.] Dhāt al-Ṣawārī
see also al-ʿAwāṣim; Cilicia; Ṣāʾifa.1; Sayf al-Dawla

C

CALIPHATE Ahl al-Ḥall wa ʾl-ʿAḳd; Bayʿa; Ḥādjib.i; Ḥarb.ii; Hiba.i; Imāma; Ḳaḍīb; Kātib.i; **Khalīfa**; Libās.i; Madjlis.1; Marāsim.1; Mawākib.1; Shūrā.1
see also Amīr al-Muʾminīn; Ghulām.i; Khilʿa.ii; Laḳab.2; Māl al-Bayʿa; *and* → COURT CEREMONY

ʿAbbāsids (750-1258) **ʿAbbāsids**; Baghdād; Dīwān.i; Ḥādjib.i; Khalīfa.i.B; Marāsim.1; Mawākib.1; Muṣādara.2; Musawwida; Naḳīb.1; Naḳīb al-Ashrāf.1; Sāmarrāʾ
see also al-Abnaʾ.III; ʿAlī b. ʿAbd Allāh b. al-ʿAbbās; ʿAlids; Architecture.I.3; Ḍarība; Hāshimiyya; al-Hāshimiyya; Laḳab.2; Libās.i.4; Riḍā.2; al-Shuʿūbiyya; Sikka.2; *and* → DYNASTIES.PERSIA

caliphs Abu ʾl-ʿAbbās al-Saffāḥ; al-Amīn; al-Hādī ila ʾl-Ḥaḳḳ; Hārūn al-Rashīd; al-Ḳādir bi ʾllāh; al-Ḳāhir bi ʾllāh; al-Ḳāʾim bi-amr Allāh; al-Mahdī; al-Maʾmūn; al-Manṣūr; al-Muhtadī; al-Muḳtadī; al Muḳtadir; al-Muḳtafī bi-llāh; al-Muḳtafī li Amr Allāh; al-Muntaṣir; al-Mustaḍīʾ; al-Mustaʿīn (I); al-Mustaʿīn (II); al-Mustakfī; al-Mustandjid (I); al-Mustandjid (II); al-Mustanṣir (I); al-Mustanṣir (II); al-Mustarshid; al-Mustaʿṣim bi ʾllāh; al-Mustaẓhir bi ʾllāh; al-Muʿtaḍid bi ʾllāh; al-Muʿtamid ʿalā ʾllāh; al-Muʿtaṣim bi ʾllāh; al-Mutawakkil ʿalā ʾllāh; al-Muʿtazz bi ʾllāh; al-Muṭīʿ li ʾllāh; al-Muttaḳī li ʾllāh; al-Nāṣir li-Dīn Allāh, Abu ʾl-ʿAbbās; al-Rāḍī bi ʾllāh; al-Rāshid
see also ʿAbd Allāh b. ʿAlī; Būrān; al-Khayzurān bint ʿAṭāʾ al-Djurashiyya; Muḥammad b. ʿAlī b. ʿAbd Allāh; al-Muwaffaḳ; al-Ruṣāfa.2

viziers Abū ʿAbd Allāh Yaʿḳūb; Abū Salāma al-Khallāl; Abū ʿUbayd Allāh; ʿAḍud al-Dīn; ʿAlī b. ʿĪsa; al-Barāmika.3; al-Barīdī; al-Djardjarāʾī.1-3; al-Faḍl b. Marwān; al-Faḍl b. al-Rabīʿ; al-Faḍl b. Sahl b. Zadhānfarūkh; al-Fayḍ b. Abī Ṣāliḥ; Ḥamīd; Hibat Allāh b. Muḥammad; Ibn al-Alḳamī; Ibn al-Baladī; Ibn al-Furāt; Ibn Hubayra; Ibn Khāḳan.2 and 3; Ibn Makhlad; Ibn Muḳla; Ibn al-Muslima; Ibn al-Zayyāt; al-Iskāfī, Abu ʾl-Faḍl; al-Iskāfī, Abū Isḥāḳ; Ismāʿīl b. Bulbul; al-Khaṣībī; al-Rabīʿ b. Yūnus; Rabīb al-Dawla; al-Rūdhrāwarī
see also al-Djahshiyārī; Hilāl al-Ṣābiʾ; Khātam

secretaries Aḥmad b. Abī Khālid al-Aḥwal; Aḥmad b. Yūsuf; ʿAmr b. Masʿada; al-Ḥasan b. Sahl; Ibn al-Djarrāḥ; Ibn Khāḳan.1 and 4; Ibn al-Māshiṭa; al-Mūriyānī

historians of al-Djahshiyārī; Ibn Abi ʾl-Dam; Ibn Abī Ṭāhir Ṭayfūr; Ibn al-Djawzī; Ibn al-Naṭṭāḥ; Ibn al-Sāʿī; Ibn al-Ṭiḳṭaḳā; al-Madāʾinī; Ṣābiʾ.(3).4

other personages al-ʿAbbās b. ʿAmr al-Ghanawī; al-ʿAbbās b. al-Maʾmūn; al-ʿAbbās b. Muḥammad; ʿAbd Allāh b. ʿAlī; ʿAbd al-Djabbār b. ʿAbd al-

Raḥmān; ʿAbd al-Malik b. Ṣāliḥ; Abū ʿAwn; Abū Muslim; ʿAlī al-Riḍā; Badjkam; Badr al-Kharshanī; Bughā al-Kabīr; Bughā al-Sharābī; Dulafids; al-Fatḥ b. Khāḳān; Harthama b. Aʿyan; al-Ḥasan b. Zayd b. al-Ḥasan; Ḥātim b. Harthama; Ḥumayd b. ʿAbd al-Ḥamīd; Ibn Abi ʾl-Shawārib; Ibn Buhlūl; Ibn al-Djaṣṣāṣ.II; Ibn Ḥamdūn; Ibn Māhān; Ibn al-Mudabbir; Ibn al-Muʿtazz; Ibn Rāʾiḳ; Ibn Thawāba; Ibrāhīm b. ʿAbd Allāh; ʿĪsā b. Mūsā; ʿĪsā b. al-Shaykh; Ḳaḥṭaba; al-Ḳāsim b. ʿĪsā; Maʿn b. Zāʾida; al-Mubarḳaʿ; Muhallabids; Muḥammad b. ʿAbd Allāh (al-Nafs al-Zakiyya); Muḥammad b. Ṭughdj al-Ikhshīd; Muḥammad b. Yāḳūt; Muʾnis al-Faḥl; Muʾnis al-Muẓaffar; al-Muwaffaḳ; Naṣr b. Shabath; al-Nāṭiḳ bi ʾl-Ḥaḳḳ; al-Nūsharī; Rāfiʿ b. Harthama; Rāfiʿ b. al-Layth b. Naṣr b. Sayyār; al-Rāwandiyya; Rawḥ b. Ḥātim; Sādjids; Ṣāliḥ b. ʿAlī; al-Sarakhsī, Abu ʾl-ʿAbbās; al-Sarī; Shabīb b. Shayba; Sulaymān b. ʿAlī b. ʿAbd Allāh; Sunbādh; [in Suppl.] Abū Manṣūr b. Yūsuf; Aytākh al-Turkī; Badr al-Muʿtaḍidī; al-Dāmaghānī, Abū ʿAbd Allāh; al-Dāmaghānī, Abu ʾl-Ḥasan; al-Ghiṭrīf b. ʿAṭāʾ; Ibn Dirham

Fāṭimids (909-1171) Dīwān.i and ii.(2); **Fāṭimids**; Ḥādjib.iv; Ḥidjāb.II; al-Ḳāhira; Khalīfa.i.D; Libās.i.5; Marāsim.1; Mawākib.1

see also Laḳab.2; Ṣāḥib al-Bāb; Sitr

caliphs Abū ʿAbd Allāh al-Shīʿī; al-ʿĀḍid li-Dīn Allāh; al-Āmir; al-ʿAzīz bi ʾllāh; al-Ḥāfiẓ; al-Ḥākim bi-Amr Allāh; al-Ḳāʾim; al-Mahdī ʿUbayd Allāh; al-Manṣūr bi ʾllāh; al-Muʿizz li-Dīn Allāh; al-Mustaʿlī bi ʾllāh; al-Mustanṣir (bi ʾllāh)

viziers ʿAbbās b. Abi ʾl-Futūḥ; al-ʿĀdil b. al-Salār; al-Afḍal b. Badr al-Djamālī; al-Afḍal (Kutayfāt); Badr al-Djamālī; Bahrām; al-Baṭāʾiḥī; Ḍirghām; Djabr Ibn al-Ḳāsim; al-Djardjarāʾī.4; Ibn Killis; Ibn Maṣāl; Ruzzīk b. Ṭalāʾiʿ; Shāwar; Shīrkūh; [in Suppl.] Ibn Khalaf.2

secretaries Ibn Mammātī; Ibn al-Ṣayrafī; [in Suppl.] Ibn Khalaf, Abu ʾl-Ḥasan

historians of Ibn al-Ṭuwayr; al-Maḳrīzī; al-Musabbiḥī

see also Djawdhar

other personages Abū Yazīd al-Nukkārī; Bardjawān; Djawdhar; Djawhar al-Ṣiḳillī; Khalaf b. Mulāʿib al-Ashhabī; al-Kirmānī; Nizār b. al-Mustanṣir; al-Nuʿmān; Sitt al-Mulk

see also al-Farghānī

Rightly-Guided Caliphs (632-661) Khalīfa.i.A; Shūrā.1

caliphs Abū Bakr; ʿAlī b. Abī Ṭālib

see also Ḥarūrāʾ; Ibn Muldjam; Khalīfa.i.A; al-Saḳīfa; al-Ṣiddīḳ

other personages Abān b. ʿUthmān; ʿAbd Allāh b. al-ʿAbbās; ʿAbd Allāh b. ʿĀmir; ʿAbd Allāh b. Saʿd; ʿAbd Allāh b. Salām; ʿAbd Allāh b. Wahb; ʿAbd al-Raḥmān b. ʿAwf; ʿAbd al-Raḥmān b. Samura; Abu ʾl-Aswad al-Duʾalī; Abū Ayyūb al-Anṣārī; Abu ʾl-Dunyā; Abū ʿUbayda al-Djarrāḥ;

al-Aḥnaf b. Ḳays; al-Aḳraʿ b. Ḥābis; ʿAmr b. al-ʿĀṣ; al-As̲h̲ʿarī, Abū Mūsā; al-As̲h̲ʿat̲h̲; al-As̲h̲tar; al-Bāhilī; Ḥabīb b. Maslama; al-Ḳaʿḳāʿ b. ʿAmr; K̲h̲ālid b. al-Walīd; Muḥammad b. Abī Bakr; al-Mut̲h̲annā b. Ḥārit̲h̲a; Saʿīd b. al-ʿĀṣ; Sulaymān b. Ṣurad
and → MUḤAMMAD, THE PROPHET.COMPANIONS OF THE PROPHET *and* FAMILY OF THE PROPHET
Umayyads (661-750) Dimas̲h̲ḳ; Dīwān.i; Ḥād̲j̲ib.i; K̲h̲alīfa.i.A; Mawlā.2.b; [in Suppl.] Bādiya
see also Architecture.I.2; Ḳays ʿAylān; Libās.i.4; Marwānids; Sufyanids; *and* → DYNASTIES.SPAIN AND NORTH AFRICA
caliphs ʿAbd al-Malik b. Marwān; His̲h̲ām; Marwān I b. al-Ḥakam; Marwān II; Muʿāwiya I; Muʿāwiya II; Sulaymān b. ʿAbd al-Malik
see also Būṣīr; al-Ruṣāfa.3; al-S̲h̲ām.2(a)
historians of ʿAwāna b. al-Ḥakam al-Kalbī; al-Azdī
other personages ʿAbbād b. Ziyād; al-ʿAbbās b. al-Walīd; ʿAbd Allāh b. ʿAbd al-Malik; ʿAbd Allāh b. Hammām; ʿAbd Allāh b. Ḥanẓala; ʿAbd Allāh b. K̲h̲āzim; ʿAbd Allāh b. Muṭīʿ; ʿAbd Allāh b. al-Zubayr; ʿAbd al-ʿAzīz b. al-Ḥad̲j̲d̲j̲ād̲j̲; ʿAbd al-ʿAzīz b. Marwān; ʿAbd al-ʿAzīz b. al-Walīd; ʿAbd al-Raḥmān b. K̲h̲ālid; ʿAmr b. Saʿīd; Asad b. ʿAbd Allāh; al-Aṣamm.1; Bald̲j̲ b. Bis̲h̲r; Bis̲h̲r b. Marwān; Bis̲h̲r b. al-Walīd; Bukayr b. Māhān; Bukayr b. Wis̲h̲āḥ; Busr; al-Ḍaḥḥāḳ b. Ḳays al-Fihrī; al-D̲j̲arrāḥ b. ʿAbd Allāh; al-D̲j̲unayd b. ʿAbd Allāh; al-Ḥad̲j̲d̲j̲ād̲j̲ b. Yūsuf; Ḥanẓala b. Ṣafwān; al-Ḥārit̲h̲ b. Surayd̲j̲; Ḥassān b. Mālik; Ḥassān b. al-Nuʿmān al-G̲h̲assānī; al-Ḥurr b. Yazīd; al-Ḥusayn b. Numayr; Ibn al-As̲h̲ʿat̲h̲; Ibn al-Ḥaḍramī; Ibn Hubayra; K̲h̲ālid b. ʿAbd Allah al-Ḳasrī; K̲h̲ālid b. Yazīd b. Muʿāwiya; Kult̲h̲ūm b. ʿIyāḍ al-Ḳus̲h̲ayrī; Ḳurra b. S̲h̲arīk; Ḳutayba b. Muslim; Maʿn b. Zāʾida; Masāmiʿa; Maslama b. ʿAbd al-Malik b. Marwān; Maymūn b. Mihrān; Muʿāwiya b. His̲h̲ām; al-Mug̲h̲īra b. S̲h̲uʿba; Muhallabids; Muḥammad b. al-Ḳāsim; Muslim b. ʿUḳba; Naṣr b. Sayyār; al-Nuʿmān b. Bas̲h̲īr; Rawḥ b. Zinbāʿ; Salm b. Ziyād b. Abīhi; S̲h̲abīb b. Yazīd; Sulaymān b. Kat̲h̲īr; [in Suppl.] ʿAdī b. Arṭāt
see also al-Baṭṭāl; Iyās b. Muʿāwiya
treatises on al-Ḳalḳas̲h̲andī.1

CARTOGRAPHY K̲h̲arīṭa
and → GEOGRAPHY; NAVIGATION
cartographers al-Falakī; Ibn Sarābiyūn; Meḥmed Reʾīs; Pīrī Reʾīs

CAUCASUS Ād̲h̲arbayd̲j̲ān.ii; Armīniya; Dāg̲h̲istān; **al-Ḳabḳ**; al-Kurd̲j̲
see also D̲j̲arīda.iv; Ḳarā Bāg̲h̲; Muhād̲j̲ir.2; S̲h̲īrwān S̲h̲āh
physical geography
mountains al-Ḳabḳ

waters Alindjaḳ; Gökče-tengiz; Ḳarā Deniz; Ḳïzïl-üzen; Ḳuban; Kur; al-Rass; Safīd Rūd

population Abkhāz.2; Alān; Andi; Arči; Avars; Balkar; Čečens; Čerkes; Darghin; Dido; Ingush; Kabards; Ḳapuča; Ḳaračay; Ḳarata; Ḳaytaḳ; Khaputs; Khemshin; Khinalug; Khunzal; Khvarshï; Ḳrïz; Ḳubači; Kwanadi; Laḳ; Laz; Lezgh; Noghay; Ossetians; Rūs; Rutul; [in Suppl.] Demography.VI
see also Ḳumuḳ

resistance to Russian conquest Ḥamza Beg; Shāmil
see also Ḥizb.iv

toponyms
ancient Alindjaḳ; Arrān; Bādjarwān.1; Balandjar; Dwin; Saray; Shammākha; Shimshāṭ; Shīrwān; Shīz
present-day Akhiskha; Astrakhān; Bāb al-Abwāb; Bākū; Bardhaʿa; Batumi; Derbend; Gandja; Ḳubba; Lankoran; Makhač-ḳalʿe; Nakhčiwān; Shakkī; [in Suppl.] Djulfā.I

CENTRAL ASIA Badakhshān; Čaghāniyān; Khʷārazm; **Mā warāʾ al-Nahr**; Mogholistān
see also Hayāṭila; Ismāʿīl b. Aḥmad; Ḳarā Khiṭāy; Ḳazaḳ; Nīzak, Ṭarkhān; [in Suppl.] Atalïḳ; Djulfā.II; *and* → DYNASTIES.MONGOLS; MONGOLIA; ONOMASTICS

architecture → ARCHITECTURE.REGIONS

belles-lettres → LITERATURE.DRAMA *and* POETRY.TURKISH.IN EASTERN TURKISH

former Soviet Union al-ʿArab.iii.Appendix; Basmačis; Djarīda.iv; Fiṭrat; Ḥizb.v; Khodjaev; Ṣadr al-Dīn ʿAynī; [in Suppl.] Demography.VI
and → *the section Toponyms in this entry*

historians of ʿAbd al-Karīm Bukhārī
see also Ḥaydar b. ʿAlī

mysticism → MYSTICISM; SAINTHOOD

physical geography
deserts Ḳaraḳum; Ḳïzïl-ḳum
mountains Ala Dagh; Altai; Balkhān; Pamirs
see also Čopan-ata
waters Aḳ Ṣu; Amū Daryā; Aral; Atrek; Baḥr al-Khazar; Balkhash; Čaghān-rūd; Ču; Ili; İssïk-kul; Ḳarā-köl; Murghāb; Sïr Daryā
see also Su

population Balūč; Čāwdors (*and* [in Suppl.] Čawdor); Emreli; Gagauz; Ḳaraḳalpaḳ; Khaladj; Ḳungrāt; Ḳurama; Özbeg; [in Suppl.] Demography.VI
see also Altaians; al-ʿArab.iii.Appendix; Ghalča; Ghuzz; Ḳarluḳ; Ḳazaḳ; Ḳipčaḳ; Ḳïrgïz; Ḳumān; Kumīdjīs; Ḳun; [in Suppl.] Ersarï

toponyms
ancient Abaskūn; Abīward; Akhsīkath; Ardjīsh; Balāsāghūn; Banākat; Fārāb; Firabr; Gurgandj; Kāth; Ḳayalïḳ; Marw al-Rudh; Marw al-Shāhidjān; Mashhad-i Miṣryān; Nakhshab; Pishpek; Sayrām; Shūmān; Sïghnāḳ; al-Ṣughd; Sūyāb; [in Suppl.] Dandānḳān; Djand; Īlāḳ
present-day
districts Atek; Ḳaratigin; Shughnān
see also Ākhāl Tekke
regions Farghānā; Khwārazm; Khuttalan; Labāb; Mangïshlak; [in Suppl.] Dasht-i Ḳïpčaḳ
towns Aḳ Masdjid.2; Alma Ata; Āmul.2; Andidjān; ʿAshḳābād; Awliyā Ata; Bayram ʿAlī; Bukhārā; Čimkent; Djalālābād; Ghudjduwān; Hazārasp; Ḥiṣār; Kash; Khīwa; Khoḳand; Khudjand(a); Kish; Ḳubādhiyān; Marghīnān; Mayhana; Ordūbād; Özkend; Pandjdih; Samarḳand

CHAD Abeshr; Bagirmi; Borkou; Kanem; Kanuri; [in Suppl.] **Čad**
and → AFRICA.CENTRAL AFRICA

CHARMS Afsūn; Ḥidjāb.IV; Kabid.4; Māshāʾ Allāh; [in Suppl.] Budūḥ
see also Kahrubā; Ḳarwasha; *and* → MAGIC

CHILDHOOD → LIFE STAGES

CHINA Djarīda.v; Masdjid.V, **al-Ṣīn**
see also Bahādur; Khoḳand; Ṣīnī
dynasties Ḳarā Khiṭāy
see also Faghfūr; Gūrkhān
personages
for leaders in uprisings, see below
literary figures Liu Chih; Ma Huan
officials P'u Shou-keng
physical geography
waters Aḳ Ṣu; Ili
population Salar
toponyms
ancient Bishbalïḳ; Khansā; Shūl.1
present-day Aḳ Ṣu; Alti Shahr; Kansu; Kāshghar; Khānbalïḳ; Khānfū; Khotan; Ḳuldja; Ning-hsia; Shansi; Shen-si; Sinkiang; Szechuan
see also Sandābil; Ṣīn (Čīn) Kalān
treatises on ʿAlī Akbar Khiṭāʾī

uprisings Panthay
leaders Ma Chung-ying; Ma Hua-lung; Ma Ming-hsin; Pai Yen-hu

CHRISTIANITY Ahl al-Kitāb; Dayr; Dayṣāniyya; ʿĪsā; Kanīsa; Maryam; **Naṣārā**; Rāhib; al-Ṣalīb
see also Dhimma; Djizya; Ghiyār; al-Ḥākim bi-Amr Allāh; Ifrandj; Karshūnī; Ḳūmis; Lāhūt and Nāsūt.2; Maʿalthāyā; [in Suppl.] Dāwiyya and Isbitāriyya; Fidāʾ; *and* → BIBLE; CRUSADE(R)S; LANGUAGES.AFRO-ASIATIC.ARABIC.CHRISTIAN ARABIC; NUBIA
apologetics Ibn Zurʿa; al-Kindī, ʿAbd al-Masīḥ
churches **Kanīsa**; Sihyawn
see also Masdjid.I.B.3
communities Anadolu.iii.4; al-Andalus.iv; Istanbul.vii.b; Mozarab; al-Shām.2(a) (271b-2a)
see also Fener
denominations Ḳibṭ; Nasṭūriyyūn
and → JUDAISM.JEWISH SECTS
Catholics Bashīr Shihāb II; Isḥāḳ, Adīb; Ṣābundjī; Ṣāyigh, Fatḥ Allāh; Shaykhū, Luwīs; [in Suppl.] Buṭrus Karāma
Copts Ibn al-ʿAssāl; Ibn Mammātī; Ibn al-Muḳaffaʿ; **Ḳibṭ**; al-Makīn b. al-ʿAmīd; Māriya; al-Mufaḍḍal b. Abi 'l-Faḍāʾil; [in Suppl.] Ibn Kabar; Ibn al-Rāhib
see also Sullam; *and* → EGYPT.TOPONYMS; NUBIA
Greek orthodox Gagauz
see also Paṭrīk
Jacobites Ibn al-ʿIbrī; Ibn Zurʿa
see also al-Kindī, ʿAbd al-Masīḥ; Paṭrīk
Maronites Farḥāt; Isṭifān al-Duwayhī; al-Rayḥānī; Salīm al-Naḳḳāsh; [in Suppl.] Abū Shabaka; al-Bustānī
see also Bsharrā; Durūz.ii; Paṭrīk; *and* → LEBANON
Melkites Abū Ḳurra; al-Antāḳī; Mīkhāʾīl al-Ṣabbāgh; al-Muḳawḳis; Saʿīd b. al-Biṭrīḳ; [in Suppl.] Ibn al-Ḳuff
see also Mashāḳa; Paṭrīk
Monophysites al-Akhṭal; al-Ḳuṭāmī
Nestorians Ibn Buṭlān; Ibn al-Ṭayyib; al-Kindī, ʿAbd al-Masīḥ; Mattā b. Yūnus; **Nasṭūriyyūn**; Sābūr b. Sahl
Protestants Fāris al-Shidyāḳ; Mashāḳa; Ṣarrūf; Ṣāyigh, Tawfīḳ; [in Suppl.] al-Bustānī.2
see also Nimr
unspecified Baḥdal; Ibn al-Tilmīdh; al-Masīḥī; Petrus Alfonsi; [in Suppl.] Ḥubaysh b. al-Ḥasan al-Dimashḳī; Ibn al-Ṣuḳāʿī

monasteries **Dayr**; Dayr al-Djāthalīḳ; Dayr Kaʿb; Dayr Ḳunnā; Dayr Murrān; Dayr Samʿān
see also Khānḳāh; Rāhib
writings on al-Shābushtī
polemics Ahl al-Kitāb
anti-Jewish Petrus Alfonsi
Christian-Muslim al-Suʿūdī, Abu 'l-Faḍl
pre-Islamic Abraha; ʿAdī b. Zayd; ʿAmr b. ʿAdī; ʿAmr b. Hind; Baḥīrā; Bahrām
see also Ghassān; Lakhmids
saints Djirdjīs; Djuraydj
20th-century al-Khūrī; Ṣarrūf; Shaykhū, Luwīs; [in Suppl.] Abū Shabaka; Abyaḍ
see also al-Maʿlūf

CIRCUMCISION Khafḍ; **Khitān**
see also ʿAbdī; ʿAlī; Kurds.iv.A.i; Mawākib.4.11

CLOTHING Banīḳa; Djallāb; Farw; Ḳumāsh; **Libās**; Sirwāl
see also Ghiyār; Iḥrām; Khayyāṭ; Khilʿa; Kurds.iv.C.1; Shiʿār.4; *and* → MYSTICISM.DRESS
accessories Mandīl; Mirwaḥa
see also Shadd
headwear Ḳawuḳlu
see also Sharīf.(5)
veils Ḥidjāb.I; Lithām
materials Farw; Ḥarīr; Kattān; Khaysh; Ḳuṭn; Ṣūf
see also Fanak; Ḳalamkārī; Ḳumāsh; Lubūd; Mukhattam

COLOUR **Lawn**; Musawwida
and → DYEING
colours Asfar
see also Sharīf.(5)

COMMERCE Bayʿ; Imtiyāzāt; Kasb; Ḳirāḍ
see also Inshāʾ; Sūḳ; *and* → INDUSTRY; LAW.LAW OF OBLIGATIONS
commercio-legal terms Mufāwaḍa; Mushāraka
functions Dallāl; Malik al-Tudjdjār; Shāh Bandar
trade Ḳahwa; Kārimī; Ḳuṭn; Lubān
see also Kalah; Kārwān; Ḳaysāriyya; Kirmān; Mīnāʾ; Ṣafawids.II; Szechuan

COMMONWEALTH OF INDEPENDENT STATES → CAUCASUS; CENTRAL ASIA; COMMUNISM; EUROPE.EASTERN EUROPE

COMMUNICATIONS Barīd; Ḥamām; Manār
see also Anadolu.iii.(5); *and* → TRANSPORT

COMMUNISM Ḥizb.i; **Shuyūʿiyya**
see also Lāhūtī

CONGO **Congo**; al-Murdjibī

COSMETICS al-Kuḥl
see also Khiḍāb

COSMOGRAPHY ʿAdjāʾib; ʿĀlam; Falak; Ḳāf; Samāʾ.1
see also Djughrāfiyā; al-Khaḍir; Kharīṭa; al-Kura; Makka.4; *and* → ASTROLOGY; ASTRONOMY; GEOGRAPHY
treatises on al-Dimashḳī; al-Ḳazwīnī, Zakariyyāʾ; al-Kharaḳī
see also Kitāb al-Djilwa

COURT CEREMONY **Marāsim**; Mawākib
see also Hiba; Khilʿa; Miẓalla; Naḳḳāra-khāna; Nithār; Sitr; *and* → MONARCHY.ROYAL INSIGNIA

CREATION **Ibdāʿ**; **Khalḳ**
see also Ḥudūth al-ʿĀlam; Insān

CRETE **Iḳrīṭish**
see also Abū Ḥafṣ ʿUmar al-Ballūṭī
toponyms
towns Ḳandiya

CRUSADE(R)S **Crusades**; [in Suppl.] Dāwiyya and Isbitāriyya
see also al-ʿĀdil.1; al-Afḍal b. Badr al-Djamālī; (Sīrat) ʿAntar; Ayyūbids; Balak; Baybars I; Fāṭimids.5; Ifrandj; Ḳalāwūn; Ḳilidj Arslan I; Nūr al-Dīn Maḥmūd b. Zankī; Ṣalāḥ al-Dīn; al-Shām.2(a); *and* → *the section Toponyms under* PALESTINE *and* SYRIA
battles al-Manṣūra; Mardj al-Ṣuffar; Nīkbūlī
castles al-Dārūm; Ḥārim; Ḥiṣn al-Akrād; Ḳalʿat al-Shaḳīf; Ṣāfītha
conquests ʿAkkā; Anadolu.iii.1; ʿĀsḳalān; Ayla; Ghazza; Ḥayfā; Ḳayṣariyya; al-Khalīl; Ḳubrus.2; al-Ḳuds.10; Ludd; Maʿarrat al-Nuʿmān
historians of Ibn al-Ḳalānisī
see also al-Nuwayrī, Muḥammad

CRYPTOGRAPHY **Muʿammā**; Ramz.2

see also Kitābāt.5; al-Sīm

CUISINE **Maṭbakh**
drinks Čay; Ḳahwa; Khamr; Kumis; **Mashrūbāt**; Nabīdh; Sherbet
see also Naḥl; [in Suppl.] Čāy-khāna
food **Ghidhā'**; Kabid.5; Khubz; Kuskusū; Mishmish; Nārandj; al-Ruzz; al-Samn; Sawīḳ; Sha'īr; Sikbādj; Sukkar; [in Suppl.] Basbās; Djawz; Ḥays; Hindibā'
see also Baḳḳāl; Filāḥa; Ḳamḥ; Maḍīra; Milḥ; Naḥl; Pist; Simsim; [in Suppl.] Ibn Shaḳrūn al-Miknāsī
herbs Shibithth; [in Suppl.] Basbās
see also Shīḥ
prohibitions Ghidhā'.iii and iv.7; Ḳahwa; Khamr; Mashrūbāt; Mayta; Nabīdh
see also Dhabīḥa.1; Ḥayawān.4; Nadjis; *and* → *individual articles under* ANIMALS
spices Kammūn; Ḳaranful; [in Suppl.] **Afāwīh**; Dār Ṣīnī
see also Kārimī; Ḳūṣ; Milḥ

CUSTOM **'Āda**; Adab
see also Abd al-Raḥmān al-Fāsī; 'Āshūrā'.II; Hiba; Ḥidjāb.I; Īdjāra; Khil'a; Mandīl; *and* → LAW.CUSTOMARY LAW
tribal customs 'Abābda; al-Dhunūb, Dafn; Khāwa; Muwāraba; [in Suppl.] 'Ār
see also Īdjāra

CYPRUS **Ḳubrus**; Madjlis.4.A.xxiv
toponyms
towns Lefḳosha; Maghōsha

(former) CZECHOSLOVAKIA [in Suppl.] **Čeh**

D

DEATH Djanāza; Ḥināṭa; Intiḥār; Ḳabr; Maḳbara; **Mawt**; Niyāḥa; [in Suppl.] Ghassāl
see also Ghā'ib; Ghusl; Ḳatl; Marthiya; Shahīd; *and* → ARCHITECTURE.MONUMENTS.TOMBS; ESCHATOLOGY

DESERTS al-Aḥḳāf; Biyābānak; al-Dahnā'; Ḳaraḳum; Ḳizil-ḳum; Nafūd; al-Naḳb; al-Rub' al-Khālī; Sāḥil; al-Ṣaḥrā'; Sīnā'
see also (Djazīrat) al-'Arab.ii; Badw.II; Ḥarra; Khabrā'; Reg; Samūm

DICTIONARY **Ḳāmūs**
see also Fāris al-Shidyāḳ; Sullam; *and* → LEXICOGRAPHY

DIPLOMACY Imtiyāzāt; Mübādele
see also Amān; Bālyōs; Berātlî; Daftar; Hiba; Inshāʾ; Kātib; Ḳawwās; Mandates
diplomatic accounts Aḥmad Rasmī; Ibn Faḍlān; Meḥmed Yirmisekiz; [in Suppl.] al-Ghazzāl; Ibn ʿUthmān al-Miknāsī
see also Ṣubḥī Meḥmed
diplomats Consul; Elči; Safīr.2

DIVINATION **Kihāna**
see also Djafr; Ibn Barradjān; Malāḥim; Nudjūm (Aḥkām al-); Shāma; *and* → ASTROLOGY; DREAMS
diviners ʿArrāf; Kāhin
practices Faʾl; Firāsa; Ghurāb; Ḥisāb al-Djummal; Ḥurūf; Ikhtilādj; Istiḳsām; ʿIyāfa; al-Kaff; Katif; Khaṭṭ; Khawāṣṣ al-Ḳurʾān; Ḳiyāfa; Ḳurʿa; Māʾ.1; Riyāfa
see also Būḳalā; Ikhtiyārāt; Mirʾāt
treatises on Fāl-nāma; Ibn al-Bannāʾ al-Marrākushī; Malḥama; [in Suppl.] Ibn ʿAzzūz
see also Djafr; Nudjūm (Aḥkām al-)

(DIVINE) PUNISHMENT **ʿAdhāb**; ʿAdhāb al-Ḳabr; Djazāʾ.ii; Falaḳa; Ḥadd; Maskh; Ṣalb
see also ʿAbd.3.i; ʿĀd; Kaffāra; Ḳiyāma; Munkar wa-Nakīr; Murtadd; Siyāsa.1; *and* → LAW

DIVORCE Barāʾa.I; Faskh; Suknā; al-Suraydjiyya
see also ʿAbd.3; ʿĀda; Ghāʾib; Ḥaḍāna; Ibn Suraydj; ʿIdda; ʿIwaḍ; Ḳasam; Liʿān; al-Marʾa.2; Rapak

DOCUMENTS ʿAlāma; **Diplomatic**; Farmān; Inshāʾ; Kātib; Manshūr; Papyrus; **Sidjill**; [in Suppl.] Dabīr
see also Barāʾa.I; Ḳaṭʿ; Sharṭ.1; *and* → ADMINISTRATION.RECORDS; WRITING
Ottoman ʿArḍ Ḥāl; Berāt; **Diplomatic**.iv; Farmān.ii; Irāde; Khaṭṭ-i Humāyūn and Khaṭṭ-i Sherīf; **Sidjill**.3
and → OTTOMAN EMPIRE.ADMINISTRATION

DREAMS **Ruʾyā**
see also Istikhāra; Nubuwwa; *and individual articles on animals, in particular* Ayyil; Baghl; Ḍabb; Fīl; Ghurāb; Saraṭān.5

treatises on al-Dīnawarī, Abū Saʿīd; Ibn Ghannām; Ibn Shāhīn al-Ẓāhirī; Ibn Sīrīn

DRUGS **Adwiya**; [in Suppl.] Anzarūt
see also Kahrubā; al-Kuḥl; *and* → MEDICINE; PHARMACOLOGY
narcotics Afyūn; Bandj; Ḥashīsh; Ḳāt; Shahdānadj
see also Filāḥa.iii
tobacco Bahāʾī Meḥmed Efendi

DRUZES al-Darazī; **Durūz**; Ḥamza b. ʿAlī; al-Muḳtanā; Shakīb Arslān; [in Suppl.] Binn
see also Ḥadd; Maḥkama.4.ii, iii and v; Maʿn; [in Suppl.] Dawr; Ḥinn; *and* → LEBANON
historians of Ṣāliḥ b. Yaḥyā

DYEING ʿAfṣ; Ḥinnāʾ; Ḳalamkārī; **Khiḍāb**; Nīl
see also Shaʿr.1
dyer **Ṣabbāgh**

DYNASTIES **Dawla**; Ḥādjib; Mushīr
see also Čāshna-gīr; Khādim al-Ḥaramayn; Laḳab; Libās.i; Malik; Marāsim; Mashwara; Mawākib; Pādishāh; Parda-dār; *and* → ADMINISTRATION; ONOMASTICS.TITLES
Afghanistan and India ʿĀdil-Shāhs; Arghūn; Bahmanīs; Barīd Shāhīs; Dihlī Sultanate; Fārūḳids; Ghaznawids; Ghūrids; Hindu-shāhīs; ʿImād Shāhī; Kart; Khaldjīs; Ḳuṭb Shāhī; Lōdīs; Mughals; Niẓām Shāhīs; Sayyids; Sharḳīs; Sūrs; [in Suppl.] Bānīdjūrids
see also Afghānistān.v.2 and 3; Awadh; Dāwūdpōtrās; Dīwān.v; Hind.iv; Khʷādja-i Djahān; Lashkar; Marāsim.5; Mawākib.5; Nithār; Rānā Sāngā; Sammā; *and* → ARCHITECTURE.REGIONS; MILITARY.INDO-MUSLIM; ONOMASTICS.TITLES.INDO-MUSLIM
ʿĀdil-Shāhs (1490-1686) **ʿĀdil-Shāhs**; Bīdjāpūr; Hind.vii.ix
rulers Muḥammad b. Ibrāhīm II
historians of Shīrāzī, Rafīʿ al-Dīn
Awadh Nawwābs (1722-1856) **Awadh**
rulers Burhān al-Mulk; Ghāzi ʾl-Dīn Ḥaydar; Saʿādat ʿAlī Khān; Ṣafdar Djang; Shudjāʿ al-Dawla
viziers Mahdī ʿAlī Khān
Bahmanids (1347-1527) **Bahmanīs**; Hind.vii.vii
see also Bīdar; Gulbargā; Pēshwā
rulers Humāyūn Shāh Bahmanī; Maḥmūd Shihāb al-Dīn; Muḥammad I; Muḥammad II; Muḥammad III

other personages Khalīl Allāh; Maḥmūd Gāwān
Bārakzays (1819-1973) Afghānistān.v.3.B
kings ʿAbd al-Raḥmān Khān; Dūst Muḥammad; Ḥabīb Allāh Khān; Shīr ʿAlī; [in Suppl] Amān Allāh
Bengal Nawwābs
rulers ʿAlī Werdī Khān; Djaʿfar; Sirādj al-Dawla
see also Murshidābād
Bengal Sultans (1336-1576)
sultans Dāwūd Khān Kararānī; Fakhr al-Dīn Mubārakshāh; Ḥusayn Shāh; Maḥmūd; Rādjā Ganesh; Rukn al-Dīn Bārbak Shāh; Sikandar Shāh
historians of [in Suppl.] ʿAbbās Sarwānī
Dihlī Sultans (1206-1555) Ḍarība.6.a; **Dihlī Sultanate**; Dīwān.v; Khaldjīs; Lōdīs; Nāʾib.1; Naḳīb.2; Sayyids; Sūrs
see also Burdj.III.2
sultans Fīrūz Shāh Tughluḳ; Ghiyāth al-Dīn Tughluḳ I; Ghiyāth al-Dīn Tughluḳ Shāh II; Iltutmish; Kayḳubād; Khiḍr Khān; Ḳuṭb al-Dīn Aybak; Maḥmūd; Ibrāhīm Lōdī; Mubārak Shāh; Muḥammad b. Tughluḳ; Muḥammad Shāh I Khaldjī; Raḍiyya; Shir Shāh Sūr; [in Suppl.] Balban; Dawlat Khān Lōdī
viziers Kāfūr (*and* Malik Kāfūr); Khān-i Djahān Maḳbūl; Miʾān Bhuʾā
historians of Baranī; al-Djuzdjānī; Niẓāmī (*and* [in Suppl.] Ḥasan Niẓāmī); Shams al-Dīn-i Sirādj ʿAfīf
other personages Mallū Iḳbāl Khān; [in Suppl.] ʿAbd al-Wahhāb Bukhārī; ʿAyn al-Mulk Multānī; Daryā Khān Noḥānī; Ikhtisān
see also ʿAlī Mardān; Hūlāgū; Khaldjīs; Sammā
Durrānīs (1747-1842) Afghānistān.v.3
kings Aḥmad Shāh Durrānī
historians of ʿAbd al-Karīm Munshī
other personages Kāmrān Shāh Durrānī
Fārūḳids (1370-1601) **Fārūḳids**
rulers Mīrān Muḥammad Shāh I
Ghaznawids (977-1186) ʿAmīd; Dīwān.v; **Ghaznawids**
see also Ḥiṣār.iii
rulers Alp Takīn; Bahrām Shāh; Ismāʿīl b. Sebüktigin; Maḥmūd b. Sebüktigin; Masʿūd b. Maḥmūd; Mawdūd b. Masʿūd; Muḥammad b. Maḥmūd b. Sebüktigin; Sebüktigin
viziers Aḥmad b. Muḥammad; Altūntāsh; al-Faḍl b. Aḥmad al-Isfarāʾinī; Ḥasanak; Maymandī
historians of Bayhaḳī
see also al-Ḳāshānī; Shabānkāraʾī; [in Suppl.] Fakhr-i Mudabbir
other personages Muḥammad Bakhtiyār Khaldjī; Shāh Malik

Ghūrids (ca. 1000-1215) **Ghūrids**
rulers Djahān-sūz; Muḥammad b. Sām; Sayf al-Dīn
see also Niẓāmī
Gudjarāt Sultans (1391-1583) Gudjarāt.c
sultans Bahādur Shāh Gudjarātī; Maḥmūd
historians of [in Suppl.] Ḥādjdjī al-Dabīr
other personages Malik Ayāz
Kālpī Sultans Kalpī
sultans Maḥmūd Khān
Kashmīr Sultans (1346-1589) Kashmīr.i.4
sultans Sikandar (But-Shikan); [in Suppl.] Čaks
see also [in Suppl.] Gul Khātūn
historians of [in Suppl.] Ḥaydar Malik
other personages [in Suppl.] Bayḥaḳī Sayyids
Langāh dynasty of Multān (1437-1526) Multān
sultans Ḥusayn Shāh Langāh I; Ḥusayn Shāh Langāh II
Madura Sultans
sultans Djalāl al-Dīn Aḥsan
Mālwā Sultans (1401-1531) Mālwā
sultans Dilāwar Khān; Hūshang Shāh Ghūrī; Maḥmūd
see also Bāz Bahādur
viziers Mēdinī Rā'ī
other personages Malik Mughīth
Mughals (1526-1858) Ḍarība.6.b and c; Dīwān.v; Manṣab; **Mughals**; [in Suppl.] Ilāhī Era
see also Fawdjdār; Kōtwāl; Maṭbakh.4; Nithār; Ṣadr.5; Ṣūba; Ṣūbadār; Ṣūfiyāna; Ṣulḥ-i kull; Suwār; [in Suppl.] Dāgh u taṣḥīḥa; ʿIbādat Khāna
emperors Aḥmad Shāh.I; Akbar; Awrangzīb; Bābur; Bahādur Shāh I; Bahādur Shāh II; Djahāndār Shāh; Djahāngīr; Farrukh-siyar; Humāyūn; Muḥammad Shāh; Shāh ʿĀlam II; Shāh Djahān
see also Darshan; Mumtāz Maḥall; Nūr Djahān
viziers Iʿtimād al-Dawla
secretaries Abu 'l-Faḍl ʿAllāmī; Muḥammad Kāẓim
historians of ʿAbd al-Ḥamīd Lāhawrī; Abu 'l Faḍl ʿAllāmī; Bakhtāwar Khān; Djawhar; Ghulām Ḥusayn Khān Ṭabāṭabā'ī; ʿInāyat Allāh Khān; Īsar-dās; Khʷāfī Khān; Muḥammad Kāẓim; Muḥammad Sharīf; Mustaʿidd Khān; Muʿtamad Khān; Niʿmat Allāh b. Ḥabīb Allāh Harawī; Nūr al-Ḥaḳḳ al-Dihlawī; [in Suppl.] ʿĀḳil Khān Rāzī
see also Aẓfarī; Badā'ūnī; Ma'āthir al-Umarā'
other personages ʿAbd al-Raḥīm Khān; ʿAlī Werdī Khān; Āṣaf Khān; Bakhtāwar Khān; Bayram Khān; Burhān al-Mulk; Dāniyāl; Ghulām Ḳādir Rohilla; Hindāl; Iʿtibār Khān; Iʿtiḳād Khān; ʿIwaḍ Wadjīh;

Kāmrān; K̲h̲ān Djahān Lōdī; K̲h̲usraw Sulṭān; Mahābat K̲h̲ān; Mak̲h̲dūm al-Mulk (*and* [in Suppl.] 'Abd Allāh Sulṭānpūrī); Mān Singh; Mīr Djumla; Mīrzā 'Askarī; Mīrzā 'Azīz "Kōka"; Murād; Murād Bak̲h̲s̲h̲; Murs̲h̲id Ḳulī K̲h̲ān; Niẓām al-Mulk; S̲h̲afī'ā Yazdī; S̲h̲āh Manṣūr S̲h̲īrāzī; S̲h̲arīf Āmulī; al-Siyālkūtī; [in Suppl.] Akbar b. Awrangzīb; 'Āḳil K̲h̲ān Rāzī; G̲h̲āzī K̲h̲ān; Gūran; 'Ināyat K̲h̲ān (2x) *see also* Bāra Sayyids (*and* [in Suppl.] Bārha Sayyids); Marāt̲h̲ās
Niẓām S̲h̲āhids (1491-1633)   **Niẓām S̲h̲āhīs**
 see also Aḥmadnagar
 rulers   Ḥusayn Niẓām S̲h̲āh; Malik Aḥmad Baḥrī
 other personages   Malik 'Ambar
S̲h̲arḳī Sultans of Djawnpūr (1394-1479)   **S̲h̲arḳīs**
 sultans   Ḥusayn S̲h̲āh; Ibrāhīm S̲h̲āh S̲h̲arḳī; Maḥmūd S̲h̲āh S̲h̲arḳī; Malik Sarwar
Africa   Fundj; Gwandu; S̲h̲īrāzī
 see also Bū Sa'īd; Dār Fūr; Kilwa; Songhay
Anatolia and the Turks   Artuḳids; Aydin-og̲h̲lu; Dānis̲h̲mendids; D̲h̲u 'l-Ḳadr; Eretna; Germiyān-og̲h̲ullari̊; Ḥamīd Og̲h̲ullari̊; Īnāl; Isfendiyār Og̲h̲lu; Ḳarāmān-og̲h̲ullari̊; Ḳarasi̊; Mentes̲h̲e-og̲h̲ullari̊; 'Ot̲h̲mānli̊; Saltuḳ Og̲h̲ullari̊; Ṣarūk̲h̲ān; S̲h̲āh-i Arman
 see also Būrids; Derebey; Mangi̊ts; Mengüček; Ramaḍān Og̲h̲ullari̊; *and* → ONOMASTICS.TITLES
Artuḳids (1102-1408)   **Artuḳids**
 rulers   Īlg̲h̲āzī; Nūr al-Dīn Muḥammad
Aydin-og̲h̲lu (1308-1425)   **Aydin-og̲h̲lu**
 amīrs   Djunayd
Ottomans (1281-1924)   **'Ot̲h̲mānli**
 see also 'Ot̲h̲mān I; *and* → OTTOMAN EMPIRE; TURKEY.OTTOMAN PERIOD
 sultans   'Abd al-'Azīz; 'Abd al-Ḥamīd I; 'Abd al-Ḥamīd II; 'Abd al-Madjīd I; 'Abd al-Madjīd II; Aḥmad I; Aḥmad II; Aḥmad III; Bāyazīd I; Bāyazīd II; Ibrāhīm; Maḥmūd; Meḥemmed I; Meḥemmed II; Meḥemmed III; Meḥemmed IV; Meḥemmed V Res̲h̲ād; Meḥemmed VI Waḥīd al-Dīn; Murād I; Murād II; Murād III; Murād IV; Murād V; Muṣṭafā I; Muṣṭafā II; Muṣṭafā III; Muṣṭafā IV; Orkhan; 'Ot̲h̲mān I; 'Ot̲h̲mān II; 'Ot̲h̲mān III; Selīm I; Selīm II; Selīm III; Süleymān; Süleymān II
 see also Bāb-i Humāyūn; Djem; Ertog̲h̲rul; K̲h̲ādim al-Ḥaramayn; K̲h̲alīfa.i.E; K̲h̲urrem; Kösem Wālide; Mas̲h̲wara; Muhr.1; Muṣṭafā.1 and 2; Müteferriḳa; Nīlūfer K̲h̲ātūn; Nūr Bānū; Rikāb; Ṣafiyye Wālide Sulṭān; S̲h̲ehzāde; Ṣolaḳ
 grand viziers   **Ṣadr-ı A'ẓam**
 see also Bāb-i 'Ālī; Bas̲h̲vekil; Ḳapi̊; 'Ot̲h̲mān-zāde

14th century ʿAlī Pasha Čandārli̊-zāde; Djandarli̊
15th century Aḥmad Pasha Gedik; Dāwūd Pasha, Ḳodja; Djandarli̊; Khalīl Pasha Djandarli̊; Maḥmūd Pasha; Meḥmed Pasha, Ḳaramānī; Meḥmed Pasha, Rūm; Sinān Pasha, Khodja.1
16th century Aḥmad Pasha, Ḳara; ʿAlī Pasha Khādim; ʿAlī Pasha Semiz; Ayās Pasha; Čighāla-zāde Sinān Pāshā; Derwīsh Pasha; Ferhād Pasha; Hersek-zāde; Ibrāhīm Pasha; Ibrāhīm Pasha, Dāmād; Khādi̊m Ḥasan Pasha Ṣoḳolli̊; Khādi̊m Süleymān Pasha; Lala Meḥmed Pasha (*and* Meḥmed Pasha, Lālā, Shāhīnoghlu); Luṭfī Pasha; Meḥmed Pasha, Lālā, Melek-Nihād; Mesīḥ Meḥmed Pasha; Mesīḥ Pasha; ʿOthmān Pasha; Pīrī Meḥmed Pasha; Rüstem Pasha; Sinān Pasha, Khādi̊m; Sinān Pasha, Khodja.2; Siyāwush Pasha.1; Soḳollu Meḥmed Pasha
17th century ʿAlī Pasha ʿArabadji̊; ʿAlī Pasha Güzeldje; ʿAlī Pasha Sürmeli; Dāwūd Pasha, Ḳara; Derwīsh Meḥmed Pasha; Dilāwar Pasha; Ḥāfiẓ Aḥmed Pasha; Ḥusayn Pasha; Ibrāhīm Pasha, Kara; Ipshir Muṣṭafā Pasha; Ismāʿīl Pasha, Nishāndji̊; Ḳarā Muṣṭafā Pasha; Kemānkesh; Khalīl Pasha Ḳayṣariyyeli; Khosrew Pasha, Bosniak; Köprülü.I-III; Meḥmed Pasha, Čerkes; Meḥmed Pasha, Elmās; Meḥmed Pasha, Gürdjü, Khādi̊m; Meḥmed Pasha, Gürdjü II; Meḥmed Pasha, Öküz; Meḥmed Pasha, Sulṭān-zāde; Meḥmed Pasha, Tabani̊-yassi̊; Murād Pasha, Ḳuyudju; Naṣūḥ Pasha; Redjeb Pasha; Siyāwush Pasha.2; Süleymān Pasha, Malaṭyali̊
18th century ʿAbd Allāh Pasha; ʿAlī Pasha Čorlulu; ʿAlī Pasha Dāmād; ʿAlī Pasha Ḥakīm-oghlu; Derwīsh Meḥmed Pasha; Ḥamza Ḥāmid Pasha; Ḥamza Pasha; (Dāmād) Ḥasan Pasha; (Seyyid) Ḥasan Pasha; (Sherīf) Ḥasan Pasha; Ibrāhīm Pasha, Nevshehirli; Kaḥyā Ḥasan Pasha; Khalīl Pasha Ḥādjdjī Arnawud; Köprülü.V; Meḥmed Pasha, Balṭadji̊; Meḥmed Pasha, ʿIwaḍ; Meḥmed Pasha, Melek; Meḥmed Pasha, Muḥsin-zāde; Meḥmed Pasha Rāmī (*and* Rāmī Meḥmed Pasha); Meḥmed Pasha, Tiryāḳī; Meḥmed Pasha, Yegen, Gümrükčü; Meḥmed Pasha, Yegen, Ḥādjdjī; Rāghib Pasha; Saʿīd Efendi
19th century and on Aḥmad Wafīḳ Pasha; ʿAlī Pasha Muḥammad Amīn; Dāmād Ferīd Pasha; Derwīsh Meḥmed Pasha; Djawād Pasha; Fuʾād Pasha; Ḥusayn ʿAwnī Pasha; Ḥusayn Ḥilmī Pasha; Ibrāhīm Edhem Pasha; Ibrāhīm Ḥaḳḳī Pasha; ʿIzzet Pasha; Kečiboynuzu; Khayr al-Dīn Pasha; Khosrew Pasha, Meḥmed; Küčük Saʿīd Pasha; Maḥmūd Nedīm Pasha; Maḥmūd Shewḳat Pasha; Meḥmed Saʿīd Ghālib Pasha; Midḥat Pasha; Muṣṭafā Pasha, Bayraḳdār; Reshīd Pasha, Muṣṭafā; [in Suppl.] Esʿad Pasha

grand muftis **Shaykh al-Islām**.2
see also Bāb-i Mashīkhat; Fatwā.ii

15th century Fenārī-zāde; Gūrānī; Khosrew
16th century Abu ʾl-Suʿūd; Bostānzāde.2; Čiwi-zāde; Djamālī; Kemāl Pasha-zāde; Khōdja Efendi
17th century Bahāʾī Meḥmed Efendi; Esʿad Efendi, Meḥmed; Ḳarā-Čelebi-zāde.4; Ṣunʿ Allāh
18th century Čelebi-zāde; Dürrīzāde.1-4; Esʿad Efendi, Meḥmed (2x); Ḥayātī-zāde.2; Meḥmed Ṣāliḥ Efendi; Pīrī-zāde
19th century ʿĀrif Ḥikmet Bey; Dürrīzāde.5; Esʿad Efendi, Aḥmed; Ḥasan Fehmī Efendi
20th century Djamāl al-Dīn Efendi; Dürrīzāde,ʿAbd Allāh; Muṣṭafā Khayrī Efendi

high admirals ʿAlī Pasha Güzeldje; Čighāla-zāde Sinān Pasha; Djaʿfar Beg; Djezāʾirli Ghāzī Ḥasan Pasha; Ḥasan Pasha; Ḥusayn Pasha; Kenʿān Pasha; Khalīl Pasha Ḳayṣariyyeli; Khayr al-Dīn Pasha; Piyāle Pasha
see also Raʾīs.3

historians of ʿAbdī; ʿAbdī Efendi; ʿAbdī Pasha; Aḥmad Djewdet Pasha; Aḥmad Rasmī; ʿAlī; ʿAlī Amīrī; ʿĀshi̊ḳ-pasha-zāde; ʿĀṣim; ʿAṭāʾ Bey; al-Bakrī.1; Bidlīsī; Bihishtī; Čelebi-zāde; Česhmīzāde; Djalālzāde Muṣṭafā Čelebi; Djalālzāde Ṣāliḥ Čelebi; Enwerī; Esʿad Efendi, Meḥmed; Ḥasan Bey-zāde; ʿIzzī; Ḳarā-čelebi-zāde.4; Kātib Čelebi; Kemāl, Meḥmed Nāmi̊ḳ; Kemāl Pasha-zāde; Khayr Allāh Efendi; Luḳmān b. Sayyid Ḥusayn; Luṭfī Efendi; Maṭrāḳčī; Meḥmed Ḥākim Efendi; Meḥmed Khalīfe b. Ḥüseyn; Meḥmed Pasha, Ḳaramānī; Meḥmed Zaʿīm; Muḥyi ʾl-Dīn Meḥmed; Naʿīmā; ʿOthmān-zāde; Pečewī; Ramaḍān-zāde; Rāshid, Meḥmed; Rūḥī; Selānīkī; Shefīḳ Meḥmed Efendi; Shemʿdānī-zāde; Sheref, ʿAbd al-Raḥmān; Silāḥdār, Fi̊ndi̊ḳli̊li̊ Meḥmed Agha; Ṣolaḳ-zāde; Ṣubḥī Meḥmed
see also Ḥadīdī; Shāhnāmedji

other personages
see also Shehzāde
13th century Sawdji̊.1
14th century ʿAlāʾ al-Dīn Beg; Badr al-Dīn b. Ḳāḍī Samāwnā; Ḳāsim.1; Sawdji̊.3; Shāhīn, Lala; Süleymān Pasha
15th century Aḥmad Pasha Khāʾin; Ewrenos; Ewrenos Oghullari̊; Fenārī-zāde; Ibn ʿArabshāh; Ḳāsim.2 and 3; Ḳāsim Pasha, Djazarī; Mūsā Čelebi; Muṣṭafā.1 and 2; Suleymān Čelebi
16th century Bostānzāde; Čiwi-zāde; Derwīsh Pasha; Djaʿfar Čelebi; Djalālzāde Muṣṭafā Čelebi; Ferīdūn Beg; Hāmōn; Ḳāsim.4; Ḳāsim Agha; Ḳāsim Pasha; Kemāl Reʾīs; Khosrew Pasha; Ḳorḳud b. Bayazīd; Maḥmūd Pasha; Maḥmūd Tardjumān; Meḥmed Pasha, Bi̊yi̊ḳli̊; Muṣṭafā.3; Muṣṭafā Pasha, Ḳara Shāhīn; Muṣṭafā Pasha,

Lala; Muṣṭafā Pa<u>sh</u>a al-Na<u>sh</u><u>sh</u>ār; Özdemir Pa<u>sh</u>a; Pertew Pa<u>sh</u>a.I; Pīrī Reʾīs; Ramaḍān-zāde; Riḍwān Pa<u>sh</u>a; Ṣari Kürz; Selmān Reʾīs; <u>Sh</u>āh Sulṭān; <u>Sh</u>āhīn, Āl; Sīdī ʿAlī Reʾīs; Sinān

17th century Ābāza; Ḥaydar-og<u>h</u>lu, Meḥmed; Ḥusayn Pa<u>sh</u>a; Ḳāsim.5; Ḳāṭirdjī-og<u>h</u>li Meḥmed Pa<u>sh</u>a; Maʿn-zāda; Meḥmed <u>Kh</u>alīfe b. Ḥüseyn; ʿO<u>th</u>mān Pa<u>sh</u>a, Yegen; <u>Sh</u>āhīn, Āl; [in Suppl.] Aḥmad Pa<u>sh</u>a Küčük; Čōbān-og<u>h</u>ullari

18th century Ābāza; Aḥmad Pa<u>sh</u>a; Aḥmad Pa<u>sh</u>a Bonneval; Aḥmad Rasmī; <u>Dj</u>ānīkli Ḥā<u>dj</u><u>dj</u>i ʿAlī Pa<u>sh</u>a; Meḥmed Ḥākim Efendi; Meḥmed Yirmisekiz; Paswan-og<u>h</u>lu; Patrona <u>Kh</u>alīl; Ṣari Meḥmed Pa<u>sh</u>a

19th century Aḥmad <u>Dj</u>ewdet Pa<u>sh</u>a; ʿAlī Pa<u>sh</u>a Tepedelenli; Ayyūb Ṣabrī Pa<u>sh</u>a; Bah<u>dj</u>at Muṣṭafā Efendi; Dāwūd Pa<u>sh</u>a (2x); <u>Dj</u>awād Pa<u>sh</u>a; Fāḍil Pa<u>sh</u>a; Ḥālet Efendi; Ḥusayn Pa<u>sh</u>a; Ibrāhīm Derwī<u>sh</u> Pa<u>sh</u>a; Kabakči-og<u>h</u>lu Muṣṭafā; Ḳōzān-og<u>h</u>ullari; Muṣṭafā Pa<u>sh</u>a, Bu<u>sh</u>atli; Pertew Pa<u>sh</u>a.II; Riḍwān Begović; Ṣādiḳ Rifʿat Pa<u>sh</u>a; <u>Sh</u>ebṣefa Ḳadin; [in Suppl.] Camondo

20th century ʿAbd al-Ḥaḳḳ Ḥāmid; <u>Dj</u>āwīd; <u>Dj</u>emāl Pa<u>sh</u>a; Enwer Pa<u>sh</u>a; Fehīm Pa<u>sh</u>a; Ḥasan Fehmī; ʿIzzet Pa<u>sh</u>a; Kāẓim Ḳadrī; Kāẓim Karabekir; Mu<u>kh</u>tār Pa<u>sh</u>a; Münīf Pa<u>sh</u>a

Sal<u>dj</u>ūḳs of Rūm (1077-1307) **Sal<u>dj</u>ūḳids**

rulers Kaykāʾūs; Kay<u>kh</u>usraw; Kayḳubād; Ḳili<u>dj</u> Arslan I; Ḳili<u>dj</u> Arslan II; Ḳili<u>dj</u> Arslan III; Ḳili<u>dj</u> Arslan IV; Malik-<u>Sh</u>āh.4; Sulaymān b. Ḳutulmi<u>sh</u>

historians of Ibn Bībī

other personages A<u>sh</u>raf Og<u>h</u>ullari; Muʿīn al-Dīn Sulaymān Parwāna; Saʿd al-Dīn Köpek

Arabian Peninsula Bū Saʿīd; Hamdānids; Hā<u>sh</u>imids (2x); āl-<u>Kh</u>alīfa; Mahdids; Na<u>dj</u>āḥids; Ra<u>sh</u>īd, Āl; Rasūlids; Ṣabāḥ, Āl, Ṣulayḥids; Suʿūd, Āl; [in Suppl.] <u>Dj</u>abrids

Āl Saʿūd (1746-) **Suʿūd, Āl**

rulers [in Suppl.] ʿAbd al-ʿAzīz; Fayṣal b. ʿAbd al-ʿAzīz

see also Muḥammad b. Suʿūd

Bū Saʿīd (1741-) **Bū Saʿīd**

sultans Barg<u>h</u>a<u>sh</u>; Saʿīd b. Sulṭān

Carmathians (894-end 11th century) **Ḳarmaṭī**

rulers al-<u>Dj</u>annābī, Abū Saʿīd; al-<u>Dj</u>annābī, Abū Ṭāhir

Hā<u>sh</u>imids (1908-1925) **Hā<u>sh</u>imids**

rulers Ḥusayn (b. ʿAlī)

see also ʿAbd Allāh b. al-Ḥusayn; Fayṣal I; Fayṣal II

Rasūlids (1229-1454) **Rasūlids**

historians of al-<u>Kh</u>azra<u>dj</u>ī

other personages [in Suppl.] Ibn Ḥātim
see also al-Sharīf Abū Muḥammad Idrīs
Ṭāhirids (1454-1517)
rulers ʿĀmir I; ʿĀmir II
Zaydīs (860-) Rassids
imāms Ḥasan al Uṭrūsh; al-Mahdī li-Dīn Allāh Aḥmad; al-Manṣūr bi ’llāh, ʿAbd Allāh; al-Manṣūr bi ’llāh, al-Ḳāsim b. ʿAlī; al-Manṣūr bi ’llāh, al-Ḳāsim b. Muḥammad; al-Muʾayyad bi ’llāh Muḥammad; Muḥammad al-Murtaḍā li-Dīn Allāh; al-Mutawakkil ʿalā ’llāh, Ismāʿīl; al-Mutawakkil ʿalā ’llāh, Sharaf al-Dīn; al-Nāṣir li-Dīn Allāh, Aḥmad; al-Rassī; [in Suppl.] al-Ḥādī ila ’l-Ḥaḳḳ
see also Imāma
other personages al-Muṭahhar; al-Nāṣir li-Dīn Allāh; al-Sharīf Abū Muḥammad Idrīs
Zurayʿids (1138-1174)
viziers Bilāl b. Djarīr al-Muḥammadī
Egypt and the Fertile Crescent ʿAbbāsids; ʿAnnāzids; Ayyūbids; Bābān; Būrids; Fāṭimids; Ḥamdānids; Ḥasanwayh; Mamlūks; Marwānids; Mazyad; Mirdās
see also ʿAmmār; Begteginids; Djalīlī; Ṣadaḳa, Banū; *and* → EGYPT. MODERN PERIOD.MUḤAMMAD ʿALĪ’S LINE; ONOMASTICS.TITLES.ARABIC
ʿAbbāsids (749-1258) → CALIPHATE
Ayyūbids (1169-end 15th century) **Ayyūbids**
see also Rank
rulers al-ʿĀdil; al-Afḍal; Bahrām Shāh; al-Kāmil; al-Muʿaẓẓam; al-Nāṣir; Ṣalāḥ al-Dīn; (al-Malik) al-Ṣāliḥ ʿImād al-Dīn; (al-Malik) al-Ṣāliḥ Nadjm al-Dīn Ayyūb
see also Dīwān.ii.(3)
viziers Ibn al-ʿAdīm; Ibn al-Athīr.3; Ibn Maṭrūḥ
secretaries ʿImād al-Dīn; al-Ḳāḍī al-Fāḍil
historians of Abu ’l-Fidā; Abū Shāma; Ibn Shaddād; ʿImād al-Dīn; al-Maḳrīzī; al-Manṣūr, al-Malik
other personages Abu ’l-Fidā; Aybak; Ibn al-ʿAssāl; Ḳarāḳūsh, Bahāʾ al-Dīn; Ḳarāḳūsh, Sharaf al-Dīn; al-Muẓaffar, al-Malik
Fāṭimids (909-1171) → CALIPHATE
Ḥamdānids (905-1004) **Ḥamdānids**
rulers Nāṣir al-Dawla; Sayf al-Dawla; [in Suppl.] Abū Taghlib
other personages Ḥusayn b. Ḥamdān; Luʾluʾ
Ikhshīdids (935-969)
rulers Kāfūr
viziers Ibn al-Furāt.5
other personages al-Ṣayrafī
Mamlūks (1250-1517) Dhu ’l-Faḳāriyya; Dīwān.ii.(4); Ḥādjib.iv; Hiba.ii;

Khādim al-Ḥaramayn; Khaznadār; **Mamlūks**; Mashwara; Nāʾib.1
see also Ḥarfūsh; Ḳumāsh; Mamlūk; Manshūr; Rank; *and* → MILITARY.

MAMLUK

sultans Barḳūḳ; Barsbāy; Baybars I; Baybars II; Čaḳmaḳ; Faradj; Ḥasan; Īnāl al-Adjrūd; Ḳāʾit Bāy; Ḳalāwūn; Ḳānṣawh al-Ghawrī; Khalīl; Khushḳadam; Ḳuṭuz; Lādjīn; al-Muʾayyad Shaykh; al-Nāṣir; (al-Malik) al-Ṣāliḥ; Shaʿbān; Shadjar al-Durr

administrators Faḍl Allāh; Ibn ʿAbd al-Ẓāhir; Ibn Faḍl al-ʿUmarī; Ibn Ghurāb; Ibn Ḥidjdja; Ibn al-Sadīd (Ibn al-Muzawwiḳ); Ibn al-Sadīd, Karīm al-Dīn; al-Ḳalḳashandī.1 [in Suppl.] Ibn al-Ṣuḳāʿ

historians of Abu ʾl-Maḥāsin b. Taghrībirdī; Baybars al-Manṣūrī; Ibn ʿAbd al-Ẓāhir; Ibn Duḳmāk; Ibn Ḥabīb, Badr al-Dīn; Ibn Iyās; Ibn Shāhīn al-Ẓāhirī; al-Maḳrīzī; al-Mufaḍḍal b. Abi ʾl-Faḍāʾil; al-Nuwayrī, Shihāb al-Dīn; al-Ṣafadī, al-Ḥasan; Shāfiʿ b. ʿAlī; al-Shudjāʿī

other personages Abu ʾl-Fidāʾ; al-ʿAynī; Ibn Djamāʿa; Ibn al-Mundhir

Marwānids (983-1085) **Marwānids**

rulers Naṣr al-Dawla

Mazyadids (ca. 961-1150) **Mazyad**; Ṣadaḳa, Banū

rulers Ṣadaḳa b. Manṣūr

Mirdāsids (1023-1079) **Mirdās**

see also Asad al-Dawla

Ṭūlūnids (868-905)

rulers Aḥmad b. Ṭūlūn; Khumārawayh

see also Ibn al-Mudabbir.1

historians of al-Balawī; Ibn al-Dāya

other personages [in Suppl.] al-ʿAbbās b. Aḥmad b. Ṭūlūn

ʿUḳaylids (ca. 990-1096)

rulers Muslim b. Ḳuraysh

Mongols Batuʾids; Čaghatay Khānate; Čingizids; Djalāyir; Djānids; Girāy; Īlkhāns; Ḳarā Khiṭāy; **Mongols**; Shībānids
see also Čūbānids; Ḳāzān; Soyūrghāl; [in Suppl.] Āgahī; Dīwān-begi; Djamāl Ḳarshī; Ordu.2; *and* → ONOMASTICS.TITLES.MONGOLIAN

Batuʾids (1236-1502) **Batuʾids**

see also Saray

rulers Batu; Berke; Mangū-tīmūr

other personages Masʿūd Beg

Čaghatayids (1227-1370) **Čaghatay Khānate**

rulers Burāḳ Khān; Čaghatay Khān

historians of Ḥaydar Mīrzā

Djānids (1598-1785) **Djānids**

rulers Nadhr Muḥammad

see also Bukhārā
Girāy Khāns (ca. 1426-1792) **Girāy**
rulers Dawlat Giray; Ghāzī Girāy I; Ghāzī Girāy II; Ghāzī Girāy III; Ḥādjdjī Girāy; Islām Girāy; Ḳaplan Girāy I; Ḳaplan Girāy II; Meḥmed Girāy I; Mengli Girāy I; Ṣāḥib Girāy Khān I; Selīm Girāy I
see also Ḳalghay; Meḥmed Baghčesarāyī; Meḥmed Girāy
Great Khāns (1206-1634) Čingizids
rulers Čingiz Khān; Ḳubilay; Möngke; Ögedey
other personages Ḳaydu; Maḥmūd Yalawač
Ilkhānids (1256-1353) **Īlkhāns**
see also Ṣadr.2
rulers Baydu; Gaykhātū; Ghāzān; Hūlāgū; Öldjeytü
viziers Saʿd al-Dawla
historians of Ḥamd Allāh al-Mustawfī al-Ḳazwīnī; Rashīd al-Dīn Ṭabīb
other personages Djuwaynī, ʿAlāʾ al-Dīn; Ḳutlugh-Shāh Noyan
Shaybānids (1500-1598) **Shībānids**
rulers ʿAbd Allāh b. Iskandar; Abu ʾl-Khayr; Shībānī Khān
historians of Abu ʾl-Ghāzī Bahādur Khān; [in Suppl.] Ḥāfiẓ Tanïsh

Persia Afrāsiyābids; Aḥmadīlīs; Aḳ Ḳoyunlu; Bādūsbānids; Bāwand; Buwayhids; Dulafids; Faḍlawayh; Farīghūnids; Ḥasanwayh; Hazāraspids; Ildeñizids; Ilek-Khāns; Ilyāsids; Īndjū; Ḳādjār; Kākūyids; Ḳarā-ḳoyunlu; Ḳārinids; Kāwūs; Khʷārazm-shāhs; Ḳutlugh-khānids; Lur-i Buzurg; Lur-i Kūčik; Mangïts; Marʿashīs; Muḥtādjids; Musāfirids; Mushaʿshaʿ; Muẓaffarids; Rawwādids; Ṣafawids; Ṣaffārids; Saldjūḳids; Salghurids; Sāmānids; Sarbadārids; Sāsānids; Shaddādids; Shīrwān Shāh
see also Ardalān; Atabak; ʿAwfī; Čāshna-gīr; Daylam; Dīwān.iv; Djalāyir; Ghulām.ii; Ḥādjib.iii; Ḥarb.v; al-Ḥasan b. Zayd b. Muḥammad; Hiba.iv; Ḥiṣār.iii; Īlkhāns; Iran.v; Kayānids; Marāsim.3; Mawākib.3; Shāhī; *and* → ONOMASTICS.TITLES.PERSIAN
Afshārids (1736-1795) **Afshār**
rulers Nādir Shāh Afshār
historians of ʿAbd al-Karīm Kashmīrī; Mahdī Khān Astarābādī
Buwayhids (932-1062) **Buwayhids**
rulers Abū Kālīdjār; ʿAḍud al-Dawla; Bakhtiyār; Djalāl al-Dawla; Fakhr al-Dawla; ʿImād al-Dawla; Khusraw Fīrūz (*and* al-Malik al-Raḥīm); Madjd al-Dawla; Muʾayyid al-Dawla; Muʿizz al-Dawla; Rukn al-Dawla; Ṣamṣām al-Dawla; Shams al-Dawla; Sharaf al-Dawla; Sulṭān al-Dawla; [in Suppl.] Bahāʾ al-Dawla wa-Ḍiyāʾ al-Milla
viziers al-ʿAbbās b. al-Ḥusayn; Ibn ʿAbbād; Ibn al-ʿAmīd; Ibn Baḳiyya; Ibn Mākūlā.1 and 2; al-Muhallabī, Abū Muḥammad; Sābūr b.

Arda<u>sh</u>īr; [in Suppl.] ʿAbd al-ʿAzīz b. Yūsuf; Ibn <u>Kh</u>alaf.1; Ibn Saʿdān
secretaries Hilāl al-Ṣābiʾ (*and* Ṣābiʾ.(3).9); Ibn Hindū; Ṣābiʾ.(3).7
historians of Ṣābiʾ.(3).7
other personages al-Basāsīrī; Fasand̲j̲us; Ḥasan b. Ustā<u>dh</u>-hurmuz; Ibn
 Ḥād̲j̲ib al-Nuʿmān; ʿImrān b. <u>Sh</u>āhīn; al-Malik al-ʿAzīz; [in Suppl.]
 Ibrāhīm <u>Sh</u>īrāzī
Dābūyids (660-760)
 rulers Dābūya
Ildeñizids (1137-1225) **Ildeñizids**
 rulers Ildeñiz; Özbeg b. Muḥammad Pahlawān; Pahlawān
Ḳād̲j̲ārs (1779-1924) **Ḳād̲j̲ār**; Mu<u>sh</u>īr al-Dawla
 see also Ḳāʾim-maḳām-i Farāhānī; Mad̲j̲lis al-<u>Sh</u>ūrā; *and* → IRAN.
 MODERN PERIOD
 rulers Ā<u>gh</u>ā Muḥammad <u>Sh</u>āh; Fatḥ ʿAlī <u>Sh</u>āh; Muḥammad ʿAlī <u>Sh</u>āh
 Ḳād̲j̲ār; Muḥammad <u>Sh</u>āh; Muẓaffar al-Dīn <u>Sh</u>āh Ḳād̲j̲ār; Nāṣir al-Dīn
 <u>Sh</u>āh
 other personages ʿAbbās Mīrzā; [in Suppl.] Amīr Niẓām; Ḥād̲j̲d̲j̲ī
 Ibrāhīm <u>Kh</u>ān Kalāntar
Khanate of K̲h̲īwa <u>Kh</u>īwa
 rulers Abu ʾl-<u>Gh</u>āzī Bahādur <u>Kh</u>ān
Kh^wārazm-<u>Sh</u>āhs (ca. 995-1231) **Kh^wārazm-<u>sh</u>āhs**
 rulers Atsiz b. Anū<u>sh</u>tigin; Djalāl al-Dīn <u>Kh</u>^wārazm-<u>sh</u>āh; Maʾmūn b.
 Muḥammad
 historians of D̲j̲uwaynī; al-Nasawī
 other personages Burāḳ Ḥād̲j̲ib
Muẓaffarids (1314-1393) **Muẓaffarids**
 rulers <u>Sh</u>āh-i <u>Sh</u>ud̲j̲āʿ
 historians of Muʿīn al-Dīn Yazdī
Pahlawīs (1926-1979) **Pahlawi**
 and → IRAN.MODERN PERIOD
 rulers Muḥammad Riḍā <u>Sh</u>āh Pahlawī; Riḍā <u>Sh</u>āh
Sād̲j̲ids (ca. 856- ca. 930) **Sād̲j̲ids**
 rulers Abu ʾl-Sād̲j̲; Muḥammad b. Abi ʾl-Sād̲j̲
Ṣafawids (1501-1732) Bārūd.v; Ī<u>sh</u>īk-āḳāsī; Iʿtimād al-Dawla; Kūrčī; Libās.
 iii; **Ṣafawids**
 see also Ḥaydar; Ḳi̇zi̇l-bā<u>sh</u>; Nuḳṭawiyya; Ṣadr.4; Ṣadr al-Dīn Ardabīlī;
 Ṣadr al-Dīn Mūsā; Ṣafī al-Dīn Ardabīlī; Soyūr<u>gh</u>āl
 rulers ʿAbbās I; Ḥusayn (*and* Sulṭān Ḥusayn); Ismāʿīl I; Ismāʿīl II;
 Sulaymān (<u>Sh</u>āh)
 historians of Ḥasan-i Rūmlū; Iskandar Beg; Ḳummī
 see also [in Suppl.] Ibn al-Bazzāz al-Ardabīlī
 other personages Alḳāṣ Mīrzā; Ḥamza Mīrzā; al-Karakī; Mad̲j̲lisī

Ṣaffārids (867-ca. 1495) **Ṣaffārids**
rulers ʿAmr b. al-Layth
Saldjūḳs (1038-1194) Amīr Dād; Arslan b. Saldjūḳ; Atabak; **Saldjūḳids**
see also Sarāparda; *and* → DYNASTIES.ANATOLIA AND THE TURKS.SALDJŪḲS OF RŪM
rulers Alp Arslan; Bahrām Shāh; Barkyārūḳ; Maḥmūd b. Muḥammad b. Malik-Shāh; Malik-Shāh.1-3; Masʿūd b. Muḥammad b. Malik-Shāh; Muḥammad b. Maḥmūd b. Muḥammad b. Malik-Shāh; Muḥammad b. Malik-Shāh; Riḍwān; Sandjar
see also Čaghri̊-beg; Silāḥdār
viziers Anūshirwān b. Khālid; Djahīr; al-Kundurī; Madjd al-Mulk al-Balāsānī; al-Maybudī.3; Niẓām al-Mulk; Rabīb al-Dawla; [in Suppl.] Ibn Dārust
historians of al-Bundārī; ʿImād al-Dīn; Nīshāpūrī; Rāwandī; [in Suppl.] al-Ḥusaynī
other personages Āḳ Sunḳur al-Bursuḳī; Arslan-Arghūn; Ayāz; al-Basāsīrī; Būrī-bars; Bursuḳ; Büz-abeh; Ḳāwurd; Khalaf b. Mulāʿib al-Ashhabī; Khāṣṣ Beg; Kurbuḳa; Niẓāmiyya; [in Suppl.] Ekinči
Salghurids (1148-1270) **Salghurids**
rulers Saʿd (I) b. Zangī
Sāmānids (819-1005) **Sāmānids**
rulers Ismāʿīl b. Aḥmad; Ismāʿīl b. Nūḥ; Manṣūr b. Nūḥ; Naṣr b. Aḥmad b. Ismāʿīl; Nūḥ (I); Nūḥ (II)
viziers Balʿamī; al-Muṣʿabī; [in Suppl.] al-Djayhānī
historians of Narshakhī
see also al-Sallāmī
other personages Arslan b. Saldjūḳ; Sīmdjūrids; [in Suppl.] al-Djayhānī
Ṭāhirids (821-873)
rulers ʿAbd Allāh b. Ṭāhir; Muḥammad b. Ṭāhir
historians of Ibn al-Daybaʿ
other personages Muḥammad b. ʿAbd Allāh (b. Ṭāhir)
Tīmūrids (1370-1506)
see also Ṣadr.3; Soyūrghāl
rulers Abū Saʿīd b. Tīmūr; Bāyḳarā; Bāysonghor; Ḥusayn; Shāh Rukh
see also Khān-zāda Bēgum
historians of Ibn ʿArabshāh; Khʷāfī Khān; Shāmī, Niẓām al-Dīn; Sharaf al-Dīn ʿAlī Yazdī
other personages Mīr ʿAlī Shīr Nawāʾī; Mīrānshāh b. Tīmūr
Zands (1750-1794)
rulers Karīm Khān Zand; Luṭf ʿAlī Khān
see also Lak

Zangids (1127-1222)

 rulers Masʿūd b. Mawdūd b. Zangī; Mawdūd b. ʿImād al-Dīn Zankī; Nūr al-Dīn Arslān S͟hāh; Nūr al-Dīn Maḥmūd b. Zankī

 viziers al-D͟jawād al-Iṣfahānī

 see also Begteginids; Karīm K͟hān Zand; Luʾluʾ, Badr al-Dīn

 historians of Ibn al-At͟hīr.2

 other personages S͟hīrkūh

Ziyārids (927-ca. 1090)

 rulers Kābūs b. Wus͟hmagīr b. Ziyār; Kay Kāʾūs b. Iskandar; Mardāwīd͟j

Spain and North Africa ʿAbbādids; ʿAbd al-Wādids; Afṭasids; Ag͟hlabids; ʿAlawīs; ʿĀmirids; ʿAmmār; D͟hu ʾl-Nūnids; D͟jahwarids; Ḥafṣids; Ḥammādids; Ḥammūdids; Hūdids; Ḥusaynids; Idrīsids; (Banū) K͟hurāsān; Marīnids; Midrār; al-Murābiṭūn; al-Muwaḥḥidūn; Naṣrids; Razīn, Banū; Rustamids; Saʿdids

 see also ʿAlāma; Dīwān.iii; Ḥād͟jib.ii and v; Hiba.iii; Ḥiṣār.ii; al-Ḥulal al-Maws͟hiyya; Karamānlī; K͟halīfa.i.C and D; Lakab.3; Marāsim.2; Mawākib.2; Parias; S͟hurafāʾ.1.III; *and* → CALIPHATE.FĀṬIMIDS

ʿAbbādids (1023-1091) **ʿAbbādids**; Is͟hbīliya

 rulers al-Muʿtaḍid bi ʾllāh; al-Muʿtamid ibn ʿAbbād

 see also al-Rundī

 viziers Ibn ʿAmmār, Abū Bakr

ʿAbd al-Wādids (1236-1550) **ʿAbd al-Wādids**

 rulers Abū Ḥammū I; Abū Ḥammū II; Abū Tās͟hufīn I; Abū Tās͟hufīn II; Abū Zayyān I; Abū Zayyān II; Abū Zayyān III

 historians of Ibn K͟haldūn, Abū Zakariyyāʾ

Afṭasids (1022-1094) **Afṭasids**

 rulers al-Mutawakkil ʿalā ʾllāh, Ibn al-Afṭas

 viziers Ibn Kuzmān.II

 secretaries Ibn ʿAbdūn; Ibn Kabṭūrnu

Ag͟hlabids (800-909) al-ʿAbbāsiyya; **Ag͟hlabids**; Rakkāda

 rulers Ibrāhīm I; Ibrāhīm II

ʿAlawids (1631-) **ʿAlawīs**; Kāʾid; Mawlāy; S͟hurafāʾ.1.III

 rulers ʿAbd Allāh b. Ismāʿīl; ʿAbd al-ʿAzīz b. al-Ḥasan; ʿAbd al-Raḥmān b. His͟hām; Ḥafīẓ (ʿAbd al-); (Mawlāy) al-Ḥasan; Mawlāy Ismāʿīl; Muḥammad III b. ʿAbd Allāh; Muḥammad IV b. ʿAbd al-Raḥmān; Muḥammad b. Yūsuf (Muḥammad V); al-Ras͟hīd (Mawlāy); Sulaymān (Mawlāy)

 viziers Akanṣūs; Ibn Idrīs (I); [in Suppl.] Bā Ḥmād; Ibn ʿUt͟hmān al-Miknāsī

 historians of Akanṣūs; Ibn Zaydān; al-Kardūdī

 other personages Aḥmad al-Nāṣirī al-Salāwī (*and* al-Nāṣir al-Salāwī); Ibn Idrīs (II); K͟hunāt͟ha

Almohads (1130-1269) Hargha; al-ʿIḳāb; Mizwār; **al-Muwaḥḥidūn**
rulers ʿAbd al-Muʾmin; Abū Yaʿḳūb Yūsuf; Abū Yūsuf Yaʿḳūb al-Manṣūr; Ibn Tūmart; al-Maʾmūn; al-Nāṣir
historians of ʿAbd al-Wāḥid al-Marrākushī; al-Baydhaḳ; Ibn Ṣāḥib al-Ṣalāt
see also al-Ḥulal al-Mawshiyya
other personages [in Suppl.] Ibn al-Ḳaṭṭān
see also Abū Ḥafṣ ʿUmar al-Hintātī; Ibn Mardanīsh
Almoravids (1056-1147) Amīr al-Muslimīn; **al-Murābiṭūn**
rulers ʿAlī b. Yūsuf b. Tāshufīn; al-Lamtūnī
secretaries Ibn ʿAbdūn
historians of Ibn al-Ṣayrafī
see also al-Ḥulal al-Mawshiyya
other personages Ibn Bādjdja; Ibn Ḳasī
ʿĀmirids (1021-1096) **ʿĀmirids**
rulers ʿAbd al-Malik b. Abī ʿĀmir; al-Muẓaffar
viziers Ibn al-Ḳaṭṭāʿ
other personages ʿAbd al-Raḥmān b. Abī ʿĀmir
Djahwarids (1030-1070) **Djahwarids**
other personages (al-)Ḥakam ibn ʿUk(k)āsha; Ibn ʿAbdūs
Ḥafṣids (1228-1574) **Ḥafṣids**
secretaries Ḥāzim
historians of al-Ḥādjdj Ḥammūda
other personages Ibn ʿArafa
Ḥammādids (972-1152) **Ḥammādids**
rulers Bādīs; al-Manṣūr; al-Nāṣir
see also Ḳalʿat Banī Ḥammād
Ḥammūdids (1010-1057) **Ḥammūdids**
viziers Ibn Dhakwān
Hūdids (1039-1142) **Hūdids**
rulers al-Muʾtamin
Ḥusaynids (1705-1957) **Ḥusaynids**
rulers Aḥmad Bey; al-Ḥusayn (b. ʿAlī); Muḥammad Bey; Muḥammad al-Ṣādiḳ Bey
ministers Khayr al-Dīn Pasha; Muṣṭafā Khaznadār
Idrīsids (789-926) **Idrīsids**
rulers Idrīs I; Idrīs II
Marīnids (1196-1465) **Marīnids**
rulers Abu ʾl-Ḥasan; Abū ʿInān Fāris
Naṣrids (1230-1492) **Naṣrids**
viziers Ibn al-Khaṭīb
other personages [in Suppl.] Ibn al-Sarrādj

Rustamids (777-909) **Rustamids**
historians of Ibn al-Ṣag͟hīr
Saʿdids (1511-1659) **Saʿdids**; S͟hurafāʾ.1.III
rulers ʿAbd Allāh al-G͟hālib; Aḥmad al-Manṣūr; Mawlāy Maḥammad al-S͟hayk͟h
see also Mawlāy
viziers Ibn ʿĪsā
historians of ʿAbd al-ʿAzīz b. Muḥammad; al-Ifrānī
other personages [in Suppl.] Abū Maḥallī
Tud͟jībids (1019-1039)
rulers Maʿn b. Muḥammad; al-Muʿtaṣim
ʿUbaydids
historians of Ibn Ḥamādu
Umayyads (756-1031)
amīrs and caliphs ʿAbd Allah b. Muḥammad; ʿAbd al-Raḥmān; al Ḥakam I; al-Ḥakam II; His͟hām I; His͟hām II; His͟hām III; al-Mahdī; al-Mund͟hir b. Muḥammad
see also Madīnat al-Zahrāʾ; Muʿāwiya b. His͟hām; Rabaḍ; al-Ruṣāfa.4; [in Suppl.] Bubas͟htru
viziers Ibn ʿAlḳama.2; Ibn S͟huhayd
secretaries ʿArīb b. Saʿd al-Kātib al-Ḳurṭubī; Ibn Burd.I
other personages ʿAbd al-Raḥmān b. Marwān; G͟hālib b. ʿAbd al-Raḥmān; Ḥabīb b. ʿAbd al-Malik; Ḥasdāy b. S͟haprūṭ; Ibn ʿAlḳama.1; Ibn D͟hakwān; Ibn al-Ḥannāṭ; Ibn Ḳasī; Ibn al-Ḳiṭṭ; al-Manṣūr; Rabīʿ b. Zayd; Ṣubḥ
Zīrids (972-1152)
rulers Buluggīn b. Zīrī; al-Muʿizz b. Bādīs
other personages Ibn Abi ʾl-Rid͟jāl
see also Ḳurhub
Zīrids of Granada (1012-1090)
rulers ʿAbd Allāh b. Buluggīn

E

EARTHQUAKES *see* Ag͟hrï Dag͟h; Amasya; Anṭākiya; ʿAs͟hḳābād; Čankïrï; Cilicia; Daybul; Djidjelli; Erzind͟jan; Ḥarra; Ḥulwān; Istanbul.VI.f; Ḳalhāt; Kāńgṛā; Ḳazwīn; Kilāt; Nīs͟hāpūr; al-Ramla

ECONOMICS Bayʿ; Kasb; Māl
see also Muḍāraba

EDUCATION **Maʿārif**

see also ʿArabiyya.B.IV; Idjāza

educational reform → REFORM

institutions of learning Dār al-Ḥadīth; Djāmiʿa; Köy Enstitüleri; Kuttāb; Madrasa; Maktab; Pesantren

see also Kulliyya; Ṣadr.(c); Samāʿ.2; Shaykh; *and* → EDUCATION.LIBRARIES

individual establishments al-Azhar; Bayt al-Ḥikma; Dār al-Ḥikma; Dār al-ʿUlūm; Ghalaṭa-sarāyi̊; Ḥarbiye; al-Ḳarawiyyīn.ii; al-Khaldūniyya; Makhredj; Mulkiyya; al-Ṣādiḳiyya; [in Suppl.] Institut des hautes études marocaines; Institut des hautes études de Tunis

see also Aligarh; Deoband; Filāḥa.iii; al-Ḳāhira; Lakhnaw; al-Madīna.ii; Makka.3; Muṣṭafā ʿAbd al-Rāziḳ; al-Mustanṣir (I); Nadwat al-ʿUlamāʾ; [in Suppl.] ʿAbd al-Bārī; ʿAbd al-Wahhāb; Farangī Maḥall

learned societies and academies Andjuman; Djamʿiyya; Djemʿiyyet-i ʿIlmiyye-i ʿOthmāniyye; Institut d'Égypte; Khalḳevi; Madjmaʿ ʿIlmī

libraries Dār al-ʿIlm; **Maktaba**

see also ʿAlī Pasha Mubārak; Khāzin; al-Madīna.ii

collections ʿAlī Amīrī (*and* [in Suppl.] ʿAlī Emīrī); Esʿad Efendi, Meḥmed; Khudā Bakhsh; [in Suppl.] ʿAbd al-Wahhāb

see also Geniza

librarians Ibn al-Fuwaṭī; Ibn Ḥadjar al-ʿAsḳalānī; Ibn al-Sāʿī; al-Kattānī

treatises on Ergin, Osman

EGYPT al-Azhar; al-Ḳāhira; Ḳibṭ; **Miṣr**; Nūba; al-Ṣaʿīd

see also al-ʿArab.iv; al-Fusṭāṭ; *and* → DYNASTIES.EGYPT AND THE FERTILE CRESCENT; NUBIA

administration Dār al-Maḥfūẓāt al-ʿUmūmiyya; Dīwān.ii; Ḳabāla; Kharādj.I; Rawk

see also Miṣr.D.1.b; *and* → CALIPHATE.ʿABBĀSIDS *and* FĀṬIMIDS; DYNASTIES.EGYPT AND THE FERTILE CRESCENT.MAMLŪKS; OTTOMAN EMPIRE.ADMINISTRATION

architecture → ARCHITECTURE.REGIONS

before Islam Firʿawn; Manf; Miṣr.D.1; Nūba.2; Saḳḳāra; [in Suppl.] Abū Sinbil

dynasties ʿAbbāsids; Ayyūbids; Fāṭimids; Mamlūks; Muḥammad ʿAlī Pasha

and → DYNASTIES.EGYPT AND THE FERTILE CRESCENT

historians of Abu 'l-Maḥāsin b. Taghrībirdī; ʿAlī Pasha Mubārak; al-Bakrī.2; al-Balawī; al-Damurdāshī; al-Djabartī; Ibn ʿAbd al-Ḥakam.4; Ibn Duḳmāk; Ibn Iyās; Ibn Muyassar; al-Kindī, Abū ʿUmar Muḥammad; al-Maḳrīzī; al-Nuwayrī, Muḥammad; Rifāʿa Bey al-Ṭahṭāwī; al-Ṣafadī, al-Ḥasan; Salīm al-Naḳḳāsh; al-Suyūṭī

and → DYNASTIES.EGYPT AND THE FERTILE CRESCENT

modern period Ḍarība.4; Djarīda.i.A; Djāmiʿa; Dustūr.iii; Ḥizb.i; Ḥukūma.iii;

al-Ikhwān al-Muslimūn; Iltizām; Imtiyāzāt.iv; Institut d'Égypte; Maʿārif.1.ii; Madjlis.4.A.xvi; Madjmaʿ ʿIlmī.i.2.b; Maḥkama.4.i; Miṣr.D.7; Salafiyya.2(a)

see also Baladiyya.2; al-Bannāʾ; Madjlis al-Shūrā

influential persons Djamāl al-Dīn al-Afghānī; al-Marṣafī; Muḥammad ʿAbduh; Muṣṭafā Kāmil Pasha; al-Muwayliḥī.1; Rifāʿa Bey al-Ṭahṭāwī; Salāma Mūsā; al-Sanhūrī, ʿAbd al-Razzāḳ; Sayyid Ḳuṭb; Shākir, Aḥmad Muḥammad; Shaltūt, Maḥmūd; al-Subkiyyūn; [in Suppl.] Abu 'l-ʿAzāʾim; al-ʿAdawī; al-Bakrī; al-Biblāwī; Djawharī, Ṭanṭāwī; al-ʿIdwī al-Ḥamzāwī; ʿIllaysh

Muḥammad ʿAlī's line ʿAbbās Ḥilmī I; ʿAbbās Ḥilmī II; Fuʾād al-Awwal; Ḥusayn Kāmil; Ibrāhīm Pasha; Ismāʿīl Pasha; Muḥammad ʿAlī Pasha; Saʿīd Pasha; [in Suppl.] Bakhīt al-Muṭīʿī al-Ḥanafī; Fārūḳ

see also ʿAzīz Miṣr; Khidīw; [in Suppl.] Dāʾira Saniyya; Ibʿādiyya

statesmen ʿAlī Pasha Mubārak; al-Bārūdī; Fikrī; Ismāʿīl Ṣidḳī; Luṭfī al-Sayyid; Muḥammad Farīd Bey; Muḥammad Nadjīb; al-Naḥḥās; Nūbār Pasha; Saʿd Zaghlūl; al-Sādāt; Sharīf Pasha; [in Suppl.] ʿAbd al-Nāṣir

see also Muṣṭafā Kāmil Pasha

Ottoman period (1517-1798) Dhu 'l-Faḳāriyya; Ḳāsimiyya; Ḳāzdughliyya; Miṣr.D.6; Muḥammad ʿAlī Pasha; Shaykh al-Balad

see also Ḥurriyya.ii

beys ʿAlī Bey; Muḥammad Abu 'l-Dhahab (*and* [in Suppl.] Abu 'l-Dhahab)

physical geography

waters Burullus; al-Nīl

see also Miḳyās; Rawḍa; al-Suways

population ʿAbābda; Ḳibṭ

see also [in Suppl.] Demography.IV; *and* → CHRISTIANITY.DENOMINATIONS.COPTS

toponyms

ancient Adfū; Bābalyūn; al-Bahnasā; Burullus; Dabīḳ; al-Ḳulzum; Manf; Shaṭā

see also al-Sharḳiyya

present-day

regions Buḥayra; al-Fayyūm; al-Gharbiyya; Girgā; al-Sharḳiyya; Sīnāʾ

see also al-Ṣaʿīd

towns ʿAbbāsa; Abūḳīr; Akhmīm; al-ʿAllāḳī; al-ʿArīsh; Asyūṭ; Aṭfīḥ; ʿAyn Shams; Banhā; Banī Suwayf; Bilbays; Būlāḳ; Būṣīr; Dahshūr; Daḳahliyya; Damanhūr; Dimyāṭ; al-Farāfra; al-Fusṭāṭ; Girgā; Ḥulwān; al-Iskandariyya; Ismāʿīliyya; Isna; al-Ḳāhira; Ḳalyūb; Ḳanṭara.3; Ḳifṭ; Ḳunā; Ḳūṣ; Ḳuṣayr; al-Maḥalla al-Kubrā; al-Manṣūra; Manūf; Port Saʿīd; Rafaḥ; Rashīd; Saḳḳāra; Samannūd; Sīwa.1; al-Suways; [in Suppl.] Abū Zaʿbal

see also al-Muḳaṭṭam; Rawḍa

EMANCIPATION Ḥurriyya
for manumission, see ʿAbd; *and for women* → WOMEN

EMIGRATION Djāliya; **Hidjra**
see also al-Mahdjar; Muhādjir; al-Muhādjirūn; Pārsīs; Ṣiḥāfa.3; *and* → NEW WORLD

EPIGRAPHY **Kitābāt**
see also Eldem, Khalīl Edhem; Ḥisāb al-Djummal; Khaṭṭ; Musnad.1
sites of inscriptions Lībiyā.2; Liḥyān; Orkhon; al-Sawdāʾ; Ṣiḳilliya.4; Ṣirwāḥ.1
see also Ḥaḍramawt; Sabaʾ; Ṣafaitic

ESCHATOLOGY ʿAdhāb al-Ḳabr; Ākhira; al-Aʿrāf; Barzakh; Baʿth; Djahannam; Djanna; Djazāʾ; Dunyā; Ḥawḍ; Ḥisāb; Isrāfīl; ʿIzrāʾīl; Ḳiyāma; Maʿād; al-Mahdī; Mawḳif.2; Munkar wa-Nakīr; Sāʿa.3
see also Ḳayyim; Shafāʿa; Shaḳāwa; *and* → DEATH; PARADISE
hereafter Adjr.1; **Ākhira**
see also Dunyā
signs ʿAṣā; Dābba; al-Dadjdjāl
see also Baʿth; Sāʿa.3

ETERNITY **Abad**; Ḳidam

ETHICS Adab; **Akhlāḳ**; Ḥisba
see also Ḥurriyya; al-Maḥāsin wa ʾl-Masāwī; Miskawayh; *and* → VIRTUES

ETHIOPIA Adal; Aḥmad Grāñ; Awfāt; Bāli; Dawāro; Djabart; Djimmā; **Ḥabash**; Ḥabashat; al-Nadjāshī
see also Ḥabesh; Kūsh; Shaykh Ḥusayn; *and* → LANGUAGES.AFRO-ASIATIC
historians of ʿArabfaḳih
population ʿĀmir; Diglal; Djabart; Galla; Māryā; Oromo; Rashāʾida
toponyms Assab; Dahlak; Dire Dawa; Eritrea; Harar; Maṣawwaʿ; Ogādēn

ETHNICITY Maghāriba; Mashāriḳa; Sārt
see also Fatā; Ibn Gharsiya; Ismāʿīl b. Yasār; Mawlā; Saracens

ETIQUETTE **Adab**
see also Āʾīn; Hiba; *and* → LITERATURE

EUNUCH **Khāṣī**
see also Khādim; Mamlūk.3

EUROPE
Eastern Europe Arnawutluḳ; Balkan; Bulgaria; Iḳrīṭis͟h; Itil; Ḳubrus; Leh; [in Suppl.] Čeh
see also Bulg͟hār; Ḥizb.v; Ibrāhīm b. Yaʿḳūb; Muhād͟jir.2; Muslimūn.1; Rūmeli; al-Ṣaḳāliba
for individual countries → ALBANIA; BULGARIA; CRETE; CYPRUS; (former) CZECHOSLOVAKIA; GREECE; HUNGARY; POLAND; (former) YUGOSLAVIA
Russia Ḳi̊ri̊m
see also Bulg͟hār; D͟jadīd; Ḥizb.v; Ḳayyūm Nāṣirī
dynasties Girāy
population Bas͟hd͟jirt; Besermyans; Beskesek-abaza; Buk͟hārli̊k; Burṭās; Čeremiss; Čuli̊m; Čuwas͟h; Gagauz; Ḳarapapak͟h; Lipḳa; Rūs
see also Ḳang͟hli; K͟hazar; Kimäk; Pečenegs; al-Ṣaḳāliba
toponyms
ancient Atil; Saḳsīn
present-day Aḳ Kirmān; Aḳ Masd͟jid.1; Azaḳ; Bāg͟hče Sarāy; Ismāʿīl; Ḳamāniča; Ḳaraṣū-bāzār; Ḳāsimov; Ḳāzān; Kefe; Kerč; K͟hotin; Ḳi̊lburun; Sug͟hdāḳ
Western Europe al-Bas͟hkunis͟h; Ifrand͟j; Īṭaliya; Malta; Nemče; Sardāniya
see also Ibn Idrīs (II); Ibrāhīm b. Yaʿḳūb; al-Mad͟jūs; Muslimūn.2
for individual countries → AUSTRIA; FRANCE; ITALY; PORTUGAL; SPAIN

EVIL EYE ʿ**Ayn**
see also Karkaddan; *and* → CHARMS; ISLAM.POPULAR BELIEFS

F

FAITH ʿAḳīda; **Īmān**
and → ISLAM; RELIGION

FALCONRY **Bayzara**; Čaki̊rd͟ji̊-bas͟hi̊; Dog͟hand͟ji̊

FASTING ʿĀs͟hūrāʾ; Ramaḍān; **Ṣawm**
see also ʿĪd al-Fiṭr; Ṣūfiyāna

FĀṬIMIDS → CALIPHATE

FESTIVAL **ʿĪd**; Kandūrī; Mawlid; Mawsim; S͟henlik
see also Maṭbak͟h.2
festivals ʿAnṣāra; ʿĀs͟hūrāʾ.II; Bara Wafāt; ʿĪd al-Aḍḥā; ʿĪd al-Fiṭr; K͟hiḍr-ilyās; Mihragān; Nawrūz; Sulṭān al-Ṭalaba

see also G̲h̲adīr K̲h̲umm; Kurds.iv.C.3; Lālis̲h̲; Lĕbaran; Ra's al-ʿĀm

FLORA (D̲j̲azīrat) al-ʿArab.v; Būstān; Filāḥa; Hind.i.k
  and → BOTANY
flowers Nard̲j̲is; S̲h̲aḳīḳat al-Nuʿmān; Sūsan; [in Suppl.] Bābūnad̲j̲; D̲j̲ullanār
  see also Filāḥa.iv; Lāle Devri; Lālezarī; Nawriyya; *and* → ARCHITECTURE.
  MONUMENTS.GARDENS; LITERATURE.POETRY.NATURE
plants Ad̲h̲argūn; Afsantīn; Afyūn; Ḥalfā'; Ḥinnā'; Kammūn; Ḳaranful; Karm;
  Ḳaṣab; Naʿām; **Nabāt**; Ṣabr; S̲h̲ibit̲h̲t̲h̲; S̲h̲īḥ; S̲h̲ukāʿā; Sidr; Simsim; Sirād̲j̲
  al-Ḳuṭrub; Sūs; [in Suppl.] Aḳūnīṭun; Ās; Bābūnad̲j̲; Basbās; D̲j̲āwars;
  Fūd̲h̲and̲j̲; Hindibā'; Iklīl al-Malik
  see also Maryam; Naḥl; Namir and Nimr; Naṣr; Ṣamg̲h̲; Sinnawr; Sirwāl;
  and → DRUGS.NARCOTICS
trees Abanūs; ʿAfṣ; Argan; Baḳḳam; Bān; K̲h̲as̲h̲ab; Nak̲h̲l; Sād̲j̲; Ṣandal; Sidr;
  [in Suppl.] D̲j̲awz; D̲j̲ullanār
  see also ʿAyn S̲h̲ams; G̲h̲āba; Kāfūr; Kahrubā; Ḳaṭrān; Lubān; Ṣamg̲h̲; [in
  Suppl.] Halīlad̲j̲

FRANCE Arbūna; Fraxinetum
  see also Balāṭ al-S̲h̲uhadā'; Muslimūn.2; Rifāʿa Bey al-Ṭaḥṭāwī; Ṣāyig̲h̲, Fatḥ
  Allāh; al-S̲h̲ām.2(b)

FRANKS **Ifrand̲j̲**
  and → CRUSADE(R)S

FURNISHINGS Mafrūs̲h̲āt; Sirād̲j̲; [in Suppl.] **At̲h̲āt̲h̲**

G

GAMBLING **Ḳimār**; al-Maysir
  and → ANIMALS.SPORT; RECREATION.GAMES

GENEALOGY **Ḥasab wa-Nasab**; **Nasab**; S̲h̲arīf; S̲h̲urafā'
  see also ʿIrḳ; Naḳīb al-As̲h̲rāf; S̲h̲araf; *and* → LITERATURE.GENEALOGICAL;
  ONOMASTICS

GEOGRAPHY **D̲j̲ug̲h̲rāfiyā**; Iḳlīm; Istiwā'; K̲h̲arīṭa; al-Ḳubba
  see also Mag̲h̲rib; Makka.4; Mas̲h̲riḳ

for the detailed geography of areas, see Adamawa; Ādharbaydjān.i; Afghānistān.i; Aḳ Ṣu; Algeria.i; Anadolu.ii; al-Andalus.ii and iii.2; (Djazīrat) al-ʿArab.ii; Armīniya; Arnawutluḳ.3; ʿAsīr; Baḥr; Djazīra; Filāḥa; Ḥammāda; Indonesia; ʿIrāḳ; Iran; Lībiyā; al-Maghrib; Māzandarān.2; Mūrītāniyā.1; Nadjd.1; al-Shām.1; Sīstān.2; Somali.2

administrative Kūra; Mamlaka; Mikhlāf; Rustāḳ.1; Ṣūba
see also Djund; Iḳlīm

geographers Abu ʾl-Fidāʾ; Abū ʿUbayd al-Bakrī; ʿĀshiḳ; al-Balkhī, Abū Zayd; al-Dimashḳī; Ibn ʿAbd al-Munʿim al-Ḥimyarī; Ibn al-Faḳīh; Ibn Ghālib; Ibn Ḥawḳal; Ibn Khurradādhbih; Ibn Mādjid; Ibn Rusta; Ibn Sarābiyūn; al-Idrīsī; al-Iṣṭakhrī; al-Ḳazwīnī; al-Masʿūdī; al-Muhallabī, Abu ʾl-Ḥusayn; al-Muḳaddasī
see also Baṭlamiyūs; Istibṣār; Ḳāsim b. Aṣbagh; al-Masālik wa ʾl-Mamālik; al-Sarakhsī, Abu ʾl-ʿAbbās; [in Suppl.] al-Djayhānī; Ḥudūd al-ʿĀlam

literature Djughrāfiyā.IV.c and V; Ṣurat al-Arḍ
and → Literature.travel-literature

physical geography
deserts → Deserts
mountains → Mountains
salt flats **Sabkha**
see also Shaṭṭ
springs ʿAyn Dilfa; ʿAyn Mūsā; al-Ḥamma; Ḥasan Abdāl
see also Ḳaplîdja
volcanoes *see* ʿAdan; Aghrî Dagh; Damāwand; Ḥarra; Ladjāʾ; al-Ṣafā.2; [in Suppl.] Djabal Says
waters
lakes Baikal; Bakhtigān; Balkhash; Burullus; Gökče-tengiz; Hāmūn; al-Ḥūla; Issîk-kul; Ḳarā-köl
see also Buḥayra; al-Ḳulzum; *and* → Oceans and Seas
rivers → Rivers
straits Bāb al-Mandab; Boghaz- iči; Čanaḳ-ḳalʿe Boghazi

terms Ḥarra; Khabrāʾ; Nahr; Reg; Rīf; Sabkha; Shaṭṭ
see also Ṣanf; Sarḥadd

urban Ḳarya; Ḳaṣaba; Khiṭṭa; Maḥalle; Medina; Rabaḍ; Shahr; Shahristān
see also Fener; Ḥayy; Khiṭaṭ; Mallāḥ; *and* → Architecture.urban; Sedentarism

Gifts **Hiba**; Ṣila.3
see also Bakhshīsh; Nithār; Pīshkash; Rashwa; *and* → Payments

Greece
see also Muhādjir.2; Muslimūn.1.B.3; Pomaks

toponyms

districts Karlı̊-īli

islands Čoka Adası̊; Eğriboz; Körfüz; Levkas; Limni; Midilli; Naḳshe; On Iki Ada; Para; Rodos; Ṣaḳı̊z; Santurin Adası̊; Semedirek; Sheytānlı̊ḳ ; Shire; Sisām

see also Djazāʾir-i Baḥr-i Safīd

regions Mora

towns Atīna; Aynabakhtı̊; Baliabadra; Dede Aghač; Dimetoḳa; Karaferye; Ḳawāla; Kerbenesh; Kesriye; Ḳordos; Ḳoron; Livadya; Menekshe; Modon; Nauplion; Navarino; Olendirek; Preveze; Selānīk; Siroz

see also [in Suppl.] Gümüldjine

GUILDS **Ṣinf**

Arabic Amīn; ʿArīf; Futuwwa.ii and iii; Ḥammāl; Ḥarfūsh; Khātam; Khayyāṭ; Ṣinf.1

see also Shadd; Shaykh; Sirwāl

Persian Ṣinf.2

Turkish Akhī; Akhī Baba; Anadolu.iii.6; Ḥarīr.ii; Ketkhudā.ii; Ṣinf.3; [in Suppl.] Ikhtiyāriyya; Inḥiṣār

see also Akhī Ewrān; ʿĀlima; Čāʾūsh; Kannās; Mawākib.4.4; Muhr.1

GUINEA Fūta Djallon; **Guinea**; Konakry

see also Sūdān (Bilād al-).2

GYPSIES **Čingāne**; **Lūlī**; Nūrī

H

HADITH → LITERATURE.TRADITION-LITERATURE

HAGIOGRAPHY **Manāḳib**

and → SAINTHOOD

hagiographers Aflākī; ʿAṭāʾī; al-Bādisī.2; "Djamālī"; Ḥasan Dihlawī; Ibn ʿAskar; Ibn Maryam; al-Ifrānī; al-Ḳādirī al-Ḥasanī, Abū ʿAbd Allāh; al-Sharrāṭ; al-Sulamī, Abū ʿAbd al-Raḥmān

see also Aḥmad Bābā; Bāḳı̊khānlı̊; al-Kattānī; Sinān Pasha, Khodja.1

HELL Aṣḥāb al-Ukhdūd; **Djahannam**; Saʿīr; Saḳar; Ṣirāṭ

see also al-Aʿrāf; Shayṭān.1

HEPHTHALITES Hayāṭila; Nīzak, Ṭarkhān

HERALDRY al-Asad; Rank

HERESY Bidʿa; Dahriyya; Dīn-i Ilāhī; Ghulāt; Ḳābiḍ; Kāfir; Khūbmesīḥīs; Mulḥid
see also al-Ṣalīb
heretics Abū ʿĪsā al-Warrāḳ; Abu 'l-Khattāb al-Asadī; Bashshār b. Burd; Bishr b. Ghiyāth al-Marīsī; Ibn Dirham; Ibn al-Rawandī; Mollā Ḳābiḍ; Muḥammad b. ʿAlī al-Shalmaghānī
and → SECTS
refutations of Ibn al-Djawzī, ʿAbd al-Raḥmān; [in Suppl.] Afḍal al-Dīn Turka

HOSTELRY **Funduḳ**; **Khān**; Manzil
see also Ribāṭ.1.b

HUMOUR al-Djidd wa 'l-Hazl; Nādira
see also Hidjāʾ.ii; Mudjūn
comic figures Djuḥā; Ibn al-Djaṣṣāṣ.II; Naṣr al-Dīn Khodja
humourists Ashʿab; al-Ghāḍirī; Ibn Abī ʿAtīḳ; Ibn Dāniyāl; Ḳaṣāb, Teodor; Sīfawayh al-Ḳāṣṣ; [in Suppl.] Abu 'l-ʿAnbas al-Ṣaymarī

HUNGARY Budīn; Eğri; Esztergom; Istolnī (Istōnī) Belghrād; **Madjar**; Mohács; Pécs; Pest; Sigetwār; Szeged; Székesfehérvár
see also Bashdjirt; Kanizsa; Maḥmūd Tardjumān; Mezőkeresztes; Muslimūn. 1.B.1; Ofen

HUNTING **Ṣayd**
see also Kurds.iv.C.5; Samak; Shikārī; *and* → ANIMALS; FALCONRY
treatises on Kushādjim; [in Suppl.] Ibn Manglī
see also al-Shamardal
wild animals Fahd; Khinzīr; Mahāt; Naʿām; Namir and Nimr; Salūḳī; [in Suppl.] Ḍabuʿ

HYDROLOGY Biʾr; Ḳanāt; Māʾ; Maʾṣir
see also Filāḥa; Ḳanṭara.5 and 6; Madjrīṭ; al-Mīzān.2; Sāʿa.1; *and* → ARCHITECTURE.MONUMENTS.DAMS; GEOGRAPHY.WATERS

I

IDOLS Nuṣub; **Ṣanam**
see also Shaman; *and* → PRE-ISLAM.IN ARABIAN PENINSULA

ILLNESS Ma<u>dj</u>nūn; Malāryā; Ramad; Saraṭān.7; [in Suppl.] <u>Dj</u>u<u>dh</u>ām
  see also Kalb; Ḳuṭrub; Summ
treatises on Ḥayātī-zāde; Ibn Buṭlān; Ibn <u>Dj</u>azla
  and → MEDICINE

INDIA **Hind**; Hindī
  see also ʿĀda.iii; Balharā; Imām-bārā; Maṭbaʿa.4; Sikkat al-Ḥadīd.1; *and* → LITERATURE; MILITARY; MUSIC
administration Baladiyya.5; Ḍarība.6; Dīwān.v; <u>Dj</u>izya.iii; Ḥisba.iv; Kātib.iii; <u>Kh</u>arā<u>dj</u>.IV; Pargana; Safīr.3
  see also Kitābāt.10; Māʾ.9; *and* → MILITARY.INDO-MUSLIM
agriculture Filāḥa.v
architecture → ARCHITECTURE.REGIONS
belles-lettres → LITERATURE.IN OTHER LANGUAGES *and* POETRY.INDO-PERSIAN
dynasties ʿĀdil-<u>Sh</u>āhs; Bahmanīs; Barīd <u>Sh</u>āhīs; Dihlī Sultanate; Farūḳids; <u>Gh</u>aznavids; <u>Gh</u>ūrids; Hindū-<u>Sh</u>āhīs; ʿImād <u>Sh</u>āhī; <u>Kh</u>al<u>dj</u>īs; Ḳuṭb <u>Sh</u>āhīs; Lodīs; Mu<u>gh</u>als; Niẓām <u>Sh</u>āhīs; Sayyids; <u>Sh</u>arḳīs
  see also Awadh; Dār al-Ḍarb; Rānā Sāngā; *and* → DYNASTIES.AFGHANISTAN AND INDIA
education Dār al-ʿUlūm.c and d; <u>Dj</u>āmiʿa; Ma<u>dj</u>maʿ ʿIlmī.iv; Madrasa.II; Nadwat al-ʿUlamāʾ; [in Suppl.] Farangī Maḥall
  see also Aḥmad <u>Kh</u>ān; Deoband; Maḥmūdābād Family
historians of <u>Gh</u>ulām Ḥusayn <u>Kh</u>ān Ṭabāṭabāʾī; Niẓām al-Dīn Aḥmad b. al-Harawī; Su<u>dj</u>ān Rāy Bhandārī
  see also <u>Dj</u>aʿfar <u>Sh</u>arīf; al-Maʿbarī; Mīr Muḥammad Maʿṣūm; *and* → DYNASTIES.AFGHANISTAN AND INDIA; LITERATURE.HISTORICAL
languages Gu<u>dj</u>arātī; Hindī; Hindustānī.i and ii; Lahndā; Marāthī; Pan<u>dj</u>ābī.1; Sind.3.a
  see also Kitābāt.10; *and* → LANGUAGES.INDO-IRANIAN
modern period <u>Dj</u>amʿiyya.v; Hindustānī.iii; Ḥizb. vi; Indian National Congress; Iṣlāḥ.iv; Ka<u>sh</u>mīr.ii; Ḳawmiyya.vi; <u>Kh</u>āksār; <u>Kh</u>ilāfa; Ma<u>dj</u>lis.4.C; al-Marʾa.5; Nikāḥ.II.3; [in Suppl.] <u>Dj</u>arīda.vii
  see also Mahsūd; Mappila; [in Suppl.] Faḳīr of Ipi; *and* → INDIA.EDUCATION
  Indian Mutiny Aẓim Allāh <u>Kh</u>ān; Ba<u>kh</u>t <u>Kh</u>ān; Imdād Allāh; Kānpur
  Khilāfat movement **<u>Kh</u>ilāfa**; Muḥammad ʿAlī; Mu<u>sh</u>īr Ḥusayn Ḳidwāʾī; <u>Sh</u>awkat ʿAlī; [in Suppl.] ʿAbd al-Bārī; Ḥasrat Mohānī
    see also Amīr ʿAlī
  statesmen Nawwāb Sayyid Ṣiddīḳ Ḥasan <u>Kh</u>ān; Sālār <u>Dj</u>ang; [in Suppl.] Āzād, Abu ʾl-Kalām
    see also Maḥmūdābād Family
mysticism → MYSTICISM.MYSTICS; SAINTHOOD

physical geography
waters Djamnā; Gangā
see also Nahr.2
population Bhaṭṭi; Bohorās; Dāwūdpōtrās; Djāt́; Gakkhaŕ; Gandāpur; Güdjar; Ḥabshī; Hind.ii; Khaṭak; Khokars; Lambadis; Mappila; Mēd; Memon; Mēʾō; Naitias; Pārsīs; Rādjpūts; Rohillas; Shikārī; Sidi; [in Suppl.] Demography.VII
see also Khōdja; Marāt́hās
Tamils Ceylon; Labbai; Marakkayar; Rawther
religion Ahl-i Ḥadīth; Barāhima; Djayn; Hindū; Ibāḥatiya; Mahdawīs; Pandj Pīr; Sikhs
see also Khʷādja Khiḍr; Pārsīs; [in Suppl.] Andjuman-i Khuddām-i Kaʿba;
and → MYSTICISM; SAINTHOOD; THEOLOGY
reform Aḥmad Brēlwī; al-Dihlawī, Shāh Walī Allāh; Ismāʿīl Shahīd; Karāmat ʿAlī; Nanak
toponyms
ancient Arūr; Čāmpānēr; Čhat; Djāba; Djandjīra; Fatḥpūr-sikrī; Hampī; Ḥusaynābād; Kūlam; Lakhnawtī; al-Manṣūra; Mēwāŕ; Nandurbār; Nārnawl; Pānd́uʾā; Shikārpūr.2; Sidhpūr; Sindābūr; Sindān; Sūmanāt
present-day
regions Assam; Bihār; Bombay State; Dakhan; Djaypur; Doʾāb; Gudjarat; Hariyānā; Ḥaydarābād.b; Kāmrūp; Kashmīr; Khāndēsh; Ḳūhistān.4; Ladākh; Lūdhiāna; Maʿbar; Mahisur; Malabar; Mēwāt; Muẓaffarpur; Nāgpur; Palamāw; Pālānpur; Pandjāb; Rādhanpūr; Rāmpur; Rohilkhand; Sundarban; [in Suppl.] Djammū
see also Alwār; Banganapalle; Bāonī; Berār; Djōdhpur; Hunza and Nagir
towns Adjmēr; Āgra; Aḥmadābād; Aḥmadnagar; Aligarh; Allāhābād; Ambāla; Amritsar; Anhalwāra; Arcot; Awadh; Awrangābād; Awrangābād Sayyid; Aʿẓamgarh; Badāʾūn; Bālā-ghāt; Bāndā; Bānkīpūr; Banūr; Bareilly; Barōda; Benares; Bharatpūr; Bharoč; Bhattinda; Bhōpāl; Bīdar; Bīdjāpūr; Bidjnawr; Bilgrām; Bombay City; Bulandshahr; Burhānpūr; Buxar; Calcutta; Čandērī; Dawlatābād; Deoband; Dhār; Dhārwār; Dihlī; Diū; Djālor; Djawnpur; Djūnāgaŕh; Djunnar; Dwārkā; Farīdkōt́; Farrukhābād; Fayḍābād; Fīrūzpūr; Gulbargā; Gwāliyār; Hānsī; Ḥaydarābād.a; Ḥiṣār Fīrūza; Īdar; Islāmābād; Itāwā; Kalpī; Kalyāni; Kanawdj; Kāńgŕā; Kannanūr; Kānpur; Karnāl; Karnāt́ak; Katahr; Khambāyat; Khayrābād; Khuldābād; Kōŕā; Koyl; Lakhnaw; Lalitpur; Lūdhiāna; Madras; Mahīm; Māhīm; Māhūr; Mālda; Mālwā; Mānd́ū; Manēr; Mangrōl; Mathurā; Mīrat́h; Mīrzāpur; Multān; Mungīr; Murādābad;

Murs̲h̲idābād; Muẓaffarpur; Nad̲j̲ībābād; Nagar; Nāgawr; Nāgpur; Naldrug; Nānder; Pānīpat; Parendā; Pāṭan; Paṭnā; Pūna; Rād̲j̲mahāl; Rāyču̇r; Sahāranpūr; Sahsarām; Sārangpur; Sardhanā; Sark̲h̲ēd̲j̲; S̲h̲akark̲h̲elda; S̲h̲ikārpūr.3; S̲h̲ōlāpur; Sirhind; Srīnagar; Śrīanga-paṭṭanam; Sūrat; [in Suppl.] Amrōhā; Eličpur; G̲h̲āzīpur

and → ASIA.SOUTH

INDONESIA   Baladiyya.7; D̲j̲āmiʿa; Dustūr.xi; Ḥizb.vii; Ḥukūma.vi; **Indonesia**; Maḥkama.6; Malays; Masjumi; [in Suppl.] Ḍarība.7; Hoesein Djajadiningrat
    see also ʿĀda.iv; Nikāḥ.II.4; Pasisir; Prang Sabīl
architecture   → ARCHITECTURE.REGIONS
education   Pesantren
literature   Indonesia.vi; Ḳiṣṣa.6; Miʿrād̲j̲.4; S̲h̲āʿir.7
    see also Kitābāt.8; Malays; *and* → LITERATURE.POETRY.MYSTICAL
Muslim movements   Padri; Sarekat Islam
    see also Sulawesi
population   Malays; Minangkabau; [in Suppl.] Demography.VIII
    see also Sayābid̲j̲a
religion   → MYSTICISM.MYSTICS
    festivals   Kandūrī; Lĕbaran
toponyms   Ambon; At̲j̲èh; Banda Islands; Band̲j̲armasin; Bangka; Batjan; Billiton; Borneo (*and* [in Suppl.]); D̲j̲akarta; Kubu; Kutai; Lombok; Madura; Makassar; Palembang; Pasè; Pasir; Pontianak; Riau; Sambas; Sulawesi (*and* Celebes); Sumatra; Sunda Islands; Surakarta

INDUSTRY   Ḥarīr; Kattān; Ḳuṭn; Lubūd; Milḥ
    see also Bursa; al-Iskandariyya; Ḳayṣariyya

INHERITANCE   ʿĀda.iii; Akdariyya; ʿAwl; **Farāʾiḍ**; **Mīrāt̲h̲**; al-Sahm.2
    see also Ḳassām; K̲h̲āl; Mak̲h̲red̲j̲; Muk̲h̲allefāt
works on   al-Sad̲j̲āwandī, Sirād̲j̲ al-Dīn

INVENTIONS   ʿAbbās b. Firnās; Ibn Mād̲j̲id; Mūsā (Banū); Sāʿa.1

IRAN   al-Furs; **Iran**; Kurds; Lur
    see also al-ʿArab.iii; Ḥarb.v; Kitābāt.9; Libās.iii; *and* → DYNASTIES.PERSIA; SHIITES; ZOROASTRIANS
administration   Ḍarība.5; Diplomatic.iii; Dīwān.iv; G̲h̲ulām.ii; Imtiyāzāt.iii; Kātib.ii; K̲h̲āliṣa; K̲h̲arād̲j̲.II; Maḥkama.3; Parwānačī
    see also Kalāntar; *and* → IRAN.MODERN PERIOD
agriculture   Filāḥa.iii
architecture   → ARCHITECTURE.REGIONS

before Islam Anūsharwān; Ardashīr; Bahrām; Dārā; Dārābdjird; Dihḳan; Djamshīd; Farīdūn; al-Ḥaḍr; Hayāṭila; Hurmuz; al-Hurmuzān; Ḳārinids; Kayānids; Kay Kāʾūs; Kay Khusraw; Khurshīd; Kisrā; Marzpān; Mazdak; Mulūk al-Ṭawāʾif.1; Parwīz, Khusraw (II); Pīshdādids; Sāsānids; Shāpūr; [in Suppl.] Farrukhān
see also Afrāsiyāb; Buzurgmihr; Hamadhān; Ikhshīd; Iran.iv; Ispahbadh; Ḳaṣr-i Shīrīn; Ḳūmis; al-Madāʾin; al-Rayy; Rustam b. Farrukh Hurmuzd; Sarpul-i Dhuhāb; [in Suppl.] Dabīr; *and* → ZOROASTRIANS

historians of Ḥamza al-Iṣfahānī; Ibn Manda; al-Māfarrūkhī; al-Rāfiʿī
and → DYNASTIES.PERSIA

language → LANGUAGES.INDO-IRANIAN

literature → LITERATURE

modern period Baladiyya.4; Djāmiʿa; Djamʿiyya.iii; Djarīda.ii; Dustūr.iv; Ḥizb.iii; Ḥukūma.ii; Iran.v.b; Iṣlāḥ.ii; Ḳawmiyya.iii; Maʿārif.3; Madjlis.4.A.iii; Madjmaʿ ʿIlmī.ii; al-Marʾa.3; Shuyūʿiyya.2; [in Suppl.] Demography.III
see also Khazʿal Khān; Madjlis al-Shūrā; Maḥkama.3; [in Suppl.] Amīr Niẓām; *and* → DYNASTIES.PERSIA.ḲĀDJĀRS *and* PAHLAWĪS; SHIITES

activists Fidāʾiyyān-i Islām; Kāshānī, Āyātullāh; Kasrawī Tabrīzī; Khʷānsārī, Sayyid Muḥammad; Khiyābānī, Shaykh Muḥammad; Khurāsānī; Kūčak Khān Djangalī; Lāhūtī; Maḥallātī; Malkom Khān; Muṣaddiḳ; Muṭahharī; Nāʾīnī; Nūrī, Shaykh Faḍl Allāh; Ṣamṣām al-Salṭana; Sharīʿatī, ʿAlī; [in Suppl.] Āḳā Khān Kirmānī; Āḳā Nadjafī; Amīr Kabīr; Ḥaydar Khān ʿAmū Ughlī
see also Djangalī; Kurds.iii. C; [in Suppl.] Āzādī; Faramush-khāna

physical geography

deserts Biyābānak

mountains Ala Dagh; Alburz; Alwand Kūh; Bīsutūn; Damāwand; Hamrīn; Hawrāmān
see also Sarḥadd

waters Bakhtigān, Hāmūn; Karkha; Kārūn; Mānd; Ruknābād; Safīd Rūd; Shāh Rūd.1; Shāpūr; Shaṭṭ al-ʿArab
see also Baḥr Fāris

population Bakhtiyārī; Bāzūkiyyūn; Bilbās; Djāf; Eymir.3; Göklän; Gūrān; (Banū) Kaʿb; Ḳarā Gözlu; Ḳāshḳāy; Kurds; Lām; Lur; Shabānkāra; Shāhsewan; Shakāk; Shaḳāḳī; Sindjābī
see also Daylam; Dulafids; Eymir.2; Fīrūzānids; Iran.ii; Ḳufṣ; Shūlistān; [in Suppl.] Demography.III

religion Iran.vi; Ṣafawids.IV
and → MYSTICISM.MYSTICS; SAINTHOOD

toponyms

ancient Abarshahr; Ardalān; Arradjān; ʿAskar Mukram; Bādj; Bākusāyā;

Bayhaḳ; Dārābdjird; Daskara; Dawraḳ; Dihistān; Dīnawar; al-Djazīra; Djibāl; Djīruft; Gurgān; Ḥafrak; Ḥulwān; Īdhadj; Iṣṭakhr; (al-)Karadj; Khargird.2; Ḳūmis; Ḳurḳūb; Mihragān.iv.1; Narmāshīr; Nasā; Nawbandadjān; al-Rayy; Rūdhbār.2; Rūdhrāwar; Ṣaymara; Shāpūr; Shūlistān; al-Sīradjān; Sīrāf; Sīsar; Suhraward; al-Sūs; [in Suppl.] Arghiyān; Ghubayrā

present-day

islands al-Fārisiyya

provinces Ādharbaydjān; Balūčistān; Fārs; Gīlān; Hamadhān; Iṣfahān; Khurāsān; Khūzistān; Kirmān; Kirmānshāh; Kurdistān; Māzandarān

see also Astarābādh.2; Rūyān

regions Bākharz; Hawrāmān; Ḳūhistān.1; Makrān; Sarḥadd; Sīstān; [in Suppl.] Bashkard

see also Gulistān

towns and districts Ābādah; Abarḳūh; ʿAbbādān; ʿAbbāsābād; Abhar; al-Ahwāz; Āmul.1; Ardakān; Ardistān; Asadābādh; Ashraf; Astarābādh.1; Āwa; Bam; Bampūr; Bandar ʿAbbās; Bandar Pahlawī; Bārfurūsh; Barūdjird; Barzand; Bīrdjand; Bisṭām; Būshahr; Dāmghān; Dizfūl; Djannāba; Djuwayn.1 and 2; Faraḥābād; Faryāb; Fasā; Fīrūzābād; Fūman; Gulpāyagān; Gunbadh-i Ḳābūs; Hurmuz; Iṣfahān; Isfarāyīn; Kāshān; Ḳaṣr-i Shīrīn; Kāzarūn; Ḳazwīn; Khʷāf; Khalkhāl; Khʷār; Khārag; Khargird.1; Khōī; Khurramābād; Khurramshahr; Kinkiwar; Ḳishm; Ḳūčān; Ḳūhistān.2; Ḳuhrūd; Ḳum; Lāhīdjān; Lār (2x); Linga; Luristān; Mahābād; Mākū; Marāgha; Marand; Mashhad; Miyāna; Narāḳ; Naṭanz; Nayrīz; Nihāwand; Nīshāpūr; Rafsandjān; Rām-hurmuz; Rasht; Rūdhbār.3; Sabzawār.1; Ṣaḥna; Ṣāʾīn Ḳalʿa; Saḳḳiz; Salmās; Sanandadj; Sarakhs; Sārī; Sarpul-i Dhuhāb; Sarwistān; Sāwa; Shāh Rūd.3; Shīrāz; Shushtar; Simnān; al-Sīradjān; Ṣōmāy; Suldūz; Sulṭānābād; Sulṭāniyya; Sunḳur; al-Sūs; [in Suppl.] Bashkard; Biyār; Djārdjarm; Djulfa.II; Hawsam

see also Shahr; Shahristān; *and* → KURDS.TOPONYMS

IRAQ **ʿIrāḳ**; Kurds

see also al-ʿArabiyya; Djalīlī; Lakhmids; Sawād; Shahāridja; *and* → CALIPHATE.ʿABBĀSIDS; DYNASTIES.EGYPT AND THE FERTILE CRESCENT

architecture → ARCHITECTURE.REGIONS

before Islam → PRE-ISLAM.IN FERTILE CRESCENT

historians of al-Azdī; Baḥshal; Ibn Abī Ṭāhir Ṭayfūr; Ibn al-Bannāʾ; Ibn al-Dubaythī; al-Khaṭīb al-Baghdādī

see also Ibn al-Nadjdjār; *and* → CALIPHATE.ʿABBĀSIDS; DYNASTIES.EGYPT AND THE FERTILE CRESCENT

modern period Djarīda.i.A; Djāmiʿa; Dustūr.vi; Ḥizb.i; Ḥukūma.iii; Kurds.iii.C;

Madjlis.4.A.iv; Madjmaʿ ʿIlmī.i.2.c; Maḥkama.4.iv; Mandates
see also Bābān; Kūt al-ʿAmāra; al-Mawṣil.2
monarchy Fayṣal I; Fayṣal II; Ghazī
see also Hāshimids
opposition leaders Ḳāsim ʿAbd al-Karīm; Muṣṭafā Barzānī
politicians al-Shahrastānī, Sayyid Muḥammad; Shīnā
prime ministers Nūrī al-Saʿīd; Rashīd ʿAlī al-Gaylānī
physical geography
mountains Sindjār
waters Abu ʾl-Khaṣīb; al-ʿAḍaym; Didjla; Diyālā; al-Furāt; Khābūr; al-Khāzir; Shaṭṭ al-ʿArab
population Bādjalān; Bilbās; Djubūr; Dulaym; Lām; al-Manāṣir
see also Shammar; [in Suppl.] Demography.III; *and* → KURDS
toponyms
ancient Abarḳubādh; ʿAḳarḳūf; ʿAlth; al-Anbār; Bābil; Badjimzā; Bādjisrā; Bādūrayā; Bākhamrā; Baradān; Barāthā; Bawāzīdj; Bihḳubādh; Birs; Dayr ʿAbd al-Raḥmān; Dayr al-ʿĀḳūl; Dayr al-Aʿwar; Dayr al-Djamādjim; Diyār Rabīʿa; Djabbul; al-Djazīra; Fallūdja; Ḥadītha.I; Ḥarbāʾ; Ḥarūrāʾ; Ḥawīza; al-Ḳādisiyya; Kalwādhā; Kaskar; Ḳaṣr ibn Hubayra; Khāniḳīn; al-Khawarnaḳ; Kūthā; Ḳuṭrabbul; al-Madāʾin; Niffar; Nimrūd; Nīnawā; al-Nukhayla; al-Ruṣāfa.1; Sāmarrāʾ
see also al-Karkh; Nuṣratābād; Senkere
present-day
regions Bahdīnān; al-Baṭīḥa; Maysān
see also Lālish
towns Altīn Köprü; ʿAmādiya; ʿAmāra; ʿĀna; ʿAyn al-Tamr; Badra; Baghdād; Baʿḳūba; Balāwāt; Bārzān; al-Baṣra; Daḳūḳāʾ; Daltāwa; Dīwāniyya; al-Fallūdja; Ḥadītha.II; al-Ḥilla; Hīt; Irbil; Karbalāʾ; Kāẓimayn; Kirkūk; al-Kūfa; Kūt al-ʿAmāra; Maʿalthāyā; al-Mawṣil; al-Nadjaf; al-Nāṣiriyya; Nuṣratābād; Rawāndiz; Sāmarrāʾ; al-Samāwa.2; Senkere; Shahrazūr; Sindjār; Sūḳ al-Shuyūkh; Sulaymāniyya; [in Suppl.] Athūr
see also Djalūlāʾ; *and* → KURDS.TOPONYMS

IRRIGATION Band; Ḳanāt; Māʾ; Nāʿūra
see also Filāḥa; Kārūn; al-Nahrawān; *and* → RIVERS
water **Māʾ**
see also Ḥawḍ; Sabīl.2; Saḳḳāʾ; *and* → ARCHITECTURE.MONUMENTS; HYDROLOGY; NAVIGATION; OCEANS AND SEAS; RIVERS

ISLAM ʿAḳīda; Dīn; Djamaʿa; **Islām**; Masdjid; Muḥammad; Murtadd; Muslim; Rukn.1; Shīʿa

see also Iṣlāḥ; Iʿtikāf; Nubuwwa; Rahbāniyya; Shirk; *and* → ALMS; FASTING; KORAN; PILGRIMAGE; PRAYER
conversion to Islām.ii
European converts Pickthall
five pillars of Islam Ḥadjdj; Ṣalāt; Ṣawm; Shahāda
see also al-Ḳurṭubī, Yaḥyā; Rukn.1
formulas Allāhumma; Basmala; Ḥamdala; In Shāʾ Allāh; Māshāʾ Allāh; Salām; Subḥān
see also [in Suppl.] Abbreviations
popular beliefs ʿAyn; Dīw; Djinn; Ghūl; Muḥammad.2; [in Suppl.] ʿĀʾisha Ḳandīsha; Ḥinn
see also ʿAnḳāʾ; Shafāʿa.2; *and* → LAW.CUSTOMARY LAW

ISRAEL → PALESTINE

ITALY **Īṭaliya**; Ḳawṣara; Ḳillawriya; Rūmiya; Sardāniya; Ṣiḳilliya
and → SICILY

IVORY COAST **Côte d'Ivoire**; Kong

J

JACOBITES → CHRISTIANITY.DENOMINATIONS

JEWELRY [in Suppl.] **Djawhar**
see also Khātam
pearls and precious stones ʿAḳīḳ; al-Durr; Kūh-i Nūr; Luʾluʾ; Mardjān
see also Dhahab; Fiḍḍa; Ḥadjar; Kahrubā; Maʿdin.2.3

JORDAN Dustūr.x; Ḥukūma.iii; Madjlis.4.A.vii; Maḥkama.4.vi; Mandates
physical geography
mountains al-Djibāl
population al-Ḥuwayṭāt; al-Manāṣir
see also [in Suppl.] Demography.III
statesmen ʿAbd Allāh b. al-Ḥusayn
see also Hāshimids
toponyms
ancient Adhrūḥ; Ayla; al-Balḳāʾ; Djarash; al-Djarbāʾ; al-Djibāl; Faḥl; al-Ḥumayma; al-Muwaḳḳar
present-day ʿAdjlūn; al-ʿAḳaba; ʿAmmān; Bayt Rās; al-Ghawr.1; Irbid.I; Maʿān; al-Salṭ; al-Shawbak

JUDAISM Ahl al-Kitāb; Banū Isrā'īl
see also Filasṭīn; Hūd; Nasī'; al-Sāmira; *and* → BIBLE; PALESTINE
communities al-Andalus.iv; al-Fāsiyyūn; Iran.ii and vi; Iṣfahān.1; al-Iskandariyya; Istanbul.vii.b; al-Ḳuds; Lār.2; Mallāḥ; Marrākush; Ṣufrūy
influences in Islam ʿĀshūrā'.I
see also Ḳibla; Muḥammad.i.I.C.2
Jewish personages in Muslim world ʿAbd Allāh b. Salām; Abū ʿĪsā al-Iṣfahānī; Abū Naḍḍāra; Dhū Nuwās; Hāmōn; Ḥasdāy b. Shaprūṭ; Ibn Abi 'l-Bayān; Ibn Djāmiʿ; Ibn Djanāḥ; Ibn Gabirol; Ibn Kammūna; Ibn Maymūn; Ibn Yaʿīsh; Ibrāhīm b. Yaʿḳūb; Isḥāḳ b. Sulaymān al-Isrā'īlī; Kaʿb b. al-Ashraf; al-Kōhēn al-ʿAṭṭār; Māsardjawayh; Māshā' Allāh; Mūsā b. ʿAzra; al-Rādhāniyya; Saʿadyā Ben Yōsēf; Saʿd al-Dawla; al-Samaw'al b. ʿĀdiyā; Shabbatay Ṣebī; Shā'ūl; Shīnā; [in Suppl.] Camondo; Ibn Biklārish
see also Abu 'l-Barakāt; Kaʿb al-Aḥbār; Ḳaynuḳāʿ; Ḳurayẓa
Jewish sects ʿĀnāniyya; al-ʿĪsāwiyya; Karaites
Judaeo-Christian sects Ṣābi'a.1
see also Naṣārā
Judaeo-Muslim sects Shabbatay Ṣebī
Jewish-Muslim relations
persecution Dhimma; Djizya; Ghiyār; al-Ḥākim bi-Amr Allāh; al-Maghīlī
polemics Abū Isḥāḳ al-Ilbīrī; Ibn Ḥazm, Abū Muḥammad; al-Suʿūdī, Abu 'l-Faḍl
see also Ahl al-Kitāb
with Muḥammad Fadak; Ḳaynuḳāʿ; Khaybar; Ḳurayẓa; al-Madīna.i.1; Naḍīr
see also Muḥammad.1.I.C
language and literature Judaeo-Arabic; Judaeo-Berber; Judaeo-Persian; Ḳiṣṣa.8; Risāla.1.VII
see also Geniza; Mukhtaṣar; Musammaṭ; Muwashshaḥ; *and* → LEXICOGRAPHY; LITERATURE.IN OTHER LANGUAGES

K

KENYA Gede; **Kenya**; Kilifi; Lamu; Malindi; Manda; Mazrūʿī; Mombasa; Pate; Siu
see also Nabhān; [in Suppl.] Djarīda.viii
Swahili literature Ḳiṣṣa.7; Madīḥ.5; Marthiya.5; Mathal.5; [in Suppl.] Ḥamāsa.vi
see also Miʿrādj.3
poets Shaaban Robert
song Siti Binti Saad

KORAN   Allāh.i; Āya; Fāṣila; Iʿd̲j̲āz; Ḳirāʾa; **al-Ḳurʾān**; Muḳaṭṭaʿāt; Muṣḥaf; Nask̲h̲; Sūra

    see also ʿArabiyya.A.ii; Basmala; Faḍīla; Hamza; Ind̲j̲īl; Iṣlāḥ.i.B.1; K̲h̲alḳ.II; K̲h̲awāṣṣ al-Ḳurʾān

commentaries   Muk̲h̲taṣar; S̲h̲arḥ.III

    in Arabic   ʿAbd al-Razzāḳ al-Kās̲h̲ānī; Abu 'l-Faḍl ʿAllāmī; Abū Ḥayyān al-G̲h̲arnāṭī; Abu 'l-Layt̲h̲ al-Samarḳandī; Abu 'l-Suʿūd; Abū ʿUbayda; al-ʿAskarī.ii; al-Bag̲h̲awī; Baḳī b. Mak̲h̲lad; al-Bayḍāwī; al-Bulḳīnī.4; al-Dāmād; al-Dārimī; D̲j̲īwan; Fak̲h̲r al-Dīn al-Rāzī; Fayḍī; G̲h̲ulām Ḥusayn K̲h̲ān Ṭabāṭabāʾī; Gīsū Darāz; Gūrānī; Ibn Abi 'l-Rid̲j̲āl; Ibn ʿAd̲j̲iba; Ibn Barrad̲j̲ān; Ibn Kat̲h̲īr, ʿImād al-Dīn; Ismāʿīl Ḥaḳḳi; al-Kalbī.I; Kalīm Allāh al-D̲j̲ahānābādī; Kemāl Pas̲h̲a-zāde; al-Ḳurṭubī, Abū ʿAbd Allāh; al-Ḳus̲h̲ayrī.1; al-Maḥallī; al-Māturīdī; Mud̲j̲āhid b. D̲j̲abr al-Makkī; Mud̲j̲īr al-Dīn al-ʿUlaymī; Muḥsin-i Fayḍ-i Kās̲h̲ānī; Muḳātil b. Sulaymān; al-Nīsābūrī; al-Rāg̲h̲ib al-Iṣfahānī; al-Rummānī; Sahl al-Tustarī; al-S̲h̲aḥḥām; al-S̲h̲ahrastānī, Abu 'l-Fatḥ; al-S̲h̲arīf al-Raḍī; al-Suhrawardī, S̲h̲ihāb al-Dīn Abū Ḥafṣ; al-Sulamī, Abū ʿAbd al-Raḥmān; al-Suyūṭī; [in Suppl.] ʿAbd al-Wahhāb Buk̲h̲ārī; Abu 'l-Fatḥ al-Daylamī; al-Aṣamm

        see also ʿAbd Allāh b. al-ʿAbbās; Abū Nuʿaym al-Mulāʾī; Aḥmadiyya; al-ʿAlamī; al-Dihlawī, S̲h̲āh Walī Allāh; D̲j̲afr; D̲j̲ilwatiyya; Ḥād̲j̲d̲j̲ī Pas̲h̲a; Hind.v.e; Ibn Masʿūd; Ḳuṭb al-Dīn S̲h̲īrāzī; al-Manār; al-Suddī; Sufyān b. ʿUyayna; al-Sulamī, ʿIzz al-Dīn

        late 19th and 20th centuries   al-Ālūsī.2; Aṭfiyās̲h̲; Mawdūdī; Muḥammad b. Aḥmad al-Iskandarānī; Muḥammad Abū Zayd; Muḥammad Farīd Wad̲j̲dī; Sayyid Ḳuṭb; S̲h̲altūt, Maḥmūd; [in Suppl.] D̲j̲awharī, Ṭanṭāwī

    in Persian   Abu 'l-Futūḥ al-Rāzī; al-Dawlatābādī; D̲j̲āmī; Kās̲h̲ifī; al-Maybudī.1; Muṣannifak

    in Turkish   Aḳ Ḥiṣārī.b

    in Urdu   As̲h̲raf ʿAlī

createdness of   Miḥna

    see also D̲j̲ahmiyya

readers   ʿAbd Allāh b. Abī Isḥāḳ; Abū ʿAmr b. al-ʿAlāʾ; al-Aʿmas̲h̲; ʿĀṣim; al-Dānī; Ḥamza b. Ḥabīb; Ibn ʿĀmir; ʿĪsā b. ʿUmar; al-Kisāʾī; Nāfiʿ al-Layt̲h̲ī; al-Sad̲j̲āwandī, Abū ʿAbd Allāh

    see also Abu 'l-ʿĀliya al-Riyāḥī; al-Dāraḳuṭnī; Ḥafṣ b. Sulaymān; Ibn al-D̲j̲azarī; Ibn al-Faḥḥām; Ibn Mud̲j̲āhid; Ibn S̲h̲anabūd̲h̲; al-Ḳasṭallānī; Makkī; al-Malaṭī; Mud̲j̲āhid b. D̲j̲abr al-Makkī; [in Suppl.] Ibn Miḳsam

reading   Adāʾ; Ḥarf; Ḳaṭʿ; K̲h̲atma; **Ḳirāʾa**

    see also al-S̲h̲āṭibī, Abu 'l-Ḳāsim; al-Sid̲j̲istānī

recensions   ʿAbd Allāh b. al-Zubayr; ʿAbd al-Malik b. Marwān; Abu 'l-Dardāʾ; ʿĀʾis̲h̲a bint Abī Bakr; ʿĀṣim; al-Dimyāṭī; al-Ḥad̲j̲d̲j̲ād̲j̲ b. Yūsuf; Ibn

Masʿūd; Nāfiʿ al-Laythī
see also Abu ʾl-Aswad al-Duʾalī; ʿArabiyya.ii.1 and 2; al-Ḥuṣrī.II
stories ʿĀd; Ādam; Aṣḥāb al-Kahf; Ayyūb; Bilkīs; Dāwūd; Djālūt; Firʿawn; Ḥābīl wa Ḳābīl; Ḥawwāʾ; Ibrāhīm; ʿĪsā; al-Iskandar; al-Khaḍir; Lūṭ; Maryam; Mūsā; Nūḥ; Sulaymān b. Dāwūd
see also Ḳiṣaṣ al-Anbiyāʾ; Shayṭān.2; *and* → BIBLE.BIBLICAL PERSONAGES
suras al-Aḥḳāf; Aṣḥāb al-Kahf; Fātiḥa; al-Fīl; Ghāshiya; Kawthar; Luḳmān; al-Muʿawwidhatān[i]; al-Muddaththir and al-Muzzammil; al-Musabbiḥāt; Sadjda; al-Ṣāffāt
see also Ḥayawān.3; **Sūra**
terms Aḥkām; ʿĀlam; Amr; al-Aʿrāf; ʿAṣa; Aṣḥab al-Kahf; Aṣḥāb al-Rass; Aṣḥāb al-Ukhdūd; Āya; Baḥīra; al-Baḥrayn; Baʿl; Barāʾa; Baraka; Barzakh; Birr; Dābba; Daʿwa; Dharra; Dīn; Djahannam; Djāhiliyya; Djanna; Djinn; Dunyā; Faḳīr; Farāʾiḍ; Fitna; Fiṭra; Furḳān; al-Ghayb; Ḥadd; Ḥaḳḳ; Ḥanīf; Hātif; Ḥawārī; Ḥayāt; Ḥidjāb; Ḥisāb; Ḥizb; Ḥudjdja; Ḥūr; Iblīs; Īlāf; Ilhām; ʿIlliyyūn; Kaffāra; Kāfir; Kalima; Ḳarīn; Ḳarya; Ḳawm; Ḳayyim; Khalḳ; Khaṭīʾa; Ḳiyāma; Kursī; Ḳuwwa.2; Lawḥ; Madjnūn; Maḳām Ibrāhīm; Milla; Millet; Miskīn; Mīthāḳ; al-Munāfiḳūn.1; Nadhīr; Nafs.I; Nār; Raḥma; Rizḳ; Rudjūʿ; Rukn; Ṣabr; Ṣadr; al Ṣāffāt; Ṣaḥīfa; Sakīna; Salām; al-Ṣāliḥūn; Shaḳāwa; Shakk.1; Shirk; al-Ṣiddīḳ; Sidjdjīl; Sidjdjīn; Sidrat al-Muntahā; Sirādj;; Ṣirāṭ; Subḥān; Sulṭān; [in Suppl.] Asāṭīr al-Awwalīn
see also Ḥikāya.I; Sabab.1; Samāʾ.1
translations Ḳurʾān.9
see also Aljamía
into English Aḥmadiyya; Pickthall
into Malay ʿAbd al-Raʾūf al-Sinkilī
into Persian al-Dihlawī, Shāh Walī Allāh
see also Khaṭṭ.ii
into Swahili Kenya (891a)
into Urdu ʿAbd al-Ḳādir Dihlawī; Djawān; Rafīʿ al-Dīn

KURDS **Kurds**
see also Kitāb al-Djilwa; *and* → IRAN; IRAQ; TURKEY
dynasties ʿAnnāzids; Bābān; Faḍlawayh; Ḥasanwayh; Marwānids; Rawwādids; Shaddādids
see also Kurds.iii.B
Kurdish national movement Badrkhānī; Ḳāḍī Muḥammad; Kurds.iii.C; Muṣṭafā Barzānī
see also Bārzān; Mahābād
sects Ṣārliyya; Shabak
toponyms Ardalān; Bahdīnān; Barādūst; Bārzān; Djawānrūd; Hakkārī.2; Rawāndiz; Saḳḳiz; Sanandadj; Sāwdj-Bulāḳ; Shahrazūr; Shamdīnān; Ṣōmāy; Sulaymāniyya

see also Kirkūk; Kurds.ii; Orāmār; Shabānkāra; Sīsar
tribes Djāf; Hakkārī.1; Hamawand; Kurds.iii.B and iv.A.2; Lak.1; Shabānkāra; Shakāk; Shaḳāḳī; Sindjābī

KUWAIT Djarīda.i.A; Dustūr.xvi; **al-Kuwayt**; Madjlis.4.A.ix; Maḥkama.4.ix; Ṣabāḥ, Āl
see also (Djazīrat) al-ʿArab; al-ʿArabiyya; Djāmiʿa
toponyms al-Dibdiba; [in Suppl.] Aḥmadī
see also Ḳarya al-ʿUlyā

L

LAMENTATION Bakkāʾ; **Niyāḥa**; Rawḍa-khʷānī

LAND → TAXATION
in the sense of agriculture, see Filāḥa
in the sense of surveying, see Misāḥa; Rawk

LANGUAGES **Lugha**
and → LINGUISTICS
Afro-Asiatic Ḥām; Sām.2
see also Karshūnī; Maʿlūlā.2; Sullam
Arabic Algeria.v; Aljamía; al-Andalus.x; **Arabiyya**.A; ʿIrāḳ.iv.a; Judaeo-Arabic.i and ii; Lībiyā.2; al-Maghrib.VII; Malta.2; Mūrītāniyā.6
see also Ibn Makkī; Ḳarwasha; Khaṭṭ; Madjmaʿ ʿIlmī.i; al-Sīm; [in Suppl.] Ḥaḍramawt.iii
Arabic dialects Arabiyya.A.iii; al-Ṣaʿīd.2; al-Shām.3; Shāwiya.3; Shuwa; Siʿird; Sūdān.2; Sūdān (Bilād al-).3
and → LINGUISTICS.PHONETICS; LITERATURE.POETRY.VERNACULAR
Christian Arabic Karshūnī; Shaykhū, Luwīs
see also ʿArabiyya.A.ii.1
Bantu Swahili
Berber **Berbers**.V; Judaeo-Berber; Mūrītāniyā.6; Sīwa.2
see also Mzāb
Berber words in Arabic Āfrāg; Agadir; Āgdāl; Aménokal; Amghar; Argan; Ayt; Imẓad
see also Ḳallala; Rīf.I.2(a)
Chadic Hausa.ii
Cushitic Kūsh; Somali.5
Ethiopian-Semitic Eritrea.iv; Ḥabash.iv
Hebrew Ibn Djanāḥ
North Arabian Ṣafaitic

see also Liḥyān; *and* → EPIGRAPHY
South Arabian Saba᾽
see also Ḥaḍramawt (*and* [in Suppl.] Ḥaḍramawt.iii); al-Ḥarāsīs; al-Sawdā᾽; *and* → EPIGRAPHY
Modern South Arabian Mahrī; Shiḥrī; Suḳuṭra.3
see also al-Baṭāḥira; al-Ḥarāsīs; [in Suppl.] Ḥaḍramawt.iii
Teda-Daza Kanuri
Austronesian Atjèh; Indonesia.iii; Malays
Ibero-Caucasian Andi; Beskesek-abaza; Čerkes; Dāghistān; Darghin; al-Ḳabḳ; Ḳayyūm Nāṣirī
see also al-Kurdj
Indo-European Arnawutluḳ.1
see also al-Ḳabḳ
Indo-Iranian
Indian Afghānistān.iii; Bengali.i; Ceylon; Chitral.II; Dardic and Kāfir Languages; Gudjarātī; Hind.iii; Hindī; Hindustānī; Kashmīrī; Lahndā; Maldives.2; Marāthī; Pandjābī.1; Sind.3.a
see also Madjma῾ ῾Ilmī.iv; Sidi; [in Suppl.] Burushaski
Iranian Afghān.ii; Afghānistān.iii; Balūčistān.B; Darī; Gūrān; Hind.iii; ῾Irāḳ.iv.b; Judaeo-Persian.ii; Kurds.v; Lur
see also Dāghistān; al-Ḳabḳ; Khʷārazm; Madjma῾ ῾Ilmī.ii; Ossetians; Shughnān; al-Ṣughd
Persian dialects Simnān.3
(Niger-)Kordofanian Nūba.3
Nilo-Saharan Nūba.3; Songhay.1; Sūdān.2
Turkic Ādharī; Balkar; Bulghār; Gagauz; Khaladj.2
see also Afghānistān.iii; Dāghistān; al-Ḳabḳ; Khazar; Madjma῾ ῾Ilmī.iii

LAW ῾Āda; Dustūr; **Fiḳh**; Idjmā῾; **Ḳānūn**.i and iii; Ḳiyās; Maḥkama; **Sharī῾a**
see also Aṣḥāb al-Ra᾽y; Ḥuḳūḳ; *and* → INHERITANCE
for questions of law, see ῾Abd.3; Djāsūs; Filāḥa.i.4; Ḥarb.i; Ḥarīr; In Shā᾽ Allāh; Intiḥār; Ḳabr; Kāfir; Khāliṣa; Khiṭba; Mā᾽; al-Mar᾽a; Murtadd; Raḍā῾; Rāḳid; Rashwa; Safar.1; Sha῾r.2; Ṣūra; al-Suraydjiyya
Anglo-Mohammedan law ῾Āda.iii; Amīr ῾Alī; Munṣif
see also Ḥanafiyya
customary law **῾Āda**; Dakhīl; Ḳānūn.iv; [in Suppl.] Djirga
see also Baranta; Berbers.IV; al-Māmī; al-Mar᾽a.2; Mushā῾
early religious law Abū Ḥanīfa; Abū Yūsuf; al-Ash῾arī, Abū Burda; ῾Aṭā᾽ b. Abī Rabāḥ; al-Awzā῾ī; Ibn Abī Laylā.II; Ibn Shubruma; al-Layth b. Sa῾d; Mālik b. Anas; Maymūn b. Mihrān; al-Nakha῾ī, Ibrāhīm; al-Sha῾bī; al-Shāfi῾ī; Shurayḥ; Sufyān al-Thawrī; [in Suppl.] Fuḳahā᾽ al-Madīna al-Sab῾a; Ibn Abi ᾽l-Zinād
Ibāḍī law ῾Abd al-῾Azīz b. al-Ḥādjdj Ibrāhīm; Abū Ghānim al-Khurāsānī; Abū

Muḥammad b. Baraka (*and* Ibn Baraka); Abū Zakariyyāʾ al-Djanāwunī; Ibn Djaʿfar
see also al-Djayṭālī; Maḥkama.4.ix (Oman)

in South-east Asia Penghulu; Rapak; Sharīʿa (In South-East Asia)

inheritance → INHERITANCE

jurisprudence Fatwā; **Fiḳh**; Īdjāb; Idjmāʿ; Idjtihād; Ikhtilāf; Istiḥsān; Ḳiyās; Maṣlaḥa; Nāzila
see also Sadd al-Dharāʾīʿ

jurist **Faḳīh**; Mardjaʿ-i Taḳlīd; Mudjtahid
see also Sharḥ.III

Ḥanafī Abū Ḥanīfa al-Nuʿmān; Abu ʾl-Layth al-Samarḳandī; Abu ʾl-Suʿūd; al-ʿAmīdī; al-Bihārī; al-Djaṣṣāṣ; al-Ḥalabī; Ḥamza al-Ḥarrānī; Ibn ʿĀbidīn; Ibn Buhlūl; Ibn Ghānim; Ibn Ḳuṭlūbughā; Ibn Nudjaym; Ibn al-Shiḥna; Ḳāḍī Khān; al-Kāsānī; Ḳasṭallānī; al-Ḳudūrī, Abu ʾl-Ḥusayn Aḥmad; al-Marghīnānī; al-Nasafī.4; al-Sadjāwandī, Sirādj al-Dīn; al-Sarakhsī, Muḥammad b. Aḥmad; al-Shaybānī, Abū ʿAbd Allāh; al-Shiblī, Abū Ḥafs; [in Suppl.] Abū ʿAbd Allāh al-Baṣrī; Abu ʾl-Barakāt; al-Dāmaghānī, Abū ʿAbd Allāh Muḥammad b. ʿAlī; al-Dāmaghānī, Abu ʾl-Ḥasan ʿAlī b. Muḥammad
see also ʿAbd al-Ḳādir al-Ḳurashī; al-Fatāwā al-ʿĀlamgīriyya; Ibn Duḳmāḳ; al-Ṣayrafī

Ḥanbalī Aḥmad b. Ḥanbal; al-Bahūtī; al-Barbahārī; Ghulām al-Khallāl; Ibn ʿAḳīl; Ibn al-Bannāʾ; Ibn Baṭṭa al-ʿUkbarī; Ibn al-Djawzī; Ibn al-Farrāʾ; Ibn Ḥāmid; Ibn Ḳayyim al-Djawziyya; Ibn Ḳudāma al-Maḳdisī; Ibn Mufliḥ; Ibn Radjab; Ibn Taymiyya; al-Kalwadhānī; al-Khallāl; al-Khiraḳī; al-Marwazī
and → THEOLOGY

Mālikī Aḥmad Bābā; Asad b. al-Furāt; al-Bādjī; al-Bāḳillānī; Bannānī; al-Burzulī; al-Dānī; al-Fāsī; Ibn ʿAbd al-Ḥakam; Ibn Abī Zamanayn; Ibn Abī Zayd al-Ḳayrawānī; Ibn ʿAmmār, Abu ʾl-ʿAbbās; Ibn ʿArafa; Ibn ʿĀṣim; Ibn al-Faraḍī; Ibn Farḥūn; Ibn Ḥabīb, Abū Marwān; Ibn al-Ḥādjdj; Ibn al-Ḥādjib; Ibn al-Ḳāsim; Ibn Maḍāʾ; Ibn Rushayd; Ibn Sūda; al-Ibshīhī(1); ʿĪsā b. Dīnār; ʿIyāḍ b. Mūsā; al-Ḳābisī; al-Ḳalaṣādī; al-Kardūdī; Ḳaṣṣāra; Khalīl b. Isḥāḳ; al-Khushanī; al-Ḳurṭubī, Abū ʿAbd Allāh; al-Ḳurṭubī, Yaḥyā; Mālik b. Anas; al-Manūfī.4 and 5; al-Māzarī; Muḥammad b. Saḥnūn; Saḥnūn; Sālim b. Muḥammad; al-Sanhūrī, Abu ʾl-Ḥasan; Shabṭūn; al-Shāṭibī, Abū Isḥāḳ; Shihāb al-Dīn al-Ḳarāfī; [in Suppl.] Abū ʿImrān al-Fāsī; al-Azdī; Ibn Daḳīḳ al-ʿĪd; Ibn Dirham; Ibn Rushd
see also Ibn ʿAbd al-Barr; al-Ḳaṣṣār; Laḳīṭ; al-Sharīf al-Tilimsānī

Shāfiʿī al-ʿAbbādī; Abū Shudjāʿ; Bādjūrī; al-Baghawī; al-Bulḳīnī; Daḥlān; al-Djanadī; al-Djīzī; al-Djuwaynī; Ibn Abī ʿAṣrūn; Ibn Abi ʾl-Dam; Ibn

ʿAḳīl; Ibn ʿAsākir; Ibn Djamāʿa; Ibn Ḥabīb, Badr al-Dīn; Ibn Ḥadjar al-Haytamī; Ibn Ḳāḍī Shuhba.1; Ibn Ḳāsim al-Ghazzī; Ibn al-Ṣalāḥ; Ibn Suraydj; al-Ḳalḳashandī; al-Ḳalyūbī; al-Ḳazwīnī, Abū Ḥātim; al-Ḳazwīnī, Djalāl al-Dīn; al-Ḳazwīnī, Nadjm al-Dīn; al-Kiyā al-Harrāsī; Makhrama; al-Māwardī; al-Mutawallī; al-Muzanī; al-Nawawī; al-Rāfiʿī; al-Ramlī; al-Shāfiʿī; al-Shahrazūrī; al-Shīrāzī, Abū Isḥāḳ; al-Subkī; al-Sulamī, ʿIzz al-Dīn; al-Ṣuʿlūkī; [in Suppl.] Abū Zurʿa; Ibn Daḳīḳ al-ʿĪd
see also Abū Thawr; Dāwūd b. Khalaf; al-Isfarāyīnī

Shiite → SHIITES

Ẓāhirī Dāwūd b. Khalaf; al-Ḥumaydī; Ibn Dāwūd; Ibn Ḥazm, Abū Muḥammad; (al-)Mundhir b. Saʿīd
see also Ṣāʿid al-Andalusī; [in Suppl.] Ibn al-Rūmiyya

law of obligations ʿAḳd; ʿĀriyya; Bayʿ; Ḍamān; Dhimma; Fāsid wa Bāṭil; Faskh; Hiba; Īdjāb; Idjār; Inkār; ʿIwaḍ; Kafāla; Khiyār; Ḳirāḍ; Muʿāmalāt; Muʿāwaḍa.3; Muḍāraba; Mufāwaḍa; Mughārasa; Mushāraka; Rahn; Ṣulḥ; [in Suppl.] Dayn; Gharūḳa
see also ʿAmal.4; Djāʾiz; Ghasb; Ḳabḍ.i; Ḳasam; Maḍmūn; Suftadja; [in Suppl.] Ikrāh

contract of hire and lease Adjr; **Īdjār**; Kirāʾ; Musāḳāt; Muzāraʿa; [in Suppl.] Ḥikr; Inzāl

contract of sale Barāʾa.I; **Bayʿ**; Iḳāla; ʿIwaḍ; Muʿāwaḍa.1; Muwāḍaʿa.1; Salam; Shirāʾ; [in Suppl.] Darak
see also Ḍarūra; Ildjāʾ; Mukhāṭara; Ṣafḳa; Salaf; Sawm

law of procedure ʿAdl; Amīn; Bayyina; Daʿwā; Ghāʾib; Ḥakam; Iḳrār; Ḳaḍāʾ; Maẓālim; Shāhid; Sidjill.2

offices Faḳīh; Ḥakam; Ḳāḍī; Ḳāḍī ʿAskar; Ḳassām; Mardjaʿ-i Taḳlīd; Nāʾib.1; Shaykh al-Islām
see also Amīn; Fatwā; Khalīfa.ii; Maḥkama; Shurṭa

Ottoman Bāb-i Mashīkhat; Djazāʾ.ii; Djurm; Fatwā.ii; ʿIlmiyye; Ḳānūn.iii; Ḳānūnnāme; Ḳassām; Maḥkama.2; Makhredj; Medjelle; Medjlis-i Wālā; Mewlewiyyet; Narkh; Shaykh al-Islām.2; Sidjill.3
see also Ḥanafiyya; al-Ḥaramayn; *and* → DYNASTIES.ANATOLIA AND THE TURKS.OTTOMANS.GRAND MUFTIS

penal law ʿĀḳila; Diya; Ḥadd; Ḳadhf; Ḳatl; Khaṭaʾ; Ḳiṣāṣ.5; Ṣalb; Sariḳa
see also Muḥṣan; al-Ṣalīb; Shubha; Sidjn; [in Suppl.] Ikrāh

reform → REFORM

schools Ḥanābila; Ḥanafiyya; Mālikiyya; al-Shāfiʿiyya
see also Ibn Abī Laylā; Sufyān al-Thawrī

terms Adāʾ; Adjr.2; ʿAdl; Aḥkām; Ahl al-Ḥall wa ʾl-ʿAḳd; ʿAḳd; Akdariyya; ʿAḳīḳa; ʿĀḳila; ʿAmal.3 and 4; Amān; ʿĀmil; Amīn; ʿĀriyya; ʿArsh; ʿAwl; ʿAzīma.1; Baʿl.2.b; Bāligh; Barāʾa.I; Bayʿ; Bayʿa; Bayyina; Burhān; Ḍamān; Dār al-ʿAhd; Dār al-Ḥarb; Dār al-Islām; Dār al-Ṣulḥ; Ḍarūra; Daʿwā;

D͟habīḥa; D͟himma; Diya; Djāʾiz; Djanāba; Djazāʾ.ii; Djihād; Djizya; Djurm; Fakīh; Farāʾiḍ; Farḍ; Fāsid wa-Bāṭil; Fāsiḳ; Fas͟kh; Fatwā; Fayʾ; Fiḳh; G͟hāʾib; G͟hanīma; G͟hārim; G͟haṣb; G͟husl; Ḥaḍāna; Ḥadat͟h; Ḥadd; Ḥad͟jr; Hady; Ḥakam; Ḥaḳḳ; Ḥawāla; Ḥayḍ; Hiba; Ḥiyal.4; Ḥuḳūḳ; Ḥulūl; ʿIbādāt; Ibāḥa.I; ʿIdda; Id͟hn; Īd͟jāb; Īd͟jār; Idjmāʿ; Idjtihād; Iḥrām; Iḥyāʾ; Iḳāla; Ik͟htilāf; Iḳrār; Ild͟jāʾ; Inkār; Inṣāf; Istibrāʾ; Istiḥsān; Istiʾnāf; Istis͟hāb; ʿIwaḍ; Ḳabāla; Ḳabḍ.i; Ḳaḍāʾ; Ḳad͟hf; Kafāʾa; Kafāla; Ḳānūn; Ḳānūnnāme; Ḳasam; Ḳatl; K͟haṭaʾ; K͟hiyār; Kirāʾ; Ḳirāḍ; Ḳiṣāṣ; Ḳiyās; Liʿān; Liṣṣ; Luḳaṭa; Maḍmūn; Mafṣūl; Mahr; Maṣlaḥa; Mawāt; Mawlā.5; Maẓālim; Milk; Muʿāmalāt; Muʿāwaḍa; Muḍāraba; Mud͟jtahid; Mufāwaḍa; Mug͟hārasa; Muḥṣan; Muk͟hāṭara; Munāṣafa; Musāḳāt; Mus͟hāraka; Mutʿa; Muṭlaḳ; Muwāḍaʿa.1; Muzāraʿa; Nad͟jis; Nāfila; Naṣṣ; Nāzila; Niyya; Rahn; Ribā; Ruk͟hṣa.1; Sabab.2; Ṣadaḳa; Sadd al-D͟harāʾīʿ; Ṣafḳa; Ṣaḥīḥ.2; al-Sahm.2; Salaf; Salam; Sariḳa; Sawm; S͟hāhid; S͟hak͟hṣ; S͟hakk.1; S͟harika; S͟harṭ.1; S͟hirāʾ; S͟hubha; S͟hufʿa; Sid͟jn; Suftad͟ja; Suknā; Sukūt; Ṣulḥ; Sunna.2; [in Suppl.] ʿAḳār; Darak; Dayn; D͟jabr; G͟hārūḳa; Ḥikr; Ikrāh; Inzāl *see also* Bayt al-Māl; Hudna; Ṣag͟hīr; S͟hukr.2; S͟hūrā.2; Siyāsa.3

LEBANON   D͟jarīda.i.A; D͟jāmiʿa; Dustūr.ix; Ḥizb.i; Ḥukūma.iii; **Lubnān**; Mad͟jlis.4.A.vi; Maḥkama.4.iii; Mandates; Mutawālī
   see also Baladiyya.2; D͟jāliya; Ḳays ʿAylān; al-Maʿlūf; [in Suppl.] Aḥmad Pas͟ha Küčük; al-Bustānī; Demography.III; *and* → DRUZES
governors   Bas͟hīr S͟hihāb II; Dāwūd Pas͟ha; D͟jānbulāt; Fak͟hr al-Dīn; Ḥarfūs͟h; S͟hihāb
   see also Maʿn; Maʿn-zāda
historians of   Iskandar Ag͟ha
religious leaders   S͟haraf al-Dīn
   see also Mutawālī
toponyms
   ancient   ʿAyn al-D͟jarr
   present-day
      regions   al-Biḳāʿ; al-S͟hūf
      towns   Baʿlabakk; Batrūn; Bayrūt; Bs͟harrā; Bteddīn; D͟jubayl; Karak Nūḥ; Ṣaydā; Ṣūr

LEGENDS   Ḥikāya
   and → BIBLE.BIBLICAL PERSONAGES; ESCHATOLOGY; KORAN.STORIES
legendary beings   ʿAnḳāʾ; al-Burāḳ; Dīw; al-D͟jassāsa; D͟jinn; G͟hūl; Hātif; ʿIfrīt; Ḳuṭrub; Parī; Sīmurg͟h
   see also al-Ruk͟hk͟h
legendary locations   Damāwand; D͟jūdī; Ergenekon; Ḥūs͟h; Ḳîzîl-elma; Sāwa.3
legendary people   Abū Rig͟hāl; Abū Safyān; Abū Zayd; ʿAdnān; Afrāsiyāb; Ahl

al-Ṣuffa; Amīna; Āṣāf b. Barakhyā; Asḥāb al-Kahf; Barṣīṣā; al-Basūs; Bilḳīs; al-Dadjdjāl; Djamshīd; Ḥabīb al-Nadjdjār; Ḥanẓala b. Ṣafwān; Hind bint al-Khuss; Hirmis; Hūshang; Ibn Buḳayla; al-Kāhina; Ḳaḥṭān; Kāwah; al-Khaḍir; Luḳmān; Masʿūd; Naṣr al-Dīn Khodja; Sām; Saṭīḥ b. Rabīʿa; Shiḳḳ; Siyāwush; Sulaymān b. Dāwūd
see also Akhī Ewrān; ʿAmr b. ʿAdī; ʿAmr b. Luḥayy; Aṣḥāb al-Rass; Ḳuss b. Sāʿida; Muʿammar; Ṣarï Ṣalṭūḳ Dede; *and* → KORAN.STORIES

legendary stories ʿAbd Allāh b. Djudʿān; Aktham b. Ṣayfī; Almās; al-Baṭṭāl; Buhlūl; Damāwand; Djirdjīs; Djūdī; al-Durr; Fāṭima; al-Ghazāl; al-Ḥaḍr; Ḥāʾiṭ al-ʿAdjūz; Haram; Hārūt wa-Mārūt; Hudhud; Isrāʾīliyyāt; Khālid b. Yazīd b. Muʿāwiya; Ḳiṣaṣ al-Anbiyāʾ; Nūḥ

LEXICOGRAPHY **Ḳāmūs**; Laḥn al-ʿĀmma
see also Sharḥ.I; Sullam; *and* → LINGUISTICS

lexicographers

Arabic Abū Zayd al-Anṣārī; al-Azharī; al-Djawālīḳī; al-Djawharī; Farḥāt; al-Fīrūzābādī; Ibn al-Birr; Ibn Durayd; Ibn Fāris; Ibn Makkī; Ibn Manẓūr; Ibn Sīda; Ibn al-Sikkīt; al-Ḳazzāz; al-Khalīl b. Aḥmad; Muḥammad Murtaḍā; Nashwān b. Saʿīd; al-Ṣaghānī, Raḍiyy al-Dīn; al-Shaybānī, Abū ʿAmr (*and* [in Suppl.] Abū ʿAmr al-Shaybānī); [in Suppl.] Abū Isḥāḳ al-Fārisī; al-Bustānī.1 and 2; al-Fārābī
see also Abū Ḥātim al-Rāzī; Akhtarī; al-Rāghib al-Iṣfahānī; [in Suppl.] Ibn Kabar

Hebrew Ibn Djanāḥ
see also Judaeo-Arabic.iii.B

Persian ʿAbd al-Rashīd al-Tattawī; Aḥmad Wafīḳ Pasha; Burhān; Surūrī Kāshānī; [in Suppl.] Dehkhudā
see also Ārzū Khān; Mahdī Khān Astarābādī; Riḍā Ḳulī Khān

Turkish Akhtarī; al-Kāshgharī; Kāẓim Ḳadrī; Niʿmat Allāh b. Aḥmad; Sāmī
see also Esʿad Efendi, Meḥmed; Luṭfī Efendi; Riyāḍī; Shināsī

terms Fard.b

LIBYA Djāmiʿa; Djarīda.i.B; Dustūr.xii; **Lībiyā**; Madjlis.4.A.xviii
see also ʿArabiyya.A.iii.3; al-Bārūnī; Ḳaramānlī; Khalīfa b. ʿAskar; Sanūsiyya; *and* → DYNASTIES.SPAIN AND NORTH AFRICA

population → AFRICA.NORTH AFRICA; BERBERS

toponyms

ancient Ṣabra; Surt

present-day

oases Awdjila; Baḥriyya; al-Djaghbūb; Djawf Kufra; al-Djufra; Ghadamès; Kufra

regions Barḳa; al-Djufra; Fazzān

see also Nafūsa
towns Adjdābiya; Benghāzī; Darna; Djādū; Murzuḳ
see also Ghāt

LIFE STAGES **Ḥayāt**
childbirth ʿAḳīḳa; Āl; Liʿān; al-Marʾa.2.c; Mawākib.4.2
see also Raḍāʿ
pregnancy Rāḳid
suckling Raḍāʿ
treatises on ʿArīb b. Saʿd al-Kātib al-Ḳurṭubī
childhood Bāligh; **Ṣaghīr**
see also Ḥaḍāna; al-Shayb wa ʼl-Shabāb; *and* → CIRCUMCISION; EDUCATION; MARRIAGE
old age **Muʿammar**
see also al-Shayb wa ʼl-Shabāb; Shaykh; *and* → DEATH

LINGUISTICS **Lugha**; Naḥw
see also Balāgha; Bayān; Laḥn al-ʿĀmma; Sharḥ.I; *and* → LANGUAGES; LEXICOGRAPHY
grammarians/philologists
8th century ʿAbd Allāh b. Abī Isḥāḳ; Abū ʿAmr al-ʿAlāʾ; al-Akhfash.I; ʿĪsā b. ʿUmar; al-Khalīl b. Aḥmad; Ḳuṭrub; al-Mufaḍḍal al-Ḍabbī; Sībawayhi; al-Shaybānī, Abū ʿAmr (*and* [in Suppl.] Abū ʿAmr al-Shaybānī)
see also [in Suppl.] Abu ʼl-Bayḍāʾ al-Riyāḥī
9th century Abū Ḥātim al-Sidjistānī; Abū ʿUbayd al-Ḳāsim b. Sallām; Abū ʿUbayda; Abū Zayd al-Anṣārī; al-Akhfash.II; al-Aṣmaʿī; al-Bāhilī, Abū Naṣr; Djūdī al-Mawrūrī; al-Farrāʾ; Ibn al-Aʿrābī, Muḥammad; Ibn Sallām al-Djumaḥī; Ibn al-Sikkīt; al-Kisāʾī, Abu ʼl-Ḥasan; al-Layth b. al-Muẓaffar; al-Māzinī, Abū ʿUthmān; al-Mubarrad; Muḥammad b. Ḥabīb; al-Ruʾāsī; [in Suppl.] Abu ʼl-ʿAmaythal
10th century al-Akhfash.III; al-Anbārī, Abū Bakr; al-Anbārī, Abū Muḥammad; al-ʿAskarī.i; Djaḥẓa; al-Fārisī; Ghulām Thaʿlab; Ḥamza al-Iṣfahānī; Ibn al-ʿArīf, al-Ḥusayn; Ibn Djinnī; Ibn Durayd; Ibn Durustawayh; Ibn Kaysān; Ibn Khālawayh; Ibn al-Khayyāṭ, Abū Bakr; Ibn al-Ḳūṭiyya; Ibn al-Naḥḥās; Ibn al-Sarrādj; al-Ḳālī; Ḳudāma; Nifṭawayh; al-Rummānī; al-Sīrāfī; [in Suppl.] Abū Isḥāḳ al-Fārisī; Abū Riyāsh al-Ḳaysī; Abu ʼl-Ṭayyib al-Lughawī; al-Ḥātimī; Ibn Kaysān; Ibn Miḳsam
11th century al-Adjdābī; al-ʿAskarī. ii; Ibn al-Birr; Ibn Fāris; Ibn al-Ḥādjdj; Ibn al-Iflīlī; Ibn Makkī; Ibn Sīda; al-Ḳazzāz; al-Marzūḳī; al-Rabaḥī; al-Rabaʿī; al-Shantamarī; [in Suppl.] Abū Usāma al-Harawī; al-Djurdjānī
12th century al-Anbārī, Abu ʼl-Barakāt; al-Baṭalyawsī; al-Djawālīḳī; al-Djazūlī, Abū Mūsā; al-Ḥarīrī; Ibn Barrī, Abū Muḥammad; Ibn Maḍāʾ;

Ibn al-Shadjarī al-Baghdādī; al-Maydānī; [in Suppl.] Abu 'l-Barakāt; Ibn Hishām al-Lakhmī
13th century al-Astarābādhī, Raḍī al-Dīn; Ibn al-Adjdābī; Ibn al-Athīr.1; Ibn al-Ḥādjdj; Ibn al-Ḥādjib; Ibn Mālik; Ibn Muʿṭī; al-Muṭarrizī; al-Shalawbīn; al-Sharīshī; [in Suppl.] al-Balaṭī, Abu 'l-Fatḥ ʿUthmān; Ibn al-Adjdābī
14th century Abū Ḥayyān al-Gharnāṭī; al-Astarābādhī, Rukn al-Dīn; Fakhrī; Ibn Ādjurrūm; Ibn ʿAḳīl, ʿAbd Allāh; Ibn Barrī, Abu 'l-Ḥasan; Ibn Hishām, Djamāl al-Dīn; Ibn Khātima; Ibn al-Ṣāʾigh; al-Sharīf al-Gharnatī
15th century al-Azharī, Khālid; Ibn ʿĀṣim; al-Sanhūrī, Abu 'l-Ḥasan; al-Suyūṭī
17th century ʿAbd al-Ḳādir al-Baghdādī
18th century Farḥāt
19th century Fāris al-Shidyaḳ; Ibn al-Ḥādjdj; al-Nabarāwī
see also Fuʾād Pasha
20th century [in Suppl.] Arat
phonetics Ḥurūf al-Hidjāʾ.II; Makhāridj al-Ḥurūf; Mushtarik; Ṣawtiyya
see also Ḍād; Dāl; Dhāl; Djīm; Fāʾ; Ghayn; Haʾ; Ḥāʾ; Hamza; Hāwī; Ḥurūf al-Hidjāʾ; Imāla; Kāf; Ḳāf; Khāʾ; Lām; Mīm; Nūn; Pāʾ; Rāʾ; Ṣād; Sīn and Shīn
for Arabic dialects, see Algeria.v; Andalus.x; ʿIrāḳ.iv; Lībīya.2; al-Maghrib.VII; Mahrī; Malta.2
terms Aḍdād; Āla.i.; ʿĀmil; ʿAṭf; Dakhīl; Djāmiʿ, Fard, Fiʿl; Gharīb; Ḥaraka wa Sukūn.ii; Ḥarf; Hāwī; Ḥikāya.I; Ḥukm.II; Ḥulūl; Ibdāl; Iḍāfa; Idghām; Iḍmār; ʿIlla.i; Imāla; Iʿrāb; Ishtiḳāḳ; Ism; Istifhām; Istithnāʾ; Kasra; Ḳaṭʿ; Khabar; Ḳiyās.2; Māḍī; Maʿnā.1; Muʿarrab; Mubālagha.a; Mubtadaʾ.1; Muḍāriʿ; Mudhakkar; Muḍmar; Musnad.2; Muṭlaḳ; Muwallad.2; Muzdawidj; Nafy; Naṣb; Naʿt; Nisba.1, Rafʿ.1; Sabab.4; Ṣaḥīḥ.3; Sālim.2; Ṣarf; Sharṭ.3; Ṣifa.1; Ṣila.1; [in Suppl.] Ḥāl
see also Basīṭ wa-Murakkab; Ghalaṭāt-i Meshhūre; Ḥurūf al-Hidjāʾ

LITERATURE **Adab**; ʿArabiyya.B; ʿIrāḳ.v; Iran.vii; ʿOthmānli.III
autobiographical Nuʿayma, Mīkhāʾīl; Sālim; Shāʾūl
see also Shaybānī
biographical Faḍīla; **Manāḳib**; Mathālib
see also ʿIlm al-Ridjāl; Maʾāthir al-Umarāʾ; Mughals.10; Shurafāʾ.2 Ṣila.2.II.c; *and* → HAGIOGRAPHY; LITERATURE.HISTORICAL *and* POETRY; MEDICINE.PHYSICIANS.BIOGRAPHIES OF; MUḤAMMAD, THE PROPHET
criticism Ibn al-Athīr.3; Ibn Rashīḳ; Ḳudāma; [in Suppl.] al-Djurdjānī; al-Ḥātimī
modern Kemāl, Meḥmed Nāmiḳ; Köprülü; Kurd ʿAlī; al-Māzinī; Olghun, Meḥmed Ṭāhir; [in Suppl.] Alangu; Atač

terms Mubālagha.b

drama **Masraḥ**

Arabic Khayāl al-Ẓill; Masraḥ.1 and 2

see also ʿArabiyya.B.V

playwrights Abū Naḍḍāra; Faraḥ Anṭūn; Ibn Dāniyāl; al-Ḳusanṭīnī; al-Maʿlūf; Nadjīb al-Ḥaddād; Nadjīb Muḥammad Surūr; al-Naḳḳāsh; Ṣalāḥ ʿAbd al-Ṣabūr; Salīm al-Naḳḳāsh; al-Sharḳāwī; Shawḳī; [in Suppl.] al-Bustānī.1

see also Isḥāḳ, Adīb; Ismāʿīl Ṣabrī; Khalīl Muṭrān; Shumayyil, Shiblī

Central Asian Masraḥ.5

Persian Masraḥ.4

playwrights Muḥammad Djaʿfar Ḳaradja-dāghī; [in Suppl.] Amīrī

Turkish Ḳaragöz; Ḳawuḳlu; Masraḥ.3; Orta Oyunu

playwrights ʿAbd al-Ḥaḳḳ Ḥāmid; Aḥmad Wafīḳ Pasha; Ākhund-zāda; Djewdet; Karay, Refīḳ Khālid; Ḳaṣāb, Teodor; Kemāl, Meḥmed Nāmiḳ; Khayr Allāh Efendi; Manāṣtirli Meḥmed Rifʿat; Meḥmed Raʾūf; Mīzāndji Meḥmed Murād; Muḥibb Aḥmed "Diranas"; Muṣāḥib-zāde Djelāl; Oktay Rifat; Shināsī; [in Suppl.] Alus; Bashḳut; Čamlibel; Ḥasan Bedr al-Dīn

see also Djanāb Shihāb al-Dīn; Ebüzziya Tevfik; Ekrem Bey; Kaygili, ʿOthmān Djemāl; Khālide Edīb; Muʿallim Nādjī

Urdu Masraḥ.6

playwrights Amānat; [in Suppl.] Āghā Ḥashar Kashmīrī

epistolary **Inshāʾ**; Kātib; **Risāla**

see also Ṣadr.(b)

letter-writers ʿAbd al-Ḥamīd; Aḥmad Sirhindī; ʿAmr b. Masʿada; al-Babbaghāʾ; Ghālib; Ḥāletī; al-Hamadhānī; Harkarn; Ibn ʿAmīra; Ibn al-Athīr.3; Ibn Idrīs.I; Ibn Ḳalāḳis; Ibn al-Khaṣīb; Ibn al-Ṣayrafī; al-Ḳabtawrī; al-Ḳāḍī al-Fāḍil; Kānī; Khalīfa Shāh Muḥammad; Khʷāndamīr; al-Khʷārazmī; al-Maʿarrī; Makhdūm al-Mulk Manīrī; Meḥmed Pasha Rāmī (*and* Rāmī Meḥmed Pasha); Muḥammad b. Hindū-Shāh; Oḳčuzāde; Rashīd al-Dīn (Waṭwāṭ); Saʿīd b. Ḥumayd; al-Shaybānī, Ibrāhīm; [in Suppl.] ʿAbd al-ʿAzīz b. Yūsuf; Amīr Niẓām; Ibn Khalaf

see also Aljamía; al-Djunayd; Ibn al-ʿAmīd.1; Ibn al-Khaṭīb; Mughals.10; Sudjān Rāy Bhandārī

etiquette-literature **Adab**; al-Maḥāsin wa 'l-Masāwī

see also al-Djidd wa 'l-Hazl; Djins; Ḥiyal; Iyās b. Muʿāwiya; Kalīla wa-Dimna; Kātib; Marzban-nāma; Nadīm; Sulūk.1

authors Abū Ḥayyān al-Tawḥīdī; al-Bayhaḳī; Djāḥiẓ; al-Ghuzūlī; Hilāl al-Ṣābiʾ; al-Ḥuṣrī.I; Ibn ʿAbd Rabbih; Ibn Abi 'l-Dunyā; Ibn al-Muḳaffaʿ; al-Ḳalyūbī; al-Ḳāshānī; al-Kisrawī; al-Marzubānī; Merdjümek; al-Nīsābūrī; al-Rāghib al-Iṣfahānī; al-Shimshāṭī; al-Ṣūlī

see also al-Djahshiyārī; al-Ḳalḳashandī.1; Shabīb b. Shayba
genealogical Mathālib
genealogists al-Abīwardī; al-Djawwānī; al-Hamdānī; al-Kalbī.II; al-Ḳalḳashandī.1; Ḳāsim b. Aṣbagh; al-Marwazī; Muṣʿab; al-Rushāṭī; [in Suppl.] Fakhr-i Mudabbir
see also Ibn Daʾb; al-Ḳādirī al-Ḥasanī; al-Khwārazmī; Mihmindār
genres
poetry Ghazal; Hidjāʾ; Ḳaṣīda; Khamriyya; Madīḥ; Marthiya; Mathnawī; Mufākhara; Munṣifa; Musammaṭ; Muwashshaḥ; Nawriyya; Shahrangīz; Sharḳī
see also ʿArabiyya.B; Iran.vii; Rabīʿiyyāt; Sāḳī.2; Shawāhid
prose Adab; Adjāʾib; Awāʾil; Badīʿ; Bilmedje; Djafr; Faḍīla; Fahrasa; Ḥikāya; Ilāhī; Inshāʾ; Isrāʾīliyyāt; Kān wa-Kān; Khiṭaṭ; Ḳiṣṣa; al-Ḳūmā; Laḥn al-ʿĀmma; Lughz; al-Maghāzī; al-Maḥāsin wa ʾl-Masāwī; Maḳāla; Maḳāma; Malḥūn; Manāḳib; Masāʾil wa-Adjwiba; al-Masālik wa ʾl-Mamālik; Mathālib; Mawsūʿa; Muḳaddima; Mukhtaṣar; Munāẓara; Nādira; Naḳāʾiḍ; Naṣīḥat al-Mulūk; Risāla; Sharḥ; Ṣila.2; Sīra; Sunan; [in Suppl.] Arbaʿūn Ḥadīth; Ḥabsiyya
see also Alf Layla wa-Layla (363b); ʿArabiyya.B; Bibliography; Djughrāfiyā; Fatḥnāme; Ḥayawān; Ḥiyal; Iran.vii; Malāḥim; Mathal; Shāhnāmedji; *and* → CHRISTIANITY.MONASTERIES.WRITINGS ON
historical Isrāʾīliyyāt; al-Maghāzī
see also Fatḥnāme; Ṣaḥāba; Ṣila.2.II; *and* → *the sections* BIOGRAPHICAL, MAGHĀZĪ-LITERATURE, *and* TRADITION-LITERATURE *under this entry*
Andalusian → ANDALUSIA
Arabic
on countries/cities → *individual countries*
on dynasties/caliphs → *individual dynasties under* DYNASTIES
universal histories Abu ʾl-Fidāʾ; Abū Mikhnaf; Akanṣūs; al-Anṭāḳī; ʿArīb b. Saʿd al-Kātib al-Ḳurṭubī; al-ʿAynī; al-Bakrī.1 and 2; al-Balādhurī; Baybars al-Manṣūrī; al-Birzālī; Daḥlān; al-Dhahabī; al-Diyārbakrī; al-Djannābī; al-Djazarī; al-Farghānī; Ḥamza al-Iṣfahānī; Ḥasan-i Rūmlū; al-Haytham b. ʿAdī; Ibn Abī Shayba; Ibn Abī Ṭayyiʾ; Ibn Aʿtham al-Kūfī; Ibn al-Athīr.2; Ibn al-Dawādārī; Ibn al-Djawzī (Sibṭ); Ibn al-Furāt; Ibn Kathīr; Ibn Khaldūn; Ibn Khayyāṭ al-ʿUṣfurī; Ibn al-Saʿī; al-Kalbī.II; Kātib Čelebi; al-Kutubī; al-Makīn b. al-ʿAmīd; al-Masʿūdī; Miskawayh; Münedjdjim Bashī; al-Muṭahhar b. Ṭāhir al-Maḳdisī; al-Nuwayrī, Shihāb al-Dīn; Saʿīd b. al-Biṭrīḳ
see also Akhbār Madjmūʿa
8th-century authors Abū Mikhnaf; ʿAwāna b. al-Ḥakam al-Kalbī; Sayf b. ʿUmar
9th-century authors al-Balādhurī; al-Fāḳihī; al-Farghānī; al-Haytham

b. ʿAdī; Ibn ʿAbd al-Ḥakam.4; Ibn Abī S̲h̲ayba; Ibn Abī Ṭāhir Ṭayfūr; Ibn Aʿt̲h̲am al-Kūfī; Ibn K̲h̲ayyāṭ al-ʿUṣfurī; Ibn al-Naṭṭāḥ; al-Kalbī.II; al-Madāʾinī; Naṣr b. Muzāḥim

10th-century authors   ʿArīb b. Saʿd al-Kātib al-Ḳurṭubī; al-Azdī; Bah̲shal; al-Balawī; al-D̲j̲ah̲s̲h̲iyārī; Ḥamza al-Iṣfahānī; Ibn al-Dāya; Ibn al-Ḳūṭiyya; Ibn Manda; Ibn al-Ṣag̲h̲īr; al-Kindī, Abū ʿUmar Muḥammad; al-Masʿūdī

11th-century authors   al-Antāḳī, Abu ʾl-Farad̲j̲; Ibn al-Bannāʾ; Ibn Burd.I; Ibn Ḥayyān; Ibn al-Raḳīḳ; al-Māfarrūk̲h̲ī

12th-century authors   al-ʿAẓīmī; Ibn al-D̲j̲awzī; Ibn G̲h̲ālib; Ibn al-Ḳalānisī; Ibn Ṣāḥib al-Ṣalāt; Ibn al-Ṣayrafī, Abū Bakr; Ibn S̲h̲addād, Abū Muḥammad; ʿImād al-Dīn ; S̲h̲īrawayh

     see also al-Bayd̲h̲aḳ; Ibn Manda

13th-century authors   ʿAbd al-Wāḥid al-Marrākus̲h̲ī; Abū S̲h̲āma; al-Bundārī; al-D̲j̲anadī; Ibn Abi ʾl-Dam; Ibn Abī Ṭayyiʾ; Ibn al-ʿAdīm; Ibn al-At̲h̲īr.2; Ibn al-D̲j̲awzī (Sibṭ); Ibn Ḥamādu; Ibn al-Mud̲j̲āwir; Ibn Muyassar; Ibn al-Nad̲j̲d̲j̲ār; Ibn al-Sāʿī; Ibn Saʿīd al-Mag̲h̲ribī; Ibn S̲h̲addād, ʿIzz al-Dīn; Ibn S̲h̲addād, Bahāʾ al-Dīn; Ibn al-Ṭuwayr; al-Makīn b. al-ʿAmīd; al-Manṣūr, al-Malik; al-Rāfiʿī; [in Suppl.] Ibn ʿAskar; Ibn Ḥātim

14th-century authors   Abu ʾl-Fidā; Baybars al-Manṣūrī; al-Birzālī; al-D̲h̲ahabī; al-D̲j̲azarī; Ibn Abī Zarʿ; Ibn al-Dawādārī; Ibn Duḳmāk; Ibn al-Furāt, Nāṣir al-Dīn; Ibn Ḥabīb, Badr al-Dīn; Ibn ʿId̲h̲ārī; Ibn Kat̲h̲īr, ʿImād al-Dīn; Ibn K̲h̲aldūn; Ibn al-K̲h̲aṭīb; Ibn al-Ṭiḳṭaḳā; al-K̲h̲azrad̲j̲ī, Muwaffaḳ al-Dīn; al-Kutubī; al-Mufaḍḍal b. Abi ʾl-Faḍāʾil; al-Ṣafadī, Ṣalāḥ al-Dīn; S̲h̲āfiʿ b. ʿAlī

15th-century authors   Abu ʾl-Maḥāsin b. Tag̲h̲rībirdī; ʿArabfaḳih; al-ʿAynī; al-Fāsī; Ibn ʿArabs̲h̲āh; Ibn S̲h̲āhīn al-Ẓāhirī; al-Maḳrizī; al-Sak̲h̲āwī

16th-century authors   al-Diyārbakrī; al-D̲j̲annābī, Abū Muḥammad; Ḥasan-i Rūmlū; Ibn al-Daybaʿ; Ibn Iyās; Mud̲j̲īr al-Dīn al-ʿUlaymī; al-Suyūṭī

17th-century authors   ʿAbd al-ʿAzīz b. Muḥammad; al-Bakrī (b. Abi ʾl-Surūr); Ibn Abī Dīnār; Kātib Čelebi; al-Maḳḳarī; al-Mawzaʿī

18th-century authors   al-Damurdās̲h̲ī; al-Ḥād̲j̲d̲j̲ Ḥammūda; al-Ifrānī; Müned̲j̲d̲j̲im Bas̲h̲ï

19th-century authors   Aḥmad al-Nāṣirī al-Salāwī (*and* al-Nāṣir al-Salāwī); Akansūs; ʿAlī Pas̲h̲a Mubārak; Daḥlān; al-D̲j̲abartī; G̲h̲ulām Ḥusayn K̲h̲ān Ṭabāṭabāʾī; Ibn Abi ʾl-Ḍiyāf

     see also al-Kardūdī

20th-century authors   Ibn Zaydān; Kurd ʿAlī

Indo-Persian   Mug̲h̲als.10

on countries/cities → INDIA
on dynasties/caliphs → *individual dynasties under* DYNASTIES.AFGHANISTAN AND INDIA
13th and 14th-century authors Baranī; al-Djuzdjānī; Shams al-Dīn-i Sirādj ʿAfīf
15th and 16th-century authors Abu ʾl-Faḍl ʿAllāmī; Djawhar; Gulbadan Bēgam; Niẓām al-Dīn Aḥmad b. al-Harawī; [in Suppl.] ʿAbbās Sarwānī
17th-century authors ʿAbd al-Ḥamīd Lāhawrī; Bakhtāwar Khan; Firishta; Ināyat Allāh Kańbū; Mīr Muḥammad Maʿṣūm; Niʿmat Allāh b. Ḥabīb Allāh Harawī; Nūr al-Ḥaḳḳ al-Dihlawī; Shīrāzī, Rafīʿ al-Dīn; [in Suppl.] ʿĀḳil Khān Rāzī; Ḥādjdjī al-Dabīr; Ḥaydar Malik
see also Badāʾūnī
18th-century authors ʿAbd al-Karīm Kashmīrī; Ḳāniʿ; Khʷāfī Khān; Niʿmat Khān
19th-century authors ʿAbd al-Karīm Munshī; Ghulām Ḥusayn Khān Ṭabāṭabāʾī; Ghulām Ḥusayn "Salīm"
see also Aẓfarī

Persian [in Suppl.] Čač-nāma
on Iran → IRAN
on dynasties/caliphs → *individual dynasties under* DYNASTIES.PERSIA
universal histories Mīrkhʷānd; Niẓām-shāhī; Sipihr
10th-century authors Balʿamī.2
11th-century authors Bayhaḳī; Gardīzī
12th-century authors Anūshirwān b. Khālid; al-Bayhaḳī, Ẓahīr al-Dīn; [in Suppl.] Ibn al-Balkhī
13th-century authors Djuwaynī; Ibn Bībī; Ibn-i Isfandiyār; [in Suppl.] Ḥasan Niẓāmī; al-Ḥusaynī
14th-century authors Banākitī; Ḥamd Allāh al-Mustawfī al-Ḳazwīnī; Shabānkāraʾī; [in Suppl.] al-Aḳsarāyī
15th-century authors ʿAbd al-Razzāḳ al-Samarḳandī; Ḥāfiẓ-i Abrū
16th-century authors Bidlīsī, Sharaf al-Dīn; Djamāl al-Ḥusaynī; Ghaffārī; Ḥaydar Mīrzā; Khʷāndamīr; Ḳum(m)ī; al-Lārī; Shāmī, Niẓām al-Dīn; [in Suppl.] Ḥāfiẓ Tanīsh
see also ʿAlī b. Shams al-Dīn
17th-century authors ʿAbd al-Fattāh Fūmanī; Ḥaydar b. ʿAlī; Iskandar Beg; Rāzī, Amīn Aḥmad
18th-century authors Mahdī Khān Astarābādī
see also Īsar-dās
19th and 20th-century authors ʿAbd al-Karīm Bukhārī; [in Suppl.] Fasāʾī

Turkish Shāhnāmedji

on the Ottoman Empire → DYNASTIES.ANATOLIA AND THE TURKS.
OTTOMANS.HISTORIANS OF

universal histories   S̲h̲āriḥ ül-Menār-zāde
   see also Nes̲h̲rī

15th-century authors   ʿĀs̲h̲iḳ-pas̲h̲a-zāde; Meḥmed Pas̲h̲a, Ḳaramānī

16th-century authors   ʿAlī; Bihis̲h̲tī; D̲j̲alālzāde Muṣṭafā Čelebi; D̲j̲alāl-
   zāde Ṣāliḥ Čelebi; Kemāl Pas̲h̲a-zāde; Luḳmān b. Sayyid Ḥusayn;
   Maṭrāḳči; Meḥmed Zaʿīm; Nes̲h̲rī; Selānīkī; Seyfī
   see also Ḥadīdī; Med̲j̲dī

17th-century authors   ʿAbdī; ʿAbdī Pas̲h̲a; Ḥasan Bey-zāde; Ḥibrī;
   Ḳarā-čelebi-zāde.4; Kātib Čelebi; Meḥmed K̲h̲alīfe b. Hüseyn; S̲h̲āriḥ
   ül-Menār-zāde

18th-century authors   ʿAbdī Efendi; Aḥmad Rasmī; Čelebi-zāde;
   Čes̲h̲mīzāde; Enwerī; ʿIzzī; Müned̲j̲d̲j̲im Bas̲h̲ı̊; ʿOt̲h̲mān-zāde

19th-century authors   Aḥmad D̲j̲ewdet Pas̲h̲a; ʿĀṣim; ʿAṭāʾ Bey,
   Ṭayyārzāda; Esʿad Efendi, Meḥmed; Kemāl, Meḥmed Nāmı̊ḳ; K̲h̲ayr
   Allāh Efendi

20th-century authors   Aḥmad Rafīḳ; ʿAlī Amīrī; (Meḥmed) ʿAṭāʾ Beg;
   Luṭfī Efendi; Mīzānd̲j̲ı̊ Meḥmed Murād; S̲h̲ems al-Dīn Günaltay;
   S̲h̲eref, ʿAbd al-Raḥmān
   see also Ḥilmī

in Eastern Turkish   Abu ʾl-G̲h̲āzī Bahādur K̲h̲ān; Bāḳı̊k̲h̲ānlı̊; Muʾnis

in other languages   Afg̲h̲ān.iii; Aljamía; Bengali.ii; Berbers.VI; Beskesek-abaza;
   Bosna.3; Hausa.iii; Hindī; Indonesia.vi; Judaeo-Arabic.iii; Judaeo-Persian.i;
   Kano; Ḳiṣṣa.8; Lahndā.2; Laḳ; Masraḥ.6; Pand̲j̲ābī.2; S̲h̲iʿr.7; Sind.3.b;
   Somali.6

   for Swahili → KENYA; *for Malaysian* → MALAYSIA; *and* → LITERATURE.
   POETRY.MYSTICAL

Bengali authors   Nad̲h̲r al-Islām; Nūr Ḳuṭb al-ʿĀlam

Hindi authors   Malik Muḥammad D̲j̲āyasī; Nihāl Čand Lāhawrī; Prēm Čand;
   Sud̲j̲ān Rāy Bhandārī
   see also ʿAbd al-Raḥīm K̲h̲ān; Ins̲h̲āʾ; Lallūd̲j̲ī Lāl

Judaeo-Arabic authors   Mūsā b. ʿAzra; al-Samawʾal b. ʿĀdiyā
   and → JUDAISM.LANGUAGE AND LITERATURE

Judaeo-Persian authors   S̲h̲āhīn-i S̲h̲īrāzī
   and → JUDAISM.LANGUAGE AND LITERATURE

Pashto authors   K̲h̲us̲h̲ḥāl K̲h̲ān K̲h̲aṭak

Tatar authors   G̲h̲afūrī, Med̲j̲īd

mag̲h̲āzī-literature   Abū Maʿs̲h̲ar al-Sindī; Ibn ʿĀʾid̲h̲; al-Kalāʿī; **al-Mag̲h̲āzī**;
   Mūsā b. ʿUḳba
   see also al-Baṭṭāl; Sīra

personages in literature   Abū Ḍamḍam; Abu ʾl-Ḳāsim; Abū Zayd; Ali Baba;

Ayāz; Aywaz.2; al-Basūs; al-Baṭṭāl; Bekrī Muṣṭafā Agha; Buzurgmihr; Dhu 'l-Himma; Djamshīd; Djuḥā; al-Ghāḍirī; Ḥamza b. ʿAbd al-Muṭṭalib; Ḥātim al-Ṭāʾī; Ḥayy b. Yaḳẓān; Köroghlu; Manas; Naṣr al-Dīn Khodja; Rustam; Sām; Ṣarı̊ Ṣalṭūḳ Dede; Shahrazād; al-Sīd; Sindbād; Siyāwush

picaresque Maḳāma; Mukaddī

poetry ʿArūḍ; Ḥamāsa; Ḳāfiya; Lughz; Maʿnā.3; Mukhtārāt; Muzdawidj; Shāʿir; **Shiʿr**

see also Rāwī; Sharḥ.II; *for poetical genres* → LITERATURE.GENRES.POETRY; *and* → METRICS

Andalusian ʿArabiyya.B.Appendix; Khamriyya.vi; Muwashshaḥ; Nawriyya; Shāʿir.1.D

anthologies al-Fatḥ b. Khaḳān; al-Fihrī; Ibn Bassām; Ibn Diḥya; Ibn Faradj al-Djayyānī; al-Shaḳundī

8th-century poets Ghirbīb b. ʿAbd Allāh

9th-century poets ʿAbbās b. Firnās; ʿAbbas b. Nāṣiḥ; al-Ghazāl

see also Ibn ʿAlḳama.2

10th-century poets Ibn ʿAbd Rabbih; Ibn Abī Zamanayn; Ibn Faradj al-Djayyānī; Ibn Ḳuzmān.I; Muḳaddam b. Muʿāfā; al-Ramādī; al-Sharīf al-Ṭalīḳ

11th-century poets Abū Isḥāḳ al-Ilbīrī; Ibn al-Abbār; Ibn ʿAbd al-Ṣamad; Ibn ʿAmmār; Ibn Burd.II; Ibn Darrādj al-Ḳasṭallī; Ibn Gharsiya; Ibn al-Ḥaddād; Ibn al-Ḥannāṭ; Ibn al-Labbāna; Ibn Māʾ al-Samāʾ; Ibn al-Shahīd; Ibn Shuhayd; Ibn Zaydūn; al-Muʿtamid ibn ʿAbbād

see also Ṣāʿid al-Baghdādī

12th-century poets al-Aʿmā al-Tuṭīlī; Ḥafṣa bint al-Ḥādjdj; Ibn ʿAbdūn; Ibn Baḳī; Ibn Ḳabṭūrnu; Ibn Khafādja; Ibn Ḳuzmān.II and V; Ibn al-Ṣayrafī; al-Ḳurṭubī; al-Ruṣāfī; Ṣafwān b. Idrīs

see also Mūsā b. ʿAzra

13th-century poets Ḥāzim; Ibn al-Abbār; Ibn ʿAmīra; Ibn Sahl; Ibn Saʿīd al-Maghribī; al-Ḳabtawrī; al-Shushtarī

14th-century poets Ibn al-Ḥādjdj; Ibn Khātima; Ibn Luyūn; Ibn al-Murābiʿ; al-Sharīf al-Gharnāṭī

Arabic ʿAtāba; Ghazal.i; Ḥamāsa.i; Hidjāʾ; Kān wa-Kān; Ḳaṣīda.1; al-Ḳūmā; Madīḥ.1; Maḳṣūra; Malḥūn; Marthiya.1; Mawāliyā; Mawlidiyya; Mukhtārāt.1; Musammaṭ.1; Muwashshaḥ; Naḳāʾiḍ; Nasīb; Rubāʿī.3; Shāʿir.1; **Shiʿr**.1

see also ʿArabiyya.B.II; Bānat Suʿād; Burda.2; ʿIlm al-Djamāl; Ḳalb.II; Madjnūn Laylā.1; Mawlid; al-Muʿallaḳāt; Muwallad.2; Ṣuʿlūk; *and* → LITERATURE.POETRY.ANDALUSIAN *and* POETRY.MYSTICAL

anthologies al-Muʿallaḳāt; al-Mufaḍḍaliyyāt; **Mukhtārāt**.1

anthologists Abu 'l-Faradj al-Iṣbahānī; Abū Tammām; al-ʿAlamī;

al-Bā<u>kh</u>arzī; al-Buḥturī; Diʿbil; al-Hamdānī; Ḥammād al-Rāwiya; Ibn Abī Ṭāhir Ṭayfūr; Ibn Dāwūd; Ibn al-Ḳutayba; Ibn al-Muʿtazz; Ibn al-Ṣayrafī; ʿImād al-Dīn; al-Nawā<u>dj</u>ī; al-Sarī al-Raffāʾ; al-<u>Sh</u>ayzarī; al-<u>Sh</u>im<u>sh</u>āṭī; [in Suppl.] Abū Zayd al-Ḳura<u>sh</u>ī; al-Bustānī.3

pre-Islamic poets ʿAbīd b. al-Abraṣ; Abū <u>Dh</u>uʾayb al-Hu<u>dh</u>alī; Abū Duʾād al-Iyādī; Abū Kabīr al-Hu<u>dh</u>alī; ʿAdī b. Zayd; al-Afwah al-Awdī; al-A<u>gh</u>lab al-ʿI<u>dj</u>lī; ʿAlḳama; ʿĀmir b. al-Ṭufayl; ʿAmr b. al-Ahtam; ʿAmr b. Ḳamīʾa; ʿAmr b. Kul<u>th</u>ūm; ʿAntara; al-Aʿ<u>sh</u>ā; al-Aswad b. Yaʿfur; Aws b. Ḥa<u>dj</u>ar; Bi<u>sh</u>r b. Abī <u>Kh</u>āzim; Bisṭām b. Ḳays; Durayd b. al-Ṣimma; al-Ḥādira; al-Ḥāri<u>th</u> b. Ḥilliza; Ḥassān b. <u>Th</u>ābit; Ḥātim al-Ṭāʾī; Ibn al-Iṭnāba al-<u>Kh</u>azra<u>dj</u>ī; Imruʾ al-Ḳays b. Ḥu<u>dj</u>r; Ḳays b. al-<u>Kh</u>aṭīm; al-<u>Kh</u>ansāʾ; Laḳīṭ al-Iyādī; Laḳīṭ b. Zurāra; al-Muna<u>khkh</u>al al-Ya<u>sh</u>kurī; Muraḳḳi<u>sh</u>; al-Mutalammis; al-Nābi<u>gh</u>a al-<u>Dh</u>ubyānī; Salāma b. <u>Dj</u>andal; al-Samawʾal b. ʿĀdiyā; al-<u>Sh</u>anfarā
see also ʿArabiyya.B.I; <u>Gh</u>azal; Hu<u>dh</u>ayl; al-Muʿallaḳāt; al-Mufaḍḍaliyyāt; Mufā<u>kh</u>ara.2; Nasīb.2.a; <u>Sh</u>āʿir.1A; al-<u>Sh</u>antamarī; Ṣuʿlūk.II.4

mu<u>kh</u>aḍramūn poets (6th-7th centuries) al-ʿAbbās b. Mirdās; ʿAbd Allāh b. Rawāḥa; Abū <u>Kh</u>irā<u>sh</u>; Abū Miḥ<u>dj</u>ān; ʿAmr b. Maʿdīkarib; Ḍirār b. al-<u>Kh</u>aṭṭāb; Ḥassān b. <u>Th</u>ābit; al-Ḥuṭayʾa; Ibn (al-)Aḥmar; Kaʿb b. Mālik; Kaʿb b. Zuhayr; <u>Kh</u>idā<u>sh</u> b. Zuhayr al-Aṣ<u>gh</u>ar; Labīd b. Rabīʿa; Maʿn b. Aws al-Muzanī; **Mu<u>kh</u>aḍram**; Mutammim b. Nuwayra; al-Nābi<u>gh</u>a al-<u>Dj</u>aʿdī; al-Namir b. Tawlab al-ʿUklī; al-<u>Sh</u>ammā<u>kh</u> b. Ḍirār; Suḥaym; [in Suppl.] Abu ʾl-Ṭamaḥān al-Ḳaynī; Ibn Muḳbil
see also Hu<u>dh</u>ayl; Nasīb.2.b

7th and 8th-century poets al-ʿAbbās b. al-Aḥnaf; ʿAbd Allāh b. Hammān; Abū ʿAṭāʾ al-Sindī; Abū Dahbal al-<u>Dj</u>umaḥī; Abū Dulāma; Abu ʾl-Na<u>dj</u>m al-ʿI<u>dj</u>lī; Abū Ṣa<u>kh</u>r al-Hu<u>dh</u>alī; Abu ʾl-<u>Sh</u>amaḳmaḳ; Adī b. al-Riḳāʿ; al-ʿA<u>djdj</u>ā<u>dj</u>; al-Aḥwaṣ; al-A<u>kh</u>ṭal; al-ʿAr<u>dj</u>ī; Aʿ<u>sh</u>ā Hamdān; al-A<u>sh</u><u>dj</u>aʿ b. ʿAmr al-Sulamī; Ayman b. <u>Kh</u>uraym; al-Baʿī<u>th</u>; Ba<u>shsh</u>ār b. Burd; <u>Dh</u>u ʾl-Rumma; <u>Dj</u>amīl; <u>Dj</u>arīr; Dukayn al-Rā<u>dj</u>iz; al-Farazdaḳ; al-Ḥakam b. ʿAbdal; al-Ḥakam b. Ḳanbar; Ḥammād ʿA<u>dj</u>rad; Ḥamza b. Bīḍ; Ḥāri<u>th</u>a b. Badr al-<u>Gh</u>udānī; al-Ḥuḍayn; Ḥumayd b. <u>Th</u>awr; Ḥumayd al-Arḳaṭ; Ibn Abī ʿUyayna; Ibn al-Dumayna; Ibn Harma; Ibn Ḳays al-Ruḳayyāt; Ibn La<u>dj</u>aʾ; Ibn al-Mawlā; Ibn Mayyāda; Ibn Mufarri<u>gh</u>; Ibn Muṭayr; Ibn Sayḥān; ʿImrān b. Ḥiṭṭān; ʿInān; Ismāʿīl b. Yasār; Kaʿb b. <u>Dj</u>uʿayl al-Ta<u>gh</u>labī; Ḳaṭarī b. al-Fu<u>dj</u>āʾa; al-Kumayt b. Zayd al-Asadī; al-Ḳuṭāmī; Ku<u>th</u>ayyir b. ʿAbd al-Raḥmān; Laylā al-A<u>kh</u>yaliyya; Manṣūr al-Namarī; Marwān b. Abī Ḥafṣa and Marwān b. Abi ʾl-<u>Dj</u>anūb; Miskīn al-Dārimī; Mūsā <u>Sh</u>ahawātin; Musāwir al-Warrāḳ; Muṭīʿ b. Iyās; Nubāta b. ʿAbd Allāh; Nuṣayb; Nuṣayb b. Rabāḥ; al-Rāʿī; Ruʾba b. al-ʿA<u>djdj</u>ā<u>dj</u>; Ṣafī al-Dīn

al-Ḥillī; Ṣafwān al-Anṣārī; Saḥbān Wā'il; Ṣāliḥ b. ʿAbd al-Ḳuddūs; Salm al-Khāsir; al-Sayyid al-Ḥimyarī; al-Shamardal; Sudayf b. Maymūn; Sufyān al-ʿAbdī; Sulaymān b. Yaḥyā; Surāḳa b. Mirdās al-Aṣghar; [in Suppl.] ʿAbd al-Raḥmān b. Ḥassān; Abū ʿAmr al-Shaybānī (*and* al-Shaybānī, Abū ʿAmr); Abū Ḥayyā al-Numayrī; Abū Ḥuzāba; Abū Nukhayla; Bakr b. al-Naṭṭāḥ
see also Nasīb.2.c and d; Ṣuʿlūk.III.2

9th and 10th-century poets Abān b. ʿAbd al-Ḥamīd; ʿAbd Allāh b. Ṭāhir; Abu 'l-ʿAtāhiya; Abu 'l-ʿAynā'; Abū Dulaf; Abu 'l-Faradj al-Iṣbahānī; Abū Firās; Abū Nuwās; Abu 'l-Shīṣ; Abū Tammām; Abū Yaʿḳūb al-Khuraymī; al-ʿAkawwak; ʿAlī b. al-Djahm; al-ʿAttābī; al-Babbaghā'; al-Baṣīr; al-Buḥturī; al-Bustī; Diʿbil; Dīk al-Djinn; al-Ḥimṣī; al-Djammāz; al-Hamdānī; (al-)Ḥusayn b. al-Ḍaḥḥāk; Ibn al-ʿAllāf; Ibn Bassām; Ibn al-Ḥadjdjādj; Ibn Kunāsa; Ibn Lankak; Ibn al-Muʿadhdhal; Ibn Munādhir; Ibn al-Muʿtazz; Ibn al-Rūmī; al-Ḳāsim b. ʿĪsa; Khālid b. Yazīd al-Kātib al-Tamīmī; al-Khālidiyyāni; al-Khaṭṭābī; al-Khubza'aruzzī; al-Kisrawī; Kushādjim; al-Ma'mūnī; Muḥammad b. ʿAbd al-Raḥmān al-ʿAṭawī; Muḥammad b. Ḥāzim al-Bāhilī; Muḥammad b. Umayya; Muḥammad b. Yasīr al-Riyāshī; al-Muṣʿabī; Muslim b. al-Walīd; al-Mutanabbī; Naṣr b. Nuṣayr; Sahl b. Hārūn b. Rāhawayh; Saʿīd b. Ḥumayd; al-Ṣanawbarī; al-Sarī al-Raffā'; al-Shimshāṭī; [in Suppl.] Abu 'l-ʿAmaythal; Abu 'l-Asad al-Ḥimmānī; Abu 'l-Ḥasan al-Maghribī; Abū Hiffān; Abu 'l-ʿIbar; Abū Riyāsh al-Ḳaysī; Abū Saʿd al-Makhzūmī; Abū Shurāʿa; ʿAlī b. Muḥammad al-Tūnīsī al-Iyādī; Faḍl al-Shāʿira; al-Fazārī; al-Ḥamdawī
see also al-Hamadhānī; Ibn Abī Zamanayn; Nasīb.2.d; Shahīd; al-Ṣūlī

11th-13th-century poets al-Abīwardī; ʿAmīd al-Dīn al-Abzārī; al-Arradjānī; al-Badīʿ al-Asṭurlābī; Bahā' al-Dīn Zuhayr; al-Bākharzī; Ḥayṣa Bayṣa; al-Ḥuṣrī.II; Ibn Abi 'l-Ḥadīd; Ibn Abī Ḥaṣīna; Ibn al-ʿAfīf al-Tilimsānī; Ibn al-Habbāriyya; Ibn Ḥamdīs; Ibn Ḥayyūs; Ibn Hindū; Ibn al-Ḳaṭṭān; Ibn al-Ḳaysarānī.2; Ibn Khamīs; Ibn Maṭrūḥ; Ibn al-Nabīh; Ibn Rashīḳ; Ibn Sanā' al-Mulk; Ibn al-Shadjarī al-Baghdādī; Ibn Sharaf al-Ḳayrawānī; Ibn Shibl; Ibn al-Taʿāwīdhī; al-Kammūnī; Ḳurhub; al-Maʿarrī; al-Marwazī; Mihyār; Muḥammad b. ʿAlī b. ʿUmar; al-Rūdhrāwarī; al-Ṣaghānī, ʿAbd al-Mu'min; Ṣāʿid al-Baghdādī; al-Sharīf al-ʿAḳīlī; al-Sharīf al-Raḍī; Shumaym; [in Suppl.] Abu 'l-Ḥasan al-Anṣārī; al-Balaṭī, Abu 'l-Fatḥ ʿUthmān; al-Būṣīrī; al-Ghazzī
see also al-Khazradjī; Nasīb.2.d

14th-18th-century poets ʿAbd al-ʿAzīz b. Muḥammad; ʿAbd al-Ghanī; al-Bakrī; al-Būrīnī; Farḥāt; Ibn Abī Ḥadjala; Ibn ʿAmmār; Ibn

Ḥidjdja; Ibn Nubāta; Ibn al-Ṣāʾigh; Ibn al-Wannān; al-Ṣanʿānī, Ḍiyāʾ al-Dīn; Suʿūdī

see also Khiḍr Beg; al-Shirbīnī

19th and 20th-century poets al-Akhras; al-Bārūdī; Fāris al-Shidyāḳ; al-Fārūḳī; Fikrī; Ḥāfiẓ Ibrāhīm; Ibn Idrīs (I); Ismāʿīl Ṣabrī; Ismāʿīl Ṣabrī Pasha; Ḳaddūr al-ʿAlamī; al-Kāẓimī, ʿAbd al-Muḥsin; Khalīl Muṭrān; al-Khūrī; al-Maʿlūf; al-Manfalūṭī; Mardam.2; Maʿrūf al-Ruṣāfī; al-Māzinī; Nādjī; Nadjīb al-Ḥaddād; Nadjīb Muḥammad Surūr; Saʿīd Abū Bakr; Ṣalāḥ ʿAbd al-Ṣabūr; Ṣāyigh, Tawfīḳ; al-Shābbī; al-Sharḳāwī; Shāʾūl; Shawḳī; Shukrī; [in Suppl.] Abū Māḍī; Abū Shādī; al-ʿAḳḳād; al-Bustānī; Buṭrus Karāma; Ibn ʿAmr al-Ribāṭī; Ibn al-Ḥādjdj

see also Shāʿir.1.C; Shiʿr.1.b

transmission of **Rāwī**

transmitters Ḥammād al-Rāwiya; Ibn Daʾb; Ibn Kunāsa; Khalaf b. Ḥayyān al-Aḥmar; Khālid b. Ṣafwān b. al-Ahtam; al-Kisrawī; al-Mufaḍḍal al-Ḍabbī; Muḥammad b. al-Ḥasan b. Dīnār; al-Sharḳī b. al-Ḳuṭāmī; al-Sukkarī; al-Ṣūlī; [in Suppl.] Abū ʿAmr al-Shaybānī (*and* al-Shaybānī, Abū ʿAmr)

and → LINGUISTICS.GRAMMARIANS.8TH *and* 9TH CENTURY

Indo-Persian Mughals.10; Sabk-i Hindī; Shāʿir.4

see also Pandjābī.2; *and* → LITERATURE.POETRY.MYSTICAL

11th-century poets Masʿūd-i Saʿd-i Salmān; [in Suppl.] Abu ʾl-Faradj b. Masʿūd Rūnī

14th-century poets Amīr Khusraw; Ḥasan Dihlawī; [in Suppl.] Ḥamīd Ḳalandar

16th-century poets Fayḍī

see also ʿAbd al-Raḥīm Khān

17th and 18th-century poets Ārzū Khān; Ashraf ʿAlī Khān; Bīdil; Dard; Ghanī; Ghanīmat; Ḥazīn; Idrākī Bēglārī; Ḳāniʿ; Ḳudsī, Muḥammad Djān; Makhfī; Malik Ḳummi; Munīr Lāhawrī; Nāṣir ʿAlī Sirhindī; Naẓīrī; Salīm, Muḥammad Ḳulī; Shaydā, Mullā; [in Suppl.] Ghanīmat Kundjāhī

19th-century poets Aẓfarī; Ghālib; Rangīn; [in Suppl.] Adīb Pīshāwarī

see also Afsūs

love **Ghazal**; **Nasīb**; Raḳīb; Shahrangīz

see also Ibn Sahl; al-Marzubānī; Muraḳḳish; Shawḳ.1(a); Shawḳ, Taṣadduḳ Ḥusayn; Suḥaym; *and* → LOVE.PLATONIC LOVE

mystical

Arabic ʿAbd al-Ghanī; al-Bakrī, Muḥammad; al-Bakrī, Muṣṭafā; al-Dimyāṭī; al-Ḥallādj; Ibn ʿAdjība; Ibn ʿAlīwa; Ibn al-ʿArabī; al-Madjdhūb; Makhrama.3; al-Shushtarī *see also* ʿAbd al-Ḳādir al-<u>Dj</u>īlānī; Abū Madyan; al-Ḳādirī al-Ḥasanī; [in Suppl.] al-Hilālī

Central Asian Aḥmad Yasawī

Indian Bāḳī bi 'llāh; Bīdil; Dard; "<u>Dj</u>amālī"; Hānsawī; Ḥusaynī Sādāt Amīr; Imdād Allāh; Malik Muḥammad <u>Dj</u>āyasī; [in Suppl.] Ḥamīd Ḳalandar

    see also Bhitāʾī; Pan<u>dj</u>ābī.2; <u>Sh</u>āʿir.4

Indonesian Ḥamza Fanṣūrī

Persian Aḥmad-i <u>Dj</u>ām; ʿAṭṭār; Bābā-Ṭāhir; <u>Dj</u>alāl al-Dīn Rūmī; Faḍl Allāh Ḥurūfī; <u>Gh</u>u<u>dj</u>duwānī; Humām al-Dīn b. ʿAlāʾ Tabrīzī; ʿIrāḳī; Kamāl <u>Kh</u>u<u>dj</u>andī; Ḳāsim-i Anwār; Kirmānī; Lāhi<u>dj</u>ī; Maḥmūd <u>Sh</u>abistarī; Sanāʾī; <u>Sh</u>īrīn Ma<u>gh</u>ribī, Muḥammad; Sulṭān Walad; [in Suppl.] ʿĀrif Čelebī; ʿImād al-Dīn ʿAlī, Faḳīh-i Kirmānī

    see also Abū Saʿīd b. Abi 'l-<u>Kh</u>ayr; <u>Kh</u>araḳānī; <u>Sh</u>awḳ; [in Suppl.] Aḥmad-i Rūmī

Turkish ʿĀ<u>sh</u>iḳ Pa<u>sh</u>a; Faṣīḥ Dede; Gul<u>sh</u>anī; Gül<u>sh</u>ehrī; Hüdāʾī; Müne<u>dj</u><u>dj</u>im Ba<u>sh</u>i; Nefes; Nesīmī; Refīʿī; Ṣarì ʿAbd Allāh Efendī; Sezāʾī, Ḥasan Dede; <u>Sh</u>eyyād Ḥamza; [in Suppl.] E<u>sh</u>refo<u>gh</u>lu; Esrār Dede

    see also Ḥusām al-Dīn Čelebi; Ismāʿīl al-Anḳarawī; Ismāʿīl Ḥaḳḳī; Ḳay<u>gh</u>usuz Abdāl; <u>Kh</u>alīlī; Sulṭān Walad

nature Ibn <u>Kh</u>afā<u>dj</u>a; Nawriyya; Rabīʿiyyāt; al-Ṣanawbarī

Persian <u>Gh</u>azal.ii; Ḥamāsa.ii; Hi<u>dj</u>āʾ.ii; Ḳaṣīda.2; <u>Kh</u>amsa; Madīḥ.2; Malik al-<u>Sh</u>uʿarāʾ; Marthiya.2; Mathnawī.2; Mu<u>kh</u>tārāt.2; Musammaṭ; Mustazād; Rubāʿī.1; <u>Sh</u>ahrangīz.1; <u>Sh</u>āʿir.2; **Shiʿr**.2; [in Suppl.] Ḥabsiyya

    see also Barzū-nāma; Farhād wa-<u>Sh</u>īrīn; Iskandar Nāma.ii; Kalīla wa-Dimna; Ma<u>dj</u>nūn Laylā.2; Radīf.2; Ṣafawids.III; Sāḳī.2; <u>Sh</u>aman; <u>Sh</u>aʿr.3; <u>Sh</u>arīf; *and →* LITERATURE.POETRY.INDO-PERSIAN *and* POETRY. MYSTICAL

anthologies **Mu<u>kh</u>tārāt**.2

    anthologists ʿAwfī; Dawlat-<u>Sh</u>āh; Luṭf ʿAlī Beg; [in Suppl.] <u>Dj</u>ā<u>dj</u>armī.2

biographies Sām Mīrzā

9th-century poets Muḥammad b. Waṣīf

    see also Sahl b. Hārūn b. Rāhawayh

10th-century poets Bābā-Ṭāhir; Daḳīḳī; Kisāʾī; al-Muṣʿabī; Rūdakī; <u>Sh</u>ahīd; [in Suppl.] Abū <u>Sh</u>akūr Bal<u>kh</u>ī

11th-13th-century poets ʿAbd al-Wāsiʿ <u>Dj</u>abalī; Anwarī; Asadī; ʿAṭṭār; Azraḳī; Bābā Afḍal; <u>Dj</u>alāl al-Dīn Rūmī; Falakī <u>Sh</u>irwānī; Farru<u>kh</u>ī; Firdawsī; Gurgānī; Humām al-Dīn b. ʿAlāʾ Tabrīzī; ʿImādī (*and* [in Suppl.]); ʿIrāḳī; Kamāl al-Dīn Ismāʿīl; Ḳaṭrān; <u>Kh</u>^wā<u>dj</u>ū; <u>Kh</u>āḳānī;

Labībī; Lāmiʿī; Mahsatī; Manūčihrī; Muʿizzī; Mukhtārī; Niẓāmī Gandjawī; Pūr-i Bahāʾ; Ṣābir; Saʿdī; Sanāʾī; Sayyid Ḥasan Ghaznawī; Shufurwa; Sūzanī; [in Suppl.] ʿAmʿaḳ; Djādjarmī; Djamāl al-Dīn Iṣfahānī

see also Shams-i Ḳays; Sūdī

14th and 15th-century poets ʿAṣṣār; Awḥadī; Banākitī; Bushāḳ; Djāmī; Faḍl Allāh Ḥurūfī; Fattāḥī; Ḥāfiẓ; Ḥāmidī; Ibn-i Yamīn; ʿIṣāmī; Kātibī; Nizārī Ḳuhistānī; Rāmī Tabrīzī; Salmān-i Sāwadjī; Sayfī ʿArūḍī Bukhārī; Sharaf al-Dīn ʿAlī Yazdī; Shīrīn Maghribī, Muḥammad; [in Suppl.] ʿĀrifī; Badr-i Čāčī; ʿImād al-Dīn ʿAlī, Faḳīh-i Kirmānī

see also Djem; Ḥamd Allāh al-Mustawfī al-Ḳazwīnī; Sūdī

16th-century poets Bannāʾī; Baṣīrī; Fighānī; Hātifī; Hilālī; Muḥtasham-i Kāshānī; Mushfiḳī; Nawʿī; Saḥābī Astarābādī; Sām Mīrzā

see also Luḳmān b. Sayyid Ḥusayn

17th-century poets Asīr; al-Dāmād; Ḳadrī; Ḳalīm Abū Ṭālib; Kāshif; Lāhīdjī.2; Nāẓim Farrukh Ḥusayn; Ṣāʾib; Saʿīdā Gīlānī; Shawkat Bukhārī; Shifāʾī Iṣfahānī

see also al-ʿĀmilī; Ghanīmat; Khushḥāl Khān Khaṭak; [in Suppl.] Findiriskī; *and* → LITERATURE.POETRY.INDO-PERSIAN

18th-century poets Hātif; Ḥazīn; Luṭf ʿAlī Beg; Nadjāt; Shihāb Turshīzī

see also Āzād Bilgrāmī

19th and 20th-century poets Bahār; Furūgh; Furūghī; Ḳāʾānī; Ḳurrat al-ʿAyn; Lāhūtī; Nafīsī, Saʿīd; Nashāṭ; Nīmā Yūshīdj; Parwīn Iʿtiṣāmī; Pūr-i Dāwūd; Rashīd Yāsimī; Riḍā Ḳulī Khān; Ṣabā; Sabzawārī; Shahriyār; Shaybānī; Shihāb Iṣfahānī; Shūrīda, Muḥammad Taḳī; Sipihrī; Surūsh; [in Suppl.] ʿĀrif, Mīrzā; Ashraf al-Dīn Gīlānī; Dehkhudā

see also Ghālib; Iḳbāl; Ḳāʾim-maḳām-i Farāhānī; Sipihr

Turkish Ḥamāsa.iii; Hidjāʾ.iii; Ḳaṣīda.3; Khamsa; Ḳoshma; Madīḥ.3; Māni; Marthiya.3; Mathnawī.3; Mukhtārāt.3; Musammaṭ.1; Rabīʿiyyāt; Rubāʿī.2; Shahrangīz.2; Sharḳi̊; **Shiʿr**.3; [in Suppl.] Ghazal.iii

see also Alpami̊sh; ʿĀshiḳ; Farhād wa-Shirīn; Ilāhī; Iskandar Nāma.iii; Karadja Oghlan; Madjnūn Laylā.3; Ozan; Shāhnāmedji; Shāʿir.3; *and* → LITERATURE.POETRY. MYSTICAL

anthologies **Mukhtārāt**.3

biographies ʿĀshi̊ḳ Čelebi; Laṭīfī; Riḍā; Riyāḍī; Sālim; Sehī Bey

11th and 12th-century poets Aḥmad Yuknakī; Ḥakīm Ata; Ḳutadghu Bilig

13th and 14th-century poets Aḥmadī; ʿĀshi̊ḳ Pasha; Burhān al-Dīn; Dehhānī; Gülshehrī; Sheykh-oghlu; Sheyyād Ḥamza

15th-century poets Āhī; Aḥmad Pasha Bursali̊; Dāʿī; Firdewsī;

Gulshanī; Ḥamdī, Ḥamd Allāh; Ḳāsim Pasha; Ḳayghusuz Abdāl; Khalīlī; Khiḍr Beg; Süleymān Čelebi, Dede
see also Djem; Ḥāmidī
16th-century poets Āgehī; ʿAzīzī; Bāḳī; Baṣīrī; Bihishtī; Dhātī; Djaʿfar Čelebi; Djalāl Ḥusayn Čelebi; Djalālzāde Muṣṭafā Čelebi; Djalālzāde Ṣāliḥ Čelebi; Faḍli; Faḳīrī; Fawrī; Ferdī; Fighānī; Fuḍūlī; Ghazālī; Gulshanī; Ḥadīdī; Ḳarā-čelebi-zāde; Kemāl Pasha-zāde; Khāḳānī; Khayālī; Ḳorḳud b. Bāyazīd; Lāmiʿī; Laṭīfī; Luḳmān b. Sayyid Ḥusayn; Meʾalī; Medjdī; Mesīḥī; Mihrī Khātūn; Naẓmī, Edirneli; Nedjātī Bey; Newʿī; Rewānī; Sehī Bey; Surūrī.1; Sūzī Čelebi
17th-century poets ʿAṭāʾī; ʿAzmī-zāde; Bahāʾī Meḥmed Efendi; Faṣīḥ Dede; Fehīm, Undjuzāde Muṣṭafā; Ḥāletī; Ḳarā-čelebi-zāde; Ḳul Muṣṭafā; Ḳuloghlu; Nāʾilī; Nāẓim, Muṣṭafā; Naẓmī, Sheykh Meḥmed; Nefʿī; Niyāzī; ʿÖmer ʿĀshiḳ; Riyāḍī; Ṣarı ʿAbd Allāh Efendī
18th-century poets Belīgh, Ismāʿīl; Belīgh, Meḥmed Emīn; Čelebi-zāde; Česhmīzāde; Fiṭnat; Gevherī; Ghālib; Ḥāmī-i Āmidī; Ḥashmet; Kānī; Meḥmed Pasha Rāmī (*and* Rāmī Meḥmed Pasha); Nābī; Naḥīfī; Naẓīm; Nedīm; Neshʾet; Newres.1; ʿOthmān-zāde; Rāghib Pasha; Sezāʾī, Ḥasan Dede
19th-century poets ʿĀrif Hikmet Bey; ʿAynī; Dadaloghlu; Derdli; Dhihnī; Fāḍil Bey; Faṭīn; Fehīm, Süleymān; Ismāʿīl Ṣafā; ʿIzzet Molla; Kemāl, Meḥmed Nāmıḳ; Laylā Khānım; Menemenli-zāde Meḥmed Ṭāhir; Muʿallim Nādjī; Newres.2; Pertew Pasha.II; Redjāʾī-zāde; Shināsī; Sünbül-zāde Wehbī; Surūrī.2
20th-century poets ʿAbd al-Ḥāḳḳ Ḥāmid; Djanāb Shihāb al-Dīn; Djewdet; Ekrem Bey; Hāshim; Kanık; Köprülü (Meḥmed Fuad); Ḳoryürek; Laylā Khānım; Meḥmed ʿĀkif; Meḥmed Emīn; Muḥibb Aḥmed "Diranas"; Nāẓim Ḥikmet; Oktay Rifat; Orkhan Seyfī; Ortač, Yūsuf Ḍiyā; Sāhir, Djelāl; [in Suppl.] ʿĀshıḳ Weysel; Bölükbashı; Čamlıbel; Eshref; Eyyūboghlu; Gövsa
see also [in Suppl.] Ergun; Fındıḳoghlu
in Eastern Turkish Ādharī.ii; Bābur; Bāḳıkhānlı; Dhākir; Djambul Djabaev; Ghāzī Girāy II; Ḥamāsa.iv; Hidjāʾ.iii; Iskandar Nāma.iii; Ismāʿīl I; Ḳayyūm Nāṣirī; Ḳutadghu Bilig; Luṭfī; Mīr ʿAlī Shīr Nawāʾī; Muʾnis; Sakkākī; Shahriyār
translations from Western langs. Ismāʿīl Ḥaḳḳi ʿĀlīshān; Kanık; Shināsī
Urdu Ghazal.iv; Ḥamāsa.v; Hidjāʾ.iv; Ḳaṣīda.4; Madīḥ.4; Madjnūn Laylā.4; Marthiya.4; Mathnawī.4; Mukhtārāt.4; Musammaṭ.2; Mushāʿara; Shahrangīz.3; **Shiʿr**.4
17th-century poets Nuṣratī
18th-century poets Ashraf ʿAlī Khān; Dard; Djurʾat; Maẓhar; Sawdā;

Sūz; [in Suppl.] Ḥasan, Mīr Ghulām
see also Ārzū Khān
19th-century poets Amānat; Anīs; Aẓfarī; Dabīr, Salāmat ʿAlī; Dāgh; Dhawḳ; Ghālib; Faḳīr Muḥammad Khān; Ḥālī; Ilāhī Bakhsh "Maʿrūf"; Inshāʾ; Mīr Muḥammad Taḳī; Muḥsin ʿAlī Muḥsin; Muʾmin; Muṣḥafī; Nāsikh; Nasīm; Rangīn; Shawḳ, Taṣadduḳ Ḥusayn; [in Suppl.] Ātish
see also [in Suppl.] Āzād
20th-century poets Akbar, Ḥusayn Allāhābādī; Āzād; Djawān; Iḳbāl; Muḥammad ʿAlī; Rāshid, N.M.; Ruswā; Shabbīr Ḥasan Khān Djosh; Shiblī Nuʿmānī; [in Suppl.] Ḥasrat Mohānī
see also Āzurda
vernacular Nabaṭī
see also al-Shām.3
prose Adab; Ḥikāya; Ḳiṣṣa; Maḳāma; Muḳaddima; Naṣīḥat al-Mulūk; Risāla; Sharḥ
and → LITERATURE.ETIQUETTE-LITERATURE *and* HISTORICAL; PRESS
Arabic ʿArabiyya.B.V; Ḥikāya.i; Ḳiṣṣa.2; Maḳāla.1; Maḳāma; Nahḍa; Naṣīḥat al-Mulūk.1; Risāla.1; Sadjʿ.3; Sīra Shaʿbiyya
and → LITERATURE.DRAMA; PRESS
works Alf Layla wa-Layla; ʿAntar; Baybars; Bilawhar wa-Yūdāsaf; Dhu 'l-Himma; Kalīla wa-Dimna; Luḳmān.3; Sayf Ibn Dhī Yazan; Sindbād al-Ḥakīm
see also Sindbād
9th and 10th-century authors al-Djāḥiẓ; al-Hamadhānī; Ibn al-Muḳaffaʿ; [in Suppl.] Abu 'l-ʿAnbas al-Ṣaymarī
11th-13th-century authors al-Ḥarīrī; Ibn Nāḳiyā; al-Ṣaymarī; [in Suppl.] Abu 'l-Muṭahhar al-Azdī; al-Djazarī
see also al-Sharīshī
14th-18th-century authors Ibn Abī Ḥadjala; al-Shirbīnī
see also al-Ibshīhī
19th and 20th-century authors Aḥmad Amīn; Faraḥ Anṭūn; Ḥāfiẓ Ibrāhīm; Maḥmūd Taymūr; al-Maʿlūf; al-Manfalūṭī; Mayy Ziyāda; al-Māzinī; Muḥammad Ḥusayn Haykal; al-Muwayliḥī.2; Nuʿayma, Mīkhāʾīl; al-Rayḥānī; Salāma Mūsā; Sayyid Ḳuṭb; al-Sharḳāwī; Shāʾūl; [in Suppl.] Abū Shādī; al-ʿAḳḳād; al-Bustānī.6
see also Djamīl al-Mudawwar; al-Khālidī; Kurd ʿAlī; Shumayyil, Shiblī
Persian Ḥikāya.ii; Iran.vii; Ḳiṣṣa.4; Maḳāla.2; Naṣīḥat al-Mulūk.2; Risāla.2
see also Ṣafawids.III; *and* → LITERATURE.DRAMA; PRESS
works Bakhtiyār-nāma; Dabistān al-Madhāhib; Ḳahramān-nāma; Kalīla wa-Dimna; Madjnūn Laylā.2; Marzbān-nāma

see also Niẓām al-Mulk; Niẓāmī ʿArūḍī Samarḳandī
11th and 12th-century authors Ḥamīdī; al-Ḳāshānī; Kay Kāʾūs b. Iskandar; Nāṣir-i Khusraw; Naṣr Allāh b. Muḥammad; Niẓāmī ʿArūḍī Samarḳandī; Rashīd al-Dīn (Waṭwāṭ); al-Samʿānī, Abu ʾl-Ḳāsim
13th-century authors Saʿdī
14th-century authors Nakhshabī
15th-century authors Kāshifī
16th-century authors
see also Shemʿī
17th and 18th-century authors ʿInāyat Allāh Kańbū; Mumtāz
19th and 20th-century authors Bahar; Hidayat, Ṣādiḳ; Nafīsī, Saʿīd; Shaybānī; Shaykh Mūsā Nathrī; [in Suppl.] Āl-i Aḥmad; Bihrangī; Dehkhuda
see also Furūgh.2
Turkish Ḥikāya.iii; Ḳiṣṣa.3; Maddāḥ; Maḳāla.3; Risāla.3
see also Bilmedje; *and* → LITERATURE.DRAMA; PRESS
works Alpamïsh; Billur Köshk; Dede Ḳorḳut; Ḳahramān-nāma; Oghuz-nāma
see also Merdjümek; Ṣarï Ṣaltūḳ Dede
14th-century authors Sheykh-oghlu
15th-century authors Sheykh-zāde.3
16th-century authors
see also Shemʿī
17th-century authors Nergisī
18th-century authors ʿAlī ʿAzīz, Giridli; Nābī
19th and 20th-century authors Aḥmad Ḥikmet; Aḥmad Midḥat; Aḥmad Rāsim; Djanāb Shihāb al-Dīn; Ebüzziya Tevfik; Ekrem Bey; Fiṭrat; Hïsar; Ḥusayn Djāhid; Ḥusayn Raḥmī; Karay, Refīḳ Khālid; Ḳaṣāb, Teodor; Kaygïlï, ʿOthmān Djemāl; Kemāl; Kemāl, Meḥmed Nāmïḳ; Kemal Tahir; Khālid Ḍiyāʾ; Khālide Edīb; Laylā Khānïm; Meḥmed Raʾūf; Oktay Rifat; ʿÖmer Seyf ül-Dīn; Orkhan Kemāl; Reshād Nūrī; Sabahattin Ali; Sāmī; Sezāʾī, Sāmī; [in Suppl.] Atač; Atay; Čaylaḳ Tewfīḳ; Esendal; Haliḳarnas Balïḳčïsï
see also Aḥmad Iḥsān; Ileri, Djelāl Nūrī; İnal; Ismāʿīl Ḥaḳḳi ʿĀlīshān; Ḳiṣṣa.3(b); [in Suppl.] Eyyūboghlu
in Eastern Turkish Rabghūzī
Urdu Ḥikāya.iv; Ḳiṣṣa.5
and → LITERATURE.DRAMA; PRESS
19th and 20th-century authors Amān, Mīr; Djawān; Faḳīr Muḥammad Khān; Iḳbāl; Nadhīr Aḥmad Dihlawī; Prēm Čand; Ruswā; Shabbīr Ḥasan Khān Djosh; Shiblī Nuʿmānī; Surūr; [in Suppl.] Āzād
proverbs in Mathal.4

see also Ḥamza al-Iṣfahānī; Rashīd al-Dīn (Waṭwāṭ); Shināsī

terms ʿArūḍ; ʿAtāba; Badīʿ; Balāgha; Bayān; Dakhīl; Fard; Faṣāḥa; Fāṣila; Ibtidāʾ; Idjāza; Iḍmār; Iḳtibās; Intihāʾ; Irtidjāl; Istiʿāra; Ḳabḍ.iii; Ḳāfiya; Ḳaṭʿ; Kināya; Luzūm mā lā yalzam; al-Maʿānī wa ʾl-Bayān; Madjāz; Maʿnā.3; Muʿāraḍa; Muzāwadja; Radīf.2; Radjaz.4; Shawāhid; Ṣila.2

and → LITERATURE.GENRES; METRICS

topoi Bukhl; Bulbul; Ghurāb; Gul; Ḥamām; Ḥayawān.5; Inṣāf; al-Ḳamar.II; Ḳaṭā; Nardjis; Raḥīl; Sāḳī; Shamʿa; Shaʿr.3; al-Shayb wa ʾl-Shabāb

see also Ghazal.ii; ʿIshḳ; Khamriyya; Rabīʿiyyāt

tradition-literature Athar; **Ḥadīth**; Ḥadīth Ḳudsī; Hind.v.e; Sunan; Sunna; [in Suppl.] Arbaʿūn Ḥadīth

see also Ahl al-Ḥadīth; Ḥashwiyya; Khabar; Mustamlī; Naskh; Riwāya; Sharḥ.III

authoritative collections Abū Dāʾūd al-Sidjistānī; Aḥmad b. Ḥanbal; Anas b. Mālik; al-Bayhaḳī; al-Bukhārī, Muḥammad b. Ismāʿīl; al-Dāraḳuṭnī; al-Dārimī; Ibn Ḥibbān; Ibn Mādja; Muslim b. al-Ḥadjdjādj; al-Nasāʾī

see also al-ʿAynī; Ibn Hubayra

terms al-Djarḥ wa ʾl-Taʿdīl; Fard; Gharīb; Ḥikāya.I; Idjāza; Isnād; Khabar al-Wāḥid; Mashhūr; Matn; Muʿanʿan; Munkar; Mursal; Muṣannaf; Musnad.3; Mustamlī; Mutawātir.(a); Rafʿ.2; Ridjāl; Ṣaḥīḥ.1; Ṣāliḥ; Sunan

see also Ḥadīth

traditionists Rāwī; Ridjāl

see also al-Rāmahurmuzī

7th century ʿAbd Allāh b. ʿUmar b. al-Khaṭṭāb; Abū Bakra; Abū Hurayra; al-Aʿmash; Ibn Abī Laylā.I; Ibn Masʿūd; Kaʿb al-Aḥbār; al-Khawlānī, Abū Idrīs; al-Khawlānī, Abū Muslim; [in Suppl.] Djābir b. ʿAbd Allāh

8th century Abu ʾl-ʿĀliya al-Riyāḥī; Abū Mikhnaf; al-Ashʿarī, Abū Burda; Djābir b. Zayd; al-Fuḍayl b. ʿIyāḍ; Ghundjār; al-Ḥasan b. Ṣāliḥ b. Ḥayy al-Kūfī; al-Ḥasan al-Baṣrī; Ibn Abī Laylā.II; Ibn Daʾb; Ibn Isḥāḳ; Ibn al-Naṭṭāḥ; Ibn Shubruma; Ibn Sīrīn; ʿIkrima; al-Layth b. Saʿd; Maymūn b. Mihrān; Muḳātil b. Sulaymān; Nāfiʿ; al-Nakhaʿī, Ibrāhīm; Saʿīd b. Abī Arūba; al-Shaʿbī; Shuʿba b. al-Ḥadjdjādj; al-Suddī; [in Suppl.] Abū ʿAmr al-Shaybānī (*and* al-Shaybānī, Abū ʿAmr); Ibn Djuraydj

9th century Abū Nuʿaym al-Mulāʾī; Baḳī b. Makhlad; Ibn Abī Khaythama; Ibn Abi ʾl-Shawārib; Ibn Abī Shayba; Ibn ʿĀʾisha.IV; Ibn Rāhwayh; Ibn Saʿd; Ibn Sallām al-Djumaḥī; Ibrāhīm al-Ḥarbī; al-Karābīsī.2; al-Marwazī; Muslim b. al-Ḥadjdjādj; Nuʿaym b. Ḥammād; al-Ṣanʿānī, ʿAbd al-Razzāḳ; Sufyān b. ʿUyayna; [in Suppl.] Abū ʿĀṣim al-Nabīl; Asad b. Mūsā b. Ibrāhīm *see also* Ibn Khayyāṭ al-ʿUṣfurī; Ibn Ḳuṭlūbughā

10th century Abū ʿArūba; al-Anbārī, Abū Bakr; al-Anbārī, Abū Muḥammad; Ghulām Thaʿlab; Ibn al-ʿAllāf; Ḳāsim b. Aṣbagh; al-Khaṭṭābī; al-Saraḳusṭī; al-Sidjistānī; [in Suppl.] Ibn ʿUḳda

11th century al-Ḥākim al-Naysābūrī; Ibn ʿAbd al-Barr; Ibn al-Bannāʾ; Ibn Fūrak; Ibn Mākūlā.3; al-Ḳābisī; al-Khaṭīb al-Baghdādī; al-Sahmī

12th century al-Baghawī; Ibn al-ʿArabī; Ibn ʿAsākir; Ibn Ḥubaysh; Ibn al-Ḳaysarānī.1; Ibn al-Nadjdjār; al-Lawātī; Razīn b. Muʿāwiya; al-Rushāṭī; al-Ṣadafī; al-Sarrādj, Abū Muḥammad; Shīrawayh; al-Silafī

see also al-Samʿānī, Abū Saʿd

13th century al-Dimyāṭī al-Shāfiʿī; Ibn al-Athīr.1; Ibn Diḥya; Ibn Faraḥ al-Ishbīlī; al-Ṣaghānī, Raḍiyy al-Dīn; [in Suppl.] Ibn Daḳīḳ al-ʿĪd

14th century al-Dhahabī; Ibn Kathīr; al-Mizzī

15th century Ibn Ḥadjar al-ʿAsḳalānī; al-Ibshīhī.2; al-Ḳasṭallānī; Muʿīn al-Miskīn; al-Suyūṭī

see also Ibn Ḳuṭlūbughā

19th and 20th centuries Shākir, Aḥmad Muḥammad

Shiite ʿAbd Allāh b. Maymūn; Dindān; Djaʿfar al-Ṣādiḳ; Ibn Bābawayh(i); al-Kashshī; al-Kāẓimī, ʿAbd al-Nabī; al-Kulaynī, Abū Djaʿfar Muḥammad; Madjlisī; Muḥammad b. Makkī; Shāh ʿAbd al-ʿAẓīm al-Ḥasanī; [in Suppl.] Akhbāriyya; al-Barḳī; Djābir al-Djuʿfī

see also Asmāʾ

translations from Western languages

into Arabic Muḥammad Bey ʿUthmān Djalāl; Shaʾul; Shumayyil, Shiblī

into Persian Muḥammad Ḥasan Khān; Nafīsī, Saʿīd; Sharīʿatī, ʿAlī

into Turkish Ismāʿīl Ḥaḳḳi ʿĀlīshān; Kanık; Khālide Edīb; Shināsī

travel-literature Djughrāfiyā.(d); **Riḥla**

authors ʿAbd al-Ghanī; al-ʿAbdarī; Abū Dulaf; Abū Ṭālib Khān; Aḥmad Iḥsān; ʿAlī Bey al-ʿAbbāsī; ʿAlī Khān; al-ʿAyyāshī; Ewliyā Čelebi; Fāris al-Shidyāḳ; al-Ghassānī; Ghiyāth al-Dīn Naḳḳāsh; Ibn Baṭṭūṭa; Ibn Djubayr; Ibn Idrīs(II); Kurd ʿAlī; Ma Huan; Meḥmed Yirmisekiz; Nāṣir-i Khusraw; Shiblī Nuʿmānī; Sīdī ʿAlī Reʾīs; [in Suppl.] al-Ghazzāl; Ibn Nāṣir.3

see also Hārūn b. Yaḥyā; Ibn Djuzayy; Ibn Rushayd; Ibn Saʿīd al-Maghribī; Ibrāhīm b. Yaʿḳūb; Khayr Allāh Efendi; Leo Africanus

narratives [in Suppl.] Akhbār al-Ṣīn wa ʾl-Hind

wisdom-literature al-Aḥnaf b. Ḳays; ʿAlī b. Abī Ṭālib; Buzurgmihr; Hūshang; Luḳmān; Sahl b. Hārūn b. Rāhawayh; [in Suppl.] Djāwīdhān Khirad

see also Aktham b. Ṣayfī; Buhlūl; al-Ibshīhī

wondrous literature Abū Ḥāmid al-Gharnāṭī; **ʿAdjāʾib**; Buzurg b. Shahriyār; al-Ḳazwīnī

see also Ibn Sarābiyūn; Ḳiṣaṣ al-Anbiyāʾ; Sindbād

LOVE   ʿIs̲h̲ḳ
  see also Is̲h̲āra; Kalb.II; *and* → LITERATURE.POETRY.LOVE
mystical love   ʿĀs̲h̲iḳ; ʿIs̲h̲ḳ; S̲h̲awḳ
    and → LITERATURE.POETRY.MYSTICAL; MYSTICISM
platonic love   Djamīl al-ʿUd̲h̲rī; G̲h̲azal.i.3; Ibn Dāwūd; Kut̲h̲ayyir b. ʿAbd al-
    Raḥmān; Laylā al-Ak̲h̲yaliyya; Nuṣayb b. Rabāḥ; al-Ramādī
    and → LITERATURE.POETRY.LOVE
treatises on   al-Antākī, Dāʾūd; Ibn Ḥazm, Abū Muḥammad; Rafīʿ al-Dīn
    see also Buk̲h̲tīs̲h̲ūʿ

M

MADAGASCAR   **Madagascar**; Massalajem

MAGIC   ʿAzīma.2; Djadwal; Istinzāl; K̲h̲āṣṣa; Nīrandj; Ruḳya; **Siḥr**; Sīmiyāʾ; [in
    Suppl.] Budūḥ
    see also Djinn.III; Ḥadjar; Ḥurūf; Istik̲h̲āra; Istiḳsām; Istisḳāʾ; Kabid.4; al-
    Kamar.II; Ḳatl.ii.2; K̲h̲awāṣṣ al-Ḳurʾān; Kihāna; Kitābāt.5; Rūḥāniyya; Sidr
magicians   ʿAbd Allāh b. Hilāl; S̲h̲aʿbad̲h̲a
    see also Antemuru
treatises on   al-Maḳḳarī; [in Suppl.] Ibn ʿAzzūz; al-Būnī

MALAWI   Kota Kota

MALAYSIA   Malacca; **Malay Peninsula**; Malays; **Malaysia**
    see also Baladiyya.6; Djāmiʿa; Indonesia; Kandūrī; Kitābāt.8; Partai Islam se
    Malaysia (Pas); Rembau
architecture → ARCHITECTURE.REGIONS
literature   ʿAbd Allāh b. ʿAbd al-Ḳādir; Dāwūd al-Faṭānī; Ḥikāya.v; Ḳiṣṣa.6;
    Malays; S̲h̲āʿir.7
    see also Indonesia.vi
states   Penang; Perak; Sabah; Sarawak

MALI   Adrar.2; Aḥmad al-S̲h̲ayk̲h̲; Aḥmadu Lobbo; Ḥamāliyya; Kaʿti; **Mali**;
    Mansa Mūsā
    see also Mande; Sūdān (Bilād al-).2
historians of   al-Saʿdī
toponyms
  regions   Kaarta
  towns   Bamako; Dienné; Gao; Segu

MAMLUKS **Mamlūks**
see also Ḥarfūsh; Manshūr; Mihmindār; Rank; *and* → DYNASTIES.EGYPT AND THE FERTILE CRESCENT; MILITARY.MAMLUK

MARONITES → CHRISTIANITY.DENOMINATIONS; LEBANON

MARRIAGE Djilwa; Khiṭba; Mutʿa; **Nikāḥ**; [in Suppl.] Djabr
see also ʿAbd.3.e; ʿĀda.iii and iv.4; ʿArūs Resmi; Fāsid wa-Bāṭil.III; Ghāʾib; Ḥaḍāna; Kafāʾa; Kurds.iv.A.1; al-Marʾa.2; Mawākib.4.3 and 5; Raḍāʿ; Shawwāl; Suknā; Sukūt
dowry **Mahr**; Ṣadāḳ

MARTYRDOM Fidāʾī; Maẓlūm; Shahīd
see also Ḥabīb al-Nadjdjār; (al-)Ḥusayn b. ʿAlī b. Abī Ṭālib; Khubayb; Madjlis.3; Mashhad; Masʿūd; [in Suppl.] ʿAbd Allāh b. Abī Bakr al-Miyānadjī

MATHEMATICS Algorithmus; al-Djabr wa ʾl-Muḳābala; Farḍ; Ḥisāb al-ʿAḳd; Ḥisāb al-Ghubār; **ʿIlm al-Ḥisāb**; Kasr; Ḳaṭʿ; Ḳuṭr; Māl; Manshūr; Misāḥa; Muḳaddam; Muṣādara.1; Muthallath; **al-Riyāḍiyyāt**; al-Sahm.1.a; [in Suppl.] ʿIlm al-Handasa
see also al-Mīzān; [in Suppl.] Halīladj
algebra **al-Djabr wa ʾl-Muḳābala**
geometry **Misāḥa**; [in Suppl.] **ʿIlm al-Handasa**
mathematicians Abū Kāmil Shudjāʿ; Abu ʾl-Wafāʾ al-Būzadjānī; ʿAlī al-Ḳūshdjī; al-Bīrūnī; Ibn al-Bannāʾ al-Marrākushī; Ibn al-Haytham; Ibn ʿIrāḳ; Isḥaḳ Efendi; al-Ḳalaṣādī; al-Karābīsī.1; al-Karadjī; al-Kāshī; al-Khʷārazmī; al-Khāzin; al-Khudjandī; Kushiyār b. Labān; al-Madjrīṭī; al-Mārdīnī; Muḥammad b. ʿĪsā al-Māhānī; Muḥammad b. ʿUmar; al-Shīrāzī, Abu ʾl-Ḥusayn
see also Balīnūs; Ḳusṭā b. Lūḳā

MAURITANIA Adrar.3; Atar; Ḥawḍ; Māʾ al-ʿAynayn al-Ḳalḳamī; Madjlis.4.A. xxii; **Mūrītāniyā**
see also Dustūr.xv; Lamtūna; al-Māmī; Sūdān (Bilād al-).2
historians of al-Shinḳīṭī
toponyms
ancient Awdaghost; Ghāna; Ḳunbi Ṣāliḥ; Shinḳīṭ
present-day Nouakchott

MECHANICS Ḥiyal.2; al-Ḳarasṭūn; [in Suppl.] al-Djazarī; **Ḥiyal**
see also Ibn al-Sāʿātī; *and* → HYDROLOGY

Medicine

and → Anatomy; Drugs; Illness; Pharmacology

centres of Bīmāristān; Gondēshāpūr; Ḳalāwūn; [in Suppl.] Abū Zaʿbal

see also Baghdād; Dimashḳ; al-Madīna

dentistry

dental care Miswāk

see also ʿAḳīḳ; Mardjān

treatises on Hāmōn

see also Ibn Abi ʾl-Bayān

medical handbooks/encyclopaedias ʿAlī b. al-ʿAbbās; al-Djurdjānī, Ismāʿīl b. al-Ḥusayn; Ibn al-Nafīs; Ibn Sīnā; al-Masīḥī; Shānī-zāde

medicines Almās; ʿAnbar; al-Dahnadj; Dhahab; al-Durr; Fiḍḍa; Kāfūr; Ḳaṭrān; al-Ḳily; al-Kuḥl; Lubān; Maghnāṭīs.1; Mardjān; Milḥ.2; Misk; Mūmiyāʾ; Ṣābūn; Ṣamgh; [in Suppl.] Bawraḳ; Halīladj

see also Bāzahr; al-Iksīr; Kabid.3; [in Suppl.] Afāwīh; Dam; *for medicinal use of animal parts and plants, see articles on specific animals and plants under* Animals *and* Flora, *respectively*

obstetrics ʿArīb b. Saʿd al-Kātib al-Ḳurṭubī

and → Life Stages.childbirth

ophthalmologists ʿAlī b. ʿĪsā; ʿAmmār al-Mawṣilī; al-Ghāfiḳī; Ibn Dāniyāl; Khalīfa b. Abi ʾl-Maḥāsin

see also ʿAyn; Ḥunayn b. Isḥāḳ al-ʿIbādī; Ibn al-Nafīs; Ibn Zuhr.V; *and* → Anatomy.eye

physicians Djarrāḥ; Ḥāwī; [in Suppl.] Faṣṣād

see also ʿAyn; Constantinus Africanus; Ḥikma; Kabid.3; Masāʾil wa-Adjwiba; *and* → Medicine.ophthalmologists; Pharmacology

biographies of Ibn Abī Uṣaybiʿa; Ibn Djuldjul; Ibn al-Ḳāḍī; Isḥāḳ b. Ḥunayn

see also Ibn al-Ḳifṭī

7th century [in Suppl.] al-Ḥārith b. Kalada

9th century Bukhtīshūʿ; Ḥunayn b. Isḥāḳ al-ʿIbādī; Ibn Māsawayh; Sābūr b. Sahl

see also Māsardjawayh

10th century ʿAlī b. al-ʿAbbās; ʿArīb b. Saʿd al-Kātib al-Ḳurṭubī; Ibn Djuldjul; Isḥāḳ b. Ḥunayn; Isḥāḳ b. Sulaymān al-Isrāʾīlī; Ḳusṭā b. Lūḳā; al-Rāzī, Abū Bakr; Ṣābiʾ.(3); Saʿīd al-Dimashḳī; [in Suppl.] Ibn Abi ʾl-Ashʿath

11th century al-Anṭākī, Abu ʾl-Faradj; Ibn Buṭlān; Ibn Djanāḥ; Ibn Djazla; Ibn al-Djazzār; Ibn Riḍwān; Ibn Sīnā; Ibn al-Ṭayyib; Ibn Wāfid; Ibn Zuhr.II; al-Masīḥī

12th century Abu ʾl-Barakāt; al-Djurdjānī, Ismāʿīl b. al-Ḥusayn; Ibn Djāmiʿ; Ibn al-Tilmīdh; Ibn Zuhr.III and IV; al-Marwazī, Sharaf al-Zamān; [in Suppl.] Ibn Biklārish

see also Ibn Rushd

13th century Ibn Abi 'l-Bayān; Ibn Abī Uṣaybiʿa; Ibn Hubal; Ibn al-Nafīs; Ibn Ṭumlūs; Saʿd al-Dawla; al-Suwaydī; [in Suppl.] Ibn al-Ḳuff
14th century Ḥādjdjī Pasha; Ibn al-Khaṭīb; Isḥāḳ b. Murād; Ḳuṭb al-Dīn Shīrāzī
15th century Bashīr Čelebi
16th century al-Anṭākī, Dāʾūd; Hāmōn
17th century Ḥayātī-zāde
18th century al-Ṣanʿānī, Ḍiyāʾ al-Dīn; [in Suppl.] Ādarrāḳ; Ibn Shaḳrūn al-Miknāsī
19th century and on Bahdjat Muṣṭafā Efendi; Muḥammad b. Aḥmad al-Iskandarānī; Shānī-zāde; Shumayyil, Shiblī; [in Suppl.] ʿAbd al-Salām b. Muḥammad
Greek Diyusḳuridīs; Djālīnūs; Rūfus al-Afsīsī; [in Suppl.] Ahrun; Buḳrāṭ
see also Ḥunayn b. Isḥāḳ al-ʿIbādī; Ibn Riḍwān; Ibn al-Ṭayyib; Isḥāḳ b. Ḥunayn; Iṣṭifān b. Basīl; [in Suppl.] Ḥubaysh b. al-Ḥasan al-Dimashḳī; Ibn Abi 'l-Ashʿath
Jewish Hāmōn; Ibn Abi 'l-Bayān; Ibn Djāmiʿ; Ibn Djanāḥ; Isḥāḳ b. Sulaymān al-Isrāʾīlī; Māsardjawayh; Saʿd al-Dawla; [in Suppl.] Ibn Biklārish
see also Abu 'l-Barakāt; Ḥayātī-zāde.1
Ottoman Bahdjat Muṣṭafā Efendi; Bashīr Čelebi; Ḥādjdjī Pasha; Hāmōn; Ḥayātī-zāde; Isḥāḳ b. Murād; Shānī-zāde
see also Ḥekīm-bashi̊
terms Bīmāristān; Djarrāḥ; Ḥidjāb; Ḳuwwa.5; Sabab.1
see also Ḥāl
veterinary Bayṭār; Ibn Hudhayl; Ibn al-Mundhir

MELKITES → CHRISTIANITY.DENOMINATIONS

MESOPOTAMIA → IRAQ

METALLURGY Ḳalʿī; Khārṣīnī; **Maʿdin**
see also Kalah; al-Mīzān.1; *and* → MINERALOGY.MINES
metals Dhahab; Fiḍḍa; al-Ḥadīd; Nuḥās
and → MINERALOGY.MINERALS; PROFESSIONS.CRAFTSMEN AND TRADESMEN.ARTISANS

METAPHYSICS **Mā baʿd al-Ṭabīʿa**
see also ʿAbd al-Laṭīf al-Baghdādī; Māhiyya; Muṭlaḳ

METEOROLOGY al-Āthār al-ʿUlwiyya
see also Anwāʾ; Sadjʿ.2; [in Suppl.] Ibn al-Adjdābī
winds **Rīḥ**; Samūm

METRICS **ʿArūḍ**
and → LITERATURE.POETRY
metres Mudjtathth; Mutadārik; Mutaḳārib; Mutawātir.(b); Radjaz; Ramal.1; Sarīʿ
terms Dakhīl; Fard; Ḳaṭʿ; Sabab.3; Ṣadr.(a); Sālim.3
treatises on al-Djawharī; al-Khalīl b. Aḥmad; al-Khazradjī, Ḍiyāʾ al-Dīn; Shams-i Ḳays

MILITARY Baḥriyya; Djaysh; **Ḥarb**; [in Suppl.] Baḥriyya
see also Dār al-Ḥarb; Djihād; Fatḥnāme; Ghazw; Naḳḳāra-khāna
architecture Ribāṭ
and → ARCHITECTURE.MONUMENTS.STRONGHOLDS
army **Djaysh**; Istiʿrāḍ (ʿArḍ); **Lashkar**; Radīf.3
see also Djāsūs; Ṣaff.2; *and* → MILITARY.MAMLUK *and* OTTOMAN
contingents Bāzinḳir; Djāndār; Djaysh.iii.2; Djund; Ghulām; Gūm; Ḳūrčī; Maḥalla; Mamlūk; Mutaṭawwiʿa; Sipāhī.2
see also Almogávares; Fāris
battles
see also Shiʿār.1; *and* → MILITARY.EXPEDITIONS
before 622 Buʿāth; Dhū Ḳār; Djabala; Fidjār; Ḥalīma; Shiʿb Djabala; [in Suppl.] Dāḥis
see also Ayyām al-ʿArab; Ḥanẓala b. Mālik
622-632 Badr; Biʾr Maʿūna; Buzākha; Ḥunayn; Khandaḳ; Khaybar; Muʾta
see also Mālik b. ʿAwf
633-660 Adjnādayn; ʿAḳrabāʾ; al-Djamal; Djisr; Faḥl; Ḥarūrāʾ; al-Ḳādisiyya.2; Mardj al-Ṣuffar; Ṣiffīn; [in Suppl.] Dhāt al-Ṣawārī
see also ʿAbd Allāh b. Saʿd; ʿĀʾisha bint Abī Bakr; ʿAlī b. Abī Ṭālib; al-Hurmuzān; al-Nahrawān; Rustam b. Farrukh Hurmuzd
661-750 ʿAyn al-Warda; Balāṭ al-Shuhadāʾ; Baldj b. Bishr; al-Bishr; Dayr al-Djamādjim; Dayr al-Djāthalīḳ; al-Ḥarra; al-Khāzir; Mardj Rāhiṭ
see also (al-)Ḥusayn b. ʿAlī b. Abī Ṭālib; Kulthūm b. ʿIyāḍ al-Ḳushayrī; (al-)Ḳusṭanṭīniyya
751-1258 al-Arak; Bākhamrā; Dayr al-ʿĀḳūl; Fakhkh; Ḥaydarān; Hazārasp; al-ʿIḳāb; Köse Dāgh; Malāzgird.2; Shant Mānkash; [in Suppl.] Dandānḳān
see also Ḥadjar al-Nasr; al-Madjūs; al-Manṣūr bi ʾllāh, Ismāʿīl; Mardj Dābiḳ
1258-18th century ʿAyn Djālūt; Čāldirān; Dābiḳ; Djarba; Ḥimṣ; Ḳoṣowa; Mardj Dābiḳ; Mardj Rāhiṭ; Mardj al-Ṣuffar; Mezőkeresztes; Mohács.a and b; Nīkbūlī; Pānīpat
see also Baḥriyya.iii; Fatḥnāme; Ḥarb; Nahr Abī Fuṭrus; ʿOthmān Pasha
after 18th century Abuklea; Atjèh; Česhme; Farwān; Gök Tepe; Isly; Kūt al-

ʿAmāra; Maysalūn; Nizīb; Rīf.II
see also al-ʿAḳaba; Gulistān

bodies ʿAyyār; Dawāʾir; Djaysh.iii.1; Futuwwa; Ghāzī; al-Shākiriyya
see also ʿAlī b. Muḥammad al-Zandjī; al-Ikhwān; Khashabiyya; Sarhang

booty Fayʾ; **Ghanīma**
see also Baranta; Ghazw; Khāliṣa; Pendjik; *and* → MILITARY.PRISONERS

decorations **Nishān**

expeditions Ghāzī; **Ṣāʾifa**
see also Ghazw

Indo-Muslim Bārūd.vi; Ghulām.iii; Ḥarb.vi; Ḥiṣār.vi; Lashkar; Sipāhī.3; Suwār
see also Istiʿrāḍ (Arḍ)

Mamluk al-Baḥriyya; Baḥriyya.II; Bārūd.iii; Burdjiyya; Ḥalḳa; Ḥarb.iii; Ḥiṣār.iv; **Mamlūk**
see also Amīr Ākhūr; al-Amīr al-Kabīr; Atābak al-ʿAsākir; ʿAyn Djālūt; Čerkes.ii; Ḥimṣ; ʿĪsa b. Muhannā; Khāṣṣakiyya; Ḳumāsh; Rikābdār; Silāḥdār

navy **Baḥriyya**; Dār al-Ṣināʿa; Daryā-begi; Ḳapudan Pasha; Lewend.1; Nassads; Raʾīs.3; Riyāla; [in Suppl.] **Baḥriyya**
see also ʿAzab; Gelibolu; Kātib Čelebi; [in Suppl.] Dhāt al-Ṣawārī; *and* → DYNASTIES.ANATOLIA AND THE TURKS.OTTOMANS.HIGH ADMIRALS; NAVIGATION.SHIPS; PIRACY

offices Amīr; ʿArīf; Atābak al-ʿAsākir; Fawdjdār; Ispahbadh; Ispahsālār; Istiʿrāḍ (ʿArḍ); Ḳāʾid; Manṣab; Sālār; Sardār; Sarhang; Shiḥna; Silāḥdār
see also Amīr al-Umarāʾ; Dārūgha; Ḳāḍī ʿAskar; Ḳūrčī; *and* → MILITARY.OTTOMAN

Ottoman Bāb-i Serʿaskeri; Baḥriyya.iii; Balyemez; Bārūd.iv; Devshirme; Djebeli; Ghulām.iv; Ḥarb.iv; Ḥarbiye; Ḥiṣār.v; Müsellem; Radīf.3; Sandjaḳ; Sipāhī.1; [in Suppl.] Djebedji
see also ʿAskarī; Ḍabṭiyya; Gelibolu; Gūm; Ḥareket Ordusu; Istiʿrāḍ (Arḍ); Ḳapïdji; Karakol; Martolos; Mensūkhāt; Mondros; Nefīr; Ordu; Pendjik; *and* → MILITARY.NAVY

army contingents al-Abnāʾ.V; ʿAdjamī Oghlān; Akïndjï; Alay; ʿAzab; Bashïbozuḳ; Bölük; Deli; Devedji; Djānbāzān; Eshkindji; Ghurabāʾ; Gönüllü; Khāṣṣekī; Khumbaradjï; Lewend; Niẓām-ï Djedīd; Odjaḳ; Orta; [in Suppl.] Djebedji
see also Akhī; Nefīr; Sipāhī.1

officers Bayraḳdār; Biñbashï; Bölük-bashï; Čāʾūsh; Čorbadjï.1; Ḍābiṭ; Daryā-begi; Ḳapudan Pasha; Mushīr; Rikābdār; Riyāla
see also Sandjaḳ; Silāḥdār

pay ʿAṭāʾ; Inʿām; Māl al-Bayʿa; Rizḳ.3

police Aḥdāth; ʿAsas; Ḍabṭiyya; Karakol; **Shurṭa**
see also Dawāʾir; Futuwwa; Kōtwāl; Martolos; Naḳīb.2

prisoners   Lamas-ṣū; Mübādele.ii; [in Suppl.] Fidāʾ
    see also Sidjn; *and* → MILITARY.BOOTY
reform   → REFORM.MILITARY
tactics   Ḥarb; Ḥiṣār; Ḥiyal.1
    see also Fīl; *and* → ARCHITECTURE.MONUMENTS.STRONGHOLDS
treatises on   Ibn Hudhayl; [in Suppl.] Fakhr-i Mudabbir
    see also Ḥarb.ii; Ḥiyal.1
weapons   ʿAnaza; ʿArrāda; Balyemez; Bārūd; Dūrbāsh; Ḳaws; Mandjanīḳ; Nafṭ.2
    see also ʿAlam; Asad Allāh Iṣfahānī; Hilāl.ii; Ḥiṣār; Ḳalʿī; Lamṭ; Marātib

MINERALOGY   **Maʿdin**
    see also al-Mīzān.1
minerals   Abū Ḳalamūn; ʿAḳīḳ; Almās; Bārūd; Billawr; al-Dahnadj; Fīrūzadj; al-
    Kibrīt; al-Kuḥl; Maghnāṭīs.1; Milḥ; Mūmiyāʾ; Naṭrūn; [in Suppl.] Bawrak
    see also al-Andalus.v; Damāwand; Golkondā; Ḥadjar; Kirmān; Maʿdin;
    Malindi; *and* → JEWELRY; METALLURGY
mines   al-ʿAllāḳī; Anadolu.iii.6; al-Andalus.v.2; ʿAraba; Armīniya.III; Azalay;
    Badakhshān; Billiton; Bilma; Čankîrî; al-Djabbūl; Djayzān; al-Durūʿ;
    Farghānā; Firrīsh; Gümüsh-khāne; Kalah; Ḳarā Ḥiṣār.2 and 3; Ḳayṣariyya;
    al-Ḳily; Ḳishm; Maʿdin.2; al-Maʿdin; Sofāla
    see also Fāzūghlī; Filasṭīn; Milḥ
treatises on   al-Suwaydī

MIRACLES   **Karāma**; **Muʿdjiza**
    see also Āya; Dawsa; Māʾ al-ʿAynayn al-Ḳalḳamī; Miʿrādj; *and* → SAINTHOOD

MONARCHY   Malik; Mamlaka
    see also Darshan; Shāh; *and* → COURT CEREMONY
royal insignia   Miẓalla; Sandjaḳ; Sarāparda; Shamsa
    see also Shams.3

MONASTICISM   **Rahbāniyya**
    and → CHRISTIANITY.MONASTERIES

MONGOLIA   Ḳaraḳorum; Khalkha; **Mongolia**; Mongols
Mongols   Batuʾids; Čaghatay Khānate; Čūbānids; Djalāyir; Djānids; Giray;
    Hayāṭila; Ilkhāns; Kalmuk; Ḳarā Khiṭāy; Ḳūrīltāy; Mangît; **Mongols**
    see also ʿAyn Djālūt; Dūghlāt; Ergenekon; Ḥimṣ; Khānbalîk; Ḳūbčūr;
    Ḳungrāt; Libās.iii; Ötüken; *and* → DYNASTIES.MONGOLS
historians of   Rashīd al-Dīn Ṭabīb
        and → DYNASTIES.MONGOLS *and the section Historians Of under individ-*
        ual dynasties

physical geography
  waters   Ork̲h̲on

MONOPHYSITES   → CHRISTIANITY.DENOMINATIONS

MOROCCO   **al-Mag̲h̲rib**
  see also ʿArabiyya.A.iii.3; Ḥimāya.ii; Mallāḥ; Rīf.II; Sulṭān al-Ṭalaba
  architecture   → ARCHITECTURE.REGIONS.NORTH AFRICA
  dynasties   ʿAlawīs; Idrīsids; Marīnids; Saʿdids
    see also Bū Ḥmāra; Ḥasanī; S̲h̲urafāʾ.1.III; [in Suppl.] Aḥmad al-Hība; *and*
    → DYNASTIES.SPAIN AND NORTH AFRICA
  historians of   Aḥmad al-Nāṣirī al-Salāwī (*and* al-Nāṣir al-Salāwī); Akansūs; Ibn
    Abī Zarʿ; Ibn al-Ḳāḍī
    see also Ibn al-Raḳīḳ; al-Kattānī; [in Suppl.] ʿAllāl al-Fāsī; *and* →
    DYNASTIES.SPAIN AND NORTH AFRICA
  modern period   Baladiyya.3; Djāmiʿa; Djarīda.i.B; Djays̲h̲.iii.2; Dustūr.xvii;
    Ḥizb.i; Ḥukūma.iv; Maʿārif.2.C; Madjlis.4.A.xxi; Madjmaʿ ʿIlmī.i.2.d;
    Maḥkama.4.x; Mak̲h̲zan; [in Suppl.] Institut des hautes études marocaines
  reform   Salafiyya.1(c)
  statesmen   [in Suppl.] ʿAllāl al-Fāsī
  population   Dukkāla; Glāwā; Ḥarṭānī; K̲h̲ult; S̲h̲āwiya.1; [in Suppl.] Awraba
    see also al-Fasiyyūn; al-Maʿḳil; *and* → BERBERS
  religion   al-Mag̲h̲rib.VI
    mystical orders   Darḳāwa; Hansaliyya; Hazmīriyyūn; ʿIsāwā; al-Nāṣiriyya;
      S̲h̲ādhiliyya; [in Suppl.] Ḥamādis̲h̲a
      for Djazūliyya, *see* al-Djazūlī, Abū ʿAbd Allāh
      see also S̲h̲arḳawa; [in Suppl.] ʿĀʾis̲h̲a Ḳandīs̲h̲a; *and* → MYSTICISM;
      SAINTHOOD
  toponyms
    ancient   Anfā; Bādis; al-Baṣra; Fāzāz; al-Ḳaṣr al-Ṣag̲h̲īr; Nakūr; S̲h̲alla;
      Sidjilmāsa
    present-day
      islands   [in Suppl.] al-Ḥusayma
      regions   Darʿa; Figuig; G̲h̲arb; Ḥawz; Ifni; Rīf.I.2; Spartel; al-Sūs al-
        Aḳṣā
      towns   Agadir-ighir; Āg̲h̲māt; al-ʿArāʾis̲h̲; Aṣfī; Aṣīla; Azammūr;
        Damnāt; (al-)Dār al-Bayḍāʾ; al-Djadīda; Dubdū; Faḍāla; Fās; Garsīf;
        al-Ḳaṣr al-Kabīr; al-Mahdiyya; Marrākus̲h̲; Mawlāy Idrīs; Melilla;
        Miknās; Ribāṭ al-Fatḥ; Sabta; Salā; S̲h̲afs̲h̲āwan; Ṣufrūy; al-Suwayra;
        [in Suppl.] Azrū; Benī Mellāl
        see also al-Ḥamrāʾ

MOUNTAINS   Adja' and Salmā; Adrar.2; Ag̲h̲rî Dag̲h̲; Aïr; Ala Dag̲h̲; Alad̲j̲a Dag̲h̲; Alburz; Altai; Alwand Kūh; ʿAmūr; Atlas; Awrās; Balk̲h̲ān; Bes̲h̲-parmak̲; Bībān; Bingöl Dag̲h̲; Bīsutūn; Čopan-ata; Damāwand; Deve Boynu; D̲j̲abala; al-D̲j̲ibāl; D̲j̲ūdī; D̲j̲urd̲j̲ura; Elma Dag̲h̲î; Erd̲j̲iyas Dag̲h̲î; Fūta D̲j̲allon; Gāwur Dag̲h̲larî; Ḥadūr; Ḥamrīn; Ḥarāz; Hawrāmān; Hindū Kus̲h̲; Ḥiṣn al-G̲h̲urāb; Ḥufās̲h̲; al-Ḳabk̲; Kabylia; Ḳarakorum; Ḳāsiyūn; K̲h̲umayr; Kūh-i Bābā; al-Lukkām; Nafūsa; Pamirs; Safīd Kūh; al-Sarāt; al-S̲h̲ārāt; Sind̲j̲ār; Sulaymān

    see also Hind.i.i; Ḳarā Bāg̲h̲; *and* → *the section Physical Geography under individual countries*

MOZAMBIQUE   Kerimba; Makua; **Mozambique**; Pemba; Sofāla

MUḤAMMAD, THE PROPHET   Hid̲j̲ra; Ḥirā'; al-Ḥudaybiya; K̲h̲aybar; K̲h̲uzāʿa; Ḳudāʿa; Ḳurays̲h̲; al-Madīna.i.2; Mawlid; Miʿrād̲j̲; **Muḥammad**; Ṣaḥāba; Sunna

    see also al-Ḳurʾān; Muʾāk̲h̲āt; al-Muʾallafa Ḳulūbuhum; Nubuwwa; Nūr Muḥammadī; Sayyid; S̲h̲araf; S̲h̲arīf; [in Suppl.] Bayʿat al-Riḍwān

belongings of   At̲h̲ar; al-Burāḳ; Burda.1; D̲h̲u 'l-Faḳār; Duldul; Emānet-i Muḳaddese; Ḳadam S̲h̲arīf; K̲h̲irḳa-yi S̲h̲erīf; Liḥya-yi S̲h̲erīf

biographies of   **al-Mag̲h̲āzī**; **Sīra**
    biographers   Abd al-Ḥaḳḳ b. Sayf al-Dīn; al-Bakrī, Abu 'l-Ḥasan; Daḥlān; al-Diyārbakrī; al-D̲j̲awwānī; al-Ḥalabī, Nūr al-Dīn; Ibn His̲h̲ām; Ibn Isḥāḳ; Ibn Sayyid al-Nās; ʿIyāḍ b. Mūsā; Ḳarā-čelebi-zāde.4; al-Ḳasṭallānī; Liu Chih; Mug̲h̲ulṭāy; Muḥammad Ḥusayn Haykal; Muʿīn al-Miskīn; [in Suppl.] Dinet
    see also Hind.v.e; Ibn Saʿd; al-K̲h̲arg̲h̲ūs̲h̲ī
companions of   Abū Ayyūb al-Anṣārī; Abū Bakra; Abu 'l-Dardā'; Abū D̲h̲arr; Abū Hurayra; ʿAdī b. Ḥātim; ʿAmmār b. Yāsir; Anas b. Mālik; al-Arḳam; al-As̲h̲ʿarī, Abū Mūsā; ʿAttāb; al-Barā' (b. ʿĀzib); al-Barā' (b. Maʿrūr); Bas̲h̲īr b. Saʿd; Bilāl b. Rabāḥ; Bis̲h̲r b. al-Barā'; Burayda b. al-Ḥuṣayb; Diḥya; D̲j̲āriya b. Ḳudāma; G̲h̲asīl al-Malāʾika; Hās̲h̲im b. ʿUtba; Ḥurḳūṣ b. Zuhayr al-Saʿdī; Ibn Masʿūd; Kaʿb b. Mālik; K̲h̲abbāb b. al-Aratt; K̲h̲ālid b. Saʿīd; Ḳut̲h̲am b. al-ʿAbbās; Maslama b. Muk̲h̲allad; al-Miḳdād b. ʿAmr; Muʿāwiya b. Ḥudayd̲j̲; al-Mug̲h̲īra b. S̲h̲uʿba; Muḥammad b. Abī Ḥud̲h̲ayfa; Muṣʿab b. ʿUmayr; al-Nābig̲h̲a al-D̲j̲aʿdī; al-Nuʿmān b. Bas̲h̲īr; Saʿd b. Abī Waḳḳāṣ; Ṣafwān b. al-Muʿaṭṭal; Saʿīd b. Zayd; S̲h̲addād b. ʿAmr; S̲h̲uraḥbīl b. Ḥasana; [in Suppl.] D̲j̲ābir b. ʿAbd Allāh; Ibn Mīt̲h̲am
    see also Ahl al-Ṣuffa; al-Ḳaʿḳāʿ; K̲h̲awlān.2; Ḳuss b. Sāʿida; Rawḥ b. Zinbāʿ; al-Salaf wa 'l-K̲h̲alaf
family of   al-ʿAbbās b. ʿAbd al-Muṭṭalib; ʿAbd Allāh b. ʿAbd al-Muṭṭalib; ʿAbd al-Muṭṭalib b. Hās̲h̲im; Abū Lahab; Abū Ṭālib; ʿAḳīl b. Abī Ṭālib; ʿAlī b. Abī

Ṭālib; Āmina; Dja'far b. Abī Ṭālib; Fāṭima; Ḥalīma bint Abī Dhu'ayb; Ḥamza b. 'Abd al-Muṭṭalib; (al-)Ḥasan b. 'Alī b. Abī Ṭālib; al-Ḥasan b. Zayd b. al-Ḥasan; Hāshim b. 'Abd Manāf; (al-)Ḥusayn b. 'Alī b. Abī Ṭālib; Rukayya

see also Ahl al-Bayt; Sharīf; Shurafā'

wives of 'Ā'isha bint Abī Bakr; Ḥafṣa; Khadīdja; Māriya; Maymūna bint al-Ḥārith; Ṣafiyya; Sawda bt. Zam'a

MUSIC Ghinā'; Ḳayna; Maḳām; Malāhī; **Mūsīḳī**; Ramal.2; Shashmaḳom; [in Suppl.] Īḳā'

see also Kurds.iv.C.4; Lamak; Naḳḳāra-khāna; al-Rashīdiyya; Samā'.1

composers Ibrāhīm al-Mawṣilī; Ismā'īl Ḥaḳḳi; al-Ḳusanṭını; Lāhūtī; Laylā Khānim; Ma'bad b. Wahb; Ṣafī al-Dīn al-Urmawī; Shewḳī Beg; Ṣolaḳ-zāde; [in Suppl.] 'Allawayh al-A'sar; al-Dalāl; Ḥabba Khātūn

instruments Būḳ; Darabukka; Duff; Ghayṭa; Imzad; Ḳithāra; Mi'zaf; Mizmār; Nefīr; Rabāb; Ṣandj; Sanṭūr; Saz

see also Mehter; Mūrisṭus; Naḳḳāra-khāna

musicians 'Azza al-Maylā'; Djaḥẓa; Ibn Djāmi'; Ibn Muḥriz; Ibrāhīm al-Mawṣilī; Isḥāḳ b. Ibrāhīm al-Mawṣilī; Ṣafī al-Dīn al-Urmawī; [in Suppl.] 'Allawayh al-A'sar; Barṣawmā al-Zāmir; al-Dalāl; Faḍl al-Shā'ira

see also al-Ḳāsim b. 'Īsā

regional

Andalusian al-Ḥā'ik

Indian **Hind**.viii; Khayāl

see also Bāyazīd Anṣārī; [in Suppl.] Ḥabba Khātūn

Persian Mihragān.iv.3

see also Lāhūtī; Naḳḳāra-khāna

Turkish Ilāhī; Ḳoshma; Mehter; Sharḳī

see also Laylā Khānim; Māni; Nefīr; Shewḳı Beg

song **Ghinā'**; Ḳayna; Khayāl; Nashīd; Nawba; Shashmaḳom

see also Abu 'l-Faradj al-Iṣbahānī; Ḥawfī; Ilāhī; Mawāliyā.3; Shā'ir.1.E

singers 'Ālima; 'Azza al-Maylā'; Djamīla; al-Gharīḍ; Ḥabāba; Ibn 'Ā'isha.I; Ibn Bāna; Ibn Djāmi'; Ibn Misdjaḥ; Ibn Muḥriz; Ibn Suraydj; Ibrāhīm al-Mawṣilī; Ḳayna; Ma'bad b. Wahb; Mālik b. Abi 'l-Samḥ; Mukhāriḳ; Nashīṭ; Rā'iḳa; Sā'ib Khāthir; Sallāma al-Zarḳā'; Shāriya; Siti Binti Saad; [in Suppl.] Badhl al-Kubrā; al-Dalāl; al-Djarādatāni; Faḍl al-Shā'ira; Ḥabba Khātūn

see also 'Āshiḳ; al-Barāmika.5

treatises on 'Abd al-Ḳādir b. Ghaybī; Abu 'l-Faradj al-Iṣbahānī; al-Ḥā'ik; Ibn Bāna; Ibn Khurradādhbih; Mashāḳa; (Banu 'l-) Munadjdjim.4; Mūrisṭus; Mushāḳa; Ṣafī al-Dīn al-Urmawī; al-Ṣaydawı

see also Abu 'l-Maḥāsin b. Taghrībirdī; İnal; Malāhī

MYSTICISM   Allāh.III.4; Darwīs̲h̲; D̲h̲ikr; Ibāḥa.II; Karāma; Murīd; Murs̲h̲id; Pīr;
    Samāʿ.1; S̲h̲ayk̲h̲
    see also Sadjdjāda.3; Saʿīd al-Suʿadāʾ; *and* → DYNASTIES.PERSIA.ṢAFAWIDS
concepts   Baḳāʾ wa-Fanāʾ; al-Insān al-Kāmil; Is̲h̲rāḳ; Lāhūt and Nāsūt
    see also Allāh.III.4; al-Ḥallādj.IV; Ibn al-ʿArabī; al-Niffarī
dervishes   **Darwīs̲h̲**; Raḳṣ
    see also [in Suppl.] Buḳʿa; *and* → MYSTICISM.ORDERS
dress   K̲h̲irḳa; Pālāhang; S̲h̲add.1
early ascetics   ʿĀmir b. ʿAbd al-Ḳays al-ʿAnbarī; al-Ḥasan al-Baṣrī; al-Fuḍayl b.
    ʿIyāḍ; Ibrāhīm b. Adham; Maʿrūf al-Kark̲h̲ī; Sarī al-Saḳaṭī
    see also Bakkāʾ
mystical poetry   → LITERATURE.POETRY
mystics   Darwīs̲h̲
    see also Pist; *and* → HAGIOGRAPHY
    African (excluding North Africa)   [in Suppl.] al-Duwayḥī
        see also Ṣāliḥiyya; Sūdān (Bilād al-).2
    Andalusian   Abū Madyan; Ibn al-ʿArabī; Ibn al-ʿArīf, Abu ʾl-ʿAbbās; Ibn
        ʿĀs̲h̲ir; Ibn Barradjān; Ibn Ḳasī; Ibn Masarra; al-S̲h̲us̲h̲tarī
    Arabic (excluding Andalusian and North African)   ʿAbd al-G̲h̲anī; ʿAbd al-
        Ḳādir al-Djīlānī; ʿAbd al-Karīm al-Djīlī; ʿAdī b. Musāfir; Aḥmad al-
        Badawī; ʿAydarūs; al-Bakrī, Muḥammad; al-Bakrī, Muṣṭafā; Bis̲h̲r al-
        Ḥāfī; al-Bisṭāmī, ʿAbd al-Raḥmān; al-Damīrī; al-Dasūḳī, Ibrāhīm b. ʿAbd
        al-ʿAzīz; al-Dasūḳī, Ibrāhīm b. Muḥammad; D̲h̲u ʾl-Nūn, Abu ʾl-Fayḍ;
        al-Dimyāṭī, al-Bannāʾ; al-Dimyāṭī, Nūr al-Dīn; al-Djunayd; al-G̲h̲azālī,
        Abū Ḥāmid; al-G̲h̲azālī, Aḥmad; al-Ḥallādj; al-Harawī al-Mawṣilī; Ibn
        ʿAṭāʾ Allāh; al-Ḳazwīnī, Nadjm al-Dīn; al-K̲h̲arrāz; al-Kurdī; al-
        Kus̲h̲as̲h̲ī; Mak̲h̲rama; al-Manūfī; al-Muḥāsibī; al-Munāwī; al-Niffarī;
        al-Nūrī; Rābiʿa al-ʿAdawiyya al-Ḳaysiyya; al-Rifāʿī; Sahl al-Tustarī; al-
        Sarrādj, Abū Naṣr; al-S̲h̲aʿrānī; al-S̲h̲iblī, Abū Bakr; Sumnūn; [in Suppl.]
        Abu ʾl-ʿAzāʾim; al-ʿAdawī; al-ʿAfīfī; al-Ḥiṣāfī
        see also Abū Nuʿaym al-Iṣfahānī; Abū Ṭālib al-Makkī; Bā ʿAlawī;
        Baḥrak; Bakriyya; Bayyūmiyya; Faḍl, Bā; Faḳīh, Bā; Faḳīh, Bal;
        Hurmuz, Bā; Ḳādiriyya; Marwāniyya; Saʿdiyya; al-Ṣiddīḳī; [in Suppl.]
        al-Bakrī; Demirdās̲h̲iyya; *and* → MYSTICISM.EARLY ASCETICS
    Central Asian   Aḥmad Yasawī; Ḥakīm Ata; Naḳs̲h̲band; [in Suppl.] Aḥrār
        see also Ḳalandariyya; Pārsāʾiyya
    Indian   Abū ʿAlī Ḳalandar; Aḥmad Sirhindī; As̲h̲raf ʿAlī; Bahāʾ al-Dīn
        Zakariyyā; Bāḳī bi ʾllāh (*and* [in Suppl.]); al-Banūrī; Budhan; Burhān al-
        Dīn G̲h̲arīb; Burhān al-Dīn Ḳuṭb-i ʿĀlam; Čirāg̲h̲-i Dihlī; Čis̲h̲tī;
        Djahānārā Bēgam; Djalāl al-Dīn Ḥusayn al-Buk̲h̲ārī; "Djamālī"; Farīd
        al-Dīn Masʿūd "Gandj-i-S̲h̲akar"; Gīsū Darāz; Hānsawī; Ḥusaynī Sādāt
        Amīr; Imdād Allāh; Kalīm Allāh al-Djahānābādī; Ḳuṭb al-Dīn Bak̲h̲tiyār

Kākī; Malik Muḥammad Djāyasī; Miyān Mīr, Miyādjī; Mubārak Ghāzī; Muḥammad Ghawth Gwāliyārī; al-Muttaḳī al-Hindī; Muẓaffar Shams Balkhī; Niẓām al-Dīn Awliyā'; Niẓām al-Dīn, Mullā Muḥammad; Nūr Ḳuṭb al-ʿĀlam; Shāh Muḥammad b. ʿAbd Aḥmad; [in Suppl.] ʿAbd al-Bārī; ʿAbd al-Wahhāb Bukhārī; Bulbul Shāh; Farangī Maḥall; Gadā'ī Kambō; Ḥamīd Ḳalandar; Ḥamīd al-Dīn Ḳāḍī Nāgawrī; Ḥamīd al-Dīn Ṣūfī Nāgawrī Siwālī; Ḥamza Makhdūm

see also ʿAydarūs; Čishtiyya; Dārā Shukōh; Dard; Djīwan; Hind.v; Khalīl Allāh (*and* Khalīl Allāh But-shikan); Malang; Mughals.6; Naḳshbandiyya.3; Shaṭṭāriyya; Suhrawardiyya.2

Indonesian ʿAbd al-Ra'ūf al-Sinkilī; ʿAbd al-Ṣamad al-Palimbānī; Ḥamza Fanṣūrī; Shams al-Dīn al-Samaṭrānī

North African ʿAbd al-Ḳādir al-Fāsī; ʿAbd al-Salām b. Mashīsh; Abu 'l-Maḥāsin al-Fāsī; Abū Muḥammad Ṣāliḥ; Aḥmad b. Idrīs; ʿAlī b. Maymūn; al-ʿAyyāshī; al-Daḳḳāḳ; al-Djazūlī; al-Hāshimī; Ḥmād u-Mūsā; Ibn ʿAbbād; Ibn ʿAdjība; Ibn ʿAlīwa; Ibn ʿArūs; Ibn Ḥirzihim; al-Ḳādirī al-Ḥasanī; al-Kūhin; al-Lamaṭī; Mā' al-ʿAynayn al-Ḳalḳamī; al-Madjdhūb; al-Sanūsī, Abū ʿAbd Allāh; al-Sanūsī, Muḥammad b. ʿAlī; al-Sanūsī, Shaykh Sayyid Aḥmad; al-Shādhilī; [in Suppl.] al-Asmar; al-Dilā'; al-Fāsī; Ibn ʿAzzūz

see also ʿAmmāriyya; ʿArūsiyya; Darkāwa; Hansaliyya; Hazmīriyyūn; al-Ifrānī; ʿĪsāwa; Madaniyya; al-Nāṣiriyya; Raḥmāniyya; Shādhiliyya; [in Suppl.] Ḥamādisha

Persian ʿAbd al-Razzāḳ al-Ḳāshānī; Abū Saʿīd b. Abi 'l-Khayr; Abū Yazīd al-Bisṭāmī; Aḥmad-i Djām, ʿAlā' al-Dawla al-Simnānī; ʿAlī al-Hamadānī; al-Anṣārī al-Harawī; Ashraf Djahāngīr; Bābā-Ṭāhir; Djalāl al-Dīn Rūmī; Faḍl Allah Ḥurūfī; Ghudjduwānī; Ḥamdūn al-Ḳaṣṣār; Hudjwīrī; Ibn Khafīf; ʿIrāḳī; al-Kalābādhī; Kamāl Khudjandī; Ḳāsim-i Anwār; Kāzarūnī; Khalīl Allāh (*and* Khalīl Allāh But-shikan); Kharaḳānī; al-Khargūshī; Kirmānī; Kubrā; al-Ḳushayrī.1; Lāhīdjī.1; Maḥmūd Shabistarī; Nadjm al-Dīn Rāzī Dāya; Naḳshband; Rūzbihān; Saʿd al-Dīn al-Ḥammū'ī; Saʿd al-Dīn Kāshgharī; Ṣadr al-Dīn Ardabīlī; Ṣadr al-Dīn Mūsā; Ṣafī; Saʿīd al-Dīn Farghānī; Sayf al-Dīn Bākharzī; Shams-i Tabrīz(ī); al-Suhrawardī, Abu 'l-Nadjīb; al-Suhrawardī, Shihāb al-Dīn Abū Ḥafṣ; Sulṭān Walad; [in Suppl.] ʿAbd Allāh b. Abī Bakr al-Miyānadjī; Abū ʿAlī; Aḥmad-i Rūmī; ʿAyn al-Ḳuḍāt al-Hamadhānī; Ibn al-Bazzāz al-Ardabīlī

see also Djāmī; Madjlisī-yi Awwal; Naḳshbandiyya.1; Niʿmat-Allāhiyya; Ṣafawids.I.ii

Turkish Aḳ Shams al-Dīn; Altî Parmak; ʿĀshîḳ Pasha; Badr al-Dīn b. Ḳāḍī Samāwnā; Baraḳ Baba; Bīdjān; Emīr Sulṭān; Faṣīḥ Dede; Fehmī; Gulshanī; Gülshehrī; Ḥādjdjī Bayrām Walī; Hüdā'ī; Ḥusām al-Dīn

Čelebi; Ismāʿīl al-Anḳarawī; Ismāʿīl Ḥaḳḳi; Ḳayg̲h̲usuz Abdāl; K̲h̲alīlī; Ḳuṭb al-Dīn-zāde; Merkez; Niyāzī; Sezāʾī, Ḥasan Dede; [in Suppl.] ʿĀrif Čelebī; Es̲h̲refog̲h̲lu; Esrār Dede

see also As̲h̲rafiyya; Bakriyya; Bayrāmiyya; Bektās̲h̲iyya; Djilwatiyya; Gülbaba; Ilāhī; K̲h̲alwatiyya; Mawlawiyya; Naḳs̲h̲bandiyya.2; S̲h̲aʿbāniyya; S̲h̲amsiyya; Sunbuliyya

orders ʿAmmāriyya; ʿArūsiyya; As̲h̲rafiyya; Bakriyya; Bayrāmiyya; Bayyūmiyya; Bektās̲h̲iyya; Čis̲h̲tiyya; Darḳāwa; Djilwatiyya; Hansaliyya; Hazmīriyyūn; ʿĪsāwā; Ḳādiriyya; Ḳalandariyya; K̲h̲alwatiyya; Madaniyya; Marwāniyya; Mawlawiyya; Mīrg̲h̲aniyya; Murīdiyya; Naḳs̲h̲bandiyya; al-Nāṣiriyya; Niʿmat-Allāhiyya; Pārsāʾiyya; Raḥmāniyya; Rifāʿiyya; Saʿdiyya; Ṣāliḥiyya; Sanūsiyya; S̲h̲aʿbāniyya; S̲h̲ādhiliyya; S̲h̲amsiyya; S̲h̲aṭṭāriyya; Suhrawardiyya; Sunbuliyya; [in Suppl.] Demirdās̲h̲iyya; Ḥamādis̲h̲a

for ʿAdawiyya, *see* ʿAdī b. Musāfir; *for* ʿAfīfiyya, *see* [in Suppl.] al-ʿAfīfī; *for* Aḥmadiyya (Badawiyya), *see* Aḥmad al-Badawī; *for* Dasūḳiyya (Burhāmiyya), *see* al-Dasūḳī, Ibrāhīm b. ʿAbd al-ʿAzīz; *for* al-Djazūliyya, *see* al-Djazūlī; *for* Guls̲h̲aniyya, *see* Guls̲h̲anī; for Idrīsiyya, *see* Aḥmad b. Idrīs; *for* Kāzarūniyya (Murs̲h̲idiyya, Ishāḳiyya), *see* Kāzarūnī; *for* Kubrawiyya, *see* Kubrā

see also Nūrbak̲h̲s̲h̲iyya; Ṣafawids.I.ii

terms Abdāl; ʿĀs̲h̲iḳ; Awtād; Baḳāʾ wa-Fanāʾ; Basṭ; Bīs̲h̲arʿ; Čāʾus̲h̲; Darwīs̲h̲; Dawsa; Dede; Dhawḳ; Dhikr; Djilwa; Faḳīr; Fikr; al-G̲h̲ayb; G̲h̲ayba; G̲h̲ufrān; Ḥaḍra; Ḥaḳīḳa.3; Ḥaḳḳ; Ḥāl; Ḥidjāb.III; Ḥuḳūḳ; Ḥulūl; Ḥurriyya; Huwa huwa; Ik̲h̲lāṣ; Ilhām; ʿInāya; al-Insān al-Kāmil; Is̲h̲ān; Is̲h̲āra; ʿIs̲h̲ḳ; Is̲h̲rāḳ; Ithbāt; Ittiḥād; Ḳabḍ.ii; Kāfir; Ḳalb.I; Kalima; Karāma; Kas̲h̲f; K̲h̲alīfa.iii; K̲h̲alwa; K̲h̲ānḳāh; K̲h̲irḳa; al-Ḳuṭb; Lāhūt and Nāsūt; Madjdhūb; Manzil; Maʿrifa; Muḥāsaba.1; Munādjāt; Murīd; Murs̲h̲id; Nafs; Odjaḳ; Pālāhang; Pīr; Pūst; Pūst-nes̲h̲īn; Rābiṭa; Ramz.3; Rātib; Ribāṭ; Riḍā.1; Rind; Rūḥāniyya; Ruk̲h̲ṣa.2; Ṣabr; Ṣadr; S̲h̲aṭḥ; S̲h̲awḳ; S̲h̲ayk̲h̲; S̲h̲ukr.1; Ṣidḳ; Silsila; Sulṭān.4; Sulūk.2; [in Suppl.] Buḳʿa; G̲h̲awth

see also Čelebī; Futuwwa; Gülbaba; Lawḥ; Lawn

N

NATIONALISM Istiḳlāl; **Ḳawmiyya**

see also Djangalī; K̲h̲ilāfa; Pās̲h̲tūnistān; al-S̲h̲uʿūbiyya; *and* → POLITICS. MOVEMENTS

NATURAL SCIENCE **al-Āthār al-ʿUlwiyya; Ḥikma**; Masāʾil wa-Adjwiba
see also Nūr.1

natural scientists al-Bīrūnī; al-Dimas̲h̲ḳī; Ibn Bādjdja; Ibn al-Hayt̲h̲am; Ibn

Rushd; Ibn Sīnā; Ikhwān al-Ṣafāʾ; al-Ḳazwīnī; al-Marwazī, Sharaf al-Zamān
and → ALCHEMY; ASTRONOMY; BOTANY; METAPHYSICS; ZOOLOGY

NATURE → BOTANY; FLORA; LITERATURE.POETRY.NATURE

NAVIGATION Djughrāfiyā; Iṣbaʿ; Kharīṭa; Maghnāṭīs.2; Manār; **Milāḥa**; Mīnāʾ
see also al-Khashabāt; Rīḥ
ships Milāḥa (esp. 4); Nassads; **Safīna**; Shīnī
see also Baḥriyya.2; Kelek; *and* → MILITARY.NAVY
shipyards Dār al-Ṣināʿa
treatises on Ibn Mādjid; Sīdī ʿAlī Reʾīs; Sulaymān al-Mahrī
see also Djughrāfiyā.IV.d; Milāḥa.1 and 3

NEPAL **Nepal**

NESTORIANS → CHRISTIANITY.DENOMINATIONS

NEW WORLD Djāliya; Djarīda.i.C.; **al-Mahdjar**
emigrants Djabrān Khalīl Djabrān; al-Maʿlūf; Nuʿayma, Mīkhāʾīl; al-Rayḥānī; [in Suppl.] Abū Māḍī; Abū Shādī
see also Pārsīs

NIGER **Niger**
see also Sūdān (Bilād al-).2
toponyms Bilma; Djādū; Kawār

NIGERIA Hausa; **Nigeria**
see also Djarīda.vi; Fulbe; al-Kānemī; Kanuri; Nikāḥ.II.6; Sūdān (Bilād al-).2; *and* → AFRICA.CENTRAL AFRICA *and* WEST AFRICA
leaders Muḥammad Bello
see also Gwandu
toponyms
provinces Adamawa; Bornū
towns Ibadan; Kano; Katsina; Kūkawa; Sokoto

NOMADISM **Badw**; Horde; Īlāt; Khāwa; Khayma; Marʿā
see also Baḳḳāra; Baranta; Dakhīl; Dawār; Ḥayy; Ḳayn; *and* → BEDOUINS; GYPSIES; TRIBES
nomadic possessions Khayma; Mifrash
see also Khayl

NUBIA ʿAlwa; Barābra; Dongola; al-Marīs; **Nūba**
see also Baḳṭ; Dār al-Ṣulḥ; Ibn Sulaym al-Aswānī; al-Muḳurra; Sōba; *and* → EGYPT.TOPONYMS; SUDAN.TOPONYMS
languages Nūba.3
peoples Nūba.4

NUMBER Abdjad; Ḥisāb al-ʿAḳd; Ḥisāb al-Djummal; Ḥurūf; ʿIlm al-Ḥisāb *and* → MATHEMATICS
numbers Khamsa; Sabʿ
see also al-Ṣifr

NUMISMATICS Dār al-Ḍarb; Sikka
see also ʿAlī Pasha Mubārak; Ismāʿīl Ghālib; Makāyil; Nithār
coinage Aḳče; Bālish; Čao; Čeyrek; Dīnār; Dirham.2; Fals; Ḥasanī; Larin; Mohur; Pāʾī; Pāra; Pawlā; Paysā; Riyāl; Rūpiyya; Ṣadīḳī; Ṣāḥib Ḳirān; Shāhī
see also Dhahab; Fidda; Filori; Hilāl.ii; Sanadjāt; *and* → DYNASTIES
for coinage in the name of rulers, see al-Afḍal (Kutayfāt); ʿAlī Bey; Ghāzi ʾl-Dīn Ḥaydar; Ḳaṭarī b. al-Fudjāʾa; Khurshīd; al-Manṣūr, al-Malik Muḥammad; Muṣṭafā.1; [in Suppl.] Farrukhān.2
for coinage under dynasties, see in particular Artuḳids; Barīd Shāhīs; Kh^{w}ārazm-shāhs; Lōdīs.5; Mughals.10; al-Muwaḥḥidūn; ʿOthmānli̊.IX; Rasūlids.2; Ṣafawids.VI; Saldjūḳids.VIII; Ṣiḳilliya.3; Ṣulayḥids.2
mint localities Abarshahr; al-Abbāsiyya; Andarāb.1; Ānī; Bāghče Sarāy; Islāmābād; Iṣṭakhr; al-Kurdj; Māh al-Baṣra; Mawlāy Idrīs; Māzandarān.7; [in Suppl.] Biyār; Firrīm
reform ʿAbd al-Malik b. Marwān; [in Suppl.] al-Ghiṭrīf b. ʿAṭāʾ
terms ʿAdl.2; Salām (*and* Sālim.1)

O

OBSCENITY **Mudjūn**; **Sukhf**

OCEANS AND SEAS **Baḥr**; al-Madd wa ʾl-Djazr
see also Kharīṭa; *and* → CARTOGRAPHY; NAVIGATION
waters Aral; Baḥr Adriyās; Baḥr Bunṭus; Baḥr Fāris; Baḥr al-Hind; Baḥr al-Khazar; Baḥr al-Ḳulzum; Baḥr Lūṭ; Baḥr Māyuṭis; al-Baḥr al-Muḥīṭ; Baḥr al-Rūm; Baḥr al-Zandj; Marmara Deñizi

OIL **Nafṭ**.3
oilfields ʿAbbādān; Abḳayḳ; Alti̊n Köprü; al-Baḥrayn; al-Dahnāʾ; al-Ghawār; al-Ḥasā; al-Ḳaṭīf; Khārag; Khūzistān; Kirkūk; Kirmānshāh; al-Kuwayt;

Lībiyā; Nadjd.3; Rām-hurmuz; Ra'ʾs (al-)Tannūra; [in Suppl.] Aḥmadī
see also Djannāba; Fārs; al-Khubar

OMAN Bū Saʿīd; Madjlis.4.A.xiii; Maḥkama.4.ix; Nabhān
see also [in Suppl.] al-Ḥārithī
population ʿAwāmir; al-Baṭāḥira; al-Djanaba; al-Durūʿ; Hinā; al-Ḥubūs; al-ʿIfār; (Banū) Kharūṣ; Mahra; Mazrūʿī; Nabhān
and → TRIBES.ARABIAN PENINSULA
toponyms
islands Khūryān-mūryān; Maṣīra
regions al-Bāṭina; Raʾs Musandam; al-Rustāḳ; al-Sharḳiyya
towns al-Buraymī; Ḥāsik; ʿIbrī; Ḳalhāt; Masḳaṭ; Maṭraḥ; al-Mirbāṭ; Nizwa; al-Rustāḳ; Ṣalāla; Ṣuḥār
see also (Djazīrat) al-ʿArab; [in Suppl.] Gwādar

ONOMASTICS Bā; Ibn; Ism; Kisrā; Kunya; Laḳab; Nisba.2
see also al-Asmāʾ al-Ḥusnā; Oghul; Ṣiḳilliya.2
epithets Ata; Baba; Ghufrān; Humāyūn; al-Ṣiddīḳ
in form of address Agha; Ākhūnd; Beg; Begum; Čelebi; Efendi; Khwādja; Khātūn; Khudāwand; Shaykh
see also Akhī; Sharīf.(3)
proper names Aḥmad; Dhu 'l-Faḳār; Humā; Marzpān; Meḥemmed; Mihragan. iv.2; Sonḳor
see also al-Asad; Payghū
titles
African Diglal; Sulṭān.3
Arabic ʿAmīd; Amīr al-Muʾminīn; Amīr al-Muslimīn; Asad al-Dawla; ʿAzīz Miṣr; ʿIzz al-Dawla; ʿIzz al-Dīn; Khādim al-Ḥaramayn; Khidīw; Malik; Mihmindār; Mushīr; Sardār; Sayyid, Shaykh al-Balad; Shaykh al-Islām.1; Sulṭān.1
see also Dawla.2
Central Asian Afshīn; Ikhshīd; Ḳosh-begi; Shār; [in Suppl.] Atalïḳ; Dīwān-begi; İnaḳ
Indo-Muslim Āṣāf-Djāh; Khwādja-i Djahān; Khān Khānān; Nawwāb; Niẓām; Pēshwā; Ṣāḥib Ḳirān; Sardār; Shār
Mongolian Noyan; Ṣāḥib Ḳirān
Persian Agha Khān; Ispahbadh; Ispahsālār; Iʿtimād al-Dawla; Khwādja; Marzpān; Mīr; Mīrzā; Mollā; Pādishāh; Ṣadr; Sālār; Sardār; Sarkār Āḳā; Shāh
South-east Asian Penghulu; Sulṭān.2
Turkish Alp; Beglerbegi; Dāmād; Daryā-begi; Dayi̊; Gülbaba; Khwādjegān-i Dīwān-i Humāyūn; Khāḳān; Khān; Khudāwendigār; Mīr-i Mīrān;

Mushīr; Pasha; Payghū; Ṣadr-i Aʿẓam; Shaykh al-Islām.2; Ṣu Bashi
see also Čorbadji

OPTICS Ḳaws Ḳuzaḥ; **Manāẓir**
see also Mirʾāt; Sarāb
works on Ibn al-Haytham; Kamāl al-Dīn al-Fārisī
see also Ḳuṭb al-Dīn Shīrāzī

OTTOMAN EMPIRE Anadolu.iii.2 and 3; Ertoghrul.1; Istanbul; Lāle Devri; **ʿOthmānli**
see also Bāb-i ʿĀlī; Ḥidjāz Railway; Maṭbakh.2; Pasha Ḳapusu; Shenlik; *and* → DYNASTIES.ANATOLIA AND THE TURKS; EUROPE.EASTERN; LAW.OTTOMAN; MILITARY.OTTOMAN; *and the section Ottoman Period under individual countries*
administration Berātli; Ḍabṭiyya; Dīwān-i Humāyūn; Eyālet; Imtiyāzāt.ii; Khāṣṣ; Khazīne; Mashwara; Millet.3; Mukhtār; Mülāzemet; Mulāzim; Mulkiyya; Nāḥiye; Nishāndji; Reʾīs ül-Küttāb; Sandjaḳ; [in Suppl.] Dāʾira Saniyya
see also Ḳaḍāʾ; Maʾmūr; Odjaḳ; *and* → DOCUMENTS.OTTOMAN; LAW.OTTOMAN; MILITARY.OTTOMAN
archives and registers Başvekalet Arşivi; Daftar-i Khāḳānī; Ḳānūn.iii; Maṣraf Defteri; Mühimme Defterleri; Sāl-nāme; **Sidjill**.3
see also Daftar.III; Ferīdūn Beg; Maḥlūl
financial Arpaliḳ; Ashām; Bayt al-Māl.II; Daftardār; Dār al-Ḍarb; Dirlik; Djayb-i Humāyūn; Duyūn-i ʿUmūmiyye; Irsāliyye; Ḳāʾime; Khazīne; Māliyye; Muḥāsaba.2; Mukhallefāt; Muṣādara.3; Rūznāmedji; Sāliyāne; Siyāḳat
see also Bakhshīsh; Ṣurra
fiscal Ḍarība.3; Djizya.ii; Ḥisba.ii; Kharādj.III; Muḥaṣṣil; Mültezim; ʿOthmānli.II; Resm
see also Mutaṣarrif; Shehir Ketkhüdāsi
agriculture Filāḥa.iv; Māʾ.8; Raʿiyya.2
and → AGRICULTURE
court ceremony Čāʾūsh; Khirḳa-yi Sherīf; Marāsim.4; Mawākib.4; Mehter; Selāmliḳ
diplomacy Bālyōs; Consul; Elči; Hiba.v; Penče
see also Berātli; Imtiyāzāt.ii; Ḳawwās; *and* → DIPLOMACY
education Ghalaṭa-sarāyi; Külliyye; Maʿārif.I.i; Makhredj; Mulkiyya; Ṣaḥn-i Thamān; Ṣofta
see also Ḥarbiye; *and* → EDUCATION; REFORM.EDUCATIONAL
functionaries Āmeddji; Aʿyān; Bazirgan; Bostāndji; Bostāndji-bashi; Čakirdji-bashi; Čāshnagīr-bashi; Ḍābiṭ; Ḍabṭiyya; Daftardār; Dilsiz; Doghandji;

Elči; Emīn; G̲h̲ulām.iv; Ḥekīm-bas̲h̲î; Ič-og̲h̲lanî; ʿIlmiyye; Ḳāʾim-maḳām; Ḳapu Ag̲h̲asî; Ḳawwās; Ketk̲h̲udā.1; K̲h̲aznadār; K̲h̲ʷādjegān-i Dīwān-i Humāyūn; Maʾmūr; Mewḳūfātči; Mīr-Āk̲h̲ūr; Mus̲h̲īr; Mustas̲h̲ār; Mutaṣarrif; Nis̲h̲āndjî; Reʾīs ül-Küttāb; Rūznāmedji; Ṣadr-ı Aʿẓam; S̲h̲āhnāmedji; S̲h̲ehir Emāneti; S̲h̲ehir Ketk̲h̲üdāsî

see also ʿAdjamī og̲h̲lān; ʿAsas; Bālā; Balṭadjî; Bālyōs; Bīrūn; Enderūn; al-Ḥaramayn; K̲h̲āṣī.III; K̲h̲āṣṣ Oda; K̲h̲āṣṣekī; Mābeyn; *and* → LAW.OTTOMAN; MILITARY.OTTOMAN

history ʿOt̲h̲mānlî.I

   and → DYNASTIES.ANATOLIA AND THE TURKS; LITERATURE.HISTORICAL. TURKISH; TURKEY.OTTOMAN PERIOD

industry and trade Ḥarīr.ii; Kārwān; Ḳuṭn.2; Milḥ.3; ʿOt̲h̲mānlî.II; Sūḳ.7

   see also Maʿdin.3

law → LAW.OTTOMAN

literature → LITERATURE

military → MILITARY.OTTOMAN

modernisation of Baladiyya.1; Ḥukūma.i; Ḥurriyya.ii; Iṣlāḥ.iii; Ittiḥād we Teraḳḳī Djemʿiyyeti; Madjlis.4.A.i; Madjlis al-S̲h̲ūrā

   and → TURKEY.OTTOMAN PERIOD

P

PAKISTAN Djināḥ; Dustūr.xiv; Ḥizb.vi; Ḥukūma.v; Madjlis.4.C; al-Marʾa.5; **Pākistān**; [in Suppl.] Djarīda.vii

   see also Ahl-i Ḥadīt̲h̲; Dār al-ʿUlūm.c; Djamʿiyya.v; Djūnāgaŕh; Hind.ii and iv; Kas̲h̲mīr.ii; Ḳawmiyya.vi; K̲h̲aybar; Muhādjir.3; Pas̲h̲tūnistān; Sind.2; *and* → INDIA

architecture → ARCHITECTURE.REGIONS

education Djāmiʿa

physical geography

   mountains Sulaymān

   waters Kurram; Mihrān

population Afrīdī; Dāwūdpōtrās; Mahsūd; Mohmand; Mullagōrī; [in Suppl.] Demography.VII; Gurčānī

   see also Djirga

statesmen Djināḥ; Liyāḳat ʿAlī K̲h̲ān

   see also Mawdūdī

toponyms

   ancient Čīnīōt; Daybul; Ḳandābīl; K̲h̲ayrābād.ii

   present-day

      districts Chitral; Ḥāfiẓābād; Hazāra; K̲h̲ārān; K̲h̲ayrpūr; Kilāt.2;

Kōhāt; Kwát́a; Mastūd̲j̲; Sībī
regions   Balūčistān; Dardistān; Dērad̲j̲āt; Dīr; D̲j̲ahlāwān; Kaččhī; Las
   Bēla; Makrān; Pand̲j̲āb; Sind; Swāt
towns   Amarkot; Bād̲j̲awr; Bahāwalpūr; Bakkār; Bannū; Bhakkar;
   Gūd̲j̲rāṅwāla; Gud̲j̲rāt; Ḥasan Abdāl; Ḥaydarābād; Islāmābād; Karāčī;
   Kilāt.1; Ḳuṣdār; Kwát́a; Lāhawr; Mastūd̲j̲; Pes̲h̲āwar; Rāwalpindi;
   S̲h̲ikārpūr.1; Sībī; Siyālkūt; [in Suppl.] Gilgit; Gwādar

PALESTINE   D̲j̲arīda.i.A; **Filasṭīn**; Ḥizb.i; Mad̲j̲lis.4.A.xxiii; Maḥkama.4.v; Mandates
   see also D̲j̲arrāḥids; Ḳays ʿAylān; al-K̲h̲ālidī; al-Sāmira; S̲h̲āhīn, Āl; [in Suppl.]
   Demography.III; and → CRUSADE(R)S
architecture   Ḳubbat al-Ṣak̲h̲ra; al-Ḳuds; al-Masd̲j̲id al-Aḳṣā
   see also Kawkab al-Hawāʾ
historians of   Mud̲j̲īr al-Dīn al-ʿUlaymī
physical geography
   waters   Baḥr Lūṭ; al-Ḥūla; Nahr Abī Futrus
toponyms
   ancient   Arsūf; ʿAt̲h̲līt̲h̲; ʿAyn D̲j̲ālūt; Bayt D̲j̲ibrīn; al-Dārūm; Irbid.II;
      Sabasṭiyya.1; Subayta
   present-day
      regions   al-G̲h̲awr.1; Mard̲j̲ Banī ʿĀmir; al-Naḳb
      towns   ʿAkkā; ʿAmwās; ʿĀsḳalān; Baysān; Bayt Laḥm; Bīr al-Sabʿ;
         G̲h̲azza; Ḥayfā; Ḥiṭṭīn; al-K̲h̲alīl; al-Ḳuds; Lad̲j̲d̲j̲ūn; Ludd; Nābulus;
         al-Nāṣira; Rafaḥ; al-Ramla; Rīḥā.1; Ṣafad
         see also Ḳayṣariyya; Ṣihyawn
under British mandate   Filasṭīn.2; Muḥammad ʿIzzat Darwaza; [in Suppl.] Amīn
   al-Ḥusaynī
   see also Mandates

PANARABISM   Ḳawmiyya; **Pan-Arabism**; [in Suppl.] al-D̲j̲āmiʿa al-ʿArabiyya
partisans of   al-Kawākibī; Nūrī al-Saʿīd; Ras̲h̲īd Riḍā; [in Suppl.] ʿAbd al-Nāṣir
   see also al-Kāẓimī, ʿAbd al-Muḥsin

PANISLAMISM   Ḳawmiyya; **Pan-Islamism**; **al-Rābiṭa al-Islāmiyya**
   see also Dustūr.xviii; Iṣlāḥ.ii; K̲h̲ilāfa; Muʾtamar
partisans of   ʿAbd al-Ḥamīd II; D̲j̲amāl al-Dīn al-Afg̲h̲ānī; Fiṭrat; Gasprali
   (Gasprinski), Ismāʿīl; Ḥālī; Kūčak K̲h̲ān D̲j̲angalī; Māʾ al-ʿAynayn al-
   Ḳalḳamī; Meḥmed ʿĀkif; Ras̲h̲īd Riḍā; Ṣafar; [in Suppl.] And̲j̲uman-i
   K̲h̲uddām-i Kaʿba; al-Bakrī
   see also D̲j̲adīd

PANTURKISM Ḳawmiyya.iv; **Pan-Turkism**
partisans of Gasprali (Gasprinski), Ismāʿīl; Gökalp, Ziya; Riḍā Nūr; Suʿāwī, ʿAlī

PAPYROLOGY Ḳirṭās; Papyrus
see also Diplomatic.i.15; *and* → DOCUMENTS

PARADISE al-ʿAs͟hara al-Mubas͟hs͟hara; Dār al-Salām; **Dj̲anna**; Ḥūr; Kawt͟har; Riḍwān; Salsabīl
see also al-Aʿrāf

PAYMENTS ʿAṭāʾ; Dj̲āmakiyya; Ḥawāla; Inʿām; Māl al-Bayʿa; Maʿūna; Ṣila.3; Soyurg͟hal; Ṣurra
bribery Marāfiḳ; **Ras͟hwa**

PERFUME Bān; Ḥinnāʾ; Kafur; Misk
see also al-ʿAṭṭār; Maʿdin.4

PERSIA → IRAN

PHARMACOLOGY Adwiya; Aḳrābād͟hīn; **al-Ṣaydana**
see also Diyusḳuridīs; Dj̲ālīnūs; Nabāt; *and* → BOTANY; DRUGS; MEDICINE
pharmacologists Ibn al-Bayṭār; Ibn Samadj̲ūn; Ibn al-Tilmīd͟h; Ibn Wāfid; al-Kōhēn al-ʿAṭṭār; Sābūr b. Sahl; [in Suppl.] al-G͟hāfiḳī; Ibn Biklāris͟h; Ibn al-Rūmiyya
see also al-ʿAs͟hs͟hāb; al-ʿAṭṭār; al-Bīrūnī; al-Suwaydī

PHILATELY **Posta**
and → TRANSPORT.POSTAL SERVICE

PHILOSOPHY Falāsifa; **Falsafa**; Ḥikma; Mā baʿd al-Ṭabīʿa; Manṭiḳ; Naẓar
see also ʿĀlam.1; Allāh.iii.2; al-Maḳūlāt; Muk͟htaṣar; S͟harḥ.IV
logic **Manṭiḳ**
terms Āla.iii; ʿAraḍ; Dalīl; Faṣl; Fiʿl; Ḥadd; Ḥaḳīḳa.2; Ḥudj̲dj̲a; Ḥukm.I; Huwa huwa.A; Muḳaddam; Natīdj̲a; S͟harṭ.2
see also Ḳaṭʿ; al-Sūfisṭāʾiyyūn
philosophers **Falāsifa**
Christian Ibn al-Ṭayyib; Ibn Zurʿa; Mattā b. Yūnus
Greek Aflāṭūn; Anbaduḳlīs; Arisṭūṭālīs; Balīnūs; Baṭlamiyūs; Buruḳlus; Dj̲ālīnūs; Fīt͟hāg͟hūras; Furfūriyūs; al-Iskandar al-Afrūdīsī; al-Sūfisṭāʾiyyūn; Suḳrāṭ
see also Ḥunayn b. Isḥāḳ al-ʿIbādī; Īsāg͟hūdj̲ī; Isḥāḳ b. Ḥunayn; Lawn; al-Maḳūlāt; Mattā b. Yūnus; Nīḳūlāʾūs; al-S͟hayk͟h al-Yūnānī

Islamic

biographers of al-Shahrazūrī, Shams al-Dīn

9th century Abu 'l-Hudhayl al-ʿAllāf; al-Kindī, Abū Yūsuf; al-Sarakhsī, Abu 'l-ʿAbbās

see also Dahriyya; Falāsifa; Lawn

10th century Abū Sulaymān al-Manṭiḳī; al-Fārābī; Ibn Masarrā; al-Mawṣilī; al-Rāzī, Abū Bakr; [in Suppl.] al-ʿĀmirī

11th century Abū Ḥayyān al-Tawḥīdī; Bahmanyār; Ibn Ḥazm; Ibn Sīnā; Miskawayh

12th century Abu 'l-Barakāt; al-Baṭalyawsī; Ibn Bādjdja; Ibn Rushd; Ibn Ṭufayl; al-Suhrawardī, Shihāb al-Dīn Yaḥyā

see also al-Ghazālī; Ḥayy b. Yaḳẓān; Ishrāḳiyyūn; al-Shahrastānī, Abu 'l-Fatḥ

13th century al-Abharī; Ibn Sabʿīn; al-Kātibī;; Ṣadr al-Dīn al-Ḳūnawī; al-Shahrazūrī, Shams al-Dīn

see also Fakhr al-Dīn al-Rāzī

14th century Djamāl al-Dīn Aḳsarayī

16th century al-Maybudī.2

17th century al-Dāmād; al-Fārūḳī, Mullā; Lāhīdjī.2; [in Suppl.] Findiriskī

19th century Sabzawārī; [in Suppl.] Abu 'l-Ḥasan Djilwa

Jewish Ibn Gabirol; Ibn Kammūna; Isḥāḳ b. Sulaymān al-Isrāʾīlī; Judaeo-Arabic.iii; Saʿadyā Ben Yōsēf

see also Abu 'l-Barakāt

terms Abad; ʿAdam; ʿAḳl; ʿAmal.1 and 2; Anniyya; Awwal; Basīṭ wa-Murakkab; Dhāt; Dhawḳ; Ḍidd; Djawhar; Djins; Djism; Djuzʾ; Fard; Ḥadd; Ḥaraka wa-Sukūn.I.1; Hayʾa; Ḥayāt; Hayūlā; Ḥiss; Ḥudūth al-ʿĀlam; Ḥulūl; Huwiyya; Ibdāʿ; Idrāk; Iḥdāth; Ikhtiyār; ʿIlla.ii; ʿInāya; Inṣāf; ʿIshḳ; Ishrāḳ; al-Ḳaḍāʾ wa 'l-Ḳadar.A.3; Kawn wa-Fasād; Ḳidam; Ḳuwwa.4, 6 and 7; Maʿād; Māhiyya; Maḥsūsāt; Malaka; Maʿnā.2; Nafs; Nihāya; Nūr.2; Saʿāda; Sabab.1; Shakhṣ; Shakk.2; Shayʾ; Shubha

see also Athar.3; ʿAyn; Dahriyya; Insān; Ḳaṭʿ; Ḳiyāma; Siyāsa.2; *and* → PHILOSOPHY.LOGIC.TERMS

PHYSIOGNOMY Firāsa; Ḳiyāfa; Shāma; [in Suppl.] Aflīmūn

and → ANATOMY

PILGRIMAGE ʿArafa; al-Djamra; **Ḥadjdj**; Hady; Iḥrām; Kaʿba; Minā; Muṭawwif; al-Muzdalifa; Radjm; al-Ṣafā.1; Saʿy; Shiʿār.1

see also Amīr al-Ḥādjdj; Ḥidjāz Railway; Kārwān; Kāẓimayn; Makka; [in Suppl.] ʿAtabāt; Darb Zubayda; Fayd; *and* → ISLAM

PIRACY **Ḳurṣān**
see also al-ʿAnnāba; ʿArūdj; Ḥasan Baba; Ḥusayn Pasha, Mezzomorto; Kemāl Reʾīs; Khayr al-Dīn Pasha; Lewend

PLAGUE ʿAmwās
see also Ibn Khaldūn, Walī al-Dīn
treatises on Ibn Khātima; Ibn Riḍwān; al-Masīḥī

POLAND **Leh**
see also Islām Girāy; Ḳamāniča; Köprülü; Lipḳa; Muslimūn.1.A.1; *and* → OTTOMAN EMPIRE

POLITICS Baladiyya; Dawla; Djumhūriyya; Dustūr; Ḥimāya.2; Ḥizb; Ḥukūma; Ḥurriyya.ii; Istiḳlāl; Ḳawmiyya; Madjlis; Makhzan; Mandates; Mashyakha; Medeniyyet; Musāwāt; Muwaṭin; Nāʾib.2; Shūrā.3; Siyāsa; [in Suppl.] Āzādī; al-Djāmiʿa al-ʿArabiyya
see also Ahl al-Ḥall wa ʾl-ʿAḳd; Imtiyāzāt; Mashwara; Salṭana; *and* → ADMINISTRATION; DIPLOMACY; OTTOMAN EMPIRE
doctrines Ḥizb.i; Ishtirākiyya; Mārk(i)siyya; Shuyūʿiyya; [in Suppl.] Hidjra
see also Musāwāt; Muslimūn.4; Radjʿiyya; *and* → PANARABISM; PANISLAMISM; PANTURKISM
movements Djadīd; Djangalī; Istiḳlāl; Ittiḥād we Teraḳḳī Djemʿiyyeti; Khāksar; Khilāfa; al-Rābiṭa al-Islāmiyya
see also Fiṭrat; Ḥamza Beg; Ḥizb; Ḥurriyya.ii; Kūčak Khān Djangalī; [in Suppl.] ʿAbd al-Bārī; *and* → PANARABISM; PANISLAMISM; PANTURKISM
parties Demokrat Parti; **Ḥizb**; Ḥürriyet we Iʾtilāf Fîrḳasî; Partai Islam se Malaysia (Pas); Shuyūʿiyya.1.2
see also Andjuman; Djamʿiyya; (Tunalî) Ḥilmī; Ḥizb.i; Ishtirākiyya; Khīyābānī, Shaykh Muḥammad; Leff; Luṭfī al-Sayyid; Mārk(i)siyya; Muṣṭafā Kāmil Pasha; Sarekat Islam; [in Suppl.] ʿAbd al-Nāṣir; *and* → COMMUNISM; REFORM
reform → REFORM
terms Shaʿb.2

PORTUGAL **Burtuḳāl**; Gharb al-Andalus
see also Ḥabesh; *and* → SPAIN
toponyms Bādja; Ḳulumriya; al-Maʿdin; Mīrtula; Shantamariyyat al-Gharb; Shantarīn; Shilb; Shintara

PRAYER Adhān; Dhikr; Djumʿa; **Duʿāʾ**; Fātiḥa; Iḳāma; Khaṭīb; Khuṭba; Ḳibla; Ḳunūt; Ḳuʿūd; Maḥyā; Masdjid; Miḥrāb; Mīḳāt; Muṣallā; Rakʿa; Rātib; **Ṣalāt**; Ṣalāt al-Khawf; Subḥa; Sutra

see also Amīn; Dikka; G̲h̲āʾib; Gulbāng; Istiʾnāf; Maḳām Ibrāhīm; al-Masḥ ʿalā ʾl-K̲h̲uffayn; Namāzgāh; *and* → Ablution; Architecture.mosques; Islam
bowing Sad̲j̲da
carpet Sad̲j̲d̲j̲āda
of petition Istisḳāʾ; Munās̲h̲ada

Pre-Islam al-ʿArab.i; (D̲j̲azīrat) al-ʿArab.vii; Armīniya.II.1; Badw.III; D̲j̲āhiliyya; G̲h̲assān; Kinda.1 and Appendix; Lak̲h̲mids; Liḥyān; Maʿin; Makka.1; Nabaṭ; Rūm
see also Ḥayawān.2; Ilāh; al-Kalbī.II; Lībiyā.2; *and* → Assyria; Byzantine Empire; Military.battles; Zoroastrians
customs/institutions ʿAtīra; Baliyya; G̲h̲id̲h̲āʾ.i and ii; Ḥad̲j̲d̲j̲.i; Ḥilf; Ḥimā; Ḥimāya; Istisḳāʾ; Kāhin; K̲h̲afāra; Mawlā; Nuṣub; Raḍāʿ.2; Sādin
see also Fayʾ; G̲h̲anīma; Īlāf; Karkūr; Nār; Ṣadā; S̲h̲ayba
gods D̲h̲u ʾl-K̲h̲alaṣa; Hubal; Isāf wa-Nāʾila; Ḳaws Ḳuzaḥ; al-Lāt; Manāf; Manāt; Nasr; S̲h̲ams.1; S̲h̲ayʿ al-Ḳawm; Suʿayr; al-Sud̲j̲d̲j̲a; Suwāʿ
see also ʿAmr b. Luḥayy; D̲j̲āhiliyya; Ilāh; Kaʿba.V; al-Ḳamar.II; Mawḳif.3; Rabb; Ṣanam; S̲h̲ayṭān
in Arabian peninsula Abraha; (D̲j̲azīrat) al-ʿArab.i and vi; Bakr b. Wāʾil; D̲j̲ad̲h̲īma al-Abras̲h̲; G̲h̲umdān; Ḥabas̲h̲at; Ḥād̲j̲ib b. Zurāra; Ḥaḍramawt; Hās̲h̲im b. ʿAbd Manāf; Hind bint al-K̲h̲uss; Ḥums; Ḳatabān; Ḳayl; Ḳuṣayy; Ḳuss b. Sāʿida; Mārib; Nuṣub; Sabaʾ; Sad̲j̲ʿ.1; Salḥīn; [in Suppl.] Ḥaḍramawt.i
see also Badw.III; Dār al-Nadwa; Ḥanīf.4; Kinda.Appendix; *and* → Literature.poetry.arabic; Oman.toponyms; Saudia Arabia.toponyms; Tribes.arabian peninsula; Yemen.toponyms
in Egypt → Egypt.before islam
in Fertile Crescent K̲h̲ursābād; Manbid̲j̲; Maysān; Nabaṭ; [in Suppl.] At̲h̲ūr
see also Biṭrīḳ.I; Ḥarrān; S̲h̲ahārid̲j̲a; S̲h̲ahrazūr
G̲h̲assānids D̲j̲abala b. al-Ayham; D̲j̲illiḳ; **G̲h̲assān**; al-Ḥārit̲h̲ b. D̲j̲abala; [in Suppl.] D̲j̲abala b. al-Ḥārit̲h̲
Lak̲h̲mids ʿAmr b. ʿAdī; ʿAmr b. Hind; al-Ḥīra; **Lak̲h̲mids**; al-Mund̲h̲ir IV; al-Nuʿmān (III) b. al-Mund̲h̲ir
in Iran → Iran.before islam

Predestination Ad̲j̲al; Allāh.II.B; Iḍṭirār; Ik̲h̲tiyār; Istiṭāʿa; **al-Ḳaḍāʾ wa ʾl-Ḳadar**; Ḳadariyya; Kasb; Ḳisma
see also ʿAbd al-Razzāḳ al-Ḳās̲h̲ānī; Badāʾ; Dahr; Duʿāʾ.II.b; Ḳaḍāʾ; S̲h̲aḳāwa
advocates of D̲j̲abriyya; D̲j̲ahmiyya; al-Karābīsī.2 ; Sulaymān b. D̲j̲arīr al-Raḳḳī
opponents of G̲h̲aylān b. Muslim; **Ḳadariyya**; Ḳatāda b. Diʿāma; Maʿbad al-D̲j̲uhanī

PRESS **Djarīda**; Maḳāla; **Maṭbaʿa**; **Ṣiḥāfa**

Arabic ʿArabiyya.B.V.a; Baghdād (906b); Būlāḳ; **Djarīda**.i; Ḳiṣṣa.2; Maḳāla.1; al-Manār; **Maṭbaʿa**.1; al-Rāʾid al-Tūnusī; **Ṣiḥāfa**
see also Nahḍa
journalism Abū Naḍḍāra; al-Bārūnī; Djabrān Khalīl Djabrān; Djamāl al-Dīn al-Afghānī; Djamīl; Fāris al-Shidyāḳ; Ibn Bādīs; Isḥāḳ, Adīb; al-Kawākibī; al-Khaḍir; Khalīl Ghānim; Khalīl Muṭrān; Kurd ʿAlī; Luṭfī al-Sayyid; al-Maʿlūf; Mandūr; al-Manūfī.7; al-Māzinī; Muṣṭafā ʿAbd al-Rāziḳ; al-Muwayliḥī; al-Nadīm, ʿAbd Allāh; Nadjīb al-Ḥaddād; Nimr; Rashīd Riḍā; Ṣafar; Saʿīd Abū Bakr; Salāma Mūsā; Salīm al-Naḳḳāsh; Ṣarrūf; Shāʾūl; Shaykhū, Luwis; Shinā; Shumayyil, Shiblī; [in Suppl.] Abū Shādī; al-Bustānī
see also al-Mahdjar

Indian **Maṭbaʿa**.4; [in Suppl.] **Djarīda**.vii
journalism Muḥammad ʿAlī; Ruswā; Shabbīr Ḥasan Khān Djosh; [in Suppl.] Āzād; Ḥasrat Mohānī
see also Nadwat al-ʿUlamāʾ

Persian **Djarīda**.ii; Maḳāla; **Maṭbaʿa**.3
journalism Furūghī.3; Lāhūtī; Malkom Khān; Rashīd Yāsimī; [in Suppl.] Amīrī

Turkish **Djarīda**.iii; Djemʿiyyet-i ʿIlmiyye-i ʿOthmāniyye; Ibrāhīm Müteferriḳa; Maḳāla; **Maṭbaʿa**.2; Meshʿale; Mīzān
see also Ādharī.ii
journalism Aḥmad Iḥsān; Aḥmad Midḥat; Djewdet; Ebüzziya Tevfik; Gasprali (Gasprinski), Ismāʿīl; Ḥasan Fehmī; (Aḥmed) Ḥilmī; Hiṣar; Ḥusayn Djāhid; Ileri, Djelāl Nūrī; İnal; Ḳaṣāb, Teodor; al-Kāẓimī, Meḥmed Sālim; Kemāl; Kemāl, Meḥmed Nāmiḳ; Khālid Ḍiyāʾ; Köprülü (Meḥmed Fuad); Manāṣtirli Meḥmed Rifʿat; Meḥmed ʿĀkif; Mīzāndji Meḥmed Murād; Örik, Nahīd Ṣirrī; Orkhan Seyfī; Ortač, Yūsuf Ḍiyā; Riḍā Nūr; Sāhir, Djelāl; Sāmī; Shināsī; Suʿāwī, ʿAlī; [in Suppl.] Aghaoghlu; Atay; Čaylaḳ Tewfīḳ; Eshref
see also Badrkhānī; Fedjr-i Ātī; Khalīl Ghānim; Saʿīd Efendi

PROFESSIONS al-ʿAṭṭār; Baḳḳāl; Bayṭār; Dallāl; Djānbāz; Djarrāḥ; Ḥammāl; Kannās; Kātib; Ḳayn; Ḳayna; Khayyāṭ; Mukārī; Munādī; Munadjdjim; al-Nassādj; Ṣabbāgh; Ṣāʾigh; Saḳḳāʾ; Sāsān; Shaʿbadha; Shāʿir; Shammāʿ; [in Suppl.] Dabbāgh; Djammāl; Djazzār; Faṣṣād; Ghassāl; Ḥāʾik; Ḥallāḳ
see also Asad Allāh Iṣfahānī; Aywaz.1; Khādim; Shāwiya; Ṣinf; *and* → LAW.OFFICES; MILITARY.OFFICES

craftsmanship **Ṣināʿa**

craftsmen and tradesmen
artisans Ṣabbāgh; Ṣāʾigh; [in Suppl.] Ḥāʾik

labourers Ḥammāl; Kannās; Ḳayn; Khayyāṭ; Shammāʿ; [in Suppl.] Dabbāgh; Djazzār; Ghassāl; Ḥallāḳ
merchants al-ʿAṭṭār; Baḳḳāl; Mukārī; [in Suppl.] Djammāl
performers Djānbāz; Ḳayna; Shāʿir.1.E
see also al-Sīm

PROPERTY **Māl**; Milk; [in Suppl.] ʿAḳār
see also Munāṣafa; Shufʿa; Soyūrghāl; *and* → TAXATION.TAXES

PROPHETHOOD **Nubuwwa**; Rasūl
and → MUḤAMMAD, THE PROPHET
prophets Ādam; Alīsaʿ; Ḥā-Mīm; Hārūn b. ʿImrān; Hūd; Ibrāhīm; Idrīs; Lūṭ; Muḥammad; Mūsā; Nūḥ; Sadjāḥ; Ṣāliḥ; Shaʿyā; Shīth; Shuʿayb
see also Fatra; ʿIṣma; Khālid b. Sinān; al-Kisāʾī, Ṣāḥib Ḳiṣaṣ al-Anbiyāʾ; Ḳiṣaṣ al-Anbiyāʾ; Luḳmān; *and* → MUḤAMMAD, THE PROPHET

PROVERBS **Mathal**; al-Maydānī
see also Iyās b. Muʿāwiya; Nār; *and* → ANIMALS.AND PROVERBS; LITERATURE

Q

QATAR al-Dawḥa; Hādjir; **Ḳaṭar**; Madjlis.4.A.xi; Maḥkama.4.ix

R

RAIDS Baranta; Ghanīma; **Ghazw**
and → BEDOUINS; MILITARY.EXPEDITIONS

RECREATION Cinema; Ḳaragöz; Khayāl al-Ẓill; Masraḥ; Orta Oyunu
games Djerīd; Kharbga; Ḳimār; **Laʿib**; al-Maysir; Mukhāradja; Nard; Shaṭrandj
see also Ishāra; Kurds.iv.C.5; Maydān; *and* → ANIMALS.SPORT
sports Čawgān; Pahlawān

REFORM Djamʿiyya; **Iṣlāḥ**
see also Baladiyya; Ḥukūma; al-Manār; *and* → WOMEN.EMANCIPATION
educational Aḥmad Djewdet Pasha; Aḥmad Khān; al-Azhar.IV; Ḥabīb Allāh Khān; Maʿārif; Münīf Pasha; Nadwat al-ʿUlamāʾ; [in Suppl.] al-ʿAdawī
see also al-Marṣafī

financial Muḥaṣṣil
legal Abu ’l-Suʿūd; Aḥmad Djewdet Pasha; Küčük Saʿīd Pasha; Medjelle; Mīrāth.2; Nikāḥ.II; al-Sanhūrī, ʿAbd al-Razzāḳ
see also Djazāʾ.ii; Ileri, Djelāl Nūrī; Imtiyāzāt.iv; Khayr al-Dīn Pasha; Maḥkama
military Niẓām-i̊ Djedīd
numismatic → NUMISMATICS
politico-religious Atatürk; Djamāl al-Dīn al-Afghānī; Ileri, Djelāl Nūrī; Ibn Bādīs; (al-)Ibrāhīmī; Ismāʿīl Ṣidḳī; Ḳāsim Amīn; Khayr al-Dīn Pasha; Midḥat Pasha; Muḥammad ʿAbduh; Muḥammad Bayram al-Khāmis; Nurculuk; Padri; Rashīd Riḍā; Shaltūt, Maḥmūd; al-Subkiyyūn; [in Suppl.] ʿAbd al-Nāṣir
see also Baladiyya; Bast; Djamʿiyya; Dustūr; Ḥarbiye; Ibrāhīm Müteferriḳa; al-Ikhwān al-Muslimūn; Iṣlāḥ; Mappila.5.ii; Salafiyya; Shaʿb; al-Shawkānī; [in Suppl.] Abu ’l-ʿAzaʾim; *and* → POLITICS
militant al-Bannāʾ; Fidāʾīyyān-i Islām; Ḥamāliyya; Ibn Bādīs; al Ikhwān al-Muslimūn; Mawdūdī; Sayyid Ḳuṭb
see also Ibn al-Muwaḳḳit; Mudjāhid; [in Suppl.] al-Djanbīhī

RELIGION ʿAḳīda; **Dīn**; al-Milal wa’l-Niḥal; Milla; Millet.1
see also Ḥanīf; *and* → CHRISTIANITY; ISLAM; JUDAISM
other than the major three Bābīs; Bahāʾīs; Barāhima; Budd; Dhu ’l-Sharā; Djayn; Gabr; Hindū; Ibāḥatiya; Ṣābiʾ; Ṣābiʾa; al-Sāmira; Sikhs; Sumaniyya
see also Aghāthūdhīmūn; Bakhshī; al-Barāmika.1; Hirmis; Hurmuz; Khʷādja Khiḍr; Kitāb al-Djilwa; Mānī; al-Milal wa’l-Niḥal; Millet; Nānak; al-Shahrastānī, Abu ’l-Fatḥ; *and* → BAHAIS; DRUZES; ZOROASTRIANS
pantheism ʿAmr b. Luḥayy; Djahiliyya; Kaʿba.V
see also Ḥarīriyya; Ḥadjdj.i; Ibn al-ʿArabī; Ibn al-ʿArīf; Kāfiristān; Kamāl Khudjandī; *and* → PRE-ISLAM.GODS
popular → ISLAM.POPULAR BELIEFS

RHETORIC Badīʿ; Balāgha; Bayān; Faṣāḥa; Ḥaḳīḳa.1; Ibtidāʾ; Idjāza; Iḳtibās; Intihāʾ; Istiʿāra; Kināya; al-Maʿānī wa ’l-Bayān; Madjāz; Mubālagha; Muḳābala.3; Muwāraba; Muzāwadja; Muzdawidj; Ramz.1
see also Ishāra
treatises on al-ʿAskarī.ii; Ḥāzim; Ibn al-Muʿtazz; al-Ḳazwīnī (Khaṭīb Dimashḳ); al-Rādūyānī; al-Sakkākī; al-Sidjilmāsī; [in Suppl.] al-Djurdjānī; Ibn Wahb

RHYME **Ḳāfiya**; Luzūm mā lā yalzam
and → LITERATURE.POETRY; METRICS

RITUALS ʿAḳīḳa; ʿAnṣāra; ʿĀshūrāʾ; Khitān; Rawḍa-khʷānī

see also Bakkā'; Ḥammām; 'Ibādāt; al-Maghrib.VI; [in Suppl.] Dam; *and* → CUSTOMS

RIVERS **Nahr**
see also Ma'ṣir; *and* → NAVIGATION
waters al-'Aḍaym; 'Afrīn; Alindjaḳ; al-'Alḳamī; Amū Daryā; al-'Āṣī; Atbara; Atrek; Baḥr al-Ghazāl.1; Baradā; Čaghān-rūd; Congo; Čoruh; Ču; Dar'a; Daw'an; Dehās; Didjla; Diyālā; Djamnā; Djayḥān; al-Furāt; Gangā; Gediz Čayi̊; Göksu; al-Ḥamma; Harī Rūd; Ibruh; Ili; Isly; Itil; Kābul.1; Karkha; Kārūn; Khābūr; Khalkha; al-Khāzir; Ḳi̊zi̊l-irmāḳ; Ḳi̊zi̊l-üzen; Ḳuban; Ḳunduz; Kur; Kurram; Lamas-ṣū; Mānd; Menderes; Merič; Mihrān; al-Mudawwar; Nahr Abī Fuṭrus; Niger; al-Nīl; Ob; Orkhon; Özi; al-Rass; Safīd Rūd; Sakarya; Sandja; Sayḥān; Shaṭṭ al-'Arab; Shebelle; Si̊r Daryā; [in Suppl.] Gūmāl
see also Hind.i.j; 'Īsā, Nahr; *and* → *the section Physical Geography under individual countries*

ROMANIA Ada Ḳal'e; Babadaghi̊; Bender; Boghdān; Budjāḳ; Bükresh; Deli-Orman; Dobrudja; Eflāḳ; Erdel; Ibrail; Isakča; Köstendje; Medjīdiyye; Nagyvárad
see also Muslimūn.1.B.2

RUSSIA → EUROPE.EASTERN EUROPE

S

SACRED PLACES Abū Ḳubays; al-Ḥaram al-Sharīf; Ḥudjra; Ka'ba; Karbalā'; Kāẓimayn; al-Khalīl; al-Ḳuds.II; al-Madīna; Makka; al-Muḳaṭṭam; al-Nadjaf
see also Ḥawṭa; Ḥimā; Ḳāsiyūn; Mawlāy Idrīs; Mudjāwir; Shāh 'Abd al-'Aẓīm al-Ḥasanī; Shayba; *and* → ARCHITECTURE.MONUMENTS; SAINTHOOD

SACRIFICES 'Aḳīḳa; 'Atīra; Baliyya; Dhabīḥa; Fidya; Hady; Ḳurbān; Shi'ār.2 and 3
see also Ibil; 'Īd al-Aḍḥā; Kaffāra; Nadhr; [in Suppl.] Dam

SAINTHOOD Mawlid
see also 'Abābda; Mawlā.I; *and* → CHRISTIANITY; HAGIOGRAPHY; MYSTICISM
saints
African Shaykh Ḥusayn
Arabic Aḥmad b. 'Īsā; Aḥmad al-Badawī; Nafīsa

see also Ḳunā; *and* → MYSTICISM
North African Abū Muḥammad Ṣāliḥ; Abū Yaʿazzā; ʿĀʾisha al-Mannūbiyya; al-Bādisī.1; al-Daḳḳāḳ; al-Djazūlī, Abū ʿAbd Allāh; Ḥmād u-Mūsā; Ibn ʿArūs; al-Ḳabbāb; Ḳaddūr al-ʿAlamī; al-Khaṣāṣī; Muḥriz b. Khalaf; al-Sabtī; al-Shāwī; [in Suppl.] Ḥamādisha
see also al-Maghrib.VI; Sabʿatu Ridjāl; *and* → MYSTICISM
Central Asian Aḥmad Yasawī
Indian Abū ʿAlī Ḳalandar; Ashraf Djahāngīr; Badīʿ al-Dīn; Badr; Bahāʾ al-Dīn Zakariyyā; Čishtī; Farīd al-Dīn Masʿūd "Gandj-i Shakar"; Ghāzī Miyān; Gīsū Darāz; Imām Shāh; Khʷādja Khiḍr; Maghribī; Makhdūm al-Mulk Manīrī; Masʿūd; Niẓām al-Dīn Awliyāʾ; Nūr Ḳuṭb al-ʿĀlam; Ratan; Shāh Muḥammad b. ʿAbd Aḥmad; [in Suppl.] Bābā Nūr al-Dīn Rishī; Gadāʾī Kambō; Gangōhī; Ḥamīd al-Dīn Ḳāḍī Nāgawrī; Ḥamīd al-Dīn Ṣūfī Nāgawrī Siwālī
see also Ḥasan Abdāl; Pāk Pāťan
Persian ʿAlī al-Hamadānī; Bābā-Ṭāhir
Turkish Akhī Ewrān; Emīr Sulṭān; Ḥādjdjī Bayrām Walī; Ḥakīm Ata; Ḳoyun Baba; Merkez; Ṣarı̊ Ṣalṭūḳ Dede
terms Abdal; Ilhām

SAUDI ARABIA (Djazīrat) al-ʿArab; Djarīda.i.A; Djāmiʿa; Dustūr.vii; al-Hidjar; al-Ikhwān; Madjlis.4.A.viii; Maḥkama.4.vii; **al-Suʿūdiyya, al-Mamlaka al-ʿArabiyya**
see also Bā ʿAlawī; Badw; Baladiyya.2; Barakāt; Makka; [in Suppl.] Demography.III; *and* → PRE-ISLAM.IN ARABIAN PENINSULA; TRIBES.ARABIAN PENINSULA
before Islam → PRE-ISLAM.IN ARABIAN PENINSULA
dynasties Hāshimids (2x); Rashīd, Āl; Suʿūd, Āl
and → DYNASTIES.ARABIAN PENINSULA
historians of al-Azraḳī; Daḥlān; al-Fāḳihī; al-Fāsī; Ibn Fahd; Ibn Manda; Ibn al-Mudjāwir; Ibn al-Nadjdjār; al-Samhūdī
see also al-Diyārbakrī
physical geography
deserts al-Aḥḳāf; al-Dahnāʾ; Nafūd; al-Rubʿ al-Khālī
see also Badw.II; Ḥarra
mountains Djabala; Ḥufāsh; Raḍwā; al-Sarāt
see also Adjaʾ and Salmā
plains ʿArafa; al-Dibdiba; al-Ṣammān
wadis al-ʿAtk; al-Bāṭin; Bayḥān; Bayḥān al-Ḳaṣāb; Djayzān; Fāʾw; Ḥamḍ, Wādī al-; al-Rumma; al-Sahbāʾ; Sirḥān
waters Dawʿan

population → TRIBES.ARABIAN PENINSULA

toponyms

ancient Badr; al-Djār; Fadak; al-Ḥidjr; al-Ḥudaybiya; Ḳurḥ; Madyan Shuʿayb; al-Rabadha
see also Fāʾw

present-day

districts al-Aflādj; al-Djawf; al-Ḳaṣīm; al-Khardj

islands Farasān

oases al-Dirʿiyya; Dūmat al-Djandal; al-Ḥasā; al-Khurma

regions ʿAsīr; ʿAwlaḳī; Bayḥān; al-Ḥāḍina; Ḥaly; al-Ḥawṭa; al-Ḥidjāz; Ḳurayyāt al-Milḥ; Nadjd; Nafūd; Raʾs (al-)Tannūra; al-Rubʿ al-Khālī

towns Abhā; Abḳayḳ; Abū ʿArīsh; Burayda; al-Dammām; al-Djawf; Djayzān; al-Djubayl; al-Djubayla; Djudda; Fakhkh; Ghāmid; Ḥāyil; al-Hufūf; Ḥuraymilā; Ḳarya al-Suflā; Ḳarya al-ʿUlyā; al-Ḳaṣāb; al-Ḳaṭīf; Khamīs Mushayṭ; Khaybar; al-Khubar; al-Ḳunfudha; al-Madīna; Makka; Minā; al-Mubarraz; Nadjrān; Rābigh; al-Riyāḍ; [in Suppl.] Fayd
see also (Djazīrat) al-ʿArab; al-ʿĀriḍ; Bīsha; Ḍariyya

SCIENCE **ʿIlm**; Mawṣūʿa
see also Ibn Abī Uṣaybīʿa; Shumayyil, Shiblī; [in Suppl.] al-Bustānī; Ibn al-Akfānī.3; Ibn Farīghūn; *and* → ALCHEMY; ASTROLOGY; ASTRONOMY; BOTANY; MATHEMATICS; MECHANICS; MEDICINE; OPTICS; PHARMACOLOGY; ZOOLOGY

SECTS ʿAdjārida; Ahl-i Ḥadīth; Ahl-i Ḥaḳḳ; Aḥmadiyya; ʿAlids; Azāriḳa; al-Badjalī; Baḳliyya; Bihʾāfrīd b. Farwardīn; Bohorās; Burghūthiyya; Djabriyya; Djahmiyya; al-Djanāḥiyya; al-Djārūdiyya; Durūz; Farāʾiḍiyya; Ghurābiyya; Ḥarīriyya; Ḥashīshiyya; Ḥulmāniyya; Ḥurūfiyya; al-Ibāḍiyya; Ḳarmaṭī; Karrāmiyya; Kaysāniyya; al-Khalafiyya; Khāridjites; Khashabiyya; Khaṭṭābiyya; Khōdja; Khūbmesīḥīs; Khurramiyya; Kuraybiyya; Mahdawīs; Manṣūriyya; al-Mughīriyya; Muḥammadiyya; Mukhammisa; Muṭarrifiyya; al-Muʿtazila; Nadjadāt; Nāwūsiyya; al-Nukkār; Nuḳṭawiyya; Nūrbakhshiyya; Nuṣayriyya; al-Rāwandiyya; Rawshaniyya; Salmāniyya; Ṣārliyya; Satpanthīs; Shabak; Shābāshiyya; Shaykhiyya; Shumayṭiyya; Ṣufriyya; [in Suppl.] Dhikrīs
see also Abu ʾl-Maʿālī; ʿAlī Ilāhī; Bābāʾī; Bābīs; Bāyazīd Anṣārī; Bīsharʿ; Dahriyya; al-Dhammiyya; Dīn-i Ilāhī; Ghassāniyya; Ghulāt; Ḥā-Mīm; Imām Shāh; ʿIrāḳ.vi; Kasrawī Tabrīzī; al-Kayyāl; Kāẓim Rashtī; Ḳi̊zi̊l-bāsh; al-Malaṭī; Mazdak; Mudjtahid.III; Sālimiyya; Sulṭān Sehāk; *and* → MYSTICISM.ORDERS

Alids ʿAbd Allāh b. Muʿāwiya; Abū ʿAbd Allāh Yaʿḳūb; Abu ʾl-Aswad al-Duʾalī; Abū Hāshim; Abū Nuʿaym al-Mulāʾī; Abū Salāma al-Khallāl; Abu ʾl-Sarāyā al-Shaybānī; ʿAlī b. Muḥammad al-Zandjī; **ʿAlids**; al-Djawwānī; Hāniʾ b.

ʿUrwa al-Murādī; al-Ḥasan b. Zayd b. Muḥammad; Ḥasan al-Uṭrūsh; Ḥudjr; al-Ḥusayn b. ʿAlī, Ṣāḥib Fakhkh; Ibrāhīm b. al-Ashtar; Khidāsh; Muḥammad b. ʿAbd Allāh (al-Nafs al-Zakiyya); al-Mukhtār b. Abī ʿUbayd; Muslim b. ʿAḳīl b. Abī Ṭālib; Sulaym b. Ḳays; Sulaymān b. Ṣurad
see also Dhu 'l-Faḳār; al-Djanāḥiyya; al-Djārūdiyya; Ghadīr Khumm; al-Ma'mūn; Sharīf; *and* → SHIITES

Bābism Bāb; **Bābīs**; Kāshānī; Ḳurrat al-ʿAyn; Maẓhar; Muḥammad ʿAlī Bārfurūshī; Muḥammad ʿAlī Zandjānī; Muḥammad Ḥusayn Bushrū'ī; Ṣubḥ-i Azal
see also al-Aḥsā'ī; Mudjtahid.III; Nuḳṭat al-Kāf; al-Sābiḳūn

Druzes → DRUZES

Ibāḍīs ʿAbd al-ʿAzīz b. al-Ḥādjdj Ibrāhīm; Abū Ghānim al-Khurāsānī; Abū Ḥafṣ ʿUmar b. Djamīʿ; Abū Ḥātim al-Malzūzī (*and* al-Malzūzī); Abu 'l-Khaṭṭāb al-Maʿāfirī; Abū Muḥammad b. Baraka; Abu 'l-Mu'thir al-Bahlawī; Abū Zakariyyā' al-Djanāwunī; Abū Zakariyyā' al-Wardjlānī; Aṭfiyāsh; al-Barrādī; al-Bughṭūrī; al-Dardjīnī; Djābir b. Zayd; al-Djayṭālī; al-Djulandā; **al-Ibāḍiyya**; Ibn Baraka; Ibn Djaʿfar; al-Irdjānī; al-Lawātī; Maḥbūb b. al-Raḥīl al-ʿAbdī; al-Mazātī; al-Nafūsī; al-Shammākhī al-Īfranī; [in Suppl.] Abū ʿAmmār; al-Ḥārithī
see also ʿAwāmir; Azd; Ḥalḳa; al-Khalafiyya; (Banū) Kharūṣ; *and* → DYNASTIES.SPAIN AND NORTH AFRICA.RUSTAMIDS; LAW; SECTS.KHARIDJITES

historians of Abu 'l-Mu'thir al-Bahlawī; Abū Zakariyyā' al-Wardjlānī; al-Barrādī; al-Bughṭūrī; al-Dardjīnī; Ibn al-Ṣaghīr; Ibn Salām; al-Lawātī; Maḥbūb b. al-Raḥīl al-ʿAbdī; al-Mazātī; al-Sālimī
see also al-Nafūsī

Jewish → JUDAISM

Kharidjites Abū Bayhas; Abū Fudayk; Abū Yazīd al-Nukkārī; al-Ḍaḥḥāk b. Ḳays al-Shaybānī; Ḥurḳūṣ b. Zuhayr al-Saʿdī; ʿImrān b. Ḥiṭṭān; Ḳaṭarī b. al-Fudjā'a; **Khāridjites**; Ḳurrā'; Ḳuʿūd; Mirdās b. Udayya; Nāfiʿ b. al-Azraḳ; al-Nukkār; Shabīb b. Yazīd
see also ʿAdjārida; Azāriḳa; Ḥarūrā'; al-Ibāḍiyya; Ibn Muldjam; Imāma; Istiʿrāḍ; al-Manṣūr bi 'llāh; Nadjadāt; Ṣufriyya

Shiite → SHIITES

Uṣūlīs Mudjtahid.III

SEDENTARISM Sārt
see also Shaʿb.1; *and* → ARCHITECTURE.URBAN; GEOGRAPHY.URBAN

SENEGAL Djolof; **Senegal**
see also Murīdiyya
toponyms [in Suppl.] Dakar

SEXUALITY ʿAzl; Bāh; Djins; Khitān; Liwāṭ; Siḥāḳ; [in Suppl.] Bighāʾ
see also Djanāba; Khāṣī

SHIITES ʿAbd Allāh b. Sabaʾ; ʿAlids; Ghulāt; Imāma; Ismāʿīliyya; Ithnā ʿAshariyya; Sabʿiyya; **Shīʿa**
see also Abu ʾl-Sarāyā al-Shaybānī; ʿAlī b. Abī Ṭālib; ʿAlī Mardān; Madjlis.3; [in Suppl.] Batriyya; *and* → SHIITES.SECTS

branches Ismāʿīliyya; Ithnā ʿAshariyya; Ḳarmaṭī; Nizāriyya
see also Hind.v.d; Imāma; Sabʿiyya; *and* → SHIITES.SECTS

Carmathians (Djazīrat) al-ʿArab.vii.2; al-Djannābī, Abū Saʿīd; al-Djannābī, Abū Ṭāhir; Ḥamdān Ḳarmaṭ; al-Ḥasan al-Aʿṣam; **Ḳarmaṭī**
see also ʿAbdān; al-Baḥrayn; Baḳliyya; Daʿwa; Shābāshiyya

Ismāʿīliyya ʿAbd Allāh b. Maymūn; Abū ʿAbd Allāh al-Shīʿī; Abu ʾl-Khattāb al-Asadī; Allāh.iii.1; (Djazīrat) al-ʿArab.vii.2; Bāb; Bāṭiniyya; Dāʿī; Daʿwa; Fāṭimids; Ḥaḳāʾiḳ; Hind.v.d; Ibn ʿAttāsh; Ikhwān al-Ṣafāʾ; Imāma; **Ismāʿīliyya**; Lanbasar; Madjlis.2; al-Mahdī ʿUbayd Allāh; Malāʾika.2; Manṣūr al-Yaman; Maymūn-diz; Sabʿiyya; Shahriyār b. al-Ḥasan; [in Suppl.] Dawr
see also Ḥawwāʾ; Ikhlāṣ; Maṣyād; Sabʿ; Salamiyya; Ṣulayḥids; *and* → CALIPHATE.FĀṬIMIDS; SHIITES.IMAMS

authors Abū Ḥātim al-Rāzī; Abū Yaʿḳūb al-Sidjzī; al-Kirmānī; al-Muʾayyad fi ʾl-Dīn; al-Nasafī.1; Nāṣir-i Khusraw; [in Suppl.] Djaʿfar b. Manṣūr al-Yaman
and → MUSTAʿLĪS-ṬAYYIBĪS *and* NIZĀRĪS *under this entry*

Mustaʿlī-Ṭayyibīs Bohorās; al-Ḥāmidī; Luḳmāndjī; al-Makramī; Makramids; Muḥammad b. Ṭāhir al-Ḥārithī; Shaykh Ādam; Sulaymān b. Ḥasan; Sulaymānīs; [in Suppl.] ʿAlī b. Ḥanzala b. Abī Sālim; ʿAlī b. Muḥammad b. Djaʿfar; Amīndjī b. Djalāl b. Ḥasan; Ḥasan b. Nūḥ; Idrīs b. al-Ḥasan
see also Ismāʿīliyya

Nizārīs Agha Khān; Alamūt.ii; Buzurg-ummīd; Fidāʾī; Ḥasan-i Ṣabbāḥ; Ḥashīshiyya; Khōdja; Maḥallātī; Nizār b. al-Mustanṣir; **Nizāriyya**; Nūr al-Dīn Muḥammad II; Pīr Ṣadr al-Dīn; Pīr Shams; Rāshid al-Dīn Sinān; Rukn al-Dīn Khurshāh; Sabz ʿAlī; Shāh Ṭāhir; al-Shahrastānī, Abu ʾl-Fatḥ; Shams-al-Dīn Muḥammad; Shihāb al-Dīn al-Ḥusaynī
see also Sarkār Āḳā; Satpanthīs

Sevener **Sabʿiyya**
see also Sabʿ

Twelver Imāma; **Ithnā ʿAshariyya**; Mudjtahid.II; Mutawālī; al-Rāfiḍa
see also Buwayhids; *and* → SHIITES.IMAMS
authors Ibn Bābawayh(i); al-Māmaḳānī; al-Shahīd al-Thānī

and → SHIITES.THEOLOGIANS

Zaydīs al-Ḥasan b. Ṣāliḥ b. Ḥayy al-Kūfī; Ibn Abi 'l-Ridjāl; al-Mahdī li-Dīn Allāh Aḥmad; Muḥammad b. Zayd; al-Nāṣir li-Dīn Allāh; al-Rassī; Sulaymān b. Djarīr al-Rakkī; [in Suppl.] Abu 'l-Barakāt; Abu 'l-Fatḥ al-Daylamī; Aḥmad b. ʿĪsā; Djaʿfar b. Abī Yaḥyā; al-Ḥākim al-Djushamī

see also Imāma; Muṭarrifiyya; Rassids; *and* → DYNASTIES.ARABIAN PENINSULA

doctrines and institutions Bāṭiniyya; Djafr; Ḳāʾim Āl Muḥammad; Khalḳ.VII; Madjlis.2 and 3; al-Mahdī; Malāʾika.2; Mardjaʿ-i Taḳlīd; Maẓhar; Maẓlūm; Mudjtahid.II; Mutʿa.V; Radjʿa; Safīr.1; [in Suppl.] Āyatullāh

see also Adhān; Ahl al-Bayt; ʿAḳīda; Bāb; Ghayba; Ḥudjdja; Imāma; ʿIlm al-Ridjāl; Imām-bārā; Imāmzāda; Mollā; *and* → THEOLOGY.TERMS.SHIITE

dynasties Buwayhids; Fāṭimids; Ṣafawids

see also Mushaʿshaʿ

imams ʿAlī b. Abī Ṭālib; ʿAlī al-Riḍā; al-ʿAskarī; Djaʿfar al-Ṣādiḳ; (al-)Ḥasan b. ʿAlī b. Abī Ṭālib; (al-)Ḥusayn b. ʿAlī b. Abī Ṭālib; Muḥammad b. ʿAlī al-Riḍā; Muḥammad b. ʿAlī (al-Bāḳir); Muḥammad al-Ḳāʾim; Mūsā al-Kāẓim

see also Bāb; Ghayba; Imāmzāda; Malāʾika.2; Maẓlūm; Riḍā.2; Safīr.1

jurists al-ʿĀmilī; al-Ḥillī.2; al-Māmaḳānī; al-Mufīd; Muḥammad b. Makkī; al-Shahīd al-Thānī; Shīrāzī; [in Suppl.] Anṣārī; Bihbihānī

see also ʿĀḳila; Madjlisī; Madjlisī-yi Awwal; Mardjaʿ-i Taḳlīd; Mudjtahid.II; Mutʿa.V

places of pilgrimage Karbalāʾ; Kāẓimayn; al-Nadjaf; [in Suppl.] ʿAtabāt

see also Shāh ʿAbd al-ʿAẓīm al-Ḥasanī

rituals Rawḍa-khwānī

sects Ahl-i Ḥaḳḳ; ʿAlids; Baḳliyya; Bohorās; Djābir b. Ḥayyān; al-Djanāḥiyya; al-Djārūdiyya; Ghurābiyya; Ḥurūfiyya; Ibaḥa.II; Kaysāniyya; Khashabiyya; Khaṭṭābiyya; Khōdja; Khurramiyya; Kuraybiyya; Manṣūriyya; al-Mughīriyya; Muḥammadiyya; Mukhammisa; Muṭarrifiyya; al-Muʿtazila; Nāwūsiyya; Nūrbakhshiyya; Nuṣayriyya; al-Rāwandiyya; Salmāniyya; Satpanthīs; Shaykhiyya; Shumayṭiyya

see also ʿAbd Allāh b. Sabaʾ; Bāṭiniyya; Bayān b. Samʿān al-Tamīmī; Bektāshiyya; Ghulāt; Hind.v.d; Imām Shāh; Ḳaṭʿ; al-Kayyāl; Kāẓim Rashtī; Ḳîzîl-bāsh; Mushaʿshaʿ; [in Suppl.] Ibn Warsand; *and* → DRUZES; SECTS.ʿALIDS

Kaysāniyya Abū Hāshim; Kaysān; **Kaysāniyya**

see also al-Sayyid al-Ḥimyarī

Khaṭṭābiyya Abu 'l-Khaṭṭāb al-Asadī; Bashshār al-Shaʿīrī; Bazīgh b. Mūsā; **Khaṭṭābiyya**

see also Mukhammisa; al-Ṣāmit

Khurramiyya Bābak; [in Suppl.] Bādhām

Mukhammisa **Mukhammisa**
 see also al-Muḥassin b. ʿAlī
Shaykhism al-Aḥsāʾī; Ra<u>sh</u>tī, Sayyid Kāẓim; **Shaykhiyya**
terms → THEOLOGY.TERMS.SHIITE
theologians al-Dāmād; al-Ḥillī.1; Hi<u>sh</u>ām b. al-Ḥakam; al-Ḥurr al-ʿĀmilī; Ibn
 Bābawayh(i); Ibn <u>Sh</u>ahrā<u>sh</u>ūb; al-Karakī; Kā<u>sh</u>if al-<u>Gh</u>iṭāʾ; <u>Kh</u>^wānsārī,
 Sayyid Mīrzā; al-Kulaynī, Abū Djaʿfar Muḥammad; Lāhīdjī.2; Mīr Lawḥī;
 al-Mufīd; Mullā Ṣadrā <u>Sh</u>īrāzī; al-Nasafī.1; <u>Sh</u>ayṭān al-Ṭāḳ; [in Suppl.]
 A<u>kh</u>bāriyya; Anṣārī; Fayḍ-i Kā<u>sh</u>ānī; Ibn Abī Djumhūr al-Aḥsāʾī; Ibn
 Mī<u>th</u>am
 see also al-ʿAyyā<u>sh</u>ī; Ḥudjdja; Imāma; <u>Kh</u>alḳ.VII; Mollā
20th-century Kā<u>sh</u>ānī; <u>Kh</u>^wānsārī, Sayyid Muḥammad; <u>Kh</u>iyābānī, <u>Sh</u>ay<u>kh</u>
 Muḥammad; <u>Kh</u>urāsānī; Muṭahharī; Nāʾīnī; <u>Sh</u>araf al-Dīn; <u>Sh</u>arīʿatī,
 ʿAlī; <u>Sh</u>arīʿatmadārī; [in Suppl.] Āḳā Nadjafī; Burūdjirdī; Ḥāʾirī
traditionists → LITERATURE.TRADITION-LITERATURE.TRADITIONISTS.SHIITES

SIBERIA **Sibīr**
physical geography
 waters Ob
population Bu<u>kh</u>ārlĭk

SICILY Benavert; Ibn al-Ḥawwās; Ibn al-<u>Kh</u>ayyāṭ; Ibn al-<u>Th</u>umna; Kalbids;
 Ṣiḳilliya
 see also A<u>gh</u>labids.iii; Asad b. al-Furāt; Fāṭimids; Ibn Ḥamdīs; Ibn al-Ḳaṭṭāʿ;
 Ibn Makkī
toponyms Balarm; Benavent; Djirdjent; Ḳaṣryānnih; Siraḳūsa
 see also al-<u>Kh</u>āliṣa

SLAVERY **ʿAbd**; <u>Gh</u>ulām; ʿĪtḳnāme; Ḳayna; <u>Kh</u>āṣī; Mamlūk; Mawlā; al-Ṣaḳāliba
 see also Ḥaba<u>sh</u>.i; Ḥab<u>sh</u>ī; Hausa; ʿIdda.5; Istibrāʾ; <u>Kh</u>ādim; Ḳul; Maṭmūra;
 Sidi; *and* → MUSIC.SONG.SINGERS

SOMALIA **Somali**
 see also Ḥabe<u>sh</u>; Muḥammad b. ʿAbd Allāh Ḥassān; Ogādēn
religious orders Ṣāliḥiyya
 see also Somali.4
toponyms
 regions Guardafui
  see also Ogādēn
 towns Barawa; Berberā; Hargeisa; Maḳdi<u>sh</u>ū; Merka; <u>Sh</u>ungwaya

SOUTH(-EAST) ASIA → ASIA

SOVIET UNION → CAUCASUS; CENTRAL ASIA.FORMER SOVIET UNION; COMMUNISM; EUROPE.EASTERN EUROPE; SIBERIA

SPAIN Aljamía; Almogávares; al-Burt; al-Bushārrāt; Moriscos
see also Ibn al-Ḳiṭṭ; Ifni; al-ʿIḳāb; *and* → ANDALUSIA; DYNASTIES.SPAIN AND NORTH AFRICA
physical geography
mountains al-Shārāt
waters al-Ḥamma; Ibruh; al-Mudawwar; Shaḳūra; [in Suppl.] Araghūn
toponyms
ancient Barbashturu; Bulāy; Ḳasṭīliya.1; Labla; al-Madīna al-Zāhira; Shadūna; Shaḳunda; Shaḳūra; Shantabariyya; [in Suppl.] Āfrāg; Balyūnash
see also Rayya
present-day
islands al-Djazāʾir al-Khālida; Mayūrḳa; Minūrḳa
regions Ālaba wa ʾl-Ḳilāʿ; Djillīḳiyya; Faḥṣ al-Ballūṭ; Firrīsh; Ḳanbāniya; Ḳashtāla; Navarra; [in Suppl.] Araghūn
towns Alsh; Arkush; Arnīṭ; Badjdjāna; Balansiya; Bālish; Banbalūna; Barshalūna; al-Basīt; Basta; Baṭalyaws; Bayyāna; Bayyāsa; Biṭrawsh; al-Bunt; Burghush; Dāniya; Djarunda; Djayyān; al-Djazīra al-Khaḍrāʾ; Djazīrat Shuḳr; Finyāna; Gharnāṭa; Ifrāgha; Ilbīra; Ishbīliya; Istidja; Ḳabra; Ḳādis; Ḳalʿat Ayyūb; Ḳalʿat Rabāḥ; Ḳanṭara.2; Ḳarmūna; Ḳarṭādjanna; al-Ḳulayʿa; Ḳūnka; Ḳūriya; Ḳurṭuba; Laḳant; Lārida; Lawsha; Liyūn; Lūrḳa; al-Maʿdin; Madīnat Sālim; Madīnat al-Zahrāʾ; Madjrīṭ; Mālaḳa; Mārida; al-Mariyya; Mawrūr; al-Munakkab; Mursiya; Runda; Saraḳusṭa; Shaḳūbiya; Shalamanḳa; Shalṭīsh; Shant Mānkash; Shant Yāḳub; Shantamariyyat al-Sharḳ; Sharīsh; Shāṭiba; [in Suppl.] Ashturḳa
see also al-Andalus.iii.3; Balāṭ; Djabal Ṭāriḳ; al-Ḳalʿa; *and* → PORTUGAL

SRI LANKA **Ceylon**; Sarandīb
and → INDIA.POPULATION.TAMILS

SUDAN Dār Fūr; Dustūr.xiii; Ḥizb.i; Madjlis.4.A.xvii; al-Mahdiyya; **Sūdān**
see also Baladiyya.2; Fundj; Ḥabesh; Nūba
Mahdist period ʿAbd Allāh b. Muḥammad al-Taʿāʾishī; Khalīfa.iv; **al-Mahdiyya**
see also Awlād al-Balad; Dār Fūr; Emīn Pasha; Rābiḥ b. Faḍl Allāh
physical geography
waters al-Nīl
population ʿAbābda; ʿAlwa; (Banū) ʿĀmir; Baḳḳāra; Barābra; Djaʿaliyyūn;

Ghuzz.iii; Nūba.4; Rashā'ida; Shāyḳiyya
see also Fallāta
religious orders Mīrghaniyya
toponyms
ancient ʿAydhāb; Sōba
present-day
provinces Baḥr al-Ghazāl.3; Berber.2; Dār Fūr; Fāshōda; Kasala
regions Fāzūghlī; Kordofān
towns Atbara; Berber.3; Dongola; al-Fāshir; Kasala; Ḳerrī; al-Khurṭūm; Omdurman; Sawākin; Shandī; Sinnār

SUPERSTITION ʿAyn; Faʾl; Ghurāb; Ḥinnāʾ; Khamsa; Ṣadā
see also ʿAḳīḳ; Bāriḥ; Laḳab

SYRIA **al-Shām**
and → LEBANON
architecture → ARCHITECTURE.REGIONS
before Islam → PRE-ISLAM.IN FERTILE CRESCENT
dynasties ʿAmmār; Ayyūbids; Būrids; Fāṭimids; Ḥamdānids; Mamlūks
see also [in Suppl.] al-Djazzār Pasha; *and* → DYNASTIES.EGYPT AND THE FERTILE CRESCENT; LEBANON
historians of al-ʿAẓīmī; Ibn Abī Ṭayyiʾ; Ibn al-ʿAdīm; Ibn ʿAsākir; Ibn al-Ḳalānisī; Ibn Kathīr; Ibn Shaddād; Kurd ʿAlī; al-Kutubī
and → DYNASTIES.EGYPT AND THE FERTILE CRESCENT
modern period Djarīda.i.A; Djāmiʿa; Dustūr.ix; Ḥizb.i; Ḥukūma.iii; Madjlis.4.A.v; Madjmaʿ ʿIlmī.i.2.a; Maḥkama.4.ii; Mandates; Maysalūn; Salafiyya.2(b); al-Shām.2, esp. (b) and (c)
see also Baladiyya.2; Kurd ʿAlī; Mardam.2; [in Suppl.] Demography.III
statesmen al-Khūrī; Mardam.1
physical geography al-Shām.1
mountains Ḳāsiyūn; al-Lukkām
waters ʿAfrīn; al-ʿĀṣī; Baradā
toponyms
ancient Afāmiya; ʿArbān; al-Bakhrāʾ; al-Bāra; Barḳaʿīd; Dābiḳ; Diyār Muḍar; Diyār Rabīʿa; al-Djābiya; al-Djazīra; Djilliḳ; Manbidj; Namāra.1; al-Raḥba; Raʾs al-ʿAyn; Rīḥā.2; al-Ruṣāfa.3; Shayzar
present-day
districts al-Bathaniyya; al-Djawlān
regions al-Ghāb; Ḥawrān; Ḳinnasrīn.2; Ladjāʾ; al-Ṣafā.2
see also Ghūṭa
towns Adhriʿāt; Bāniyās; Boṣrā; Buzāʿā; Dayr al-Zōr; Dimashḳ; Djabala; al-Djabbūl; Djisr al-Shughr; Ḥalab; Ḥamāt; Ḥārim; Ḥimṣ;

Ḥuwwārīn; Ḳanawāt; Ḳarḳīsiyā; Khawlān.2; Ḳinnasrīn.1; al-Lādhiḳiyya; Maʿarrat Maṣrīn; Maʿarrat al-Nuʿmān; Maʿlūlā; Maskana; Maṣyād; al-Mizza; Namāra.2 and 3; al-Raḳḳa; Ṣāfītha; Salamiyya; Ṣalkhad
see also al-Marḳab

T

TANZANIA Dar-es-Salaam; Kilwa; Mikindani; Mkwaja; Mtambwe Mkuu

TAXATION Bādj; **Bayt al-Māl**; Ḍarība; Djizya; Ḳānūn.ii and iii; Kharādj; [in Suppl.] Ḍarība.7
see also Ḍabṭ; Djahbadh; Māʾ; Maʾṣir; Raʿiyya
collectors ʿĀmil; Dihḳan; Muḥaṣṣil; Mültezim; Mustakhridj
see also Amīr
taxes ʿArūs Resmi; ʿAwāriḍ; Bād-i Hawā; Badal; Bādj; Djawālī; Djizya; Filori; Furḍa; Ispendje; Ḳūbčūr; Maks; Mālikāne; Muḳāṭaʿa; Pīshkash; Resm
see also Ḥisba.ii; Ḳaṭīʿa
land taxes Bashmaḳlïḳ; Bennāk; Čift-resmi; **Kharādj**; Mīrī; Muḳāsama
see also Daftar; Daftar-i Khāḳānī; Ḳabāla; Ḳānūn.iii.1; Rawk
tithe-lands Ḍayʿa; Īghār; Iḳṭāʿ; Iltizām; Khāliṣa; Khāṣṣ; Ṣafī
see also Baʿl.2.b; Dār al-ʿAhd; Fayʾ; Filāḥa.iv
treatises on al-Makhzūmī

THAILAND Patani

THEOLOGY ʿAḳīda; Allāh; Dīn; Djanna; **ʿIlm al-Kalām**; Imāma; Īmān; Kalām; al-Mahdī
see also ʿĀlam.1; Hilāl.i; *and* → ISLAM
disputation Masāʾil wa-Adjwiba; Munāẓara; Radd; [in Suppl.] ʿIbādat Khāna
see also Mubāhala
treatises on al-Samarḳandī, Shams al-Dīn
schools
Shiite Ismāʿīliyya; Ithnā ʿAshariyya; Ḳarmaṭī; [in Suppl.] Akhbāriyya
see also Muʿtazila
Sunni Ashʿariyya; Ḥanābila; Māturīdiyya; Muʿtazila
see also ʿIlm al-Kalām.II; Ḳadariyya; Karāmat ʿAlī; Murdjiʾa; al-Nadjdjāriyya
terms Adjal; Adjr; ʿAdl; ʿAhd; Ahl al-ahwāʾ; Ahl al-kitāb; Ākhira; ʿAḳīda; ʿAḳl; ʿAḳliyyāt; ʿĀlam.2.; ʿAmal.2; Amr; al-Aṣlaḥ; Baʿth; Bāṭiniyya; Bidʿa; Birr; Daʿwa; Dīn; Djamāʿa; Djazāʾ; Djism; Duʿāʾ; Fard; Fāsiḳ; Fiʿl; Fitna; Fiṭra;

al-Ghayb; Ghayba; Ghufrān; Ḥadd; Ḥaḳḳ; Ḥaraka wa-Sukūn.I.2 and 3; Ḥisāb; Ḥudjdja; Ḥudūth al-ʿĀlam; Ḥulūl; Iʿdjāz; Iḍṭirār; Ikhlāṣ; Ikhtiyār; ʿIlla.ii.III; Imāma; Īmān; Islām; ʿIṣma; Istiṭāʿa; Ittiḥād; al-Ḳaḍāʾ wa ʾl-Ḳadar; Kaffāra; Kāfir; Kalima; Karāma; Kasb; Kashf; Khalḳ; Khaṭīʾa; Khidhlān; Ḳidam; Kumūn; Ḳunūt; Ḳuwwa.3; Luṭf; Maʿād; al-Mahdī; al-Manzila bayn al-Manzilatayn; al-Mughayyabāt al-Khams; al-Munāfiḳūn.2; Murtadd; Muṭlaḳ; Nāfila; Nafs; Nāmūs.1; Nūr Muḥammadī; Riyāʾ; Rizḳ; Rudjūʿ; Ruʾyat Allāh; Sabīl.1; Shubha; Ṣifa.2; [in Suppl.] Ḥāl

see also Abad; Allāh.ii; In Shāʾ Allāh; ʿInāya; Ṣūra; *and* → ESCHATOLOGY; KORAN.TERMS

Shiite Badāʾ; Ghayba; Ibdāʿ; Kashf; Lāhūt and Nāsūt.5; Maẓhar; Maẓlūm; al-Munāfiḳūn.2; Naḳḍ al-Mīthāḳ; Radjʿa; al-Sābiḳūn; Safīr.1; al-Ṣāmit; Sarkār Āḳā

and → SHIITES.DOCTRINES AND INSTITUTIONS

theologians

see also Sharḥ.III

in early Islam Djahm b. Ṣafwān; al-Ḥasan al-Baṣrī; [in Suppl.] al-Aṣamm; al-Ḥasan b. Muḥammad b. al-Ḥanafiyya; Ibn Kullāb

Ashʿarī al-Āmidī; al-Ashʿarī, Abu ʾl-Ḥasan; al-Baghdādī; al-Bāḳillānī; al-Bayhaḳī; al-Djuwaynī; al-Faḍālī; Fakhr al-Dīn al-Rāzī; al-Ghazālī, Abū Ḥāmid; Ibn Fūrak; al-Īdjī; al-Isfarāyīnī; al-Kiyā al-Harrāsī; al-Ḳushayrī; al-Sanūsī, Abū ʿAbd Allāh; al-Simnānī

see also Allāh.ii; ʿIlm al-Kalām.II.C; Imāma; Īmān; [in Suppl.] Ḥāl

Ḥanbalī ʿAbd al-Ḳādir al-Djīlānī; Aḥmad b. Ḥanbal; al-Anṣārī al-Harawī; al-Barbahārī; Ibn ʿAbd al-Wahhāb; Ibn ʿAḳīl; Ibn Baṭṭa al-ʿUkbarī; Ibn al-Djawzī; Ibn Ḳayyim al-Djawziyya; Ibn Ḳudāma al-Maḳdisī; Ibn Taymiyya; al-Khallāl

see also Īmān; *and* → LAW

Māturīdī ʿAbd al-Ḥayy; Bishr b. Ghiyāth; al-Māturīdī

see also Allāh.ii; ʿIlm al-Kalām.II.D; Imāma; Īmān

Muʿtazilī ʿAbbād b. Sulaymān; ʿAbd al-Djabbār b. Aḥmad; Abu ʾl-Hudhayl al-ʿAllāf; Aḥmad b. Abī Duʾād; Aḥmad b. Ḥābiṭ; ʿAmr b. ʿUbayd; al-Balkhī; Bishr b. al-Muʿtamir; Djaʿfar b. Ḥarb; Djaʿfar b. Mubashshir; Djāḥiẓ; al-Djubbāʾī; Hishām b. ʿAmr al-Fuwaṭī; Ibn al-Ikhshīd; Ibn Khallād; al-Iskāfī; al-Khayyāṭ; Muʿammar b. ʿAbbād; al-Murdār; al-Nāshiʾ al-Akbar; al-Naẓẓām; al-Shaḥḥām; [in Suppl.] Abū ʿAbd Allāh al-Baṣrī; Abu ʾl-Ḥusayn al-Baṣrī; Abū Rashīd al-Nīsābūrī; Ḍirār b. ʿAmr; al-Ḥākim al-Djushamī; Ibn Mattawayh

see also Ahl al-Naẓar; Allāh.ii; Ḥafṣ al-Fard; Ibn Abi ʾl-Ḥadīd; Ibn al-Rāwandī; ʿIlm al-Kalām.II.B; Imāma; Khalḳ.V; Lawn; Luṭf; al-Maʾmūn; al-Manzila bayn al-Manzilatayn; [in Suppl.] al-Aṣamm; Ḥāl

Shiite → SHIITES

Wahhābī Ibn ʿAbd al-Wahhāb; Ibn Ghannām
Indo-Muslim ʿAbd al-ʿAzīz al-Dihlawī; ʿAbd al-Ḳādir Dihlawī; Ashraf ʿAlī; Baḥr al-ʿUlūm; al-Dihlawī, Shāh Walī Allāh; al-ʿImrānī; ʿIwaḍ Wadjīh; [in Suppl.] ʿAbd Allāh Sulṭānpūrī; Farangī Maḥall
see also Hind.v.b; al-Maʿbarī; Mappila; Ṣulḥ-i kull
Jewish Ibn Maymūn; Saʿadyā Ben Yōsēf
19th and 20th centuries Muḥammad ʿAbduh; Muḥammad Abū Zayd
see also Sunna.3

TIME Abad; Dahr; Ḳidam
see also Ibn al-Sāʿātī
calendars Djalālī; Hidjra; Nasīʾ; [in Suppl.] Ilāhī Era
see also Nawrūz; Rabīʿ b. Zayd; Sulaymān al-Mahrī
day and night ʿAṣr; ʿAtama; Layl and Nahār; al-Shafaḳ
days of the week Djumʿa; Sabt
months
see also al-Ḳamar
Islamic al-Muḥarram; Rabīʿ; Radjab; Ramaḍān; Ṣafar; Shaʿbān; Shawwāl
Syrian Nīsān
Turkish Odjaḳ
timekeeping Anwāʾ; al-Ḳamar; Mīḳāt; Mizwala; Sāʿa.1
see also Asṭurlāb; Ayyām al-ʿAdjūz; Hilāl.i; Rubʿ

TOGO Kabou; Kubafolo

TRANSPORT **Naḳl**
and → ANIMALS.CAMELS *and* EQUINES; HOSTELRY; NAVIGATION
caravans Azalay; **Kārwān**; Maḥmal; [in Suppl.] Djammāl
see also Anadolu.iii.5; Darb al-Arbaʿīn; Khān
mountain passes Bāb al-Lān; Bībān; Dār-i Āhanīn; Deve Boynu; Khaybar
see also Chitral
postal service **Barīd**; Fuyūdj; Ḥamām; Posta; Raḳḳāṣ
see also Anadolu.iii.5
stamps **Posta**
railways Ḥidjāz Railway; **Sikkat al-Ḥadīd**
see also Anadolu.iii.5; al-Ḳāhira (442a); Khurramshahr
wheeled vehicles ʿAdjala; Araba

TRAVEL **Riḥla**; Safar
and → LITERATURE.TRAVEL-LITERATURE
supplies Mifrash
and → NOMADISM

TREASURY   **Bayt al-Māl**; K̲h̲azīne; Mak̲h̲zān
      and → ADMINISTRATION.FINANCIAL

TREATIES   Bak̲t̲; Küčük Ḳaynardja; Mandates; Mondros; **Muʿāhada**
      see also Dār al-ʿAhd; Ḥilf al-Fuḍūl; Mīt̲h̲āḳ-i Millī
    tributes   Bak̲t̲; Parias
          and → TAXATION

TRIBES   ʿĀʾila; ʿAs̲h̲īra; Ḥayy; **Ḳabīla**; Sayyid
      see also ʿAṣabiyya; Ḥilf; K̲h̲aṭīb; S̲h̲arīf.(1); S̲h̲ayk̲h̲; [in Suppl.] Bisāṭ.iii; *and* →
      NOMADISM
    Afghanistan and India   Abdālī; Afrīdī; Bhaṭṭi; Čahar Aymaḳ; Dāwūdpōtrās; Djāt̲;
          Durrānī; Gakkhaŕ; Gandāpur; G̲h̲alzay; Güdjar; K̲h̲aṭak; Khokars;
          Lambadis; Mahsūd; Mēʾō; Mohmand; Mullagorī; Sammā; Sumerā; [in
          Suppl.] Gurčānī
          see also Afg̲h̲ān.i; Afg̲h̲ānistān.ii
    Africa   ʿAbābda; ʿĀmir; Antemuru; Bedja; Beleyn; Bis̲h̲ārīn; Dankalī;
          Djaʿaliyyūn; Kunta; Makua; Māryā; Mazrūʿī; S̲h̲āyḳiyya
          see also Diglal; Fulbe; al-Manāṣir; Mande
    Arabian peninsula
        ancient   ʿAbd al-Ḳays; al-Abnāʾ.I; ʿĀd; ʿAkk; ʿĀmila; ʿĀmir b. Ṣaʿṣaʿa; al-
              Aws; Azd; Badjīla; Bāhila; Bakr b. Wāʾil; Ḍabba; Djad̲h̲īma b. ʿĀmir;
              Djurhum; Fazāra; G̲h̲anī b. Aʿṣur; G̲h̲assān; G̲h̲aṭafān; G̲h̲ifār; Hamdān;
              Ḥanīfa b. Ludjaym; Ḥanẓala b. Mālik; Ḥārit̲h̲ b. Kaʿb; Hawāzin; Hilāl;
              ʿId̲j̲l; Iram; Iyād; Kalb b. Wabara; al-Ḳayn; K̲h̲afādja; K̲h̲at̲h̲ʿam; al-
              K̲h̲azradj; Kilāb b. Rabīʿa; Kināna; Kinda; K̲h̲uzāʿa; Ḳurays̲h̲; Ḳus̲h̲ayr;
              Laʿaḳat al-Dam; Lak̲h̲m; Liḥyān.2; Maʿadd; Maʿāfir; Māzin; Muḥārib;
              Murād; Murra; Naḍīr; Nawfal; Riyām; Saʿd b. Bakr; Saʿd b. Zayd Manāt
              al-Fizr; Salīḥ; Salūl; S̲h̲aybān; Sulaym
              see also Asad (Banū); Ḥabas̲h̲ (Aḥābīs̲h̲); al-Ḥidjāz; Mak̲h̲zūm;
              Mustaʿriba; Mutaʿarriba; Nizār b. Maʿadd; Numayr; Rabīʿa (and Muḍar);
              S̲h̲ayba; [in Suppl.] Aʿyās̲
        present-day   ʿAbdalī; ʿAḳrabī; ʿAwāmir; ʿAwāzim; Banyar; al-Baṭāhira;
              Buḳūm; al-Dawāsir; al-D̲h̲īʾāb; Djaʿda (ʿĀmir); al-Djanaba; al-Durūʿ;
              G̲h̲āmid; Hādjir; Ḥakam b. Saʿd; Hamdān; al-Ḥarāsīs; Ḥarb; Hās̲h̲id wa-
              Bakīl; Ḥassān, Bā; Ḥaws̲h̲abī; Hinā; al-Ḥubūs; Hud̲h̲ayl; Ḥudjriyya;
              Hutaym; al-Ḥuwayṭāt; al-ʿIfār; Ḳaḥṭān; K̲h̲ālid; (Banū) K̲h̲arūṣ;
              K̲h̲awlān; Ḳudāʿa; Mad̲h̲ḥidj; Mahra; al-Manāṣir; Mazrūʿī; Murra;
              Muṭayr; Muzayna; Nabhān; Ruwala; S̲h̲ammar; S̲h̲ararāt; Subayʿ;
              Ṣubayḥī; Sudayri; Ṣulayb
              see also (Djazīrat) al-ʿArab.vi; Badw; al-Ḥidjāz; S̲h̲āwiya.2
    Central Asia and Mongolia   Čāwdors; Dūg̲h̲lāt; Emreli; Gagauz; Göklän; Ḳarluḳ;

Ḳungrāt; Mangït; Mongols; Özbeg; Pečenegs; Salur; Sulduz
see also Ghuzz; Īlāt; Ḳāyï; Khaladj
Egypt and North Africa ʿAbābda; Ahaggar; al-Butr; Djazūla; Dukkāla; Ifoghas; Khulṭ; Kūmiya; al-Maʿḳil; Mandīl; Riyāḥ
see also Khumayr; *and* → BERBERS
Fertile Crescent
ancient Asad; Bahrāʾ; Djarrāḥids; Djudhām; Muhannā; al-Muntafiḳ.1
present-day ʿAnaza; Asad (Banū); Bādjalān; Bilbās; Ḍafīr; Djāf; Djubūr; Dulaym; Hamawand; al-Ḥuwayṭāt; Kurds.iv.A; Lām; al-Manāṣir; al-Muntafiḳ.2; Ṣakhr; Shammar
see also al-Baṭīḥa; Shāwiya.2
Iran Bāzūkiyyūn; Bilbās; Djāf; Eymir.2 and 3; (Banū) Kaʿb; Ḳarā Gözlū; Kurds.iv.A; Lak; Lām; Shahsewan; Shakāk; Shaḳāḳī; Sindjābī
see also Daylam; Dulafids; Fīrūzānids; Göklän; Īlāt; Shūlistān
Turkey Afshār; Bayat; Bayïndïr; Begdili; Čepni; Döger; Eymir.1; Ḳadjar; Ḳāyï; [in Suppl.] Čawdor
see also Shakāk; Shaḳāḳī

TUNISIA Baladiyya.3; Djāmiʿa; Djamʿiyya.iv; Djarīda.i.B; Dustūr.i; Ḥizb.i; Ḥukūma.iv; Istiḳlāl; al-Khaldūniyya; Maʿārif.2.A; Madjlis.4.A.xix; Salafiyya.1(a); [in Suppl.] Demography.IV
see also Fallāḳ; Ḥimāya.ii; Khalīfa b. ʿAskar; Ṣafar; [in Suppl.] al-Ḥaddād, al-Ṭāhir; Inzāl; *and* → BERBERS; DYNASTIES.SPAIN AND NORTH AFRICA
historians of Ibn Abī Dīnār; Ibn Abi ʾl-Ḍiyāf; Ibn ʿIdhārī; [in Suppl.] ʿAbd al-Wahhāb
see also Ibn al-Raḳīḳ; *and* → DYNASTIES.SPAIN AND NORTH AFRICA
institutions
educational al-Ṣādiḳiyya; [in Suppl.] Institut des hautes études de Tunis
see also [in Suppl.] ʿAbd al-Wahhāb
musical al-Rashīdiyya
press al-Rāʾid al-Tūnusī
language ʿArabiyya.A.iii.3
literature Malḥūn; *and* → LITERATURE
Ottoman period (1574-1881) Aḥmad Bey; al-Ḥusayn (b. ʿAlī); Ḥusaynids; Khayr al-Dīn Pasha; Muḥammad Bayram al-Khāmis; Muḥammad Bey; Muḥammad al-Ṣādiḳ Bey; Muṣṭafā Khaznadār; [in Suppl.] Ibn Ghidhāhum
pre-Ottoman period ʿAbd al-Raḥmān al-Fihrī; Aghlabids; Ḥafṣids; Ḥassān b. al-Nuʿmān al-Ghassānī; (Banū) Khurāsān
and → BERBERS; DYNASTIES.SPAIN AND NORTH AFRICA
toponyms
ancient al-ʿAbbāsiyya; Ḥaydarān; Ḳalʿat Banī Ḥammād; Manzil Bashshū; Raḳḳāda; Ṣabra (al-Manṣūriyya); Subayṭila

present-day
districts Djarīd
islands Djarba; Ḳarḳana
regions Djazīrat Sharīk; Ḳasṭīliya.2; Nafzāwa; Sāḥil.1
towns Bādja; Banzart; Ḥalḳ al-Wādī; Ḳābis; al-Kāf; Ḳafsa; Ḳallala; al-Ḳayrawān; al-Mahdiyya; Monastir; Nafṭa; Safāḳus; Sūsa

TURKEY Anadolu; Armīniya; Istanbul; Ḳarā Deniz
see also Libās.iv; *and* → OTTOMAN EMPIRE
architecture → ARCHITECTURE.REGIONS
dynasties → DYNASTIES.ANATOLIA AND THE TURKS; OTTOMAN EMPIRE
language → LANGUAGES.TURKIC
literature → LITERATURE
modern period (1920-) Baladiyya.1; Demokrat Parti; Djāmiʿa; Djarīda.iii; Djümhūriyyet Khalḳ Fïrḳasï; Dustūr.ii; Ḥizb.ii; Ishtirākiyya; Khalḳevi; Köy Enstitüleri; Kurds.iii.C; Madjlis.4.A.ii; Mīthāḳ-i Millī; Shuyūʿiyya.3; [in Suppl.] Demography.III
see also Djamʿiyya.ii; Iskandarūn; Iṣlāḥ.iii; Ittiḥād we Teraḳḳī Djemʿiyyeti; Karakol Djemʿīyyetī; Ḳawmiyya.iv; Kemāl; Kirkūk; Maʿārif.1.i; Māliyye; Nurculuk; *and* → LITERATURE
religious leaders Nursī
statesmen/women Atatürk; Çakmak; Ḥusayn Djāhid; Ileri, Djelāl Nūrī; Kāẓïm Karabekir; Khālide Edīb; Köprülü (Mehmed Fuad); Meḥmed ʿĀkif; Menderes; Okyar; Orbay, Ḥüseyin Raʾūf; Shems al-Dīn Günaltay; Sheref, ʿAbd al-Raḥmān; [in Suppl.] Adïvar; Aghaoghlu; Atay; Esendal
see also Čerkes Edhem; Gökalp, Ziya; Hïsar; *and* → TURKEY.OTTOMAN PERIOD.YOUNG TURKS
mysticism → MYSTICISM.MYSTICS; SAINTHOOD
Ottoman period (1342-1924) Ḥizb.ii; Istanbul; Ittiḥād-i Muḥammedī Djemʿiyyeti; Ittiḥād we Teraḳḳī Djemʿiyyeti; Maʿārif.1.i; Madjlis.4.A.i; Madjlis al-Shūrā; Maṭbakh.2; **ʿOthmānli**
see also Aywaz.1; Derebey; Djamʿiyya.ii; Khalīfa.i.E; [in Suppl.] Demography.II; Djalālī; *and* → OTTOMAN EMPIRE
Young Turks Djawīd; Djemāl Pasha; Enwer Pasha; (Tunalï) Ḥilmī; Isḥāḳ Sükutī; Kemāl, Meḥmed Nāmïḳ; Mīzāndjï Meḥmed Murād; Niyāzī Bey; Ṣabāḥ al-Dīn; Shükrü Bey
see also Djamʿiyya; Djewdet; Dustūr.ii; Fāḍil Pasha; Ḥukūma.i; Ḥurriyya.ii; Ittiḥād we Teraḳḳī Djemʿiyyeti
physical geography
mountains Aghrï Dagh; Ala Dagh; Aladja Dagh; Beshparmaḳ; Bingöl Dagh; Deve Boynu; Elma Daghï; Erdjiyas Daghï; Gāwur Daghlarï
waters Boghaz-iči; Čanaḳ-ḳalʿe Boghazï; Čoruh.I; Djayḥān; Gediz Čayï;

Göksu; Ḳi̊zi̊l-irmāḳ; Lamas-ṣū; Marmara Deñizi; Menderes; al-Rass; Sakarya; Sayḥān

population [in Suppl.] Demography.II

see also Muhādjir.2

pre-Ottoman period Mengüček

see also Kitābāt.7; *and* → DYNASTIES.ANATOLIA AND THE TURKS; TURKEY. TOPONYMS

toponyms

ancient ʿAmmūriya; Ānī; Arzan; ʿAyn Zarba; Baghrās; Bālis; Beshike; Būḳa; al-Djazīra; Dulūk; Dunaysir; Ḥarrān; Lādhiḳ.1; Shabakhtān; Sīs; Sulṭān Öñü

see also Diyār Bakr; Shimshāṭ

present-day

districts Shamdīnān

islands Bozdja-ada; Imroz

provinces Aghri̊; Čoruh; Diyar Bakr; Hakkārī; Ičil; Kars; Ḳasṭamūnī; Khanzīt; Ḳodja Eli; Mūsh; Newshehir

regions al-ʿAmḳ; Cilicia; Dersim; Diyār Muḍar; Djānīk; Menteshe-eli

towns Ada Pāzāri̊; Adana; Adiyaman; Afyūn Ḳara Ḥiṣār; Aḳ Ḥiṣār.1 and 2; Aḳ Shehr; Akhlāṭ; Ala Shehir; Alanya; Alti̊ntash; Amasya; Anadolu; Anamur; Ankara; Antākiya; Antalya; ʿArabkīr; Ardahān; Artvin; Aya Solūk; Āyās; Aydi̊n; ʿAynṭāb; Aywali̊k; Babaeski; Bālā; Bālā Ḥiṣār; Balāṭ; Bālikesrī; Bālṭa Līmānī; Bandirma; Bāyazīd; Bāybūrd; Baylān; Bergama; Besni; Beyshehir; Bidlīs; Bīgha; Biledjik; Bingöl; Bīredjik; Birge; Bodrum; Bolu; Bolwadin; Bozanti; Burdur; Bursa; Čanki̊ri̊; Čatāldja; Česhme; Čölemerik; Čorlu; Čorum; Deñizli; Diwrīgī; Diyār Bakr; Edirne; Edremit; Eğin; Eğridir; Elbistan; Elmali̊; Enos; Ereğli; Ergani; Ermenak; Erzindjan; Erzurum; Eskishehir; Gebze; Gelibolu; Gemlik; Giresun; Göksun; Gördes; Gümüsh-khāne; al-Hārūniyya; Ḥiṣn Kayfā; Iskandarūn; Isparta; Istanbul; Iznīḳ; Ḳarā Ḥiṣār; Ḳaradja Ḥiṣār; Kars; Ḳasṭamūnī; Ḳayṣariyya; Kemākh; Killiz; Ḳi̊rḳ Kilise; Kirmāstī; Ḳi̊rshehir; Ḳoč Ḥiṣār; Konya; Köprü Ḥiṣāri̊; Ḳoylu Ḥiṣār; Ḳōzān; Ḳūla; Kutāhiya; Lādhiḳ.2 and 3; Lāranda; Lüleburgaz; Maghnisa; Malaṭya; Malāzgird.1; Malkara; Maʿmūrat al-ʿAzīz; Marʿash; Mārdīn; al-Maṣṣīṣa; Mayyāfāriḳīn; Menemen; Mersin; Merzifūn; Mīlās; Mudanya; Mughla; Mūsh; Naṣībīn; Newshehir; Nīgde; Nīksār; Nizīb; Orāmār; ʿOthmāndji̊ḳ; Payās; Rize; al-Ruhā; Ṣabandja; Ṣāmsūn; Ṣart; Sarūdj; Siʿird; Silifke; Simaw; Sīnūb; Sīwās; Siwri Ḥiṣār; Sögüd; Sumaysāṭ; al-Suwaydiyya; [in Suppl.] Ghalaṭa

see also Fener; Ḳarasi̊.2; (al-)Ḳusṭanṭīniyya

U

UMAYYADS → CALIPHATE; DYNASTIES.SPAIN AND NORTH AFRICA

UNITED ARAB EMIRATES al-Ḳawāsim; Madjlis.4.A.xii; Maḥkama.4.ix; [in Suppl.] **al-Imārāt al-ʿArabiyya al-Muttaḥida**
population Mazrūʿī
and → TRIBES.ARABIAN PENINSULA
toponyms Abū Ẓabī; al-Djiwāʾ; Dubayy; al-Fudjayra; Raʾs al-Khayma; al-Shārika; Ṣīr Banī Yās; [in Suppl.] ʿAdjmān
see also (Djazīrat) al-ʿArab; al-Khaṭṭ

(former) USSR → CAUCASUS; CENTRAL ASIA.FORMER SOVIET UNION; COMMUNISM; EUROPE.EASTERN EUROPE; SIBERIA

V

VIRTUES ʿAdl; Ḍayf; Futuwwa; Ḥasab wa-Nasab; Ḥilm; ʿIrḍ; Murūʾa; Ṣabr
see also Sharaf; Sharīf
vices Bukhl

W

WEIGHTS AND MEASUREMENTS Aghač; Arpa; Dhirāʿ; Dirham.1; Farsakh; Ḥabba; Iṣbaʿ; Istār; **Makāyil**; Marḥala; Miḳyās; **Misāḥa**; al-Mīzān; Ṣāʿ; Sanadjāt; [in Suppl.] Gaz
see also al-Ḳarasṭūn

WINE **Khamr**; Sāḳī
see also Karm
bacchic poetry **Khamriyya**
Arabic Abū Nuwās; Abū Miḥdjan; Abu ʾl-Shīṣ; ʿAdī b. Zayd; Ḥāritha b. Badr al-Ghudānī; (al-)Ḥusayn b. al-Ḍaḥḥāk; Ibn al-ʿAfīf al-Tilimsānī; Ibn Sayḥān
see also al-Babbaghāʾ; Ibn al-Fāriḍ; Ibn Harma; al-Nawādjī
Turkish Rewānī; Riyāḍī
boon companions Ibn Ḥamdūn; al-Ḳāshānī; Khālid b. Yazīd al-Kātib al-Tamīmī
see also Abu ʾl-Shīṣ; ʿAlī b. al-Djahm

WOMEN ʿAbd; Ḥarīm; Ḥayḍ; Ḥidjāb.I; ʿIdda; Istibrāʾ; Khafḍ; **al-Marʾa**; Nikāḥ;

Siḥāḳ; [in Suppl.] Bighā᾽
see also ʿArūs Resmi; Bas̲h̲maḳlïḳ; K̲h̲ayr; K̲h̲iḍr-ilyās; Lit̲h̲ām; *and* → Divorce; Life Stages.childbirth *and* childhood; Marriage
and literature al-Mar᾽a.1
see also Ḳiṣṣa; S̲h̲ahrazād
Arabic authors al-Bāʿūni.6; Ḥafṣa bint al-Ḥād̲j̲d̲j̲; ʿInān; al-K̲h̲ansā᾽; Laylā al-Ak̲h̲yaliyya; Mayy Ziyāda; [in Suppl.] Faḍl al-S̲h̲āʿira
see also ʿAbbāsa; ʿĀtika; K̲h̲unātha; Ḳiṣṣa.2; S̲h̲ilb
Persian authors Ḳurrat al-ʿAyn; Mahsatī; Parwīn Iʿtiṣāmī
see also Gulbadan Bēgam; Mak̲h̲fī
Turkish authors Fiṭnat; K̲h̲ālide Edīb; Laylā K̲h̲ānïm (2x); Mihrī K̲h̲ātūn
see also Ḳiṣṣa.3(b)
concubinage ʿAbd.3.f; K̲h̲aṣṣekī
emancipation Ḳāsim Amīn; Malak Ḥifnī Nāṣif; Saʿīd Abū Bakr; Salāma Mūsā; [in Suppl.] al-Ḥaddād, al-Ṭāhir
see also Ḥid̲j̲āb; Ileri, D̲j̲elāl Nūrī; al-Mar᾽a; [in Suppl.] As̲h̲raf al-Dīn Gīlānī
influential women
Arabic ʿĀ᾽is̲h̲a bint Ṭalḥa; Asmā᾽; Barīra; Būrān; Hind bint ʿUtba; al-K̲h̲ayzurān bint ʿAṭā᾽ al-D̲j̲uras̲h̲iyya; K̲h̲unāt̲h̲a; Shad̲j̲ar al-Durr; Sitt al-Mulk; Ṣubḥ; Sukayna bt. al-Ḥusayn; [in Suppl.] Asmā᾽
see also al-Maʿāfirī; *and* → Muhammad, the Prophet.wives of
Indo-Muslim Nūr D̲j̲ahān; Samrū
Mongolian Bag̲h̲dād K̲h̲ātūn; K̲h̲ān-zāda Bēgum
Ottoman ʿĀdila K̲h̲ātūn; K̲h̲urrem; Kösem Wālide; Mihr-i Māh Sulṭān; Nīlūfer K̲h̲ātūn; Nūr Bānū; Ṣafiyye Wālide Sulṭān; S̲h̲āh Sulṭān; S̲h̲ebṣefa Ḳadïn
legendary women al-Basūs; Bilḳīs; Hind bint al-K̲h̲uss
see also Āsiya
musicians/singers ʿAzza al-Maylā᾽; D̲j̲amīla; Ḥabāba; Rā᾽iḳa; Sallāma al-Zarḳā᾽; S̲h̲āriya; Siti Binti Saad; [in Suppl.] Bad̲h̲l al-Kubrā; al-D̲j̲arādatān[i]; Faḍl al-S̲h̲āʿira; Ḥabba K̲h̲ātūn
see also ʿĀlima; Ḳayna
mystics ʿĀ᾽is̲h̲a al-Mannūbiyya; D̲j̲ahānārā Bēgam; Nafīsa; Rābiʿa al-ʿAdawiyya al-Ḳaysiyya

Writing **K̲h̲aṭṭ**
see also Ibn Muḳla; Kitābāt; *and* → Art.calligraphy; Epigraphy
manuscripts and books Daftar; Ḥāshiya; **Kitāb**; Muḳābala.2; **Nusk̲h̲a**; [in Suppl.] Abbreviations
see also Ḳaṭʿ; Maktaba
bookbinding Īlk̲h̲āns; Kitāb; Nusk̲h̲a; ʿOt̲h̲mānlï.VII.c
materials D̲j̲ild; Kāg̲h̲ad; Ḳalam; K̲h̲ātam; Ḳirṭās; Midād; Papyrus; Raḳḳ; [in

Suppl.] Dawāt
see also ʿAfṣ; Afsantīn; Diplomatic; Īlkhāns; Maʿdin.4
scripts Khaṭṭ; Siyāḳat
see also Nuskha; Swahili; *and* → ART.CALLIGRAPHY; EPIGRAPHY

Y

YEMEN Djarīda.i.A; Dustūr.viii; Madjlis.4.A.xiv and xv; Maḥkama.4.viii
see also ʿAsīr; Ismāʿīliyya; Mahrī; Makramids; [in Suppl.] Abū Mismār
architecture → ARCHITECTURE.REGIONS
before Islam al-Abnāʾ.II; Abraha; Dhū Nuwās; (Djazīrat) al-ʿArab; Ḥabashat; Ḥaḍramawt; Ḳatabān; Ḳayl; Mārib; al-Mathāmina; Sabaʾ; al-Sawdāʾ; [in Suppl.] Ḥaḍramawt
see also [in Suppl.] Bādhām
dynasties Hamdānids; Mahdids; Rasūlids; Ṣulayḥids
see also Rassids; *and* → DYNASTIES.ARABIAN PENINSULA
historians of al-Djanadī; al-Khazradjī; al-Mawzaʿī; al-Nahrawālī; al-Rāzī, Aḥmad b. ʿAbd Allāh; al-Sharīf Abū Muḥammad Idrīs; al-Shillī
see also Ibn al-Mudjāwir
Ottoman period (1517-1635) Maḥmūd Pasha; al-Muṭahhar; Özdemir Pasha; Riḍwān Pasha
see also Baladiyya.2; Khādim Süleymān Pasha
physical geography
mountains Ḥaḍūr; Ḥarāz; Ḥiṣn al-Ghurāb; al-Sarāt; Shahāra; Shibām.4
wadis Barhūt; al-Khārid; al-Saḥūl
population ʿAbdalī; ʿAḳrabī; Banyar; Hamdān; Ḥāshid wa-Bakīl; Ḥawshabī; Ḥudjriyya; Ḳaḥṭān; Khawlān; Madhḥidj; Mahra
and → TRIBES.ARABIAN PENINSULA
toponyms
ancient al-ʿĀra; Shabwa; Ṣirwāḥ
see also Nadjrān
present-day
districts Abyan; ʿAlawī; ʿĀmiri; ʿAwdhalī; Dathīna; Faḍlī; Ḥarāz; Ḥarīb; al-Ḥayma; Ḥudjriyya
islands Ḳamarān; Mayyūn; Suḳuṭra
regions ʿAwlaḳī; Ḥaḍramawt; Laḥdj; al-Shiḥr; [in Suppl.] Ḥaḍramawt.ii
towns ʿAdan; ʿAthr; Bayt al-Faḳīh; Dhamār; Ghalāfiḳa; Ḥabbān; Hadjarayn; Ḥāmī; Ḥawra; al-Ḥawṭa; al-Ḥudayda; Ibb; ʿIrḳa; Ḳaʿṭaba; Kawkabān; Ḳishn; Laḥdj; al-Luḥayya; Mārib; al-Mukallā; al-Mukhā; Rayda; Ṣaʿda; al-Saḥūl; Ṣanʿāʾ; Sayʾūn; Shahāra; al-Shaykh Saʿīd;

Shibām; al-Shiḥr; [in Suppl.] ʿĪnāt
see also (Djazīrat) al-ʿArab

(former) YUGOSLAVIA Džabić; Khosrew Beg; Muslimūn.1.B.6; Pomaks; Riḍwān Begović; [in Suppl.] Handžić
see also ʿÖmer Efendi
toponyms
republics Bosna; Ḳaradagh; Ḳoṣowa; Māḳadūnyā; Ṣirb
see also [in Suppl.] Dalmatia
towns Aḳ Ḥiṣār.3; Aladja Ḥiṣār; Banjaluka; Belgrade; Eszék; Ishtib; Ḳarlofča; Livno; Manāṣtir; Mostar; Nish; Okhrī; Pasarofča; Pirlepe; Prishtina; Prizren; Raghūsa; Sarajevo; Sisḳa

Z

ZAIRE Katanga; Kisangani

ZANZIBAR Barghash; Bū Saʿīd; Kizimkazi

ZOOLOGY **Ḥayawān**.7
and → ANIMALS
writers on al-Damīrī; al-Marwazī, Sharaf al-Zamān
see also al-Djāḥiẓ

ZOROASTRIANS Gabr; Iran.vi; **Madjūs**; Mōbadh
see also Bihʾāfrīd b. Farwardīn; Ghazal.ii; Gudjarāt.a; Pārsīs; Pūr-i Dāwūd; Sarwistān; Shīz; al-Ṣughd; Sunbādh
dynasties Maṣmughān
gods Bahrām

PRÉFACE À LA QUATRIÈME ÉDITION

Cette édition de l'Index des Matières inclut les références jusqu'au dernier volume publié de l'*Encyclopédie de l'Islam* (vol. IX), paru en février 1998.

Une Liste d'Entrées précéde l'index des matières proprement dit. La Liste des Entrées renvoie le lecteur aux articles particuliers de l'*Encyclopédie de l'Islam*. Pour se faire une idée générale de ce que l'*Encyclopédie* propose sur un sujet plus développé, le lecteur doit consulter l'Index des Matières proprement dit. Ainsi, pour trouver l'article sur le jeu d'échecs dans l'*Encyclopédie*, on consultera la Liste des Entrées, laquelle renvoie le lecteur à Shaṭrandj, tandis qu'une référence à cet article dans son contexte plus grand est à trouver dans l'Index des Matières sous RÉCRÉATION.JEUX.

Des observations et suggestions pour l'amélioration de cet Index sont toujours bienvenues.

Mai 1998 — Peri Bearman

LISTE DES ENTRÉES

Les références concernent soit l'article de base de l'*Encyclopédie*, soit l'Index des Matières proprement dit, lequel rassemble tous les articles concernés par le sujet sous un seul intitulé. Une flèche renvoie le lecteur à l'entrée existant dans l'Index des Matières, qui suit la Liste des Entrées à la p.169. Les noms de pays, de dynasties et de califats, figurant *in extenso* dans l'Index des Matières, ne sont pas donnés dans la liste qui suit.

A

Abatteur [au Suppl.] D̲j̲azzār
Abeille Naḥl
Ablution → ABLUTION
Abrégement Muk̲h̲taṣar
Abréviations [au Suppl.] Abréviations
Abricot Mishmis̲h̲
Abstinence Istibrā'
Académie Mad̲j̲ma' 'Ilmī
Accident 'Araḍ
Accouchement → PHASES DE LA VIE
Acquisition Kasb
Acrobate D̲j̲ānbāz
Action 'Amal; Fi'l
Activisme → RÉFORME.POLITICO-RELIGIEUSE.MILITANTE
Addax Mahāt
Administration → ADMINISTRATION
Administration (d'un Etat) Siyāsa
Adoption → ADOPTION
Adultère → ADULTÈRE
Agriculture → AGRICULTURE
Agrumes Nārand̲j̲
Aiguière [au Suppl.] Ibrīḳ
Album Muraḳḳa'
Alchimie → ALCHIMIE
Alfa Ḥalfā'
Algèbre → MATHÉMATIQUES
Aliments → CUISINE
Allaitement → PHASES DE LA VIE
Aloès Ṣabr
Alphabet → ALPHABET
Ambre gris 'Anbar
Ambre jaune Kahrubā
Âme Nafs
Amende D̲j̲urm
Amérique → NOUVEAU MONDE
Ameublement → MOBILIER
Amiral Ḳapudan Pas̲h̲a
Amour → AMOUR
Amusement → RÉCRÉATION
Analogie Ḳiyās
Anatomie → ANATOMIE
Anche (instrument à) G̲h̲ayṭa
Âne Ḥimār
Anecdote Nādira
Anémone S̲h̲aḳīḳat al-Nu'mān
Aneth S̲h̲ibit̲h̲t̲h̲
Angélologie → ANGÉLOLOGIE
Animal → ANIMAUX
Anthologie Muk̲h̲tārāt
Anthropomorphisme → ANTHROPOMORPHISME
Antilope → ANIMAUX
Antinomianisme Ibāḥa.II
Apostasie → APOSTASIE

Appel Duʿāʾ; Istiʾnāf
Appel à la prière Adhān
Aqueduc → ARCHITECTURE. MONUMENTS
Arabe → LANGUES.AFRO-ASIATIQUES; LINGUISTIQUE
Arachnides → ANIMAUX
Araignée ʿAnkabūt
Araire Miḥrāth
Arbitre Ḥakam
Arbres → FLORE
Arc Ḳaws
Arc-en-ciel Ḳaws Ḳuzaḥ
Archéologie → ARCHÉOLOGIE
Architecture → ARCHITECTURE
Archives → ADMINISTRATION
Argent Fiḍḍa; *et* → NUMISMATIQUE
Arithmétique → MATHÉMATIQUES
Armée → MILITAIRES
Armes → MILITAIRES
Armoise Afsantīn
Arsenal Dār al-Ṣināʿa
Art → ART
Artemisia Shīḥ
Article Maḳāla
Artisanat → ART
Artisans → PROFESSIONS
Artistes → PROFESSIONS
Ascensions al-Maṭāliʿ
Ascétisme → ASCÉTISME
Asphalte Mūmiyāʾ
Association Andjuman; Djamʿiyya
Association (en droit) Sharika
Associationnisme Shirk
Astrolabe Asṭurlāb
Astrologie → ASTROLOGIE
Astronomie → ASTRONOMIE
Atomism Djuzʾ
l'Au-delà → ESCHATOLOGIE
Aumônes → AUMÔNES
Autruche Naʿām
Avant l'Islam → PÉRIODE PRÉISLAMIQUE
Avant-propos Muḳaddima
Avarice Bukhl

B

Bābisme → SECTES
Bachisme → VIN.POÉSIE BACHIQUE
Baguette ʿAṣā; Ḳaḍīb
Bahāʾīs → BAHĀʾĪS
Bain → ARCHITECTURE.MONUMENTS
Balance al-Mīzān
Balayeur Kannās
Banque → BANQUE
Barbier [au Suppl.] Ḥallāḳ
Barrage → ARCHITECTURE.MONUMENTS
Basques → BASQUES
Bateau Safīna
Baudrier Shadd
Beauté ʿIlm al-Djamāl
Bécassine-des-marais Shunḳub
Bédouin → BÉDOUINS
Belette Ibn ʿIrs
Bélomancie Istiḳsām
Bénédiction Baraka
Benjoin, noisetier à Bān
Berbères → BERBÈRES
Bestiaux Baḳar
Beurre al-Samn
Bible → BIBLE
Bibliographie → BIBLIOGRAPHIE
Bibliothèque → EDUCATION
Bien-être Maṣlaḥa

Bijoux → BIJOUX
Biographie → LITTÉRATURE.BIOGRAPHIQUE
Bitume Mūmiyā'
Bivalve Ṣadaf
Blanchisseur [au Suppl.] Ghassāl
Blé Ḳamḥ
Bois Khashab
Bois de santal Ṣandal
Boissons → CUISINE
Botanique → BOTANIQUE
Boucher [au Suppl.] Djazzār
Bouddhisme Budd; Sumaniyya
Bouquetin Ayyil
Boussole Maghnāṭīs.II
Brigand Ṣuʿlūk
Brique Labin
Brosse à dents Miswāk
Buffle [au Suppl.] Djāmūs
Bure Khirḳa
Butin → MILITAIRES
Byzantins → BYZANTINS

C

Cadavre Djanāza
Cadeau → CADEAUX
Cadran Rubʿ
Cadran solaire Mizwala
Café Ḳahwa
Caille Salwā
Calame Ḳalam
Calendrier → TEMPS
Califat → CALIFAT
Calife Khalīfa
Calligraphie → ART
Calomnie Ḳadhf
Caméléon Ḥirbā'
Camomille [au Suppl.] Bābūnadj
Camphre Kāfūr
Canal Ḳanāt
Canne à sucre Ḳaṣab al-Sukkar
Cannelle [au Suppl.] Dār Ṣīnī
Capitulations Imtiyāzāt
Caprins [au Suppl.] Ghanam
Caravane → TRANSPORT
Carte Kharīṭa
Cartographie → CARTOGRAPHIE
Cause ʿIlla
Cautionnement Kafāla
Cavalier Faris
Céramique → ART.POTERIE
Cérémonies de la cour → CÉRÉMONIES DE LA COUR
Cession Ḥawāla
Chacal Ibn Āwā
Chaire Minbar
Chaise Kursī
Chalumeau Mizmār
Chambellan Ḥādjib
Chambre souterraine Sardāb
Chameau → ANIMAUX
Chamelier [au Suppl.] Djammāl
Chamito-sémitique Ḥām
Chancellerie → DOCUMENTS
Chandelier Shammāʿ
Chandelle Shamʿa
Chant → MUSIQUE
Chanteur → MUSIQUE
Chanvre Ḥashīsh
Chapelet Subḥa
Chapiteau ʿAmūd
Chardon Shukāʿā
Chariot ʿAdjala; Araba
Charité → ALMS
Charmes → CHARMES
Charmeur de serpents Ḥāwī
Charrette ʿAdjala; Araba
Charrue Miḥrāth

Chasse → CHASSE
Châtiment → CHÂTIMENT (DIVIN);
    DROIT.DROIT PÉNAL
Chef d'un tribu Sayyid
Chemins de fer → TRANSPORT
Chêne ʿAfṣ
Chènevis S̲h̲ahdānad̲j̲
Cheval Faras
Chevaux → ANIMAUX.ÉQUINES
Cheveux → ANATOMIE
Chien Kalb
Chiffre → NUMÉRO
Chiisme → CHIITES
Chirognomie al-Kaff
Chirurgien D̲j̲arrāḥ
Chrétiens → CHRISTIANISME
Christianisme → CHRISTIANISME
Ciel Samāʾ
Cimetière Maḳbara
Cinéma Cinématographe
Cinq K̲h̲amsa
Circoncision → CIRCONCISION
Circoncision des filles K̲h̲afḍ
Citadelle → ARCHITECTURE.
    MONUMENTS.FORTERESSES
Citerne Ḥawḍ
Citoyen Muwāṭin
Citron Nārand̲j̲
Civière D̲j̲anāza
Civilisation Medeniyyet
Clan Āl
Climat Iḳlīm
Clou de girofle Ḳaranful
Codes → CRYPTOGRAPHIE
Coeur Ḳalb
Coiffeur [au Suppl.] Ḥallāk̲
Coiffure → VÊTEMENTS
Coït Bāh
Coitus interruptus ʿAzl
Collyre Kuḥl
Colombe Ḥamām
Colonne ʿAmūd

Commensal Nadīm
Commentaire (coranique) S̲h̲arḥ; et
    → CORAN
Commerce → COMMERCE
Commissionnaire Dallāl
Communications → COMMUNICA-
    TIONS
Communisme → COMMUNISME
Compagnons (du Prophète) →
    MUḤAMMAD, LE PROPHÈTE
Comptabilité → COMPTABILITÉ
Concubinage → FEMMES
Conférence Muʾtamar
Confrérie → MYSTICISME
Congrès Muʾtamar
Conjonction Ḳirān
Connaissance ʿIlm; Maʿrifa
Constellation → ASTRONOMIE
Constitution Dustūr
Construction Bināʾ
Consul Consul
Consultation S̲h̲ūrā
Conte Ḥikāya
Conteur Ḳāṣṣ; Maddāḥ
Contrainte [au Suppl.] Ikrāh
Contraires Aḍdād; Ḍidd
Contrat → DROIT.DROIT CONTRAC-
    TUEL
Coptes → CHRISTIANISME.CON-
    FESSIONS
Coq Dīk
Cor Būḳ
Corail Mard̲j̲ān
Coran → CORAN
Corbeau G̲h̲urāb
Cornaline ʿAḳīḳ
Corporation → CORPORATIONS
Corps D̲j̲ism
Corruption → PAIEMENTS
Cosmétique → COSMÉTIQUE
Cosmographie → COSMOGRAPHIE
Costume → VÊTEMENTS

Coton Ḳuṭn
Cotonnade (indienne) Ḳalamkārī
Coudée Dhirāʿ
Couleur → COULEUR
Cours d'eau → GÉOGRAPHIE.GÉOGRAPHIE PHYSIQUE.EAUX
Courtier Dallāl
Courtisan Nadīm
Couscous Kuskusū
Coutume → COUTUME
Couturier Khayyāṭ
Couvent → CHRISTIANISME
Couverture → ART.TAPISSERIE
Créancier Ghārim
Création → CRÉATION
Crépuscule al-Shafaḳ
Cristal Billawr
Critique, littéraire → LITTÉRATURE
Croisades → CROISADES
Croissant Hilāl
Croix al-Ṣalīb
Croyance ʿAḳīda
Crucifixion Ṣalb
Crustacés → ANIMAUX
Cryptographie → CRYPTOGRAPHIE
Cuir Djild
Cuisine → CUISINE
Cuivre Nuḥās; *et voir* Malachite
Culture (agriculture) → AGRICULTURE
Cumin Kammūn
Cure-dents Miswāk
Cymbale Ṣandj

D

Dactylonomie Ḥisāb al-ʿAḳd
Daim Ayyil
Danse Raḳṣ
Datte Nakhl
Débat → THÉOLOGIE
Débit d'eau → ARCHITECTURE.MONUMENTS
Débiteur Ghārim
Déclinaison (grammaire) Iʿrāb
Déclinaison (astronomie) al-Mayl
Décoration → ARCHITECTURE; ART.DÉCORATIF; MILITAIRES
Décret divin al-Ḳadāʾ wa-l-Ḳadar
Demeure Bayt; Dār
Démographie [au Suppl.] Démographie
Démon Djinn
Dents → MÉDECINE.DENTAIRE
Derviche → MYSTICISME
Désert → DÉSERTS
Dessin → ART
Destin → PRÉDESTINATION
Détroits → GÉOGRAPHIE. GÉOGRAPHIE PHYSIQUE.EAUX
Dette [au Suppl.] Dayn
Diable Iblīs; Shayṭān
Dialecte → LANGUES.AFRO-ASIATIQUES.ARABE; LINGUISTIQUE.PHONÉTIQUE
Diamant Almās
Dictionnaire → DICTIONNAIRE
Dieu Allāh; Ilāh
Dieux préislamiques → PÉRIODE PRÉISLAMIQUE
Dîme → TAXATION
Diplomatie → DIPLOMATIE
Dissolution Faskh
Divination → DIVINATION
Divorce → DIVORCE
Documents → ADMINISTRATION; DOCUMENTS
Domaine Ḍayʿa

Dot → MARIAGE
Doute Shakk
Drame → LITTÉRATURE
Drapeau ʿAlam; Sandjaḳ
Drogues → DROGUES
Droguiste al-ʿAṭṭār
Droit → DROIT
Droit coutumier → DROIT
Dromadaire → ANIMAUX.CHAMEAUX
Druzes → DRUZES
Dulcimer Sanṭūr
Duodécimains → CHIITES.BRANCHES
Dynastie → DYNASTIES

E

Eau Māʾ
Ebène Abanūs
Echecs Shaṭrandj
Eclipse Kusūf
Ecliptique Minṭaḳat al-Burūdj
Ecole élémentaire Kuttāb
Economique → ECONOMIQUE
Ecriture → ECRITURE
Edit Farmān
Education → EDUCATION
Eglise Kanīsa
Elégie Marthiya
Eléphant Fīl
Elixir al-Iksīr
Eloge Madīḥ
Eloquence Balāgha; Bayān; Faṣāḥa
Emancipation → EMANCIPATION
Embaumement Ḥināṭa
Emigration → EMIGRATION
Empire byzantin → BYZANTINS
Empire ottoman → EMPIRE OTTOMAN
Encens Lubān
Encre Midād
Encrier [au Suppl.] Dawāt
Encyclopédie Mawsūʿa
Endive [au Suppl.] Hindibāʾ
Enfance → PHASES DE LA VIE
Enfant trouvé Laḳīṭ
Enfer → ENFER
Enigme Lughz
Enterrement Djanāza
Envoyé Rasūl
Epices → CUISINE
Epicier Baḳḳāl
Epigraphie → EPIGRAPHIE
Epique Ḥamāsa
Epistolographie → LITTÉRATURE.EPISTOLAIRE
Epithète → ONOMASTIQUE
Equateur Istiwāʾ
Equines → ANIMAUX
Equitation Furūsiyya
Erreur Khaṭaʾ
Escargot Ṣadaf
Eschatologie → ESCHATOLOGIE
Esclavage → ESCLAVAGE
Esclave ʿAbd
Espion Djāsūs
Espionnage *voir* Espion
Esthétique ʿIlm al-Djamāl
Etable Iṣṭabl
Étendard Sandjaḳ; Sandjaḳ-i Sherīf
Eternité Abad; Ḳidam
Ethique → ETHIQUE
Ethnicité → ETHNICITÉ
Etiquette → ETIQUETTE
Etoile → ASTRONOMIE
Etymologie Ishtiḳāḳ

Eunuque → EUNUQUE
Evangile Indjīl
Eventail Mirwaḥa
Exorde Ibtidā'
Expédition → MILITAIRES
Expiation Kaffāra

F

Faculté Kulliyya
Faïence Kāshī
Famille ʿĀ'ila
Fauconnerie → FAUCONNERIE
Faune → ANIMAUX
Félins → ANIMAUX
Femmes → FEMMES
Fennec Fanak
Fenouil [au Suppl.] Basbās
Fer Ḥadīd
Fête → FÊTE
Feu Nār
Feutre Lubūd
Fiançailles Khiṭba
Fief Iḳṭāʿ
Film Cinématographe
Fils Ibn
Finance → ADMINISTRATION
Fisc → TAXATION
Flamant-rose Nuḥām
Fleurs → FLORE
Flore → FLORE
Foi → FOI
Foi, profession de *voir* Profession de foi
Foie Kabid
Fondamentalisme → RÉFORME. POLITICO-RELIGIEUSE.MILITANTE
Fontaine Shadirwān
Forêt Ghāba
Forgeron Ḳayn
Formules → ISLAM
Forteresse → ARCHITECTURE. MONUMENTS
Fossé Khandaḳ
Fou Madjnūn
Fourmis Naml
Fourrure Farw
Fraction Kasr
Franc-maçonnerie [au Suppl.] Farāmūsh-khāna; Farmāsūniyya
Fruit *voir* Agrumes

G

Gage Rahn
Gain Kasb
Gangas Ḳaṭā
Garde (de l'enfant) Ḥaḍāna
Garde-robe → VÊTEMENTS
Gazelle Ghazāl
Gemmes → BIJOUX
Généalogie → GÉNÉALOGIE
Géographie → GÉOGRAPHIE
Géométrie → MATHÉMATIQUES
Geste Ishāra
Gitans → GITANS
Glose Ḥāshiya
Gomme-résine Ṣamgh
Goudron Ḳaṭrān
Gouvernement Ḥukūma
Grammaire → LINGUISTIQUE
Gratitude Shukr

Grenadier (fleur de) Djullanār
Grossesse → PHASES DE LA VIE
Guépard Fahd
Guerre Ḥarb
Gynécologie → PHASES DE LA VIE

H

Habillement → VÊTEMENTS
Hagiographie → HAGIOGRAPHIE
Hautbois Ghayṭa
Hémérologie Ikhtiyārāt
Henné Ḥinnāʾ
Héraldique → HÉRALDIQUE
Hérésie → HÉRÉSIE
Hérisson Ḳunfudh
Héritage → HÉRITAGE
Hippopotame [au Suppl.] Faras al-Māʾ
Historiographie → LITTÉRATURE. HISTORIQUE
Homicide Ḳatl
Homme Insān
Homonyme Aḍdād
Homosexualité Liwāṭ
Honneur ʿIrḍ
Horloge Sāʿa
Horticulture → ARCHITECTURE. MONUMENTS.JARDINS; FLORE
Hôtel (monnaies) Dār al-Ḍarb
Hôtellerie → HÔTELLERIE
Houris Ḥūr
Humoristes → HUMOUR
Humour → HUMOUR
Huppe Hudhud
Hydrologie → HYDROLOGIE
Hydromancie Istinzāl
Hyène [au Suppl.] Ḍabuʿ
Hymne Nashīd
Hyperbole Mubālagha
Hypnotisme Sīmiyāʾ.1
Hypocrisie Riyāʾ

I

Iconographie → ART
Idole → IDOLES
Image Ṣūra
Impôt de capitation Djizya
Imprimerie Maṭbaʿa
Inclination → PRIÈRE
Incubation Istikhāra
Indépendance Istiḳlāl
Indigo Nīl
Individu Shakhṣ
Industrie → INDUSTRIE
Infidèle Kāfir
Inflexion Imāla
Inimitabilité (du Ḳurʾān) Iʿdjāz
Innovation Bidʿa
Inscriptions → EPIGRAPHIE
Insectes → ANIMAUX
Insignes → MILITAIRES.DÉCORATIONS; MONARCHIE.INSIGNE ROYAL
Inspection (des troupes) Istiʿrāḍ
Instrument Āla
Instrument (de musique) → MUSIQUE
Insulte rimée Hidjāʾ
Intellect ʿAḳl
Intercession Shafāʿa
Interdiction Ḥadjr
Intérêt Ribā

Interrogation Istifhām
Introduction Ibtidā'; Muḳaddima
Inventions → INVENTIONS
Invocation Du'ā'
Ipséité Huwiyya
Iris Sūsan
Irrigation → IRRIGATION
Islam → ISLAM
Ivoire 'Ādj

J

Jardin → ARCHITECTURE. MONUMENTS.JARDINS
Javelot Djerīd
Jeu → JEU
Jeûne → JEÛNE
Jeunes Turcs → TURQUIE.PÉRIODE OTTOMANE
Jeux → RÉCRÉATION
Jouets → RÉCRÉATION.JEUX
Jour → TEMPS
Journal Djarīda
Journalisme → PRESSE
Judaïsme → JUDAÏSME
Juge Ḳāḍī
Jurisconsulte → DROIT.JURISTE
Jurisprudence → DROIT
Juriste → DROIT
Jusquiame Bandj
Justice 'Adl

K

Kat Ḳāt
Kurdes → KURDES

L

Lacs → GÉOGRAPHIE.GÉOGRAPHIE PHYSIQUE.EAUX
Laine Ṣūf
Lamentation → LAMENTATION
Lampe Sirādj
Langue → LANGUES
Lavage → ABLUTION
Lavage (des morts) Ghusl
Laveur (des morts) [au Suppl.] Ghassāl
Lecture (Coranique) → CORAN
Légende → LÉGENDES
Lèpre [au Suppl.] Djudhām
Lesbianisme Siḥāḳ
Lettre(s) Ḥarf; Ḥurūf al-Hidjā'
Lévrier Salūḳī
Lexicographie → LEXICOGRAPHIE
Lézard Ḍabb
Liberté Ḥurriyya; [au Suppl.] Āzādī
Libre arbitre → PRÉDESTINATION
Lièvre [au Suppl.] Arnab
Lin Kattān
Linguistique → LINGUISTIQUE
Lion al-Asad
Lis Sūsan
Literie Mafrūshāt; Mifrash
Lithographie → IMPRIMERIE
Littérature → LITTÉRATURE

Livre Kitāb
Logique → PHILOSOPHIE
Longévité Muʿammar
Louage Kirāʾ
Louage, contrat de → DROIT
Loup Dhiʾb
Loup-garou Ḳuṭrub
Lumière Nūr
Lune Hilāl; al-Ḳamar
Luth Sāz
Lutte Pahlawān
Lyre Ḳithāra

M

Maçonnerie Bināʾ
Magie → MAGIE
Magnétite Maghnāṭīs.I
Maire Raʾīs
Maison *voir* Demeure; Thé, maison de
Malachite al-Dahnadj
Maladie → MALADIES
Malaria Malāryā
Malheur Shaḳāwa
Mandragore Sirādj al-Ḳuṭrub
Mangouste Nims
Manuscrit Nuskha
Marchandage Sawm
Marchands → PROFESSIONS
Marché Sūḳ
Marée al-Madd wa-l-Djazr
Mariage → MARIAGE
Marine → MILITAIRES
Martyr Shahīd
Martyre → MARTYRE
Marxisme Mārk(i)siyya
Masse Dūrbāsh
Mathématiques → MATHÉMATIQUES
Matière Hayūlā
Mausolée → ARCHITECTURE. MONUMENTS.TOMBEAUX
Mécanique → MÉCANIQUE
Médecin → MÉDECINE
Médecine → MÉDECINE
Médecine dentaire → MÉDECINE
Melilot [au Suppl.] Iklīl al-Malik
Mendiant Sāsān
Menstrues Ḥayḍ
Menthe [au Suppl.] Fūdhandj
Mer → OCÉANS ET MERS
Messie al-Masīḥ
Mesures → POIDS ET MESURES
Métal → ART
Métallurgie → MÉTALLURGIE
Métamorphose → ANIMAUX.TRANS-FORMATION EN
Métaphore Istiʿāra
Métaphysique → MÉTAPHYSIQUE
Météorologie → MÉTÉOROLOGIE
Métonymie Kināya
Métrique → MÉTRIQUE
Meurtre Ḳatl
Migration → EMIGRATION
Militaires → MILITAIRES
Millet [au Suppl.] Djāwars
Minaret Manāra
Minéralogie → MINÉRALOGIE
Miniatures → ART.PEINTURE
Miracle → MIRACLES
Mirage Sarāb
Miroir Mirʾāt
Mise à part Istithnāʾ
Misère Shaḳāwa
Mobilier → MOBILIER
Modernisme → RÉFORME
Modes musicaux Maḳām
Moine Rāhib
Mois → TEMPS

Mollusques → ANIMAUX
Monachisme Rahbāniyya
Monarchie → MONARCHIE
Monastère → CHRISTIANISME. COUVENTS
Monde ʿĀlam
Mongols → MONGOLIE
Monnaies → NUMISMATIQUE
Montagne → MONTAGNES
Morphologie Ṣarf
Mort → MORT
Mosaïque → ART
Mosquée → ARCHITECTURE.MONUMENTS
Mouche Dhubāb
Mouchoir Mandīl
Mouillage Mīnāʾ
Moutons, éleveur de Shāwiya
Mulet Baghl
Municipalité Baladiyya
Musc Misk
Musique → MUSIQUE
Myrobolan [au Suppl.] Halīladj
Myrte [au Suppl.] Ās
Mysticisme → MYSTICISME
Mystique → MYSTICISME
Mythes → LÉGENDES

N

Nacre Ṣadaf
Naevi Shāma
Narcisse Nardjis
Narcotiques → DROGUES
Nationalisme → NATIONALISME
Natron [au Suppl.] Bawraḳ
Nature → LITTÉRATURE.POÉSIE.DE LA NATURE
Navigation → NAVIGATION
Navire → NAVIGATION
Nilomètre Miḳyās
Noix [au Suppl.] Djawz
Nom Ism
Nomadisme → NOMADISME
Noria Nāʿūra
Nourriture → CUISINE
Nouveau Monde → NOUVEAU MONDE
Nuit Layl et Nahār
Nullité Fāsid wa-Bāṭil
Numéraux → NUMÉRO
Numismatique → NUMISMATIQUE

O

Obélisque → ARCHITECTURE.MONUMENTS
Obscénité → OBSCÉNITÉ
Observatoire → ASTRONOMIE
Obstétrique → MÉDECINE
Océan → OCÉANS ET MERS
Octogone Muthamman
Oeil → ANATOMIE; MAUVAIS OEIL
Oiseau → ANIMAUX
Ombre, théâtre d' Ḳaragöz; Khayāl al-Ẓill
Omoplatoscopie Katif
Oncle Khāl
Onirocritique → RÊVES
Onomastique → ONOMASTIQUE
Onomatomancie Ḥurūf, ʿIlm al-
Ophtalmologie → MÉDECINE
Opium Afyūn

Optique → OPTIQUE
Or Dhahab
Orange Nārandj
Orchestre Mehter
Orfèvre Ṣā'igh
Organes (corps) → ANATOMIE
Orge Shaʿīr
Orientalisme Mustashriḳūn
Ornithomancie ʿIyāfa
Orthodoxie Sunna
Oryx Lamṭ; Mahāt
Ostentation Riyāʾ
Ouvriers → PROFESSIONS
Ovins [au Suppl.] Ghanam

P

Paganisme → PÉRIODE PRÉ-ISLAMIQUE
Paiement → PAIEMENTS
Pain Khubz
Paix Ṣulḥ
Palais → ARCHITECTURE.MONUMENTS
Palanquin Maḥmal
Paléographie → ECRITURE; EPIGRAPHIE
Palmier Nakhl
Palmomancie Ikhtilādj
Paludisme Malāryā
Panarabisme → PANARABISME
Panégyrique Madīḥ
Panislamisme → PANISLAMISME
Pantalon Sirwāl
Panthéisme → RELIGION
Panthère Namir
Panturquisme → PANTURQUISME
Papier Kāghad
Papyrologie → PAPYROLOGIE
Papyrus Papyrus
Paradis → PARADIS
Parasol Miẓalla
Parchemin Raḳḳ
Parenté Ḳarāba
Parfum → PARFUM
Parlement Madjlis
Paronomase Muzāwadja
Partenariat Sharika
Parti politique → POLITIQUE
Passé Māḍī
Patronyme Kunya
Pâturage Marʿā
Pauvre Faḳīr; Miskīn
Pavillon → ARCHITECTURE.MONUMENTS
Pêche Samak.3
Péché Khaṭīʾa
Pédiatrie → PHASES DE LA VIE
Peinture → ART
Pèlerinage → PÈLERINAGE
Pensée Fikr
Périodiques → PRESSE
Perle al-Durr; Luʾluʾ
Perroquet Babbaghāʾ
Perruche Babbaghāʾ
Persan → LANGUES.INDO-EUROPÉENNES.IRANIENNES; LINGUISTIQUE
Perse → IRAN
Personne Shakhṣ
Peste → PESTE
Pétrole → PÉTROLE
Peuple Ḳawm; Shaʿb
Phare → ARCHITECTURE.MONUMENTS
Pharmacologie → PHARMACOLOGIE
Philatélie → PHILATÉLIE
Philologie → LINGUISTIQUE
Philosophie → PHILOSOPHIE

Phlébotomiste [au Suppl.] Faṣṣād
Phonétique → LINGUISTIQUE
Physiognomancie Ḳiyāfa
Physionomie → PHYSIONOMIE
Pierre Ḥadjar
Pierres précieuses → BIJOUX
Pigeon Ḥamām
Pilier Rukn
Pirate → PIRATERIE
Piraterie → PIRATERIE
Plan Kharīṭa
Planche Lawḥ
Planète → ASTRONOMIE
Plantes → FLORE
Plaques → ART
Plâtre Djiṣṣ
Pluie (prière de la) Istisḳā᾽
Pluriel Djamʿ
Poème → LITTÉRATURE.GENRES. POÉSIE
Poésie → LITTÉRATURE
Poète Shāʿir
Poids → POIDS ET MESURES
Poison Summ
Poisson → ANIMAUX
Poitrine → ANATOMIE
Pôle Ḳuṭb
Police → MILITAIRES
Politique → POLITIQUE
Polythéisme Shirk
Pont → ARCHITECTURE.MONUMENTS
Porc Khinzīr
Porc-épic Ḳunfudh
Port Mīnā᾽
Porte → ARCHITECTURE.MONUMENTS
Portefaix Ḥammāl
Porteur Ḥammāl
Porteur d'eau Saḳḳā᾽
Possession Milk
Poste (histoire de la) → PHILATÉLIE
Poste (services postaux) → TRANSPORT
Potasse Ḳily
Poterie → ART
Pou *voir* Poux
Poudre Bārūd
Poule Dadjādja
Poule sultane [au Suppl.] Abū Barāḳish.II
Poux Ḳaml
Pré-Islam → PÉRIODE PRÉISLAMIQUE
Prédestination → PRÉDESTINATION
Préemption Shufʿa
Préface Muḳaddima
Présage Fa᾽l
Presse → PRESSE
Preuve Bayyina
Prière → PRIÈRE
Prière (direction de la) Ḳibla
Prière (niche) Miḥrāb
Prison Sidjn
Prisonnier → MILITAIRES
Procédure légale → DROIT.DROIT DE LA PROCÉDURE
Processions Mawākib
Profession de foi Shahāda
Professions → PROFESSIONS
Profit Kasb
Prophétat → PROPHÉTAT
Prophète → MUḤAMMAD, LE PROPHÈTE; PROPHÉTAT
Prophétie → PROPHÉTAT
Propriété → PROPRIÉTÉ
Prose → LITTÉRATURE
Prosodie → LITTÉRATURE.POÉSIE; METRIQUE; RIME
Prostitution [au Suppl.] Bighā᾽
Protection Ḥimāya; Idjāra
Proverbe → LITTÉRATURE; PROVERBES
Puit → ARCHITECTURE.MONUMENTS
Pyramide Haram

Q

Qarmates → CHIITES.BRANCHES
Quiddité Māhiyya

R

Radiodiffusion Idhāʿa
Rage *voir* Chien
Raid → RAIDS
Rançon [au Suppl.] Fidāʾ
Rapports, sexuels Bāh
Récitation → CORAN.LECTURE
Reconnaissance Shukr
Récréation → RÉCRÉATION
Réflexion Fikr
Réforme → RÉFORME
Registre → ADMINISTRATION. DOCUMENTS
Réglisse Sūs
Religion → RELIGION
Reliure → ECRITURE
Renard Fanak
Reptiles → ANIMAUX
République Djumhūriyya
Ressemblance Shubha
Résurrection Ḳiyāma
Retraite Khalwa
Rêve → RÊVES
Révélation Ilhām
Rhapsodomancie Ḳurʿa
Rhétorique → RHÉTORIQUE
Rhinocéros Karkaddan
Rime → RIME
Rituel → RITUELS
Rivière → RIVIÈRES
Riz al-Ruzz
Robe d'honneur Khilʿa
Roi Malik; Shāh
Roman Ḳiṣṣa
Ronde de nuit ʿAsas
Rongeurs → ANIMAUX
Rosaire Subḥa
Rose Gul
Roseau Ḳaṣab
Rossignol Bulbul
Route Shāriʿ
Royaume Mamlaka
Rue Shāriʿ

S

Sable Raml
Sagesse Ḥikma
Saignée [au Suppl.] Faṣṣād
Saint → SAINT
Sainteté Ḳadāsa
Salamandre Samandal
Sang [au Suppl.] Dam
Sang, vengeance du Ḳiṣāṣ
Sanglier Khinzīr
Santé → MÉDECINE
Sappan, bois de Baḳḳam
Satire Hidjāʾ
Sauterelle Djarād
Savon Ṣābūn
Scapulomancie Katif
Sceau Khātam; Muhr
Science → SCIENCES; SCIENCES NATURELLES
Scorpion ʿAḳrab
Scribe Kātib; [au Suppl.] Dabīr

Secrétaire Kātib; [au Suppl.] Dabīr
Sel Milḥ
Selle (du cheval) Sardj
Semaine → TEMPS
Sémitique (langues) Sām.2
Sens Ḥiss; Maḥsūsāt
Sept Sabʿ
Septimains → CHIITES.BRANCHES
Serment Ḳasam
Sermon Khuṭba
Sermonnaire Ḳāṣṣ
Serpent Ḥayya
Serviteur Khādim
Sésame Simsim
Sexe Djins
Sexualité → SEXUALITÉ
Siège, guerre de Ḥiṣār
Siège, machinerie de Ḥiṣār; Mandjanīḳ
Singe Ḳird
Socialisme Ishtirākiyya
Société Djamʿiyya
Sodium Naṭrūn; *et voir* Natron
Sodomie Liwāṭ
Soie Ḥarīr
Soleil Shams
Sorcellerie → MAGIE
Soude Ḳily; *et voir* Natron
Soufisme → MYSTICISME
Soufre Kibrīt
Sources → GÉOGRAPHIE.GÉOGRAPHIE PHYSIQUE
Souterrain Sardāb
Sphère Falak; Kura
Sport → ANIMAUX.SPORT; RÉCRÉATION
Substance Djawhar
Succession → HÉRITAGE
Sucre Sukkar
Suicide Intiḥār
Superstition → SUPERSTITION
Surnom Laḳab
Swahili → KENYA
Symbolisme Ramz.3
Syndicat Niḳāba

T

Tablette Lawḥ
Tabouret Kursī
Tache de peau Shāma
Tailleur Khayyāṭ
Talion Ḳiṣāṣ
Talisman → CHARMES
Tambour Darabukka
Tambourin Duff
Tanneur [au Suppl.] Dabbāgh
Tapis → ART.TAPISSERIE
Tapisserie → ART
Taxation → TAXATION
Teck Sādj
Teinture → TEINTURE
Teinturier → TEINTURE
Témoin Shāhid
Temps → MÉTÉOROLOGIE; TEMPS
Tente Khayma
Terre → TERRE
Textiles → ART; VÊTEMENTS.MATÉRIAUX
Thé Čay
Thé, maison de [au Suppl.] Čāy-khāna
Théâtre → LITTÉRATURE.DRAME
Théâtre d'ombre Ḳaragöz; Khayāl al-Ẓill
Théologie → THÉOLOGIE
Théophanie Maẓhar
Thrène Marthiya

Timbres → PHILATELIE
Tissage → ART.TEXTILES
Tisserand al-Nassādj; [au Suppl.] Ḥā'ik
Tisserin [au Suppl.] Abū Barāḳish.1
Titres → ONOMASTIQUE
Toile Kattān; Khaysh
Tombeau → ARCHITECTURE.MONUMENTS
Tortue Sulaḥfā
Tour Burdj
Tradition → LITTÉRATURE.TRADITION
Traduction → LITTÉRATURE.TRADUCTIONS
Traité → TRAITÉS
Transfert Ḥawāla
Transport → TRANSPORT
Travail *voir* Syndicat
Tremblements de terre → TREMBLEMENTS DE TERRE
Trésor → TRÉSOR
Triangle Muthallath
Tribu → TRIBUS
Tribunal Maḥkama
Tribut → TRAITÉS
Trictrac, jeu de Nard
Troc Muʿāwaḍa
Trompette Būḳ
Trope Madjāz
Turquoise Fīrūzadj
Tziganes → GITANS

U

Université Djāmiʿa
Urbanisation → ARCHITECTURE; GÉOGRAPHIE
Usure Ribā
Usurpation Ghaṣb

V

Vautour Humā; Nasr
Véhicule → TRANSPORT
Vengeance (du sang) Ḳiṣāṣ
Vent → MÉTÉOROLOGIE
Vente, contrat de → DROIT
Ventilation → ARCHITECTURE. URBAINE
Ventouseur [au Suppl.] Faṣṣād
Verbe Fiʿl
Verre → Art
Verset Āya
Vêtements → VÊTEMENTS
Vétérinaire → MÉDECINE
Vices → VERTUS
Vie Ḥayāt
Vigne Karm
Vikings al-Madjūs
Village Ḳarya
Ville Ḳarya; Ḳaṣaba
Vin → VIN
Viol Rabāb
Vipère Afʿā
Voeu Nadhr
Voie Lactée al-Madjarra
Voile → VÊTEMENTS.COIFFURES
Vol Sariḳa
Volcans → GÉOGRAPHIE. GÉOGRAPHIE PHYSIQUE
Voleur Liṣṣ
Voyage → VOYAGE

W

Wagon *voir* Charrette

Z

Zaydites → CHIITES
Zéro al-Ṣifr
Zodiaque Minṭaḳat al-Burūdj
Zoologie → ZOOLOGIE
Zoroastriens → ZOROASTRIENS

INDEX DES MATIÈRES

Le monde musulman dont il est question dans l'Index des Matières est le monde actuel. Ce qui jadis constituait le royaume de Perse est représenté ici par l'Asie centrale, le Caucase et l'Afghanistan, de même qu'une partie des territoires autrefois gouvernés par l'empire Ottoman englobe à présent des pays individuels de l'Europe de l'est et du Moyen-Orient. Des pays modernes, tels que la Jordanie et le Liban, ont la place qui leur revient. Pour les pays où l'islam est installé de longue date, on trouve une subdivision 'période moderne', tandis qu'on a réuni les articles de l'*Encyclopédie* qui traitent du 19e et du 20e siècles. Lorsqu'un individu est classé au '15e siècle', cette datation indique l'année de sa mort A.D.

Les références en caractères réguliers renvoient aux articles de l'*Encyclopédie*. Toutefois celles qui sont imprimées en caractères gras indiquent l'article principal. Les entrées en lettres capitales précédées d'une flèche renvoient à des rubriques dans l'Index des Matières. Ainsi dans le cas de

> BÉDOUINS **Badw**; Biʾr; Dawār; G͟hanīma; G͟hazw; al-Hid͟jar
> *voir aussi* Liṣṣ; *et* → ARABIE SÉOUDITE; NOMADISME; TRIBUS.PÉNINSULE ARABIQUE

Badw, Biʾr, Dawār; G͟hanīma; Ghazw; al-Hid͟jar renvoient à des articles de l'*Encyclopédie* qui traitent principalement des Bédouins, Badw étant l'article sur les Bédouins. Liṣṣ fait allusion à un article de l'*Encyclopédie* qui contient des informations sur les Bédouins, et ARABIE SÉOUDITE, NOMADISME, TRIBUS.PÉNINSULE ARABIQUE renvoient le lecteur à des rubriques analogues dans l'Index des Matières.

A

ʿABBĀSIDES → CALIFAT

ABLUTION **G͟hus͟l**; Istind͟jāʾ; Istins͟hāḳ; al-Masḥ ʿalā l-K͟huffayn
voir aussi D͟janāba; Ḥadat͟h; Ḥammām; Ḥawḍ; Ḥayḍ

ABYSSINIE → ÉTHIOPIE

ADMINISTRATION Barīd; Bayt al-Māl; Daftar; Diplomatique; **Dīwān**; D͟jizya; Kātib; [au Suppl.] Démographie.I
voir aussi al-Ḳalḳas͟handī.I; al-Ṣūlī
pour les califats ou dynasties spécifiques → CALIFAT; DYNASTIES; EMPIRE OTTOMAN

diplomatique → Diplomatie
documents **Daftar**.I
et → Documents; Empire Ottoman.administration
archives Dār al-Maḥfūẓāt al-ʿUmūmiyya; Geniza
et → Empire Ottoman.administration
financière ʿAṭāʾ; Bayt al-Māl; Daftar; Dār al-Ḍarb; Ḳānūn.II; Kasb; Khāzin; Khaznadār; Makhzan; Muṣādara.2; Mustawfī; Rūznāma; Siyāḳat
voir aussi Dhahab; Fiḍḍa; Ḥisba; *et* → Empire Ottoman.administration; Numismatique
fiscale → Taxation
fonctionnaires ʿĀmil; Amīn; Amīr; Amīr al-Ḥādjdj; ʿArīf; Dawādār; Djahbadh; Ḥisba; Īshīk-āḳāsī; Kalāntar; Kātib; Khāzin; Mushīr; Mushrif; Mustakhridj; Mustawfī; Parwānačī; Raʾīs; Ṣāḥib al-Madīna; [au Suppl.] Dabīr
voir aussi Barīd; Consul; Fatwā; Fuyūdj; Koṫwāl; Malik al-Tudjdjār; Mawlā; Muwāḍaʿa; *et* → Droit.fonctions; Empire Ottoman; Militaires.fonctions
géographie → Géographie.administrative
juridique → Droit
militaire → Militaires
ottomane → Empire Ottoman

Adoption [au Suppl.] ʿĀr
voir aussi ʿĀda.III

Adultère Ḳadhf; Liʿān
voir aussi al-Marʾa.II
sanctions Ḥadd

Afghanistan Afghān; **Afghānistān**
architecture → Architecture.régions
dynasties Aḥmad Shāh Durrānī; Ghaznawides; Ghūrides; Kart
et → Dynasties.afghanistan et inde
géographie physique Afghānistān.I
eaux Dehās; Hāmūn; Harī Rūd; Kābul.I; Ḳunduz; Kurram; Murghāb; Pandjhīr; [au Suppl.] Gūmāl
voir aussi Afghānistān.I
montagnes Hindū Kush; Kūh-i Bābā; Safīd Kūh
voir aussi Afghānistān.I
historiens Sayfī Harawī
langue → Langues.indo-iraniennes.iraniennes
période moderne Djāmiʿa; Dustūr.V; Khaybar; Madjlis.IV.B; Maṭbaʿa.V
voir aussi Muhādjir.3

hommes d'état ʿAbd al-Raḥmān Khān; Ayyūb Khān; Dūst Muḥammad; Ḥabīb Allāh Khān; Muḥammad Dāwūd Khān; Shīr ʿAlī; [au Suppl.] Amān Allāh
voir aussi [au Suppl.] Faḳīr d'Ipi

population Abdālī; Čahār Aymaḳ; Durrānī; Ghalča; Ghalzay; Moghols; Mohmand; [au Suppl.] Démographie.III; Hazāra
voir aussi Afghān.I; Afghānistān.II; Khaladj; Özbeg.I.d; [au Suppl.] Djirga

toponymes
- *anciens* Būshandj; Bust; Dihistān; Djuwayn.3; Farmūl; Fīrūzkūh.I; Khōst; Khudjistān; Marw al-Rūdh; al-Rukhkhadj
- *actuels*
  - *districts* Andarāb.1; Bādghīs; Farwān; Ḳuhistān.III; Lamghānāt
  - *régions* Badakhshan; Dardistān; Djūzdjān; Ghardjistān; Ghūr; Kāfiristān; Khōst; Nangrahār; Sīstān; [au Suppl.] Hazāradjāt
    voir aussi Pandjhīr
  - *villes* Andkhūy; Balkh; Bāmiyān; Djām; Farāh; Faryāb.I; Gardīz; Ghazna; Girishk; Harāt; Kābul.II; Ḳandahār; Karūkh; Khulm; Ḳunduz; Maymana; Mazār-i Sharīf; Rūdhbār.1; Sabzawār.2; Sar-i Pul; Shibarghān; [au Suppl.] Djalālābād

Afrique Lamlam

Afrique centrale Cameroun; Congo; Gabon; [au Suppl.] Čad
voir aussi Hausa; Muḥammad Bello; al-Murdjibī; [au Suppl.] Démographie.V
pour les pays individuels → Congo; Niger; Nigéria; Tchad; Zaïre
- *géographie physique*
  - *déserts* Sāḥil.2
- *littérature* Hausa.III; Kano; Shāʿir.5 et 6; Shiʿr.5
- *population* Kanuri; Kotoko; Shuwa

Afrique du Nord Algérie; Atlas; Ifrīḳiya; Lībiyā; Maghāriba; al-Maghrib (2x); Mashāriḳa
voir aussi al-ʿArab.V; ʿArabiyya.A.III.3; Badw.II.D; Djaysh.III; Ghuzz.II; Ḥawz; Kharbga; Kitābāt.IV; Lamṭ; Léon l'Africain; Libās.II; Maḥalla; Mānū; Ṣaff.3; Sipāhī.2; [au Suppl.] ʿĀr; *et* → Dynasties.espagne et afrique du nord
pour les pays individuels → Algérie; Libye; Maroc; Tunisie
- *architecture* → Architecture.régions
- *géographie physique* Reg; Rīf; Sabkha; al-Ṣaḥrāʾ; Shaṭṭ
  et → *l'entrée Géographie Physique sous pays individuels*
- *mysticisme* → Mysticisme
- *période moderne* Baladiyya.III; Djamāʿa; Djarīda.I.B; Hilāl; Ḳawmiyya.II
  et → Algérie; Libye; Maroc; Tunisie

population Ahaggar; Berbères; Dukkāla; Khulṭ; al-Maʿḳil; Shāwiya.1; [au Suppl.] Démographie.IV

voir aussi Khumayr; Kūmiya; al-Manāṣīr; Mandīl; Maures; *et* → BERBÈRES

Afrique méridionale Mozambique; South Africa

voir aussi [au Suppl.] Djarīda.IX

pour les pays individuels → MOZAMBIQUE

Afrique occidentale Côte d'Ivoire; Dahomey; Gambie; Ghāna; Guinée; Libéria; Mali; Mūrītāniyā; Niger; Nigeria; Sénégal; Sierra Leone

voir aussi Kitābāt.V; Ḳunbi Ṣāliḥ; al-Maghīlī; Malam; Murīdiyya; Sūdān (Bilād al-).2; Sulṭān.3

pour les pays individuels → BÉNIN; CÔTE D'IVOIRE; GUINÉE; MALI; MAURITANIE; NIGER; NIGERIA; SÉNÉGAL; TOGO

architecture Ḳunbi Ṣāliḥ; Masdjid.VII

empires Mande; Oyo; Songhay.3

voir aussi Muḥammad b. Abī Bakr; Samori Ture

géographie physique

déserts Sāḥil.2

eaux Niger

montagnes Fūta Djallon

langue Hausa; Nūba.III; Shuwa.2; Songhay.1; Sūdān (Bilād al-).3

voir aussi Fulbé; Kanuri; Sénégal; *et* → LANGUES.AFRO-ASIATIQUES.ARABE

littérature → AFRIQUE.AFRIQUE CENTRALE

population Fulbé; Ḥarṭānī; Ifoghas; Kunta; Songhay.2; [au Suppl.] Démographie.V

voir aussi Lamlam; Mande

Afrique orientale Djibūtī; Érythrée; Ḥabesh; Ḳumr; Madagascar; Mafia; Somali; Sūdān

voir aussi Emīn Pasha; Muṣāḥib; Nikāḥ.II.5; al-Nudjūm; Shīrāzī; [au Suppl.] Djarīda.VIII

pour les pays individuels → ÉTHIOPIE; KENYA; MADAGASCAR; MALAWI; SOMALIE; SOUDAN; TANZANIE; ZANZIBAR

architecture Manāra.III; Masdjid.VI; Mbweni; Minbar.IV

voir aussi Shungwaya

fêtes Mawlid.2; Nawrūz.II

géographie physique

eaux Atbara; Baḥr al-Ghazāl.1; Shebelle

voir aussi Baḥr al-Hind; Baḥr al-Zandj

langue Érythrée; Ḥabash.IV; Kūsh; Nūba.III; Somali.5; Sūdān. 2; Swahili

voir aussi Ḳumr; Madagascar

littérature Miʿrādj.III; Somali.6

voir aussi Kitābāt.VI; *et* → KENYA.LITTÉRATURE SWAHILIE
population ʿAbābda; ʿĀmir; Antemuru; Bedja; Beleyn; Bishārīn; Danḳalī; Djaʿaliyyūn; Galla; Māryā; Mazrūʿī; Oromo; Somali.1; [au Suppl.] Démographie.V
voir aussi Diglal; Lamlam; al-Manāṣīr

AGRICULTURE **Filāḥa**; Marʿā; Raʿiyya
voir aussi Mazraʿa; Mughārasa; Musāḳāt; Muzāraʿa; [au Suppl.] Akkār; *et* → BOTANIQUE; FLORE; IRRIGATION
outils Miḥrāth
produits Ḳahwa; Ḳamḥ; Karm; Ḳaṣab al-Sukkar; Khamr.II; Ḳuṭn; [au Suppl.] Djāwars; Hindibāʾ
voir aussi Ḥarīr; *et* → CUISINE
termes Āgdāl; Baʿl.2.b; Čiftlik; Ghūṭa; Maṭmūra
traités sur Abū l-Khayr al-Ishbīlī; Ibn Wāfid; Ibn Waḥshiyya

ALBANIE **Arnawutluḳ**; Iskender Beg; Ḳarā Maḥmūd Pasha
voir aussi Muslimūn.I.B.4; Sāmī; *et* → EMPIRE OTTOMAN
toponymes Aḳ Ḥiṣār.IV; Awlonya; Delvina; Drač; Elbasan; Ergiri; Korča; Krujë; Lesh

ALCHIMIE Dhahab; Fiḍḍa; al-Iksīr; Kibrīt; **al-Kīmiyāʾ**
voir aussi Ḳārūn; Maʿdin; al-Nūshādir; *et* → MÉTALLURGIE; MINÉRALOGIE
alchimistes Djābir b. Ḥayyān; Ibn Umayl; Ibn Waḥshiyya; al-Rāzī, Abū Bakr; [au Suppl.] Abū l-Ḥasan al-Anṣārī; al-Djildakī
voir aussi Hirmis; Khālid b. Yazīd b. Muʿāwiya; [au Suppl.] al-Djawbarī, ʿAbd al-Raḥīm; Findiriskī; Ibn Daḳīḳ al-ʿĪd
outillage al-Anbīḳ
termes Rukn.2

ALGÉRIE **Algérie**
voir aussi ʿArabiyya.A.III.3; ʿArsh; Ḥalḳa; *et* → BERBÈRES; DYNASTIES. ESPAGNE ET AFRIQUE DU NORD
architecture → ARCHITECTURE.RÉGIONS.AFRIQUE DU NORD
dynasties ʿAbd al-Wādides; Fāṭimides; Ḥammādides; Rustamides
et → DYNASTIES.ESPAGNE ET AFRIQUE DU NORD
géographie physique Algérie.I
montagnes ʿAmūr; Atlas; Awrās; Bībān; Djurdjura; Kabylie
littérature Ḥawfī
période moderne Djāmiʿa; Djarīda.I.B; Ḥizb.I; Ḥukūma.IV; Maʿārif.II; Madjlis. IV.A.20
réforme Ibn Bādīs; (al-)Ibrāhīmī; Salafiyya.1(b)
voir aussi Fallāḳ

période ottomane (1518-1830) ʿAbd al-Ḳādir b. Muḥyī l-Dīn; Algérie.II.b; ʿArūdj; Ḥasan Agha; Ḥasan Baba; Ḥasan Pasha; al-Ḥusayn; Ḥusayn Pasha, Mezzomorto; Khayr al-Dīn Pasha
population Ahaggar; Algérie.III; Berbères
voir aussi Kabylie; *et* → BERBÈRES
religion Algérie.III; Shāwiya.1
confréries religieuses ʿAmmāriyya; Raḥmāniyya
voir aussi Darḳāwa; *et* → MYSTICISME
toponymes
anciens Arshgūl; Ashīr; al-Manṣūra; Sadrāta; [au Suppl.] Hunayn
actuels
oasis Biskra; Ḳanṭara.1; al-Ḳulayʿa.II.1; Laghouat; Sūf; [au Suppl.] Gourara
régions Ḥuḍna; Mzab; Sāḥil.1.b
villes Adrar.1; al-ʿAnnāba; Ārzāw; ʿAyn Temushent; Bidjāya; Biskra; Bulayda; Colomb-Béchar; al-Djazāʾir; Djidjelli; Ghardāya; Ḳalʿat Banī ʿAbbās; Ḳalʿat Huwwāra; al-Ḳulayʿa.II.2; Ḳusṭanṭīna; Laghouat; al-Madiyya; Masīla; Milyāna; al-Muʿaskar; Mustaghānim; Nadrūma; Saʿīda; Sharshal; Sīdī Bū l-ʿAbbās

ALPHABET **Abdjad**; Ḥarf; Ḥisāb; **Ḥurūf al-Hidjāʾ**
voir aussi Djafr; Khaṭṭ; [au Suppl.] Budūḥ; *et* → ÉCRITURE.ÉCRITURES
pour les lettres de l'alphabet arabe et persan, voir Ḍād; Dāl; Dhāl; Djīm; Fāʾ; Ghayn; Hāʾ; Ḥāʾ; Hamza; Kāf; Ḳāf; Khāʾ; Lām; Mīm; Nūn; Pāʾ; Rāʾ; Ṣād; Sīn et Shīn
secret → CRYPTOGRAPHIE

AMOUR **ʿIshḳ**
voir aussi Ishāra; Ḳalb.II; *et* → LITTÉRATURE.POÉSIE.D'AMOUR
mystique ʿĀshiḳ; ʿIshḳ; Shawḳ
et → LITTÉRATURE.POÉSIE.MYSTIQUE; MYSTICISME
platonique Djamīl al-ʿUdhrī; Ghazal.I.3; Ibn Dāwūd; Kuthayyir b. ʿAbd al-Raḥmān; Laylā al-Akhyaliyya; Nuṣayb b. Rabāḥ; al-Ramādī
et → LITTÉRATURE.POÉSIE.D'AMOUR
traités sur al-Antāḳī, Dāwūd; Ibn Ḥazm, Abū Muḥammad; Rafīʿ al-Dīn
voir aussi Bukhtīshūʿ

ANATOMIE Djism; Katif; [au Suppl.] Aflīmūn
voir aussi Ishāra; Khiḍāb; Ḳiyāfa; Shāma; [au Suppl.] Dam
cheveux ʿAfṣ; Afsantīn; Ḥinnāʾ; Liḥya-yi Sherīf; **Shaʿr**
voir aussi [au Suppl.] Ḥallāḳ

dents → MÉDECINE.DENTAIRE
oeil **ʿAyn**; Kuḥl; Manāẓir; Ramad
et → MÉDECINE.OPHTALMOLOGISTES; OPTIQUE
organes Kabid; Ḳalb
poitrine **Ṣadr**
traités sur
en turc Shānī-zāde
et → MÉDECINE.MANUELS/ENCYCLOPÉDIES DE MÉDECINE

ANDALOUSIE **al-Andalus**; Gharb al-Andalus; Morisques; Mozárabe; Mudéjar; Shark al-Andalus
voir aussi Kitābāt.III; Libās.II; Māʾ.VII; al-Madjūs; Maures; Muwallad; Safīr.2.b; Ṣāʾifa.2; *et* → DYNASTIES.ESPAGNE ET AFRIQUE DU NORD; ESPAGNE
administration Dīwān.III; Ḳūmis; Ṣāḥib al-Madīna
voir aussi Fatā
architecture → ARCHITECTURE.RÉGIONS
dynasties al-Murābiṭūn.IV; al-Muwaḥḥidūn; [au Suppl.] ʿAzafī
voir aussi al-Andalus.VI; (Banū) Ḳasī; *et* → DYNASTIES.ESPAGNE ET AFRIQUE DU NORD
période des "reyes de taifas" (11e siècle) ʿAbbādides; Afṭasides; ʿĀmirides; Dhū l-Nūnides; Djahwarides; Ḥammūdides; Hūdides; **Mulūk al-Ṭawāʾif**.II; Razīn, Banū
voir aussi Balansiya; Dāniya; Gharnāṭa; Ibn Ghalbūn; Ibn Rashīḳ, Abū Muḥammad; Ishbīliya; Ḳurṭuba; Mudjāhid al-ʿĀmirī; Parias; al-Sīd
géographie physique → ESPAGNE
gouverneurs jusqu'à la conquête umayyade ʿAbd al-Malik b. Ḳaṭan; ʿAbd al-Raḥmān al-Ghāfiḳī; Abū l-Khaṭṭār; al-Ḥurr b. ʿAbd al-Raḥmān al-Thaḳafī; al-Ḥusām b. Ḍirār
voir aussi Kalb b. Wabara; Mūsā b. Nuṣayr; al-Ṣumayl b. Ḥātim
grammarians Abū Ḥayyān al-Gharnāṭī; al-Baṭalyawsī; Djūdī al-Mawrūrī; Ibn al-ʿArīf, al-Ḥusayn; Ibn ʿĀṣim; Ibn al-Iflīlī; Ibn Khātima; Ibn al-Ḳūṭiyya; Ibn Maḍāʾ; Ibn Mālik; Ibn Sīda; al-Rabaḥī; al-Shalawbīn; al-Shantamarī; al-Sharīf al-Gharnatī; al-Sharīshī; [au Suppl.] Ibn Hishām al-Lakhmī
voir aussi al-Shāṭibī, Abū Isḥāḳ
historiens al-Ḍabbī, Abū Djaʿfar; Ibn al-Abbār, Abū ʿAbd Allāh; Ibn ʿAbd al-Malik al-Marrākushī; Ibn Bashkuwāl; Ibn Burd.I; Ibn al-Faraḍī; Ibn Ghālib; Ibn Ḥayyān; Ibn ʿIdhārī; Ibn al-Khaṭīb; Ibn al-Ḳūṭiyya; Ibn Saʿīd al-Maghribī; al-Maḳḳarī; al-Rushāṭī
voir aussi al-Shaḳundī; *et* → DYNASTIES.ESPAGNE ET AFRIQUE DU NORD
juristes al-Bādjī; al-Dānī; al-Ḥumaydī; Ibn Abī Zamanayn; Ibn ʿĀṣim; Ibn al-Faraḍī; Ibn Ḥabīb, Abū Marwān; Ibn Ḥazm, Abū Muḥammad; Ibn Maḍāʾ;

Ibn Rushayd; ʿĪsā b. Dīnār; ʿIyāḍ b. Mūsā; al-Ḳalaṣādī; al-Ḳurṭubī, Abū ʿAbd Allāh; al-Ḳurṭubī, Yaḥyā; (al-)Mundhir b. Saʿīd; Shabṭūn; [au Suppl.] Ibn Rushd

voir aussi al-Khushanī; Mālikiyya; Ṣāʿid al-Andalusī; Shūrā.2; Shurṭa.2; [au Suppl.] Ibn al-Rūmiyya

littérature Aljamía; ʿArabiyya.B.Appendice; Fahrasa

et → ANDALOUSIE.HISTORIENS; LITTÉRATURE.POÉSIE

mysticisme → MYSTICISME.MYSTIQUES

toponymes → ESPAGNE

ANGÉLOLOGIE **Malāʾika**

voir aussi ʿAdhāb al-Ḳabr; Dīk; Iblīs; Ḳarīn; Rūḥāniyya; Siḥr

anges ʿAzāzīl; Djabrāʾīl; Hārūt wa-Mārūt; Isrāfīl; ʿIzrāʿīl; Mīkāl; Munkar wa-Nakīr; Riḍwān

ANIMAUX Dābba; **Ḥayawān**

voir aussi Badw; (Djazīrat) al-ʿArab.V; Farw; Hind.I.l; Khāṣī; Marbaṭ; [au Suppl.] Djazzār; *et* → ZOOLOGIE

animaux aquatiques

crustacés **Saraṭān**

mollusques **Ṣadaf**

poisson **Samak**

animaux terrestres

antilopes Ghazāl; Lamṭ; Mahāt

arachnides ʿAḳrab; ʿAnkabūt

canidés Dhiʾb; Fanak; Ibn Āwā; Kalb; Salūḳī; [au Suppl.] Ḍabuʿ

chameaux **Ibil**

voir aussi (Djazīrat) al-ʿArab.V; Badw.II.c et d; Kārwān; Raḥīl; [au Suppl.] Djammāl; *et* → TRANSPORT.CARAVANES

domestiqués Baḳar; Fīl; Ibil; Kalb; Khinzīr; Nims; [au Suppl.] Djāmūs; Ghanam

voir aussi Shāwiya.2; *et* → ANIMAUX.ÉQUINES

équines Badw.II; Baghl; **Faras**; Ḥimār; **Khayl**

voir aussi Fāris; Furūsiyya; Ḥazīn; Ibn Hudhayl; Ibn al-Mundhir; Iṣṭabl; Marbaṭ; Maydān; Mīr-Ākhūr; Sardj

félins ʿAnāḳ; al-Asad; Fahd; Namir et Nimr; Sinnawr

insectes Dhubāb; Djarād; Ḳaml; Naḥl; Naml; Nāmūs.2

oiseaux Babbaghāʾ; Dadjādja; Dīk; Ghurāb; Ḥamām; Hudhud; Humā; Ḳaṭā; Naʿām; Nasr; Nuḥām; al-Rukhkh; Salwā; Shunḳub; [au Suppl.] Abū Barāḳish

voir aussi Bayzara; Bulbul; ʿIyāfa; al-Ramādī; Sonḳor

reptiles Afʿā; Ḍabb; Ḥayya; Ḥirbāʾ; Samandal; Sulaḥfā

voir aussi Ādam; Almās
rongeurs [au Suppl.] Fa'r
et l'art al-Asad; Fahd; Fīl; Ḥayawān.VI; Karkaddan; Maʿdin; Namir et Nimr; [au Suppl.] Arnab
et proverbes Ḥayawān.II; Mathal
voir aussi les articles sur les animaux individuels, en particulier Afʿā; Dhiʾb; Fahd; Ghurāb; Ḳaṭā; Khinzīr; Ḳird; Lamṭ; Naml
sauvages *outre les articles ci-dessus, voir aussi* Ayyil; Fanak; Fīl; Ibn ʿIrs; Karkaddan; Ḳird; Ḳunfudh; [au Suppl.] Arnab; Faras al-Māʾ
et → CHASSE
sport Bayzara; Fahd; Furūsiyya; Ḥamām; Khinzīr; Mahāt; [au Suppl.] Ḍabuʿ
voir aussi Čakïrdjï-bashï; Doghandjï; Kurdes et Kurdistān.IV.C.5; *et* → CHASSE
transformation en Ḥayawān.III; Ḳird; **Maskh**

ANTHROPOMORPHISME Ḥashwiyya; Karrāmiyya
voir aussi Bayān b. Samʿān; Djism; Hishām b. al-Ḥakam; Ḥulmāniyya

APOSTASIE Mulḥid; Murtadd
voir aussi Ḳatl; *et* → HÉRÉSIE

ARABIE SÉOUDITE (Djazīrat) al-ʿArab; Djarīda.I.A; Djāmiʿa; Dustūr.VII; al-Hidjar; al-Ikhwān; Madjlis.IV.A.8; Maḥkama.IV.7; **al-Suʿūdiyya, al-Mamlaka al-ʿArabiyya**
voir aussi Bā ʿAlawī; Badw; Baladiyya.II; Barakāt; Makka; [au Suppl.] Démographie.III; *et* → PÉRIODE PRÉISLAMIQUE.DANS LA PÉNINSULE ARABIQUE; TRIBUS.PÉNINSULE ARABIQUE
avant l'Islam → PÉRIODE PRÉISLAMIQUE.DANS LA PÉNINSULE ARABIQUE
dynasties Hāshimides (2x); Rashīd, Āl; Suʿūd, Āl
et → DYNASTIES.PÉNINSULE ARABIQUE
géographie physique
déserts al-Aḥḳāf; al-Dahnāʾ; Nafūd; al-Rubʿ al-Khālī
voir aussi Badw.II; Ḥarra
eaux Dawʿan
montagnes Djabala; Ḥufāsh; Raḍwā; al-Sarāt
voir aussi Adjaʾ et Salmā
plaines ʿArafa; al-Dibdiba; al-Ṣammān
wadis al-ʿAtk; al-Bāṭin; Bayḥān; Bayḥān al-Ḳaṣāb; Djayzān; Fāʾw; (Wādī l-) Ḥamḍ; Rumma, Wādī; al-Sahbāʾ; Sirḥān
historiens al-Azraḳī; Daḥlān; al-Fāḳihī; al-Fāsī; Ibn Fahd; Ibn Manda; Ibn al-Mudjāwir; Ibn al-Nadjdjār; al-Samhūdī
voir aussi al-Diyārbakrī

population   → TRIBUS.PÉNINSULE ARABIQUE
toponymes
   anciens   Badr; al-Ḏjār; Fadak; al-Ḥidjr; al-Ḥudaybiya; Ḳurḥ; Madyan Shuʿayb; al-Rabaḏha
      voir aussi Fāʾw
   actuels
      districts   al-Aflāḏj; al-Ḏjawf; al-Ḳaṣīm; al-Khardj
      îles   Farasān
      oasis   al-Dirʿiyya; Dūmat al-Ḏjandal; al-Ḥasā; al-Khurma
      régions   ʿAsīr; ʿAwlaḳī; Bayḥān; al-Ḥāḏina; Ḥaly; al-Ḥawṭa; al-Ḥidjāz; Ḳurayyāt al-Milḥ; Naḏjd; Nafūd; Raʾs (al-)Tannūra; al-Rubʿ al-Khālī
      villes   Abhā; Abḳayḳ; Abū ʿArīsh; Burayda; al-Dammām; al-Ḏjawf; Ḏjayzān; al-Ḏjubayl; al-Ḏjubayla; Ḏjudda; Fakhkh; Ghāmid; Ḥāyil; al-Hufūf; Ḥuraymilā; Ḳarya al-Suflā; Ḳarya al-ʿUlyā; al-Ḳaṣāb; al-Ḳaṭīf; Khamīs Mushayṭ; Khaybar; al-Khubar; al-Ḳunfudha; al-Madīna; Makka; Minā; al-Mubarraz; Naḏjrān; Rābigh; al-Riyāḍ; [au Suppl.] Fayd
         voir aussi (Ḏjazīrat) al-ʿArab; al-ʿĀriḍ; Bīsha; Ḍariyya

ARCHÉOLOGIE
   et → ARCHITECTURE.RÉGIONS; ÉPIGRAPHIE; *et l'entrée Toponymes sous les pays individuels*
   archéologues turques   ʿOthmān Ḥamdī

ARCHITECTURE   **Architecture**; Bināʾ
   voir aussi Kitābāt; *et* → MILITAIRES
architectes   Ḳāsim Agha; Khayr al-Dīn; Sinān
décorative   Fusayfisāʾ; Kāshī; Khaṭṭ; Parčīn-kārī
matériaux   Ḏjiṣṣ; Labin
      voir aussi Bināʾ
monuments
   aqueducs   Ḳanṭara.5 et 6
      voir aussi Faḳīr; Sinān
   bains   **Ḥammām**; Ḥammām al-Ṣarakh
   barrages   **Band**
      voir aussi Dizfūl; Sāwa.2.I; Shushtar; [au Suppl.] Abū Sinbil; *et* → HYDROLOGIE
   débits d'eau   **Sabīl**.2
      fontaines   Shadirwān
   églises   → CHRISTIANISME
   forteresses   Burḏj; Ḥiṣār; **Ḥiṣn**; Ḳaṣaba; Sūr
      voir aussi Bāb.2; al-Ḳalʿa; Ribāṭ

forteresses individuelles Abū Safyān; Āgra; Alamūt.I; Alindjaḳ; ʿAmādiya; Anadolu Ḥiṣārî; Anamur; Anapa; Asīrgarh; Atak; al-ʿAwāṣim; Bāb al-Abwāb; Bālā Ḥiṣār; Balāṭunus; Barzūya; Baynūn; Bhakkar; Čandērī; Čirmen; al-Dārūm; Djaʿbar; al-Djarbāʾ; Gaban; Gāwilgaṙh; Ghumdān; Gök Tepe; Golkonḍā; Ḥadjar al-Nasr; Hānsī; Ḥarrān.II.a; Ḥiṣn al-Akrād; Ḥiṣn Kayfā; Iṣṭakhr; Kakhtā; Ḳalʿat Nadjm; Ḳalʿat al-Shaḳīf; Ḳalāwdhiya; Ḳalʿe-i Sefīd; Ḳandahār; Kanizsa; al-Karak; Kawkab; Kharāna; Khartpert; Khērla; Khotin; Khunāṣira; Kilāt-i Nādirī; Ḳoron; Ḳoyul Ḥiṣār; Lanbasar; Lüleburgaz; Mānḍū; Manōhar; al-Marḳab; Muḍgal; Narnālā; Parendā; al-Rāwandān; Rōhtās; Rūm Ḳalʿesi; Rūmeli Ḥiṣārî; Ṣahyūn; Shalbaṭarra; Softa; al-Ṣubayba; [au Suppl.] Bādiya; Bubashtru; al-Dīkdān; Firrīm

voir aussi Ashīr; Bahmanides; Bīdar; Dawlatābād; Diyār Bakr; Ḥimṣ; Kawkabān.II; Khursābād; Maḥall; Māhūr

jardins **Būstān**; Ḥaʾir

voir aussi Bostāndjî; Gharnāṭa.B; Ḥawḍ; Māʾ.XI; Srīnagar.2; *et* → Flore; Littérature.poésie.de la nature

mausolées → Architecture.monuments.tombeaux

monastères → Christianisme.couvents

mosquées Ḥawḍ; Külliyye; Manāra; **Masdjid**; Miḥrāb; Minbar

voir aussi ʿAnaza; Bāb.1; Bahw; Balāṭ; Dikka; Khaṭīb; Muṣallā.2

mosquées individuelles Aya Sofya; al-Azhar; Ḥarrān.II.b; Ḥusaynī Dālān; Kaʿba; al-Ḳarawiyyīn; Ḳubbat al-Ṣakhra; Ḳuṭb Mīnār; al-Masdjid al-Aḳṣā; al-Masdjid al-Ḥarām

voir aussi Anḳara; Architecture; Bahmanides; Dhār; Djām; Edirne; Ḥamāt; Ḥimṣ; Kāẓimayn; Ḳazwīn; Maʿarrat al-Nuʿmān; Makka.IV; Sinān

obélisques **Misalla**

palais **Sarāy**

voir aussi Balāṭ

palais individuels Čirāghān; Ḳaṣr al-Ḥayr al-Gharbī; Ḳaṣr al-Ḥayr al-Sharḳī; Kayḳubādiyya; Khirbat al-Mafdjar; Khirbat al-Minya; Ḳubādābād; Maḥall; al-Mushattā; [au Suppl.] Djabal Says

voir aussi Gharnāṭa.B; Khirbat al-Bayḍāʾ; Ḳubbat al-Hawāʾ; Lashkar-i Bāzār

pavillons Köshk

phares **Manār**; al-Nāẓūr

ponts **Djisr**; Djisr Banāt Yaʿḳūb; Djisr al-Ḥadīd; Djisr al-Shughr

voir aussi Dizfūl; Ḳanṭara; Sayḥān

portes **Bāb**; Bāb-i Humāyūn; Ḥarrān.II.d

puits Bāʾolī; **Biʾr**; Biʾr Maymūn

voir aussi Ḥawḍ
tombeaux **Ḳabr**; **Ḳubba**; **Maḳbara**; Mas͟hhad
voir aussi Mut͟hamman
constructions individuelles Baḳīʿ al-G͟harḳad; Golkonḍā; Ḥarrān.II.c; Maklī; Nafīsa; Rādkān; Sahsarām
voir aussi Abarḳūh; Abū Ayyūb al-Anṣārī; Abū Madyan; Āgra; Aḥmad al-Badawī; Aḥmad Yasawī; Bahmanides; Barīd S͟hāhides; D͟jahāngīr; G͟hāzī Miyān; Gunbad͟h-i Ḳābūs; Ḥimṣ; Imāmzāda; Karak Nūḥ; Karbalāʾ; Ḳazwīn; al-K͟halīl; Ḳubbat al-Hawāʾ; Maʿarrat al-Nuʿmān; al-Madīna; Sulṭāniyya.2
régions
Afghanistan et le sous-continent indien Āgra; Bahmanides; Barīd S͟hāhides; Bharōč; Bīdar; Bīd͟jāpūr; Bihār; Čāmpānēr; Dawlatābād; Dihlī.II; D͟jūnāgaṛh; G͟haznawides; G͟hūrides; Golkonḍā; Hampī; Hānsī; Ḥaydarābād; Hind.VII; Ḥusaynī Dālān; Ḳuṭb Mīnār; Lāhawr; Lak͟hnaw; Maḥall; Mahisur; Māndū.2; Mug͟hals.VII; Multān.2; Nāgawr; Sind.4; Srīnagar.2
voir aussi Burd͟j.3; Būstān.II; Imām-bārā; Las͟hkar-i Bāzār; Māʾ.XI; Maḳbara.V; Maklī; Manāra.II; Masd͟jid.II; Miḥrāb; Minbar.III; Miẓalla.5; Mut͟hamman; Parčīn-kārī; Pīs͟hṭāḳ
Afrique → AFRIQUE; *pour l'architecture d'Afrique du Nord, voir ci-dessous*
Afrique du Nord Fās; Fāṭimides.L'art fāṭimide; Ḥiṣn.I; Ḳalʿat Banī Ḥammād; al-Ḳarawiyyīn
voir aussi ʿAnaza; Bid͟jāya; Miḥrāb
Andalousie al-Andalus.IX; Burd͟j.II; G͟harnāṭa; Is͟hbīliya; Ḳurṭuba; Naṣrides.B
voir aussi al-Nāẓūr
Asie centrale Buk͟hārā; Ḥiṣn.III; Īlk͟hāns; Samarḳand.2
voir aussi Miḥrāb
Asie du Sud-Est Ḥiṣn.IV; Indonésie.V; Masd͟jid.III-V
Croissant fertile Bag͟hdād; Dimas͟hḳ; Ḥarrān.II; Ḥimṣ; ʿIrāḳ.VII; Ḳubbat al-Ṣak͟hra; al-Ḳuds; Maʿarrat al-Nuʿmān; al-Marḳab; al-Masd͟jid al-Aḳṣā; al-Raḳḳa; [au Suppl.] Bādiya; Dār al-Ḥadīt͟h.I
voir aussi Ḳaṣr al-Ḥayr al-G͟harbī; Ḳaṣr al-Ḥayr al-S͟harḳī; K͟hirbat al-Mafd͟jar; Miḥrāb; al-Rāwandān
Égypte Abū l-Hawl; al-Azhar; Haram; al-Ḳāhira; Mas͟hrabiyya.1; Nafīsa
voir aussi Miḥrāb; Misalla; Miṣr; Saʿīd al-Suʿadāʾ; [au Suppl.] Abū Sinbil
Iran Ḥisn.II; Iṣfahān.II; Iṣṭak͟hr; Ḳazwīn; K͟hursābād; Mas͟hrabiyya.2; Rādkān; al-Rayy.2; Ṣafawides.V; Sald͟jūḳides.VI; Sāmānides.2(b); Sulṭāniyya.2
voir aussi Ḳaṣr-i S͟hīrīn; Miḥrāb; Ribāṭ-i S͟haraf
Péninsule arabique al-Ḥid͟jr; Kaʿba; al-Masd͟jid al-Ḥarām

voir aussi Makka.IV; Ṣanʿāʾ
Turquie Adana; Anḳara; Aya Sofya; Diwrīgī; Diyār Bakr; Edirne; Ḥarrān.II; Ḥiṣn Kayfā; Istanbul; Konya.II; Lāranda; ʿOthmānli̊.V
voir aussi Ḳapli̊dja; Ḳāsim Agha; Khayr al-Dīn; Köshk; Miḥrāb; Rūm Ḳalʿesi; Sinān
termes ʿAmūd; ʿAnaza; Bahw; Balāṭ; Īwān; Muḳarbaṣ; Muḳarnas; Muthamman; Pīshṭāḳ; Riwāḳ; Sarāy; Sardāb; Shadirwān
urbaine Dār; Funduḳ; Ḥammām; Īwān; Ḳaysāriyya; Khān.II; Madrasa.III; Masdjid; Muṣallā.2; Rabʿ; Selāmli̊ḳ; Shāriʿ; Sūḳ; Sūr
voir aussi Kanīsa; Sarāy; *et* → SÉDENTARISATION
ventilation Mirwaḥa; [au Suppl.] Bādgīr
voir aussi Khaysh

ARMÉNIE **Armīniya**; Rewān; Shimshāṭ
et → CAUCASE

ART Arabesque; Fann; Fusayfisāʾ; Kāshī; Khaṭṭ; Khazaf; Kitābāt; Lawn; Maʿdin.IV; Parčīn-kārī; Rasm
voir aussi Architecture; Billawr; Dhahab; Fiḍḍa; ʿIlm al-Djamāl; Khātam; Muhr; Ṣūra; *et* → ANIMAUX.ET L'ART; ARCHITECTURE
artisanat Ḳalamkārī; [au Suppl.] Bisaṭ; Dawāt
voir aussi Ḥalfāʾ
calligraphie **Khaṭṭ**
voir aussi ʿAlī; Inal; Ḳum(m)ī; Muraḳḳaʿ; Nuskha; *et* → ÉCRITURE
calligraphes ʿAlī Riḍā-i ʿAbbāsī; Ḥamza al-Ḥarrānī; Ibn al-Bawwāb; Ibn Muḳla; Muḥammad Ḥusayn Tabrīzī; Müstaḳīm-zāde
céramique → ART.POTERIE
décoratif ʿĀdj; al-Asad; Djiṣṣ; Fahd; Ḥayawān.VI; Hilāl.II; Īlkhāns; al-Ḳamar.II; Mashrabiyya; Parčīn-kārī; Shams.3
voir aussi Kāshī; Maʿdin.IV
découpage de silhouettes Fakhrī
dessin **Rasm**
métal Bīdar; Īlkhāns; Maʿdin.IV; ʿOthmānli̊.VII.b; Sāmānides.2(a); [au Suppl.] Ibrīḳ
mosaïque **Fusayfisāʾ**; Kāshī
peinture
miniatures Īlkhāns; Mughals.IX; Naḳḳāsh-khāna; ʿOthmānli̊.VIII
voir aussi Fīl; Kalīla wa-Dimna.16; Māndū.3; Miʿrādj.V; al-Mīzān.III; Muraḳḳaʿ; Rustam.2; Sāḳī.3; [au Suppl.] Djawhar; *et* → ANIMAUX.ET L'ART; ART.DESSIN
miniaturistes Bihzād; Manṣūr; Maṭrāḳči̊; Naḳḳāsh Ḥasan (Pasha); Riḍā ʿAbbāsī; Riḍāʾī; Siyāh-ḳalem

voir aussi ʿAlī; Luḳmān b. Sayyid Ḥusayn
peinture moderne Djabrān Khalīl Djabrān; ʿOthmān Ḥamdī; Sipihrī; [au Suppl.] Dinet; Eyyūboghlu, Bedrī
et → ANIMAUX.ET L'ART
plaques **Kāshī**
poterie Anadolu.III.6; al-Andalus.IX; **Fakhkhār**; Īlkhāns; Iznīḳ; Ḳallala; **Khazaf**; Minā'ī; ʿOthmānli̊.VII.a; Sāmānides.2(a); Ṣīnī
régional et d'époque al-Andalus.IX; Berbères.VI; Fāṭimides.L'art fāṭimide; Īlkhāns; ʿIrāḳ.VII; Mughals.VIII et IX; ʿOthmānli̊.VII; Saldjūḳides.VI; Sāmānides.2(a)
tapisserie ʿOthmānli̊.VI; Sadjdjāda.2; [au Suppl.] **Bisāṭ**
voir aussi Karkaddan; Mafrūshāt; Mifrash; Mīlās
textiles Anadolu.III.6; al-Andalus.IX; al-Bahnasā; Bursa; Dabīḳ; Ḥarīr; Īlkhāns; Ḳumāsh; Mughals.VII; ʿOthmānli̊.VI; al-Rayy.2; Sāmānides.2(a); [au Suppl.] Ḥā'ik
voir aussi Ḳalamkārī; Ḳaṣab; Kattān; Ḳurḳūb; Mandīl; al-Nassādj; *et* → VÊTEMENTS
verre Ḳily; ʿOthmānli̊.VII.d; Sāmānides.2(a)

ASCÉTISME Bakkā'; Malāmatiyya
voir aussi Khalwa; Manāḳib; [au Suppl.] Asad b. Mūsā
pour les ascètes → MYSTICISME.MYSTIQUES; SAINT

ASIE Almali̊gh; Baikal
voir aussi Baraba; Mogholistān
Centrale → ASIE CENTRALE
du Sud Birmanie; Ceylan; Hind; Laquedives; Maldives; Maurice; Minicoy; Népal; Nicobar; Seychelles
voir aussi Ruhmī
pour les pays individuels → BANGLADESH; BIRMANIE; INDE; PAKISTAN; SRI LANKA
Eurasie → EUROPE
Occidentale Čam; Djāwī; Indochine; Indonésie; Ḳimār; (Péninsule) Malaise; Malaisie; Patani; Philippines; al-Shīlā; al-Ṣīn; Singapour; [au Suppl.] Brunei
voir aussi Kitābāt.VIII; Ṣanf; Shāh Bandar.2; [au Suppl.] Démographie.VIII; *et* → ARCHITECTURE.RÉGIONS.ASIE DU SUD-EST; DROIT.EN ASIE DU SUD-EST; ONOMASTIQUE.TITRES
pour les pays individuels → CHINE; INDONÉSIE; MALAISIE; MONGOLIE; THAÏLANDE

ASIE CENTRALE Badakhshān; Čaghāniyān; Khwārazm; **Mā warā' al-Nahr**; Mogholistān *voir aussi* Hayāṭila; Ismāʿīl b. Aḥmad; Ḳarā Khiṭāy; Ḳazaḳ; Nīzak, Ṭarkhān; [au Suppl.] Atalîḳ; Djulfā.II; *et* → DYNASTIES.MONGOLES; MONGOLIE; ONOMASTIQUE

architecture → ARCHITECTURE.RÉGIONS

belles-lettres → LITTÉRATURE.DRAME *et* POÉSIE.TURQUE.EN TURC ORIENTAL

géographie physique

déserts Ḳaraḳum; Ḳîzîl-ḳum

eaux Aḳ Ṣu; Amū Daryā; Aral; Atrek; Baḥr al-Khazar; Balkhash; Čaghān-rūd; Ču; Ili; İssîk-kul; Ḳarā-köl; Murghāb; Sîr Daryā

voir aussi Su

montagnes Ala Dagh; Altaï; Balkhān; Pamir

voir aussi Čopan-ata

historiens ʿAbd al-Karīm Bukhārī

voir aussi Ḥaydar b. ʿAlī

mysticisme → MYSTICISME; SAINT

population Balūč; Čāwdors (*et* [au Suppl.] Čawdor); Emreli; Gagauz; Ḳara-ḳalpaḳ; Khaladj; Ḳungrāt; Kurama; Özbeg; [au Suppl.] Démographie.VI

voir aussi Altaï; al-ʿArab.III.Appendice; Ghalča; Ghuzz; Ḳarluḳ; Ḳazaḳ; Ḳipčaḳ; Ḳîrgîz; Ḳumān; Kumīdjīs; Ḳun; [au Suppl.] Ersarî

toponymes

anciens Abaskūn; Abīward; Akhsīkath; Ardjīsh; Balāsāghūn; Banākat; Fārāb; Firabr; Gurgandj; Kāth; Ḳayalîḳ; Marw al-Rūdh; Marw al-Shāhidjān; Mashhad-i Miṣriyān; Nakhshab; Pishpek; Sayrām; Shūmān; Sîghnāḳ; al-Ṣughd; Sūyāb; [au Suppl.] Dandānḳān; Djand; Īlāḳ

actuels

districts Atek; Ḳaratigin; Shughnān

voir aussi Ākhāl Tekke

régions Farghānā; Khwārazm; Khuttalān; Labāb; Mangîshlak; [au Suppl.] Dasht-i Ḳîpčaḳ

villes Aḳ Masdjid.2; Alma Ata; Āmul.2; Andidjān; ʿAshḳābād; Awliyā Ata; Bayram ʿAlī; Bukhārā; Čimkent; Djalālābād; Ghudjduwān; Hazārasp; Ḥiṣār; Kash; Khīwa; Khoḳand; Khudjand(a); Kish; Ḳubādhiyān; Marghīnān; Mayhana; Ordūbād; Özkend; Pandjdih; Samarḳand

Union Soviétique ancienne al-ʿArab.III.Appendice; Basmačis; Djarīda.IV; Fiṭrat; Ḥizb.V; Khodjaev; Ṣadr al-Dīn ʿAynī; [au Suppl.] Démographie.VI

et → *l'entrée Toponymes dans cette rubrique*

ASSYRIE Khursābād; Nimrūd; Nīnawā.1; [au Suppl.] Athūr

ASTROLOGIE Ikhtiyārāt; Ḳaws Ḳuzaḥ; al-Kayd; Ḳirān; Minṭaḳat al-Burūdj; Munadjdjim; **Nudjūm (Aḥkām al-)**

voir aussi Khaṭṭ
astrologues Abū Maʿshar al-Balkhī; al-Bīrūnī; Ibn Abī l-Ridjāl, Abū l-Ḥasan; Ibn al-Khaṣīb, Abū Bakr; al-Ḳabīṣī; al-Khayyāṭ, Abū ʿAlī; Māshāʾ Allāh
voir aussi Baṭlamiyūs; *et* → ASTRONOMIE; DIVINATION
termes al-Djawzahar; Ḥadd; Ḳaṭʿ; Muthallath; Saʿd wa-Naḥs (*et* al-Saʿdān[i]; Shaḳāwa); al-Sahm.1.b

ASTRONOMIE Anwāʾ; Asṭurlāb; Falak; Hayʾa; **ʿIlm al-Hayʾa**; al-Ḳamar.I; al-Kayd; Kusūf; Ḳuṭb; al-Madd wa-l-Djazr; al-Madjarra; al-Manāzil; Minṭaḳat al-Burūdj; al-Nudjūm
voir aussi Djughrāfiyā; Ḳibla.II; al-Ḳubba; Kura; Makka.IV; Mīḳāt.2; Mizwala
astronomes ʿAbd al-Raḥmān al-Ṣūfī; Abū l-Ṣalt; ʿAlī al-Ḳūshdjī; al-Badīʿ al-Asṭurlābī; al-Battānī; al-Bīrūnī; al-Biṭrūdjī; Djābir b. Aflaḥ; al-Djaghmīnī; al-Farghānī; Ḥabash al-Ḥāsib al-Marwazī; Ibn Amādjūr; Ibn al-Bannāʾ al-Marrākushī; Ibn ʿIrāḳ; Ibn al-Ṣaffār; Ibn al-Samḥ; Ibn Yūnus; al-Kāshī; al-Kh^{w}ārazmī, Abū Djaʿfar; al-Khāzin; al-Khazīnī; al-Khudjandī; Kushiyār; Ḳuṭb al-Dīn Shīrāzī; al-Madjrīṭī; al-Mārdīnī; al-Marrākushī; Muḥammad b. ʿĪsā b. Aḥmad al-Māhānī; Muḥammad b. ʿUmar; al-Nayrīzī; al-Shayzarī; [au Suppl.] ʿAbd al-Salām b. Muḥammad
voir aussi Baṭlamiyūs; al-Falakī; Falakī Shirwānī; Ibn al-Haytham; Ḳusṭā b. Lūḳā; Sindhind; [au Suppl.] Ibn al-Adjdābī; *et* → ASTROLOGIE
corps célestes
comètes **al-Nudjūm**.III.b
étoiles et constellations ʿAḳrab; ʿAnāḳ; al-Asad; Dadjādja; Fard; Kalb; Ḳird; Mahāt; Minṭaḳat al-Burūdj; Muthallath; Naʿām; Nasr; **al-Nudjūm**; Radīf.1; al-Sahm.1.c; Samak.9; Saraṭān.VI; Shams.2; al-Shiʿrā; [au Suppl.] Arnab; Ghanam
voir aussi al-Kayd; Saʿd wa-Naḥs (*et* al-Saʿdān[i]; Shaḳāwa); al-Sāḳ; Sulaḥfā
planètes al-Ḳamar.I; al-Mirrīkh; al-Mushtarī; **al-Nudjūm**.II
voir aussi Minṭaḳat al-Burūdj; Ruʾyat al-Hilāl; al-Saʿdān[i]
observatoire Marṣad
termes al-Djawzahar; Istiḳbāl; al-Maṭāliʿ; al-Maṭlaʿ; Mayl; Muḳābala.I; Muḳanṭarāt; Niṣf al-Nahār; Radīf.1; Rubʿ; Ruʾyat al-Hilāl; al-Sāḳ; al-Samt; Shakkāziyya

AUMÔNES Khayr; **Ṣadaḳa**

AUTRICHE Beč; **Nemče**
voir aussi Muslimūn.II.2

B

BĀBISME → SECTES

BAHĀʾĪS Bāb; Bābīs; Bahāʾ Allāh; **Bahāʾīs**; Mas<u>h</u>riḳ al-Ad<u>h</u>kār; Naḳḍ al-Mīt<u>h</u>āḳ; <u>Sh</u>awḳī Efendi Rabbānī
voir aussi Lawḥ; Maẓhar; [au Suppl.] Anṣārī

BAHRAIN **al-Baḥrayn**; āl-<u>Kh</u>alīfa; Ma<u>dj</u>lis.IV.A.10; Maḥkama.IV.9
voir aussi Ḳarmaṭī
toponymes al-Manāma; al-Muḥarraḳ
voir aussi al-Mu<u>sh</u>aḳḳar

BALKANS **Balḳan**; **Rumeli**; al-Ṣaḳāliba
et → EUROPE

BANGLADESH **Bangāla**; Ma<u>dj</u>lis.IV.C
voir aussi Bengali; Na<u>dh</u>r al-Islām; Satya Pīr; [au Suppl.] <u>Dj</u>arīda.VII
littérature → LITTÉRATURE.EN D'AUTRES LANGUES
toponymes Bāḳargan<u>dj</u>; Bangāla; Bōgrā; Chittagong; Ḍhākā; Dīna<u>dj</u>pur; <u>Dj</u>assawr; Farīdpur; Sātgāʾon; Silhet; Sundarban
voir aussi Ruhmī; Sonārgāʾon

BANQUE Muḍāraba; Ribā.5; Sufta<u>dj</u>a
voir aussi <u>Dj</u>ahba<u>dh</u>; <u>Sh</u>arika

BASQUES **al-Ba<u>sh</u>kuni<u>sh</u>**
voir aussi Ibn <u>Gh</u>arsiya

BÉDOUINS **Badw**; Biʾr; Dawār; <u>Gh</u>anīma; <u>Gh</u>azw; al-Hi<u>dj</u>ar
voir aussi Liṣṣ; *et* → ARABIE SÉOUDITE; NOMADISME; TRIBUS.PÉNINSULE ARABIQUE
traités sur Rzewuski

BÉNIN Kandi; Kotonou; Kouandé

BERBÈRES **Berbères**; Judéo-berbère
voir aussi Ḥimāya.II.2; Imẓad; al-Ir<u>dj</u>ānī; Ḳallāla; Ḳiṣṣa.VIII; Leff; Libās.II; Lit<u>h</u>ām; Mafā<u>kh</u>ir al-Barbar; Ṣaff.3; <u>Sh</u>āwiya.1; Ṣufriyya.2; *et* → ALGÉRIE
droit coutumier ʿĀda.II; Ḳānūn.IV
dynasties ʿAbd al-Wādides; ʿAmmār; Marīnides; Midrār; al-Murābiṭūn; al-Muwaḥḥidūn; Razīn, Banū

langue → LANGUES.AFRO-ASIATIQUES
religion al-Baḏjalī; Berbères.III; Ḥā-Mīm; Ṣāliḥ b. Ṭarīf
résistance Berbères.I.c; al-Kāhina; Kusayla; Maysara
tribus al-Barānis; Barg̲h̲awāṭa; Birzāl; al-Butr; Ḏjazūla; G̲h̲āniya; G̲h̲ubrīnī; G̲h̲umāra; Glāwā; Gudāla; Ḥāḥā; Harg̲h̲a; Hawwāra; Hintāta; Ifog̲h̲as; Īfran; Iraten; Kutāma; Lamṭa; Lamtūna; Lawāta; Mag̲h̲īla; Mag̲h̲rāwa; Malzūza; Maṣmūda; Māssa; Matg̲h̲ara; Maṭmāṭa; Mazāta; Midyūna; Misrāta; al-Nafūsa; Nafza; Nafzāwa; Ṣanhāḏja; [au Suppl.] Awraba

BIBLE **Indjil**
   et → CHRISTIANISME; JUDAÏSME
personnages bibliques Ādam; ʿAmālīk̲; Ayyūb; Āzar; ʿAzāzīl; Balʿam; Bilḳīs; Binyāmīn; Buk̲h̲t-naṣ(ṣ)ar; Dāniyāl; Dāwūd; Ḏjabrāʾīl; Ḏjālūt; Firʿawn; Ḥābīl wa-Ḳābīl; Ḥām; Hāmān; Hārūn b. ʿImrān; Hārūt wa-Mārūt; Ḥawwāʾ; Ḥizḳīl; Ilyās; ʿImrān; Irmiyā; ʿĪsā; Isḥāḳ; Ismāʿīl; Kanʿān; Ḳārūn; Ḳiṭfīr; Kūs̲h̲; Lamak; Lazare; Lūṭ; Maryam; al-Masīḥ; Namrūd; Nūḥ; Rāḥīl; Sām.1; al-Sāmirī; Sāra; S̲h̲amsūn; S̲h̲amwīl; S̲h̲aʿyā; S̲h̲īth; Sulaymān b. Dāwūd
   voir aussi Ḏhū l-Kifl; al-Fayyūm; Hūd; Idrīs
toponymes bibliques Ṣihyawn
   voir aussi Ḏjūdī
traductions
   en arabe Fāris al-S̲h̲idyāḳ; Saʿadyā; [au Suppl.] al-Bustānī.2
      voir aussi ʿArabiyya.A.II.1; Judéo-arabe.III.B
   en persan Abū l-Faḍl ʿAllāmī
      voir aussi Judéo-persan.I.2

BIBLIOGRAPHIE **Bibliographie**; Fahrasa

BIJOUX [au Suppl.] **Djawhar**
   voir aussi K̲h̲ātam
perles et pierres précieuses ʿAḳīḳ; Durr; Kūh-i Nūr; Luʾluʾ; Marḏjān
   voir aussi Ḏhahab; Fiḍḍa; Ḥaḏjar; Kahrubā; Maʿdin.II

BIRMANIE Arakan; **Birmanie**; Mergui; Rangoun

BOTANIQUE Adwiya; al-ʿAs̲h̲s̲h̲āb; Nabāt
   et → AGRICULTURE; FLORE; MÉDECINE; PHARMACOLOGIE
botanistes Abū ʿUbayd al-Bakrī; al-Dīnawarī; Abū Ḥanīfa; Ibn al-Bayṭār; [au Suppl.] al-G̲h̲āfiḳī; Ibn al-Rūmiyya
   voir aussi Abū l-K̲h̲ayr al-Is̲h̲bīlī; Filāḥa; Nīḳūlāʾūs; al-Suwaydī

BULGARIE **Bulgarie**; Pomáks
   voir aussi Küčük Ḳaynarḏja; Muhāḏjir.2; Muslimūn.I.B.5

fleuves Merič

toponymes Burgas; Deli-Orman; Dobrudja; Filibe; Hezārg̲h̲rad; Küstendil; Newrokop; Nīkbūlī; ʿOt̲h̲mān Pazar; Plewna; Rusčuk; Selwi; S̲h̲umnu; Sofia

BYZANTINS Biṭrīḳ; Ḳayṣar; **Rūm**
> *voir aussi* Anadolu.III.1 et 2; Hiba.I; Iznīḳ; Ḳalāwd̲h̲iya; Ḳubrus; (al-) Ḳus-ṭanṭīniyya; al-Maṣṣīṣa; Muʾta; Nauplion; Saracens; *et* → PALESTINE; SYRIE; TURQUIE

alliés Djarādjima; D̲j̲arrāḥides; G̲h̲assān; al-Ḥārit̲h̲ b. Djabala; Kinda.1; Salīḥ; [au Suppl.] D̲j̲abala b. al-Ḥārit̲h̲
> *et* → TRIBUS

militaires Alay; Lamas-ṣū; Malāzgird.II; Naft.II; [au Suppl.] D̲h̲āt al-Ṣawārī
> *voir aussi* al-ʿAwāṣim; Cilicie; Ṣāʾifa.1; Sayf al-Dawla

C

CADEAUX **Hiba;** Ṣila.3
> *voir aussi* Bak̲h̲s̲h̲īs̲h̲; Nit̲h̲ār; Pīs̲h̲kas̲h̲; Ras̲h̲wa; *et* → PAIEMENTS

CALIFAT Ahl al-Ḥall wa-l-ʿAḳd; Bayʿa; Ḥādjib.I; Ḥarb.II; Hiba.I; Imāma; Ḳaḍīb; Kātib; **K̲h̲alifa**; Libās.I; Madjlis.I; Marāsim.1; Mawākib.I; S̲h̲ūrā.1
> *voir aussi* Amīr al-Muʾminīn; G̲h̲ulām.I; K̲h̲ilʿa.2; Laḳab.II; Māl al-Bayʿa; *et* → CÉRÉMONIES DE LA COUR

ʿAbbāsides (750-1258) **ʿAbbāsides**; Bag̲h̲dād; Dīwān.I; Ḥādjib.I; K̲h̲alīfa.I.B; Marāsim.1; Mawākib.I; Muṣadara.2; Musawwida; Naḳīb.1; Naḳīb al-As̲h̲rāf.1; Sāmarrāʾ
> *voir aussi* al-Abnāʾ.3; ʿAlī b. ʿAbd Allāh b. al-ʿAbbās; ʿAlides; Architec-ture.I.3; Dāriba; Hās̲h̲imiyya, al-Hās̲h̲imiyya; Laḳab.II; Libās.I.D; Riḍā.2; al-S̲h̲uʿūbiyya; Sikka.2; *et* → DYNASTIES.PERSE

califes Abū l-ʿAbbās al-Saffāḥ; al-Amīn; al-Hādī ilā l-Ḥaḳḳ; Hārūn al-Ras̲h̲īd; al-Ḳādir bi-llāh; al-Ḳāhir bi-llāh; al-Ḳaʾim bi-Amr Allāh; al-Mahdī; al-Maʾmūn; al-Manṣūr; al-Muhtadī; al-Muḳtadī; al-Muḳtadir; al-Muktafī bi-llāh; al-Muktafī li-Amr Allāh; al-Muntaṣir; al-Mustaḍīʾ; al-Mustaʿīn (Iᵉʳ); al-Mustaʿīn (II); al-Mustakfī; al-Mustandjid (Iᵉʳ); al-Mustandjid (II); al-Mustanṣir (Iᵉʳ); al-Mustanṣir (II); al-Mustars̲h̲id; al-Mustaʿṣim bi-llāh; al-Mustaẓhir bi-llāh; al-Muʿtaḍid bi-llāh; al-Muʿtamid ʿalā llāh; al-Muʿtaṣim bi-llāh; al-Mutawakkil ʿalā llāh; al-Muʿtazz bi-llāh; al-Muṭīʿ li-llāh; al-Muttaḳī li-llāh; al-Nāṣir li-Dīn Allāh, Abū l-ʿAbbās; al-Rāḍī bi-llāh; al-Rās̲h̲id
> *voir aussi* ʿAbd Allāh b. ʿAlī; Būrān; al-K̲h̲ayzurān; Muḥammad b. ʿAlī b. ʿAbd Allāh; al-Muwaffaḳ; al-Ruṣāfa.2

vizirs Abū ʿAbd Allāh Yaʿḳūb; Abū Salāma al-Khallāl; Abū ʿUbayd Allāh; ʿAḍud al-Dīn; ʿAlī b. ʿĪsā; al-Barāmika.3; al-Barīdī; al-Djardjarāʾī.1-3; al-Faḍl b. Marwān; al-Faḍl b. al-Rabīʿ; al-Faḍl b. Sahl; al-Fayḍ b. Abī Ṣāliḥ; Ḥamīd b. al-ʿAbbās; Hibat Allāh b. Muḥammad; Ibn al-Alḳamī; Ibn al-Baladī; Ibn al-Furāt; Ibn Hubayra; Ibn Khāḳan.II et III; Ibn Makhlad; Ibn Muḳla; Ibn al-Muslima; Ibn al-Zayyāt; al-Iskāfī, Abū l-Faḍl; al-Iskāfī, Abū Isḥāḳ; Ismāʿīl b. Bulbul; al-Khaṣībī; al-Rabīʿ b. Yūnus; Rabīb al-Dawla; al-Rūdhrāwarī

voir aussi al-Djahshiyārī; Hilāl al-Ṣābiʾ; Khātam

secrétaires Aḥmad b. Abī Khālid; Aḥmad b. Yūsuf; ʿAmr b. Masʿada; al-Ḥasan b. Sahl; Ibn al-Djarrāḥ; Ibn Khāḳan.I et IV; Ibn al-Māshiṭa; al-Mūriyānī

historiens des al-Djahshiyārī; Ibn Abī l-Dam; Ibn Abī Ṭāhir Ṭayfūr; Ibn al-Djawzī; Ibn al-Naṭṭāḥ; Ibn al-Sāʿī; Ibn al-Ṭiḳṭaḳā; al-Madāʾinī; Ṣābiʾ.3.4

autres personnages al-ʿAbbās b. ʿAmr; al-ʿAbbās b. al-Maʾmūn; al-ʿAbbās b. Muḥammad; ʿAbd Allāh b. ʿAlī; ʿAbd al-Djabbār b. ʿAbd al-Raḥmān; ʿAbd al-Malik b. Ṣāliḥ; Abū ʿAwn; ʿAlī al-Riḍā; Badjkam; Badr al-Kharshanī; Bughā al-Kabīr; Bughā al-Sharābī; Dulafides; al-Fatḥ b. Khāḳān; Harthama b. Aʿyan; al-Ḥasan b. Zayd b. al-Ḥasan; Ḥātim b. Harthama; Ḥumayd b. ʿAbd al-Ḥamīd; Ibn Abī l-Shawārib; Ibn Buhlūl; Ibn al-Djaṣṣāṣ.II; Ibn Ḥamdūn; Ibn Māhān; Ibn al-Mudabbir; Ibn al-Muʿtazz; Ibn Rāʾiḳ; Ibn Thawāba; Ibrāhīm b. ʿAbd Allāh; ʿĪsā b. Mūsā; ʿĪsā b. al-Shaykh; Ḳaḥṭaba; al-Ḳāsim b. ʿĪsā; Maʿn b. Zāʾida; al-Mubarḳaʿ; Muhallabides; Muḥammad b. ʿAbd Allāh (al-Nafs al-Zakiyya); Muḥammad b. Ṭughdj al-Ikhshīd; Muḥammad b. Yāḳūt; Muʾnis al-Faḥl; Muʾnis al-Muẓaffar; al-Muwaffaḳ; Naṣr b. Shabath; al-Nāṭiḳ bi-l-Ḥaḳḳ; al-Nūsharī; Rāfiʿ b. Harthama; Rāfiʿ b. al-Layth b. Naṣr b. Sayyār; al-Rāwandiyya; Rawḥ b. Ḥātim; Sādjides; Ṣāliḥ b. ʿAlī; al-Sarakhsī, Abū l-ʿAbbās; al-Sarī; Shabīb b. Shayba; Sulaymān b. ʿAlī b. ʿAbd Allāh; Sunbādh; [au Suppl.] Abū Manṣūr Ibn Yūsuf; Aytākh al-Turkī; Badr al-Muʿtaḍidī; al-Dāmaghānī.1 et 2; al-Ghiṭrīf b. ʿAṭāʾ; Ibn Dirham

Fāṭimides (909-1171) Dīwān.I et II.II; **Fāṭimides**; Ḥādjib.IV; Ḥidjāb.II; al-Ḳāhira; Khalīfa.I.D; Libās.I.E; Marāsim.1; Mawākib.I

voir aussi Laḳab.II; Ṣāḥib al-Bāb; Sitr

califes Abū ʿAbd Allāh al-Shīʿī; al-ʿĀḍid li-Dīni llāh; al-Āmir; al-ʿAzīz bi-llāh; al-Ḥāfiẓ; al-Ḥākim bi-Amr Allāh; al-Ḳāʾim bi-Amr Allāh; al-Mahdī ʿUbayd Allāh; al-Manṣūr bi-llāh; al-Muʿizz li-Dīn Allāh; al-Mustaʿlī bi-llāh; al-Mustanṣir (Ier)

vizirs ʿAbbās b. Abī l-Futūḥ; al-ʿĀdil b. al-Salār; al-Afḍal b. Badr al-Djamālī; al-Afḍal (Kutayfāt); Badr al-Djamālī; Bahrām; al-Baṭāʾiḥī; Ḍirghām; Djabr b. al-Ḳāsim; al-Djardjarāʾī.4; Ibn Killis; Ibn Maṣāl; Ruzzīk Ibn

Ṭalāʾiʿ; Shāwar; Shīrkūh; [au Suppl.] Ibn Khalaf.II

secrétaires Ibn Mammātī; Ibn al-Ṣayrafī; [au Suppl.] Ibn Khalaf, Abū l-Ḥasan

historiens des Ibn al-Ṭuwayr; al-Maḳrīzī; al-Musabbiḥī

voir aussi Djawdhar

autres personnages Abū Yazīd al-Nukkārī; Bardjawān; Djawdhar; Djawhar al-Ṣiḳillī; Khalaf b. Mulāʿib; al-Kirmānī; Nizār b. al-Mustanṣir; al-Nuʿmān; Sitt al-Mulk

voir aussi al-Farghānī

les Califes orthodoxes (632-661) Khalīfa.I.A; Shūrā.1

califes Abū Bakr; ʿAlī b. Abī Ṭālib

voir aussi Ḥarūrāʾ; Ibn Muldjam; Khalīfa.I.A; al-Saḳīfa; al-Ṣiddīḳ

autres personnages Abān b. ʿUthmān; ʿAbd Allāh b. al-ʿAbbās; ʿAbd Allāh b. ʿĀmir; ʿAbd Allāh b. Saʿd; ʿAbd Allāh b. Salām; ʿAbd Allāh b. Wahb; ʿAbd al-Raḥman b. ʿAwf; ʿAbd al-Raḥmān b. Samura; Abū l-Aswad al-Duʾalī; Abū Ayyūb al-Anṣārī; Abū l-Dunyā; Abū ʿUbayda al-Djarrāḥ; al-Aḥnaf b. Ḳays; al-Aḳraʿ b. Ḥābis; ʿAmr b. al-ʿĀṣ; al-Ashʿarī, Abū Mūsā; al-Ashʿath; al-Ashtar; al-Bāhilī; Ḥabīb b. Maslama; al-Ḳaʿḳāʿ b. ʿAmr; Khālid b. al-Walīd; Muḥammad b. Abī Bakr; al-Muthannā b. Ḥāritha; Saʿīd b. al-ʿĀṣ; Sulaymān b. Ṣurad

et → MUḤAMMAD, LE PROPHÈTE.COMPAGNONS DU PROPHÈTE *et* FAMILLE DU PROPHÈTE

Umayyades (661-750) Dimashḳ; Dīwān.I; Hādjib.I; Khalīfa.I.A; Mawlā.II.2; [au Suppl.] Bādiya

voir aussi Architecture.I.2; Ḳays ʿAylān; Libās.I.D; Marwānides; Sufyānides; *et* → DYNASTIES.ESPAGNE ET AFRIQUE DU NORD

califes ʿAbd al-Malik b. Marwān; Hishām; Marwān Ier b. al-Ḥakam; Marwān II; Muʿāwiya Ier; Muʿāwiya II; Sulaymān b. ʿAbd al-Malik

voir aussi Būṣīr; al-Ruṣāfa.3; al-Shaʾm.2(a)

historiens des ʿAwāna b. al-Ḥakam; al-Azdī

autres personnages ʿAbbād b. Ziyād; al-ʿAbbās b. al-Walīd; ʿAbd Allāh b. ʿAbd al-Malik; ʿAbd Allāh b. Hammām; ʿAbd Allāh b. Ḥanẓala; ʿAbd Allāh b. Khāzim; ʿAbd Allāh b. Muṭīʿ; ʿAbd Allāh b. al-Zubayr; ʿAbd al-ʿAzīz b. al-Ḥadjdjādj; ʿAbd al-ʿAzīz b. Marwān; ʿAbd al-ʿAzīz b. al-Walīd; ʿAbd al-Raḥmān b. Khālid b. al-Walīd; ʿAmr b. Saʿīd; Asad b. ʿAbd Allāh; al-Aṣamm.1; Baldj; Bishr b. Marwān; Bishr b. al-Walīd; Bukayr b. Māhān; Bukayr b. Wishāḥ; Busr b. Abī Arṭāt; al-Ḍaḥḥāḳ b. Ḳays al-Fihrī; al-Djarrāḥ b. ʿAbd Allāh; al-Djunayd b. ʿAbd Allāh; al-Ḥadjdjādj b. Yūsuf; Ḥanẓala b. Ṣafwān; al-Ḥārith b. Suraydj; Ḥassān b. Mālik; Ḥassān b. al-Nuʿmān al-Ghassānī; al-Ḥurr b. Yazīd; al-Ḥusayn b. Numayr; Ibn al-Ashʿath; Ibn al-Ḥaḍramī; Ibn Hubayra; Khālid al-Ḳasrī; Khālid b. Yazīd; Kulthūm b. ʿIyāḍ; Ḳurra b. Sharīk; Ḳutayba b. Muslim;

Maʿn b. Zāʾida; Masāmiʿa; Maslama b. ʿAbd al-Malik b. Marwān; Maymūn b. Mihrān; Muʿāwiya b. Hishām; al-Mughīra b. Shuʿba; Muhallabides; Muḥammad b. al-Ḳāsim; Muslim b. ʿUḳba; Naṣr b. Sayyār; al-Nuʿmān b. Bashīr; Rawḥ b. Zinbāʿ; Salm b. Ziyād b. Abīhi; Shabīb b. Yazīd; Sulaymān b. Kathīr al-Khuzāʿī; [au Suppl.] ʿAdī b. Arṭāt
voir aussi al-Baṭṭāl; Iyās b. Muʿāwiya
traités sur al-Ḳalḳashandī.I

CARTOGRAPHIE Kharīṭa
et → GÉOGRAPHIE; NAVIGATION
cartographes al-Falakī; Ibn Sarābiyūn; Meḥmed Reʾīs; Pīrī Reʾīs

CAUCASE Ādharbaydjān.II; Armīniya; Dāghistān; **al-Ḳabḳ**; al-Kurdj
voir aussi Djarīda.IV; Ḳarā Bāgh; Muhādjir.2; Shīrwān Shāh
géographie physique
eaux Alindjaḳ; Gökče-tengiz; Ḳarā Deniz; Ḳizil-üzen; Ḳuban; Kur; al-Rass; Safīd Rūd
montagnes al-Ḳabḳ
population Abkhāz.2; Alān; Andi; Arči; Avares; Balkar; Čečens; Čerkesses; Darghins; Dido; Ingush; Kabard; Ḳapuča; Ḳaračay; Ḳarata; Ḳaytaḳ; Khaput; Khemshin; Khinalug; Khunzal; Khvarshi; Ḳriz; Ḳubači; Kwanadi; Laḳ; Laz; Lezgh; Noghay; Ossètes; Rūs; Rutul; [au Suppl.] Démographie.VI
voir aussi Ḳumuḳ
résistance à la conquête russe Ḥamza Beg; Shāmil
voir aussi Ḥizb.IV
toponymes
anciens Alindjaḳ; Arrān; Bādjarwān.1; Balandjar; Dwin; Saray; Shammākha; Shimshāṭ; Shīrwān; Shīz
actuels Akhiskha; Astrakhān; Bāb al-Abwāb; Bākū; Bardhaʿa; Batumi; Derbend; Gandja; Ḳubba; Lankoran; Makhač-ḳalʿe; Nakhčiwān; Shakkī; [au Suppl.] Djulfā.I

CÉRÉMONIES DE LA COUR **Marāsim**; Mawākib
voir aussi Hiba; Khilʿa; Miẓalla; Naḳḳāra-khāna; Nithār; Sitr; *et* → MONARCHIE.INSIGNE ROYAL

CHARMES Afsūn; Ḥidjāb.IV; Kabid.4; Māshāʾ Allāh; [au Suppl.] Budūḥ
voir aussi Kahrubā; Ḳarwasha; *et* → MAGIE

CHASSE **Ṣayd**
voir aussi Kurdes et Kurdistān.IVC.5; Samak; Shikārī; *et* → ANIMAUX; FAUCONNERIE

animaux sauvages Fahd; Khinzīr; Mahāt; Naʿām; Namir et Nimr; Salūḳī; [au Suppl] Ḍabuʿ
traités sur Kushādjim; [au Suppl.] Ibn Manglī
voir aussi al-Shamardal

CHĀTIMENT (DIVIN) **ʿAdhāb**; ʿAdhāb al-Ḳabr; Djazāʾ; Falaḳa; Ḥadd; Maskh; Ṣalb
voir aussi ʿAbd.3.i; ʿĀd; Kaffāra; Ḳiyāma; Munkar wa-Nakīr; Murtadd; Siyāsa.1; *et* → DROIT

CHIITES ʿAbd Allāh b. Sabaʾ; ʿAlides; Ghulāt; Imāma; Ismāʿīliyya; Ithnā ʿAshariyya; Sabʿiyya; **Shīʿa**
voir aussi Abū l-Sarāyā al-Shaybānī; ʿAlī b. Abī Ṭālib; ʿAlī Mardān; Madjlis.III; [au Suppl.] Batriyya; *et* → CHIITES.SECTES
branches Ismāʿīliyya; Ithnā ʿAshariyya; Ḳarmaṭī; Nizāriyya
voir aussi Hind.V.D; Imāma; Sabʿiyya; *et* → CHIITES.SECTES
Duodécimains Imāma; **Ithnā ʿAshariyya**; Mudjtahid.II; Mutawālī; al-Rāfiḍa
voir aussi Buwayhides; *et* → CHIITES.IMAMS
auteurs Ibn Bābawayh(i); al-Māmaḳānī; al-Shahīd al-Thānī
et → CHIITES.THÉOLOGIENS
Ismāʿīliyya ʿAbd Allāh b. Maymūn; Abū ʿAbd Allāh al-Shīʿī; Abū l-Khattāb al-Asadī; Allāh.III.1; (Djazīrat) al-ʿArab.VII; Bāb; Bāṭiniyya; Dāʿī; Daʿwa; Fāṭimides; Ḥaḳāʾiḳ; Hind.V.D; Ibn ʿAttāsh; Ikhwān al-Ṣafāʾ; Imāma; **Ismāʿīliyya**; Lanbasar; Madjlis.II; al-Mahdī ʿUbayd Allāh; Malāʾika.II; Manṣūr al-Yaman; Maymūn-diz; Sabʿiyya; Shahriyār b. al-Ḥasan; [au Suppl.] Dawr
voir aussi Ḥawwāʾ; Ikhlāṣ; Maṣyād; Sabʿ; Salamiyya; Ṣulayḥides; *et* → CALIFAT.FĀṬIMIDES; CHIITES.IMAMS
auteurs Abū Ḥātim al-Rāzī; Abū Yaʿḳūb al-Sidjzī; al-Kirmānī; al-Muʾayyad fī l-Dīn; Nāṣir-i Khusraw; [au Suppl.] al-Bazdawī; Djaʿfar b. Manṣūr al-Yaman
et → MUSTAʿLITES-ṬAYYIBITES *et* NIZĀRITES *ci-dessous*
Mustaʿlites-Ṭayyibites Bohorās; al-Ḥāmidī; Luḳmāndjī; al-Makramī; Makramides; Muḥammad b. Ṭāhir al-Ḥārithī; Shaykh Ādam; Sulaymān b. Ḥasan; Sulaymānīs; [au Suppl.] ʿAlī b. Ḥanẓala; ʿAlī b. Muḥammad b. Djaʿfar; Amīndjī b. Djalāl; Ḥasan b. Nūḥ; Idrīs b. al-Ḥasan
voir aussi Ismāʿīliyya
Nizārites Agha Khān; Alamūt.II; Buzurg-ummīd; Fidāʾī; Ḥasan-i Ṣabbāḥ; Ḥashīshiyya; Khōdja; Maḥallātī; Nizār b. al-Mustanṣir; **Nizāriyya**; Nūr al-Dīn Muḥammad II; Pīr Ṣadr al-Dīn; Pīr Shams; Rāshid al-Dīn Sinān; Rukn al-Dīn Khurshāh; Sabz ʿAlī; Shāh Ṭāhir;

al-Shahrastānī, Tādj al-dīn; Shams-al-Dīn Muḥammad; Shihāb al-Dīn
voir aussi Sarkār Āḳā; Satpanthīs

Qarmates (Djazīrat) al-ʿArab.VII; al-Djannābī, Abū Saʿīd; al-Djannābī, Abū Ṭāhir; Ḥamdān Ḳarmaṭ; al-Ḥasan al-Aʿṣam; **Ḳarmaṭī**
voir aussi ʿAbdān; al-Baḥrayn; Baḳliyya; Daʿwa; Shābāshiyya

Septimains **Sabʿiyya**
voir aussi Sabʿ

Zaydites al-Ḥasan b. Ṣāliḥ b. Ḥayy; Ibn Abī l-Ridjāl; al-Mahdī li-Dīn Allāh Aḥmad; Muḥammad b. Zayd; al-Nāṣir (li-Dīn Allāh); al-Rassī; Sulaymān b. Djarīr al-Raḳḳī; [au Suppl.] Abū l-Barakāt; Abū l-Fatḥ al-Daylamī; Aḥmad b. ʿĪsā; Djaʿfar b. Abī Yaḥyā; al-Ḥākim al-Djushamī
voir aussi Imāma; Muṭarrifiyya; Rassides; *et* → DYNASTIES.PÉNINSULE ARABIQUE

doctrines et institutions Bāṭiniyya; Djafr; Ḳāʾim Āl Muḥammad; Khalḳ.VII; Madjlis.II et III; al-Mahdī; Malāʾika.II; Mardjaʿ-i Taḳlīd; Maẓhar; Maẓlūm; Mudjtahid.II; Mutʿa.V; Radjʿa; Safīr.1; [au Suppl.] Āyatullāh
voir aussi Adhān; Ahl al-Bayt; ʿAḳīda; Bāb; Ghayba; Ḥudjdja; Imāma; ʿIlm al-Ridjāl; Imām-bārā; Imāmzāda; Mollā; *et* → THÉOLOGIE.TERMES.CHIITES

dynasties Buwayhides; Fāṭimides; Ṣafawides
voir aussi Mushaʿshaʿ

imams ʿAlī b. Abī Ṭālib; ʿAlī al-Riḍā; al-ʿAskarī; Djaʿfar al-Ṣādiḳ; (al-)Ḥasan b. ʿAlī b. Abī Ṭālib; (al-)Ḥusayn b. ʿAlī b. Abī Ṭālib; Muḥammad b. ʿAlī al-Riḍā; Muḥammad b. ʿAlī (al-Bāḳir); Muḥammad al-Ḳāʾim; Mūsā al-Kāẓim
voir aussi Bāb; Ghayba; Imāmzāda; Malāʾika.II; Maẓlūm; Riḍā.2; Safīr.1

juristes al-ʿĀmilī; al-Ḥillī; al-Māmaḳānī; al-Mufīd; Muḥammad b. Makkī; al-Shahīd al-Thānī; Shīrāzī; [au Suppl.] Anṣārī; Bihbihānī
voir aussi ʿĀḳila; Madjlisī; Madjlisī-ya Awwal; Mardjaʿ-i Taḳlīd; Mudjtahid.II; Mutʿa.V

lieux de pèlerinage Karbalāʾ; Kāẓimayn; al-Nadjaf; [au Suppl.] ʿAtabāt
voir aussi Shāh ʿAbd al-ʿAẓīm

rituels Rawḍa-khwānī

sectes Ahl-i Ḥaḳḳ; ʿAlides; Baḳliyya; Bohorās; Djābir b. Ḥayyān; al-Djanāḥiyya; al-Djārūdiyya; Ghurābiyya; Ḥurūfiyya; Ibāḥa.II; Kaysāniyya; Khashabiyya; Khaṭṭābiyya; Khōdja; Khurramiyya; Kuraybiyya; Manṣūriyya; al-Mughīriyya; Muḥammadiyya; Mukhammisa; Muṭarrifiyya; al-Muʿtazila; Nāwūsiyya; Nūrbakhshiyya; Nuṣayriyya; al-Rāwandiyya; Salmāniyya; Satpanthīs; Shaykhiyya; Shumayṭiyya
voir aussi ʿAbd Allāh b. Sabaʾ; Bāṭiniyya; Bayān b. Samʿān; Bektāshiyya; Ghulāt; Hind.V.D; Imām Shāh; Ḳaṭʿ; al-Kayyāl; Kāẓim Rashtī; Ḳïzïl-bāsh; Mushaʿshaʿ; [au Suppl.] Ibn Warsand; *et* → DRUZES; SECTES.ʿALIDES

Kaysāniyya Abū Hāshim; Kaysān; **Kaysāniyya**
voir aussi al-Sayyid al-Ḥimyarī

Khaṭṭābiyya Abū l-Khaṭṭāb al-Asadī; Bashshār al-Shaʿīrī; Bazīgh b. Mūsā; **Khaṭṭābiyya**
voir aussi Mukhammisa; al-Ṣāmit
Khurramiyya Bābak; [au Suppl.] Bādhām
Mukhammisa **Mukhammisa**
voir aussi al-Muḥassin b. ʿAlī
Shaykhisme al-Aḥsāʾī; Rashtī, Sayyid Kāẓim; **Shaykhiyya**
termes → THÉOLOGIE.TERMES.CHIITES
théologiens al-Dāmād; al-Ḥillī; Hishām b. al-Ḥakam; al-Ḥurr al-ʿĀmilī; Ibn Bābawayh(i); Ibn Shahrāshūb; al-Karakī; Kāshif al-Ghiṭāʾ; Khʷānsārī, Sayyid Mīrzā; al-Kulaynī; Lāhīdjī.II; Mīr Lawḥī; al-Mufīd; Mullā Ṣadrā Shīrāzī; Shayṭan al-Ṭāḳ; [au Suppl.] Akhbāriyya; Anṣārī; al-Bazdawī; Fayḍ-i Kāshānī; Ibn Abī Djumhūr al-Aḥsāʾī; Ibn Mītham
voir aussi al-ʿAyyāshī; Ḥudjdja; Imāma; Khalḳ.VII; Mollā
du vingtième siècle Kāshanī; Khʷānsārī, Sayyid Muḥammad; Khiyābānī; Khurāsānī; Muṭahharī; Nāʾīnī; Sharaf al-Dīn; Sharīʿatī, ʿAlī; Sharīʿat-madārī; [au Suppl.] Āḳā Nadjafī; Burūdjirdī; Ḥāʾirī
traditionnistes → LITTÉRATURE.TRADITION.TRADITIONNISTES.CHIITES

CHINE Djarīda.V; Masdjid.V; **al-Ṣīn**
voir aussi Bahādur; Khoḳand; Ṣīnī
dynasties Ḳarā Khiṭāy
voir aussi Faghfūr; Gūrkhān
géographie physique
eaux Aḳ Ṣu; Ili
personnages
pour les chefs de rebellions, voir ci-dessous
fonctionnaires P'u Shou-keng
littérateurs Liu Tchih; Ma Huan
population Salar
rebellions Panthay
chefs Ma Hua-lung; Ma Ming-hsin; Ma Tchung-ying; Pai Yen-hu
toponymes
anciens Bishbaliḳ; Khansā; Shūl.1
actuels Aḳ Ṣu; Alti Shahr; Kansu; Kāshghar; Khānbaliḳ; Khānfū; Khotan; Ḳuldja; Ning-hsia; Shansi; Shen-si; Sinkiang; Szechuan
voir aussi Sandābil; Ṣīn (Čīn) Kalān
traités sur ʿAlī Akbar Khiṭāʾī

CHRISTIANISME Ahl al-Kitāb; Dayr; Dayṣāniyya; ʿĪsā; Kanīsa; Maryam; **Naṣārā**; Rāhib; Ṣalīb
voir aussi Dhimma; Djizya; Ghiyār; al-Ḥākim bi-Amr Allāh; Ifrandj;

Karshūnī; Ḳūmis; Lāhūt et Nāsūt.II; Maʿalthāyā; [au Suppl.] Dāwiyya et Isbitāriyya; Fidāʾ; *et* → BIBLE; CROISADES; LANGUES.AFRO-ASIATIQUES.ARABE CHRÉTIEN; NUBIE

apologistes Ibn Zurʿa; al-Kindī, ʿAbd al-Masīḥ

communautés Anadolu.III.4; al-Andalus.IV; Istanbul.VII.2; Mozárabe; al-Shaʾm.2(a)(280a)
voir aussi Fener

confessions Ḳibṭ; Nasṭūriyyūn
et → JUDAÏSME.SECTES JUIVES

catholiques Bashīr Shihāb II; Isḥāḳ, Adīb; Ṣābundjī; Ṣāyigh, Fatḥ Allāh; Shaykhū; [au Suppl.] Buṭrus Karāma

coptes Ibn al-ʿAssāl; Ibn Mammātī; Ibn al-Muḳaffaʿ; **Ḳibṭ**; al-Makīn b. al-ʿAmīd; Māriya; al-Mufaḍḍal b. Abī l-Faḍāʾil; [au Suppl.] Ibn Kabar; Ibn al-Rāhib
voir aussi Sullam; *et* → ÉGYPTE.TOPONYMES; NUBIE

jacobites Ibn al-ʿIbrī; Ibn Zurʿa
voir aussi al-Kindī, ʿAbd al-Masīḥ; Paṭrīk

maronites Farḥāt; Isṭifān al-Duwayhī; al-Rayḥānī; Salīm al-Naḳḳāsh; [au Suppl.] Abū Shabaka; al-Bustānī
voir aussi Bsharrā; Durūz.Période ottomane; Paṭrīk; *et* → LIBAN

melkites Abū Ḳurra; al-Anṭāḳī; Mīkhāʾīl Ṣabbāgh; al-Muḳawḳis; Saʿīd b. al-Biṭrīḳ; [au Suppl.] Ibn al-Ḳuff
voir aussi Mashāḳa; Paṭrīk

monophysites al-Akhṭal; al-Ḳuṭāmī

nestoriens Ibn Buṭlān; Ibn al-Ṭayyib; al-Kindī, ʿAbd al-Masīḥ; Mattā b. Yūnus; **Nasṭūriyyūn**; Sābūr b. Sahl

non-spécifiés Baḥdal; Ibn al-Tilmīdh; al-Masīḥī; Petrus Alfonsi; [au Suppl.] Ḥubaysh b. al-Ḥasan al-Dimashḳī; Ibn al-Ṣuḳāʿī

orthodoxes grecs Gagauz
voir aussi Paṭrīk

protestants Fāris al-Shidyāḳ; Mashāḳa; Ṣarrūf; Ṣāyigh, Tawfīḳ; [au Suppl.] al-Bustānī.2
voir aussi Nimr

couvents **Dayr**; Dayr al-Djāthalīḳ; Dayr Kaʿb; Dayr Ḳunnā; Dayr Murrān; Dayr Samʿān
voir aussi Khānḳāh; Rāhib

traités sur al-Shābushtī

du vingtième siècle al-Khūrī; Ṣarrūf; Shaykhū; [au Suppl.] Abū Shabaka; Abyaḍ
voir aussi al-Maʿlūf

églises **Kanīsa**; Sihyawn
see also Masdjid.I.B.3

polémiques Ahl al-Kitāb

anti-juives Petrus Alfonsi
chrétiennes-musulmanes al-Suʿūdī, Abū l-Faḍl
pré-islamique Abraha; ʿAdī b. Zayd; ʿAmr b. ʿAdī; ʿAmr b. Hind; Baḥīrā; Bahrām
voir aussi G͟hassān; Lak͟hmides
saints D̲jird̲jīs; D̲juraydj̲

CHYPRE **Ḳubrus**; Mad̲jlis.IV.A.24
toponymes
villes Lefḳōs͟ha; Mag͟hōs͟ha

CIRCONCISION K͟hafḍ; **K͟hitān**
voir aussi ʿAbdī; ʿAlī; Kurdes et Kurdistān.IV.A.1; Mawākib.IV.11

COMMERCE Bayʿ; Imtiyāzāt; Kasb; Ḳirāḍ
voir aussi Ins͟hāʾ; Sūḳ; *et* → DROIT.DROIT CONTRACTUEL; INDUSTRIE
commerce Ḳahwa; Kārimī; Ḳuṭn; Lubān
voir aussi Kalah; Kārwān; Ḳaysāriyya; Kirmān; Mīnāʾ; Ṣafawides.II; Szechuan
fonctions Dallāl; Malik al-Tud̲jd̲jār; S͟hāh Bandar
termes juridico-commerciaux Mufāwaḍa; Mus͟hāraka

COMMUNAUTÉ DES ÉTATS INDÉPENDANTS → ASIE CENTRALE; CAUCASE; COMMUNISME; EUROPE.EUROPE ORIENTALE

COMMUNICATIONS Barīd; Ḥamām; Manār
voir aussi Anadolu.III.5; *et* → TRANSPORT

COMMUNISME Ḥizb.I; **S͟huyūʿiyya**
voir aussi Lāhūtī

COMPTABILITÉ Muḥāsaba.II; Mustawfī
voir aussi Daftar; *et* → ADMINISTRATION.FINANCIÈRE

CONGO **Congo**; al-Murd̲jibī

CORAN Allāh.I; Āya; Fāṣila; Iʿd̲jāz; Ḳirāʾa; **al-Ḳurʾān**; Muḳaṭṭaʿāt; Muṣḥaf; Nask͟h; Sūra
voir aussi ʿArabiyya.A.II; Basmala; Faḍīla; Hamza; Ind̲jīl; Iṣlāḥ.I.B.1; K͟halḳ.II; K͟hawāṣṣ al-Ḳurʾān
caractère créé Miḥna
voir aussi D̲jahmiyya

commentaires Mukhtaṣar; Sharḥ.III

en arabe ʿAbd al-Razzāḳ al-Ḳāshānī; Abū l-Faḍl ʿAllāmī; Abū Ḥayyān al-Gharnāṭī; Abū l-Layth al-Samarḳandī; Abū l-Suʿūd; Abū ʿUbayda; al-ʿAskarī.II; al-Baghawī; Baḳī b. Makhlad; al-Bayḍāwī; al-Bulḳīnī.4; al-Dāmād; al-Dārimī; Djīwan; Fakhr al-Dīn al-Rāzī; Fayḍī; Ghulām Ḥusayn Khān Ṭabāṭabāʾī; Gīsū Darāz; Gūrānī; Ibn Abī l-Ridjāl; Ibn ʿAdjība; Ibn Barradjān; Ibn Kathīr, ʿImād al-dīn; Ismāʿīl Ḥaḳḳī; al-Kalbī.I; Kalīm Allāh al-Djahānābādī; Kemāl Pasha-zāde; al-Ḳurṭubī, Abū ʿAbd Allāh; al-Ḳushayrī.I; al-Maḥallī; al-Māturīdī; Mudjāhid b. Djabr al-Makkī; Mudjīr al-Dīn al-ʿUlaymī; Muḥsin-i Fayḍ-i Kāshānī; Muḳātil b. Sulaymān; al-Nīsābūrī; al-Rāghib al-Iṣfahānī; al-Rummānī; Sahl al-Tustarī; al-Shaḥḥām; al-Shahrastānī, Tādj al-dīn; al-Sharīf al-Raḍī; al-Suhrawardī, Shihāb al-dīn Abū Ḥafṣ; al-Sulamī, Abū ʿAbd al-Raḥmān; al-Suyūṭī; [au Suppl.] ʿAbd al-Wahhāb Bukhārī; Abū l-Fatḥ al-Daylamī; al-Aṣamm

voir aussi ʿAbd Allāh b. al-ʿAbbās; Abū Nuʿaym al-Mulāʾī; Aḥmadiyya; al-ʿAlamī; al-Dihlawī, Shāh Walī Allāh; Djafr; Djilwatiyya; Ḥādjdjī Pasha; Hind.V.E; Ibn Masʿūd; Ḳuṭb al-Dīn Shīrāzī; al-Manār; al-Suddī; Sufyān b. ʿUyayna; al-Sulamī, ʿIzz al-dīn

19ᵉ-20ᵉ siècles al-Ālūsī.II; Aṭfiyāsh; Mawdūdī; Muḥammad b. Aḥmad al-Iskandarānī; Muḥammad Abū Zayd; Muḥammad Farīd Wadjdī; Sayyid Ḳuṭb; Shaltūt, Maḥmūd; [au Suppl.] Djawharī, Ṭanṭāwī

en ourdou Ashraf ʿAlī

en persan Abū l-Futūḥ al-Rāzī; al-Dawlatābādī; Djāmī; Kāshifī; al-Maybudī.I; Muṣannifak

en turque Aḳ Ḥiṣārī.b

histoires ʿĀd; Ādam; Aṣḥāb al-Kahf; Ayyūb; Bilḳīs; Dāwūd; Djālūt; Firʿawn; Ḥābīl wa-Ḳābīl; Ḥawwāʾ; Ibrāhīm; ʿĪsā; Iskandar; al-Khaḍir; Lūṭ; Maryam; Mūsā; Nūḥ; Sulaymān b. Dāwūd

voir aussi Ḳiṣaṣ al-Anbiyāʾ; Shayṭān.2; *et* → BIBLE.PERSONNAGES BIBLIQUES

lecteurs ʿAbd Allāh b. Abī Isḥāḳ; Abūʿ Amr b. al-ʿAlāʾ; al-Aʿmash; ʿĀṣim; al-Dānī; Ḥamza b. Ḥabīb; Ibn ʿĀmir; ʿĪsā b. ʿUmar; al-Kisāʾī; Nāfiʿ b. ʿAbd al-Raḥmān; al-Sadjāwandī, Abū ʿAbd Allāh

voir aussi Abū l-ʿĀliya al-Riyāḥī; al-Dāraḳuṭnī; Ḥafs b. Sulaymān; Ibn al-Djazarī; Ibn al-Faḥḥām; Ibn Mudjāhid; Ibn Shanabūdh; al-Ḳasṭallānī; Makkī b. Abī Ṭālib; al-Malaṭī; Mudjāhid b. Djabr al-Makkī; [au Suppl.] Ibn Miḳsam

lecture Adāʾ; Ḥarf; Ḳaṭʿ; Khatma; **Ḳirāʾa**

voir aussi al-Shāṭibī, Abū l-Ḳāsim; al-Sidjistānī

recensions ʿAbd Allāh b. al-Zubayr; ʿAbd al-Malik b. Marwān; Abū l-Dardāʾ; ʿĀʾisha bint Abī Bakr; ʿĀṣim; al-Dimyāṭī; al-Ḥadjdjādj b. Yūsuf; Ibn Masʿūd; Nāfiʿ b. ʿAbd al-Raḥmān *voir aussi* Abū l-Aswad al-Duʾalī; ʿArabiyya.II.1 et 2; al-Ḥuṣrī.II

sourates al-Aḥḳāf; Aṣḥāb al-Kahf; Fātiḥa; al-Fīl; G̲h̲ās̲h̲iya; Kawt̲h̲ar; Luḳmān; al-Muʿawwid̲h̲atān[i]; al-Mudda̲t̲h̲t̲h̲ir et al-Muzzammil; al-Musabbiḥāt; Sad̲j̲da; al-Ṣāffāt

voir aussi Ḥayawān.III; **Sūra**

termes Aḥkām; ʿĀlam; Amr; al-Aʿrāf; ʿAṣā; Aṣḥāb al-Kahf; Aṣḥāb al-Rass; Aṣḥāb al-Uk̲h̲dūd; Āya; Baḥīra; al-Baḥrayn; Baʿl; Barāʾa; Baraka; Barzak̲h̲; Birr; Dābba; Daʿwa; D̲h̲arra; Dīn; D̲j̲ahannam; D̲j̲āhiliyya; D̲j̲anna; D̲j̲inn; Dunyā; Faḳīr; Farāʾiḍ; Fitna; Fiṭra; Furḳān; al-G̲h̲ayb; Ḥadd; Ḥaḳḳ; Ḥanīf; Hātif; Ḥawārī; Ḥayāt; Ḥid̲j̲āb; Ḥisāb; Ḥizb; Ḥud̲j̲d̲j̲a; Ḥūr; Iblīs; Īlāf; Ilhām; ʿIlliyyūn; Kaffāra; Kāfir; Kalima; Ḳarīn; Ḳarya; Ḳawm; Ḳayyim; K̲h̲alḳ; K̲h̲aṭīʾa; Ḳiyāma; Kursī; Ḳuwwa; Lawḥ; Mad̲j̲nūn; Maḳām Ibrāhīm; Milla; Millet; Miskīn; Mīt̲h̲āḳ; al-Munāfiḳūn.1; Nad̲h̲īr; Nafs.1; Nār; Raḥma; Rizḳ; Rud̲j̲ūʿ; Rukn; Sabab.4; Ṣabr; Ṣadr; al-Ṣāffāt; Ṣaḥīfa; Sakīna; Salām; al-Ṣāliḥūn; S̲h̲aḳāwa; S̲h̲akk.1; S̲h̲irk; al-Ṣiddīḳ; Sid̲j̲d̲j̲īl; Sid̲j̲d̲j̲īn; Sidrat al-Muntahā; Sirād̲j̲;; Ṣirāṭ; Subḥān; Sulṭān; [au Suppl.] Asāṭir al-Awwalīn

voir aussi Ḥikāya.I; Samāʾ.1

traductions al-Ḳurʾān.I

voir aussi Aljamía

en anglais Aḥmadiyya; Pickthall

en malais ʿAbd al-Raʾūf al-Sinkilī

en ourdou ʿAbd al-Ḳādir Dihlawī; D̲j̲awān; Rafīʿ al-Dīn

en persan al-Dihlawī, S̲h̲āh Walī Allāh

voir aussi K̲h̲aṭṭ.II

en swahilie Kenya (923b)

Corporations **Ṣinf**

arabes Amīn; ʿArīf; Futuwwa.2 et 3; Ḥammāl; Ḥarfūs̲h̲; K̲h̲atam; K̲h̲ayyāṭ; Ṣinf.1

voir aussi S̲h̲add; S̲h̲ayk̲h̲; Sirwāl

persanes Ṣinf.2

turques Ak̲h̲ī; Ak̲h̲ī Baba; Anadolu.III.6; Ḥarīr.II; Ketk̲h̲udā.II; Ṣinf.3; [au Suppl.] Ik̲h̲tiyāriyya; Inḥiṣār

voir aussi Ak̲h̲ī Ewrān; ʿĀlima; Čāʾūs̲h̲; Kannās; Mawākib.IV.4; Muhr.1

Cosmétique Kuḥl

voir aussi K̲h̲iḍāb

Cosmographie ʿAd̲j̲āʾib; ʿĀlam; Falak; Ḳāf; Samāʾ.1

voir aussi D̲j̲ug̲h̲rāfiyā; al-K̲h̲aḍir; K̲h̲arīṭa; Kura; Makka.IV; *et* → Astrologie; Astronomie; Géographie

traités sur al-Dimas̲h̲ḳī; al-Ḳazwīnī, Zakariyyāʾ; al-K̲h̲araḳī *voir aussi* Kitāb al-Djilwa

CÔTE D'IVOIRE **Côte d'Ivoire**; Kong

COULEUR **Lawn**; Musawwida
et → TEINTURE
couleurs Asfar
voir aussi Sharīf.5

COUTUMES **ʿĀda**; Adab
voir aussi ʿAbd al-Raḥmān al-Fāsī; ʿĀshūrāʾ.II; Hiba; Ḥidjāb.I; Īdjāra; Khilʿa; Mandīl; *et* → DROIT.DROIT COUTUMIER
coutumes tribales ʿAbābda; al-Dhunūb (Dafn-); Khāwa; Muwāraba; [au Suppl.] ʿĀr
voir aussi Īdjāra

CRÉATION **Ibdāʿ**; **Khalḳ**
voir aussi Ḥudūth al-ʿĀlam; Insān

CRÉTE **Iḳrīṭish**
voir aussi Abū Ḥafṣ ʿUmar al-Ballūṭī
toponymes
villes Ḳandiya

CROISADES **Croisades**; [au Suppl.] Dāwiyya et Isbitāriyya
voir aussi al-ʿĀdil.1; al-Afḍal b. Badr al-Djamālī; ʿAntar; Ayyūbides; Balak; Baybars Ier; Fāṭimides; Ifrandj; Ḳalāwūn; Ḳilidj Arslan Ier; Nūr al-Dīn Maḥmūd b. Zankī; Ṣalāḥ al-Dīn; al-Shaʾm.2(a); *et* → *l'entrée Toponymes sous* PALESTINE *et* SYRIE
batailles al-Manṣūra; Mardj al-Ṣuffar; Nīkbūlī
châteaux al-Dārūm; Ḥārim; Ḥiṣn al-Akrād; Ḳalʿat al-Shaḳīf; Ṣāfītha
conquêtes ʿAkkā; Anadolu.III.1; ʿĀsḳalān; Ayla; Ghazza; Ḥayfā; Ḳayṣariyya; al-Khalīl; Ḳubrus.II; al-ḲudsA.I.10; Ludd; Maʿarrat al-Nuʿmān
historiens des Ibn al-Ḳalānisī
voir aussi al-Nuwayrī, Muḥammad

CRYPTOGRAPHIE **Muʿammā**; Ramz.2
voir aussi Kitābāt.V; al-Sīm

CUISINE **Maṭbakh**
aliments **Ghidhāʾ**; Kabid.5; Khubz; Kuskusū; Mishmish; Nārandj; al-Ruzz; al-Samn; Sawīḳ; Shaʿīr; Sikbādj; Sukkar; [au Suppl.] Basbās; Djawz; Ḥays; Hindibāʾ

voir aussi Baḳḳāl; Filāḥa; Ḳamḥ; Maḍīra; Milḥ; Naḥl; Pist; Simsim; [au Suppl.] Ibn Shaḳrūn

boissons Čāy; Ḳahwa; Khamr; Kumi̊s; **Mashrūbāt**; Nabīdh; Sherbet

voir aussi Naḥl; [au Suppl.] Čāy-khāna

épices Kammūn; Ḳaranful; [au Suppl.] **Afāwīh**; Dār Ṣīnī

voir aussi Kārimī; Ḳūṣ; Milḥ

herbes Shibithth; [in Suppl.] Basbās

voir aussi Shīḥ

prohibitions Ghidhāʾ.III et IV.7; Ḳahwa; Khamr; Mashrūbāt; Mayta; Nabīdh

voir aussi Dhabīḥa.1; Ḥayawān.IV; Nadjis; *et* → *articles individuels sous* ANIMAUX

D

DÉSERTS al-Aḥḳāf; Biyābānak; al-Dahnāʾ; Ḳaraḳum; Ḳi̊zi̊l-ḳum; Nafūd; al-Naḳb; al-Rubʿ al-Khālī; Sāḥil; al-Ṣaḥrāʾ; Sīnāʾ

voir aussi (Djazīrat) al-ʿArab.II; Badw.II; Ḥarra; Khabrāʾ; Reg; Samūm

DICTIONNAIRE **Ḳāmūs**

voir aussi Fāris al-Shidyāḳ; Sullam; *et* → LEXICOGRAPHIE

DIPLOMATIE Imtiyāzāt; Mübādele

voir aussi Amān; Bālyōs, Berātli̊; Daftar; Hiba; Inshāʾ; Kātib; Ḳawwās; Mandats

diplomats Consul; Elči; Safīr.2

relations diplomatiques Aḥmad Rasmī; Ibn Faḍlān; Meḥmed Yirmisekiz; [au Suppl.] al-Ghazzāl; Ibn ʿUthmān al-Miknāsī

voir aussi Ṣubḥi Meḥmed

DIVINATION **Kihāna**

voir aussi Djafr; Ibn Barradjān; Malāḥim; Nudjūm (Aḥkām al-); Shāma; *et* → ASTROLOGIE; RÊVES

devins ʿArrāf; Kāhin

pratiques Faʾl; Firāsa; Ghurāb; Ḥisāb al-Djummal; Ḥurūf; Ikhtilādj; Istiḳsām; ʿIyāfa; al-Kaff; Katif; Khaṭṭ; Khawāṣṣ al-Ḳurʾān; Ḳiyāfa; Ḳurʿa; Māʾ.I; Riyāfa

voir aussi Būḳalā; Ikhtiyārāt; Mirʾāt

traités sur Fāl-nāma; Ibn al-Bannāʾ al-Marrākushī; Malḥama; [au Suppl.] Ibn ʿAzzūz

voir aussi Djafr; Nudjūm (Aḥkām al-)

DIVORCE Barāʾa; Faskh; Suknā; al-Suraydjiyya
voir aussi ʿAbd.3; ʿĀda; Ghāʾib; Ḥaḍāna; Ibn Suraydj; ʿIdda; ʿIwaḍ; Ḳasam; Liʿān; al-Marʾa.II; Rapak

DOCUMENTS ʿAlāma; **Diplomatique**; Farmān; Inshāʾ; Kātib; Manshūr; Papyrus; **Sidjill;** [au Suppl.] Dabīr
voir aussi Barāʾa; Ḳaṭʿ; Sharṭ.1; *et* → ADMINISTRATION.DOCUMENTS; ÉCRITURE
ottomans ʿArḍ Ḥāl; Berāt; **Diplomatique**.IV; Farmān.II; Irāde; Khaṭṭ-i̊ Humāyūn et Khaṭṭ-i̊ Sherīf; **Sidjill**.3
et → EMPIRE OTTOMAN.ADMINISTRATION

DROGUES **Adwiya**; [au Suppl.] Anzarūt
voir aussi Kahrubā; Kuḥl; *et* → MÉDECINE; PHARMACOLOGIE
narcotiques Afyūn; Bandj; Ḥashīsh; Ḳāt; Shahdānadj
voir aussi Filāḥa.III
tabac Bahāʾī Meḥmed Efendi

DROIT ʿĀda; Dustūr; **Fiḳh**; Idjmāʿ; **Ḳānūn**.I; Ḳiyās; Maḥkama; **Sharīʿa**
voir aussi Aṣḥāb al-Raʾy; Ḥuḳūḳ; *et* → HÉRITAGE
pour les questions légales, voir ʿAbd.3; Djāsūs; Filāḥa.I.4; Ḥarb.I; Ḥarīr; In Shāʾ Allāh; Intiḥār; Ḳabr; Kāfir; Khāliṣa; Khiṭba; Māʾ; al-Marʾa; Murtadd; Raḍāʿ; Rāḳid; Rashwa; Safar.1; Shaʿr.2; Ṣūra; al-Suraydjiyya
ancien droit religieux Abū Ḥanīfa; Abū Yūsuf Yaʿḳūb; al-Ashʿarī, Abū Burda; ʿAṭāʾ b. Abī Rabāḥ; al-Awzāʿī; Ibn Abī Laylā.2; Ibn Shubruma; al-Layth b. Saʿd; Mālik b. Anas; Maymūn b. Mihrān; al-Nakhaʿī; al-Shaʿbī; al-Shāfiʿī; Shurayḥ; Sufyān al-Thawrī; [au Suppl.] Fuḳahāʾ al-Madīna al-Sabʿa; Ibn Abī l-Zinād
droit 'anglo-mohammedan' ʿĀda.III; Amīr ʿAlī; Munṣif
voir aussi Ḥanafiyya
droit contractuel ʿAḳd; ʿĀriyya; Bayʿ; Ḍamān; Dhimma; Fāsid wa-Bāṭil; Faskh; Hiba; Īdjāb; Īdjār; Iḳrār; Inkār; ʿIwaḍ; Kafāla; Khiyār; Ḳirāḍ; Muʿāmalāt; Muʿāwaḍa.3; Muḍāraba; Mufāwaḍa; Mughārasa; Mushāraka; Rahn; Ṣulḥ; [au Suppl.] Dayn; Ghārūḳa
voir aussi ʿAmal.4; Djāʾiz; Ghaṣb; Ḳabḍ.I; Ḳasam; Maḍmūn; Suftadja; [au Suppl.] Ikrāh
contrat de louage Adjr; **Īdjār**; Kirāʾ; Musāḳāt; Muzāraʿa; [au Suppl.] Ḥikr; Inzāl
contrat de vente Barāʾa; **Bay**ʿ; Iḳāla; ʿIwaḍ; Muʿāwaḍa.1; Muwāḍaʿa; Salam; Shirāʾ; [au Suppl.] Darak
voir aussi Ḍarūra; Ildjāʾ; Mukhāṭara; Ṣafḳa; Salaf; Sawm
droit coutumier **ʿĀda**; Dakhīl; Ḳānūn.IV; [au Suppl.] Djirga
voir aussi Baranta; Berbères.IV; al-Māmī; al-Marʾa.II; Mushāʿ

droit de la procédure ʿAdl; Amīn; Bayyina; Daʿwā; Ghāʾib; Ḥakam; Iḳrār; Ḳaḍāʾ; Maẓālim; Shāhid; Sidjill.2

droit ibāḍite ʿAbd al-ʿAzīz b. al-Ḥādjdj Ibrāhīm; Abū Ghānim; Abū Muḥammad al-ʿUmānī (*et* Ibn Baraka); Abū Zakariyyāʾ al-Djanāwunī; Ibn Djaʿfar
voir aussi al-Djayṭālī; Maḥkama.IV.9 (Oman)

droit pénal ʿĀḳila; Diya; Ḥadd; Ḳadhf; Ḳatl; Khaṭaʾ; Ḳiṣāṣ.5; Ṣalb; Sariḳa
voir aussi Muḥṣan; Ṣalīb; Shubha; Sidjn; [au Suppl.] Ikrāh

écoles Ḥanābila; Ḥanafiyya; Mālikiyya; al-Shāfiʿiyya
voir aussi Ibn Abī Laylā.2; Sufyān al-Thawrī

en Asie du Sud-est Penghulu; Rapak; Sharīʿa.7

fonctions Faḳīh; Ḥakam; Ḳāḍī; Ḳāḍī ʿAskar; Ḳassām; Mardjaʿ-i Taḳlīd; Nāʾib.1; Shaykh al-Islām
voir aussi Amīn; Fatwā; Khalīfa.II; Maḥkama; Shurṭa

héritage → HÉRITAGE

jurisprudence Fatwā; **Fiḳh**; Īdjāb; Idjmāʿ; Idjtihād; Ikhtilāf; Istiḥsān; Ḳiyās; Maṣlaḥa; Nāzila
voir aussi Sadd al-Dharāʾiʿ

juristes **Faḳīh**; Mardjaʿ-i Taḳlīd; Mudjtahid
voir aussi Sharḥ.III

ḥanafites Abū Ḥanīfa; Abū l-Layth al-Samarḳandī; Abū l-Suʿūd; al-ʿAmīdī; al-Bihārī; al-Djaṣṣāṣ; al-Ḥalabī; Ḥamza al-Ḥarrānī; Ibn ʿĀbidīn; Ibn Buhlūl; Ibn Ghānim; Ibn Ḳuṭlūbugha; Ibn Nudjaym; Ibn al-Shiḥna; Ḳāḍī Khān; al-Kāsānī; Ḳasṭallānī; al-Ḳudūrī; al-Marghīnānī; al-Nasafī.IV; al-Sadjāwandī, Sirādj al-dīn; al-Sarakhsī, Muḥammad b. Aḥmad; al-Shaybānī, Abū ʿAbd Allāh; al-Shiblī, Abū Ḥafs; [au Suppl.] Abū ʿAbd Allāh al-Baṣrī; Abū l-Barakāt; al-Dāmaghānī.1 et 2
voir aussi ʿAbd al-Ḳādir al-Ḳurashī; al-Fatāwā al-ʿĀlamgīriyya; Ibn Duḳmāḳ; al-Ṣayrafī

ḥanbalites Aḥmad b. Ḥanbal; al-Bahūtī; al-Barbahārī; Ghulām al-Khallāl; Ibn ʿAḳīl; Ibn al-Bannāʾ; Ibn Baṭṭa al-ʿUkbarī; Ibn al-Djawzī; Ibn al-Farrāʾ; Ibn Ḥāmid; Ibn Ḳayyim al-Djawziyya; Ibn Ḳudāma al-Maḳdisī; Ibn Mufliḥ; Ibn Radjab; Ibn Taymiyya; al-Kalwadhānī; al-Khallāl; al-Khiraḳī; al-Marwazī
et → THÉOLOGIE

chiites → CHIITES

mālikites Aḥmad Bābā; Asad b. al-Furāt; al-Bādjī; al-Bāḳillānī; Bannānī; al-Burzulī; al-Dānī; al-Fāsī; Ibn ʿAbd al-Ḥakam; Ibn Abī Zamanayn; Ibn Abī Zayd al-Ḳayrawānī; Ibn ʿAmmār, Abū l-ʿAbbās; Ibn ʿArafa; Ibn ʿĀṣim; Ibn al-Faraḍī; Ibn Farḥūn; Ibn Ḥabīb, Abū Marwān; Ibn al-Ḥādjdj; Ibn al-Ḥādjib; Ibn al-Ḳāsim; Ibn Maḍāʾ; Ibn Rushayd; Ibn Sūda; al-Ibshīhī; ʿĪsā b. Dīnār; ʿIyāḍ b. Mūsā; al-Ḳābisī; al-Ḳalaṣādī; al-Kardūdī; Ḳaṣṣāra; Khalīl b. Isḥāḳ; al-Khushanī; al-Ḳurṭubī, Abū ʿAbd

Allāh; al-Ḳurṭubī, Yaḥyā; Mālik b. Anas; al-Manūfī.IV et V; al-Māzarī;
Muḥammad b. Saḥnūn; Saḥnūn; Sālim b. Muḥammad; al-Sanhūrī, Abū l-
Ḥasan; S̲h̲abṭūn; al-S̲h̲āṭibī, Abū Isḥāḳ; S̲h̲ihāb al-Dīn al-Ḳarāfī; [au
Suppl.] Abū ʿImrān al-Fāsī; al-Azdī; Ibn Daḳīḳ al-ʿĪd; Ibn Dirham; Ibn
Rus̲h̲d

voir aussi Ibn ʿAbd al-Barr; al-Ḳaṣṣār; Laḳīṭ; al-S̲h̲arīf al-Tilimsānī

shāfiʿites   al-ʿAbbādī; Abū S̲h̲udjāʿ; Bādjūrī; al-Bag̲h̲awī; al-Bulḳīnī; Daḥlān;
al-Djanadī; al-Djīzī; al-Djuwaynī; Ibn Abī ʿAṣrūn; Ibn Abī l-Dam; Ibn
ʿAḳīl; Ibn ʿAsākir; Ibn Djamāʿa; Ibn Ḥabīb, Badr al-dīn; Ibn Ḥadjar al-
Haytamī; Ibn Ḳāḍī S̲h̲uhba.1; Ibn Ḳāsim al-G̲h̲azzī; Ibn al-Ṣalāḥ; Ibn
Suraydj; al-Ḳalḳas̲h̲andī; al-Ḳalyūbī; al-Ḳazwīnī, Abū Ḥātim; al-
Ḳazwīnī, Djalāl al-dīn; al-Ḳazwīnī, Nadjm al-dīn; al-Kiyā al-Harrāsī;
Mak̲h̲rama; al-Māwardī; al-Mutawallī; al-Muzanī; al-Nawawī; al-Rāfiʿī;
al-Ramlī; al-S̲h̲āfiʿī; al-S̲h̲ahrazūrī; al-S̲h̲īrāzī, Abū Isḥāḳ; al-Subkī; al-
Sulamī, ʿIzz al-dīn; al-Ṣuʿlūkī; [au Suppl.] Abū Zurʿa; Ibn Daḳīḳ al-ʿĪd

voir aussi Abū T̲h̲awr; Dāwūd b. K̲h̲alaf; al-Isfarāyīnī

Ẓāhirites   Dāwūd b. K̲h̲alaf; al-Ḥumaydī; Ibn Dāwūd; Ibn Ḥazm, Abū
Muḥammad; (al-)Mund̲h̲ir b. Saʿīd

voir aussi Ṣāʿid al-Andalusī; [au Suppl.] Ibn al-Rūmiyya

ottoman   Bāb-i Mas̲h̲īk̲h̲at; Djazāʾ; Djurm; Fatwā; ʿIlmiyye; Ḳānūnnāme;
Ḳassām; Maḥkama.II; Mak̲h̲redj; Medjelle; Medjlis-i Wālā; Mewlewiyyet;
Nark̲h̲; S̲h̲ayk̲h̲ al-Islām.2; Sidjill.3

voir aussi Ḥanafiyya; al-Ḥaramayn; *et* → DYNASTIES.ANATOLIE ET LES
TURCS.OTTOMANS.GRANDS-MUFTIS

réforme du droit   → RÉFORME

termes   Adāʾ; Adjr; ʿAdl; Aḥkām; Ahl al-Ḥall wa-l-ʿAḳd; ʿAḳd; Akdariyya;
ʿAḳīḳa; ʿĀḳila; ʿAmal.3 et 4; Amān; ʿĀmil; Amīn; ʿĀriyya; ʿArs̲h̲; ʿAwl;
ʿAzīma.1; Baʿl.2.b; Bālig̲h̲; Barāʾa; Bayʿ; Bayʿa; Bayyina; Burhān; Ḍamān;
Dār al-ʿAhd; Dār al-Ḥarb; Dār al-Islām; Dār al-Ṣulḥ; Ḍarūra; Daʿwā;
D̲h̲abīḥa; D̲h̲imma; Diya; Djāʾiz; Djanāba; Djazāʾ; Djihād; Djizya; Djurm;
Faḳīh; Farāʾiḍ; Farḍ; Fāsid wa-Bāṭil; Fāsiḳ; Fask̲h̲; Fatwā; Fayʾ; Fik̲h̲;
G̲h̲āʾib; G̲h̲anīma; G̲h̲ārim; G̲h̲aṣb; G̲h̲usl; Ḥaḍāna; Ḥadat̲h̲; Ḥadd; Ḥadjr;
Hady; Ḥakam; Ḥaḳḳ; Ḥawāla; Ḥayḍ; Hiba; Ḥiyal; Ḥuḳūḳ; Ḥulūl; ʿIbādāt;
Ibāḥa.I; ʿIdda; Id̲h̲n; Īdjāb; Īdjār; Idjmāʿ; Idjtihād; Iḥrām; Iḥyāʾ; Iḳāla;
Ik̲h̲tilāf; Iḳrār; Ildjāʾ; Inkār; Inṣāf; Istibrāʾ; Istiḥsān; Istiʾnāf; Istiṣḥāb; ʿIwaḍ;
Ḳabāla; Ḳabḍ.I; Ḳaḍāʾ; Ḳad̲h̲f; Kafāʾa; Kafāla; Ḳānūn; Ḳānūnnāme; Ḳasam;
Ḳatl; K̲h̲aṭaʾ; K̲h̲iyār; Kirāʾ; Kirād; Ḳiṣāṣ; Ḳiyās; Liʿān; Liṣṣ; Luḳaṭa;
Maḍmūn; Mafsūl; Mahr; Maṣlaḥa; Mawāt; Mawlā.E; Maẓālim; Milk;
Muʿāmalāt; Muʿāwaḍa; Muḍāraba; Mudjtahid; Mufāwaḍa; Mug̲h̲ārasa;
Muḥṣan; Muk̲h̲āṭara; Munāṣafa; Musāḳāt; Mus̲h̲āraka; Mutʿa; Muṭlaḳ;
Muwāḍaʿa; Muzāraʿa; Nadjis; Nāfila; Naṣṣ; Nāzila; Niyya; Rahn; Ribā;
Ruk̲h̲ṣa.1; Sabab.5; Ṣadaḳa; Sadd al-D̲h̲arāʾiʿ; Ṣafḳa; Ṣaḥīḥ.2; al-Sahm.2;

Salaf; Salam; Sarika; Sawm; Shāhid; Shakhs; Shakk.1; Sharika; Shart.1; Shirā'; Shubha; Shuf'a; Sidjn; Suftadja; Suknā; Sukūt; Ṣulḥ; Sunna.2; [au Suppl.] 'Akār; Darak; Dayn; Djabr; Ghārūka; Ḥikr; Ikrāh; Inzāl
voir aussi Bayt al-Māl; Hudna; Ṣaghīr; Shukr.2; Shūrā.2; Siyāsa.3

DRUZES al-Darazī; **Durūz**; Ḥamza b. 'Alī b. Aḥmad; al-Muktanā; Shakīb Arslān; [au Suppl.] Binn
voir aussi Ḥadd; Maḥkama.IV.2, 3 et 5; Ma'n; [au Suppl.] Dawr; Ḥinn; *et* → LIBAN
historiens des Ṣāliḥ b. Yaḥyā

DYNASTIES **Dawla**; Ḥādjib; Mushīr
voir aussi Čashna-gīr; Khādim al-Ḥaramayn; Lakab; Libās.I; Malik; Marāsim; Mashwara; Mawākib; Pādishāh; Parda-dār; *et* → ADMINISTRATION; ONOMASTIQUE.TITRES
Afghanistan et Inde 'Ādil-Shāhs; Arghūn; Bahmanides; Barīd Shāhides; Dihlī (Sultanat de); Fārūkides; Ghaznawides; Ghūrides; Hindū-shāhides; 'Imād Shāhides; Kart; Khaldjis; Kuṭb-Shāhides; Lōdīs; Mughals; Niẓām Shāhides; Sayyids; Sharkīs; Sūrs; [au Suppl.] Bānīdjūrides
voir aussi Afghānistān.V.2 et 3; Awadh; Dāwūdpōtrās; Dīwān.V; Hind.IV; Khʷādja-i Djahān; Lashkar; Marāsim.5; Mawākib.V; Nithār.2; Rānā Sānga; Sammā; *et* → ARCHITECTURE.RÉGIONS; MILITAIRES.INDO-MUSULMANS; ONOMASTIQUE.TITRES.INDO-MUSULMANS
'Ādil-Shāhides (1490-1686) **'Ādil-Shāhs**; Bīdjāpūr; Hind.VII.IX
souverains Muḥammad b. Ibrāhīm II
historiens des Shīrāzī, Rafī' al-dīn
Awadh (1722-1856) **Awadh**
souverains Burhān al-Mulk; Ghāzī l-Dīn Ḥaydar; Sa'ādat 'Alī Khān; Ṣafdar Djang; Shudjā' al-Dawla
vizirs Mahdī 'Alī Khān
Bahmanides (1347-1527) **Bahmanides**; Hind.VII.VII
voir aussi Bīdar; Gulbargā; Pēshwā
sultans Humāyūn Shāh Bahmanī; Maḥmūd Shihāb al-Dīn; Muḥammad Ier; Muḥammad II; Muḥammad III
autres personnages Khalīl Allāh; Maḥmūd Gāwān
Bārakzays (1819-1973) Afghānistān.V.3.b
rois 'Abd al-Raḥmān Khān; Dūst Muḥammad; Ḥabīb Allāh Khān; Shīr 'Alī; [au Suppl.] Amān Allāh
Durrānīs (1747-1842) Afghānistān.V.3
rois Aḥmad Shāh Durrānī
historiens des 'Abd al-Karīm Munshī
autres personnages Kāmrān Shāh Durrānī

Fārūḳides (1370-1601) **Fārūḳides**
souverains Mīrān Muḥammad Shāh Ier
Ghaznawides (977-1186) ʿAmīd; Dīwān.V; **Ghaznawides**
voir aussi Ḥiṣār.III
sultans Alp Takīn; Bahrām Shāh; Ismāʿīl b. Sebüktigin; Maḥmūd b. Sebüktigin; Masʿūd b. Maḥmūd; Mawdūd b. Masʿūd; Muḥammad b. Maḥmūd b. Sebüktigin; Sebüktigin
vizirs Aḥmad b. Muḥammad; Altūntāsh; al-Faḍl b. Aḥmad al-Isfarāʾinī; Ḥasanak; Maymandī
historiens des Bayhaḳī
voir aussi al-Ḳāshānī; Shabānkāraʾī; [au Suppl.] Fakhr-i Mudabbir
autres personnages Muḥammad Bakhtiyār Khaldjī; Shāh Malik
Ghūrides (circa 1000-1215) **Ghūrides**
sultans Djahān-sūz; Muḥammad b. Sām; Sayf al-Dīn
voir aussi Niẓāmī
Langāh de Multān (1437-1526) Multān
sultans Ḥusayn Shāh Langāh Ier; Ḥusayn Shāh Langāh II
Mughals (1526-1858) Ḍarība.VI.b et c; Dīwān.V; Manṣab; **Mughals**; [au Suppl.] Ilāhī
voir aussi Fawdjdār; Kōtwāl; Maṭbakh.IV; Nithār.2; Ṣadr al-Ṣudūr.3; Ṣūba; Ṣūbadār; Ṣūfiyāna; Ṣulḥ-i kull; Suwār; [au Suppl.] Dāgh u taṣḥīḥa; ʿIbādat Khāna
empereurs Aḥmad Shāh.1; Akbar; Awrangzīb; Bābur; Bahādur Shāh Ier; Bahādur Shāh II; Djahāndār Shāh; Djahāngīr; Farrukh-siyar; Humāyūn; Muḥammad Shāh; Shāh ʿĀlam II; Shāh Djahān
voir aussi Darshan; Mumtāz Maḥall; Nūr Djahān
vizirs Iʿtimād al-Dawla
secrétaires Abū l-Faḍl ʿAllāmī; Muḥammad Kāẓim
historiens des ʿAbd al-Ḥamīd Lāhawrī; Abū l-Faḍl ʿAllāmī; Bakhtāwar Khān; Djawhar; Ghulām Ḥusayn Khān Ṭabāṭabāʾī; ʿInāyat Allāh Khān; Īsar-dās; Kh^{w}āfī Khān; Muḥammad Kāẓim; Muḥammad Sharīf; Mustaʿidd Khān; Muʿtamad Khān; Niʿmat Allāh b. Ḥabīb Allāh Harawī; Nūr al-Ḥaḳḳ al-Dihlawī; [au Suppl.] ʿĀḳil Khān Rāzī
voir aussi Aẓfarī; Badāʾūnī; Maʾāthir al-Umarāʾ
autres personnages ʿAbd al-Raḥīm Khān; ʿAlī Werdī Khān; Āṣaf Khān; Bakhtāwar Khān; Bayram Khān; Burhān al-Mulk; Dāniyāl; Ghulām Ḳādir Rohilla; Hindāl; Iʿtibār Khān; Iʿtiḳād Khān; ʿIwaḍ Wadjīh; Kāmrān; Khān Djahān Lōdī; Khusraw Sulṭān; Mahābat Khān; Makhdūm al-Mulk (*et* [au Suppl.] ʿAbd Allāh Sulṭānpūrī); Mān Singh; Mīr Djumla; Mīrzā ʿAskarī; Mīrzā ʿAzīz "Kōka"; Murād; Murād Bakhsh; Murshid Ḳulī Khān; Niẓām al-Mulk; Shafīʿā Yazdī; Shāh Manṣūr Shīrāzī; Sharīf Āmulī; al-Siyālkūtī; [au Suppl.] Akbar b.

Awrangzīb; ʿĀḳil Khān Rāzī; Ghāzī Khān; Gūran; ʿInāyāt Khān (2x)
voir aussi Bāra Sayyids (*et* [au Suppl.] Bārha Sayyids); Marāthās
Nawwābs du Bengale
rulers ʿAlī Werdī Khān; Djaʿfar; Sirādj al-Dawla
voir aussi Murshidābād
Niẓām Shāhides (1491-1633) **Niẓām Shāhides**
voir aussi Aḥmadnagar
sultans Ḥusayn Niẓām Shāh; Malik Aḥmad Baḥrī
autres personnages Malik ʿAmbar
Sultans de Bengale (1336-1576)
sultans Dāwūd Khān Kararānī; Fakhr al-Dīn Mubārakshāh; Ḥusayn Shāh; Maḥmūd; Rādjā Ganesh; Rukn al-Dīn Bārbak Shāh; Sikandar Shāh
historiens des [au Suppl.] ʿAbbās Sarwānī
Sultans de Dihlī (1206-1555) Ḍarība.VI.a; **Dihlī** (Sultanat de); Dīwān.V; Khaldjīs; Lōdīs; Nāʾib.1; Naḳīb.2; Sayyids; Sūrs
voir aussi Burdj.III.2
sultans Fīrūz Shāh Tughluḳ; Ghiyāth al-Dīn Tughluḳ Ier; Ghiyāth al-Dīn Tughluḳ Shāh II; Iltutmish; Kayḳubad; Khiḍr Khān; Ḳuṭb al-Dīn Aybak; Maḥmūd; Ibrāhīm Lōdī; Mubārak Shāh; Muḥammad b. Tughluḳ; Muḥammad Shāh Ier Khaldjī; Raḍiyya; Shir Shāh Sūr; [au Suppl.] Balban; Dawlat Khān Lōdī
vizirs Kāfūr (*et* Malik Kāfūr); Khān-i Djahān Maḳbūl; Miʾān Bhuʾā
historiens des Baranī; al-Djuzdjānī; Niẓāmī (*et* [au Suppl.] Ḥasan Niẓāmī); Shams al-Dīn-i Sirādj ʿAfīf
autres personnages Mallū Iḳbāl Khān; [au Suppl.] ʿAbd al-Wahhāb Bukhārī; ʿAyn al-Mulk Multānī; Daryā Khān Noḥānī; Ikhtisān
voir aussi ʿAlī Mardān; Hūlāgū; Khaldjīs; Sammā
Sultans du Gudjarāt (1391-1583) Gudjarāt
sultans Bahādur Shāh Gudjarātī; Maḥmūd
historiens des [au Suppl.] Ḥādjdjī al-Dabīr
autres personnages Malik Ayāz
Sultans de Kālpī Kalpī
sultans Maḥmūd Khān
Sultans de Kashmīr (1346-1589) Kashmīr
sultans Sikandar (But-Shikan); [au Suppl.] Čaks
voir aussi [au Suppl.] Gul Khātūn
historiens des [au Suppl.] Ḥaydar Malik
autres personnages [au Suppl.] Bayhaḳis
Sultans de Madura
sultans Djalāl al-Dīn Aḥsan
Sultans de Mālwā (1401-1531) Mālwā

sultans Dilāwar Khān; Hūshang Shāh Ghūrī; Maḥmūd
voir aussi Bāz Bahādur
vizirs Mēdinī Rā'ī
autres personnages Malik Mughīth
Sultans sharḳides de Djawnpur (1394-1479) **Sharḳīs**
sultans Ḥusayn Shāh; Ibrāhīm Shāh Sharḳī; Maḥmūd Shāh Sharḳī; Malik Sarwar
Afrique Fundj; Gwandu; Shīrāzī
voir aussi Bū Saʿīd; Dār Fūr; Kilwa; Songhay
Anatolie et les Turcs Artuḳides; Aydi̊n-oghlu; Dānishmendides; Dhū l-Ḳadr; Eretna; Germiyān-oghullari̊; Ḥamīd Oghullari̊; Īnāl; Isfendiyār Oghlu; Ḳarāmān-oghullari̊; Ḳarasi̊; Menteshe-oghullari̊; ʿOthmānli̊; Saltuḳ Oghullari̊; Ṣarūkhān; Shāh-i Arman
voir aussi Būrides; Derebey; Mangi̊ts; Mengüček; Ramaḍān Oghullari̊; *et* → ONOMASTIQUE.TITRES
Artuḳides (1102-1408) **Artuḳides**
souverains Īlghāzī; Nūr al-Dīn Muḥammad
Aydi̊n-oghlu (1308-1425) **Aydi̊n-oghlu**
amīrs Djunayd
Ottomans (1281-1924) **ʿOthmānli̊**
voir aussi ʿOthmān Ier; *et* → EMPIRE OTTOMAN; TURQUIE.PÉRIODE OTTOMANE
sultans ʿAbd al-ʿAzīz; ʿAbd al-Ḥamīd Ier; ʿAbd al-Ḥamīd II; ʿAbd al-Madjīd Ier; ʿAbd al-Madjīd II; Aḥmad Ier; Aḥmad II; Aḥmad III; Bāyazīd Ier; Bāyazīd II; Ibrāhīm; Maḥmūd; Meḥemmed Ier; Meḥemmed II; Meḥemmed III; Meḥemmed IV; Meḥemmed V Reshād; Meḥemmed VI Waḥīd al-Dīn; Murād Ier; Murād II; Murād III; Murād IV; Murād V; Muṣṭafā Ier; Muṣṭafā II; Muṣṭafā III; Muṣṭafā IV; Orkhan; ʿOthmān Ier; ʿOthmān II; ʿOthmān III; Selīm I; Selīm II; Selīm III; Süleymān I; Süleymān II
voir aussi Bāb-i Humāyūn; Djem; Ertoghrul; Khādim al-Ḥaramayn; Khalīfa.I.E; Khurrem; Kösem Wālide; Mashwara; Muhr.1; Muṣṭafā.I et II; Müteferriḳa; Nīlūfer Khātūn; Nūr Bānū; Rikāb; Ṣafiyye Wālide Sulṭān; Shehzāde; Ṣolaḳ
grands-vizirs **Ṣadr-ı Aʿẓam**
voir aussi Bāb-i ʿĀlī; Başvekil; Ḳapi̊; ʿOthmān-zāde
14e siècle ʿAlī Pasha Čandārli̊zāde; Djandarli̊.I
15e siècle Aḥmad Pasha Gedik; Dāwūd Pasha, Kodja; Djandarli̊; Khalīl Pasha Djandarli̊; Maḥmūd Pasha; Meḥmed Pasha, Ḳaramānī; Meḥmed Pasha, Rūm; Sinān Pasha, Khodja.1
16e siècle Aḥmad Pasha Ḳara; ʿAlī Pasha Khādim; ʿAlī Pasha Semiz; Ayās Pasha; Čighāla-zāde Sinān Pasha; Derwīsh Pasha;

Ferhād Pasha; Hersek-zāde; Ibrāhīm Pasha; Ibrāhīm Pasha, Dāmād; Khādîm Ḥasan Pasha Ṣoḳollî; Khādîm Süleymān Pasha; Lala Meḥmed Pasha (*et* Meḥmed Pasha, Lālā, Shāhīnoghlu); Luṭfī Pasha; Meḥmed Pasha, Lālā, Melek-Nihād; Mesīḥ Meḥmed Pasha; Mesīḥ Pasha; ʿOthmān Pasha; Pīrī Meḥmed Pasha; Rüstem Pasha; Sinān Pasha, Khādîm; Sinān Pasha, Khodja.2; Siyāwush Pasha.1; Soḳollu

17e siècle ʿAlī Pasha ʿArabadjī; ʿAlī Pasha Güzeldje; ʿAlī Pasha Sürmeli; Dāwūd Pasha, Ḳara; Derwīsh Meḥmed Pasha; Dilāwar Pasha; Ḥāfiẓ Aḥmed Pasha; Ḥusayn Pasha; Ibrāhīm Pasha, Kara; Ipshir Muṣṭafā Pasha; Ismāʿīl Pasha, Nishāndjî; Ḳarā Muṣṭafā Pasha; Kemānkesh; Khalīl Pasha Ḳayṣariyyeli; Khosrew Pasha, Bosniak; Köprülü.I-III; Meḥmed Pasha, Čerkes; Meḥmed Pasha, Elmās; Meḥmed Pasha, Gürdjü (I); Meḥmed Pasha, Gürdjü (II); Meḥmed Pasha, Öküz; Meḥmed Pasha, Sulṭān-zāde; Meḥmed Pasha, Tabanîyassî; Murād Pasha, Kuyudju, Naṣūḥ Pasha; Redjeb Pasha; Siyāwush Pasha.2; Süleymān Pasha, Malaṭyalî

18e siècle ʿAbd Allāh Pasha; ʿAlī Pasha Čorlulu; ʿAlī Pasha Dāmād; ʿAlī Pasha Ḥakīm-oghlu; Derwīsh Meḥmed Pasha; Ḥamza Ḥāmid Pasha; Ḥamza Pasha; (Dāmād) Ḥasan Pasha; (Seyyid) Ḥasan Pasha; (Sherīf) Ḥasan Pasha; Ibrāhīm Pasha, Nevshehirli; Kaḥyā Ḥasan Pasha; Khalīl Pasha; Köprülü.V; Meḥmed Pasha, Balṭadjî; Meḥmed Pasha, ʿIwaḍ; Meḥmed Pasha, Melek; Meḥmed Pasha, Muḥsin-zāde; Meḥmed Pasha Rāmī; Meḥmed Pasha, Tiryāḳī; Meḥmed Pasha, Yegen, Gümrükčü; Meḥmed Pasha, Yegen, Ḥādjdjī; Rāghib Pasha; Saʿīd Efendi

à partir du 19e siècle Aḥmad Wafīḳ Pasha; ʿAlī Pasha Muḥammad Amīn; Dāmād Ferīd Pasha; Derwīsh Meḥmed Pasha; Djawād Pasha; Fuʾād Pasha; Ḥusayn ʿAwnī Pasha; Ḥusayn Ḥilmī Pasha; Ibrāhīm Edhem Pasha; Ibrāhīm Ḥaḳḳī Pasha; ʿIzzet Pasha; Kečiboynuzu; Khayr al-Dīn Pasha; Khosrew Pasha, Meḥmed; Küčük Saʿīd Pasha; Maḥmūd Nedīm Pasha; Maḥmūd Shewḳat Pasha; Meḥmed Saʿīd Ghālib Pasha; Midḥat Pasha; Muṣṭafā Pasha, Bayraḳdār; Reshīd Pasha, Muṣṭafā; [au Suppl.] Esʿad Pasha

grands-muftis **Shaykh al-Islām**.2

voir aussi Bāb-i Mashīkhat; Fatwā

15e siècle Fenārī-zāde; Gūrānī; Khosrew

16e siècle Abū l-Suʿūd; Bostānzāde.2; Čiwi-zāde; Djamālī, Mawlānā; Kemāl Pasha-zāde; Khōdja Efendi

17e siècle Bahāʾī Meḥmed Efendi; Esʿad Efendi, Meḥmed; Ḳarā-Čelebi-zāde.4; Ṣunʿ Allāh

18e siècle Čelebi-zāde; Dürrizāde.I IV; Esʿad Efendi, Meḥmed (2x); Ḥayātī-zāde.2; Meḥmed Ṣāliḥ Efendi; Pīrī-zāde

19e siècle ʿĀrif Ḥikmet Bey; Dürrizāde.V; Esʿad Efendi, Aḥmed; Ḥasan Fehmī

20e siècle Djamāl al-Dīn Efendi; Dürrizāde, ʿAbd Allāh; Aḥmed; Muṣṭafā Khayrī Efendi

grands-amiraux ʿAlī Pasha Güzeldje; Čighāla-zāde Sinān Pasha; Djaʿfar Beg; Djezāʾirli Ghāzī Ḥasan Pasha; Ḥasan Pasha; Ḥusayn Pasha; Kenʿān Pasha; Khalīl Pasha Ḳayṣariyyeli; Khayr al-Dīn Pasha; Piyāle Pasha

voir aussi Raʾīs.3

historiens des ʿAbdī; ʿAbdī Efendi; ʿAbdī Pasha; Aḥmad Djewdet Pasha; Aḥmad Rasmī; ʿAlī; ʿAlī Amīrī; ʿĀshi̊ḳ-Pasha-Zāde; ʿĀṣim; ʿAṭāʾ Bey; al-Bakrī.I; Bidlīsī; Bihishtī; Čelebi-zāde; Česhmīzāde; Djalālzāde Muṣṭafā Čelebi; Djalālzāde Ṣāliḥ Čelebi; Enwerī; Esʿad Efendi, Meḥmed; Ḥasan Bey-zāde; ʿIzzī; Ḳarā-čelebi-zāde.4; Kātib Čelebi; Kemāl, Meḥmed Nāmi̊ḳ; Kemāl Pasha-zāde; Khayr Allāh Efendi; Luḳmān b. Sayyid Ḥusayn; Luṭfī Efendi; Maṭrāḳči̊; Meḥmed Ḥākim Efendi; Meḥmed Khalīfe b. Ḥüseyn; Meḥmed Pasha, Ḳaramānī; Meḥmed Zaʿīm; Muḥyī l-Dīn Meḥmed; Naʿīmā; ʿOthmān-zāde; Pečewī; Ramaḍān-zāde; Rāshid, Meḥmed; Rūḥī; Selānīkī; Shefīḳ Meḥmed Efendi; Shemʿdānī-zāde; Sheref, ʿAbd al-Raḥmān; Silāḥdār Fi̊ndi̊ḳli̊li̊; Ṣolaḳ-zāde; Ṣubḥī Meḥmed

voir aussi Ḥadīdī; Shāhnāmedji

autres personnages

voir aussi Shehzāde

13e siècle Sawdji̊.1

14e siècle ʿAlāʾ al-Dīn Beg; Badr al-Dīn Ibn Ḳāḍī Samāwnā; Ḳāsim.I; Sawdji̊.3; Shāhīn, Lala; Süleymān Pasha

15e siècle Aḥmad Pasha Khāʾin; Ewrenos; Ewrenos Oghullari̊; Fenārī-zāde; Ibn ʿArabshāh; Ḳāsim.II et III; Ḳāsim Pasha; Mūsā Čelebi; Muṣṭafā.I et II; Suleymān Čelebi

16e siècle Bostānzāde; Čiwi-zāde; Derwīsh Pasha; Djaʿfar Čelebi; Djalālzāde Muṣṭafā Čelebi; Ferīdūn Beg; Hāmōn; Ḳāsim.IV; Ḳāsim Agha; Ḳāsim Pasha; Kemāl Reʿīs; Khosrew Pasha; Ḳorḳud b. Bāyazīd; Maḥmūd Pasha; Maḥmūd Tardjumān; Meḥmed Pasha, Bi̊yi̊ḳli̊; Muṣṭafā.III; Muṣṭafā Pasha, Ḳara Shāhīn; Muṣṭafā Pasha, Lala; Muṣṭafā Pasha al Nashshār; Özdemir Pasha; Pertew Pasha.I; Ramaḍān-zāde; Ri̊dwān Pasha; Ṣari̊ Kürz; Selmān Reʾīs; Shāh Sulṭān; Shāhīn, Āl; Sīdī ʿAlī Reʾīs; Sinān

17e siècle Ābāza; Ḥaydar-oghlu, Meḥmed; Ḥusayn Pasha; Ḳāsim. V; Ḳāṭi̊rdjī-oghli̊; Maʿn-zāda; Meḥmed Khalīfe b. Ḥüseyn; ʿOthmān Pasha, Yegen; Shāhīn, Āl; [au Suppl.] Aḥmad Pasha Küčük; Čōbān-oghullari̊

18e siècle Ābāza; Aḥmad Pasha; Aḥmad Pasha Bonneval; Aḥmad

Rasmī; Djānīkli Ḥādjdji ʿAlī Pasha; Meḥmed Ḥākim Efendi; Meḥmed Yirmisekiz; Paswan-oghlu; Patrona Khalīl; Ṣarî Meḥmed Pasha
19e siècle Aḥmad Djewdet Pasha; ʿAlī Pasha Tepedelenli; Ayyūb Ṣabrī Pasha; Bahdjat Muṣṭafā Efendi; Dāwūd Pasha (2x); Djawād Pasha; Fāḍil Pasha; Ḥālet Efendi; Ḥusayn Pasha; Ibrāhīm Derwīsh Pasha; Kabakčîoghlu Muṣṭafā; Ḳōzān-oghullarî; Muṣṭafā Pasha, Bushatlî; Pertew Pasha.II; Riḍwān Begovic; Ṣādîḳ Rifʿat Pasha; Shebṣefa Ḳadîn; [au Suppl.] Camondo
20e siècle ʿAbd al-Ḥaḳḳ Ḥāmid; Djāwīd; Djemāl Pasha; Enwer Pasha; Fehīm Pasha; Ḥasan Fehmī; ʿIzzet Pasha; Kāẓîm Ḳadrī; Kāẓîm Karabekir; Mukhtār Pasha; Münīf Pasha
Saldjūḳides de Rūm (1077-1307) **Saldjūḳides**
sultans Kaykāʾūs; Kaykhusraw; Kayḳubād; Ḳîlîdj Arslan Ier; Ḳîlîdj Arslan II; Ḳîlîdj Arslan III; Ḳîlîdj Arslan IV; Malik-Shāh.IV; Sulaymān b. Ḳutulmîsh
historiens des Ibn Bībī
autres personnages Ashraf Oghullarî; Muʿīn al-Dīn Sulaymān Parwāna; Saʿd al-Dīn Köpek
Égypte et le Croissant fertile ʿAbbāsides; ʿAnnāzides; Ayyūbides; Bābān; Būrides; Fāṭimides; Ḥamdānides; Ḥasanwayh; Mamlūks; Marwānides; Mazyad; Mirdās
voir aussi ʿAmmār; Begteginides; Djalīlī; Ṣadaḳa, Banū; *et* → ÉGYPTE. PÉRIODE MODERNE.LIGNE DE MUḤAMMAD ʿALĪ; ONOMASTIQUE.TITRES. ARABES
ʿAbbāsides (749-1258) → CALIFAT
Ayyūbides (1169-fin du 15e siècle) **Ayyūbides**
voir aussi Rank
souverains al-ʿĀdil; al-Afḍal; Bahrām Shāh; al-Kāmil; (al-Malik) al-Muʿaẓẓam; al-Nāṣir; Ṣalāḥ al-Dīn; (al-Malik) al-Ṣāliḥ ʿImād al-Dīn; (al-Malik) al-Ṣāliḥ Nadjm al-Dīn Ayyūb
voir aussi Dīwān.II.III
vizirs Ibn al-ʿAdīm; Ibn al-Athīr.III; Ibn Maṭrūḥ
secrétaires ʿImād al-Dīn; al-Ḳāḍī al-Fāḍil
historiens des Abū l-Fidā; Abū Shāma; Ibn Shaddād; ʿImād al-Dīn; al-Maḳrīzī; al-Manṣūr, al-Malik
autres personnages Abū l-Fidā; Aybak; Ibn al-ʿAssāl; (Bahāʾ al-dīn) Ḳarāḳūsh; (Sharaf al-dīn) Ḳarāḳūsh; (al-Malik) al-Muẓaffar
Fāṭimides (909-1171) → CALIFAT
Ḥamdānides (905-1004) **Ḥamdānides**
souverains Nāṣir al-Dawla; Sayf al-Dawla; [au Suppl.] Abū Taghlib
autres personnages Ḥusayn b. Ḥamdān; Luʾluʾ
Ikhshīdides (935-969)
souverains Kāfūr

vizirs Ibn al-Furāt.V
autres personnages al-Ṣayrafī
Mamlūks (1250-1517) Dhū l-Faḳāriyya; Dīwān.II.IV; Ḥādjib.IV; Hiba.II; Khādim al-Ḥaramayn; Khaznadār; **Mamlūks**; Mashwara; Nā'ib.1
voir aussi Ḥarfūsh; Ḳumāsh; Mamlūk; Manshūr; Rank; *et* → MILITAIRES.
MAMELUKS
sultans Barḳūḳ; Barsbāy; Baybars Ier; Baybars II; Čaḳmaḳ; Faradj; Ḥasan; Īnāl al-Adjrūd; Ḳā'it Bāy; Ḳalāwūn; Ḳānṣawh al-Ghawrī; Khalīl; Khushḳadam; Ḳuṭuz; Lādjīn; al-Mu'ayyad Shaykh; al-Nāṣir; (al-Malik) al-Ṣāliḥ ; Shaʿbān; Shadjar al-Durr
administrateurs Faḍl Allāh; Ibn ʿAbd al-Ẓāhir; Ibn Faḍl al-ʿUmarī; Ibn Ghurāb; Ibn Ḥidjdja; Ibn al-Sadīd (Ibn al-Muzawwiḳ); Ibn al-Sadīd, Karīm al-dīn; al-Ḳalḳashandī.I; [au Suppl.] Ibn al-Ṣuḳāʿ
historiens des Abū l-Maḥāsin Ibn Taghrībirdī; Baybars al-Manṣūrī; Ibn ʿAbd al-Ẓāhir; Ibn Duḳmāḳ; Ibn Ḥabīb, Badr al-dīn; Ibn Iyās; Ibn Shāhin al-Ẓāhirī; al-Maḳrīzī; al-Mufaḍḍal b. Abī l-Fadā'il; al-Nuwayrī, Shihāb al-dīn; al-Ṣafadī, al-Ḥasan; Shāfiʿ b. ʿAlī; al-Shudjāʿī
autres personnages Abū l-Fidā; al-ʿAynī; Ibn Djamāʿa; Ibn al-Mundhir
Marwānides (983-1085) **Marwānides**
souverains Naṣr al-Dawla
Mazyadides (circa 961-1150) **Mazyad**; Ṣadaḳa, Banū
souverains Ṣadaḳa b. Manṣūr
Mirdāsides (1023-1079) **Mirdās**
voir aussi Asad al-Dawla
Ṭūlūnides (868-905)
souverains Aḥmad b. Ṭūlūn; Khumārawayh
voir aussi Ibn al-Mudabbir.I
historiens des al-Balawī; Ibn al-Dāya
autres personnages [au Suppl.] al-ʿAbbās b. Aḥmad b. Tūlūn
ʿUḳaylides (circa 990-1096)
souverains Muslim b. Ḳuraysh
Espagne et Afrique du Nord ʿAbbādides; ʿAbd al-Wādides; Afṭasides; Aghlabides; ʿAlawīs; ʿĀmirides; ʿAmmār; Dhū l-Nūnides; Djahwarides; Ḥafṣides; Ḥammādides; Ḥammūdides; Hūdides; Ḥusaynides; Idrīsides; Khurāsān, Banū; Marīnides; Midrār; al-Murābiṭūn; al-Muwaḥḥidūn; Naṣrides; Razīn, Banū; Rustamides; Saʿdides
voir aussi ʿAlāma; Dīwān.III; Ḥādjib.II et V; Hiba.III; Ḥiṣār.II; al-Ḥulal al-Mawshiyya; Ḳaramānlī; Khalīfa.I.C et D; Laḳab.III; Marāsim.2; Mawākib.II; Parias; Shurafā'.III; *et* → CALIFAT.FĀṬIMIDES
ʿAbbādides (1023-1091) **ʿAbbādides**; Ishbīliya
souverains al-Muʿtaḍid bi-llāh; al-Muʿtamid ibn ʿAbbād

voir aussi al-Rundī
vizirs Ibn ʿAmmār, Abū Bakr
ʿAbd al-Wādides (1236-1550) **ʿAbd al-Wādides**
souverains Abū Ḥammū Ier; Abū Ḥammū II; Abū Tās͟hufīn Ier; Abū Tās͟hufīn II; Abū Zayyān Ier; Abū Zayyān II; Abū Zayyān III
historiens des Ibn K͟haldūn, Abū Zakariyyāʾ
Afṭasides (1022-1094) **Afṭasides**
souverains al-Mutawakkil ʿalā llāh, Ibn al-Afṭas
vizirs Ibn Ḳuzmān.II
secrétaires Ibn ʿAbdūn; Ibn Ḳabṭūrnu
Ag͟hlabides (800-909) al-ʿAbbāsiyya; **Ag͟hlabides**; Raḳḳāda
souverains Ibrāhīm Ier; Ibrāhīm II
ʿAlawides (1631-) **ʿAlawīs**; Ḳāʾid; Mawlāy; S͟hurafāʾ.III
souverains ʿAbd Allāh b. Ismāʿīl; ʿAbd al-ʿAzīz b. al-Ḥasan; ʿAbd al-Raḥmān b. His͟ham; Ḥafīẓ (ʿAbd al-); (Mawlāy) al-Ḥasan; Mawlāy Ismāʿīl; Muḥammad [III] b. ʿAbd Allāh; Muḥammad IV b. ʿAbd al-Raḥmān; Muḥammad [V] b. Yūsuf; al-Ras͟hīd (Mawlāy); Sulaymān (Mawlāy)
vizirs Akanṣūs; Ibn Idrīs [I]; [au Suppl.] Bā Ḥmād; Ibn ʿUt͟hmān al-Miknāsī
historiens des Akanṣūs; Ibn Zaydān; al-Kardūdī
autres personnages Aḥmad al-Nāṣirī (*et* al-Nāṣirī al-Salāwī); Ibn Idrīs [II]; K͟hunāt͟ha
Almohades (1130-1269) Harg͟ha; al-ʿIḳāb; Mizwār; **al-Muwaḥḥidūn**
souverains ʿAbd al-Muʾmin b. ʿAlī; Abū Yaʿḳūb Yūsuf; Abū Yūsuf Yaʿḳūb al-Manṣūr; Ibn Tūmart; al-Maʾmūn; al-Nāṣir
historiens des ʿAbd al-Wāḥid al-Marrākus͟hī; al-Bayd͟haḳ; Ibn Ṣāḥib al-Ṣalāt
voir aussi al-Ḥulal al-Maws͟hiyya
autres personnages [au Suppl.] Ibn al-Ḳaṭṭān
voir aussi Abū Ḥafṣ ʿUmar al-Hintātī; Ibn Mardanīs͟h
Almoravides (1056-1147) Amīr al-Muslimīn; **al-Murābiṭūn**
souverains ʿAlī b. Yūsuf; al-Lamtūnī
secrétaires Ibn ʿAbdūn
historiens des Ibn al-Ṣayrafī
voir aussi al-Ḥulal al-Maws͟hiyya
autres personnages Ibn Bād͟jd͟ja; Ibn Ḳasī
ʿĀmirides (1021-1096) **Āmirides**
souverains ʿAbd al-Malik b. Abī ʿĀmir; al-Muẓaffar
vizirs Ibn al-Ḳaṭṭāʿ
autres personnages ʿAbd al-Raḥmān b. Abī ʿĀmir
D͟jahwarides (1030-1070) **D͟jahwarides**

autres personnages (al-)Ḥakam ibn ʿUk(k)āsha; Ibn ʿAbdūs
Ḥafṣides (1228-1574) **Ḥafṣides**
secrétaires Ḥāzim
historiens des al-Ḥādjdj Ḥammūda
autres personnages Ibn ʿArafa
Ḥammādides (972-1152) **Ḥammādides**
souverains Bādīs; al-Manṣūr; al-Nāṣir
voir aussi Ḳalʿat Banī Ḥammād
Ḥammūdides (1010-1057) **Ḥammūdides**
vizirs Ibn Dhakwān
Hūdides (1039-1142) **Hūdides**
souverains al-Muʾtamin ibn Hūd
Ḥusaynides (1705-1957) **Ḥusaynides**
souverains Aḥmad Bey; al-Ḥusayn (b. ʿAlī); Muḥammad Bey; Muḥammad al-Ṣādiḳ Bey
ministres Khayr al-Dīn Pasha; Muṣṭafā Khaznadār
Idrīsides (789-926) **Idrīsides**
souverains Idrīs Ier; Idrīs II
Marīnides (1196-1465) **Marīnides**
souverains Abū l-Ḥasan; Abū ʿInān
Naṣrides (1230-1492) **Naṣrids**
vizirs Ibn al-Khaṭīb
autres personnages [au Suppl.] Ibn al-Sarrādj
Rustamides (777-909) **Rustamides**
historiens des Ibn al-Ṣaghīr
Saʿdides (1511-1659) **Saʿdides**; Shurafāʾ.III
sultans ʿAbd Allāh al-Ghālib billāh; Aḥmad al-Manṣūr; Mawlāy Maḥammad al-Shaykh
voir aussi Mawlāy
vizirs Ibn ʿĪsā
historiens des ʿAbd al-ʿAzīz b. Muḥammad; al-Ifrānī
autres personnages [au Suppl.] Abū Maḥallī
Tudjībides (1019-1039)
souverains Maʿn b. Muḥammad; al-Muʿtaṣim
ʿUbaydides
historiens des Ibn Ḥamādu
Umayyades (756-1031)
émirs et califes ʿAbd Allāh b. Muḥammad; ʿAbd al-Raḥmān; al-Ḥakam Ier; al-Ḥakam II; Hishām Ier; Hishām II; Hishām III; al-Mahdī; al-Mundhir b. Muḥammad
voir aussi Madīnat al-Zahrāʾ; Muʿāwiya b. Hishām; Rabaḍ; al-Ruṣāfa.4; [au Suppl.] Bubashtru

vizirs Ibn ʿAlḳama.II; Ibn Shuhayd
secrétaires ʿArīb b. Saʿd; Ibn Burd.I
autres personnages ʿAbd al-Raḥmān b. Marwān; Ghālib b. ʿAbd al-Raḥmān; Ḥabīb b. ʿAbd al-Malik; Ḥasdāy b. Shaprūṭ; Ibn ʿAlḳama.I; Ibn Dhakwān; Ibn al-Ḥannāṭ; Ibn Ḳasī; Ibn al-Ḳiṭṭ; al-Manṣūr; Rabīʿ b. Zayd; Ṣubḥ
Zīrides (972-1152)
souverains Buluggīn b. Zīrī; al-Muʿizz b. Bādīs
autres personnages Ibn Abī l-Ridjāl
voir aussi Ḳurhub
Zīrides de Granade (1012-1090)
souverains ʿAbd Allāh b. Buluggīn
Mongols Bātūʾides; Čaghatay; Čingizides; Djalāyir; Djānides; Girāy; Īlkhāns; Ḳarā Khiṭāy; **Mongols**; Shībānides
voir aussi Čubānides; Ḳāzān; Soyūrghāl; [au Suppl.] Āgahī; Dīwān-begi; Djamāl Ḳarshī; Ordu.2; *et* → ONOMASTIQUE.TITRES.MONGOLS
Bātūʾides (1236-1502) **Bātūʾides**
voir aussi Saray
souverains Bātū; Berke Khān; Mangū-tīmūr
autres personnages Masʿūd Beg
Djānides (1598-1785) **Djānides**
souverains Nadhr Muḥammad
voir aussi Bukhārā
Grands-Khāns (1206-1634) Čingizides
khāns Činghiz Khān; Ḳubilay; Möngke; Ögedey
autres personnages Ḳaydu; Maḥmūd Yalawač
Īlkhāns (1256-1353) **Īlkhāns**
voir aussi Ṣadr.1
khāns Baydu, Gaykhātū; Ghāzān; Hūlāgū; Öldjeytü
vizirs Saʿd al-Dawla
historiens des Ḥamd Allāh al-Mustawfī al-Ḳazwīnī; Rashīd al-Dīn Ṭabīb
autres personnages Djuwaynī, ʿAlāʾ al-dīn; Ḳutlugh-Shāh Noyan
Khānat de Čaghatay (1227-1370) **Čaghatay**
souverains Burāḳ Khān; Čaghatay Khān
historiens des Ḥaydar Mīrzā
Khānat de Girāy (circa 1426-1792) **Girāy**
souverains Dawlat Giray; Ghāzī Girāy Ier; Ghāzī Girāy II; Ghāzī Girāy III; Ḥādjdjī Girāy; Islām Girāy; Ḳaplan Girāy Ier; Ḳaplan Girāy II; Meḥmed Girāy Ier; Mengli Girāy Ier; Ṣāḥib Girāy Khān I; Selīm Girāy I
voir aussi Ḳalghay; Meḥmed Baghčesarāyī; Meḥmed Girāy

Shaybānides (1500-1598) **Shībānides**
souverains ʿAbd Allāh b. Iskandar; Abū l-Khayr; Shībānī Khān
historiens des Abū l-Ghāzī; [au Suppl.] Ḥāfiẓ Tanïsh
Péninsule arabique Bū Saʿīd; Hamdānides; Hāshimides (2x); āl Khalīfa; Mahdides; Nadjāḥides; Rashīd, Āl; Rasūlides; Ṣabaḥ, Āl; Ṣulayḥides; Suʿūd, Āl; [au Suppl.] Djabrides
Āl Saʿūd (1746-) **Suʿūd, Āl**
souverains [au Suppl.] ʿAbd al-ʿAzīz; Fayṣal b. ʿAbd al-ʿAzīz
voir aussi Muḥammad b. Suʿūd
Bū Saʿīd (1741-) **Bū Saʿīd**
sultans Barghash; Saʿīd b. Sulṭān
Hāshimides (1908-1925) **Hāshimides**
souverains Ḥusayn (b. ʿAlī)
voir aussi ʿAbd Allāh b. al Ḥusayn; Fayṣal Ier; Fayṣal II
Ḳarmaṭes (894-fin du 11e siècle) **Ḳarmaṭī**
souverains al-Djannābī, Abū Saʿīd; al-Djannābī, Abū Ṭāhir
Rasūlides (1229-1454) **Rasūlides**
historiens des al-Khazradjī
autres personnages [au Suppl.] Ibn Ḥātim
voir aussi al-Sharīf Abū Muḥammad Idrīs
Ṭāhirides (1454-1517)
souverains ʿĀmir Ier; ʿĀmir II
Zaydīs (860-) Rassides
imāms Ḥasan al-Uṭrūsh; al-Mahdī li-Dīn Allāh Aḥmad; al-Manṣūr bi-llāh, ʿAbd Allāh; al-Manṣūr bi-llāh, al-Ḳāsim b. ʿAlī; al-Manṣūr bi-llāh al-Ḳāsim b. Muḥammad; al-Muʾayyad bi-llāh Muḥammad; Muḥammad al-Murtaḍā li-Dīn Allāh; al-Mutawakkil ʿalā llāh, Ismāʿīl; al-Mutawakkil ʿalā llāh, Sharaf al-dīn; al-Nāṣir li-Dīn Allāh, Abū l-Ḥasan; al-Rassī; [au Suppl.] al-Ḥādī ilā l-Ḥaḳḳ
voir aussi Imāma
autres personnages al-Muṭahhar; al-Nāṣir (li-dīn Allāh); al-Sharīf Abū Muḥammad Idrīs
Zurayʿides (1138-1174)
vizirs Bilāl b. Djarīr al-Muḥammadī
Perse Afrāsiyābides; Aḥmadīlīs; Aḳ Ḳoyunlu; Bādūsbānides; Bāwand; Buwayhides; Dulafides; Faḍlawayh; Farīghūnides; Ḥasanwayh; Hazāraspides; Ildeñizides; Ilek-Khāns; Ilyāsides; Īndjū; Ḳādjār; Kākūyides; Ḳarā-ḳoyunlu; Ḳārinides; Kāwūs; Khʷārazm-shāhs; Ḳutlugh-khānides; Lur-i Buzurg; Lur-i Kūčik; Mangïts; Marʿashīs; Muḥtādjides; Musāfirides; Mushaʿshaʿ; Muẓaffarides; Rawwādides; Ṣafawides; Ṣaffārides; Saldjūḳides; Salghurides; Sāmānides; Sarbadārides; Sāsānides; Shaddādides; Shīrwān Shāh
voir aussi Ardalān; Atabak; ʿAwfī; Čāshna-gīr; Daylam; Dīwān.IV;

D̲jalāyir; G̲h̲ulām.II; Ḥād̲j̲ib.III; Ḥarb.V; al-Ḥasan b. Zayd b. Muḥammad; Hiba.IV; Ḥiṣār.III; Īlk̲h̲āns; Īrān.V; Kayānides; Marāsim.3; Mawākib.III; S̲h̲āhī; *et* → ONOMASTIQUE.TITRES.PERSANS

Afs̲h̲ārides (1736-1795) **Afs̲h̲ār**

souverains Nādir S̲h̲āh Afs̲h̲ār

historiens des ʿAbd al-Karīm Kas̲h̲mīrī; Mahdī K̲h̲ān Astarābādī

Buwayhides (932-1062) **Buwayhides**

souverains Abū Kālīd̲j̲ār; ʿAḍud al-Dawla; Bak̲h̲tiyār; D̲j̲alāl al-Dawla; Fak̲h̲r al-Dawla; ʿImād al-Dawla; K̲h̲usraw Fīrūz (*et* al-Malik al-Raḥīm); Mad̲j̲d al-Dawla; Muʾayyid al-Dawla; Muʿizz al-Dawla; Rukn al-Dawla; Ṣamṣām al-Dawla; S̲h̲ams al-Dawla; S̲h̲araf al-Dawla; Sulṭān al-Dawla; [au Suppl.] Bahāʾ al-Dawla wa-Ḍiyāʾ al-Milla

vizirs al-ʿAbbās b. al-Ḥusayn; Ibn ʿAbbād; Ibn al-ʿAmīd; Ibn Baḳiyya; Ibn Mākūlā.I et II; al Muhallabī, Abū Muḥammad; Sābūr b. Ardas̲h̲īr; [au Suppl.] ʿAbd al-ʿAzīz b. Yūsuf; Ibn K̲h̲alaf.I; Ibn Saʿdān

secrétaires Hilāl al-Ṣābiʾ (*et* Ṣābiʾ.(3).9); Ibn Hindū; Ṣābiʾ.(3).7

historiens des Ṣābiʾ.(3).7

autres personnages al-Basāsīrī; Fasand̲j̲us; Ḥasan b. Ustād̲h̲-hurmuz; Ibn Ḥād̲j̲ib al-Nuʿmān; ʿImrān b. S̲h̲āhīn; al-Malik al-ʿAzīz; [au Suppl.] Ibrāhīm S̲h̲īrāzī

Dābūyides (660-760)

souverains Dābūya

Ildeñizides (1137-1225) **Ildeñizides**

souverains Ildeñiz; Özbeg b. Muḥammad Pahlawān; Pahlawān

Ḳād̲j̲ārs (1779-1924) **Ḳād̲j̲ār**; Mus̲h̲īr al-Dawla

voir aussi Ḳāʾim-maḳām-i Farāhānī; Madjlis al-S̲h̲ūrā; *et* → IRAN. PÉRIODE MODERNE

souverains Āg̲h̲ā Muḥammad S̲h̲āh; Fatḥ ʿAlī S̲h̲āh; Muḥammad ʿAlī S̲h̲āh Ḳād̲j̲ār; Muḥammad S̲h̲āh; Muẓaffar al-Dīn S̲h̲āh Ḳād̲j̲ār; Nāṣir al-Dīn S̲h̲āh

autres personnages ʿAbbās Mīrzā; [au Suppl.] Amīr Niẓām; Ḥād̲j̲d̲j̲ī Ibrāhīm

K̲h̲ānat de K̲h̲īwa K̲h̲īwa

souverains Abū l-G̲h̲āzī

K̲h̲ʷārazm-S̲h̲āhs (circa 995-1231) **K̲h̲ʷārazm-s̲h̲āhs**

souverains Atsïz b. Anūs̲h̲tigin; D̲j̲alāl al-Dīn K̲h̲ʷārizm-s̲h̲āh; Maʾmūn b. Muḥammad

historiens des D̲j̲uwaynī; al-Nasawī

autres personnages Burāḳ Ḥād̲j̲ib

Muẓaffarides (1314-1393) **Muẓaffarides**

souverains S̲h̲āh-i S̲h̲ud̲j̲āʿ

historiens des Muʿīn al-Dīn Yazdī

Pahlawīs (1926-1979) **Pahlawī**

et → IRAN.PÉRIODE MODERNE

souverains Muḥammad Riḍā Shāh Pahlawī; Riḍā Shāh

Sādjides (circa 856-circa 930) **Sādjides**

souverains Abū l-Sādj; Muḥammad b. Abī l-Sādj

Ṣafawides (1501-1732) Bārūd.V; Īshīk-āḳāsī; Iʿtimād al-Dawla; Ḳūrčī; Libās. III; **Ṣafawides**

voir aussi Ḥaydar; Ḳizil-bāsh; Nuḳṭawiyya; Ṣadr.3; Ṣadr al-Dīn Ardabīlī; Ṣadr al-Dīn Mūsā; Ṣafī al-Dīn Ardabīlī; Soyūrghāl

souverains ʿAbbās Ier; Ḥusayn (*et* Sulṭān Ḥusayn, Shāh); Ismāʿīl Ier; Ismāʿīl II; Sulaymān, Shāh

historiens des Ḥasan-i Rūmlū; Iskandar Beg; Ḳummī

voir aussi [au Suppl.] Ibn al-Bazzāz al-Ardabīlī

autres personnages Alḳāṣ Mīrzā; Ḥamza Mīrzā; al-Karakī; Madjlisī

Ṣaffārides (867-circa 1495) **Ṣaffārides**

souverains ʿAmr b. al-Layth

Saldjūḳides (1038-1194) Amīr Dād; Arslan b. Saldjūḳ; Atabak; **Saldjūḳides**

voir aussi Sarāparda; *et* → DYNASTIES.ANATOLIE ET LES TURCS. SALDJŪḲIDES DE RŪM

souverains Alp Arslan; Bahrām Shāh; Barkyārūḳ; Maḥmūd b. Muḥammad b. Malik-shāh; Malik-Shāh.I-III; Masʿūd b. Muḥammad b. Malik-Shāh; Muḥammad b. Maḥmūd b. Muḥammad b. Malik-shāh; Muḥammad b. Malik-shāh; Riḍwān; Sandjar

voir aussi Čaghrı̊-beg; Silāḥdār

vizirs Anūshirwān b. Khālid; Djahīr; al-Kundurī; Madjd al-Mulk al-Balāsānī; al-Maybudī.III; Niẓām al-Mulk; Rabīb al-Dawla; [au Suppl.] Ibn Dārust

historiens des al-Bundārī; ʿImād al-Dīn; Nīshāpūrī; Rāwandī; [au Suppl.] al-Ḥusaynī

autres personnages Āḳ Sunḳur al-Bursuḳī; Arslan-Arghūn; Ayāz; al-Basāsīrī; Būrī-bars; Bursuḳ; Büz-abeh; Ḳāwurd; Khalaf b. Mulāʿib; Khāṣṣ Beg; Kurbuḳa; Niẓāmiyya; [au Suppl.] Ekinči

Salghurides (1148-1270) **Salghurides**

souverains Saʿd b. Zangī

Sāmānides (819-1005) **Sāmānides**

souverains Ismāʿīl b. Aḥmad; Ismāʿīl b. Nūḥ; Manṣūr b. Nūḥ; Naṣr b. Aḥmad b. Ismāʿīl; Nūḥ (Ier); Nūḥ (II)

vizirs Balʿamī; al-Muṣʿabī; [au Suppl.] al-Djayhānī

historiens des Narshakhī

voir aussi al-Sallāmī

autres personnages Arslan b. Saldjūḳ; Sīmdjūrides; [au Suppl.] al-Djayhānī

Ṭāhirides (821-873)
    souverains   ʿAbd Allāh b. Ṭāhir; Muḥammad b. Ṭāhir
    historiens des   Ibn al-Daybaʿ
    autres personnages   Muḥammad b. ʿAbd Allāh (b. Ṭāhir)
Tīmūrides (1370-1506)
    voir aussi Ṣadr.2; Soyūrghāl
    souverains   Abū Saʿīd b. Tīmūr; Bāyḳarā; Baysonghor; Ḥusayn;
      Shāhru<u>kh</u>
      voir aussi <u>Kh</u>ān-zāda Bēgum
    historiens des   Ibn ʿArab<u>sh</u>āh; <u>Kh</u>ʷāfī <u>Kh</u>ān; <u>Sh</u>āmī, Niẓām al-Dīn;
      <u>Sh</u>araf al-Dīn ʿAlī Yazdī
    autres personnages   Mīr ʿAlī <u>Sh</u>īr Nawāʾī; Mīrān<u>sh</u>āh b. Tīmūr
Zands (1750-1794)
    souverains   Karīm <u>Kh</u>ān; Luṭf ʿAlī <u>Kh</u>ān
    voir aussi Lak
Zangides (1127-1222)
    souverains   Masʿūd b. Mawdūd b. Zangī; Mawdūd b. ʿImād al-Dīn
      Zankī; Nūr al-Dīn Arslān <u>Sh</u>āh; Nur al-Dīn Maḥmūd b. Zankī
    vizirs   al-<u>Dj</u>awād al-Iṣfahānī
      voir aussi Begteginides; Ḳarīm <u>Kh</u>ān; Luʾluʾ, Badr al-dīn
    historiens des   Ibn al-A<u>th</u>īr.II
    autres personnages   <u>Sh</u>īrkūh
Ziyārides (927- circa 1090)
    souverains   Ḳābūs b. Wu<u>sh</u>magīr; Kay Kāʾūs b. Iskandar; Mardawɪ<u>dj</u>

E

ÉCONOMIQUE   Bayʿ; Kasb; Māl
    voir aussi Muḍāraba

ÉCRITURE   **<u>Kh</u>aṭṭ**
    voir aussi Ibn Muḳla; Kitābāt; *et* → ART.CALLIGRAPHIE. ÉPIGRAPHIE
    écritures   <u>Kh</u>aṭṭ; Siyāḳat
      voir aussi Nus<u>kh</u>a; Swahili; *et* → ART.CALLIGRAPHIE; ÉPIGRAPHIE
    fournitures   <u>Dj</u>ild; Kāghad; Ḳalam; <u>Kh</u>ātam; Ḳirṭās; Kitāb; Midād; Papyrus;
      Raḳḳ; [au Suppl.] Dawāt
      voir aussi ʿAfṣ; Afsantīn; Diplomatique; Īl<u>kh</u>āns; Maʿdin.IV
    manuscrits et livres   Daftar; Ḥā<u>sh</u>iya; **Kitāb**; Muḳābala.II; **Nus<u>kh</u>a**; [au Suppl.]
      Abréviations
      voir aussi Ḳaṭʿ; Maktaba
    reliure   Īl<u>kh</u>āns; Kitāb; Nus<u>kh</u>a; ʿOthmānlî.VII.c

ÉDUCATION **Maʿārif**
voir aussi ʿArabiyya.B.IV; Idjāza
bibliothèques Dār al-ʿIlm; **Maktaba**
voir aussi ʿAlī Pasha Mubārak; Khāzin; al-Madīna.I.5
bibliothécaires Ibn al-Fuwaṭī; Ibn Ḥadjar al-ʿAsḳalānī; Ibn al-Sāʿī; al-Kattānī
collections ʿAlī Amīrī (*et* [au Suppl.] ʿAlī Emīrī); Esʿad Efendi, Meḥmed; Khudā Bakhsh; [au Suppl.] ʿAbd al-Wahhāb
voir aussi Geniza
établissements d'éducation Dār al-Ḥadīth; Djāmiʿa; Köy Enstitüleri; Kuttāb; Madrasa; Maktab; Pesantren
voir aussi Kulliyya; Ṣadr.c; Samāʿ.2; Shaykh; *et* → ÉDUCATION.BIBLIOTHÈQUES
établissements individuels al-Azhar; Bayt al-Ḥikma; Dār al-Ḥikma; Dār al-ʿUlūm; Ghalaṭa-sarāyi̊; Ḥarbiye; al-Ḳarawiyyīn.II; al-Khaldūniyya; Makhredj; Mulkiyya; al-Ṣādiḳiyya; [au Suppl.] Institut des hautes études marocaines; Institut des hautes études de Tunis
voir aussi Aligarh; Deoband; Filāḥa.III; al-Ḳāhira; Lakhnaw; al-Madīna.I.5; Makka.III; Muṣṭafā ʿAbd al-Rāziḳ; al-Mustanṣir (I); Nadwat al-ʿUlamāʾ; [au Suppl.] ʿAbd al-Bārī; ʿAbd al-Wahhāb; Farangī Maḥall
sociétés savantes et académies Andjuman; Djamʿiyya; Djemʿiyyet-i ʿIlmiyye-i ʿOthmāniyye; Institut d'Égypte; Khalḳevi; Madjmaʿ ʿIlmī
réforme → RÉFORME
traités sur Ergin, Osman

ÉGYPTE al-Azhar; al-Ḳāhira; Ḳibṭ; **Miṣr**; Nūba; al-Ṣaʿīd
voir aussi al-ʿArab.IV; al-Fusṭāṭ; *et* → DYNASTIES.ÉGYPTE ET LE CROISSANT FERTILE; NUBIE
administration Dār al-Maḥfūẓāt al-ʿUmūmiyya; Dīwān.II; Ḳabāla; Kharādj.I; Rawk
voir aussi Miṣr.D.1.b; *et* → CALIFAT.ʿABBĀSIDES *et* FĀṬIMIDES; DYNASTIES.ÉGYPTE ET LE CROISSANT FERTILE.MAMLŪKS; EMPIRE OTTOMAN.ADMINISTRATION
architecture → ARCHITECTURE.RÉGIONS
avant l'Islam Firʿawn; Manf; Miṣr.D.1; Nūba.II; Saḳḳāra; [au Suppl.] Abū Sinbil
dynasties ʿAbbāsides; Ayyūbides; Fāṭimides; Mamlūks; Muḥammad ʿAlī Pasha *et* → DYNASTIES.ÉGYPTE ET LE CROISSANT FERTILE
géographie physique
eaux Burullus; al-Nīl
voir aussi Miḳyās; Rawḍa; al-Suways
historiens Abū l-Maḥāsin Ibn Taghrībirdī; ʿAlī Pasha Mubārak; al-Bakrī.II; al-Balawī; al-Damurdāshī; al-Djabartī; Ibn ʿAbd al-Ḥakam.IV; Ibn Duḳmāḳ; Ibn Iyās; Ibn Muyassar; al-Kindī, Abū ʿUmar Muḥammad; al-Maḳrīzī; al-

Nuwayrī, Muḥammad; Rifāʿa Bey; al-Ṣafadī, al-Ḥasan; Salīm al-Naḳḳāsh; al-Suyūṭī
et → DYNASTIES.ÉGYPTE ET LE CROISSANT FERTILE

période moderne Ḍarība.IV; Djarīda.I.A; Djāmiʿa; Dustūr.III; Ḥizb.I; Ḥukūma.III; al-Ikhwān al-Muslimūn; Iltizām; Imtiyāzāt.IV; Institut d'Égypte; Maʿārif.I.2; Madjlis.IV.A.16; Madjmaʿ ʿIlmī.I.2; Maḥkama.IV.1; Miṣr.D.7; Salafiyya.2a
voir aussi Baladiyya.II; al-Bannāʾ; Madjlis al-Shūrā

hommes d'état ʿAlī Pasha Mubārak; al-Bārūdī; Fikrī; Ismāʿīl Ṣidḳī; Luṭfī al-Sayyid; Muḥammad Farīd Bey; Muḥammad Nadjīb; al-Naḥḥās; Nūbār Pasha; Saʿd Zaghlūl; al Sādāt; Sharīf Pasha; [au Suppl.] ʿAbd al-Nāṣir
voir aussi Muṣṭafā Kāmil Pasha

ligne de Muḥammad ʿAlī ʿAbbās Ḥilmī Ier; ʿAbbās Ḥilmī II; Fuʾād al-Awwal; Ḥusayn Kāmil; Ibrāhīm Pasha; Ismāʿīl Pasha; Muḥammad ʿAlī Pasha; Saʿīd Pasha; [au Suppl.] Bakhīt al-Muṭīʿī; Fārūḳ
voir aussi ʿAzīz Miṣr; Khidīw; [au Suppl.] Dāʾira Saniyya; Ibʿādiyya

personnes influentes Djamāl al-Dīn al-Afghānī; al-Marṣafī; Muḥammad ʿAbduh; Muṣṭafā Kāmil Pasha; al-Muwayliḥī.I; Rifāʿa Bey; Salāma Mūsā; al-Sanhūrī, ʿAbd al-Razzāḳ; Sayyid Ḳuṭb; Shākir, Aḥmad Muḥammad; Shaltūt, Maḥmūd; al-Subkiyyūn; [au Suppl.] Abū l-ʿAzāʾim; al-ʿAdawī; al-Bakrī; al-Biblāwī; Djawharī, Ṭanṭāwī; al-ʿIdwī al-Ḥamzāwī; ʿIllaysh

période ottomane (1517-1798) Dhū l-Faḳāriyya; Ḳāsimiyya; Ḳazdughliyya; Miṣr.D.6; Muḥammad ʿAlī Pasha; Shaykh al-Balad
voir aussi Ḥurriyya.Époque moderne

beys ʿAlī Bey; Muḥammad Abū l-Dhahab (*et* [au Suppl.] Abū l-Dhahab)

population ʿAbābda; Ḳibṭ
voir aussi [au Suppl.] Démographie.IV; *et* → CHRISTIANISME.CONFESSIONS.COPTES

toponymes

anciens Adfū; Bābalyūn; al-Bahnasā; Burullus; Dabīḳ; al-Ḳulzum; Manf; Shaṭā
voir aussi al-Sharḳiyya

actuels

régions Buḥayra; al-Fayyūm; al-Gharbiyya; Girgā; al-Sharḳiyya; Sīnāʾ
voir aussi al-Ṣaʿīd

villes ʿAbbāsa; Abūḳīr; Akhmīm; al-ʿAllāḳī; al-ʿArīsh; Asyūṭ; Aṭfīḥ; ʿAyn Shams; Banhā; Banī Suwayf; Bilbays; Būlāḳ; Būṣīr; Daḥshūr; Daḳahliyya; Damanhūr; Dimyāṭ; al-Farāfra; al-Fusṭāṭ; Girgā; Ḥulwān; al-Iskandariyya; Ismāʿīliyya; Isna; al-Ḳāhira; Ḳalyūb; Ḳanṭara.3; Ḳifṭ; Ḳunā; Ḳūṣ; Ḳuṣayr; al-Maḥalla al-Kubrā; al-Manṣūra; Manūf; Port-Saïd; Rafaḥ; Rashīd; Saḳḳāra; Samannūd;

Sīwa; al-Suways; [au Suppl.] Abū Zaʿbal
voir aussi al-Mukaṭṭam; Rawḍa

ÉMANCIPATION Ḥurriyya
pour l'affranchissement, voir ʿAbd; *et pour l'émancipation des femmes* → FEMMES

ÉMIGRATION Djāliya; **Hidjra**
voir aussi al-Mahdjar; Muhādjir; al-Muhādjirūn; Pārsīs; Ṣiḥāfa.C; *et* → NOUVEAU MONDE

ÉMIRATS ARABES UNIS al-Ḳawāsim; Madjlis.IV.A.12; Maḥkama.IV.9; [au Suppl.] **al-Imārāt al-ʿArabiyya al-Muttaḥida**
population Mazrūʿī
et → TRIBUS.PÉNINSULE ARABIQUE
toponymes Abū Ẓabī; al-Djiwāʾ; Dubayy; al-Fudjayra; Raʾs al-Khayma; al-Shārika; Ṣir Banī Yās; [au Suppl.] ʿAdjmān
voir aussi (Djazīrat) al-ʿArab; al-Khaṭṭ

EMPIRE OTTOMAN Anadolu.III.2 et 3; Ertoghrul.I; Istanbul; Lāle Devri; **ʿOthmānli**
voir aussi Bāb-i ʿĀlī; Ḥidjāz; Maṭbakh.II; Pasha Ḳapusu; Shenlik; *et* → DROIT.OTTOMAN; DYNASTIES.ANATOLIE ET LES TURCS; EUROPE.EUROPE ORIENTALE; MILITAIRES.OTTOMANS; *et l'entrée Période Ottomane sous pays individuels*
administration Beratli; Ḍabṭiyya; Dīwān-i Humāyūn; Eyālet; Imtiyāzāt.II; Khāṣṣ; Khazīne; Mashwara; Millet.3; Mukhtār; Mülāzemet; Mulāzim; Mulkiyya; Nāḥiye; Nishāndji; Reʾīs ül-Küttāb; Sandjaḳ; [au Suppl.] Dāʾira Saniyya
voir aussi Ḳaḍāʾ; Maʾmūr; Odjaḳ; *et* → DOCUMENTS.OTTOMANS; DROIT.OTTOMAN; MILITAIRES.OTTOMANS
archives et registres Başvekalet Arşivi; Daftar-i Khāḳānī; Maṣraf Defteri; Mühimme Defterleri; Sāl-nāme; **Sidjill**.3
voir aussi Daftar.III; Ferīdūn Beg; Maḥlūl
financière Arpaliḳ; Ashām; Bayt al-Māl.II; Daftardār; Dār al-Ḍarb; Dirlik; Djayb-i Humāyūn; Duyūn-i ʿUmūmiyye; Irsāliyye; Ḳāʾime; Khazīne; Māliyye; Muḥāsaba.II; Mukhallefāt; Muṣādara.3; Rūznāmedji; Sāliyāne; Siyāḳat
voir aussi Bakhshīsh; Ṣurra
fiscale Ḍarība.III; Djizya.II; Ḥisba.II; Kharādj.III; Muḥaṣṣil; Mültezim; ʿOthmānli.II; Resm
voir aussi Mutaṣarrif; Shehir Ketkhüdāsi

agriculture Filāḥa.IV; Māʾ.VIII; Raʿiyya.2
et → AGRICULTURE
cérémonies de la cour Čāʾūsh; Khirḳa-i Sherīf; Marāsim.4; Mawākib.IV; Mehter; Selāmlïḳ
diplomatie Balyos; Consul; Elči; Hiba.V; Penče
voir aussi Beratlï; Imtiyāzāt.II; Ḳawwās; *et* → DIPLOMATIE
droit → DROIT.OTTOMAN
éducation Ghalaṭa-sarāyï; Külliyye; Maʿārif.I.1; Makhredj; Mulkiyya; Ṣaḥn-i Thamān; Ṣofta
voir aussi Ḥarbiye; *et* → ÉDUCATION; RÉFORME.D'ÉDUCATION
fonctionnaires Āmeddji; Aʿyān; Bazïrgan; Bostāndjï; Bostāndjï-bashï; Čakïrdjï-bashï; Čāshnagīr-bashï; Ḍābiṭ; Ḍabṭiyya; Daftardār; Dilsiz; Doghandjï; Elči; Emīn; Ghulām.IV; Ḥekīm-bashï; Ič-oghlanï; ʿIlmiyye; Ḳāʾim-maḳām; Ḳapu Aghasï; Ḳawwās; Ketkhudā; Khaznadār; Khʷādjegān-i Dīwān-i Humāyūn; Maʾmūr; Mewḳūfātčï; Mīr-Ākhūr; Mushīr; Mustashār; Mutaṣarrïf; Nishāndjï; Reʾis ül-Küttāb; Rūznāmedji; Ṣadr-ı Aʿẓam; Shāhnāmedji; Shehir-emaneti; Shehir Ketkhüdāsï
voir aussi ʿAdjamī oghlān; ʿAsas; Bālā; Balṭadjï; Balyos; Bīrūn; Enderūn; al-Ḥaramayn; Khaṣī; Khāṣṣ Oda; Khāṣṣekī; Mābeyn; *et* → DROIT.OTTOMAN; MILITARES.OTTOMANS
histoire ʿOthmānlï.I
et → DYNASTIES.ANATOLIE ET LES TURCS; LITTÉRATURE.HISTORIQUE.TURQUE; TURQUIE.PÉRIODE OTTOMANE
industrie et commerce Ḥarīr.II; Kārwān; Ḳuṭn.II; Milḥ.3; ʿOthmānlï.II; Sūḳ.7
voir aussi Maʿdin.III
littérature → LITTÉRATURE
militaires → MILITAIRES.OTTOMANS
modernisation Baladiyya.I; Ḥukūma.I; Ḥurriyya; Iṣlāḥ.III; Ittiḥād we Teraḳḳī Djemʿiyyeti; Madjlis.IV.A.1; Madjlis al-Shūrā
et → TURQUIE.PÉRIODE OTTOMANE

ENFANCE → PHASES DE LA VIE

ENFER Aṣḥāb al-Ukhdūd; **Djahannam**; Saʿīr; Saḳar; Ṣirāṭ
voir aussi al-Aʿrāf; Shayṭān.1

ÉPIGRAPHIE **Kitābāt**
voir aussi Eldem, Khalīl Edhem; Ḥisāb al-Djummal; Khaṭṭ; Musnad.1
lieux des inscriptions Lībiyā.II; Liḥyān; Orkhon; al-Sawdāʾ; Ṣiḳilliyya.4; Ṣirwāḥ.1
voir aussi Ḥaḍramawt; Sabaʾ; Ṣafaïtique

Eschatologie ʿAdhāb al-Ḳabr; Ākhira; al-Aʿrāf; Barzakh; Baʿth; Djahannam; Djanna; Djazāʾ; Dunyā; Ḥawḍ; Ḥisāb; Isrāfīl; ʿIzrāʾīl; Ḳiyāma; Maʿād; al-Mahdī; Mawḳif.2; Munkar wa-Nakīr; Sāʿa.3

voir aussi Ḳayyim; Shafāʿa; Shaḳāwa; *et* → Mort; Paradis

l'au-delà Adjr.1; **Ākhira**

voir aussi Dunyā

signes ʿAṣā; Dābba; al-Dadjdjāl

voir aussi Baʿth; Sāʿa.3

Esclavage **ʿAbd**; Ghulām; ʿİtḳnāme; Ḳayna; Khāṣī; Mamlūk; Mawlā; al-Ṣaḳāliba

voir aussi Ḥabash.I; Ḥabshī; Hausa; ʿIdda.V; Istibrāʾ; Khādim; Ḳul; Maṭmūra; Sidi; *et* → Musique.chant.chanteurs

Espagne Aljamía; Almogávares; al-Burt; al-Bushārrāt; Morisques

voir aussi Ibn al-Ḳiṭṭ; Ifni; al-ʿIḳāb; *et* → Andalousie; Dynasties.espagne et afrique du nord

géographie physique

eaux al-Ḥamma; Ibruh; al-Mudawwar; Shaḳūra; [au Suppl.] Araghūn

montagnes al-Shārāt

toponymes

anciens Barbashturu; Bulāy; Ḳasṭīliya; Labla; al-Madīna al-Zāhira; Shadūna; Shaḳunda; Shaḳūra; Shantabariyya; [au Suppl.] Āfrāg; Balyūnash

voir aussi Rayya

actuels

îles al-Djazāʾir al-Khālidāt; Mayūrḳa; Minūrḳa

régions Ālaba wa-l-Ḳilāʿ; Djillīḳiyya; Faḥṣ al-Ballūṭ; Firrīsh; Ḳanbāniya; Ḳashtāla; Navarra; [au Suppl.] Araghūn

villes Alsh; Arkush; Arnīṭ; Badjdjāna; Balansiya; Bālish; Banbalūna; Barshalūna; al-Basīt; Basta; Baṭalyaws; Bayyāna; Bayyāsa; Biṭrawsh; al-Bunt; Burghush; Dāniya; Djarunda; Djayyān; al-Djazīra al-Khaḍrāʾ; Djazīrat Shuḳr; Finyāna; Gharnāṭa; Ifrāgha; Ilbīra; Ishbīliya; Istidja; Ḳabra; Ḳādis; Ḳalʿat Ayyūb; Ḳalʿat Rabāḥ; Ḳanṭara.2; Ḳarmūna; Ḳarṭādjanna; al-Ḳulayʿa; Ḳūnka; Ḳūriya; Ḳurṭuba; Laḳant; Lārida; Lawsha; Liyūn; Lūrḳa; al-Maʿdin; Madīnat Sālim; Madīnat al-Zahrāʾ; Madjrīṭ; Mālaḳa; Mārida; al-Mariyya; Mawrūr; al-Munakkab; Mursiya; Runda; Saraḳusṭa; Shaḳūbiya; Shalamanḳa; Shalṭīsh; Shant Mānkash; Shant Yāḳub; Shantamariyyat al-Sharḳ; Sharīsh; Shāṭiba; [au Suppl.] Ashturḳa

voir aussi al-Andalus.III.3; Balāṭ; Djabal Ṭāriḳ; al-Ḳalʿa; *et* → Portugal

ÉTERNITÉ **Abad**; Ḳidam

ÉTHIOPIE Adal; Aḥmad Grāñ; Awfāt; Bāli; Dawāro; Djabart; Djimmā; **Ḥabash**; Ḥabashat; al-Nadjāshī
voir aussi Ḥabesh; Kūsh; Shaykh Ḥusayn; *et* → LANGUES.AFRO-ASIATIQUES
historiens ʿArabfaḳīh
population ʿĀmir; Diglal; Djabart; Galla; Māryā; Oromo; Rashāʾida
toponymes Assab; Dahlak; Dire Dawa; Érythrée; Harar; Maṣawwaʿ; Ogādēn

ÉTHIQUE Adab; **Akhlāḳ**; Ḥisba
voir aussi Ḥurriyya; al-Maḥāsin wa-l-Masāwī; Miskawayh; *et* → VERTUS

ETHNICITÉ Maghāriba; Mashāriḳa; Sārt
voir aussi Fatā; Ibn Gharsiya; Ismāʿīl b. Yasār; Mawlā; Saracens

ÉTIQUETTE **Adab**
voir aussi Āʾīn; Hiba; *et* → LITTÉRATURE

EUNUQUE **Khaṣī**
voir aussi Khādim; Mamlūk.3

EUROPE
Europe occidentale al-Bashkunish; Ifrandj; Īṭaliya; Malta; Nemče; Sardāniya
voir aussi Ibn Idrīs [II]; Ibrāhīm b. Yaʿḳūb; al-Madjūs; Muslimūn.II
pour les pays individuels → AUTRICHE; ESPAGNE; FRANCE; ITALIE; PORTUGAL
Europe orientale Arnawutluḳ; Balḳan; Bulgarie; Iḳrīṭish; Itil; Ḳubrus; Leh; [au Suppl.] Čeh
voir aussi Bulghar; Ḥizb.V; Ibrāhīm b. Yaʿḳūb; Muhādjir.2; Muslimūn.I; Rūmeli; al-Ṣaḳāliba
pour les pays individuels → ALBANIE; BULGARIE; CHYPRE; CRÈTE; GRÈCE; HONGRIE; POLOGNE; (ex-) TCHÉCOSLOVAQUIE; (ex-)YOUGOSLAVIE
Russie Ḳi̊ri̊m
voir aussi Bulghār; Djadīd; Ḥizb.V; Ḳayyūm Nāṣirī
dynasties Girāy
population Bashdjirt; Besermyans; Beskesek-abaza; Bukhārli̊k; Burṭās; Čeremisses; Čuli̊m; Čuwashes; Gagauz; Ḳarapapakh; Lipḳa; Rūs
voir aussi Ḳanghli; Khazar; Kimäk; Pečenegs; al-Ṣaḳāliba
toponymes
anciens Atil; Saḳsīn
actuels Aḳ Kirmān; Aḳ Masdjid.1; Astrakhān; Azaḳ; Bāghče Sarāy;

Ismāʿīl; Ḳamāniča; Ḳaraṣū-bāzār; Ḳāsimov; Ḳāzān; Kefe; Kerč; Khotin; Ḳi̊lburun; Sughdāḳ

F

FĀṬIMIDES → CALIFAT

FAUCONNERIE **Bayzara**; Čaki̊rdji̊-bashi̊; Doghandji̊

FEMMES ʿAbd; Ḥarīm; Ḥayḍ; Ḥidjāb.I; ʿIdda; Istibrāʾ; Khafḍ; **al-Marʾa**; Nikāḥ; Siḥāḳ; [au Suppl.] Bighāʾ
voir aussi ʿArūs Resmi; Bashmaḳli̊ḳ; Khayr; Khiḍr-ilyās; Lithām; *et* → DIVORCE; MARIAGE; PHASES DE LA VIE.ACCOUCHEMENT *et* ENFANCE
concubinage ʿAbd.3.f; Khaṣṣekī
émancipation des Ḳāsim Amīn; Malak Ḥifnī Nāṣif; Saʿīd Abū Bakr; Salāma Mūsā; [au Suppl.] al-Ḥaddād, al-Ṭāhir
voir aussi Ḥidjāb; Ileri, Djelāl Nūrī; al-Marʾa; [au Suppl.] Ashraf al-Dīn Gīlānī
et littérature al-Marʾa.I
voir aussi Ḳiṣṣa; Shahrazād
auteurs arabes al-Bāʿūnī.6; Ḥafṣa bint al-Ḥādjdj; ʿInān; al-Khansāʾ; Laylā al-Akhyaliyya; Mayy Ziyāda; [au Suppl.] Faḍl al-Shāʿira
voir aussi ʿAbbāsa; ʿĀtika; Khunātha; Ḳiṣṣa.II; Shilb
auteurs persanes Ḳurrat al-ʿAyn; Mahsatī; Parwīn Iʿtiṣāmī
voir aussi Gulbadan Bēgam; Makhfī
auteurs turques Fiṭnat; Khālide Edīb; Laylā Khāni̊m (2x); Mihrī Khatun
voir aussi Ḳiṣṣa.III.B
femmes influentes
arabes ʿĀʾisha bint Ṭalḥa; Asmāʾ; Barīra; Būrān; Hind bint ʿUtba; al-Khayzurān; Khunātha; Shadjar al-Durr; Sitt al-Mulk; Ṣubḥ; Sukayna; [au Suppl.] Asmāʾ
voir aussi al-Maʿāfirī; *et* → MUḤAMMAD, LE PROPHÈTE.FEMMES DU PROPHÈTE
indo-musulmanes Nūr Djahān; Samrū
mongoles Baghdād Khātūn; Khān-zāda Bēgum
ottomanes ʿĀdila Khātūn; Khurrem; Kösem Wālide; Mihr-i Māh Sulṭān; Nīlūfer Khātūn; Nūr Bānū; Ṣafiyye Wālide Sulṭān; Shāh Sulṭān; Shebṣefa Ḳadi̊n
femmes légendaires al-Basūs; Bilḳīs; Hind bint al-Khuss
voir aussi Āsiya
musiciennes/chanteuses ʿAzza al-Maylāʾ; Djamīla; Ḥabāba; Rāʾiḳa; Sallāma al-

Zarḳāʾ; S̲h̲āriya; Siti Binti Saad; [au Suppl.] Bad̲h̲l al-Kubrā; al-D̲jarādatānⁱ;
Faḍl al-S̲h̲āʿira; Ḥabba K̲h̲ātūn
   voir aussi ʿĀlima; Ḳayna
mystiques   ʿĀʾis̲h̲a al-Mannūbiyya; D̲jahānārā Bēgam; Nafīsa; Rābiʿa al-ʿAdawiyya al-Ḳaysiyya

FÊTE   ʿĪd; Kandūrī; Mawlid; Mawsim; S̲h̲enlik
   voir aussi Maṭbak̲h̲.II
fêtes   ʿAnṣāra; ʿĀs̲h̲ūrāʾ.II; Bārā Wafāt; ʿĪd al-Aḍhā; ʿĪd al-Fiṭr; K̲h̲iḍr-ilyās;
Mihragān; Nawrūz; Sulṭān al-Ṭalaba
   voir aussi G̲h̲adīr K̲h̲umm; Kurdes et Kurdistān.IV.C.3; Lālis̲h̲; Lĕbaran;
Raʾs al-ʿĀm

FLORE   (D̲jazīrat) al-ʿArab.V; Būstān; Filāḥa; Hind.I.k
   et → BOTANIQUE
arbres   Abanūs; ʿAfṣ; Argan; Baḳḳam; Bān; K̲h̲as̲h̲ab; Nak̲h̲l; Sād̲j; Ṣandal; Sidr;
[au Suppl.] D̲jawz; D̲jullanār
   voir aussi ʿAyn S̲h̲ams; G̲h̲āba; Kāfūr; Kahrubā; Ḳaṭrān; Lubān; Ṣamg̲h̲; [au
Suppl.] Halīlad̲j
fleurs   Nard̲jis; S̲h̲aḳīḳat al-Nuʿmān; Sūsan; [au Suppl.] Bābūnad̲j; D̲jullanār
   voir aussi Filāḥa.IV; Lāle Devri; Lālezarī; Nawriyya; *et* → ARCHITECTURE.
MONUMENTS.JARDINS; LITTÉRATURE.POÉSIE.DE LA NATURE
plantes   Ad̲h̲argūn; Afsantīn; Afyūn; Ḥalfāʾ; Ḥinnāʾ; Kammūn; Ḳaranful; Karm;
Ḳaṣab; Naʿām; **Nabāt**; Ṣabr; S̲h̲ibit̲h̲t̲h̲; S̲h̲īḥ; S̲h̲ukāʿā; Sidr; Simsim; Sirād̲j
al-Ḳuṭrub; Sūs; [au Suppl.] Aḳūnīṭun; Ās; Bābūnad̲j; Basbās; D̲jāwars;
Fūd̲h̲and̲j; Hindibāʾ; Iklīl al-Malik
   voir aussi Maryam; Naḥl; Namir et Nimr; Nasr; Ṣamg̲h̲; Sinnawr; Sirwāl; *et*
→ DROGUES.NARCOTIQUES

FOI   ʿAḳīda; **Īmān**
   et → ISLAM; RELIGION

FRANCE   Arbūna; Fraxinetum
   voir aussi Balāṭ al-S̲h̲uhadāʾ; Muslimūn.II; Rifāʿa Bey; Ṣāyig̲h̲, Fatḥ Allāh; al-
S̲h̲aʾm.2(b)

FRANCS   **Ifrand̲j**
   et → CROISADES

G

GÉNÉALOGIE **Ḥasab wa-Nasab**; **Nasab**; S̲h̲arīf; S̲h̲urafāʾ
voir aussi ʿIrḳ; Naḳīb al-As̲h̲rāf; S̲h̲araf; *et* → LITTÉRATURE.GÉNÉALOGIQUE;
ONOMASTIQUE

GÉOGRAPHIE **Djug̲h̲rāfiyā**; Iḳlīm; Istiwāʾ; K̲h̲arīṭa; al-Ḳubba
voir aussi Mag̲h̲rib; Makka.IV; Mas̲h̲riḳ
pour la géographie détaillée des régions, voir Adamawa; Ād̲h̲arbayd̲j̲ān.I;
Afg̲h̲ānistān.I; Aḳ Ṣu; Algérie.I; Anadolu.II; al-Andalus.II et III.2; (D̲j̲azīrat)
al-ʿArab.II; Armīniya; Arnawutluḳ.III; ʿAsīr; Baḥr; D̲j̲azīra; Filāḥa; Ḥammāda;
Indonésie; ʿIrāḳ; Īrān; Lībiyā; al-Mag̲h̲rib; Māzandarān.2; Mūrītāniyā.1;
Nad̲j̲d.1; al-S̲h̲aʾm.1; Sīstān.2; Somali.2
administrative Kūra; Mamlaka; Mik̲h̲lāf; Rustāḳ.1; Ṣūba
  voir aussi D̲j̲und; Iḳlīm
géographes Abū l-Fidā; Abū ʿUbayd al-Bakrī; ʿĀs̲h̲iḳ; al-Balk̲h̲ī, Abū Zayd; al-
  Dimas̲h̲ḳī; Ibn ʿAbd al-Munʿim al-Ḥimyarī; Ibn al-Faḳīh; Ibn G̲h̲ālib; Ibn
  Ḥawḳal; Ibn K̲h̲urradād̲h̲bih; Ibn Mād̲j̲id; Ibn Rusta; Ibn Sarābiyūn; al-
  Idrīsī; al-Iṣṭak̲h̲rī; al-Ḳazwīnī; al-Masʿūdī; al-Muhallabī, Abū l-Ḥusayn; al-
  Muḳaddasī
  voir aussi Baṭlamiyūs; Istibṣār; Ḳāsim b. Aṣbag̲h̲; al-Masālik wa-l-
  Mamālik; al-Sarak̲h̲sī, Abū l-ʿAbbās; [au Suppl.] al-D̲j̲ayhānī; Ḥudūd al-
  ʿĀlam
géographie physique
  déserts → DÉSERTS
  eaux
    détroits Bāb al-Mandab; Bog̲h̲az-ič̲i; Čanaḳ-ḳalʿe Bog̲h̲azi̊
    lacs Baikal; Bak̲h̲tigān; Balk̲h̲as̲h̲; Burullus; Gökče-tengiz; Hāmūn; al-
      Ḥūla; İssi̊ḳ-kul; Ḳarā-köl
      voir aussi Buḥayra; al-Ḳulzum; *et* → OCÉANS ET MERS
    rivières → RIVIÈRES
  lagunes salées **Sabk̲h̲a**
    voir aussi S̲h̲aṭṭ
  montagnes → MONTAGNES
  sources ʿAyn Dilfa; ʿAyn Mūsā; al-Ḥamma; Ḥasan Abdāl
    voir aussi Ḳapli̊d̲j̲a
  volcans *voir* ʿAdan; Ag̲h̲ri̊ Dag̲h̲; Damāwand; Ḥarra; Lad̲j̲āʾ; al-Ṣafā.2; [au
    Suppl.] D̲j̲abal Says
littérature D̲j̲ug̲h̲rāfiyā.IV.C et V; Ṣurat al-Arḍ
  et → LITTÉRATURE.VOYAGES, RELATIONS DE
termes Ḥarra; K̲h̲abrāʾ; Nahr; Reg; Rīf; Sabk̲h̲a; S̲h̲aṭṭ
  voir aussi Ṣanf; Sarḥadd

urbaine   Ḳarya; Ḳaṣaba; Khiṭṭa; Maḥalle; Medina; Rabaḍ; S̲h̲ahr; S̲h̲ahristān
    voir aussi Fener; Ḥayy; Khiṭaṭ; Mallāḥ; *et* → ARCHITECTURE.URBAINE;
    SÉDENTARISATION

GITANS   **Čingāne; Lūlī**; Nūrī

GRÈCE
    voir aussi Muhād̲j̲ir.2; Muslimūn.I.B.3; Pomáks
toponymes
    districts   Karlî-īli
    îles   Čoka Adasî; Eg̲ribuz, Körfüz; Levkas; Limni; Midilli; Naks̲h̲e; On Iki
        Ada; Para; Rodos; Ṣaḳiz; Santurin Adasî; Scmedirek; S̲h̲eytānlîḳ ; S̲h̲ire;
        Sisām
        voir aussi D̲j̲azā'ir-i Baḥr-i Safîd
    régions   Mora
    villes   Atīna; Aynabakhtî; Baliabadra; Dede Ag̲h̲ač; Dimetoḳa; Karaferye;
        Ḳawāla; Kerbenes̲h̲; Kesriye; Ḳordos; Ḳoron; Livadya; Meneks̲h̲e;
        Modon; Nauplion; Navarin; Olendirek; Preveze; Selānīk; Siroz
        voir aussi [au Suppl.] Gümüld̲j̲ine

GUINÉE   Fūta D̲j̲allon; **Guinée**; Konakry
    voir aussi Sūdān (Bilād al-).2

H

HADITH   → LITTÉRATURE.TRADITION

HAGIOGRAPHIE   **Manāḳib**
    et → SAINT
hagiographes   Aflākī; 'Aṭā'ī; al-Bādisī.2; D̲j̲amālī; Ḥasan Dihlawī; Ibn 'Askar;
    Ibn Maryam; al-Ifrānī; al-Ḳādirī al-Ḥasanī, Abū 'Abd Allah; al-S̲h̲arrāṭ; al-
    Sulamī, Abū 'Abd al-Raḥmān
    voir aussi Aḥmad Bābā; Bāḳîk̲h̲ānlî; al-Kattānī; Sinān Pas̲h̲a, K̲h̲od̲j̲a.1

HEPHTALITES   Hayāṭila; Nīzak, Ṭark̲h̲ān

HÉRALDIQUE   al-Asad; Rank

HÉRÉSIE   Bid'a; Dahriyya; Dīn-i Ilāhī; G̲h̲ulāt; Ḳābiḍ; Kāfir; K̲h̲ūbmesīḥī;
    Mulḥid
    voir aussi Ṣalīb

hérétiques Abū ʿĪsā al-Warrāḳ; Abū l-Khaṭṭāb al-Asadī; Bashshār b. Burd; Bishr b. Ghiyāth al-Marīsī; Ibn Dirham; Ibn al-Rāwandī; Mollā Ḳābiḍ; Muḥammad b. ʿAlī al-Shalmaghānī
et → SECTES
réfutations Ibn al-Djawzī, ʿAbd al-Raḥmān; [au Suppl.] Afḍal al-Dīn Turka

HÉRITAGE ʿĀda.III; Akdariyya; ʿAwl; **Farāʾiḍ**; **Mīrāth**; al-Sahm.2
voir aussi Ḳassām; Khāl; Makhredj; Mukhallefāt
traités sur al-Sadjāwandī; Sirādj al-dīn

HONGRIE Budīn; Eğri; Esztergom; Istolnī (Istōnī) Belghrād; **Madjar**; Mohács; Pécs; Pest; Sigetwār; Szeged; Székesfehérvár
voir aussi Bashdjirt; Kanisza; Maḥmūd Tardjumān; Mezökeresztes; Muslimūn.I.B.1; Ofen

HÔTELLERIE **Funduḳ**; **Khān**; Manzil
voir aussi Ribāṭ.1.II

HUMOUR al-Djidd wa-l-Hazl; Nādira
voir aussi Hidjāʾ.II; Mudjūn
bouffons Djuḥā; Ibn al-Djaṣṣāṣ.II; Naṣr al-Dīn Khodja
humoristes Ashʿab; al-Ghāḍirī; Ibn Abī ʿAtīḳ; Ibn Dāniyāl; Ḳaṣāb; Sīfawayh al-Ḳāṣṣ; [au Suppl.] Abū l-ʿAnbas al-Ṣaymarī

HYDROLOGIE Biʾr; Ḳanāt; Māʾ; Maʾṣir
voir aussi Filāḥa; Ḳanṭara.5 et 6; Madjrīṭ; al-Mīzān.II; Sāʿa.1; *et* → ARCHITECTURE.MONUMENTS.BARRAGES; GÉOGRAPHIE.EAUX

I

IDOLES Nuṣub; **Ṣanam**
voir aussi Shaman; *et* → PÉRIODE PRÉISLAMIQUE.DANS LA PÉNINSULE ARABIQUE

INDE **Hind**; Hindī
voir aussi ʿĀda.III; Balharā; Imām-bārā; Maṭbaʿa.IV; Sikkat al-Ḥadīd.1; *et* → LITTÉRATURE; MILITAIRES; MUSIQUE
administration Baladiyya.V; Ḍarība.VI; Dīwān.V; Djizya.III; Ḥisba.IV; Kātib; Kharādj.IV; Pargana; Safīr.2.c
voir aussi Kitābāt.X; Māʾ.IX; *et* → MILITAIRES.INDO-MUSULMANES
agriculture Filāḥa.V

architecture → ARCHITECTURE.RÉGIONS

belles-lettres → LITTÉRATURE.EN D'AUTRES LANGUES *et* POÉSIE.INDO-PERSANE

dynasties ʿĀdil-Shāhs; Bahminides; Barīd Shāhides; Dihlī (Sultanat de); Farūḳides; Ghaznawides; Ghūrides; Hindū-Shāhides; ʿImād Shāhides; Khaldjis; Ḳuṭb-Shāhides; Lōdīs; Mughals; Niẓām Shāhides; Sayyids; Sharḳīs

voir aussi Awadh; Dār al-Ḍarb; Rānā Sāngā; *et* → DYNASTIES.AFGHANISTAN ET INDE

éducation Dār al-ʿUlūm.c et d.; Djāmiʿa; Madjmaʿ ʿIlmī.IV; Madrasa.II; Nadwat al-ʿUlamāʾ; [au Suppl.] Farangī Maḥall

voir aussi Aḥmad Khān; Deoband; Maḥmūdābād

géographie physique

eaux Djamnā; Gangā

voir aussi Nahr

historiens Ghulām Ḥusayn Khān Ṭabāṭabāʾī; Niẓām al-Dīn, Aḥmad; Sudjān Rāy Bhandārī

voir aussi Djaʿfar Sharīf; al-Maʿbarī; Mīr Muḥammad Maʿṣūm; *et* → DYNASTIES.AFGHANISTAN ET INDE; LITTÉRATURE.HISTORIQUE

langues Gudjarātī; Hindī; Hindustānī.1 et 2; Lahndā; Marāṭhī; Pandjābī.1; Sind.3.a

voir aussi Kitābāt.X; *et* → LANGUES.INDO-IRANIENNES

mysticisme → MYSTICISME.MYSTIQUES; SAINT

période moderne Djamʿiyya; Hindustānī.3; Ḥizb.VI; Indian National Congress; Iṣlāḥ.IV; Kashmīr; Ḳawmiyya.VI; Khāksār; Khilāfa; Madjlis.IV.C; al-Marʾa.V; Nikāḥ.II.3; [au Suppl.] Djarīda.VII

voir aussi Mahsūd; Mappila; [au Suppl.] Faḳīr d'Ipi; *et* → INDE.ÉDUCATION

hommes d'état Nawwāb Sayyid Ṣiddīḳ Ḥasan Khān; Sālār Djang; [au Suppl.] Āzād, Abū l-Kalām

voir aussi Maḥmūdābād

le 'Mutiny' Aẓim Allāh Khān; Bakht Khān; Imdād Allāh; Kānpur

mouvement 'Khilāfat' **Khilāfa**; Muḥammad ʿAlī; Mushīr Ḥusayn Ḳidwāʾī; Shawkat ʿAlī; [au Suppl.] ʿAbd al-Bārī; Ḥasrat Mohānī

voir aussi Amīr ʿAlī

population Bhaṭṭi; Bohorās; Dāwūdpōtrās; Djāṭ; Gakkhaṛ; Gandāpur; Güdjar; Ḥabshī; Hind.II; Khaṭak; Khokars; Lambadi; Mappila; Mēd; Memon; Mēʾō; Naitias; Pārsīs; Rādjpūts; Rohillas; Shikārī; Sidi; [au Suppl.] Démographie.VII

voir aussi Khōdja; Marāṭhā

Tamils Ceylan; Labbai; Marakkayar; Rawther

religion Ahl-i Ḥadīth; Barāhima; Djayn; Hindū; Ibāḥatiya; Mahdawī; Pandj Pīr; Sikhs

voir aussi Khwādja Khiḍr; Pārsīs; [au Suppl.] Andjuman-i Khuddām-i

Kaʿba; *et* → Mysticisme; Saint; Théologie
réforme Aḥmad Brēlwī; al-Dihlawī, Shāh Walī Allāh; Ismāʿīl Shahīd; Karāmat ʿAlī; Nānak
toponymes
anciens Arūr; Čāmpānēr; Čhat; Djāba; Djandjīra; Fatḥpūr-sikrī; Hampī; Ḥusaynābād; Kūlam; Lakhnawtī; al-Manṣūra; Mēwāṙ; Nandurbār; Nārnawl; Pāṅdu'a; Shikārpūr.2; Sidhpūr; Sindābūr; Sindān; Sūmanāt
actuels
régions Assam; Bihār; Bombay; Dakhan; Djaypur; Do'āb; Gudjarāt; Hariyānā; Ḥaydarābād.II; Kāmrūp; Kashmīr; Khāndēsh; Ḳūhistān.IV; Ladākh; Lūdhiāna; Maʿbar; Mahisur; Malabar; Mēwāt; Muẓaffarpur; Nāgpur; Palamāw; Pālānpur; Pandjāb; Rādhanpūr; Rāmpur; Rohilkhand; Sundarban; [au Suppl.] Djammū
voir aussi Alwār; Banganapalle; Bāonī; Berār; Djōdhpur; Hunza et Nagir
villes Adjmēr; Āgra; Aḥmadābād; Aḥmadnagar; Aligarh; Allāhābād; Ambāla; Amritsar; Anhalwāra; Arcot; Awadh; Awrangābād; Awrangābād Sayyid; Aʿẓamgarh; Badā'ūn; Bālā-ghāt; Bāndā; Bānkīpūr; Banūr; Bareilly; Barōda; Bénarès; Bharatpūr; Bharoč; Bhattinda; Bhōpāl; Bīdar; Bīdjāpūr; Bidjnawr; Bilgrām; Bombay; Bulandshahr; Burhānpūr; Buxar; Calcutta; Čandērī; Dawlatābād; Deoband; Dhār; Dhārwār; Dihlī; Diū; Djālor; Djawnpur; Djūnāgaṙh; Djunnar; Dwārkā; Farīdkōṫ; Farrukhābād; Fayḍābād; Fīrūzpūr; Gulbargā; Gwāliyār; Hānsī; Ḥaydarābād.I; Ḥiṣār Fīrūza; Īdar; Islāmābād; Iṫāwā; Kalpī; Kalyāni; Kanawdj; Kāṅgṙā; Kannanūr; Kānpur; Karnāl; Karnāṫak; Katahr; Khambāyat; Khayrābād; Khuldābād; Kōṙā; Koyl; Lakhnaw; Lalitpūr; Lūdhiāna; Madras; Mahīm; Māhīm; Māhūr; Mālda; Mālwā; Māṅdū; Manēr; Mangrōl; Mathurā; Mīraṫh; Mīrzāpur; Multān; Mungīr; Murādābād; Murshidābād; Muẓaffarpur; Nadjībābād; Nagar; Nāgawr; Nāgpur; Naldrug; Nāndeṙ; Pānīpat; Parendā; Pāṫan; Paṫnā; Pūna; Rādjmahāl; Rāyčūr; Sahāranpūr; Sahsarām; Sārangpur; Sardhanā; Sarkhēdj; Shakarkhelda; Shikārpūr.3; Shōlāpur; Sirhind; Srīnagar; Śrīangapaṫṫanam; Sūrat; [au Suppl.] Amrōhā; Eličpur; Ghāzīpūr
et → Asie.du sud

Indonésie Baladiyya.VII; Djāmiʿa; Dustūr.XI; Ḥizb.VII; Ḥukūma.VI; **Indonésie**; Maḥkama.VI; Malais; Masjumi; [au Suppl.] Ḍarība.VII; Hoesein Djajadiningrat
voir aussi ʿĀda.IV; Nikāḥ.II.4; Pasisir; Prang Sabil
architecture → Architecture.régions
éducation Pesantren

littérature Indonésie.VI; Ḳiṣṣa.VI; Miʿrādj.IV; Shāʿir.7
voir aussi Kitābāt.VIII; Malais; *et* → LITTÉRATURE.POÉSIE.MYSTIQUE
mouvements islamiques Padri; Sarekat Islam
voir aussi Sulawesi
population Malais; Minangkabau; [au Suppl.] Démographie.VIII
voir aussi Sayābidja
religion → MYSTICISME.MYSTIQUES
fêtes Kandūrī; Lĕbaran
toponymes Ambon; Atjèh; Banda; Bandjarmasin; Bangka; Batjan; Billiton; Bornéo (*et* [au Suppl.]); Célèbes; Djakarta; Kubu; Kutai; Lombok; Madura; Makassar; Palembang; Pasè; Pasir; Pontianak; Riau; Sambas; Sonde; Sulawesi (*et* Célèbes); Sumatra; Surakarta

INDUSTRIE Ḥarīr; Kattān; Ḳuṭn; Lubūd; Milḥ
voir aussi Bursa; al-Iskandariyya; Ḳayṣariyya

INVENTIONS ʿAbbās b. Firnās; Ibn Mādjid; Mūsā (Banū); Sāʿa.1

IRAK **ʿIrāḳ**; Kurdes et Kurdistān
voir aussi al-ʿArabiyya; Djalīlī; Lakhmides; Sawād; Shahāridja; *et* → CALIFAT.ʿABBĀSIDES; DYNASTIES.ÉGYPTE ET LE CROISSANT FERTILE
architecture → ARCHITECTURE.RÉGIONS
avant l'Islam → PÉRIODE PRÉISLAMIQUE.DANS LE CROISSANT FERTILE
géographie physique
eaux Abū l-Khaṣīb; al-ʿAḍaym; Didjla; Diyālā; al-Furāt; Khābūr; al-Khāzir; Shaṭṭ al-ʿArab
montagnes Sindjār
historiens al-Azdī; Baḥshal; Ibn Abī Ṭāhir Ṭayfūr; Ibn al-Bannāʾ; Ibn al-Dubaythī; al-Khaṭīb al-Baghdādī
voir aussi Ibn al-Nadjdjār; *et* → CALIFAT.ʿABBĀSIDES; DYNASTIES.ÉGYPTE ET LE CROISSANT FERTILE
période moderne Djarīda.I.A; Djāmiʿa; Dustūr.VI; Ḥizb.I; Ḥukūma.III; Kurdes et Kurdistān.III.C; Madjlis.IV.A.4; Madjmaʿ ʿIlmī.I.II.3; Maḥkama.IV.4; Mandats
voir aussi Bābān; Kūt al-ʿAmāra; al-Mawṣil.2
leaders d'opposition Ḳāsim, ʿAbd al-Karīm; Muṣṭafā Barzānī
monarchie Fayṣal Ier; Fayṣal II; Ghāzī
voir aussi Hāshimides
politiciens al-Shahrastānī, Sayyid Muḥammad; Shīnā
premiers ministres Nūrī al-Saʿīd; Rashīd ʿAlī al-Gaylānī
population Bādjalān; Bilbās; Djubūr; Dulaym; Lām; al-Manāṣir
voir aussi Shammar; [au Suppl.] Démographie.III; *et* → KURDES

toponymes
    anciens   Abarḳubādh; ʿAḳarḳūf; ʿAltẖ; al-Anbār; Bābil; Badjimzā; Bādjisrā;
        Bādūrayā; Bāḵẖamrā; Baradān; Barāthā; Bawāzīdj; Bihḳubādh; Birs;
        Dayr ʿAbd al-Raḥmān; Dayr al-ʿĀḳūl; Dayr al-Aʿwar; Dayr al-
        Djamādjim; Diyār Rabīʿa; Djabbul; al-Djazīra; Fallūdja; Ḥadītha.I;
        Ḥarbāʾ; Ḥarūrāʾ; Ḥawīza; al-Ḳādisiyya; Kalwādhā; Kaskar; Ḳaṣr Ibn
        Hubayra; Ḵẖāniḵīn; al-Ḵẖawarnaḳ; Kūthā; Ḳuṭrabbul; al-Madāʾin;
        Niffar; Nimrūd; Nīnawā; al-Nuḵẖayla; al-Ruṣāfa.1; Sāmarrāʾ
        voir aussi al-Karḵẖ; Nuṣratābād; Senkere
    actuels
        régions   Bahdīnān; al-Baṭīḥa; Maysān
            voir aussi Lālisẖ
        villes   Altin Köprü; ʿAmādiya; ʿAmāra; ʿĀna; ʿAyn al-Tamr; Badrā;
            Baghdād; Baʿḳūba; Balāwāt; Bārzān; al-Baṣra; Daḳūḳāʾ; Daltāwa;
            Dīwāniyya; al-Fallūdja; Ḥadītha.II; al-Ḥilla; Hīt; Irbil; Karbalāʾ;
            Kāẓimayn; Kirkūk; al-Kūfa; Kūt al-ʿAmāra; Maʿalthāyā; al-Mawṣil;
            al-Nadjaf; al-Nāṣiriyya; Nuṣratābād; Rawāndīz; Sāmarrāʾ; al-Samā-
            wa.2; Senkere; Sẖahrazūr; Sindjār; Sūḳ al-Sẖuyūḵẖ; Sulaymāniyya;
            [au Suppl.] Athūr
            voir aussi Djalūlāʾ; *et* → KURDES.TOPONYMES

IRAN   al-Furs; **Īrān**; Kurdes et Kurdistān; Lur
    voir aussi al-ʿArab.III; Ḥarb.V; Kitābāt.IX; Libās.III; *et* → CHIITES; DYNASTIES.
    PERSE; ZOROASTRIENS
administration   Ḍarība.V; Diplomatique.III; Dīwān.IV; Ghulām.II; Imtiyāzāt.
    III; Kātib; Ḵẖāliṣa; Ḵẖarādj.II; Maḥkama.III; Parwānačī
        voir aussi Kalāntar; *et* → IRAN.PÉRIODE MODERNE
agriculture   Filāḥa.III
architecture   → ARCHITECTURE.RÉGIONS
avant l'Islam   Anūsẖirwān; Ardasẖīr; Bahrām; Dārā; Dārābdjird; Dihḳān;
    Djamsẖīd; Farīdūn; al-Ḥaḍr; Ḥayāṭila; Hurmuz; al-Hurmuzān; Ḳārinides;
    Kayānides; Kay Kāʾūs; Kay-Ḵẖusraw; Ḵẖursẖīd; Kisrā; Marzpān; Mazdak;
    Mulūk al-Ṭawāʾif.I; Parwīz, Ḵẖusraw (II); Pīsẖdādides; Sāsānides; Sẖāpūr;
    [au Suppl.] Farruḵẖān
        voir aussi Afrāsiyāb; Buzurgmihr; Hamadhān; Iḵẖsẖīd; Īrān.IV; Ispahbadh;
        Ḳaṣr-i Sẖīrīn; Ḳūmis; al-Madāʾin; al-Rayy; Rustam b. Farruḵẖ Hurmuzd;
        Sarpul-i Dhuhāb; [au Suppl.] Dabīr; *et* → ZOROASTRIENS
géographie physique
    déserts   Biyābānak
    eaux   Baḵẖtigān; Hāmūn; Karḵẖa; Kārūn; Mānd; Ruknābād; Safīd Rūd; Sẖāh
        Rūd.1; Sẖāpūr; Sẖaṭṭ al-ʿArab
        voir aussi Baḥr Fāris

montagnes Ala Dagh; Alburz; Alwand Kūh; Bīsutūn; Damāwand; Hamrīn; Hawrāmān
voir aussi Sarḥadd
historiens Ḥamza al-Iṣfahānī; Ibn Manda; al-Māfarrukhī; al-Rāfiʿī
et → DYNASTIES.PERSE
langue → LANGUES.INDO-IRANIENNES
littérature → LITTÉRATURE
période moderne Baladiyya.IV; Djāmiʿa; Djamʿiyya; Djarīda.II; Dustūr.IV; Ḥizb.III; Ḥukūma.II; Īrān.V.B; Iṣlāḥ.II; Ḳawmiyya.III; Maʿārif.III; Madjlis.IV.A.3; Madjmaʿ ʿIlmī.II; al-Marʾa.III; Shuyūʿiyya.2; [au Suppl.] Démographie.III
voir aussi Khazʿal Khān; Madjlis al-Shūrā; Maḥkama.III; [au Suppl.] Amīr Niẓām; *et* → CHIITES; DYNASTIES.PERSE.ḲĀDJĀRS *et* PAHLAWĪS
activistes Fidāʾiyyān-i Islām; Kāshānī, Āyat Allāh; Kasrawī Tabrīzī; Khwānsārī, Sayyid Muḥammad; Khiyābānī; Khurāsānī; Kūčak Khān Djangalī; Lāhūtī; Maḥallātī; Malkom Khān; Muṣaddiḳ; Muṭahharī; Nāʾīnī; Nūrī, Shaykh Faḍl Allāh; Ṣamṣām al-Salṭana; Sharīʿatī, ʿAlī; [au Suppl.] Āḳā Khān Kirmānī; Āḳā Nadjafī; Amīr Kabīr; Ḥaydar Khān ʿAmū Ughlı
voir aussi Djangalī; Kurdes et Kurdistān.III.C; [au Suppl.] Āzādī; Farāmūsh-khāna
population Bakhtiyārī; Bāzūkiyyūn; Bilbās; Djāf; Eymir.III; Göklän; Gūrān; (Banū) Kaʿb; Ḳarā Gözlu; Ḳāshḳāy; Kurdes et Kurdistān; Lam; Lur; Shabānkāra; Shāhsewan; Shakāk; Shaḳāḳī; Sindjābī
voir aussi Daylam; Dulafides; Eymir.II; Fīrūzānides; Īrān.II; Ḳufṣ; Shūlistān; [au Suppl.] Démographie.III
religion Īrān.VI; Ṣafawides.IV
et → MYSTICISME.MYSTIQUES; SAINT
toponymes
anciens Abarshahr; Ardalān; Arradjān; ʿAskar Mukram; Bādj; Bākusāyā; Bayhaḳ; Dārābdjird; Daskara; Dawraḳ; Dihistān; Dīnawar; al-Djazīra; Djibāl; Djīruft; Gurgān; Ḥafrak; Ḥulwān; Īdhadj; Iṣṭakhr; (al-)Karadj; Khargird.II; Ḳūmis; Ḳurḳūb; Mihragān.IV.1; Narmāshīr; Nasā; Nawbandadjān; al-Rayy; Rūdhbār.2; Rūdhrāwar; Ṣaymara; Shāpūr; Shūlistān; al-Sīradjān; Sīrāf; Sīsar; Suhraward; al-Sūs; [au Suppl.] Arghiyān; Ghubayrā
actuels
îles al-Fārisiyya
provinces Ādharbaydjān; Balūčistān; Fārs; Gīlān; Hamadhān; Iṣfahān; Khurāsān; Khūzistān; Kirmān; Kirmānshāh; Kurdistān; Māzandarān
voir aussi Astarābādh.2; Rūyān
régions Bākharz; Hawrāmān; Ḳūhistān.I; Makrān; Sarḥadd; Sīstān; [au

Suppl.] Bashkard
voir aussi Gulistān
villes et districts Ābādah; Abarḳūh; ʿAbbādān; ʿAbbāsābād; Abhar; al-Ahwāz; Āmul.1; Ardakān; Ardistān; Asadābādh; Ashraf; Astarābādh.1; Āwa; Bam; Bampūr; Bandar ʿAbbās; Bandar Pahlawī; Bārfurūsh; Barūdjird; Barzand; Bīrdjand; Bisṭām; Būshahr; Dāmghān; Dizfūl; Djannāba; Djuwayn.1 et 2; Faraḥābād; Faryāb; Fasā; Fīrūzābād; Fūman; Gulpāyagān; Gunbadh-i Ḳābūs; Hurmuz; Iṣfahān; Isfarāyīn; Kāshān; Ḳaṣr-i Shīrīn; Kāzarūn; Ḳazwīn; Khʷāf; Khalkhāl; Khʷār; Khārag; Khargird.I; Khōī; Khurramābād; Khurramshahr; Kinkiwar; Ḳishm; Ḳūčān; Ḳūhistān.II; Ḳuhrūd; Ḳum; Lāhīdjān; Lār (2x); Linga; Luristān; Mahābād; Mākū; Marāgha; Marand; Mashhad; Miyāna; Narāḳ; Naṭanz; Nayrīz; Nihāwand; Nīshāpūr; Rafsandjān; Rām-hurmuz; Rasht; Rūdhbār.3; Sabzawār.1; Ṣaḥna; Ṣāʾīn Ḳalʿa; Saḳḳiz; Salmās; Sanandadj; Sarakhs; Sārī; Sarpul-i Dhuhāb; Sarwistān; Sāwa; Shāh Rūd.3; Shīrāz; Shushtar; Simnān; al-Sīradjān; Ṣōmāy; Suldūz; Sulṭānābād; Sulṭāniyya; Sunḳur; al-Sūs; [au Suppl.] Bashkard; Biyār; Djārdjarm; Djulfa.II; Hawsam
voir aussi Shahr; Shahristān; *et* → KURDES.TOPONYMES

IRRIGATION Band; Ḳanāt; Māʾ; Nāʿūra
voir aussi Filāḥa; Kārūn; al-Nahrawān; *et* → RIVIÈRES
eau **Māʾ**
voir aussi Ḥawḍ; Sabīl.2; Saḳḳāʾ; *et* → ARCHITECTURE.MONUMENTS.DÉBITS D'EAU; HYDROLOGIE; NAVIGATION; OCÉANS ET MERS; RIVIÈRES

ISLAM ʿAḳīda; Dīn; Djamāʿa; **Islām**; Masdjid; Muḥammad; Murtadd; Muslim; Rukn.1; Shīʿa
voir aussi Iṣlāḥ; Iʿtikāf; Nubuwwa; Rahbāniyya; Shirk; *et* → AUMÔNES; CORAN; JEÛNE; PÈLERINAGE; PRIÈRE
cinq piliers de l'Islam Ḥadjdj; Ṣalāt; Ṣawm; Shahāda
voir aussi al-Ḳurṭubī, Yaḥyā; Rukn.1
conversion à l'Islam Islām.II
convertis européens Pickthall
croyances populaires ʿAyn; Dīw; Djinn; Ghūl; Muḥammad.II; [au Suppl.] ʿĀʾisha Ḳandīsha; Ḥinn
voir aussi ʿAnḳāʾ; Shafāʿa.2; *et* → DROIT.DROIT COUTUMIER
formules Allāhumma; Basmala; Ḥamdala; In Shāʾ Allāh; Māshāʾ Allāh; Salām; Subḥān
voir aussi [au Suppl.] Abréviations

ISRAËL → PALESTINE

ITALIE **Īṭaliya**; Ḳawṣara; Ḳillawriya; Rūmiya; Sardāniya; Ṣiḳilliyya
et → SICILE

J

JACOBITES → CHRISTIANISME.CONFESSIONS

JEU **Ḳimār**; al-Maysir
et → ANIMAUX.SPORT; RÉCRÉATION.JEUX

JEÛNE ʿĀs̲h̲ūrāʾ; Ramaḍān; **Ṣawm**
voir aussi ʿĪd al-Fiṭr; Ṣūfiyāna

JORDANIE Dustūr.X; Ḥukūma.III; Madjlis.IV.A.7; Maḥkama.IV.6; Mandats
géographie physique
montagnes al-Ḏj̲ibāl
hommes d'état ʿAbd Allāh b. al-Ḥusayn
voir aussi Hās̲h̲imides
population al-Ḥuwayṭāt; al-Manāṣīr
voir aussi [au Suppl.] Démographie.III
toponymes
anciens Ad̲h̲ruḥ; Ayla; al-Balḳāʾ; Djarash; al-Djarbāʾ; al-Ḏj̲ibāl; Faḥl; al-Ḥumayma; al-Muwaḳḳar
actuels ʿAdj̲lūn; al-ʿAḳaba; ʿAmmān; Bayt Rās; al-G̲h̲awr.1; Irbid.I; Maʿān; al-Salṭ; al-S̲h̲awbak

JUDAÏSME Ahl al-Kitāb; Banū Isrāʾīl
voir aussi Filasṭīn; Hūd; Nasīʾ; al-Sāmira; *et* → BIBLE; PALESTINE
communautés al-Andalus.IV; al-Fāsiyyūn; Īrān.II et VI; Iṣfahān.I; al-Iskandariyya; Istanbul.VII.2; al-Ḳuds; Lār et Läristān.II; Mallāḥ; Marrākus̲h̲; Ṣufrūy
influences sur l'Islam ʿĀs̲h̲ūrāʾ.I
voir aussi Ḳibla; Muḥammad.I.1.C.2
langue et littérature Judéo-arabe; Judéo-berbère; Judéo-persan; Ḳiṣṣa.VIII; Risāla.VII
voir aussi Geniza; Muk̲h̲taṣar; Musammaṭ; Muwas̲h̲s̲h̲aḥ; *et* → LEXICOGRAPHIE; LITTÉRATURE.EN D'AUTRES LANGUES
personnages juifs dans le monde islamique ʿAbd Allāh b. Salām; Abū ʿĪsā al-Iṣfahānī; Abū Naḍḍāra; D̲h̲ū Nuwās; Hāmōn; Ḥasdāy b. S̲h̲aprūṭ; Ibn Abī l-Bayān; Ibn D̲j̲āmiʿ; Ibn D̲j̲anāḥ; Ibn Gabirol; Ibn Kammūna; Ibn Maymūn; Ibn Yaʿīs̲h̲; Ibrāhīm b. Yaʿḳūb; Isḥāḳ al-Isrāʾīlī; Kaʿb b. al-As̲h̲raf; al-Kōhēn

al-ʿAṭṭār; Māsardjawayh; Māshāʾ Allāh; Mūsā b. ʿAzra; al-Rādhāniyya; Saʿadyā; Saʿd al-Dawla; al-Samawʾal b. ʿĀdiyā; Shabbatai Ṣebī; Shāʾūl, Anwar; Shīnā; [au Suppl.] Camondo; Ibn Biklārish
voir aussi Abū l-Barakāt; Kaʿb al-Aḥbār; Ḳaynuḳāʿ; Ḳurayẓa
rapports juives-musulmanes
avec Muḥammad Fadak; Ḳaynuḳāʿ; Khaybar; Ḳurayẓa; al-Madīna.I.1; Naḍīr
voir aussi Muḥammad.I.1.C
persécution Dhimma; Djizya; Ghiyār; al-Ḥākim bi-Amr Allāh; al-Maghīlī
polémique Abū Isḥāḳ al-Ilbīrī; Ibn Ḥazm, Abū Muḥammad; al-Suʿūdī, Abū l-Faḍl
voir aussi Ahl al-Kitāb
sectes juives ʿĀnāniyya; al-ʿĪsāwiyya; Karaïtes
sectes judéo-chrétiennes Ṣābiʾa.I
voir aussi Naṣārā
sectes judéo-musulmanes Shabbatai Ṣebī

K

KENYA Gedi; **Kenya**; Kilifi; Lamu; Malindi; Manda; Mazrūʿī; Mombasa; Pate; Siu
voir aussi Nabhān; [au Suppl.] Djarīda.VIII
littérature swahilie Ḳiṣṣa.VII; Madīḥ.V; Marthiya.V; Mathal.V; [au Suppl.] Ḥamāsa.VI
voir aussi Miʿrādj.III
chant Siti Binti Saad
poètes Shaaban Robert

KOWEIT Djarīda.I.A; Dustūr.XVI; **al-Kuwayt**; Madjlis.IV.A.9; Maḥkama.IV.9; Ṣabāḥ, Āl
voir aussi (Djazīrat) al-ʿArab; al-ʿArabiyya; Djāmiʿa
toponymes al-Dibdiba; [au Suppl.] Aḥmadī
voir aussi Ḳarya al-ʿUlyā

KURDES **Kurdes et Kurdistān**
voir aussi Kitāb al-Djilwa; *et* → IRAK; IRAN; TURQUIE
dynasties ʿAnnāzides; Bābān; Faḍlawayh; Ḥasanwayh; Marwānides; Rawwādides; Shaddādides
voir aussi Kurdes et Kurdistān.III.B
mouvement nationale kurde Badrkhānī; Ḳāḍī Muḥammad; Kurdes et Kurdistān.III.C; Muṣṭafā Barzānī
voir aussi Bārzān; Mahābād
sectes Ṣārliyya; Shabak

toponymes Ardalān; Barādūst; Bahdīnān; Bārzān; Djawānrūd; Hakkārī; Rawāndīz; Saḳḳiz; Sanandadj; Sāwdj-Bulāḳ; Shahrazūr; Shamdīnān; Ṣōmāy; Sulaymāniyya
voir aussi Kirkūk; Kurdes et Kurdistān.II; Orāmār; Shabānkāra; Sīsar
tribus Djāf; Hakkārī; Hamawand; Kurdes et Kurdistān.III.B et IV.A.2; Lak.I; Shabānkāra; Shakāk; Shaḳāḳī; Sindjābī

L

LAMENTATION Bakkāʾ; **Niyāḥa**; Rawḍa-khʷānī

LANGUES **Lugha**
et → LINGUISTIQUE
afro-asiatiques Ḥam; Sam.2
voir aussi Karshūnī; Maʿlūlā.II; Sullam
arabe Algérie.V; Aljamía; al-Andalus.X; ʿ**Arabiyya**.A; ʿIrāḳ.IV; Judéo-arabe.I et II; Lībiyā.II; al-Maghrib.VII; Malta.2; Mūrītāniyā.6
voir aussi Ibn Makkī; Ḳarwasha; Khaṭṭ; Madjmaʿ ʿIlmī.I; al-Sīm; [au Suppl.] Ḥaḍramawt.III
arabe chrétien Karshūnī; Shaykhū
voir aussi ʿArabiyya.A.II.1
dialectes arabes ʿArabiyya.A.III; al-Ṣaʿīd (Ṣaʿīd Miṣr).2; al-Shaʾm.3; Shāwiya.3; Shuwa; Siʿird; Sūdān.2; Sūdān (Bilād al-).3
et → LINGUISTIQUE.PHONÉTIQUE; LITTÉRATURE.POÉSIE.DIALECTALE
bantou Swahili
berbère **Berbères**.V; Judéo-berbère; Mūrītāniyā.6; Sīwa
voir aussi Mzab
mots berbères en arabe Āfrāg; Agadir, Āgdāl; Aménokal; Amghar; Argan; Ayt; Imẓad
voir aussi Ḳallala; Rīf.I.2.a
couchitique Kūsh; Somali.5
éthiopien-sémitique Érythrée; Ḥabash.IV
hébreu Ibn Djanāḥ
nordarabique Ṣafaïtique
voir aussi Liḥyān; *et* → ÉPIGRAPHIE
sud-arabique Sabaʾ
voir aussi Ḥaḍramawt (*et* [au Suppl.] Ḥaḍramawt.III); al-Ḥarāsīs; al-Sawdāʾ; *et* → ÉPIGRAPHIE
sud-arabique moderne Mahrī; Shiḥrī; Suḳuṭra
voir aussi al-Baṭāḥira; al-Ḥarāsīs; [au Suppl.] Ḥaḍramawt.III
tchadique Hausa.II
teda-daza Kanuri

austronésiennes Atjèh; Indonésie.III; Malais
ibéro-caucasiennes Andi; Beskesek-abaza; Čerkes; Dāg̲h̲istān; Darg̲h̲in; al-Ḳabḳ; Ḳayyūm Nāṣirī
voir aussi al-Kurd̲j̲
indo-européennes Arnawutluḳ.I
voir aussi al-Ḳabḳ
indo-iraniennes
indiennes Afg̲h̲ānistān.III; Bengali.I; Ceylan; Chitral.II; Dardiques et Kāfires; Gud̲j̲arātī; Hind.III; Hindī; Hindustānī; Kashmīrī; Lahndā; Maldives.II; Marāṭhī; Pand̲j̲ābī.1; Sind.3.a
voir aussi Mad̲j̲maʿ ʿIlmī.IV; Sidi; [au Suppl.] Burus̲h̲aski
iraniennes Afg̲h̲ān.II; Afg̲h̲ānistān.III; Balūčistān.II; Darī; Gūrān; Hind.III; ʿIrāḳ.IV; Judéo-persan.II; Kurdes et Kurdistān.V; Lur
voir aussi Dāg̲h̲istān; al-Ḳabḳ; K̲h̲ʷārazm; Mad̲j̲maʿ ʿIlmī.II; Ossètes; S̲h̲ug̲h̲nān; al-Ṣug̲h̲d
dialectes persans Simnān.3
(nigéro-)kordofanien Nūba.III
nilo-saharien Nūba.III; Songhay.1; Sūdān.2
turciques Ād̲h̲arī; Balkar; Bulg̲h̲ār; Gagauz; K̲h̲alad̲j̲.II
voir aussi Afg̲h̲ānistān.III; Dāg̲h̲istān; al-Ḳabḳ; K̲h̲azar; Mad̲j̲maʿ ʿIlmī.III

Légendes Ḥikāya
et → Bible.personnages bibliques; Coran.histoires; Eschatologie
endroits légendaires Damāwand; D̲j̲ūdī; Ergenekon; Ḥūs̲h̲; Ḳïzïl-elma; Sāwa.3
êtres légendaires ʿAnḳāʾ; al-Burāḳ; Dīw; al-D̲j̲assāsa; D̲j̲inn; G̲h̲ūl; Hātif; ʿIfrīt; Ḳuṭrub; Parī; Sīmurg̲h̲
voir aussi al-Ruk̲h̲k̲h̲
gens légendaires Abū Rig̲h̲āl; Abū Safyān; Abū Zayd; ʿAdnān; Afrāsiyāb; Ahl al-Ṣuffa; Amīna; Āṣāf b. Barak̲h̲yā; Asḥāb al-Kahf; Barṣīṣā; al-Basūs; Bilḳīs; al-Dad̲j̲d̲j̲āl; D̲j̲ams̲h̲īd; Ḥabīb al-Nad̲j̲d̲j̲ār; Ḥanẓala b. Ṣafwān; Hind bint al-K̲h̲uss; Hirmis; Hūs̲h̲ang; Ibn Buḳayla; al-Kāhina; Ḳaḥṭān; Kāwah; al-K̲h̲aḍir; Luḳmān; Masʿūd; Naṣr al-Dīn K̲h̲od̲j̲a; Sām; Saṭīḥ b. Rabīʿa; S̲h̲iḳḳ; Siyāwus̲h̲; Sulaymān b. Dāwūd
voir aussi Ak̲h̲ī Ewrān; Amr b. ʿAdī; ʿAmr b. Luḥayy; Aṣḥāb al-Rass; Ḳuss b. Sāʿida; Muʿammar; Ṣarï Ṣalṭuḳ Dede; *et* → Coran.histoires
histoires légendaires ʿAbd Allāh b. D̲j̲udʿān; Akt̲h̲am b. Ṣayfī; Almās; al-Baṭṭāl; Buhlūl; Damāwand; D̲j̲ird̲j̲īs; D̲j̲ūdī; Durr; Fāṭima; al-G̲h̲azāl; al-Ḥaḍr; Ḥāʾiṭ al-ʿAd̲j̲ūz; Haram; Hārūt wa-Mārūt; Hudhud; Isrāʾīliyyāt; K̲h̲ālid b. Yazīd; Ḳiṣaṣ al-Anbiyāʾ; Nūḥ

Lexicographie **Ḳāmūs**; Laḥn al-ʿĀmma
voir aussi S̲h̲arḥ.I; Sullam; *et* → Linguistique

lexicographes
arabes Abū Zayd al-Anṣārī; al-Azharī; al-Djawālīḳī; al-Djawharī; Farḥāt; al-Fīrūzābādī; Ibn al-Birr; Ibn Durayd; Ibn Fāris; Ibn Makkī; Ibn Manẓūr; Ibn Sīda; Ibn al-Sikkīt; al-Ḳazzāz; al-Khalīl b. Aḥmad; Muḥammad Murtaḍā; Nashwān b. Saʿīd; al-Ṣaghānī, Raḍī al-dīn; al-Shaybānī, Abū ʿAmr (*et* [au Suppl.] Abū ʿAmr al-Shaybānī); [au Suppl.] Abū Isḥāḳ al-Fārisī; al-Bustānī.1 et 2; al-Fārābī
voir aussi Abū Ḥātim al-Rāzī; Akhtarī; al-Rāghib al-Iṣfahānī; [au Suppl.] Ibn Kabar
hébraïques Ibn Djanāḥ
voir aussi Judéo-arabe.III.B
persans ʿAbd al-Rashīd b. ʿAbd al-Ghafūr; Aḥmad Wafīḳ Pasha; Burhān; Surūrī Kāshānī; [au Suppl.] Dehkhudā
voir aussi Ārzū Khān; Mahdī Khān Astarābādī; Riḍā Ḳulī Khān
turcs Akhtarī; al-Kashgharī; Kāẓim Ḳadrī; Niʿmat Allah b. Aḥmad; Sāmī
voir aussi Esʿad Efendi, Meḥmed; Luṭfī Efendi; Riyāḍī; Shināsī
termes Fard.2

LIBAN Djarīda.I.A; Djāmiʿa; Dustūr.IX; Ḥizb.I; Ḥukūma.III; **Lubnān**; Madjlis.IV.A.6; Maḥkama.IV.3; Mandats; Mutawālī
voir aussi Baladiyya.II; Djāliya; Ḳays ʿAylān; al-Maʿlūf; [au Suppl.] Aḥmad Pasha Küčük; al-Bustānī; Démographie.III; *et* → DRUZES
gouverneurs Bashīr Shihāb II; Dāwūd Pasha; Djānbulāt; Fakhr al-Dīn; Ḥarfūsh; Shihāb
voir aussi Maʿn; Maʿn-zāde
historiens Iskandar Agha
leaders spirituels Sharaf al-Dīn
voir aussi Mutawālī
toponymes
anciens ʿAyn al-Djarr
actuels
régions al-Biḳāʿ; al-Shūf
villes Baʿlabakk; Batrūn; Bayrūt; Bsharrā; Bteddīn; Djubayl; Karak Nūḥ; Ṣaydā; Ṣūr

LIBYE Djāmiʿa; Djarīda.I.B; Dustūr.XII; **Lībiyā**; Madjlis.IV.A.18
voir aussi ʿArabiyya.A.III.3; al-Bārūnī; Ḳarāmānlī; Khalīfa b. ʿAskar; Sanūsiyya; *et* → DYNASTIES.ESPAGNE ET AFRIQUE DU NORD
population → AFRIQUE.AFRIQUE DU NORD; BERBÈRES
toponymes
anciens Ṣabra; Surt

actuels

    oasis   Awd̲j̲ila; Baḥriyya; al-D̲j̲ag̲h̲būb; D̲j̲awf Kufra; al-D̲j̲ufra; Ghadamès; Kufra

    régions   Barḳa; al-D̲j̲ufra; Fazzān
      voir aussi Nafūsa

    villes   Ad̲j̲dābiya; Beng̲h̲āzī; Darna; D̲j̲ādū; Murzuḳ
      voir aussi G̲h̲āt

LIEUX SACRÉS   Abū Ḳubays; al-Ḥaram al-S̲h̲arīf; Ḥud̲j̲ra; Kaʿba; Karbalāʾ; Kāẓimayn; al-K̲h̲alīl; al-Ḳuds.II; al-Madīna; Makka; al-Muḳaṭṭam; al-Nad̲j̲af *voir aussi* Ḥawṭa; Ḥimā; Ḳāsiyūn; Mawlāy Idrīs; Mud̲j̲āwir; S̲h̲āh ʿAbd al-ʿAẓīm; S̲h̲ayba; *et* → ARCHITECTURE.MONUMENTS; SAINT

LINGUISTIQUE   **Lug̲h̲a**; Naḥw
   voir aussi Balāg̲h̲a; Bayān; Laḥn al-ʿĀmma; S̲h̲arḥ.I; *et* → LANGUES; LEXICO-GRAPHIE

grammairiens/philologues

    8ᵉ siècle   ʿAbd Allāh b. Abī Isḥāḳ; Abū ʿAmr al-ʿAlāʾ; al-Ak̲h̲fas̲h̲.I; ʿĪsā b. ʿUmar; al-K̲h̲alīl b. Aḥmad; Ḳuṭrub; al-Mufaḍḍal al-Ḍabbī; Sībawayhi; al-S̲h̲aybānī, Abū ʿAmr (*et* [au Suppl.] Abū ʿAmr al-S̲h̲aybānī)
      voir aussi [au Suppl.] Abū l-Baydāʾ al-Riyāḥī

    9ᵉ siècle   Abū Ḥātim al-Sid̲j̲istānī; Abū ʿUbayd al-Ḳāsim b. Sallām; Abū ʿUbayda; Abū Zayd al-Anṣārī; al-Ak̲h̲fas̲h̲.II; al-Aṣmaʿī; al-Bāhilī, Abū Naṣr; D̲j̲ūdī al-Mawrūrī; al-Farrāʾ; Ibn al-Aʿrābī, Muḥammad; Ibn Sallām al-D̲j̲umaḥī; Ibn al-Sikkīt; al-Kisāʾī, Abū l-Ḥasan; al-Layt̲h̲ b. al-Muẓaffar; al-Māzinī, Abū ʿUt̲h̲mān; al-Mubarrad; Muḥammad b. Ḥabīb; al-Ruʾāsī; [au Suppl.] Abū l-ʿAmayt̲h̲al

    10ᵉ siècle   al-Ak̲h̲fas̲h̲.III; al-Anbārī, Abū Bakr; al-Anbārī, Abū Muḥammad; al-ʿAskarī.I; D̲j̲aḥẓa; al-Fārisī; G̲h̲ulām T̲h̲aʿlab; Ḥamza al-Iṣfahānī; Ibn al-ʿArīf, al-Ḥusayn; Ibn D̲j̲innī; Ibn Durayd; Ibn Durustawayh; Ibn Kaysān; Ibn K̲h̲ālawayh; Ibn al-K̲h̲ayyāṭ, Abū Bakr; Ibn al-Ḳūṭiyya; Ibn al-Naḥḥās; Ibn al-Sarrād̲j̲; al-Ḳālī; Ḳudāma b. D̲j̲aʿfar; Nifṭawayh; al-Rummānī; al-Sīrāfī; [au Suppl.] Abū Isḥāḳ al-Fārisī; Abū Riyās̲h̲ al-Ḳaysī; Abū l-Ṭayyib al-Lug̲h̲awī; al-Ḥātimī; Ibn Kaysān; Ibn Miḳsam

    11ᵉ siècle   al-Ad̲j̲dābī; al-ʿAskarī.II; Ibn al-Birr; Ibn Fāris; Ibn al-Ḥād̲j̲d̲j̲; Ibn al-Iflīlī; Ibn Makkī; Ibn Sīda; al-Ḳazzāz; al-Marzūḳī; al-Rabāḥī; al-Rabaʿī; al-S̲h̲antamarī; [au Suppl.] Abū Usāma al-Harawī; al-D̲j̲urd̲j̲ānī

    12ᵉ siècle   al-Anbārī, Abū l-Barakāt; al-Baṭalyawsī, Ibn al-Sīd; al-D̲j̲awālīḳī; al-D̲j̲azūlī, Abū Mūsā; al-Ḥarīrī; Ibn Barrī, Abū Muḥammad; Ibn Maḍāʾ; Ibn al-S̲h̲ad̲j̲arī al-Bag̲h̲dādī; al-Maydānī; [au Suppl.] Abū l-Barakāt; Ibn His̲h̲ām al-Lak̲h̲mī

    13ᵉ siècle   al-Astarābād̲h̲ī, Raḍī al-dīn; Ibn al-Ad̲j̲dābī; Ibn al-At̲h̲īr.I; Ibn al-

Ḥādjdj; Ibn al-Ḥādjib; Ibn Mālik; Ibn Muʿṭī; al-Muṭarrizī; al-Shalawbīn; al-Sharīshī; [au Suppl.] al-Balaṭī; Ibn al-Adjdābī

14ᵉ siècle Abū Ḥayyān al-Gharnāṭī; al-Astarābādhī, Rukn al-dīn; Fakhrī; Ibn Ādjurrūm; Ibn ʿAḳīl, ʿAbd Allāh; Ibn Barrī, Abū l-Ḥasan; Ibn Hishām, Djamāl al-dīn; Ibn Khātima; Ibn al-Sāʾigh; al-Sharīf al-Gharnatī

15ᵉ siècle al-Azharī, Khālid; Ibn ʿĀṣim; al-Sanhūrī, Abū l-Ḥasan; al-Suyūṭī

17ᵉ siècle ʿAbd al-Ḳādir al-Baghdādī

18ᵉ siècle Farḥāt

19ᵉ siècle Fāris al-Shidyāḳ; Ibn al-Ḥādjdj; al-Nabarāwī

voir aussi Fuʾād Pasha

20ᵉ siècle [au Suppl.] Arat

phonétique Ḥurūf al-Hidjāʾ.II; Makhāridj al-Ḥurūf; Mushtarik; Ṣawtiyya

voir aussi Ḍād; Dāl; Dhāl; Djīm; Fāʾ; Ghayn; Hāʾ; Ḥāʾ; Hamza; Hāwī; Ḥurūf al-Hidjāʾ; Imāla; Kāf; Ḳāf; Khāʾ; Lām; Mīm; Nūn; Pāʾ; Rāʾ; Ṣād; Sīn et Shīn

pour les dialectes arabes, voir Algérie.V; al-Andalus.X; ʿIrāḳ.IV; Lībiya.II; al-Maghrib.VII; Mahrī; Malta.2

termes Aḍdād; Āla.I.; ʿĀmil; ʿAṭf; Dakhīl; Djāmʿ; Fard; Fiʿl; Gharīb; Ḥaraka wa-Sukūn.II; Ḥarf; Hāwī; Ḥikāya.I; Ḥukm.II; Ḥulūl; Ibdāl; Iḍāfa; Idghām; Iḍmār; ʿIlla.I; Imāla; Iʿrāb; Ishtiḳāḳ; Ism; Istifhām; Istithnaʾ; Kasra; Ḳaṭʿ; Khabar; Ḳiyās; Māḍī; Maʿnā.I; Muʿarrab; Mubālagha; Mubtadaʾ.I; Muḍāriʿ; Mudhakkar; Muḍmar; Musnad.2; Muṭlaḳ; Muwallad; Muzdawidj; Nafy; Naṣb; Naʿt; Nisba.1; Rafʿ; Sabab.6; Ṣaḥīḥ.3; Sālim.2; Ṣarf; Sharṭ.3; Ṣifa.1; Ṣila.1; [au Suppl.] Ḥāl

voir aussi Basīṭ wa Murakkab; Ghalaṭat-i Meshhūre; Ḥurūf al-Hidjāʾ

LITTÉRATURE **Adab**; ʿArabiyya.B; ʿIrāḳ.V; Īrān.VII; ʿOthmānli̊.III

autobiographique Nuʿayma, Mikhāʾīl; Sālim; Shāʾūl, Anwar

voir aussi Shaybānī

biographique Faḍīla; **Manāḳib**; Mathālib

voir aussi ʿIlm al-Ridjāl; Maʾāthir al-Umarāʾ; Mughals.X; Shurafāʾ (La littérature); Ṣila.2.II.c; *et* → HAGIOGRAPHIE; LITTÉRATURE.HISTORIQUE *et* POÉSIE; MÉDECINE.MÉDECINS.BIOGRAPHIES DES; MUḤAMMAD, LE PROPHÈTE

critique Ibn al-Athīr.III; Ibn Rashīḳ; Ḳudāma b. Djaʿfar; [au Suppl.] al-Djurdjānī; al-Ḥātimī

moderne Kemāl, Meḥmed Nāmi̊ḳ; Köprülü; Kurd ʿAlī; al-Māzinī; Olghun, Meḥmed Ṭāhir; [au Suppl.] Alangu; Atač

termes Mubālagha

drame **Masraḥ**

arabe Khayāl al-Ẓill; Masraḥ.I et II

voir aussi ʿArabiyya.B.V

dramaturges Abū Naḍḍāra; Faraḥ Anṭūn; Ibn Dāniyāl; al-Ḳusanṭīnī; al-

Maʿlūf; Nadjīb b. Sulaymān al-Ḥaddād; Nadjīb Muḥammad Surūr; al-Naḳḳāsh; Ṣalāḥ ʿAbd al-Ṣabūr; Salīm al-Naḳḳāsh; al-Sharḳāwī; Shawḳī; [au Suppl.] al-Bustānī.1

voir aussi Isḥāḳ, Adīb; Ismāʿīl Ṣabrī; Khalīl Muṭrān; Shumayyil, Shiblī

en Asie centrale Masraḥ.V

ourdo Masraḥ.VI

dramaturges Amānat; [au Suppl.] Āghā Ḥashar Kashmīrī

persan Masraḥ.IV

dramaturges Muḥammad Djaʿfar Ḳaradja-dāghī; [au Suppl.] Amīrī

turc Ḳaragöz; Ḳawuḳlu; Masraḥ.III; Orta Oyunu

dramaturges ʿAbd al-Ḥaḳḳ Ḥāmid; Aḥmad Wafīḳ Pasha; Ākhund-zāda; Djewdet; Karay, Refīḳ Khālid; Ḳaṣāb; Kemāl, Meḥmed Nāmïḳ; Khayr Allāh Efendi; Manāṣtïrlï Meḥmed Rifʿat; Meḥmed Raʾūf; Mīzāndjï Meḥmed Murād; Muḥibb Aḥmed "Diranas"; Muṣāhib-zāde Djelāl; Oktay Rifat; Shināsī; [au Suppl.] Alus; Bashḳut; Čamlïbel; Ḥasan Bedr al-Dīn

voir aussi Djanāb Shihāb al-Dīn; Ebüzziya Tevfik; Ekrem Bey; Kaygïlï; Khālide Edīb; Muʿallim Nādjī

en d'autres langues Afghān.III; Aljamía; Bengali.II; Berbères.VI; Beskesek-abaza; Bosna.III; Hausa.III; Hindī; Indonésie.VI; Judéo-arabe.III; Judéo-persan.I; Kano; Ḳiṣṣa.VIII; Lahndā.II; Laḳ; Masraḥ.VI; Pandjābī.2; Shiʿr.5; Sind.3.b; Somali.6

pour la littérature swahilienne → KENYA; *pour la littérature malaise* → MALAISIE; *et* → LITTÉRATURE.POÉSIE.MYSTIQUE

auteurs bengalis Nadhr al-Islām; Nūr Ḳuṭb al-ʿĀlam

auteurs hindis Malik Muḥammad Djāyasī; Nihāl Čand Lāhawrī; Prēm Čand; Sudjān Rāy Bhandārī

voir aussi ʿAbd al-Raḥīm Khān; Inshāʾ; Lallūdjī Lāl

auteurs judéo-arabes Mūsā b. ʿAzra; al-Samawʾal b. ʿĀdiyā

et → JUDAÏSME.LANGUE ET LITTÉRATURE

auteurs judéo-persans Shāhīn-i Shīrāzī

et → JUDAÏSME.LANGUE ET LITTÉRATURE

auteurs pashtōs Khushḥāl Khān Khaṭak

auteurs tatars Ghafūrī, Medjīd

épistolaire **Inshāʾ**; Kātib; **Risāla**

voir aussi Ṣadr.(b)

recueils épistolaires ʿAbd al-Ḥamīd b. Yaḥyā; Aḥmad Sirhindī; ʿAmr b. Masʿada; al-Babbaghāʾ; Ghālib; Ḥāletī; al-Hamadhānī; Harkarn; Ibn ʿAmīra; Ibn al-Athīr.III; Ibn Idrīs [I]; Ibn Ḳalāḳis; Ibn al-Khaṣīb; Ibn al-Ṣayrafī; al-Ḳabtawrī; al-Ḳāḍī al-Fāḍil; Kānī; Khalīfa Shāh Muḥammad; Khʷāndamīr; al-Khʷārazmī; al-Maʿarrī; Makhdūm al-Mulk; Meḥmed

Pa<u>sh</u>a Rāmī; Muḥammad b. Hindū-<u>Sh</u>āh; Oḵču-zāde; Ra<u>sh</u>īd al-Dīn (al-Waṭwaṭ); Saʿīd b. Ḥumayd; al-<u>Sh</u>aybānī, Ibrāhīm; [au Suppl.] ʿAbd al-ʿAzīz b. Yūsuf; Amīr Niẓām; Ibn <u>Kh</u>alaf

voir aussi Aljamía; al-<u>Dj</u>unayd; Ibn al-ʿAmīd.I; Ibn al-<u>Kh</u>aṭīb; Mu<u>gh</u>als.X; Sud<u>j</u>ān Rāy Bhandārī

étiquette, littérature de l' **Adab**; al-Maḥāsin wa-l-Masāwī

voir aussi al-<u>Dj</u>idd wa-l-Hazl; <u>Dj</u>ins; Ḥiyal; Iyās b. Muʿāwiya; Kalīla wa-Dimna; Kātib; Marzban-nāma; Nadīm; Sulūk.1

auteurs Abū Ḥayyān al-Tawḥīdī; al-Bayhaḵī; <u>Dj</u>āḥiẓ; al-<u>Gh</u>uzūlī; Hilāl al-Ṣābiʾ; al-Ḥuṣrī.I; Ibn ʿAbd Rabbih; Ibn Abī l-Dunyā; Ibn al-Muḵaffaʿ; al-Ḳalyūbī; al-Ḵā<u>sh</u>ānī; al-Kisrawī; al-Marzubānī; Merd<u>j</u>ümek; al-Nīsābūrī; al-Rā<u>gh</u>ib al-Iṣfahānī; al-<u>Sh</u>im<u>sh</u>āṭī; al-Ṣūlī

voir aussi al-<u>Dj</u>ah<u>sh</u>iyārī; al-Ḳalḵa<u>sh</u>andī.I; <u>Sh</u>abīb b. <u>Sh</u>ayba

généalogique Mathālib

généalogistes al-Abīwardī; al-<u>Dj</u>awwānī; al-Hamdānī; al-Kalbī.II; al-Ḳalḵa<u>sh</u>andī.I; Ḳāsim b. Aṣba<u>gh</u>; al-Marwazī; Muṣʿab; al-Ru<u>sh</u>āṭī; [au Suppl.] Fa<u>kh</u>r-i Mudabbir

voir aussi Ibn Daʾb; al-Ḳādirī al-Ḥasanī; al-<u>Kh</u>ʷārazmī; Mihmindār

genres

poésie <u>Gh</u>azal; Hid<u>j</u>āʾ; Ḳaṣīda; <u>Kh</u>amriyya; Madīḥ; Marthiya; Mathnawī; Mufā<u>kh</u>ara; Munṣifa; Musammaṭ; Muwa<u>sh</u><u>sh</u>aḥ; Nawriyya; <u>Sh</u>ahrangīz; <u>Sh</u>arḳī

voir aussi ʿArabiyya.B; Īrān.VII; Rabīʿiyyāt; Sāḵī.2; <u>Sh</u>awāhid

prose Adab; Ad<u>j</u>āʾib; Awāʾil; Badīʿ; Bilmed<u>j</u>e; <u>Dj</u>afr; Faḍīla; Fahrasa; Ḥikāya; Ilāhī; In<u>sh</u>āʾ; Isrāʾīliyyāt; Kān wa-Kān; <u>Kh</u>iṭaṭ; Ḳiṣṣa; al-Ḳūmā; Laḥn al-ʿĀmma; Lu<u>gh</u>z; al-Ma<u>gh</u>āzī; al-Maḥāsin wa-l-Masāwī; Maḳāla; Maḳāma; Malḥūn; Manāḳib; Masāʾil wa-Ad<u>j</u>wiba; al-Masālik wa-l-Mamālik; Mathālib; Mawsūʿa; Muḳaddima; Mu<u>kh</u>taṣar; Munāẓara; Nādira; Naḳāʾiḍ; Naṣīḥat al-Mulūk; Risāla; <u>Sh</u>arḥ; Ṣila.2; Sīra; Sunan; [au Suppl.] Arbaʿūn Ḥadī<u>th</u>; Ḥabsiyya

voir aussi Alf layla wa-Layla (374b); ʿArabiyya.B; Bibliographie; <u>Dj</u>u<u>gh</u>rāfiyā; Fatḥnāme; Ḥayawān; Ḥiyal; Īrān.VII; Malāḥim; Mathal; <u>Sh</u>āhnāmed<u>j</u>i; *et* → CHRISTIANISME.COUVENTS.TRAITÉS SUR

historique Isrāʾīliyyāt; al-Ma<u>gh</u>āzī

voir aussi Fatḥnāme; Ṣaḥāba; Ṣila.2.II; *et* → *les entrées* BIOGRAPHIQUE, MA<u>GH</u>ĀZĪ *et* TRADITION, LITTÉRATURE DE LA *sous cette rubrique*

andalouse → ANDALOUSIE

arabe

sur les pays/villes → *pays individuels*

sur les dynasties/califes → *dynasties individuelles sous* DYNASTIES

histoires universelles Abū l-Fidāʾ; Abū Mi<u>kh</u>naf; Akansūs; al-Antāḵī; ʿArīb b. Saʿd; al-ʿAynī; al-Bakrī; al-Balā<u>dh</u>urī; Baybars al-Manṣūrī;

al-Birzālī; Daḥlān; al-Dhahabī; al-Diyārbakrī; al-Djannābī; al-Djazarī; al-Farghānī; Ḥamza al-Iṣfahānī; Ḥasan-i Rūmlū; al-Haytham b. ʿAdī; Ibn Abī Shayba; Ibn Abī Ṭayyiʾ; Ibn Aʿtham al-Kūfī; Ibn al-Athīr.II; Ibn al-Dawādārī; Ibn al-Djawzī (Sibṭ); Ibn al-Furāt; Ibn Kathīr; Ibn Khaldūn; Ibn Khayyāṭ al-ʿUṣfurī; Ibn al-Sāʿī; al-Kalbī.II; Kātib Čelebi; al-Kutubī; al-Makīn b. al-Amīd; al-Masʿūdī; Miskawayh; Münedjdjm Bāshi̊; al-Muṭahhar b. Ṭāhir al-Maḳdisī; al-Nuwayrī, Shihāb al-dīn; Saʿīd b. al-Biṭrīḳ

voir aussi Akhbār Madjmūʿa

8ᵉ siècle Abū Mikhnaf; ʿAwāna b. al-Ḥakam; Sayf b. ʿUmar

9ᵉ siècle al-Balādhurī; al-Fāḳihī; al-Farghānī; al-Haytham b. ʿAdī; Ibn ʿAbd al-Ḥakam.IV; Ibn Abī Shayba; Ibn Abī Ṭāhir Ṭayfūr; Ibn Aʿtham al-Kūfī; Ibn Khayyāṭ al-ʿUṣfurī; Ibn al-Naṭṭāḥ; al-Kalbī.II; al-Madāʾinī; Naṣr b. Muzāḥim

10ᵉ siècle ʿArīb b. Saʿd; al-Azdī; Baḥshal; al-Balawī; al-Djahshiyārī; Ḥamza al-Iṣfahānī; Ibn al-Dāya; Ibn al-Ḳūṭiyya; Ibn Manda; Ibn al-Ṣaghīr; al-Kindī; Abū ʿUmar Muḥammad; al-Masʿūdī

11ᵉ siècle al-Antāḳī, Abū l-Faradj; Ibn al-Bannāʾ; Ibn Burd.I; Ibn Ḥayyān; Ibn al-Raḳīḳ; al-Māfarrūkhī

12ᵉ siècle al-ʿAẓīmī; Ibn al-Djawzī; Ibn Ghālib; Ibn al-Ḳalānisī; Ibn Ṣāḥib al-Ṣalāt; Ibn al-Ṣayrafī, Abū Bakr; Ibn Shaddād, Abū Muḥammad; ʿImād al-Dīn al-Iṣfahānī; Shīrawayh

voir aussi al-Baydhaḳ; Ibn Manda

13ᵉ siècle ʿAbd al-Wāḥid al-Marrākushī; Abū Shāma; al-Bundārī; al-Djanadī; Ibn Abī l-Dam; Ibn Abī Ṭayyiʾ; Ibn al-ʿAdīm; Ibn al-Athīr.II; Ibn al-Djawzī (Sibṭ); Ibn Ḥamādu; Ibn al-Mudjāwir; Ibn Muyassar; Ibn al-Nadjdjār; Ibn al-Sāʿī; Ibn Saʿīd al-Maghribī; Ibn Shaddād, ʿIzz al-dīn; Ibn Shaddād, Bahāʾ al-dīn; Ibn al-Ṭuwayr; al-Makīn b. al-Amīd; al-Manṣūr; al-Rāfiʿī; [au Suppl.] Ibn ʿAskar; Ibn Ḥātim

14ᵉ siècle Abū l-Fidā; Baybars al-Manṣūrī; al-Birzālī; al-Dhahabī; al-Djazarī; Ibn Abī Zarʿ; Ibn al-Dawādārī; Ibn Duḳmāḳ; Ibn al-Furāt, Nāṣir al-dīn; Ibn Ḥabīb, Badr al-dīn; Ibn ʿIdhārī; Ibn Kathīr, ʿImād al-dīn; Ibn Khaldūn; Ibn al-Khaṭīb; Ibn al-Ṭiḳṭaḳā; al-Khazradjī, Muwaffaḳ al-dīn; al-Kutubī; al-Mufaḍḍal b. Abī l-Faḍāʾil; al-Ṣafadī, Ṣalāḥ al-dīn; Shāfiʿ b. ʿAlī

15ᵉ siècle Abū l-Maḥāsin Ibn Taghrābirdī; ʿArabfaḳih; al-ʿAynī; al-Fāsī; Ibn ʿArabshāh; Ibn Shāhīn al-Ẓāhirī; al-Maḳrīzī; al-Sakhāwī

16ᵉ siècle al-Diyārbakrī; al-Djannābī, Abū Muḥammad; Ḥasan-i Rūmlū; Ibn al-Daybaʿ; Ibn Iyās; Mudjīr al-Dīn al-ʿUlaymī; al-Suyūṭī

17ᵉ siècle ʿAbd al-ʿAzīz b. Muḥammad; al-Bakrī.I et II; Ibn Abī Dīnār; Kātib Čelebi; al-Maḳḳarī; al-Mawzaʿī

18ᵉ siècle al-Damurdāshī; al-Ḥādjdj Ḥammūda; al-Ifrānī; Münedjdjim Bashi̊

19e siècle Aḥmad al-Nāṣirī (*et* al-Nāṣirī al-Salāwī); Akanṣūs; ʿAlī Pasha Mubārak; Daḥlān; al-Djabartī; Ghulām Ḥusayn Khān Ṭabāṭabāʾī; Ibn Abī l-Ḍiyāf
voir aussi al-Kardūdī
20e siècle Ibn Zaydān; Kurd ʿAlī
indo-persane Mughals.X
sur les pays/villes → INDE
sur les dynasties/califes → *dynasties individuelles sous* DYNASTIES. AFGHANISTAN ET INDE
13e-14e siècles Baranī; al-Djūzdjānī; Shams al-Dīn-i Sirādj ʿAfīf
15e-16e siècles Abū l-Faḍl ʿAllāmī; Djawhar; Gulbadan Bēgam; Niẓām al-Dīn, Aḥmad; [au Suppl.] ʿAbbās Sarwānī
17e siècle ʿAbd al-Ḥamīd Lāhawrī; Bakhtāwar Khān; Firishta; ʿInāyat Allāh Kanbū; Mīr Muḥammad Maʿṣūm; Niʿmat Allāh b. Ḥabīb Allāh Harawī; Nūr al-Ḥaḳḳ al-Dihlawī; Shīrāzī, Rafīʿ al-dīn; [au Suppl.] ʿĀḳil Khān Rāzī; Ḥādjdjī al-Dabīr; Ḥaydar Malik
voir aussi Badāʾūnī
18e siècle ʿAbd al-Karīm Kashmīrī; Ḳāniʿ; Khwāfī Khān; Niʿmat Khān
19e siècle ʿAbd al-Karīm Munshī; Ghulām Ḥusayn Khān Ṭabāṭabāʾī; Ghulām Ḥusayn "Salīm"
voir aussi Aẓfarī
persane [au Suppl.] Čač-nāma
sur Iran → IRAN
sur les dynasties/califes → *dynasties individuelles sous* DYNASTIES. PERSE
histoires universelles Mīrkhwānd; Niẓām Shāhī; Sipihr
10e siècle Balʿamī
11e siècle Bayhaḳī; Gardīzī
12e siècle Anūshirwān b. Khālid; al-Bayhaḳī, Ẓahīr al-dīn; [au Suppl.] Ibn al-Balkhī
13e siècle Djuwaynī; Ibn Bībī; Ibn Isfandiyār; [au Suppl.] Ḥasan Niẓāmī; al-Ḥusaynī
14e siècle Banākitī; Ḥamd Allāh al-Mustawfī al-Ḳazwīnī; Shabānkāraʾī; [au Suppl.] al-Aḳsarāyī;
15e siècle ʿAbd al-Razzāḳ al-Samarḳandī; Ḥāfiẓ-i Abrū
16e siècle Bidlīsī, Sharaf al-dīn; Djamāl al-Ḥusaynī; Ghaffārī; Ḥaydar Mīrzā; Khwāndamīr; Ḳum(m)ī; al-Lārī; Shāmī, Niẓām al-Dīn; [au Suppl.] Ḥāfiẓ Tanīsh
voir aussi ʿAlī b. Shams al-Dīn
17e siècles ʿAbd al-Fattāh Fūmanī; Ḥaydar b. ʿAlī; Iskandar Beg; Rāzī, Amīn Aḥmad
18e siècle Mahdī Khān Astarābādī
voir aussi Īsar-dās

19ᵉ-20ᵉ siècles ʿAbd al-Karīm Bukhārī; [au Suppl.] Fasāʾī
turque Shāhnāmedji
sur l'empire ottoman → DYNASTIES.ANATOLIE ET LES TURCS.OTTOMANS.HISTORIENS DES
histoires universelles Shāriḥ ül-Menār-zāde
voir aussi Neshrī
15ᵉ siècle ʿĀshiḳ-pasha-zāde; Meḥmed Pasha, Ḳaramānī
16ᵉ siècle ʿAlī; Bihishtī; Djalālzāde Muṣṭafā Čelebi; Djalālzāde Ṣāliḥ Čelebi; Kemāl Pasha-zāde; Luḳmān b. Sayyid Ḥusayn; Maṭrāḳčî; Meḥmed Zaʿīm; Neshrī; Selānīkī; Seyfī
voir aussi Ḥadīdī; Medjdī
17ᵉ siècle ʿAbdī; ʿAbdī Pasha; Ḥasan Bey-zāde; Ḥibrī; Ḳarā-čelebi-zāde.4; Kātib Čelebi; Meḥmed Khalīfe b. Ḥüseyn; Shāriḥ ül-Menār-zāde
18ᵉ siècle ʿAbdī Efendi; Aḥmad Rasmī; Čelebi-zāde; Česhmīzāde; Enwerī; ʿIzzī; Münedjdjim Bashî; ʿOthmān-zāde
19ᵉ siècle Aḥmad Djewdet Pasha; ʿĀṣim; ʿAṭāʾ Bey, Ṭayyārzāde; Esʿad Efendi, Meḥmed; Kemāl, Meḥmed Nāmîḳ; Khayr Allāh Efendi
20ᵉ siècles Aḥmad Rafīk; ʿAlī Amīrī; (Meḥmed) ʿAṭāʾ Bey; Luṭfī Efendi; Mīzāndjî Meḥmed Murād; Shems al-Dīn Günaltay; Sheref, ʿAbd al-Raḥmān
voir aussi Ḥilmī
en turc oriental Abū l-Ghāzī; Bāḳîkhānlî; Muʾnis
maghāzī Abū Maʿshar al Sindī; Ibn ʿĀʾidh; al-Kalāʿī; **al-Maghāzī**; Mūsā b. ʿUḳba
voir aussi al-Baṭṭāl; Sīra
merveilles, collections des Abū Ḥāmid al-Gharnāṭī; **ʿAdjāʾib**; Buzurg b. Shahriyār; al-Ḳazwīnī
voir aussi Ibn Sarābiyūn; Ḳiṣaṣ al-Anbiyāʾ; Sindbād
personnages dans la littérature Abū Ḍamḍam; Abū l-Ḳāsim; Abū Zayd; Ali Baba; Ayāz; Aywaz.2; al-Basūs; al-Baṭṭāl; Bekrī Muṣṭafā Agha; Buzurgmihr; Dhū l-Himma; Djamshīd; Djuḥā; al-Ghāḍirī; Ḥamza b. ʿAbd al-Muṭṭalib; Ḥātim al-Ṭāʾī; Ḥayy b. Yaḳẓān; Köroghlu; Manas; Naṣr al-Dīn Khodja; Rustam; Sām; Ṣarî Ṣalṭuḳ Dede; Shahrazād; al-Sīd; Sindbād; Siyāwush
picaresque Maḳāma; Mukaddī
poésie ʿArūḍ; Ḥamāsa; Ḳāfiya; Lughz; Madīḥ; Maʿnā.III; Mukhtārāt; Muzdawidj; Shāʿir; **Shiʿr**
voir aussi Rāwī; Sharḥ.II; *pour les genres poétiques* → LITTÉRATURE.GENRES.POÉSIE; *et* → MÉTRIQUE
andalouse ʿArabiyya.B.Appendice; Khamriyya.VI; Muwashshaḥ; Nawriyya; Shāʿir.1.D

anthologies al-Fatḥ b. Khāḳān; al-Fihrī; Ibn Bassām; Ibn Diḥya; Ibn Faradj al-Djayyānī; al-Shaḳundī

8e siècle Ghirbīb b. ʿAbd Allāh

9e siécle ʿAbbās b. Firnās; ʿAbbās b. Nāṣih; al-Ghazāl

voir aussi Ibn ʿAlḳama.II

10e siècle Ibn ʿAbd Rabbih; Ibn Abī Zamanayn; Ibn Faradj al-Djayyānī; Ibn Ḳuzmān.I; Muḳaddam b. Muʿāfā; al-Ramādī; al-Sharīf al-Ṭalīḳ

11e siècle Abū Isḥāḳ al-Ilbīrī; Ibn al-Abbār; Ibn ʿAbd al-Ṣamad; Ibn ʿAmmār; Ibn Burd.II; Ibn Darrādj al-Ḳasṭallī; Ibn Gharsiya; Ibn al-Ḥaddād; Ibn al-Ḥannāṭ; Ibn al-Labbāna; Ibn Māʾ al-Samāʾ; Ibn al-Shahīd; Ibn Shuhayd; Ibn Zaydūn; al-Muʿtamid Ibn ʿAbbād

voir aussi Ṣāʿid al-Baghdādī

12e siècle al-Aʿmā al-Tuṭīlī; Ḥafṣa bint al-Ḥādjdj; Ibn ʿAbdūn; Ibn Baḳī; Ibn Ḳabṭūrnu; Ibn Khafādja; Ibn Ḳuzmān.II et V; Ibn al-Ṣayrafī; al-Ḳurṭubī; al-Ruṣāfī; Ṣafwān b. Idrīs

voir aussi Mūsā b. ʿAzra

13e siècle Ḥāzim; Ibn al-Abbār; Ibn ʿAmīra; Ibn Sahl; Ibn Saʿid al-Maghribī; al-Ḳabtawrī; al-Shushtarī

14e siècle Ibn al-Ḥādjdj; Ibn Khātima; Ibn Luyūn; Ibn al-Murābiʿ; al-Sharīf al-Gharnāṭī

arabe ʿAtāba; Ghazal.I; Ḥamāsa.I; Hidjāʾ; Kān wa-Kān; Ḳaṣīda.I; al-Ḳūmā; Madīḥ.I; Maḳṣūra; Malḥūn; Marthiya.I; Mawāliyā; Mawlidiyya; Mukhtārāt.I; Musammaṭ.1; Muwashshaḥ; Naḳāʾiḍ; Nasīb; Rubāʿī.3; Shaʿir.1; **Shiʿr**.1

voir aussi ʿArabiyya.B.II; Bānat Suʿād; Burda.2; ʿIlm al-Djamāl; Ḳalb.II; Madjnūn Laylā.I; Mawlid; al-Muʿallaḳāt; Muwallad; Ṣuʿlūk; *et* → LITTÉRATURE.POÉSIE.ANDALOUSE *et* POÉSIE.MYSTIQUE

anthologies al-Muʿallaḳāt; al-Mufaḍḍaliyyāt; **Mukhtārāt**.I

anthologistes Abū l-Faradj al-Iṣbahānī; Abū Tammām; al-ʿAlamī; al-Bākharzī; al-Buḥturī; Diʿbil; al-Hamdānī; Ḥammād al-Rāwiya; Ibn Abī Ṭāhir Ṭayfūr; Ibn Dāwūd; Ibn al-Ḳutayba; Ibn al-Muʿtazz; Ibn al-Ṣayrafī; ʿImād al-Dīn al-Iṣfahānī; al-Nawādjī; al-Sarī; al-Shayzarī; al-Shimshāṭī; [au Suppl.] Abū Zayd al-Ḳurashī; al-Bustānī.3

préislamique ʿAbīd b. al-Abraṣ; Abū Dhuʾayb al-Hudhalī; Abū Duʾād al-Iyādī; Abū Kabīr al-Hudhalī; ʿAdī b. Zayd; al-Afwah al-Awdī; al-Aghlab al-ʿIdjlī; ʿAlḳama b. ʿAbada; ʿĀmir b. al-Ṭufayl; ʿAmr b. al-Ahtam; ʿAmr b. Ḳamīʾa; ʿAmr b. Kulthūm; ʿAntara; al-Aʿshā; al-Aswad b. Yaʿfur; Aws b. Ḥadjar; Bishr b. Abī Khāzim; Bisṭām b. Ḳays; Durayd b. al-Ṣimma; al-Ḥādira; al-Ḥārith b. Ḥilliza; Ḥassān b. Thābit; Ḥātim al-Ṭāʾī; Ibn al-Iṭnāba al-Khazradjī; Imruʾ al-Ḳays b. Ḥudjr; Ḳays b. al-Khaṭīm; al-Khansāʾ; Laḳīṭ al-Iyādī; Laḳīṭ b. Zurāra;

al-Munakhkhal al-Yashkurī; Murakkish; al-Mutalammis; al-Nābigha al-Dhubyānī; Salāma b. Djandal; al-Samawʾal b. ʿĀdiyā; al-Shanfarā
voir aussi ʿArabiyya.B.I; Ghazal; Hudhayl; al-Muʿallaḳāt; al-Mufaḍḍaliyyāt; Mufākhara2; Nasīb.2.A; Shāʿir.1A; al-Shantamarī; Ṣuʿlūk.II.4

mukhaḍramūn (6e-7e siècles) al-ʿAbbās b. Mirdās; ʿAbd Allāh b. Rawāḥa; Abū Khirāsh al-Hudhalī; Abū Miḥdjān; ʿAmr b. Maʿdīkarib; Ḍirār b. al-Khaṭṭāb; Ḥassān b. Thābit; al-Ḥuṭayʾa; Ibn (al-)Aḥmar; Kaʿb b. Mālik; Kaʿb b. Zuhayr; Khidāsh b. Zuhayr; Labīd b. Rabīʿa; Maʿn b. Aws al-Muzanī; **Mukhaḍram**; Mutammim b. Nuwayra; al-Nābigha al-Djaʿdī; al-Namir b. Tawlab al-ʿUklī; al-Shammākh b. Ḍirār; Suḥaym; [au Suppl.] Abū l-Ṭamaḥān al-Ḳaynī; Ibn Muḳbil
voir aussi Hudhayl; Nasīb.2.B

7e-8e siècles al-ʿAbbās b. al-Aḥnaf; ʿAbd Allāh b. Hammān; Abū ʿAṭāʾ al-Sindī; Abū Dahbal al-Djumaḥī; Abū Dulāma; Abū l-Nadjm al-ʿIdjlī; Abū Ṣakhr al-Hudhalī; Abū l-Shamaḳmaḳ; Adī b. al-Riḳāʿ; al-ʿAdjdjādj; al-Aḥwaṣ al-Anṣārī; al-Akhṭal; al-ʿArdjī; Aʿshā Hamdān; al-Ashdjaʿ b. ʿAmr al-Sulamī; Ayman b. Khuraym; al-Baʿīth; Bashshār b. Burd; Dhū l-Rumma; Djamīl al-ʿUdhrī; Djarīr; Dukayn al-Rādjiz; al-Farazdaḳ; al-Ḥakam b. ʿAbdal; al-Ḥakam b. Ḳanbar; Ḥammād ʿAdjrad; Ḥamza b. Bīḍ; Ḥāritha b. Badr al-Ghudānī; al-Ḥuḍayn; Ḥumayd b. Thawr; Ḥumayd al-Arḳaṭ; Ibn Abī ʿUyayna; Ibn al-Dumayna; Ibn Harma; Ibn Ḳays al-Ruḳayyāt; Ibn Ladjaʾ; Ibn al-Mawlā; Ibn Mayyāda; Ibn Mufarrigh; Ibn Muṭayr; Ibn Sayḥān; ʿImrān b. Ḥiṭṭān; ʿInān; Ismāʿīl b. Yasār; Kaʿb b. Djuʿayl al-Taghlabī; Ḳaṭarī b. al-Fudjāʾa; al-Kumayt b. Zayd al-Asadī; al-Ḳuṭāmī; Kuthayyir b. ʿAbd al-Raḥmān; Laylā al-Akhyaliyya; Manṣūr al-Namarī; Marwān; Miskīn al-Dārimī; Mūsā Shahawātin; Musāwir al-Warrāḳ; Muṭīʿ b. Iyās; Nubāta b. ʿAbd Allāh; Nuṣayb; Nuṣayb b. Rabāḥ; al-Rāʿī; Ruʾba b. al-ʿAdjdjādj; Ṣafī al-Dīn al-Ḥillī; Ṣafwān al-Anṣārī; Saḥbān Wāʾil; Ṣāliḥ b. ʿAbd al-Ḳuddūs; Salm al-Khāsir; al-Sayyid al-Ḥimyarī; al-Shamardal; Sudayf b. Maymūn; Sufyān al-ʿAbdī; Sulaymān b. Yaḥyā; Surāḳa b. Mirdās al-Aṣghar; [au Suppl.] ʿAbd al-Raḥmān b. Ḥassān; Abū ʿAmr al-Shaybānī; Abū Ḥayyā al-Numayrī; Abū Ḥuzāba; Abū Nukhayla; Bakr b. al-Naṭṭāḥ
voir aussi Nasīb.2.C et D; Ṣuʿlūk.III.2

9e-10e siècles Abān b. ʿAbd al-Ḥamīd; ʿAbd Allāh b. Ṭāhir; Abū l-ʿAtāhiya; Abū Dulaf; Abū l-Faradj al-Iṣbahānī; Abū Firās al Ḥamdānī; Abū Nuwās; Abū l-Shīṣ; Abū Tammām; Abū Yaʿḳūb al-Khuraymī; al-ʿAkawwak; ʿAlī b. al-Djahm; al-ʿAttābī; al-Babbaghāʾ; al-Baṣīr; al-Buḥturī; al-Bustī; Diʿbil; Dīk al-Djinn al-Ḥimṣī; al-Djammāz; al-Hamdānī; (al-)Ḥusayn b. al-Ḍaḥḥāk; Ibn al-ʿAllāf; Ibn

Bassām; Ibn al-Ḥadjdjādj; Ibn Kunāsa; Ibn Lankak; Ibn al-Muʿadhdhal; Ibn Munādhir; Ibn al-Muʿtazz; Ibn al-Rūmī; al-Ḳāsim b. ʿĪsā; Khālid b. Yazīd; al-Khālidiyyāni; al-Khaṭṭābī; al-Khubzaʾaruzzī; al-Kisrawī; Kushādjim; al-Maʾmūnī; Muḥammad b. ʿAbd al-Raḥmān al-ʿAṭawī; Muḥammad b. Ḥāzim al-Bāhilī; Muḥammad b. Umayya; Muḥammad b. Yasīr al-Riyāshī; al-Muṣʿabī; Muslim b. al-Walīd; al-Mutanabbī; Naṣr b. Nuṣayr; Sahl b. Hārūn; Saʿīd b. Ḥumayd; al-Ṣanawbarī; al-Sarī; al-Shimshāṭī; [au Suppl.] Abū l-ʿAmaythal; Abū l-Asad al-Ḥimmānī; Abū l-Ḥasan al-Maghribī; Abū Hiffān; Abū l-ʿIbar; Abū Riyāsh al-Ḳaysī; Abū Saʿd al-Makhzūmī; Abū Shurāʿa; ʿAlī b. Muḥammad; Faḍl al-Shāʿira; al-Fazārī; al-Ḥamdawī

voir aussi al-Hamadhānī; Ibn Abī Zamanayn; Nasīb.2.D; Shahīd al-Balkhī; al-Ṣūlī

11ᵉ-13ᵉ siècles al-Abīwardī; ʿAmīd al-Dīn al-Abzārī; al-Arradjānī; al-Badīʿ al-Asṭurlābī; Bahāʾ al-Dīn Zuhayr; al-Bākharzī; Ḥayṣa Bayṣa; al-Ḥuṣrī.II; Ibn Abī l-Ḥadīd; Ibn Abī Ḥaṣīna; Ibn al-ʿAfīf al-Tilimsānī; Ibn al-Habbāriyya; Ibn al-Ḥamdīs; Ibn Ḥayyūs; Ibn Hindū; Ibn al-Ḳaṭṭān; Ibn al-Ḳaysarānī.II; Ibn Khamīs; Ibn Maṭrūḥ; Ibn al-Nabīh; Ibn Rashīḳ; Ibn Sanāʾ al-Mulk; Ibn al-Shadjarī al-Baghdādī; Ibn Sharaf al-Ḳayrawānī; Ibn Shibl; Ibn al-Taʿāwīdhī; al-Kammūnī; Ḳurhub b. Djābir; al-Maʿarrī; al-Marwazī; Mihyār; Muḥammad b. ʿAlī b. ʿUmar; al-Rūdhrāwarī; al-Ṣaghānī, ʿAbd al-Muʾmin; Ṣāʿid al-Baghdādī; al-Sharīf al-ʿAḳīlī; al-Sharīf al-Raḍī; Shumaym; [au Suppl.] Abū l-Ḥasan al-Anṣārī; al-Balaṭī; al-Būṣīrī; al-Ghazzī

voir aussi al-Khazradjī; Nasīb.2.D

14ᵉ-18ᵉ siècles ʿAbd al-ʿAzīz b. Muḥammad; ʿAbd al-Ghanī b. Ismāʿīl; al-Bakrī; al-Būrīnī; Farḥāt; Ibn Abī Ḥadjala; Ibn ʿAmmār; Ibn Ḥidjdja; Ibn Nubāta; Ibn al-Ṣāʾigh; Ibn al-Wannān; al-Ṣanʿānī, Ḍiyāʾ al-Dīn; Suʿūdī

voir aussi Khiḍr Beg; al-Shirbīnī

19ᵉ-20ᵉ siècles al-Akhras; al-Bārūdī; Fāris al-Shidyāḳ; al-Fārūḳī; Fikrī; Ḥāfiẓ Ibrāhīm; Ibn Idrīs [I]; Ismāʿīl Ṣabrī; Ismāʿīl Ṣabrī Pasha; Ḳaddūr al-ʿAlamī; al-Kāẓimī; Khalīl Muṭrān; al-Khūrī; al-Maʿlūf; al-Manfalūṭī; Mardam.II; Maʿrūf al-Ruṣāfī; al-Māzinī; Nādjī; Nadjīb b. Sulaymān al-Ḥaddād; Nadjīb Muḥammad Surūr; Saʿīd Abū Bakr; Ṣalāḥ ʿAbd al-Ṣabūr; Ṣāyigh, Tawfīḳ; al-Shābbī; al-Sharḳāwī; Shāʾūl, Anwar; Shawḳī; Shukrī; [au Suppl.] Abū Māḍī; Abū Shādī; al-ʿAḳḳād; al-Bustānī; Buṭrus Karāma; Ibn ʿAmr al-Ribāṭī; Ibn al-Ḥādjdj

voir aussi Shāʿir.1.C; Shiʿr.1.b

transmetteurs Ḥammād al-Rāwiya; Ibn Daʾb; Ibn Kunāsa; Khalaf al-Aḥmar; Khālid b. Ṣafwān; al-Kisrawī; Muḥammad b. al-Ḥasan b. Dīnār; al-Sharḳī b. al-Ḳuṭāmī; al-Sukkarī; al-Ṣūlī; [au Suppl.] Abū

ʿAmr al-Shaybānī (*et* al-Shaybānī, Abū ʿAmr)
et → LINGUISTIQUE.GRAMMAIRIENS.8E *et* 9E SIÈCLE
transmission de **Rāwī**
d'amour **Ghazal**; **Nasīb**; Raḳīb; Shahrangīz
voir aussi Ibn Sahl; al-Marzubānī; Muraḳḳish; Shawḳ.1(a); Shawḳ, Taṣadduḳ Ḥusayn; Suḥaym; *et* → AMOUR.PLATONIQUE
de la nature Ibn Khafādja; Nawriyya; Rabīʿiyyāt; al-Ṣanawbarī
dialectale Nabaṭī
voir aussi al-Sha'm.3
indo-persane Mughals.X; Sabk-i Hindī; Shāʿir.4
voir aussi Pandjābī.2; *et* → LITTÉRATURE.POÉSIE.MYSTIQUE
11e siècle Masʿūd-i Saʿd-i Salmān; [au Suppl.] Abū l-Faradj Ibn Masʿūd Rūnī
14e siècle Amīr Khusraw Dihlawī; Ḥasan Dihlawī; [au Suppl.] Ḥamīd Ḳalandar
16e siècle Fayḍī
voir aussi ʿAbd al-Raḥīm Khān
17e-18e siècles Ārzū Khān; Ashraf ʿAlī Khān; Bīdil; Dard; Ghanī; Ghanīmaṭ Ḥazīn; Idrākī Bēglārī; Ḳāniʿ; Ḳudsī; Makhfī; Malik Ḳummi; Munīr Lāhawrī; Nāṣir ʿAlī Sirhindī; Naẓīrī; Salīm, Muḥammad Ḳulī; Shaydā, Mullā; [au Suppl.] Ghanīmat Kundjāhī
19e siècle Aẓfarī; Ghālib; Rangīn; [au Suppl.] Adīb Pīshāwarī
voir aussi Afsūs
mystique
arabe ʿAbd al-Ghanī b. Ismāʿīl; al-Bakrī, Muḥammad; al-Bakrī, Muṣṭafā; al-Dimyāṭī; al-Ḥallādj; Ibn ʿAdjība; Ibn ʿAlīwa; Ibn al-ʿArabī; al-Madjdhūb; Makhrama.III; al-Shushtarī
voir aussi ʿAbd al-Ḳādir al-Djīlānī; Abū Madyan; al-Ḳādirī al-Ḥasanī; [au Suppl.] al-Hilālī
en Asie centrale Aḥmad Yasawī
indienne Bāḳī bi-llāh; Bīdil; Dard; Djamālī; Ḥānsawī; Ḥusaynī Sādāt Amīr; Imdād Allāh; Malik Muḥammad Djāyasī; [au Suppl.] Ḥamīd Ḳalandar
voir aussi Bhitā'ī; Pandjābī.2; Shāʿir.4
indonésienne Ḥamza Fanṣūrī
persane Aḥmad-i Djām; ʿAṭṭār; Bābā-Ṭāhir; Djalāl al-Dīn Rūmī; Faḍl Allāh Ḥurūfī; Ghudjduwānī; Humām al-Dīn b. ʿAlā' Tabrīzī; ʿIrāḳī; Kamāl Khudjandī; Ḳāsim-i Anwār; al-Kirmānī; Lāhīdjī.I; Maḥmūd Shabistarī; Sanā'ī; Shīrīn Maghribī, Muḥammad; Sulṭān Walad; [au Suppl.] ʿĀrif Čelebī; ʿImād al-Dīn ʿAlī, Faḳīh-i Kirmānī
voir aussi Abū Saʿīd b. Abī l-Khayr; Kharaḳānī; Shawḳ; [au Suppl.] Aḥmad-i Rūmī

turque ʿĀshiḳ Pasha; Faṣīḥ Dede; Gulshanī; Gülshehrī; Hüdāʾī; Münedjdjim Bashi; Nefes; Nesīmī; Refīʿī; Ṣari ʿAbd Allāh Efendī; Sezāʾī, Ḥasan Dede; Sheyyād Ḥamza; [au Suppl.] Eshrefoghlu ʿAbd Allāh; Esrār Dede

voir aussi Ḥusām al-Dīn Čelebi; Ismāʿīl al-Anḳarawī; Ismāʿīl Ḥaḳḳī; Ḳayghusuz Abdāl; Khalīlī; Sulṭān Walad

ourdou Ghazal.IV; Ḥamāsa.V; Hidjāʾ.IV; Ḳaṣīda.IV; Madīḥ.IV; Madjnūn Laylā.IV; Marthiya.IV; Mathnawī.IV; Mukhtārāt.IV; Musammaṭ.2; Mushāʿara; Shahrangīz.3; **Shiʿr**.4

17e siècle Nuṣratī

18e siècle Ashraf ʿAlī Khān; Dard; Djurʾat; Maẓhar; Sawdā; Sūz; [au Suppl.] Ḥasan

voir aussi Ārzū Khān

19e siècle Amānat; Anīs; Aẓfarī; Dabīr, Salāmat ʿAlī; Dāgh; Dhawḳ; Ghālib; Faḳīr Muḥammad Khān; Ḥālī; Ilāhī Bakhsh; Inshāʾ; Mīr Muḥammad Taḳi; Muḥsin ʿAlī Muḥsin; Muʾmin; Muṣḥafī; Nāsikh; Nasīm; Rangīn; Shawḳ, Taṣadduḳ Ḥusayn; [au Suppl.] Ātish

voir aussi [au Suppl.] Āzād

20e siècle Akbar, Ḥusayn Allāhābādī; Āzād; Djawān; Iḳbāl; Muḥammad ʿAlī; Rāshid, N.M.; Ruswā; Shabbīr Ḥasan Khān Djosh; Shiblī Nuʿmānī; [au Suppl.] Ḥasrat Mohānī

voir aussi Āzurda

persane Ghazal.II; Ḥamāsa.II; Hidjāʾ.II; Ḳaṣīda.II; Khamsa; Madīḥ.II; Malik al-Shuʿaraʾ; Marthiya.II; Mathnawī.II; Mukhtārāt.II; Musammaṭ; Mustazād; Rubāʿī; Shahrangīz.1; Shāʿir.2; **Shiʿr**.2; [au Suppl.] Ḥabsiyya

voir aussi Barzu-nāma; Farhād wa-Shīrīn; Iskandar Nāma.II; Kalīla wa-Dimna; Madjnūn Laylā.II; Radīf.2; Ṣafawides.III; Sāḳī.2; Shaman; Shaʿr.3; Sharīf; *et* › LITTÉRATURE.POÉSIE.INDO PERSANE *et* POÉSIE. MYSTIQUE

anthologies **Mukhtārāt**.II

anthologistes ʿAwfī; Dawlat-Shāh; Luṭf ʿAlī Beg; [au Suppl.] Djādjarmī.II

biographies des poètes Sām Mīrzā

9e siècle Muḥammad b. Waṣīf

voir aussi Sahl b. Hārūn

10e siècle Bābā-Ṭāhir; Daḳīḳī; Kisāʾī; al-Muṣʿabī; Rūdakī; Shahīd al Balkhī; [au Suppl.] Abū Shakūr Balkhī

11e-13e siècles ʿAbd al-Wāsiʿ Djabalī; Anwarī; Asadī; ʿAṭṭār; Azraḳī; Bābā Afḍal; Djalāl al-Dīn Rūmī; Falakī Shirwānī; Farrukhī; Firdawsī; Gurgānī; Humām al-Dīn b. ʿAlāʾ Tabrīzī; ʿImādī (*et* [au Suppl.]); ʿIrāḳī; Kamāl al-Dīn Ismāʿīl; Ḳaṭrān; Khwādjū; Khāḳānī; Labībī; Lāmiʿī; Mahsatī; Manūčihrī; Muʿizzī; Mukhtārī; Niẓāmī Gandjawī;

Pūr-i Bahā'; Ṣābir; Sa'dī; Sanā'ī; Sayyid Ḥasan Ghaznawī; Shufurwa; Sūzanī; [au Suppl.] 'Am'aḳ; Djādjarmī; Djamāl al-Dīn Iṣfahānī
voir aussi Shams-i Ḳays; Sūdī
14e-15e siècles 'Aṣṣār; Awḥadī; Banākitī; Busḥāḳ; Djāmī; Faḍl Allāh Ḥurūfī; Fattāḥī; Ḥāfiẓ; Ḥāmidī; Ibn-i Yamīn; 'Iṣāmī; Kātibī; Nizārī Ḳuhistānī; Rāmī Tabrīzī; Salmān-i Sāwadjī; Sayfī 'Arūḍī Bukhārī; Sharaf al-Dīn 'Alī Yazdī; Shīrīn Maghribī, Muḥammad; [au Suppl.] 'Ārifī; Badr-i Čāčī; 'Imād al-Dīn 'Alī, Faḳīh-i Kirmānī
voir aussi Djem; Ḥamd Allāh al-Mustawfī al-Ḳazwīnī; Sūdī
16e siècle Bannā'ī; Baṣīrī; Fayḍī; Fighānī; Hātifī; Hilālī; Muḥtasham-i Kāshānī; Mushfiḳī; Naw'ī; Saḥābī Astarābādī; Sām Mīrzā
voir aussi Luḳmān b. Sayyid Ḥusayn
17e siècle Asīr; al-Dāmād; Ḳadrī; Ḳalīm Abū Ṭālib; Kāshif; Lāhīdjī.II; Nāẓim Farrukh Ḥusayn; Ṣā'ib; Sa'īdā Gīlānī; Shawkat Bukhārī; Shifā'ī Iṣfahānī
voir aussi al-'Āmilī; Ghanīmat; Khushḥāl Khān Khaṭak; [au Suppl.] Findiriskī; *et* → LITTÉRATURE.POÉSIE.INDO-PERSANE
18e siècle Hātif; Ḥazīn; Luṭf 'Alī Beg; Nadjāt; Shihāb Turshīzī
voir aussi Āzād Bilgrāmī
19e-20e siècles Bahār; Furūgh; Furūghī; Ḳā'ānī; Ḳurrat al-'Ayn; Lāhūtī; Nafīsī; Nashāṭ; Nīmā Yūshīdj; Parwīn I'tiṣāmī; Pūr-i Dāwūd; Rashīd Yāsimī; Riḍā Ḳulī Khān; Ṣabā; Sabzawārī, Ḥādjdj Mullā Hādī; Shahriyār; Shaybānī; Shihāb Iṣfahānī; Shūrīda; Sipihrī; Surūsh; [au Suppl.] 'Ārif, Mīrzā; Ashraf al-Dīn Gīlānī; Dehkhudā
voir aussi Ghālib; Iḳbāl; Ḳā'im-maḳām-i Farāhānī; Sipihr
turque Ḥamāsa.III; Hidjā'.III; Ḳaṣīda.III; Khamsa; Ḳoshma; Madīḥ.III; Māni; Marthiya.III; Mathnawī.III; Mukhtārāt.III; Musammaṭ.1; Rabī'iyyāt; Rubā'ī.2; Shahrangīz.2; Sharḳi; **Shi'r**.3; [au Suppl.] Ghazal.III
voir aussi Alpamish; 'Āshiḳ; Farhād wa-Shirīn; Ilāhī; Iskandar Nāma. III; Karadja Oghlan; Madjnūn Laylā.III; Ozan; Shāhnāmedji; Shā'ir.3; *et* → LITTÉRATURE. POÉSIE.MYSTIQUE
anthologies **Mukhtārāt**.III
biographies des poètes 'Āshiḳ Čelebi; Laṭīfī; Riḍā; Riyāḍī; Sālim; Sehī Bey
11e-12e siècles Aḥmad Yuknakī; Ḥakīm Ata; Ḳutadghu Bilig
13e-14e siècles Aḥmadī; 'Āshiḳ Pasha; Burhān al-Dīn; Dehhānī, Khodja; Gülshehrī; Sheykh-oghlu; Sheyyād Ḥamza
15e siècle Āhī; Aḥmad Pasha Bursali; Dā'ī; Firdewsī; Gulshanī; Ḥamdī, Ḥamd Allāh; Ḳāsim Pasha; Ḳayghusuz Abdāl; Khalīlī; Khiḍr Beg; Süleymān Čelebi, Dede
voir aussi Djem; Ḥāmidī
16e siècle Āgehī; 'Azīzī; Bāḳī; Baṣīrī; Bihishtī; Dhātī; Dja'far Čelebi;

Djalāl Ḥusayn Čelebi; Djalālzāde Muṣṭafā Čelebi; Djalālzāde Ṣāliḥ Čelebi; Faḍli; Faḳīrī; Fawrī; Ferdī; Fighānī; Fuḍūlī; Ghazālī; Gulshanī; Ḥadīdī; Ḳarā-čelebi-zāde; Kemāl Pasha-zāde; Khāḳānī; Khayālī; Ḳorḳud b. Bāyazīd; Lāmiʿī; Laṭīfī; Luḳmān b. Sayyid Ḥusayn; Meʾalī; Medjdī; Mesīḥī; Mihrī Khatun; Naẓmī, Edirneli; Nedjātī; Newʿī; Rewānī; Sehī Bey; Surūrī.1; Sūzī Čelebi

17e siècle ʿAṭāʾī; ʿAzmī-zāde; Bahāʾī Meḥmed Efendi; Faṣīḥ Dede; Fehīm, Undjuzāde Muṣṭafā; Ḥāletī; Ḳarā-čelebi-zāde; Ḳul Muṣṭafā; Ḳuloghlu; Naʾilī; Nāẓi̊m; Naẓmī; Nefʿī; Niyāzī; ʿÖmer ʿĀshi̊ḳ; Riyāḍī; Ṣari̊ ʿAbd Allāh Efendī

18e siècle Belīgh, Ismāʿīl; Belīgh, Meḥmed Emīn; Čelebi-zāde; Česhmīzāde; Fiṭnat; Gevherī; Ghālib; Ḥāmī-i Āmidī; Ḥashmet; Kānī; Meḥmed Pasha Rāmī; Nābī; Naḥīfī; Naẓīm; Nedīm; Neshʾet; Newres.I; ʿOthmān-zāde; Rāghib Pasha; Sezāʾī, Ḥasan Dede

19e siècle *ʿĀrif Hi*kmet Bey; ʿAynī; Dadaloghlu; Derdli, Ibrāhīm; Dhihnī; Fāḍil Bey; Faṭīn; Fehīm, Süleymān; Ismāʿīl Ṣafā; ʿIzzet Molla; Kemāl, Meḥmed Nāmi̊ḳ; Laylā Khāni̊m; Menemenli-zāde Meḥmed Ṭāhir; Muʿallim Nādjī; Newres.II; Pertew Pasha.II; Redjāʾī zāde; Shināsī; Sünbülzāde Wehbī; Surūrī.2

20e siècle ʿAbd al-Ḥāḳḳ Ḥāmid; Djanāb Shihāb al-Dīn; Djewdet; Ekrem Bey; Hāshim; Kanık; Köprülü (Meḥmed Fuad); Ḳoryürek; Laylā Khāni̊m; Meḥmed ʿĀkif; Meḥmed Emīn; Muḥibb Aḥmed "Diranas"; Nāẓi̊m Ḥikmet; Oktay Rifat; Orkhan Seyfī; Ortač, Yūsuf Ḍiyā; Sāhir, Djelal; [au Suppl.] ʿĀshi̊ḳ Weysel; Bölükbashi̊ Ri̊ḍā Tewfīḳ; Čamli̊bel; Eshref; Eyyūboghlu; Gövsa

voir aussi [au Suppl.] Ergun; Fi̊ndi̊ḳoghlu

en turc oriental Ādharī.II; Bābur; Bāḳi̊khānli̊; Dhākir; Djambul Djabaev; Ghafūrī, Medjīd; Ghāzī Girāy II; Ḥamāsa.IV; Hidjāʾ.III; Iskandar Nāma.III; Ismāʿīl Ier; Ḳayyūm Nāṣirī; Ḳutadghu Bilig; Luṭfī; Mīr ʿAlī Shīr Nawāʾī; Muʾnis; Sakkākī; Shahriyār

traductions de langues européennes Ismāʿīl Ḥaḳḳi ʿĀlīshān; Kanık; Shināsī

prose Adab; Ḥikāya; Ḳiṣṣa; Maḳāma; Muḳaddima; Naṣīḥat al-Mulūk; Risāla; Sharḥ

et → LITTÉRATURE.ÉTIQUETTE *et* HISTORIQUE; PRESSE

arabe ʿArabiyya.B.V; Ḥikāya; Ḳiṣṣa.II; Maḳāla.1; Maḳāma; Nahḍa; Naṣīḥat al-Mulūk.I; Risāla; Sadjʿ.3; Sīra Shaʿbiyya

et → LITTÉRATURE.DRAME; PRESSE

ouvrages Alf layla wa-Layla; ʿAntar; Baybars; Bilawhar wa-Yūdāsaf; Dhū l-Himma; Kalīla wa-Dimna; Luḳmān.3; Sayf Ibn Dhī Yazan; Sindbād al-Ḥakīm

voir aussi Sindbād

9e-10e siècles al-Djāḥiẓ; al-Hamadhānī; Ibn al-Muḳaffaʿ; [au Suppl.] Abū l-ʿAnbas al-Ṣaymarī

11e-13e siècles al-Ḥarīrī; Ibn Nāḳiyā; al-Ṣaymarī; [au Suppl.] Abū l-Muṭahhar al-Azdī; al-Djazarī

voir aussi al-Sharīshī

14e-18e siècles Ibn Abī Ḥadjala; al-Shirbīnī

voir aussi al-Ibshīhī

19e-20e siècles Aḥmad Amīn; Faraḥ Anṭūn; Ḥāfiẓ Ibrāhīm; Maḥmūd Taymūr; al-Maʿlūf; al-Manfalūṭī; Mayy Ziyāda; al-Māzinī; Muḥammad Ḥusayn Haykal; al-Muwayliḥī.II; Nuʿayma, Mikhāʾīl; al-Rayḥānī; Salāma Mūsā; Sayyid Ḳuṭb; al-Sharḳāwī; Shāʾūl, Anwar; [au Suppl.] Abū Shādī; al-ʿAḳḳād; al-Bustānī.6

voir aussi Djamīl al-Mudawwar; al-Khālidī; Kurd ʿAlī; Shumayyil, Shiblī

ourdou Ḥikāya.IV; Ḳiṣṣa.V

et → LITTÉRATURE.DRAME; PRESSE

19e-20e siècles Amān, Mīr; Djawān; Faḳīr Muḥammad Khān; Iḳbāl; Nadhīr Aḥmad Dihlawī; Prēm Čand; Ruswā; Shabbīr Ḥasan Khān Djosh; Shiblī Nuʿmānī; Surūr; [au Suppl.] Āzād

persane Ḥikāya.II; Īrān.VII; Ḳiṣṣa.IV; Maḳāla.II; Naṣīḥat al-Mulūk.II; Risāla.2

voir aussi Ṣafawides.III; *et* → LITTÉRATURE.DRAME; PRESSE

ouvrages Bakhtiyār-nāma; Dabistān al-Madhāhib; Ḳahramān-nāma; Kalīla wa-Dimna; Madjnūn Laylā.II; Marzbān-nāma

voir aussi Niẓām al-Mulk; Niẓāmī ʿArūḍī Samarḳandī

11e-12e siècles Ḥamīdī; al-Ḳāshānī; Kay Kāʾūs (b. Iskandar); Nāṣir-i Khusraw; Naṣr Allāh b. Muḥammad; Niẓāmī ʿArūḍī Samarḳandī; Rashīd al-Dīn (al-Waṭwāṭ); al-Samʿānī, Abū l-Ḳāsim

13e siècle Saʿdī

14e siècle Nakhshabī

15e siècle Kāshifī

16e siècle

voir aussi Shemʿī

17e-18e siècles ʿInāyat Allāh Kańbū; Mumtāz

19e-20e siècles Bahār; Hidāyat, Ṣādiḳ; Nafīsī; Shaybānī; Shaykh Mūsā Nathrī; [au Suppl.] Āl-i Aḥmad; Bihrangī; Dehkhudā

voir aussi Furūgh.2

turque Ḥikāya.III; Ḳiṣṣa.III; Maddāḥ; Maḳāla.III; Risāla.3

voir aussi Bilmedje; *et* → LITTÉRATURE.DRAME; PRESSE

ouvrages Alpamïsh; Billūr Köshk; Dede Ḳorḳut; Ḳahramān-nāma; Oghuz-nāma

voir aussi Merdjümek; Ṣarï Ṣalṭuḳ Dede

14e siècle Sheykh-oghlu

15ᵉ siècle   S̲h̲ey̲k̲h̲-zāde.3
16ᵉ siècle
  voir aussi S̲h̲emʿī
17ᵉ siècle   Nergisī
18ᵉ siècle   ʿAlī ʿAzīz, Giridli; Nābī
19ᵉ-20ᵉ siècles   Aḥmad Ḥikmet; Aḥmad Mid̲h̲at; Aḥmad Rāsim; D̲j̲anāb
  S̲h̲ihāb al-Dīn; Ebüzziya Tevfik; Ekrem Bey; Fiṭrat; Hîsar; Ḥusayn
  D̲j̲āhid; Ḥusayn Raḥmī; Karay, Refîk K̲h̲ālid; Ḳaṣāb; Kaygîlî; Kemāl;
  Kemāl, Meḥmed Nāmîḳ; Kemal Tahir; K̲h̲ālid Ḍiyāʾ; K̲h̲ālide Edīb;
  Laylā K̲h̲ānim; Meḥmed Raʾūf; Oktay Rifat; ʿÖmer Seyf ül-Dīn;
  Ork̲h̲an Kemāl; Res̲h̲ād Nūrī; Sabahattin Ali; Sāmī; Sezāʾī, Sāmī; [au
  Suppl.] Atač; Atay; Čaylaḳ Tewfīḳ; Esendal; Haliḳarnas Balîḳčîsî
  voir aussi Aḥmad Iḥsān; Ileri, Djelāl Nūrī; İnal; Ismāʿīl Ḥaḳḳi
  ʿĀlīs̲h̲ān; Ḳiṣṣa.III.B; [au Suppl.] Eyyūbog̲h̲lu
  en turc oriental   Rabg̲h̲ūzī
proverbes dans la littérature   Mat̲h̲al.IV
  voir aussi Ḥamza al-Iṣfahānī; Ras̲h̲īd al-Dīn (al-Waṭwāṭ); S̲h̲ināsī
sagesse, littérature de   al-Aḥnaf b. Ḳays; ʿAlī b. Abī Ṭālib; Buzurgmihr;
  Hūs̲h̲ang; Luḳmān; Sahl b. Hārūn; [au Suppl.] D̲j̲āwīd̲h̲ān K̲h̲irad
  voir aussi Akt̲h̲am b. Ṣayfī; Buhlūl; al-Ibs̲h̲īhī
termes littéraires   ʿArūḍ; ʿAtāba; Badīʿ; Balāg̲h̲a; Bayan; Dak̲h̲īl; Fard; Faṣāḥa;
  Fāṣila; Ibtidāʾ; Id̲j̲āza; Iḍmār; Iḳtibās; Intihāʾ; Irtid̲j̲āl; Istiʿāra; Ḳabḍ.III;
  Ḳāfiya; Ḳaṭʿ; Kināya; Luzūm mā lā yalzam; al-Maʿānī wa-l-Bayān; Mad̲j̲āz;
  Maʿnā.III; Muʿāraḍa; Muzāwad̲j̲a; Radīf.2; Rad̲j̲az.4; S̲h̲awāhid; Ṣila.2
  et › LITTÉRATURE.GENRES; MÉTRIQUE
topoi   Buk̲h̲l; Bulbul; G̲h̲urāb; Gul; Ḥamām; Ḥayawān.V; Inṣāf; al-Ḳamar.II;
  Ḳaṭā; Nard̲j̲is; Raḥīl; Sāḳī; S̲h̲amʿa; S̲h̲aʿr.3; al-S̲h̲ayb wa-l-S̲h̲abāb
  voir aussi G̲h̲azal.II; ʿIs̲h̲ḳ; K̲h̲amriyya; Rabīʿiyyāt
Tradition, littérature de la   At̲h̲ar; **Ḥadīt̲h̲**; Ḥadīt̲h̲ Ḳudsī; Hind.V.F; Sunan;
  Sunna; [au Suppl.] Arbaʿūn Ḥadīt̲h̲
  voir aussi Ahl al-Ḥadīt̲h̲; Ḥas̲h̲wiyya; K̲h̲abar; Mustamlī; Nask̲h̲; Riwāya;
  S̲h̲arḥ.III
  collections canoniques   Abū Dāʾūd al-Sid̲j̲istānī; Aḥmad b. Ḥanbal; Anas b.
    Mālik; al-Bayhaḳī; al-Buk̲h̲ārī; al-Dāraḳuṭnī; al-Dārimī; Ibn Ḥibbān; Ibn
    Mād̲j̲a; Muslim b. al-Ḥad̲j̲d̲j̲ād̲j̲; al-Nasāʾī
    voir aussi al-ʿAynī; Ibn Hubayra
  termes   al-D̲j̲arḥ wa-l-Taʿdīl; Fard; G̲h̲arīb; Ḥikāya.I; Id̲j̲āza; Isnād; K̲h̲abar
    al-Wāḥid; Mas̲h̲hūr; Matn; Muʿanʿan; Munkar; Mursal; Muṣannaf;
    Musnad.3; Mustamlī; Mutawātir.a; Rafʿ; Rid̲j̲āl; Ṣaḥīḥ.1; Ṣāliḥ; Sunan
    voir aussi Ḥadīt̲h̲
  traditionnistes   Rāwī; Rid̲j̲āl
    voir aussi al-Rāmahurmuzī
    7ᵉ siècle   ʿAbd Allāh b. ʿUmar b. al-K̲h̲aṭṭāb; Abū Bakra; Abū Hurayra;

al-Aʿmash; Ibn Abī Laylā.1; Ibn Masʿūd; Kaʿb al-Aḥbār; al-Khawlānī, Abū Idrīs; al-Khawlānī, Abū Muslim; [au Suppl.] Djābir b. ʿAbd Allāh

8ᵉ siècle Abū l-ʿĀliya al-Riyāḥī; Abū Mikhnaf; al-Ashʿarī, Abū Burda; Djābir b. Zayd; al-Fuḍayl b. ʿIyāḍ; Ghundjār; al-Ḥasan b. Ṣāliḥ b. Ḥayy; al-Ḥasan al-Baṣrī; Ibn Abī Laylā.2; Ibn Daʾb; Ibn Isḥāḳ; Ibn al-Naṭṭāḥ; Ibn Shubruma; Ibn Sīrīn; ʿIkrima; al-Layth b. Saʿd; Maymūn b. Mihrān; Muḳātil b. Sulaymān; Nāfiʿ; al-Nakhaʿī; Saʿīd b. Abī Arūba; al-Shaʿbī; Shuʿba b. al-Ḥadjdjādj; al-Suddī; [au Suppl.] Abū ʿAmr al-Shaybānī (*et* al-Shaybānī, Abū ʿAmr); Ibn Djuraydj

9ᵉ siècle Abū Nuʿaym al-Mulāʾī; Baḳī b. Makhlad; Ibn Abī Khaythama; Ibn Abī l-Shawārib; Ibn Abī Shayba; Ibn ʿĀʾisha.IV; Ibn Rāhwayh; Ibn Saʿd; Ibn Sallām al-Djumaḥī; Ibrāhīm al-Ḥarbī; al-Karābīsī.2; al-Marwazī; Muslim b. al-Ḥadjdjādj; Nuʿaym b. Ḥammād; al-Ṣanʿānī, ʿAbd al-Razzāḳ; Sufyān b. ʿUyayna; [au Suppl.] Abū ʿĀṣim al-Nabīl; Asad b. Mūsā
voir aussi Ibn Khayyāṭ al-ʿUṣfurī; Ibn Ḳuṭlūbughā

10ᵉ siècle Abū ʿArūba; al-Anbārī, Abū Bakr; al-Anbārī, Abū Muḥammad; Ghulām Thaʿlab; Ibn al-ʿAllāf; Ḳāsim b. Aṣbagh; al-Khaṭṭābī; al-Saraḳusṭī; al-Sidjistānī; [au Suppl.] Ibn ʿUḳda

11ᵉ siècle al-Ḥākim al-Naysābūrī; Ibn ʿAbd al-Barr; Ibn al-Bannāʾ; Ibn Fūrak; Ibn Mākūlā.III; al-Ḳābisī; al-Khaṭīb al-Baghdādī; al-Sahmī

12ᵉ siècle al-Baghawī; Ibn al-ʿArabī; Ibn ʿAsākir; Ibn Ḥubaysh; Ibn al-Ḳaysarānī.1; Ibn al-Nadjdjār; al-Lawātī; Razīn b. Muʿāwiya; al-Rushāṭī; al-Ṣadafī; al-Sarrādj, Abū Muḥammad; Shīrawayh; al-Silafī
voir aussi al-Samʿānī, Abū Saʿd

13ᵉ siècle al-Dimyāṭī; Ibn al-Athīr.I; Ibn Diḥya; Ibn Faraḥ al-Ishbīlī; al-Ṣaghānī, Raḍī al-dīn; [au Suppl.] Ibn Daḳīḳ al-ʿĪd

14ᵉ siècle al-Dhahabī; Ibn Kathīr; al-Mizzī

15ᵉ siècle Ibn Ḥadjar al-ʿAsḳalānī; al-Ibshīhī; al-Ḳasṭallānī; Muʿīn al-Miskīn; al-Suyūṭī
voir aussi Ibn Ḳuṭlūbughā

19ᵉ et 20ᵉ siècles Shākir, Aḥmad Muḥammad

chiites ʿAbd Allāh b. Maymūn; Dindān; Djaʿfar al-Ṣādiḳ; Ibn Bābawayh(i); al-Kashshī; al-Kāẓimī; al-Kulaynī; Madjlisī; Muḥammad b. Makkī; Shāh ʿAbd al-ʿAẓīm; [au Suppl.] Akhbāriyya; al-Barḳī; Djābir al-Djuʿfī
voir aussi Asmāʾ

traductions de langues européennes

en arabe Muḥammad Bey ʿUthmān Djalāl; Shāʾūl, Anwar; Shumayyil, Shiblī

en persan Muḥammad Ḥasan Khān; Nafīsī; Sharīʿatī, ʿAlī

en turc Ismāʿīl Ḥaḳḳī ʿĀlīshān; Kanık; Khālide Edīb; Shināsī

voyages, relations de Djughrāfiyā.V.E; **Riḥla**
auteurs ʿAbd al-Ghanī b. Ismāʿīl; al-ʿAbdarī; Abū Dulaf; Abū Ṭālib Khān; Aḥmad Iḥsān; ʿAlī Bey al-ʿAbbāsī; ʿAlī Khān; al-ʿAyyāshī; Ewliyā Čelebi; Fāris al-Shidyāḳ; al-Ghassānī; Ghiyāth al-Dīn Naḳḳāsh; Ibn Baṭṭūṭa; Ibn Djubayr; Ibn Idrīs [II]; Kurd ʿAlī; Ma Huan; Meḥmed Yirmisekiz; Nāṣir-i Khusraw; Shiblī Nuʿmānī; Sīdī ʿAlī Reʾīs; [au Suppl.] al-Ghazzāl; Ibn Nāṣir.III
voir aussi Hārūn b. Yaḥyā; Ibn Djuzayy; Ibn Rushayd; Ibn Saʿīd al-Maghribī; Ibrāhīm b. Yaʿḳūb; Khayr Allāh Efendi; Léon l'Africain
récits [au Suppl.] Akhbār al-Ṣīn wa-l-Hind

M

MADAGASCAR **Madagascar**; Massalajem

MAGIE ʿAzīma.2; Djadwal; Istinzāl; Khāṣṣa; Nīrandj; Ruḳya; **Siḥr**; Sīmiyāʾ; [au Suppl.] Budūḥ
voir aussi Djinn.III; Ḥadjar; Ḥurūf; Istikhara; Istiḳsām; Istisḳāʾ; Kabid.4; al-Ḳamar.II; Ḳatl.II.2; Khawāṣṣ al-Ḳurʾān; Kihāna; Kitābāt.V; Rūḥāniyya; Sidr
magiciens ʿAbd Allāh b. Hilāl; Shaʿbadha
voir aussi Antemuru
traités sur al-Makkarī; [au Suppl.] Ibn ʿAzzūz; al-Būnī

MALADIES Madjnūn; Malāryā; Ramad; Saraṭān.VII; [au Suppl.] Djudhām
voir aussi Kalb; Ḳuṭrub; Summ
traités sur Ḥayātī-zāde; Ibn Buṭlān; Ibn Djazla
et → MÉDECINE

MALAISIE Malacca; Malais; **(Péninsule) Malaise**; **Malaisie**
voir aussi Baladiyya.VI; Djāmiʿa; Indonésie; Kandūrī; Kitābāt.VIII; Partai Islam se Malaysia (Pas); Rembau
architecture → ARCHITECTURE.RÉGIONS
états Penang; Pérak; Sabah; Sarawak
littérature ʿAbd Allāh b. ʿAbd al-Ḳādir; Dāwūd al-Faṭānī; Ḥikāya.V; Ḳiṣṣa.VI; Malais; Shāʿir.7
voir aussi Indonésie.VI

MALAWI Kota Kota

MALI Adrar.2; Aḥmad al-Shaykh; Aḥmadu Lobbo; Ḥamāliyya; Kaʿti; **Mali**; Mansa Mūsā

voir aussi Mande; Sūdān (Bilād al-).2
historiens al-Saʿdī
toponymes
régions Kaarta
villes Bamako; Dienné; Gao; Segu

Mameluks **Mamlūks**
voir aussi Ḥarfūsh; Manshūr; Mihmindār; Rank; *et* → Dynasties.Égypte et le croissant fertile; Militaires.mameluks

Mariage Djilwa; Khiṭba; Mutʿa; **Nikāḥ**; [au Suppl.] Djabr
voir aussi ʿAbd.3.e; ʿĀda.III et IV.4; ʿArūs Resmi; Fāsid wa-Bāṭil.III; Ghāʾib; Ḥaḍāna; Kafāʾa; Kurdes et Kurdistān.IV.A.1; al-Marʾa.II; Mawākib.IV.3 et 5; Raḍāʿ; Shawwāl; Suknā; Sukūt
douaire **Mahr**; Ṣadāḳ

Maroc **al-Maghrib**
voir aussi ʿArabiyya.A.III.3; Ḥimāya.II; Mallāḥ; Rīf.II; Sulṭān al-Ṭalaba
architecture → Architecture.régions.afrique du nord
dynasties ʿAlawīs; Idrīsides; Marīnides; Saʿdides
voir aussi Bū Ḥmāra; Ḥasanī; Shurafāʾ.III; [au Suppl.] Aḥmad al-Hiba; *et* → Dynasties.espagne et afrique du nord
historiens Aḥmad al-Nāṣirī (*et* al-Nāṣirī al-Salāwī); Akanṣūs; Ibn Abī Zarʿ; Ibn al-Ḳāḍī
voir aussi Ibn al-Raḳīḳ; al-Kattānī; [au Suppl.] ʿAllāl al-Fāsī; *et* → Dynasties.espagne et afrique du nord
période moderne Baladiyya.III; Djāmiʿa; Djarīda.I.B; Djaysh.III.2; Dustūr. XVII; Ḥizb.I; Ḥukūma.IV; Maʿārif.II; Madjlis.IV.A.21; Madjmaʿ ʿIlmī.I.II. 4; Maḥkama.IV.10; Makhzan; [au Suppl.] Institut des hautes études marocaines
hommes d'état [au Suppl.] ʿAllāl al-Fāsī
réforme Salafiyya.1(c)
population Dukkāla; Glāwā; Ḥarṭānī; Khulṭ; Shāwiya.1; [au Suppl.] Awraba
voir aussi al-Fāsiyyūn; al-Maʿḳil; *et* → Berbères
religion al-Maghrib.VI
confréries mystiques Darḳāwa; Hansaliyya; Hazmīriyyūn; ʿĪsāwā; al-Nāṣiriyya; al-Shādhiliyya; [au Suppl.] Ḥamādisha
pour Djazūliyya, *voir* al-Djazūlī, Abū ʿAbd Allāh
voir aussi Sharḳāwa; [au Suppl.] ʿĀʾisha Ḳandīsha; *et* → Mysticisme; Saint
toponymes
anciens Anfā; Bādis; al-Baṣra; Fāzāz; al-Ḳaṣr al-Ṣaghīr; Nakūr; Shalla; Sidjilmāsa

actuels
îles [au Suppl.] al-Ḥusayma
régions Darʿa; Figuig; G͟harb; Ḥawz; Ifni; Rīf.I.2; Spartel; al-Sūs al-Akṣā
villes Agadir-ighir; Āg͟hmāt; al-ʿArāʾis͟h; Aṣfī; Aṣīla; Azammūr; Damnāt; (al-)Dār al-Bayḍāʾ; al-D̲j̲adīda; Dubdū; Faḍāla; Fās; Garsīf; al-Ḳaṣr al-Kabīr; al-Mahdiyya; Marrākus͟h; Mawlāy Idrīs; Melilla; Miknās; Ribāṭ al-Fatḥ; Sabta; Salā; S͟hafs͟hāwan; Ṣufrūy; al-Suwayra; [au Suppl.] Azrū; Benī Mellāl
voir aussi al-Ḥamrāʾ

MARONITES → CHRISTIANISME.CONFESSIONS; LIBAN

MARTYRE Fidāʾī; Maẓlūm; S͟hahīd
voir aussi Ḥabīb al-Nad̲j̲d̲j̲ār; (al-)Ḥusayn b. ʿAlī b. Abī Ṭālib; K͟hubayb; Mad̲j̲lis.III; Mas͟hhad; Masʿūd, Sayyid Sālār; [au Suppl.] ʿAbd Allāh b. Abī Bakr al-Miyānad̲j̲ī

MATHÉMATIQUES Algorithme; al-D̲j̲abr wa-l-Muḳābala; Fard; Ḥisāb al-ʿAḳd; Ḥisāb al-G͟hubār; **ʿIlm al-Ḥisāb**; Kasr; Ḳaṭʿ; Ḳuṭr; Māl; Mans͟hūr; Misāḥā; Muḳaddam; Muṣādara.1; Mut͟hallat͟h; **al-Riyāḍiyyāt**; al-Sahm.1.a; [au Suppl.] ʿIlm al-Handasa
voir aussi al-Mīzān; [au Suppl.] Halīladj
algèbre **al-D̲j̲abr wa-l-Muḳābala**
géométrie **Misāḥā**; [au Suppl.] **ʿIlm al-Handasa**
mathématiciens Abū Kāmil; Abū l-Wafāʾ al-Būzad̲j̲ānī; ʿAlī al-Ḳūs͟hd̲j̲ī; al-Bīrūnī; Ibn al-Bannāʾ al-Marrākus͟hī; Ibn al-Hayt͟ham; Ibn ʿIrāḳ; Isḥāḳ Efendi; al-Ḳalaṣādī; al-Karābīsī.1; al-Karad̲j̲ī; al-Kās͟hī; al-K͟hʷārazmī; al-K͟hāzin; al-K͟hud̲j̲andī; Kus͟hiyār; al-Mad̲j̲rīṭī; al-Mārdīnī; Muḥammad b. ʿĪsā b. Aḥmad al-Māhānī; Muḥammad b. ʿUmar; al-S͟hīrāzī, Abū l-Ḥusayn
voir aussi Balīnūs; Ḳusṭā b. Lūḳā

MAURITANIE Adrar.3; Atar; Ḥawḍ; Māʾ al-ʿAynayn; Mad̲j̲lis.IV.A.22; **Mūrītāniyā**
voir aussi Dustūr.XV; Lamtūna; al-Māmī; Sūdān (Bilād al-).2
historiens al-S͟hinḳīṭī
toponymes
anciens Awdag͟host; G͟hāna; Ḳunbi Ṣāliḥ; S͟hinḳīṭ
actuels Nouakchott

MAUVAIS OEIL **ʿAyn**
voir aussi Karkaddan; *et* → CHARMES; ISLAM.CROYANCES POPULAIRES

MÉCANIQUE   Ḥiyal.II; al-Ḳarasṭūn; [au Suppl.] al-Djazarī; **Ḥiyal**
   voir aussi Ibn al-Sāʿātī; *et* → HYDROLOGIE

MÉDECINE
   et → ANATOMIE; DROGUES; MALADIES; PHARMACOLOGIE
centres de   Bīmāristān; Gondēs̲h̲āpūr; Ḳalāwūn; [au Suppl.] Abū Zaʿbal
   voir aussi Bag̲h̲dād; Dimas̲h̲ḳ; al-Madīna
dentaire   Miswāk
   voir aussi ʿAḳīḳ; Mardjān
   traités sur   Hāmōn
      voir aussi Ibn Abī l-Bayān
manuels/encyclopédies de médecine   ʿAlī b. al-ʿAbbās; al-Djurdjānī, Ismāʿīl b. al-
   Ḥusayn; Ibn al-Nafīs; Ibn Sīnā; al-Masīḥī; S̲h̲ānī-zāde
médecins   Djarrāḥ; Ḥāwī; [au Suppl.] Faṣṣād
   voir aussi ʿAyn; Constantin l'Africain; Ḥikma; Kabid.3; Masāʾil wa-
   Adjwiba; *et* → MÉDICINE.OPHTALMOLOGISTES; PHARMACOLOGIE
   biographies des   Ibn Abī Uṣaybiʿa; Ibn Djuldjul; Ibn al-Ḳāḍī; Isḥāḳ b. Ḥunayn
      voir aussi Ibn al-Ḳifṭī
   7ᵉ siècle   [au Suppl.] al-Ḥārit̲h̲ b. Kalada
   9ᵉ siècle   Bukhtīs̲h̲ūʿ; Ḥunayn b. Isḥāḳ al-ʿIbādī; Ibn Māsawayh; Sābūr b. Sahl
      voir aussi Māsardjawayh
   10ᵉ siècle   ʿAlī b. al-ʿAbbās; ʿArīb b. Saʿd; Ibn Djuldjul; Isḥāḳ b. Ḥunayn;
      Isḥāḳ al-Isrāʾīlī; Ḳusṭā b. Lūḳā; al-Rāzī, Abū Bakr; Ṣābiʾ.(3); Saʿīd b.
      Yaʿḳūb al-Dimas̲h̲ḳī; [au Suppl.] Ibn Abī l-As̲h̲ʿath
   11ᵉ siècle   al-Anṭākī, Abū l-Faradj; Ibn Buṭlān; Ibn Djanāḥ; Ibn Djazla; Ibn
      al-Djazzār; Ibn Riḍwān; Ibn Sīnā; Ibn al-Ṭayyib; Ibn Wāfid; Ibn Zuhr.II;
      al-Masīḥī
   12ᵉ siècle   Abū l-Barakāt; al-Djurdjānī, Ismāʿīl b. al-Ḥusayn; Ibn Djāmiʿ; Ibn
      al-Tilmīd̲h̲; Ibn Zuhr.III et IV; al-Marwazī, S̲h̲araf al-Zamān; [au Suppl.]
      Ibn Biklāris̲h̲
      voir aussi Ibn Rus̲h̲d
   13ᵉ siècle   Ibn Abī l-Bayān; Ibn Abī Uṣaybiʿa; Ibn Hubal; Ibn al-Nafīs; Ibn
      Ṭumlūs; Saʿd al-Dawla; al-Suwaydī; [au Suppl.] Ibn al-Ḳuff
   14ᵉ siècle   Ḥādjdjī Pas̲h̲a; Ibn al-K̲h̲aṭīb; Isḥāḳ b. Murād; Ḳuṭb al-Dīn S̲h̲īrāzī
   15ᵉ siècle   Bas̲h̲īr Čelebi
   16ᵉ siècle   al-Anṭākī, Dāwūd; Hāmōn
   17ᵉ siècle   Ḥayātī-zāde
   18ᵉ siècle   al-Ṣanʿānī, Ḍiyāʾ al-dīn; [au Suppl.] Ādarrāḳ; Ibn S̲h̲aḳrūn
   à partir du 19ᵉ siècle   Bahdjat Muṣṭafā Efendi; Muḥammad b. Aḥmad al-
      Iskandarānī; S̲h̲ānī-zāde; S̲h̲umayyil, S̲h̲iblī; [au Suppl.] ʿAbd al-Salām
      b. Muḥammad
   grecs   Diyusḳuridīs; Djālīnūs; Rūfus al-Afsīsī; [au Suppl.] Ahrun; Buḳrāṭ

voir aussi Ḥunayn b. Isḥāḳ al-ʿIbādī; Ibn Riḍwān; Ibn al-Ṭayyib; Isḥāḳ b. Ḥunayn; Iṣṭifan b. Basīl; [au Suppl.] Ḥubaysh b. al-Ḥasan al-Dimashḳī; Ibn Abī l-Ashʿath

juifs Hāmōn; Ibn Abī l-Bayān; Ibn Djāmiʿ; Ibn Djanāḥ; Isḥāḳ al-Isrāʾīlī; Māsardjawayh; Saʿd al-Dawla; [in Suppl.] Ibn Biklārish

voir aussi Abū l-Barakāt; Ḥayātī-zāde.1

ottomans Bahdjat Muṣṭafā Efendi; Bashīr Čelebi; Ḥādjdjī Pasha; Hāmōn; Ḥayātī-zāde; Isḥāḳ b. Murād; Shānī-zāde

voir aussi Ḥekīm-bashi̊

médicaments Almās; ʿAnbar; al-Dahnadj; Dhahab; Durr; Fiḍḍa; Kāfūr; Ḳaṭrān; Ḳily; Kuḥl; Lubān; Maghnāṭīs; Mardjān; Milḥ.2; Misk; Mūmiyāʾ; Ṣābūn; Ṣamgh; [au Suppl.] Bawraḳ; Halīladj

voir aussi Bāzahr; al-Iksīr; Kabid.3; [au Suppl.] Afāwīh; Dam; *pour l'usage médicinal des parties anatomiques des animaux et des plantes, voir les articles sur les animaux individuels et sous* FLORE

obstétrique ʿArīb b. Saʿd

et → PHASES DE LA VIE.ACCOUCHEMENT

ophtalmologistes ʿAlī b. ʿĪsā (al-Kaḥḥāl); ʿAmmār al-Mawṣilī; al-Ghāfiḳī; Ibn Dāniyal; Khalīfa b. Abī l-Maḥāsin

voir aussi ʿAyn; Ḥunayn b. Isḥāḳ al-ʿIbādī; Ibn al-Nafīs; Ibn Zuhr.V; *et* → ANATOMIE.OEIL

termes Bīmāristān; Djarrāḥ; Ḥidjāb; Ḳuwwa.5; Sabab.2

voir aussi Ilāl

vétérinaire Bayṭār; Ibn Hudhayl; Ibn al-Mundhir

MELKITES → CHRISTIANISME.CONFESSIONS

MÉSOPOTAMIE → IRAK

MÉTALLURGIE Ḳalʿī; Khārṣīnī; **Maʿdin**

voir aussi Kalah; al-Mīzān.I; *et* → MINÉRALOGIE.MINES

métaux Dhahab; Fiḍḍa; Ḥadīd; Nuḥās

et → MINÉRALOGIE.MINÉRAUX; PROFESSIONS.PRODUCTEURS ET COMMERÇANTS.ARTISANS

MÉTAPHYSIQUE **Mā baʿd al-Ṭabīʿa**

voir aussi ʿAbd al-Laṭīf al-Baghdādī; Māhiyya; Muṭlaḳ

MÉTÉOROLOGIE al-Āthār al-ʿUlwiyya

voir aussi Anwāʾ; Sadjʿ.2; [au Suppl.] Ibn al-Adjdābī

vent **Rīḥ**; Samūm

MÉTRIQUE **ʿArūḍ**
et → LITTÉRATURE.POÉSIE
mètres Mudjtathth; Mutadārik; Mutaḳārib; Mutawātir.b; Radjaz; Ramal.1; Sarīʿ
termes Dakhīl; Fard; Ḳaṭʿ; Sabab.3; Ṣadr.(a); Sālim.3
traités sur al-Djawharī; al-Khalīl b. Aḥmad; al-Khazradjī, Ḍiyāʾ al-dīn; Shams-i Ḳays

MILITAIRES Baḥriyya; Djaysh; **Ḥarb**; [au Suppl.] Baḥriyya
voir aussi Dār al-Ḥarb; Djihād; Fatḥnāme; Ghazw; Naḳḳāra-khāna
architecture Ribāṭ
et → ARCHITECTURE.MONUMENTS.FORTERESSES
armée **Djaysh**; Istiʿrāḍ (Arḍ); **Lashkar**; Radīf.3
voir aussi Djāsūs; Ṣaff.2; *et* → MILITAIRES.MAMELUKS *et* OTTOMANS
contingents Bāzinḳir; Djāndār; Djaysh.III.2; Djund; Ghulām; Gūm; Ḳūrčī; Maḥalla; Mamlūk; Mutaṭawwiʿa; Sipāhī.2
voir aussi Almogávares; Fāris
armes ʿAnaza; ʿArrāda; Balyemez; Bārūd; Dūrbāsh; Ḳaws; Mandjanīḳ; Nafṭ.II
voir aussi ʿAlam; Asad Allāh Iṣfahānī; Hilāl.II; Ḥiṣār; Ḳalʿī; Lamṭ; Marātib
batailles
voir aussi Shiʿār.(a); *et* → MILITAIRES.EXPÉDITIONS
avant 622 Buʿāth; Dhū Ḳār; Djabala; Fidjār; Ḥalīma; Shiʿb Djabala; [au Suppl.] Dāḥis
voir aussi Ayyām al-ʿArab; Ḥanẓala
622-632 Badr; Biʾr Maʿūna; Buzākha; Ḥunayn; Khandaḳ; Khaybar; Muʾta
voir aussi Mālik b. ʿAwf
633-660 Adjnādayn; ʿAḳrabāʾ; al-Djamal; Djisr; Faḥl; Ḥarūrāʾ; al-Ḳādisiyya.II; Mardj al-Ṣuffar; Ṣiffīn; [au Suppl.] Dhāt al-Ṣawārī
voir aussi ʿAbd Allāh b. Saʿd; ʿĀʾisha bint Abī Bakr; ʿAlī b. Abī Ṭālib; al-Hurmuzān; al-Nahrawān; Rustam b. Farrukh Hurmuzd
661-750 ʿAyn al-Warda; Balāṭ al-Shuhadāʾ; Baldj; al-Bishr; Dayr al-Djamādjim; Dayr al-Djāthalīḳ; al-Ḥarra; al-Khāzir; Mardj Rāhiṭ
voir aussi (al-)Ḥusayn b. ʿAlī b. Abī Ṭālib; Kulthūm b. ʿIyāḍ; (al-)Ḳusṭanṭīniyya
751-1258 al-Arak; Bākhamrā; Dayr al-ʿĀḳūl; Fakhkh; Ḥaydarān; Hazārasp; al-ʿIḳāb; Köse-Dagh; Malāzgird.II; Shant Mānkash; [au Suppl.] Dandānḳān
voir aussi Ḥadjar al-Nasr; al-Madjūs; al-Manṣūr bi-llāh, Ismāʿīl; Mardj Dābiḳ
1258-18ᵉ siècle ʿAyn Djālūt; Čāldirān; Dābiḳ; Djarba; Ḥimṣ; Ḳoṣowa; Mardj Dābiḳ; Mardj Rāhiṭ; Mardj al-Ṣuffar; Mezőkeresztes; Mohács.1 et 2; Nīkbūlī; Pānīpat
voir aussi Baḥriyya.III; Fatḥnāme; Ḥarb; Nahr Abī Fuṭrus; ʿOthmān Pasha

après le 18e siècle Abuklea; Atjèh; Česhme; Farwān; Gök Tepe; Isly; Kūt al-ʿAmāra; Maysalūn; Nizīb; Rīf.II
voir aussi al-ʿAḳaba; Gulistān

butin Fayʾ; **Ghanīma**
voir aussi Baranta; Ghazw; Khāliṣa; Pendjik; *et* → MILITAIRES.PRISONNIERS

corps ʿAyyār; Dawāʾir; Djaysh.III.1; Futuwwa; Ghāzī; al-Shākiriyya
voir aussi ʿAlī b. Muḥammad al-Zandjī; al-Ikhwān; Khashabiyya; Sarhang

décorations **Nishān**

expéditions Ghāzī; **Ṣāʾifa**
voir aussi Ghazw

fonctions Amīr; ʿArīf; Atābak al-ʿAsākir; Fawdjdār; Ispahbadh; Ispahsālār; Istiʿrāḍ (Arḍ); Ḳāʾid; Manṣab; Sālār; Sardār; Sarhang; Shiḥna; Silāḥdār
voir aussi Amīr al-Umarāʾ; Dārūgha; Ḳāḍī ʿAskar; Ḳūrčī; *et* → MILITAIRES.OTTOMANS

indo-musulmans Bārūd.VI; Ghulām.III; Ḥarb.VI; Ḥiṣār.VI; Lashkar; Sipāhī.3; Suwar
voir aussi Istiʿrāḍ (Arḍ)

mameluks al-Baḥriyya; Baḥriyya.II; Bārūd.III; Burdjiyya; Ḥalḳa; Ḥarb.III; Ḥiṣār.IV; **Mamlūk**
voir aussi Amīr Ākhūr; al-Amīr al-Kabīr; Atābak al-ʿAsākir; ʿAyn Djālūt; Čerkesses; Ḥimṣ; ʿĪsā b. Muhannā; Khāṣṣakiyya; Ḳumāsh; Rikābdār; Silāḥdār

marine **Baḥriyya**; Dār al-Ṣināʿa; Daryā-begi; Ḳapudan Pasha; Lewend; Nassades; Raʾīs.3; Riyāla; [au Suppl.] **Baḥriyya**
voir aussi ʿAzab; Gelibolu; Kātib Čelebi; [au Suppl.] Dhāt al-Ṣawārī; *et* → DYNASTIES.ANATOLIE ET LES TURCS.OTTOMANS.GRANDS-AMIRAUX; NAVIGATION.NAVIRES; PIRATERIE

ottomans Bāb-i Serʿaskerī; Baḥriyya.III; Balyemez; Bārūd.IV; Devshirme; Djebeli; Ghulām.IV; Ḥarb.IV; Ḥarbiye; Ḥiṣār.V; Müsellem; Radīf.3; Sandjaḳ; Sipāhī.1; [au Suppl.] Djebedji
voir aussi ʿAskarī; Ḍabṭiyya; Gelibolu; Gūm; Ḥareket Ordusu; Istiʿrāḍ (Arḍ); Ḳapi̊dji̊; Karakol; Martolos; Mensūkhāt; Mondros; Nefīr; Ordu; Pendjik; *et* → MILITAIRES.MARINE

contingents de l'armée al-Abnāʾ.5; ʿAdjamī Oghlān; Aki̊ndji̊; Alay; ʿAzab; Bashi̊-bozuḳ; Bölük; Deli; Devedji; Djānbāzān; Eshkindji; Ghurabāʾ; Gönüllü; Khāṣṣekī; Khumbaradji̊; Lewend; Niẓām-i̊ Djedīd; Odjaḳ; Orta; [au Suppl.] Djebedji
voir aussi Akhī; Nefīr; Sipāhī.1

officiers Bayraḳdār; Biñbashi̊; Bölük-bashi̊; Čāʾūsh; Čorbadji̊.I; Ḍābiṭ; Daryā-begi; Ḳapudan Pasha; Mushīr; Rikābdār; Riyāla
voir aussi Sandjaḳ; Silāḥdār

police Aḥdāth; ʿAsas; Ḍabṭiyya; Karakol; **Shurṭa**
voir aussi Dawāʾir; Futuwwa; Kotwāl; Martolos; Naḳīb.2

prisonniers Lamas-ṣū; Mübādele.2; [au Suppl.] Fidā᾽
voir aussi Sidjn; *et* → MILITAIRES.BUTIN
réforme → RÉFORME.MILITAIRE
soldes ʿAṭā᾽; Inʿām; Māl al-Bayʿa; Rizḳ.3
tactique Ḥarb; Ḥiṣār; Ḥiyal.I
voir aussi Fīl; *et* → ARCHITECTURE.MONUMENTS.FORTERESSES
traités sur Ibn Hudhayl; [au Suppl.] Fakhr-i Mudabbir
voir aussi Ḥarb.II; Ḥiyal.I

MINÉRALOGIE **Maʿdin**
voir aussi al-Mīzān.I
minéraux Abū Ḳalamūn; ʿAḳīḳ; Almās; Bārūd; Billawr; al-Dahnadj; Fīrūzadj; Kibrīt; Kuḥl; Maghnāṭīs.I; Milḥ; Mūmiyā᾽; Naṭrūn; [au Suppl.] Bawraḳ
voir aussi al-Andalus.V; Damāwand; Golkondā; Ḥadjar; Kirmān; Maʿdin; Malindi; *et* → BIJOUX; MÉTALLURGIE
mines al-ʿAllāḳī; Anadolu.III.6; al-Andalus.V.2; ʿAraba; Armīniya.III; Azalay; Badakhshān; Billiton; Bilma; Čankiri; al-Djabbūl; Djayzān; al-Durūʿ; Farghānā; Firrīsh; Gümüsh-khāne; Kalah; Ḳarā Ḥiṣār.2 et 3; Ḳayṣariyya; Ḳily; Ḳishm; Maʿdin.II; al-Maʿdin; Sofala
voir aussi Fāzūghlī; Filasṭīn; Milḥ
traités sur al-Suwaydī

MIRACLES **Karāma**; **Muʿdjiza**
voir aussi Āya; Dawsa; Mā᾽ al-ʿAynayn; Miʿrādj; *et* → SAINT

MOBILIER Mafrūshāt; Sirādj; [au Suppl.] **Athāth**

MONACHISME **Rahbāniyya**
et → CHRISTIANISME.COUVENTS

MONARCHIE Malik; Mamlaka
voir aussi Darshan; Shāh; *et* → CÉRÉMONIES DE LA COUR
insigne royal Miẓalla; Sandjaḳ; Sarāparda; Shamsa
voir aussi Shams.3

MONGOLIE Ḳaraḳorum; Khalkha; **Mongolie**; Mongols
géographie physique
eaux Orkhon
Mongols Batu᾽ides; Čaghatay; Čūbānides; Djalāyir; Djānides; Giray; Hayāṭila; Ilkhāns; Kalmuk; Ḳarā Khiṭāy; Ḳūrīltāy; Mangit; **Mongols**
voir aussi ʿAyn Djālūt; Dūghlāt; Ergenekon; Ḥimṣ; Khānbaliḳ; Ḳūbčūr; Ḳungrāt; Libās.III; Ötüken; *et* → DYNASTIES.MONGOLS

historiens Rashīd al-Dīn Ṭabīb
et → DYNASTIES.MONGOLS *et l'entrée Historiens sous dynasties individuelles*

MONOPHYSITES → CHRISTIANISME.CONFESSIONS

MONTAGNES Adja' et Salmā; Adrar.2; Aghrì Dagh; Aïr; Ala Dagh; Aladja Dagh; Alburz; Altai; Alwand Kūh; ʿAmūr; Atlas; Awrās; Balkhān; Beshparmaḳ; Bībān; Bingöl Dagh; Bīsutūn; Čopan-ata; Damāwand; Deve Boynu; Djabala; al-Djibāl; Djūdī; Djurdjura; Elma Daghì; Erdjiyas Daghì; Fūta Djallon; Gāwur Daghlarì; Ḥaḍūr; Ḥamrīn; Ḥarāz; Hawrāmān; Hindū Kush; Ḥiṣn al-Ghurāb; Ḥufāsh; al-Ḳabḳ; Kabylie; Ḳaraḳorum; Ḳāsiyūn; Khumayr; Kūh-i Bābā; al-Lukkām; Nafūsa, Djabal; Pamirs; Safīd Kūh; al-Sarāt; al-Shārāt; Sindjār; Sulaymān
voir aussi Hind.I.i; Ḳarā Bāgh; *et* → *l'entrée Géographie Physique sous pays individuels*

MORT Djanāza; Ḥināṭa; Intiḥār; Ḳabr; Maḳbara; **Mawt**; Niyāḥa; [au Suppl.] Ghassāl
voir aussi Ghā'ib; Ghusl; Ḳatl; Marthiya; Shahīd; *et* → ARCHITECTURE.MONUMENTS.TOMBEAUX; ESCHATOLOGIE

MOZAMBIQUE Kerimba; Makua; **Mozambique**; Pemba; Sofala

MUḤAMMAD, LE PROPHÈTE Hidjra; Ḥirā'; al-Ḥudaybiya; Khaybar; Khuzāʿa; Ḳudāʿa; Ḳuraysh; al-Madīna.I.2; Mawlid; Miʿrādj; **Muḥammad**; Ṣaḥāba; Sunna
voir aussi al-Ḳur'ān; Mu'ākhāt; al-Mu'allafa Ḳulūbuhum; Nubuwwa; Nūr Muḥammadī; Sayyid; Sharaf; Sharīf; [au Suppl.] Bayʿat al-Riḍwān
biographies du Prophète **al-Maghāzī**; **Sīra**
biographes ʿAbd al-Ḥaḳḳ b. Sayf al-Dīn; al-Bakrī, Abū l-Ḥasan; Daḥlān; al-Diyārbakrī; al-Djawwānī; al-Ḥalabī, Nūr al-dīn; Ibn Hishām; Ibn Isḥāḳ; Ibn Sayyid al-Nās; ʿIyāḍ b. Mūsā; Ḳarā-čelebi-zāde.4; al-Ḳasṭallānī; Liu Tchih; al-Maghāzī; Mughulṭāy; Muḥammad Ḥusayn Haykal; Muʿīn al-Miskīn; [au Suppl.] Dinet
voir aussi Hind.V.e; Ibn Saʿd; al-Khargūshī
compagnons du Prophète Abū Ayyūb al-Anṣārī; Abū Bakra; Abū l-Dardā'; Abū Dharr al-Ghifārī; Abū Hurayra; ʿAdī b. Ḥātim; ʿAmmār b. Yāsir; Anas b. Mālik; al-Arḳam; al-Ashʿarī, Abū Mūsā; ʿAttāb b. Asīd; al-Barā' b. ʿĀzib; al-Barā' b. Maʿrūr; Bashīr b. Saʿd; Bilāl b. Rabāḥ; Bishr b. al-Barā'; Burayda b. al-Ḥuṣayb; Diḥya; Djāriya b. Ḳudāma; Ghasīl al-Malā'ika; Hāshim b. ʿUtba; Ḥurḳūṣ b. Zuhayr al-Saʿdī; Ibn Masʿūd; Kaʿb b. Mālik; Khabbāb b. al-

Aratt; Kẖālid b. Saʿīd; Ḳutẖam b. al-ʿAbbās; Maslama b. Mukẖallad; al-Miḳdād b. ʿAmr; Muʿāwiya b. Ḥudaydj; al-Mughīra b. Shuʿba; Muḥammad b. Abī Ḥudẖayfa; Muṣʿab b. ʿUmayr; al-Nābigha al-Djaʿdī; al-Nuʿmān b. Basẖīr; Saʿd b. Abī Waḳḳāṣ; Ṣafwān b. al-Muʿaṭṭal; Saʿīd b. Zayd; Shaddād b. ʿAmr; Shuraḥbīl b. Ḥasana; [au Suppl.] Djābir b. ʿAbd Allāh; Ibn Mītẖam *voir aussi* Ahl al-Ṣuffa; al-Ḳaʿḳāʿ; Kẖawlān; Ḳuss b. Sāʿida; Rawḥ b. Zinbāʿ; al-Salaf wa-l-Kẖalaf

effets du Prophète Atẖar; al-Burāḳ; Burda.1; Dẖū l-Faḳār; Duldul; Emānet-i Muḳaddese; Ḳadam Shārīf; Kẖîrḳa-i Sherīf; Liḥya-yi Sherīf

famille du Prophète al-ʿAbbās b. ʿAbd al-Muṭṭalib; ʿAbd Allāh b. ʿAbd al-Muṭṭalib; ʿAbd al-Muṭṭalib b. Hāshim; Abū Lahab; Abū Ṭālib; ʿAḳīl b. Abī Ṭālib; ʿAlī b. Abī Ṭālib; Āmina; Djaʿfar b. Abī Ṭālib; Fāṭima; Ḥalīma bint Abī Dhuʾayb; Ḥamza b. ʿAbd al-Muṭṭalib; (al-)Ḥasan b. ʿAlī b. Abī Ṭālib; al-Ḥasan b. Zayd b. al-Ḥasan; Hāshim b. ʿAbd Manāf; (al-)Ḥusayn b. ʿAlī b. Abī Ṭālib; Ruḳayya *voir aussi* Ahl al-Bayt; Sharīf; Shurafāʾ

femmes du Prophète ʿĀʾisha bint Abī Bakr; Ḥafṣa; Kẖadīdja; Māriya; Maymūna bint al-Ḥāritẖ; Ṣafiyya; Sawda bt. Zamʿa

MUSIQUE Ghināʾ; Ḳayna; Maḳām; Malāhī; **Mūsīḳī**; Ramal.2; Shashmaḳom; [au Suppl.] Īḳāʿ
voir aussi Kurdes et Kurdistān.IV.C.4; Lamak; Naḳḳāra-kẖāna; al-Rashīdiyya; Samāʿ.1

chant **Ghināʾ**; Ḳayna; Kẖayāl; Nashīd; Nawba; Shashmaḳom
voir aussi Abū l-Faradj al-Iṣbahānī; Ḥawfī; Ilāhī; Mawāliyā.3; Shāʿir.1.E

chanteurs/chanteuses ʿĀlima; ʿAzza al-Maylāʾ; Djamīla; al-Gharīḍ; Ḥabāba; Ibn ʿĀʾisha.I; Ibn Bāna; Ibn Djāmiʿ; Ibn Misdjaḥ; Ibn Muḥriz; Ibn Suraydj; Ibrāhīm al-Mawṣilī; Ḳayna; Maʿbad b. Wahb; Mālik b. Abī l-Samḥ; Mukẖāriḳ; Nashīṭ; Rāʾiḳa; Sāʾib Kẖātẖir; Sallāma al-Zarḳāʾ; Shāriya; Siti Binti Saad; [au Suppl.] Badẖl al-Kubrā; al-Dalāl; al-Djarādatāni; Faḍl al-Shāʿira; Ḥabba Kẖātūn
voir aussi ʿĀshiḳ; al-Barāmika.5

compositeurs Ibrāhīm al-Mawṣilī; Ismāʿīl Ḥaḳḳī; al-Ḳusanṭīnī; Lāhūtī; Laylā Kẖānim; Maʿbad b. Wahb; Ṣafī al-Dīn al-Urmawī; Shewḳī Beg; Ṣolaḳ-zāde; [au Suppl.] ʿAllawayh al-Aʿsar; al-Dalāl; Ḥabba Kẖātūn

instruments Būḳ; Darabukka; Duff; Ghayṭa; Imẕad; Ḳitẖāra; Miʿzaf; Mizmār; Nefīr; Rabāb; Ṣandj; Santūr; Saz
voir aussi Mehter; Mūristus; Naḳḳāra-kẖāna

musiciens ʿAzza al-Maylāʾ; Djaḥẕa; Ibn Djāmiʿ; Ibn Muḥriz; Ibrāhīm al-Mawṣilī; Isḥāḳ b. Ibrāhīm al-Mawṣilī; Ṣafī al-Dīn al-Urmawī; [au Suppl.] ʿAllawayh al-Aʿsar; Barṣawma al-Zamīr; al-Dalāl; Faḍl al-Shāʿira
voir aussi al-Ḳāsim b. ʿĪsā

régionale
andalouse al-Ḥāʾik
indienne **Hind**.VIII; K͟hayāl
voir aussi Bāyazīd Anṣārī; [au Suppl.] Ḥabba K͟hātūn
persane Mihragān.IV.3
voir aussi Lāhūtī; Naḳḳāra-k͟hāna
turque Ilāhī; Ḳos͟hma; Mehter; S͟harḳî
voir aussi Laylā K͟hānîm; Māni; Nefīr; S͟hewḳī Beg
traités sur ʿAbd al-Ḳādir b. G͟haybī; Abū l-Faradj al-Iṣbahānī; al-Ḥāʾik; Ibn Bāna; Ibn K͟hurradād͟hbih; Mas͟hāḳa; al-Munad͟jd͟jim.IV; Mūrisṭus; Mus͟hāḳa; Ṣafī al-Dīn al-Urmawī; al-Ṣaydāwī
voir aussi Abū l-Maḥāsin Ibn Tag͟hrībirdī; Inal; Malāhī

MYSTICISME Allāh.III.4; Darwīs͟h; D͟hikr; Ibāḥa.II; Karāma; Murīd; Murs͟hid; Pīr; Samāʿ.1; S͟haykh
voir aussi Sad͟jd͟jāda.3; Saʿīd al-Suʿadāʾ; *et* → DYNASTIES.PERSE.ṢAFAWIDES
ascètes primitifs ʿĀmir b. ʿAbd al-Ḳays; al-Ḥasan al-Baṣrī; al-Fuḍayl b. ʿIyāḍ; Ibrāhīm b. Adham; Maʿrūf al-Kark͟hī; Sarī al-Saḳaṭī
voir aussi Bakkāʾ
concepts Baḳāʾ wa-Fanāʾ; al-Insān al-Kāmil; Is͟hrāḳ; Lāhūt et Nāsūt
voir aussi Allāh.III.4; al-Ḥallād͟j.IV; Ibn al-ʿArabī; al-Niffarī
confréries ʿAmmāriyya; ʿArūsiyya; As͟hrafiyya; Bakriyya; Bayrāmiyya; Bayyūmiyya; Bektās͟hiyya; Čis͟htiyya; Darḳāwa; D͟jilwatiyya; Hansaliyya; Hazmīriyyūn; ʿĪsāwā; Ḳādiriyya; Ḳalandariyya; K͟halwatiyya; Madaniyya; Marwāniyya; Mawlawiyya; Mīrg͟haniyya; Murīdiyya; Naḳs͟hbandiyya; al-Nāṣiriyya; Niʿmat-Allāhiyya; Pārsāʾiyya; Raḥmāniyya; Rifāʿiyya; Saʿdiyya; Ṣāliḥiyya; Sanūsiyya; S͟haʿbāniyya; al-S͟hād͟hiliyya; S͟hamsiyya; S͟haṭṭāriyya; Suhrawardiyya; Sunbuliyya; [au Suppl.] Demirdās͟hiyya; Ḥamādis͟ha
pour ʿAdawiyya, *voir* ʿAdī b. Musāfir; *pour* ʿAfīfiyya, *voir* [au Suppl.] al-ʿAfīfī; *pour* Aḥmadiyya (Badawiyya), *voir* Aḥmad al-Badawī; *pour* Dasūḳiyya (Burhāmiyya), *voir* al-Dasūḳī, Ibrāhīm b. ʿAbd al-ʿAzīz; *pour* al-D͟jazūliyya, *voir* al-D͟jazūlī; *pour* Guls͟haniyya, *voir* Guls͟hanī; *pour* Idrīsiyya, *voir* Aḥmad b. Idrīs; *pour* Kāzarūniyya (Murs͟hidiyya, Isḥāḳiyya), *voir* Kāzarūnī; *pour* Kubrawiyya, *voir* Kubrā
voir aussi Nūrbak͟hs͟hiyya; Ṣafawides.I.B
costume K͟hirḳa; Pālāhang; Shadd.1
derviches **Darwīs͟h**; Raḳṣ
voir aussi [au Suppl.] Buḳʿa; *et* → MYSTICISME.CONFRÉRIES
mystiques Darwīs͟h
voir aussi Pist; *et* → HAGIOGRAPHIE
africains (à l'exception d'Afrique du Nord) [au Suppl.] al-Duwayḥī
voir aussi Ṣāliḥiyya; Sūdān (Bilād al-).2

andalous Abū Madyan; Ibn al-ʿArabī; Ibn al-ʿArīf; Ibn ʿĀshir; Ibn Barradjān; Ibn Ḳasī; Ibn Masarra; al-Shushtarī

arabes (à l'exception d'Afrique du Nord et Andalousie) ʿAbd al-Ghanī b. Ismāʿīl; ʿAbd al-Ḳādir al-Djīlānī; ʿAbd al-Karīm al-Djīlī; ʿAdī b. Musāfir; Aḥmad al-Badawī; ʿAydarūs; al-Bakrī, Muḥammad; al-Bakrī, Muṣṭafā; Bishr al-Ḥāfī; al-Bisṭāmī; al-Damīrī; al-Dasūḳī, Ibrāhīm b. ʿAbd al-ʿAzīz; al-Dasūḳī, Ibrāhīm b. Muḥammad; Dhū l-Nūn, Abū l-Fayḍ; al-Dimyāṭī, al-Bannāʾ; al-Dimyāṭī, Nūr al-dīn; al-Djunayd; al-Ghazālī, Abū Ḥāmid; al-Ghazālī, Aḥmad; al-Ḥallādj; al-Harawī al-Mawṣilī; Ibn ʿAṭāʾ Allāh; al-Ḳazwīnī, Nadjm al-dīn; al-Kharrāz; al-Kurdī; al-Ḳushashī; Makhrama; al-Manūfī; al-Muḥāsibī; al-Munāwī; al-Niffarī; al-Nūrī; Rābiʿa al-ʿAdawiyya al-Ḳaysiyya; al-Rifāʿī; Sahl al-Tustarī; al-Sarrādj, Abū Naṣr; al-Shaʿrānī; al-Shiblī, Abū Bakr; Sumnūn; [au Suppl.] Abū l-ʿAzāʾim; al-ʿAdawī; al-ʿAfīfī; al-Ḥiṣāfī

voir aussi Abū Nuʿaym al-Iṣfahānī; Abū Ṭālib al-Makkī; Bā ʿAlawī; Baḥraḳ; Bakriyya; Bayyūmiyya; Faḍl, Bā; Faḳīh, Bā; Faḳīh, Bal; Hurmuz, Bā; Ḳādiriyya; Marwāniyya; Saʿdiyya; al-Ṣiddīḳī; [au Suppl.] al-Bakrī; Demirdāshiyya; *et* → MYSTICISME.ASCÈTES PRIMITIFS

d'Asie centrale Aḥmad Yasawī; Ḥakīm Ata; Naḳshband; [au Suppl.] Aḥrār

voir aussi Ḳalandariyya; Pārsāʾiyya

indiens Abū ʿAlī Ḳalandar; Aḥmad Sirhindī; Ashraf ʿAlī; Bahāʾ al-Dīn Zakariyyāʾ; Bāḳī bi-llāh (*et* [au Suppl.]); al-Banūrī; Budhan; Burhān al-Dīn Gharīb; Burhān al-Dīn Ḳuṭb-i ʿĀlam; Čirāgh-i Dihlī; Čishtī; Djahānārā Bēgam; Djalāl al-Dīn Ḥusayn al-Bukhārī; Djamālī; Farīd al-Dīn Masʿūd "Gandj-i-Shakar"; Gīsū Darāz; Hānsawī; Ḥusaynī Sādāt Amīr; Imdād Allāh; Kalīm Allāh al-Djahānābādī; Ḳuṭb al-Dīn Bakhtiyār; Malik Muḥammad Djāyasī; Miyān Mīr, Miyāndjī; Mubārak Ghāzī; Muḥammad Ghawth Gwāliyārī; al-Muttaḳī al-Hindī; Muẓaffar Shams Balkhī; Niẓām al-Dīn Awliyāʾ; Niẓām al-Dīn, Mullā Muḥammad; Nūr Ḳuṭb al-ʿĀlam; Shāh Muḥammad b. ʿAbd Aḥmad; [au Suppl.] ʿAbd al-Bārī; ʿAbd al-Wahhāb Bukhārī; Bulbul Shāh; Farangī Maḥall; Gadāʾī Kambō; Ḥamīd Ḳalandar; Ḥamīd al-Dīn Ḳāḍī Nāgawrī; Ḥamīd al-Dīn Ṣūfī Nāgawrī Siwālī; Ḥamza Makhdūm

voir aussi ʿAydarūs; Čishtiyya; Dārā Shukōh; Dard; Djīwan; Hind.V; Khalīl Allāh (*et* Khalīl Allāh But-shikan); Malang; Mughals.VI; Naḳshbandiyya.III; Shaṭṭāriyya; Suhrawardiyya.2

indonésiens ʿAbd al-Raʾūf al-Sinkilī; ʿAbd al-Ṣamad al-Palimbānī; Ḥamza Fanṣūrī; Shams al-Dīn al-Samaṭrānī

nord-africains ʿAbd al-Ḳādir al-Fāsī; ʿAbd al-Salām b. Mashīsh; Abū l-Maḥāsin al-Fāsī; Abū Muḥammad Ṣāliḥ; Aḥmad b. Idrīs; ʿAlī b. Maymūn; al-ʿAyyāshī; al-Daḳḳāḳ; al-Djazūlī; al-Hāshimī; Ḥmād u-Mūsā; Ibn ʿAbbād; Ibn ʿAdjība; Ibn ʿAlīwa; Ibn ʿArūs; Ibn Ḥirzihim; al-

Ḳādirī al-Ḥasanī; al-Kūhin; al-Lamaṭī; Māʾ al-ʿAynayn; al-Madjdhūb; al-Sanūsī, Abū ʿAbd Allāh; al-Sanūsī, Muḥammad b. ʿAlī; al-Sanūsī, Shaykh Sayyid Aḥmad; al-Shādhilī; [au Suppl.] al-Asmar; al-Dilāʾ; al-Fāsī; Ibn ʿAzzūz

voir aussi ʿAmmāriyya; ʿArūsiyya; Darḳāwa; Hansaliyya; Hazmīriyyūn; al-Ifrānī; ʿĪsāwā; Madaniyya; al-Nāṣiriyya; Raḥmāniyya; al-Shādhiliyya; [au Suppl.] Ḥamādisha

persans ʿAbd al-Razzāḳ al-Ḳāshānī; Abū Saʿīd b. Abī l-Khayr; Abū Yazīd al-Bisṭāmī; Aḥmad-i Djām; ʿAlāʾ al-Dawla al-Simnānī; ʿAlī al-Hamadhānī; al-Anṣārī al-Harawī; Ashraf Djahāngīr; Bābā-Ṭāhir; Djalāl al-Dīn Rūmī; Faḍl Allāh Ḥurūfī; Ghudjduwānī; Ḥamdūn al-Ḳaṣṣār; Hudjwīrī; Ibn Khafīf; ʿIrāḳī; al-Kalābādhī; Kamāl Khudjandī; Ḳāsim-i Anwār; Kāzarūnī; Khalīl Allāh (*et* Khalīl Allāh But-shikan); Kharaḳānī; al-Khargūshī; Kirmānī; Kubrā; al-Ḳushayrī.I; Lāhīdjī.I; Maḥmūd Shabistarī; Nadjm al-Dīn Rāzī Dāya; Naḳshband; Rūzbihān; Saʿd al-Dīn al-Ḥammūʾī; Saʿd al-Dīn (Kāshgharī); Ṣadr al-Dīn Ardabīlī; Ṣadr al-Dīn Mūsā; Ṣafī; Saʿīd al-Dīn Farghānī; Sayf al-Dīn Bākharzī; Shams-i Tabrīz(ī); al-Suhrawardī, Abū l-Nadjīb; al-Suhrawardī, Shihāb al-dīn Abū Ḥafṣ; Sulṭān Walad; [au Suppl.] ʿAbd Allāh b. Abī Bakr al-Miyānadjī; Abū ʿAlī al-Farmadī; Aḥmad-i Rūmī; ʿAyn al-Ḳuḍāt al-Hamadhānī; Ibn al-Bazzāz al-Ardabīlī

voir aussi Djāmī; Madjlisī-yi Awwal; Naḳshbandiyya.I; Niʿmat-Allāhiyya; Ṣafawides.I.B

turcs Aḳ Shams al-Dīn; Altî Parmak; ʿAshîḳ Pasha; Badr al-Dīn Ibn Ḳāḍī Samāwnā; Baraḳ Baba; Bīdjān; Emīr Sulṭān; Faṣīḥ Dede; Fehmī; Gulshanī; Gülshehrī; Ḥādjdjī Bayrām Walī; Hüdāʾī; Ḥusām al-Dīn Čelebi; Ismāʿīl al-Anḳarawī; Ismāʿīl Ḥaḳḳi; Ḳayghusuz Abdāl; Khalīlī; Ḳuṭb al-Dīn-zāde; Merkez; Niyāzī; Sezāʾī, Ḥasan Dede; [au Suppl.] ʿĀrif Čelebi; Eshrefoghlu ʿAbd Allāh; Esrār Dede

voir aussi Ashrafiyya; Bakriyya; Bayrāmiyya; Bektāshiyya; Djilwatiyya; Gülbaba; Ilāhī; Khalwatiyya; Mawlawiyya; Naḳshbandiyya.II; Shaʿbāniyya; Shamsiyya; Sunbuliyya

poésie mystique → LITTÉRATURE.POÉSIE

termes Abdāl; ʿĀshiḳ; Awtād; Baḳāʾ wa-Fanāʾ; Basṭ; Bīsharʿ; Čāʾūsh; Darwīsh; Dawsa; Dede; Dhawḳ; Dhikr; Djilwa; Faḳīr; Fikr; al-Ghayb; Ghayba; Ghufrān; Ḥaḍra; Ḥaḳīḳa.3; Ḥaḳḳ; Ḥāl; Ḥidjāb.III; Ḥuḳūḳ; Ḥulūl; Ḥurriyya; Huwa huwa; Ikhlāṣ; Ilhām; ʿInāya; al-Insān al-Kāmil; Ishān; Ishāra; ʿIshḳ; Ishrāḳ; Ithbāt; Ittiḥād; Ḳabḍ.II; Kāfir; Ḳalb.I; Kalima; Karāma; Kashf; Khalīfa.III; Khalwa; Khānḳāh; Khirḳa; Ḳuṭb; Lāhūt et Nāsūt; Madjdhūb; Manzil; Maʿrifa; Muḥāsaba.I; Munādjāt; Murīd; Murshid; Nafs; Odjaḳ; Pālāhang; Pīr; Pūst; Pūst-neshīn; Rābiṭa; Ramz.3; Rātib; Ribāṭ; Riḍā.1; Rind; Rūḥāniyya; Rukhṣa.2; Ṣabr; Ṣadr; Shaṭḥ; Shawḳ; Shaykh; Shukr.1;

Ṣidḳ; Silsila; Sulṭān.4; Sulūk.2; [au Suppl.] Buḳʿa; G̲h̲awt̲h̲
voir aussi Čelebī; Futuwwa; Gülbaba; Lawḥ; Lawn

N

NATIONALISME   Istiḳlāl; **Ḳawmiyya**
   voir aussi D̲j̲angalī; K̲h̲ilāfa; Pās̲h̲tūnistān; al-S̲h̲uʿūbiyya; *et* → POLITIQUE.
MOUVEMENTS

NATURE   → BOTANIQUE; FLORE; LITTÉRATURE.POÉSIE.DE LA NATURE

NAVIGATION   D̲j̲ug̲h̲rāfiyā; Iṣbaʿ; K̲h̲arīṭa; Mag̲h̲nāṭīs.II; Manār; **Milāḥa**; Mīnāʾ
   voir aussi al-K̲h̲as̲h̲abāt; Rīḥ
chantiers   Dār al-Ṣināʿa
navires   Milāḥa; Nassades; **Safīna**; S̲h̲īnī
      voir aussi Baḥriyya.II; Kelek; *et* → MILITAIRES.MARINE
traités sur   Ibn Mād̲j̲id; Sīdī ʿAlī Reʾīs; Sulaymān al-Mahrī
      voir aussi D̲j̲ug̲h̲rāfiyā.IV.D; Milāḥa.I et III

NÉPAL   **Népal**

NESTORIENS   → CHRISTIANISME.CONFESSIONS

NIGER   **Niger**
   voir aussi Sūdān (Bilād al-).2
toponymes   Bilma; D̲j̲ādū; Kawār

NIGÉRIA   Hausa; **Nigeria**
   voir aussi D̲j̲arīda.VI; Fulbé; al-Kānemī; Kanuri; Nikāḥ.II.6; Sūdān (Bilād
   al-).2; *et* → AFRIQUE.AFRIQUE CENTRALE *et* AFRIQUE OCCIDENTALE
leaders   Muḥammad Bello
      voir aussi Gwandu
toponymes
   provinces   Adamawa; Bornū
   villes   Ibadan; Kano; Katsina; Kūkawa; Sokoto

NOMADISME   **Badw**; Horde; Īlāt; K̲h̲āwa; K̲h̲ayma; Marʿā
   voir aussi Baḳḳāra; Baranta; Dak̲h̲īl; Dawār; Ḥayy; Ḳayn; *et* → BÉDOUINS;
   GITANS; TRIBUS
effets nomades   K̲h̲ayma; Mifras̲h̲
      voir aussi K̲h̲ayl

NOUVEAU MONDE Djāliya; Djarīda.I.C.; **al-Mahdjar**
émigrants Djabrān Khalīl Djabrān; al-Maʿlūf; Nuʿayma, Mikhāʾīl; al-Rayḥānī; [au Suppl.] Abū Māḍī; Abū Shādī
voir aussi Pārsīs

NUBIE ʿAlwa; Barābra; Dongola; al-Marīs; **Nūba**
voir aussi Baḳṭ; Dār al-Ṣulḥ; Ibn Sulaym al-Aswānī; al-Muḳurra; Sōba; *et* → ÉGYPTE.TOPONYMES; SOUDAN.TOPONYMES
langues Nūba.III
peuples Nūba.IV

NUMÉRO Abdjad; Ḥisāb al-ʿAḳd; Ḥisāb al-Djummal; Ḥurūf; ʿIlm al-Ḥisāb
et → MATHÉMATIQUES
chiffres Khamsa; Sabʿ
voir aussi al-Ṣifr

NUMISMATIQUE Dār al-Ḍarb; Sikka
voir aussi ʿAlī Pasha Mubārak; Ismāʿīl Ghālib; Makāyil; Nithār
lieux d'ateliers de frappe Abarshahr; al-ʿAbbāsiyya; Andarāb.1; Ānī; Bāghčc Sarāy; Islāmābād; Iṣṭakhr; al-Kurdj; Māh al-Baṣra; Mawlāy Idrīs; Māzandarān.7; [au Suppl.] Biyār; Firrīm
monnaies Akče; Bālish; Čao; Čeyrek; Dīnār; Dirham.II; Fals; Ḥasanī; Larin; Mohur; Pāʾī; Pāra; Pawlā; Paysā; Riyāl; Rūpiyya; Ṣadīḳī; Ṣāḥib Ḳirān; Shāhī
voir aussi Dhahab; Fidda; Filori; Hilāl.II; Sanadjāt; *et* → DYNASTIES
pour les monnaies frappés à nom du souverain, voir al-Afḍal Kutayfāt; ʿAlī Bey; Ghāzī l-Dīn Ḥaydar; Ḳaṭarī b. al-Fudjāʾa; Khurshīd; al-Manṣūr; Muṣṭafā.I; [au Suppl.] Farrukhān.II
pour les monnaies sous les dynasties, voir en particulier Artuḳides; Barīd Shāhides; Khʷārazm-shahs; Lōdīs.V; Mughals.X; al-Muwaḥḥidūn; ʿOthmānli̊.IX; Rasūlides.2; Ṣafawides.VI; Saldjūḳides.VIII; Ṣiḳilliyya.3; Ṣulayḥides.2
réforme ʿAbd al-Malik b. Marwān; [au Suppl.] al-Ghiṭrīf b. ʿAṭāʾ
termes ʿAdl.2; Salām (*et* Sālim.1)

O

OBSCÉNITÉ **Mudjūn**; **Sukhf**

OCÉANS ET MERS **Baḥr**; al-Madd wa-l-Djazr
voir aussi Kharīṭa; *et* → CARTOGRAPHIE; NAVIGATION
eaux Aral; Baḥr Adriyas; Baḥr Bunṭus; Baḥr Fāris; Baḥr al-Hind; Baḥr al-

Ḵẖazar; Baḥr al-Ḳulzum; Baḥr Lūṭ; Baḥr Māyuṭis; al-Baḥr al-Muḥīṭ; Baḥr al-Rūm; Baḥr al-Zandj; Marmara Deñizi

OMAN   Bū Saʿīd; Madjlis.IV.A.13; Maḥkama.IV.9; Nabhān
    voir aussi [au Suppl.] al-Ḥārithī
population   ʿAwāmir; al-Baṭāḥira; al-Djanaba; al-Durūʿ; Hinā; al-Ḥubūs; al-ʿIfār; Ḵẖarūṣ; Mahra; Mazrūʿī; Nabhān
    et → TRIBUS.PÉNINSULE ARABIQUE
toponymes
    îles   Ḵẖūryān-mūryān; Maṣīra
    régions   al-Bāṭina; Raʾs Musandam; al-Rustāḳ; al-Sẖarḳiyya
    villes   al-Buraymī; Ḥāsik; ʿIbrī; Ḳalhāt; Masḳaṭ; Maṭraḥ; Mirbāṭ; Nizwa; al-Rustāḳ; Ṣalāla; Ṣuḥār
    voir aussi (Djazīrat) al-ʿArab; [au Suppl.] Gwādar

ONOMASTIQUE   Bā; Ibn; Ism; Kisrā; Kunya; Laḳab; Nisba.2
    voir aussi al-Asmāʾ al-Ḥusnā; Oghul; Ṣiḳilliyya.2
comme forme d'adresse   Agẖa; Āḵẖūnd; Beg; Begum; Čelebī; Efendi; Ḵẖʷādja; Ḵẖātūn; Ḵẖudāwand; Sẖaykẖ
    voir aussi Aḵẖī; Sẖarīf.3
épithètes   Ata; Baba; Gẖufrān; Humāyūn; al-Ṣiddīḳ
noms propres   Aḥmad; Dẖū l-Faḳār; Humā; Marzpān; Meḥemmed; Mihra-gān.IV.2; Sonḳor
    voir aussi al-Asad; Paygẖū
titres
    africains   Diglal; Sulṭān.3
    arabes   ʿAmīd; Amīr al-Muʾminīn; Amīr al-Muslimīn; Asad al-Dawla; ʿAzīz Miṣr; ʿIzz al-Dawla; ʿIzz al-Dīn; Ḵẖādim al-Ḥaramayn; Ḵẖidīw; Malik; Mihmindār; Musẖīr; Sardār; Sayyid; Sẖaykẖ al-Balad; Sẖaykẖ al-Islām.1; Sulṭān.1
        voir aussi Dawla
    d'Asie centrale   Afsẖīn; Iḵẖsẖīd; Ḳosẖ-begi; Sẖār; [au Suppl.] Atalîḳ; Dīwān-begi; İnaḳ
    d'Asie du Sud-est   Penghulu; Sulṭān.2
    indo-musulmans   Āṣāf-Djāh; Ḵẖʷādja-i Djahān; Ḵẖān Ḵẖānān; Nawwāb; Niẓām; Pēsẖwā; Ṣāḥib Ḳirān; Sardār; Sẖār
    mongols   Noyan; Ṣāḥib Ḳirān
    persans   Agẖa Ḵẖān; Ispahbadẖ; Ispahsālār; Iʿtimād al-Dawla; Ḵẖʷādja; Marzpān; Mīr; Mīrzā; Mollā; Pādisẖāh; Ṣadr; Sālār; Sardār; Sarkār Āḳā; Sẖāh
    turcs   Alp; Beglerbegi; Dāmād; Daryā-begi; Dayî; Gülbaba; Ḵẖʷādjegān-i Dīwān-i Humāyūn; Ḵẖāḳān; Ḵẖān; Ḵẖudāwendigār; Mīr-i Mīrān;

Mushīr; Pasha; Payghū; Ṣadr-i Aʿẓam; Shaykh al-Islām.2; Ṣu Bashî
voir aussi Čorbadjî

Optique Ḳaws Ḳuzaḥ; **Manāẓir**
voir aussi Mirʾāt; Sarāb
traités sur Ibn al-Haytham; Kamāl al-Dīn al-Fārisī
voir aussi Ḳuṭb al-Dīn Shīrāzī

P

Paiements ʿAṭāʾ; Djāmakiyya; Ḥawāla; Inʿām; Māl al-Bayʿa; Maʿūna; Ṣila.3; Soyūrghāl; Ṣurra
corruption Marāfiḳ; **Rashwa**

Pakistan Djināḥ; Dustūr.XIV; Ḥizb.VI; Ḥukūma.V; Madjlis.IV.C; al-Marʾa.V; **Pākistān**; [au Suppl.] Djarīda.VII
voir aussi Ahl-i Ḥadīth; Dār al-ʿUlūm.c; Djamʿiyya; Djūnāgaṙh; Hind.II et IV; Kashmīr; Ḳawmiyya.VI; Khaybar; Muhādjir.3; Pashtūnistān; Sind.2; *et* → Inde
architecture → Architecture.régions
éducation Djāmiʿa
géographie physique
eaux Kurram; Mihrān
montagnes Sulaymān
hommes d'état Djināḥ; Liyāḳat ʿAlī Khān
voir aussi Mawdūdī
population Afrīdī; Dāwūdpōtrās; Mahsūd; Mohmand; Mullagorī; [au Suppl.] Démographie.VII; Gurčānī
voir aussi Djirga
toponymes
anciens Čīnīōt; Daybul; Ḳandābīl; Khayrābād
actuels
districts Chitral; Ḥāfiẓābād; Hazāra; Khārān; Khayrpūr; Kilāt.II; Kōhāt; Kwaṫṫa; Mastūdj; Sībī
régions Balūčistān; Dardistān; Dēradjāt; Dīr; Djahlāwān; Kačchī; Las Bēla; Makrān; Pandjāb; Sind; Swāt
villes Amarkot; Bādjawr; Bahāwalpūr; Bakkār; Bannū; Bhakkar; Gūdjrāṅwāla; Gudjrāt; Ḥasan Abdāl; Ḥaydarābād; Islāmābād; Karāčī; Kilāt.I; Ḳuṣdār; Kwaṫṫa; Lāhawr; Mastūdj; Peshāwar; Rāwalpindi; Shikārpūr.1; Sībī; Siyālkut; [au Suppl.] Gilgit; Gwādar

PALESTINE Djarīda.I.A; **Filasṭīn**; Ḥizb.I; Madjlis.IV.A.23; Maḥkama.IV.5; Mandats
voir aussi Djarrāḥides; Ḳays ʿAylān; al-Khālidī; al-Sāmira; Shāhīn, Āl; [au Suppl.] Démographie.III; *et* → CROISADES
architecture Ḳubbat al-Ṣakhra; al-Ḳuds; al-Masdjid al-Aḳṣā
voir aussi Kawkab
géographie physique
eaux Baḥr Lūṭ; al-Ḥūla; Nahr Abī Fuṭrus
historiens Mudjīr al-Dīn al-ʿUlaymī
sous le mandat britannique Filasṭīn.II; Muḥammad ʿIzzat Darwaza; [au Suppl.] Amīn al-Ḥusaynī
voir aussi Mandats
toponymes
anciens Arsūf; ʿAthlīth; ʿAyn Djālūt; Bayt Djibrīn; al-Dārūm; Irbid.II; Sabasṭiyya.1; Subayta
actuels
régions al-Ghawr.1; Mardj Banī ʿĀmir; al-Naḳb
villes ʿAkkā; ʿAmwās; ʿĀsḳalān; Baysān; Bayt Laḥm; Bīr al-Sabʿ; Ghazza; Ḥayfā; Ḥiṭṭīn; al-Khalīl; al-Ḳuds; Ladjdjūn; Ludd; Nābulus; al-Nāṣira; Rafaḥ; al-Ramla; Rīḥā.1; Ṣafad
voir aussi Ḳayṣariyya; Ṣihyawn

PANARABISME Ḳawmiyya; **Panarabisme**; [au Suppl.] al-Djāmiʿa al-ʿArabiyya
partisans de al-Kawākibī; Nūrī al-Saʿīd; Rashīd Riḍā; [au Suppl.] ʿAbd al-Nāṣir
voir aussi al-Kāẓimī, ʿAbd al-Muḥsin

PANISLAMISME Ḳawmiyya; **Panislamisme**; **al-Rābiṭa al-Islāmiyya**
voir aussi Dustūr.XVIII; Iṣlāḥ.II; Khilāfa, Khilāfat Movement; Muʾtamar
partisans de ʿAbd al-Ḥamīd II; Djamāl al-Dīn al-Afghānī; Fiṭrat; Gasprali̊ (Gasprinski), Ismāʿīl; Ḥālī; Kūčak Khān Djangalī; Māʾ al-ʿAynayn; Meḥmed ʿĀkif; Rashīd Riḍā; Ṣafar; [au Suppl.] Andjuman-i Khuddām-i Kaʿba; al-Bakrī
voir aussi Djadīd

PANTURKISME Ḳawmiyya; **Panturquisme**
partisans de Gasprali̊ (Gasprinski), Ismāʿīl; Gökalp, Ziya; Ri̊ḍā Nūr; Suʿāwī

PAPYROLOGIE Ḳirṭās; Papyrus
voir aussi Diplomatique.I.15; *et* → DOCUMENTS

PARADIS al-ʿAshara al-Mubashshara; Dār al-Salām; **Djanna**; Ḥūr; Kawthar; Riḍwān; Salsabīl
voir aussi al-Aʿrāf

PARFUM Bān; Ḥinnāʾ; Kāfūr; Misk
voir aussi al-Aṭṭār; Maʿdin.IV.B.b

PÈLERINAGE ʿArafa; al-Djamra; **Ḥadjdj**; Hady; Iḥrām; Kaʿba; Minā; Muṭawwif; al-Muzdalifa; Radjm; al-Ṣafā.1; Saʿy; Shiʿār.a
voir aussi Amīr al-Ḥādjdj; Ḥidjāz; Kārwān; Kāẓimayn; Makka; [au Suppl.] ʿAtabāt; Darb Zubayda; Fayd; *et* → ISLAM

PÉRIODE PRÉISLAMIQUE al-ʿArab.I; (Djazīrat) al-ʿArab.VII; Armīniya.II.1; Badw.III; Djāhiliyya; Ghassān; Kinda.1 et Appendice; Lakhmides; Liḥyān; Maʿin; Makka.I; Nabaṭ; Rūm
voir aussi Ḥayawān.II; Ilāh; al-Kalbī.II; Lībiyā.II; *et* → ASSYRIE; BYZANTINS; MILITAIRES.BATAILLES; ZOROASTRIENS
coutumes/institutions ʿAtīra; Baliyya; Ghidhāʾ.I et II; Ḥadjdj.I; Ḥilf; Ḥimā; Ḥimāya; Istisḳāʾ; Kāhin; Khafāra; Mawla; Nuṣub; Raḍāʿ.2; Sādin
voir aussi Fayʾ; Ghanīma; Īlāf; Karkūr; Nār; Ṣadā; Shayba
dans la péninsule arabique Abraha; (Djazīrat) al-ʿArab.I et VI; Bakr b. Wāʾil; Djadhīma al-Abrash; Ghumdān; Ḥabashat; Ḥādjib b. Zurāra; Ḥaḍramawt; Hāshim b. ʿAbd Manāf; Hind bint al-Khuss; Ḥums; Ḳatabān; Ḳayl; Ḳuṣayy; Ḳuss b. Sāʿida; Mārib; Nuṣub; Sabaʾ; Sadjʿ.1; Salḥīn; [au Suppl.] Ḥaḍramawt.I
voir aussi Badw.III; Dār al-Nadwa; Ḥanīf.4; Kinda.Appendice; *et* → ARABIE SÉOUDITE.TOPONYMES; LITTÉRATURE.POÉSIE.ARABE; OMAN.TOPONYMES; TRIBUS.PÉNINSULE ARABIQUE; YÉMEN.TOPONYMES
dans le Croissant fertile Khursābād; Manbidj; Maysan; Nabaṭ; [au Suppl.] Athūr
voir aussi Biṭrīḳ.I; Ḥarrān; Shahāridja; Shahrazūr
Ghassānides Djabala b. al-Ayham; Djilliḳ; **Ghassān**; al-Ḥārith b. Djabala; [au Suppl.] Djabala b. al-Ḥārith
Lakhmides ʿAmr b. ʿAdī; ʿAmr b. Hind; al-Ḥīra, **Lakhmides**; al-Mundhir IV; al-Nuʿmān [III] b. al-Mundhir
dieux Dhū l-Khalaṣa; Hubal; Isāf wa-Nāʾila; Ḳaws Ḳuzaḥ; al-Lāt; Manāf; Manāt; Nasr; Shams.1; Shayʿ al-Ḳawm; Suʿayr; Sudjdja; Suwāʿ
voir aussi ʿAmr b. Luḥayy; Djāhiliyya; Ilāh; Kaʿba.V; al-Ḳamar.II; Mawḳif.3; Rabb; Ṣanam; Shayṭān
en Égypte → ÉGYPTE.AVANT L'ISLAM
en Iran → IRAN.AVANT L'ISLAM

PERSE → IRAN

PESTE ʿAmwās
voir aussi Ibn Khaldūn, Walī al-dīn
traités sur Ibn Khātima; Ibn Riḍwān; al-Masīḥī

PÉTROLE **Naft̤.III**
champs pétrolifères ʿAbbādān; Abḳayḳ; Altîn Köprü; al-Baḥrayn; al-Dahnāʾ; al-G͟hawār; al-Ḥasā; al-Ḳaṭīf; K͟hārag; K͟hūzistān; Kirkūk; Kirmāns͟hāh; al-Kuwayt; Lībiyā; Nad͟jd.3; Rām-hurmuz; Raʾs (al-)Tannūra; [au Suppl.] Aḥmadī
voir aussi D͟jannābā; Fārs; al-K͟hubar

PHARMACOLOGIE Adwiya; Aḳrābād͟hīn; **Ṣaydana**
voir aussi Diyusḳuridīs; D͟jālīnūs; Nabāt; *et* → BOTANIQUE; DROGUES; MÉDECINE
pharmacologues Ibn al-Bayṭār; Ibn Samad͟jūn; Ibn al-Tilmīd͟h; Ibn Wāfid; al-Kōhēn al-ʿAṭṭār; Sābūr b. Sahl; [au Suppl.] al-G͟hāfiḳī; Ibn Biklāris͟h; Ibn al-Rūmiyya
voir aussi al-ʿAs͟hs͟hāb; al-ʿAṭṭār; al-Bīrūnī; al-Suwaydī

PHASES DE LA VIE **Ḥayāt**
accouchement ʿAḳīḳa; Āl; Liʿān; al-Marʾa.II.3; Mawākib.IV.2
voir aussi Raḍāʿ
allaitement Raḍāʿ
grossesse Rāḳid
traités sur ʿArīb b. Saʿd
enfance Bālig͟h; **Ṣag͟hīr**
voir aussi Ḥaḍāna; al-S͟hayb wa-l-S͟habāb; *et* → CIRCONCISION; ÉDUCATION; MARIAGE
vieillesse **Muʿammar**
voir aussi al-S͟hayb wa-l-S͟habāb; S͟hayk͟h; *et* → MORT

PHILATELIE **Posta**
et → TRANSPORT.POSTALE

PHILOSOPHIE Falāsifa; **Falsafa**; Ḥikma; Mā baʿd al-Ṭabīʿa; Manṭiḳ; Naẓar
voir aussi ʿĀlam.1; Allāh.III.2; al-Maḳūlāt; Muk͟htaṣar; S͟harḥ.IV
logique **Manṭiḳ**
termes Āla.III; ʿAraḍ; Dalīl; Faṣl; Fiʿl; Ḥadd; Ḥaḳīḳa.2; Ḥud͟jd͟ja; Ḥukm.I; Huwa huwa.A; Muḳaddam; Natīd͟ja; S͟harṭ.2
voir aussi Ḳaṭʿ; al-Sūfisṭāʾiyyūn
philosophes **Falāsifa**
chrétiens Ibn al-Ṭayyib; Ibn Zurʿa; Mattā b. Yūnus
grecs Aflāṭūn; Anbaduḳlīs; Arisṭūṭālīs; Balīnūs; Baṭlamiyūs; Buruḳlus; D͟jālīnūs; Fīt͟hāg͟hūras; Furfūriyūs; al-Iskandar al-Afrūdīsī; al-Sūfisṭāʾiyyūn; Suḳrāṭ
voir aussi Ḥunayn b. Isḥāḳ al-ʿIbādī; Īsāg͟hūd͟jī; Isḥāḳ b. Ḥunayn; Lawn;

al-Maḳūlāt; Mattā b. Yūnus; Nīḳūlāʾūs; al-Shaykh al-Yūnānī
juifs Ibn Gabirol; Ibn Kammūna; Isḥāḳ al-Isrāʾīlī; Judéo-arabe.III; Saʿadyā
voir aussi Abū l- Barakāt
musulmans
biographes al-Shahrazūrī, Shams al-Dīn
9e siècle Abū l-Hudhayl al-ʿAllāf; al-Kindī, Abū Yūsuf; al-Sarakhsī, Abū l-ʿAbbās
voir aussi Dahriyya; Falāsifa; Lawn
10e siècle Abū Sulaymān al-Manṭiḳī; al-Fārābī; Ibn Masarra; al-Mawṣilī; al-Rāzī, Abū Bakr; [au Suppl.] al-ʿĀmirī
11e siècle Abū Ḥayyān al-Tawḥīdī; Bahmanyār; Ibn Ḥazm; Ibn Sīnā; Miskawayh
12e siècle Abū l-Barakāt; al-Baṭalyawsī; Ibn Bādjdja; Ibn Rushd; Ibn Ṭufayl; al-Suhrawardī, Shihāb al-dīn Yaḥyā
voir aussi al-Ghazālī; Ḥayy b. Yaḳẓān; Ishrāḳiyyūn; al-Shahrastānī, Tādj al-dīn
13e siècle al-Abharī; Ibn Sabʿīn; al-Kātibī; Ṣadr al-Dīn al-Ḳūnawī; al-Shahrazūrī, Shams al-dīn
voir aussi Fakhr al-Dīn al-Rāzī
14e siècle Djamāl al-Dīn Aḳsarayī
16e siècle al-Maybudī.II
17e siècle al-Dāmād; al-Fārūḳī, Mullā; Lāhīdjī.II; [au Suppl.] Findiriskī
19e siècle Sabzawarī, Ḥādjdj Mullā Hādī; [au Suppl.] Abū l-Ḥasan Djilwa
termes Abad; ʿAdam; ʿAḳl; ʿAmal.1; Anniyya; Awwal; Basīṭ wa-Murakkab; Dhāt; Dhawḳ; Ḍidd; Djawhar; Djins; Djism; Djuzʾ; Fard; Ḥadd; Ḥaraka wa-Sukūn.I.1; Hayʾa; Ḥayāt; Hayūlā; Ḥiss; Ḥudūth al-ʿĀlam; Ḥulūl; Huwiyya; Ibdāʿ; Idrāk; Iḥdāth; Ikhtiyār; ʿIlla.II; ʿInāya; Inṣāf; ʿIshḳ; Ishrāḳ; al-Ḳaḍāʾ wa-l-Ḳadar.A.3; Kawn wa-Fasad; Ḳidam; Ḳuwwa.4, 6 et 7; Maʿād; Māhiyya; Maḥsūsāt; Malaka; Maʿnā.II; Nafs; Nihāya; Nūr.II; Saʿāda; Sabab.1; Shakhṣ; Shakk.2; Shayʾ; Shubha
voir aussi Athar.III; ʿAyn; Dahriyya; Insān; Ḳaṭʿ; Ḳiyāma; Siyasa.2; *et* → PHILOSOPHIE.LOGIQUE.TERMES

PHYSIONOMIE Firāsa; Ḳiyāfa; Shāma; [au Suppl.] Aflīmūn
et → ANATOMIE

PIRATERIE **Ḳurṣān**
voir aussi al-ʿAnnāba; ʿArūdj; Ḥasan Baba; Ḥusayn Pasha, Mezzomorto; Kemāl Reʾīs; Khayr al-Dīn Pasha; Lewend

POIDS ET MESURES Aghač; Arpa; Dhirāʿ; Dirham.I; Farsakh; Ḥabba; Iṣbaʿ; Istār;

Makāyil; Marḥala; Miḳyās; **Misāḥa**; al-Mīzān; Ṣāʿ; Sanadjāt; [au Suppl.] Gaz
voir aussi al-Ḳarasṭūn

POLITIQUE Baladiyya; Dawla; Djumhūriyya; Dustūr; Ḥimāya.II; Ḥizb; Ḥukūma; Ḥurriyya; Istiḳlāl; Ḳawmiyya; Madjlis; Makhzan; Mandats; Mashyakha; Medeniyyet; Musāwāt; Muwāṭin; Nāʾib.2; Shūrā.3; Siyāsa; [au Suppl.] Āzādī; al-Djāmiʿa al-ʿArabiyya
voir aussi Ahl al-Ḥall wa-l-ʿAḳd; Imtiyāzāt; Mashwara; Salṭana; *et* → ADMINISTRATION; DIPLOMATIE; EMPIRE OTTOMAN
doctrines Ḥizb.I; Ishtirākiyya; Mārk(i)siyya; Shuyūʿiyya; [au Suppl.] Hidjra
voir aussi Musāwāt; Muslimūn.IV; Radjʿiyya; *et* → PANARABISME; PANISLAMISME; PANTURQUISME
mouvements Djadīd; Djangalī; Istiḳlāl; Ittiḥād we Teraḳḳī Djemʿiyyeti; Khāksār; Khilāfa; al-Rābiṭa al-Islāmiyya
voir aussi Fiṭrat; Ḥamza Beg; Ḥizb; Ḥurriyya; Kūčak Khān Djangalī; [au Suppl.] ʿAbd al-Bārī; *et* → PANARABISME; PANISLAMISME; PANTURQUISME
partis Demokrat Parti; **Ḥizb**; Ḥürriyyet we Iʾtilāf Fi̊rḳasi̊; Partai Islam se Malaysia (Pas); Shuyūʿiyya.1.B
voir aussi Andjuman; Djamʿiyya; (Tunali̊) Ḥilmī; Ḥizb.I; Ishtirākiyya; Khīyābānī; Leff; Luṭfī al-Sayyid; Mārk(i)siyya; Muṣṭafā Kāmil Pasha; Sarekat Islam; [au Suppl.] ʿAbd al-Nāṣir; *et* → COMMUNISME; RÉFORME
réforme → RÉFORME
termes Shaʿb.2

POLOGNE **Leh**
voir aussi Islām Girāy; Ḳamāniča; Köprülü; Lipḳa; Muslimūn.I.A.1; *et* → EMPIRE OTTOMAN

PORTUGAL **Burtuḳāl**; Gharb al-Andalus
voir aussi Ḥabesh; *et* → ESPAGNE
toponymes Bādja; Ḳulumriya; al-Maʿdin; Mīrtula; Shantamariyyat al-Gharb; Shantarīn; Shilb; Shintara

PRÉDESTINATION Adjal; Allāh.II.B; Iḍṭirār; Ikhtiyār; Istiṭāʿa; **al-Ḳaḍāʾ wa-l-Ḳadar**; Ḳadariyya; Kasb; Ḳisma
voir aussi ʿAbd al-Razzāḳ al-Ḳāshānī; Badāʾ; Dahr; Duʿāʾ.II.b; Ḳaḍāʾ; Shaḳāwa
adversaires Ghaylān b. Muslim; **Ḳadariyya**; Ḳatāda b. Diʿāma; Maʿbad al-Djuhanī
avocats Djabriyya; Djahmiyya; al-Karābīsī.2; Sulaymān b. Djarīr al-Raḳḳī

PRESSE **Djarīda**; Maḳāla; **Maṭbaʿa**; **Ṣiḥāfa**
arabe ʿArabiyya.B.V.a; Baghdād (934a); Būlāḳ; **Djarīda**.I; Ḳiṣṣa.II; Maḳāla.1;

al-Manār; **Maṭbaʿa**.I; al-Rāʾid al-Tūnusī; **Ṣiḥāfa**
voir aussi Nahḍa
journalisme Abū Naḍḍāra; al-Bārūnī; Djabrān Khalīl Djabrān; Djamāl al-Dīn al-Afghānī; Djamīl al-Mudawwar; Fāris al-Shidyāḳ; Ibn Bādīs; Isḥāḳ, Adīb; al-Kawākibī; al-Khaḍir; Khalīl Ghānim; Khalīl Muṭrān; Kurd ʿAlī; Luṭfī al-Sayyid; al-Maʿlūf; Mandūr; al-Manūfī.VII; al-Māzinī; Muṣṭafā ʿAbd al-Rāziḳ; al-Muwayliḥī; al-Nadīm, ʿAbd Allāh; Nadjīb b. Sulaymān al-Ḥaddād; Nimr; Rashīd Riḍā; Ṣafar; Saʿīd Abū Bakr; Salāma Mūsā; Salīm al-Naḳḳāsh; Ṣarrūf; Shāʾūl, Anwar; Shaykhū; Shīnā; Shumayyil, Shiblī; [au Suppl.] Abū Shādī; al-Bustānī
voir aussi al-Mahdjar
indienne **Maṭbaʿa**.IV; [au Suppl.] **Djarīda**.VII
journalisme Muḥammad ʿAlī; Ruswā; Shabbīr Ḥasan Khān Djosh; [au Suppl.] Āzād; Ḥasrat Mohānī
voir aussi Nadwat al-ʿUlamāʾ
persane **Djarīda**.II; Maḳāla; **Maṭbaʿa**.III
journalisme Furūghī.III; Lāhūtī; Malkom Khān; Rashīd Yāsimī; [au Suppl.] Amīrī
turque **Djarīda**.III; Djemʿiyyet-i ʿIlmiyye i ʿOthmāniyye; Ibrāhīm Müteferriḳa; Maḳāla; **Maṭbaʿa**.II; Meshʿale; Mīzān
voir aussi Ādharī.II
journalisme Aḥmad Iḥsān; Aḥmad Midḥat; Djewdet; Ebüzziya Tevfik; Gasprali̊ (Gasprinski), Ismāʿīl; Ḥasan Fehmī; (Aḥmed) Ḥilmī; Hisar; Ḥusayn Djāhid; Ileri, Djelāl Nūrī; Inal; Ḳaṣāb; al-Kāẓimī, Meḥmed Sālim; Kemāl; Kemāl, Meḥmed Nāmi̊ḳ; Khālid Ḍiyāʾ; Köprülü (Meḥmed Fuad); Manāsti̊rli̊ Meḥmed Rifʿat; Meḥmed ʿĀkif; Mīzāndji̊ Meḥmed Murād; Örik, Nahīd Ṣirrī; Orkhan Seyfī; Ortač, Yūsuf Ḍiyā; Ri̊ḍā Nūr; Sāhir, Djelal; Sāmī; Shināsī; Suʿāwī; [au Suppl.] Aghaoghlu; Atay; Čaylaḳ Tewfīḳ; Eshref
voir aussi Badrkhānī; Fedjr-i Ātī; Khalīl Ghānim; Saʿīd Efendi

PRIÈRE Adhān; Djumʿa; Dhikr; **Duʿāʾ**; Fātiḥa; Iḳāma; Khaṭīb; Khuṭba; Ḳibla; Ḳunūt; Ḳuʿūd; Maḥyā; Masdjid; Miḥrāb; Mīḳāt; Muṣallā; Rakʿa; Rātib; **Ṣalāt**; Ṣalāt al-Khawf; Subḥa; Sutra
voir aussi Amīn; Dikka; Ghāʾib; Gulbāng; Istiʾnāf; Maḳām Ibrāhīm; al-Masḥ ʿalā l-Khuffayn; Namāzgāh; *et* → ABLUTION; ARCHITECTURE.MOSQUÉES; ISLAM
de demande Istisḳāʾ; Munāshada
inclination Sadjda
tapis Sadjdjāda

PROFESSIONS al-ʿAṭṭār; Baḳḳāl; Bayṭār; Dallāl; Djānbāz; Djarrāḥ; Ḥammāl; Kannās; Kātib; Ḳayn; Ḳayna; Khayyāṭ; Mukārī; Munādī; Munadjdjim; al-

Nassā<u>dj</u>; Ṣabbā<u>gh</u>; Ṣā'i<u>gh</u>; Saḳḳā'; Sāsān; <u>Sh</u>aʿba<u>dh</u>a; <u>Sh</u>āʿir; <u>Sh</u>ammāʿ; [au Suppl.] Dabbā<u>gh</u>; <u>Dj</u>ammāl; <u>Dj</u>azzār; Faṣṣād; <u>Gh</u>assāl; Ḥā'ik; Ḥallāḳ
voir aussi Asad Allāh Iṣfahānī; Aywaz.I; <u>Kh</u>ādim; <u>Sh</u>āwiya; Ṣinf; *et* → DROIT.FONCTIONS; MILITAIRES.FONCTIONS

métier **Ṣināʿa**

producteurs et commerçants

artisans Ṣabbā<u>gh</u>; Ṣā'i<u>gh</u>; [au Suppl.] Ḥā'ik

artistes <u>Dj</u>ānbāz; Ḳayna; <u>Sh</u>āʿir.1.E
voir aussi al-Sīm

marchands al-ʿAṭṭār; Baḳḳāl; Mukārī; [au Suppl.] <u>Dj</u>ammāl

ouvriers Ḥammāl; Kannās; Ḳayn; <u>Kh</u>ayyāṭ; <u>Sh</u>ammāʿ; [au Suppl.] Dabbā<u>gh</u>; <u>Dj</u>azzār; <u>Gh</u>assāl; Ḥallāḳ

PROPHÉTAT **Nubuwwa**; Rasūl
et → MUḤAMMAD, LE PROPHÈTE

prophètes Ādam; Alīsaʿ; Ḥā-Mīm; Hārūn b. ʿImrān; Hūd; Ibrāhīm; Idrīs; Lūṭ; Muḥammad; Mūsā; Nūḥ; Sa<u>dj</u>āḥ; Ṣāliḥ; <u>Sh</u>aʿyā; <u>Sh</u>ī<u>th</u>; <u>Sh</u>uʿayb
voir aussi Fatra; ʿIṣma; <u>Kh</u>ālid b. Sinān; al-Kisā'ī; Ḳiṣaṣ al-Anbiyā'; Luḳmān; *et* → MUḤAMMAD, LE PROPHÈTE

PROPRIÉTÉ **Māl**; Milk; [au Suppl.] ʿAḳār
voir aussi Munāṣafa; <u>Sh</u>ufʿa; Soyūr<u>gh</u>āl; *et* → TAXATION.IMPÔTS

PROVERBES **Mathal**; al-Maydānī
voir aussi Iyās b. Muʿāwiya; Nār; *et* → ANIMAUX.ET PROVERBES; LITTÉRATURE

Q

QATAR al-Dawḥa; Hā<u>dj</u>ir; **Ḳaṭar**; Ma<u>dj</u>lis.IV.A.11; Maḥkama.IV.9

R

RAIDS Baranta; <u>Gh</u>anīma; **<u>Gh</u>azw**
et → BÉDOUINS; MILITAIRES.EXPÉDITIONS

RÉCRÉATION Cinématographe; Ḳaragöz; <u>Kh</u>ayāl al-Ẓill; Masraḥ; Orta Oyunu

jeux <u>Dj</u>erīd; <u>Kh</u>arbga; Ḳimār; **Laʿib**; al-Maysir; Mu<u>kh</u>āra<u>dj</u>a; Nard; <u>Sh</u>aṭran<u>dj</u>
voir aussi I<u>sh</u>āra; Kurdes et Kurdistān.IV.C.5; Maydān; *et* → ANIMAUX.SPORT

sport Čawgān; Pahlawān

RÉFORME Djamʿiyya; **Iṣlāḥ**
voir aussi Baladiyya; Ḥukūma; al-Manār; *et* → FEMMES.ÉMANCIPATION DES
d'éducation Aḥmad Djewdet Pasha; Aḥmad Khān; al-Azhar.IV; Ḥabīb Allāh Khān; Maʿārif; Münīf Pasha; Nadwat al-ʿUlamāʾ; [au Suppl.] al-ʿAdawī
voir aussi al-Marṣafī
financière Muḥaṣṣil
judiciaire Abū l-Suʿūd; Aḥmad Djewdet Pasha; Küčük Saʿīd Pasha; Medjelle; Mīrāth.II; Nikāḥ.II; al-Sanhūrī, ʿAbd al-Razzāḳ
voir aussi Djazāʾ; Ileri, Djelāl Nūrī; Imtiyāzāt.IV; Khayr al-Dīn Pasha; Maḥkama
militaire Niẓām-i̊ Djedīd
numismatique → NUMISMATIQUE
politico-religieuse Atatürk; Djamāl al-Dīn al-Afghānī; Ileri, Djelāl Nūrī; Ibn Bādīs; (al-)Ibrāhīmī; Ismāʿīl Ṣidḳī; Ḳāsim Amīn; Khayr al-Dīn Pasha; Midḥat Pasha; Muḥammad ʿAbduh; Muḥammad Bayram al-Khāmis; Nurculuk; Padri; Rashīd Riḍā; Shaltūt, Maḥmūd; al-Subkiyyūn; [au Suppl.] ʿAbd al-Nāṣir
voir aussi Baladiyya; Bast; Djamʿiyya; Dustūr; Ḥarbiye; Ibrāhīm Müteferriḳa; al-Ikhwān al-Muslimūn; Iṣlāḥ; Mappila.5.b; Salafiyya; Shaʿb; al-Shawkānī; [au Suppl.] Abu l-ʿAzāʾim; *et* → POLITIQUE
militante al-Bannāʾ; Fidāʾiyyān-i Islām; Ḥamāliyya; Ibn Bādīs; al-Ikhwān al-Muslimūn; Mawdūdī; Sayyid Ḳuṭb
voir aussi Ibn al-Muwaḳḳit; Mudjāhid; [au Suppl.] al-Djanbīhī

RELIGION ʿAḳīda; **Dīn**; al-Milal wa-l-Niḥal; Milla; Millet.1
voir aussi Ḥanīf; *et* → CHRISTIANISME; ISLAM; JUDAÏSME
autres que les trois principales Bābīs; Bahāʾīs; Barāhima; Budd; Dhū l-Sharā; Djayn; Gabr; Hindū; Ibāḥatiya; Ṣābiʾ; Ṣābiʾa; al-Sāmira; Sikhs; Sumaniyya
voir aussi Aghāthūdhīmūn; Bakhshī; al-Barāmika.1; Hirmis; Hurmuz; Khʷādja Khiḍr; Kitāb al-Djilwa; Mānī; al-Milal wa-l-Niḥal; Millet; Nānak; al-Shahrastānī, Tādj al-dīn; *et* → BAHĀʾĪS; DRUZES; ZOROASTRIENS
panthéisme ʿAmr b. Luḥayy; Djāhiliyya; Kaʿba.V
voir aussi Ḥarīriyya; Ḥadjdj.I; Ibn al-ʿArabī; Ibn al-ʿArīf; Kāfiristān; Kamāl Khudjandī; *et* → PÉRIODE PRÉISLAMIQUE.DIEUX
populaire → ISLAM.CROYANCES POPULAIRES

RÊVES **Ruʾyā**
voir aussi Istikhāra; Nubuwwa; *et les articles individuels sur les animaux, en particulier* Ayyil; Baghl; Ḍabb; Fīl; Ghurāb; Saraṭān.V
traités sur al-Dīnawarī, Abū Saʿīd; Ibn Ghannām; Ibn Shāhīn al-Ẓāhirī; Ibn Sīrīn

RHÉTORIQUE Badīʿ; Balāgha; Bayān; Faṣāḥa; Ḥaḳīḳa.1; Ibtidāʾ; Idjāza; Iḳtibās;

Intihāʾ; Istiʿāra; Kināya; al-Maʿānī wa-l-Bayān; Madjāz; Mubālagha; Muḳābala.3; Muwāraba; Muzāwadja; Muzdawidj; Ramz.1
voir aussi Ishāra
traités sur al-ʿAskarī.II; Ḥāzim; Ibn al-Muʿtazz; al-Ḳazwīnī (Khaṭīb Dimashḳ); al-Rādūyānī; al-Sakkākī; al-Sidjilmāsī; [au Suppl.] al-Djurdjānī; Ibn Wahb

RIME **Kāfiya**; Luzūm mā lā yalzam
et → LITTÉRATURE.POÉSIE; MÉTRIQUE

RITUELS ʿAḳīḳa; ʿAnṣāra; ʿĀshūrāʾ; Khitān; Rawḍa-khʷānī
voir aussi Bakkāʾ; Ḥammām; ʿIbādāt; al-Maghrib.VI; [au Suppl.] Dam; *et* → COUTUMES

RIVIÈRES **Nahr**
voir aussi Maʾṣir; *et* → NAVIGATION
eaux al-ʿAḍaym; ʿAfrīn; Alindjaḳ; al-ʿAlḳamī; Āmū Daryā; al-ʿĀṣī; Atbara; Atrek; Baḥr al-Ghazāl.1; Baradā; Čaghān-rūd; Congo; Čoruh; Ču; Darʿa; Dawʿan; Dehās; Didjla; Diyālā; Djamnā; Djayḥān; al-Furāt; Gangā; Gediz Čayi̊; Göksu; al-Ḥamma; Harī Rūd; Ibruh; Ili; Isly; Itil; Kābul.I; Karkha; Kārūn; Khābūr; Khalkha; al-Khāzir; Ḳi̊zi̊l İrmāḳ; Ḳi̊zi̊l-üzen; Ḳuban; Ḳunduz; Kur; Kurram; Lamas-ṣū; Mānd; Menderes; Merič; Mihrān; al-Mudawwar; Nahr Abī Fuṭrus; Niger; al-Nīl; Ob; Orkhon; Özi; al-Rass; Safīd Rūd; Saḳārya; Sandja; Sayḥān; Shaṭṭ al-ʿArab; Shebelle; Si̊r Daryā; [au Suppl.] Gūmāl
voir aussi Hind.I.j; ʿĪsā, Nahr; *et l'entrée Géographie Physique sous les pays individuels*

ROUMANIE Ada Ḳalʿe; Babadaghi̊; Bender; Boghdān; Budjāḳ; Bükresh; Deli-Orman; Dobrudja; Eflāḳ; Erdel; Ibrail; Isakča; Köstendje; Medjīdiyye; Nagyvárad
voir aussi Muslimūn.I.B.2

RUSSIE → EUROPE.EUROPE ORIENTALE

S

SACRIFICES ʿAḳīḳa; ʿAtīra; Baliyya; Dhabīḥa; Fidya; Hady; Ḳurbān; Shiʿār.b et c
voir aussi Ibil; ʿĪd al-Aḍḥā; Kaffāra; Nadhr; [au Suppl.] Dam

SAINT Mawlid
voir aussi ʿAbābda; Mawlā.I; *et* → CHRISTIANISME; HAGIOGRAPHIE; MYSTICISME

saints
africains Shaykh Ḥusayn
arabes Aḥmad b. ʿĪsā; Aḥmad al-Badawī; Nafīsa
voir aussi Ḳunā; *et* → Mysticisme
d'Afrique du Nord Abū Muḥammad Ṣāliḥ; Abū Yaʿazzā; ʿĀʾisha al-Mannūbiyya; al-Bādisī.1; al-Daḳḳāḳ; al-Djazūlī, Abū ʿAbd Allāh; Ḥmād u-Mūsā; Ibn ʿArūs; al-Ḳabbāb; Ḳaddūr al-ʿAlamī; al-Khaṣāṣī; Muḥriz b. Khalaf; al-Sabtī; al-Shāwī; [au Suppl.] Ḥamādisha
voir aussi al-Maghrib.VI; Sabʿatu Ridjāl; *et* → Mysticisme
d'Asie centrale Aḥmad Yasawī
indiens Abū ʿAlī Ḳalandar; Ashraf Djahangīr; Badīʿ al-Dīn; Badr; Bahāʾ al-Dīn Zakariyyā; Čishtī; Farīd al-Dīn Masʿūd "Gandj-i Shakar"; Ghāzī Miyān; Gīsū Darāz; Imām Shāh; Khwādja Khiḍr; Maghribī; Makhdūm al-Mulk; Masʿūd, Sayyid Sālār; Niẓām al-Dīn Awliyāʾ; Nūr Ḳuṭb al-ʿĀlam; Ratan; Shāh Muḥammad b. ʿAbd Aḥmad; [au Suppl.] Bābā Nūr al-Dīn Rishī; Gadāʾī Kambō; Gangōhī; Ḥamīd al-Dīn Ḳāḍī Nāgawrī; Ḥamīd al-Dīn Ṣūfī Nāgawrī Siwālī
voir aussi Ḥasan Abdāl; Pāk Pātan
persans ʿAlī al-Hamadhānī; Bābā-Ṭāhir
turcs Akhī Ewrān; Emīr Sulṭān; Ḥādjdjī Bayrām Walī; Ḥakīm Ata; Ḳoyun Baba; Merkez; Ṣarī Ṣalṭuḳ Dede
termes Abdāl; Ilhām

Sciences **ʿIlm**; Mawṣūʿa
voir aussi Ibn Abī Uṣaybiʿa; Shumayyil, Shiblī; [au Suppl.] al-Bustānī; Ibn al-Akfānī.III; Ibn Farīghūn; *et* → Alchimie; Astrologie; Astronomie; Botanique; Mathématiques; Mécanique; Médecine; Optique; Pharmacologie; Zoologie

Sciences Naturelles **al-Āthār al-ʿUlwiyya**; **Ḥikma**; Masāʾil wa-Adjwiba
voir aussi Nūr.1
scientifiques al-Bīrūnī; al-Dimashḳī; Ibn Bādjdja; Ibn al-Haytham; Ibn Rushd; Ibn Sīnā; Ikhwān al-Ṣafāʾ; al-Ḳazwīnī; al-Marwazī, Sharaf al-zamān
et → Alchimie; Astronomie; Botanique; Métaphysique; Zoologie

Sectes ʿAdjārida; Ahl-i Ḥadīth; Ahl-i Ḥaḳḳ; Aḥmadiyya; ʿAlides; Azāriḳa; al-Badjalī; Baḳliyya; Bihʾāfrīd b. Farwardīn; Bohorās; Burghūthiyya; Djabriyya; Djahmiyya; al-Djanāḥiyya; al-Djārūdiyya; Durūz; Farāʾiḍiyya; Ghurābiyya; Ḥarīriyya; Ḥashīshiyya; Ḥulmāniyya; Ḥurūfiyya; al-Ibāḍiyya; Ḳarmaṭī; Karrāmiyya; Kaysāniyya; al-Khalafiyya; Khāridjites; Khashabiyya; Khaṭṭābiyya; Khōdja; Khūbmesīḥī; Khurramiyya; Kuraybiyya; Mahdawī; Manṣūriyya; al-Mughīriyya; Muḥammadiyya; Mukhammisa; Muṭarrifiyya; al-

Muʿtazila; Nadjadāt; Nāwūsiyya; al-Nukkār; Nuḵṭawiyya; Nūrbaḵẖshiyya; Nuṣayriyya; al-Rāwandiyya; Rawshaniyya; Salmāniyya; Ṣārliyya; Satpanthīs; Shabak; Shābāshiyya; Shayḵẖiyya; Shumayṭiyya; Ṣufriyya; [au Suppl.] Dhikris

voir aussi Abū l-Maʿālī; al-Aḥsāʾī; ʿAlī Ilāhī; Bābāʾī; Bābīs; Bāyazīd Anṣārī; Bīsharʿ; Dahriyya; al-Dhammiyya; Dīn-i Ilāhī; Ghassāniyya; Ghulāt; Ḥā-Mīm; Imām Shāh; ʿIrāḳ.VI; Kasrawī Tabrīzī; al-Kayyāl; Kāẓim Rashtī; Ḳizil-bāsh; al-Malaṭī; Mazdak; Mudjtahid.III; Sālimiyya; Sulṭān Sehāk; *et* → MYSTI-CISME.CONFRÉRIES

ʿAlides ʿAbd Allāh b. Muʿāwiya; Abū ʿAbd Allāh Yaʿḳūb; Abū l-Aswad al-Duʾalī; Abū Hāshim; Abū Nuʿaym al-Mulāʾī; Abū Salama al-Khallāl; Abū l-Sarāyā al-Shaybānī; ʿAlī b. Muḥammad al-Zandjī; **ʿAlides**; al-Djawwānī; Hāniʾ b. ʿUrwa al-Murādī; al-Ḥasan b. Zayd b. Muḥammad; Ḥasan al-Uṭrūsh; Ḥudjr b. ʿAdī; al-Ḥusayn b. ʿAlī, Ṣāḥib Faḵẖḵẖ; Ibrāhīm b. al-Ashtar; Khidāsh; Muḥammad b. ʿAbd Allāh (al-Nafs al-Zakiyya); al-Mukhtār b. Abī ʿUbayd; Muslim b. ʿAḳīl b. Abī Ṭālib; Sulaym b. Ḳays; Sulaymān b. Ṣurad

voir aussi Dhū l-Faḳār; al-Djanāḥiyya; al-Djārūdiyya; Ghadīr Khumm; al-Maʾmūn; Sharīf; *et* → CHIITES

Bābisme Bāb; **Bābīs**; Kāshānī; Ḳurrat al-ʿAyn; Maẓhar; Muḥammad ʿAlī Bārfurūshī; Muḥammad ʿAlī Zandjānī; Muḥammad Ḥusayn Bushrūʾī; Ṣubḥ-i Azal

voir aussi al-Aḥsāʾī; Mudjtahid.III; Nuḵṭat al-Kāf; Sābiḳūn

Chiites → CHIITES

Druzes → DRUZES

Ibāḍites ʿAbd al-ʿAzīz b. al-Ḥādjdj Ibrāhīm; Abū Ghānim; Abū Ḥafṣ ʿUmar b. Djamīʿ; Abū Ḥātim al-Malzūzī (*et* al-Malzūzī); Abū l-Khaṭṭāb al-Maʿāfirī; Abū Muḥammad al-ʿUmānī; Abū l-Muʾthir; Abū Zakariyyāʾ al-Djanāwunī; Abū Zakariyyāʾ al-Wardjilānī; Aṭfiyāsh; al-Barrādī; al-Bārūnī; al-Bughṭūrī; al-Dardjīnī; Djābir b. Zayd; al-Djayṭālī; al-Djulandā; **al-Ibāḍiyya**; Ibn Baraka; Ibn Djaʿfar; al-Irdjānī; al-Lawātī; Maḥbūb b. al-Raḥīl; al-Mazātī; al-Nafūsī; al-Shammaḵẖī; [au Suppl.] Abū ʿAmmār; al-Ḥārithī

voir aussi al-ʿAwāmir; Azd; Ḥalḳa; al-Khalafiyya; Kharūs; *et* → DROIT; DYNASTIES.ESPAGNE ET AFRIQUE DU NORD.RUSTAMIDES; SECTES.KHĀRI-DJITES

historiens Abū l-Muʾthir; Abū Zakariyyāʾ al-Wardjilānī; al-Barrādī; al-Bughṭūrī; al-Dardjīnī; Ibn al-Ṣaghīr; Ibn Salām; al-Lawātī; Maḥbūb b. al-Raḥīl; al-Mazātī; al-Sālimī

voir aussi al-Nafūsī

juives → JUDAÏSME

Khāridjites Abū Bayhas; Abū Fudayk; Abū Yazīd al-Nukkārī; al-Ḍaḥḥāk b. Ḳays al-Shaybānī; Ḥurḳūṣ b. Zuhayr al-Saʿdī; ʿImrān b. Ḥiṭṭān; Ḳaṭarī b. al-

Fudjā'a; **Khāridjites**; Ḳurrā'; Ḳu'ūd; Mirdās b. Udayya; Nāfi' b. al-Azraḳ; al-Nukkār; Shabīb b. Yazīd
voir aussi 'Adjārida; Azāriḳa; Ḥarūrā'; al-Ibāḍiyya; Ibn Muldjam; Imāma; Isti'rāḍ; al-Manṣūr bi-llāh; Nadjadāt; Ṣufriyya
Uṣūlīs Mudjtahid.III

SÉDENTARISATION Sārt
voir aussi Sha'b.1; *et* → ARCHITECTURE.URBAINE; GÉOGRAPHIE.URBAINE

SÉNÉGAL Djolof; **Sénégal**
voir aussi Murīdiyya
toponymes [au Suppl.] Dakar

SEXUALITÉ 'Azl; Bāh; Djins; Khitān; Liwāṭ; Siḥāḳ; [au Suppl.] Bighā'
voir aussi Djanāba; Khāṣī

SHIITES → CHIITES

SIBÉRIE **Sibīr**
géographie physique
eaux Ob
population Bukhārlïk

SICILE Benavert; Ibn al-Ḥawwās; Ibn al-Khayyāṭ; Ibn al-Thumna; Kalbides; **Ṣiḳilliyya**
voir aussi Aghlabides.III; Asad b. al-Furāt; Fāṭimides; Ibn Ḥamdīs; Ibn al-Ḳaṭṭā'; Ibn Makkī
toponymes Balarm; Benavent; Djirdjent; Ḳaṣryānnih; Siraḳusa
voir aussi al-Khāliṣa

SOMALIE **Somali**
voir aussi Ḥabesh; Muḥammad b. 'Abd Allāh Ḥassān; Ogādēn
confréries Ṣāliḥiyya
voir aussi Somali.4
toponymes
régions Guardafui
voir aussi Ogādēn
villes Barawa; Berberā; Hargeisa; Maḳdishū; Merka; Shungwaya

SOUDAN Dār Fūr; Dustūr.XIII; Ḥizb.I; Madjlis.IV.A.17; al-Mahdiyya; **Sūdān**
voir aussi Baladiyya.II; Fundj; Ḥabesh; Nūba
confréries Mīrghaniyya

géographie physique
eaux al-Nīl
période mahdiste ʿAbd Allāh b. Muḥammad al-Taʿāʾishī; Khalīfa.IV; **al-Mahdiyya**
voir aussi Awlād al-Balad; Dār Fūr; Emīn Pasha; Rābiḥ b. Faḍl Allāh
population ʿAbābda; ʿAlwa; (Banū) ʿĀmir; Baḳḳāra; Barābra; Djaʿaliyyūn; Ghuzz.III; Nūba.IV; Rashāʾida; Shāyḳiyya
voir aussi Fallāta
toponymes
anciens ʿAydhāb; Sōba
actuels
provinces Baḥr al-Ghazāl.3; Berber.2; Dār Fūr; Fāshōda; Kasala
régions Fāzūghlī; Kordofān
villes Atbara; Berber.3; Dongola; al-Fāshir; Kasala; Ḳerrī; al-Khurṭūm; Omdurman; Sawākin; Shandī; Sinnār

SRI LANKA **Ceylan**; Sarandīb
et → INDE.POPULATION.TAMILS

SUPERSTITION ʿAyn; Faʾl; Ghurāb; Ḥinnāʾ; Khamsa; Ṣadā
voir aussi ʿAḳīḳ; Bāriḥ; Laḳab

SYRIE **al-Shaʾm**
et → LIBAN
architecture → ARCHITECTURE.RÉGIONS
avant l'Islam → PÉRIODE PRÉISLAMIQUE.DANS LE CROISSANT FERTILE
dynasties ʿAmmār; Ayyūbides; Būrides; Fāṭimides; Ḥamdānides; Mamlūks
voir aussi [au Suppl.] al-Djazzār Pasha; *et* → DYNASTIES.ÉGYPTE ET LE CROISSANT FERTILE; LIBAN
géographie physique al-Shaʾm.1
eaux ʿAfrīn; al-ʿĀṣī; Baradā
montagnes Ḳāsiyūn; al-Lukkām
historiens al-ʿAẓīmī; Ibn Abī Ṭayyiʾ; Ibn al-ʿAdīm; Ibn ʿAsākir; Ibn al-Ḳalānisī; Ibn Kathīr; Ibn Shaddād; Kurd ʿAlī; al-Kutubī
et → DYNASTIES.ÉGYPTE ET LE CROISSANT FERTILE
période moderne Djarīda.I.A; Djāmiʿa; Dustūr.IX; Ḥizb.I; Ḥukūma.III; Madjlis.IV.A.5; Madjmaʿ ʿIlmī.I.II.1; Maḥkama.IV.2; Mandats; Maysalūn; Salafiyya.2.b; al-Shaʾm.2, sp. (b) et (c)
voir aussi Baladiyya.II; Kurd ʿAlī; Mardam.II; [au Suppl.] Démographie.III
hommes d'état al-Khūrī; Mardam.I
toponymes
anciens Afāmiya; ʿArbān; al-Bakhrāʾ; al-Bāra; Barḳaʿīd; Dābiḳ; Diyār

Muḍar; Diyār Rabīʿa; al-Djābiya; al-Djazīra; Djilliķ; Manbidj; Namāra.I; al-Raḥba; Raʾs al-ʿAyn; Rīḥā.2; al-Ruṣāfa.3; Shayzar

actuels

districts al-Bathaniyya; al-Djawlān

régions al-Ghāb; Ḥawrān; Ķinnasrīn; Ladjāʾ; al-Ṣafā.2

voir aussi Ghūṭa

villes Adhriʿāt; Bāniyās; Boṣrā; Buzāʿā; Dayr al-Zōr; Dimashķ; Djabala; al-Djabbūl; Djisr al-Shughr; Ḥalab; Ḥamāt; Ḥārim; Ḥimṣ; Ḥuwwārīn; Ķanawāt; Ķarķīsiyā; Khawlān; Ķinnasrīn; al-Ladhiķiyya; Maʿarrat Maṣrīn; Maʿarrat al-Nuʿmān; Maʿlūlā; Maskana; Maṣyād; al-Mizza; Namāra.II et III; al-Raķķa; Ṣāfītha; Salamiyya; Ṣalkhad

voir aussi al-Marķab

T

TANZANIE Dar-es-Salaam; Kilwa; Mikindani; Mkwaja; Mtambwe Mkuu

TAXATION Bādj; **Bayt al-Māl**; Ḍarība; Djizya; Ķānūn.II; Kharādj; [au Suppl.] Ḍarība.VII

voir aussi Ḍabṭ; Djahbadh; Māʾ; Maʾṣir; Raʿiyya

impôts ʿArūs Resmi; ʿAwāriḍ; Bād-i Hawā; Badal; Bādj; Djawālī; Djizya; Filori; Furḍa; Ispendje; Ķūbčūr; Maks; Mālikāne; Muķāṭaʿa; Pīshkash; Resm

voir aussi Ḥisba.II; Ķatīʿa

impôts fonciers Bashmaķlïķ; Bennāk; Čift-resmi; **Kharādj**, Mīrī; Muķāsama

voir aussi Daftar; Daftar-ı Khaķānī; Ķabāla, Rawk

percepteurs ʿĀmil; Dihķan; Muhaṣṣil; Mültezim; Mustakhridj

voir aussi Amīr

terres de dîme Ḍayʿa; Īghār; Iķṭaʿ; Iltizām; Khāliṣa; Khāṣṣ; Ṣafī

voir aussi Baʿl.2.b; Dār al-ʿAhd; Fayʾ; Filāḥa.IV

traités fiscaux al-Makhzūmī

TCHAD Abeshr; Bagirmi; Borkou; Kanem; Kanuri; [au Suppl.] **Čad**

et → AFRIQUE.AFRIQUE CENTRALE

(ex-)TCHÉCOSLOVAQUIE [au Suppl.] **Čeh**

TEINTURE ʿAfṣ; Ḥinnāʾ; Ķalamkārī; **Khiḍāb**; Nīl

voir aussi Shaʿr.1

teinturier **Ṣabbāgh**

TEMPS Abad; Dahr; Ķidam

voir aussi Ibn al-Sāʿātī
calcul Anwāʾ; al-Ḳamar; Mīḳāt; Mizwala; Sāʿa.1
voir aussi Asṭurlāb; Ayyām al-ʿAdjūz; Hilāl.I; Rubʿ
calendriers Djalālī; Hidjra; Nasīʾ; [au Suppl.] Ilāhī
voir aussi Nawrūz; Rabīʿ b. Zayd; Sulaymān al-Mahrī
jour et nuit ʿAṣr; ʿAtama; Layl et Nahār; al-Shafaḳ
jours de la semaine Djumʿa; Sabt
mois
voir aussi al-Ḳamar
islamiques al-Muḥarram; Rabīʿ; Radjab; Ramaḍān; Ṣafar; Shaʿbān; Shawwāl
syriaques Nīsān
turques Odjaḳ

TERRE → TAXATION
pour l'agriculture, voir Filāḥa
pour le métrage, voir Misāḥa; Rawk

THAÏLANDE Patani

THÉOLOGIE ʿAḳīda; Allāh; Dīn; Djanna; **ʿIlm al-Kalām**; Imāma; Īmān; Kalām; al-Mahdī
voir aussi ʿĀlam.1; Hilāl.I; *et* → ISLAM
débats Masāʾil wa-Adjwiba; Munāẓara; Radd; [au Suppl.] ʿIbādat Khāna
voir aussi Mubāhala
traités sur al-Samarḳandī, Shams al-dīn
écoles
chiites Ismāʿīliyya; Ithnā ʿAshariyya; Ḳarmaṭī; [au Suppl.] Akhbāriyya
voir aussi Muʿtazila
sunnites Ashʿariyya; Ḥanābila; Māturīdiyya; Muʿtazila
voir aussi ʿIlm al-Kalām.II; Ḳadariyya; Karāmat ʿAlī; Murdjiʾa; al-Nadjdjāriyya
termes Adjal; Adjr; ʿAdl; ʿAhd; Ahl al-ahwāʾ; Ahl al-Kitāb; Ākhira; ʿAḳīda; ʿAḳl; ʿAḳliyyāt; ʿĀlam.2.; ʿAmal.2; Amr; al-Aṣlaḥ; Baʿth; Bāṭiniyya; Bidʿa; Birr; Daʿwa; Dīn; Djamāʿa; Djazāʾ; Djism; Duʿāʾ; Fard; Fāsiḳ; Fiʿl; Fitna; Fiṭra; al-Ghayb; Ghayba; Ghufrān; Ḥadd; Ḥaḳḳ; Ḥaraka wa-Sukūn.I.2 et 3; Ḥisāb; Ḥudjdja; Ḥudūth al-ʿĀlam; Ḥulūl; Iʿdjāz; Iḍṭirār; Ikhlāṣ; Ikhtiyār; ʿIlla.II.III; Imāma; Īmān; Islām; ʿIṣma; Istiṭāʿa; Ittiḥād; al-Ḳaḍāʾ wa-l-Ḳadar; Kaffāra; Kāfir; Kalima; Karāma; Kasb; Kashf; Khalḳ; Khaṭīʾa; Khidhlān; Ḳidam; Kumūn; Ḳunūt; Ḳuwwa; Luṭf; Maʿād; al-Mahdī; al-Manzila bayn al-Manzilatayn; al-Munāfiḳūn.2; Murtadd; Muṭlaḳ; Nāfila; Nafs; Nāmūs.1; Nūr Muḥammadī; Riyāʾ; Rizḳ; Rudjūʿ; Ruʾyat Allāh; Sabīl.1; Shubha; Ṣifa.2; [au Suppl.] Ḥāl

voir aussi Abad; Allāh.II; In Shā' Allāh; 'Ināya; Ṣūra; *et* → CORAN.TERMES; ESCHATOLOGIE

chiites Badā'; Ghayba; Ibdā'; Kashf; Lāhūt et Nāsūt.V; Maẓhar; Maẓlūm; al-Munāfiḳūn.2; Naḳḍ al-Mīthāḳ; Radj'a; al-Sābiḳūn; Safīr.1; al-Ṣāmit; Sarkār Āḳā

et → CHIITES.DOCTRINES ET INSTITUTIONS

théologiens

voir aussi Sharḥ.III

théologiens primitifs Djahm b. Ṣafwān; al-Ḥasan al-Baṣrī; [au Suppl.] al-Aṣamm; (al-)Ḥasan b. Muḥammad Ibn al-Ḥanafiyya; Ibn Kullāb

ash'arites al-Amidī; al-Ash'arī, Abū l-Ḥasan; al-Baghdādī, 'Abd al-Ḳāhir; al-Bāḳillānī; al-Bayhaḳī; al-Djuwaynī; al-Faḍālī; Fakhr al-Dīn al-Rāzī; al-Ghazālī, Abū Ḥāmid; Ibn Fūrak; al-Īdjī; al-Isfarāyīnī; al-Kiyā al-Harrāsī; al-Ḳushayrī; al-Sanūsī, Abū 'Abd Allāh; al-Simnānī

voir aussi Allāh.II; 'Ilm al-Kalām.II.C; Imāma; Īmān; [au Suppl.] Ḥāl

chiites → CHIITES

ḥanbalites 'Abd al-Ḳādir al-Djīlānī; Aḥmad b. Ḥanbal; al-Anṣārī al-Harawī; al-Barbahārī; Ibn 'Abd al-Wahhāb; Ibn 'Aḳīl; Ibn Baṭṭa al-'Ukbarī; Ibn al-Djawzī; Ibn Ḳayyim al-Djawziyya; Ibn Ḳudāma al-Maḳdisī; Ibn Taymiyya; al-Khallāl

voir aussi Īmān; *et* → DROIT

māturīdites 'Abd al-Ḥayy; Bishr b. Ghiyāth al-Marīsī; al-Māturīdī

voir aussi Allāh.II; 'Ilm al-Kalām.II.D; Imāma; Īmān

mu'tazilites 'Abbād b. Sulaymān; 'Abd al-Djabbār b. Aḥmad; Abū l-Hudhayl al-'Allāf; Aḥmad b. Abī Du'ād; Aḥmad b. Ḥābiṭ; 'Amr b. 'Ubayd; al-Balkhī; Bishr b. al-Mu'tamir; Dja'far b. Ḥarb; Dja'far b. Mubashshir; al-Djāḥiẓ; al-Djubbā'ī; Hishām b. 'Amr al-Fuwaṭī; Ibn al-Ikhshīd; Ibn Khallād; al-Iskāfī; al-Khayyāṭ; Mu'ammar b. 'Abbād; al-Murdār; al-Nāshi' al-Akbar; al-Naẓẓām; al-Shaḥḥām; [au Suppl.] Abū 'Abd Allāh al-Baṣrī; Abū l-Ḥusayn al-Baṣrī; Abū Rashīd al-Nīsābūrī; Ḍirār b. 'Amr; al-Ḥākim al-Djushamī; Ibn Mattawayh

voir aussi Ahl al-Naẓar; Allāh.II; Ḥafṣ al-Fard; Ibn Abī l-Ḥadīd; Ibn al-Rāwandī; 'Ilm al-Kalām.II.B; Imāma; Khalḳ.V; Lawn; Luṭf; al-Ma'mūn; al-Manzila bayn al-Manzilatayn; [au Suppl.] al-Aṣamm; Ḥāl

wahhābites Ibn 'Abd al-Wahhāb; Ibn Ghannām

indo-musulmans 'Abd al-'Azīz al-Dihlawī; 'Abd al-Ḳādir Dihlawī; Ashraf 'Alī; Baḥr al-'Ulūm; al-Dihlawī, Shāh Walī Allāh; al-'Imrānī; 'Iwaḍ Wadjīh; [au Suppl.] 'Abd Allāh Sulṭānpūrī; Farangī Maḥall

voir aussi Hind.v.b; al-Ma'barī; Mappila; Ṣulḥ-i kull

juifs Ibn Maymūn; Sa'adyā

du 19e et 20e siècles Muḥammad 'Abduh; Muḥammad Abū Zayd

voir aussi Sunna.3

TOGO Kabou; Kubafolo

TRAITÉS Baḳṭ; Küčük Ḳaynardja; Mandats; Mondros; **Muʿāhada**
voir aussi Dār al-ʿAhd; Ḥilf al-Fuḍūl; Mīthāḳ-i Millī
tributs Baḳṭ; Parias
et → TAXATION

TRANSPORT **Naḳl**
et → ANIMAUX.CHAMEAUX *et* ÉQUINES; HÔTELLERIE; NAVIGATION
caravanes Azalay; **Kārwān**; Maḥmal; [au Suppl.] Djammāl
voir aussi Anadolu.III.5; Darb al-Arbaʿīn; Khān
chemins de fer Ḥidjāz; **Sikkat al-Ḥadīd**
voir aussi Anadolu.III.5; al-Ḳāhira (462a); Khurramshahr
défilés Bāb al-Lān; Bībān; Dar-i Āhanīn; Deve Boynu; Khaybar
voir aussi Chitral
postal **Barīd**; Fuyūdj; Ḥamām; Posta; Raḳḳāṣ
voir aussi Anadolu.III.5
timbres **Posta**
véhicules à roues ʿAdjala; ʿAraba

TREMBLEMENTS DE TERRE *voir* Aghrî Dagh; Amasya; Anṭākiya; ʿAshḳābād; Čankîrî; Cilicia; Daybul; Djidjelli; Erzindjan; Ḥarra; Ḥulwān; Istanbul.VI.6; Ḳalhāt; Kāṅgṙā; Ḳazwīn; Kilāt; Nīshāpūr; al-Ramla

TRÉSOR **Bayt al-Māl**; Khazīne; Makhzān
et → ADMINISTRATION.FINANCIÈRE

TRIBUS ʿĀʾila; ʿAshīra; Ḥayy; **Ḳabīla**; Sayyid
voir aussi ʿAṣabiyya; Ḥilf; Khaṭīb; Sharīf.1; Shaykh; [au Suppl.] Bisāṭ.III; *et* → NOMADISME
Afghanistan et Inde Abdālī; Afrīdī; Bhaṭṭi; Čahār Aymaḳ; Dāwūdpōtrās; Djāṫ; Durrānī; Gakkhaṙ; Gandāpur; Ghalzay; Güdjar; Khaṭak; Khokars; Lambadi; Mahsūd; Mēʾō; Mohmand; Mullagori; Sammā; Sumerā; [au Suppl.] Gurčānī
voir aussi Afghān.I; Afghānistān.II
Afrique ʿAbābda; ʿĀmir; Antemuru; Bedja; Beleyn; Bishārīn; Danḳalī; Djaʿaliyyūn; Kunta; Makua; Māryā; Mazrūʿī; Shāyḳiyya
voir aussi Diglal; Fulbe; al-Manāṣīr; Mande
Asie centrale et Mongolie Čāwdors; Dūghlāt; Emreli; Gagauz; Göklän; Ḳarluḳ; Ḳungrāt; Mangît; Mongols; Özbeg; Pečenegs; Salur; Sulduz
voir aussi Ghuzz; Īlāt; Ḳāyî; Khaladj
Croissant fertile
anciens Asad; Bahrāʾ; Djarrāḥides; Djudhām; Muhannā; al-Muntafiḳ.1

actuels   'Anaza; Asad (Banū); Bādjalān; Bilbās; Dafīr; D̲j̲āf; D̲j̲ubūr; Dulaym;
Hamawand; al-Ḥuwayṭāt; Kurdes et Kurdistān.IV.A; Lām; al-Manāṣīr;
al-Muntafiḳ.2; Ṣak̲h̲r; S̲h̲ammar
voir aussi al-Baṭīḥa; S̲h̲āwiya.2

Égypte et Afrique du Nord   'Abābda; Ahaggar; al-Butr; D̲j̲azūla; Dukkāla;
Ifog̲h̲as; K̲h̲ulṭ; Kūmiya; al-Ma'ḳil; Mandīl; Riyāḥ
voir aussi K̲h̲umayr; *et* → BERBÈRES

Iran   Bāzūkiyyūn; Bilbās; D̲j̲āf; Eymir.II et III; (Banū) Ka'b; Ḳarā Gözlu; Kurdes
et Kurdistān.IV.A; Lak; Lām; S̲h̲āhsewan; S̲h̲akāk; S̲h̲aḳāḳī; Sind̲j̲ābī
voir aussi Daylam; Dulafides; Fīrūzānides; Göklän; Īlāt; S̲h̲ūlistān

Péninsule arabique

anciens   'Abd al-Ḳays; al-Abnā'; 'Ād; 'Akk; 'Āmila; 'Āmir b. Ṣa'ṣa'a; al-Aws;
Azd; Bad̲j̲īla; Bāhila; Bakr b. Wā'il; Ḍabba; D̲j̲ad̲h̲īma b. 'Āmir;
D̲j̲urhum; Fazāra; G̲h̲anī b. A'ṣur; G̲h̲assān; G̲h̲aṭafān; G̲h̲ifār; Hamdān;
Ḥanīfa b. Lud̲j̲aym; Ḥanẓala; Ḥārit̲h̲ b. Ka'b; Hawāzin; Hilāl; 'Id̲j̲l; Iram;
Iyād; Kalb b. Wabara; al-Ḳayn; K̲h̲afād̲j̲a; K̲h̲at̲h̲'am; al-K̲h̲azrad̲j̲; Kilāb
b. Rabī'a; Kināna; Kinda; K̲h̲uzā'a; Ḳurays̲h̲; Ḳus̲h̲ayr; La'aḳat al-Dam;
Lak̲h̲m; Liḥyān.II; Ma'add; Ma'āfir; Māzin; Muḥārib; Murād; Murra;
Naḍīr; Nawfal; Riyām; Sa'd b. Bakr; Sa'd al-Fizr; Ṣāliḥ; Salūl; S̲h̲aybān,
Banū; Sulaym
voir aussi Asad (Banū); Ḥabas̲h̲ (Aḥābīs̲h̲); al-Ḥid̲j̲āz; Mak̲h̲zūm;
Musta'riba; Muta'arriba; Nizār b. Ma'add b. 'Adnān; Numayr; Rabī'a (et
Muḍar); S̲h̲ayba; [au Suppl.] A'yāṣ

actuels   'Abdalī; 'Aḳrabī; 'Awāmir; 'Awazim; Banyar; al-Baṭāhira; Buḳūm;
al-Dawāsir; al-D̲h̲i'āb; D̲j̲a'da; al-D̲j̲anaba; al-Durū'; G̲h̲āmid; Hād̲j̲ir;
Ḥakam b. Sa'd; Hamdān; al-Ḥarāsīs; Ḥarb; Hās̲h̲id wa-Bakīl; Ḥassān,
Bā; Ḥaws̲h̲abī; Hinā; al-Ḥubūs; Hud̲h̲ayl; Hud̲j̲riyya; Hutaym; al-
Ḥuwayṭāt; al-'Ifār; Ḳaḥṭān; K̲h̲ālid; K̲h̲arūṣ; K̲h̲awlān; Ḳudā'a;
Mad̲h̲ḥid̲j̲; Mahra; al-Manāṣīr; Mazrū'ī; Murra; Muṭayr; Muzayna;
Nabhān; Ruwala; S̲h̲ammar; S̲h̲arārāt; Subay'; Ṣubayḥī; Sudayrīs;
Ṣulayb
voir aussi (D̲j̲azīrat) al-'Arab.VI; Badw; al-Ḥid̲j̲āz; S̲h̲āwiya.2

Turquie   Afs̲h̲ār; Bayat; Bayîndîr; Begdili; Čepni; Döger; Eymir.I; Ḳād̲j̲ār; Ḳāyî;
[au Suppl.] Čawdor
voir aussi S̲h̲akāk; S̲h̲aḳāḳī

TUNISIE   Baladiyya.III; D̲j̲āmi'a; D̲j̲am'iyya; D̲j̲arīda.I.B; Dustūr.I; Ḥizb.I;
Ḥukūma.IV; Istiḳlāl; al-K̲h̲aldūniyya; Ma'ārif.II; Mad̲j̲lis.IV.A.19; Salafiy-
ya.1.a; [au Suppl.] Démographie.IV
voir aussi Fallāḳ; Ḥimāya.II; K̲h̲alīfa b. 'Askar; Ṣafar; [au Suppl.] al-Ḥaddād;
Inzāl; *et* → BERBÈRES; DYNASTIES.ESPAGNE ET AFRIQUE DU NORD

historiens Ibn Abī Dīnār al-Ḳayrawānī; Ibn Abī l-Ḍiyāf; Ibn ʿIdhārī; [au Suppl.] ʿAbd al-Wahhāb
voir aussi Ibn al-Raḳīḳ; *et* → DYNASTIES.ESPAGNE ET AFRIQUE DU NORD
institutions
d'éducation al-Ṣādiḳiyya; [au Suppl.] Institut des hautes études de Tunis
voir aussi [au Suppl.] ʿAbd al-Wahhāb
de musique al-Rashīdiyya
de la presse al-Rāʾid al-Tūnusī
langue ʿArabiyya.A.III.3
littérature Malḥūn; *et* → LITTÉRATURE
période ottomane (1574-1881) Aḥmad Bey; al-Ḥusayn (b. ʿAlī); Ḥusaynides; Khayr al-Dīn Pasha; Muḥammad Bayram al-Khāmis; Muḥammad Bey; Muḥammad al-Ṣādiḳ Bey; Muṣṭafā Khaznadār; [au Suppl.] Ibn Ghidhāhum
période pré-ottomane ʿAbd al-Raḥmān al-Fihrī; Aghlabides; Ḥafṣides; Ḥassān b. al-Nuʿmān al-Ghassānī; Khurāsān (Banū)
et → BERBÈRES; DYNASTIES.ESPAGNE ET AFRIQUE DU NORD
toponymes
anciens al-ʿAbbāsiyya; Ḥaydarān; Ḳalʿat Banī Ḥammād; Manzil Bashshū; Raḳḳāda; Ṣabra Manṣūriyya; Subayṭila
actuels
districts Djarīd
îles Djarba; Ḳarḳana
régions Djazīrat Sharīk; Ḳasṭīliya; Nafzāwa; Sāḥil.1
villes Bādja; Banzart; Ḥalḳ al-Wādī; Ḳābis; al-Kāf; Ḳafsa; Ḳallala; al-Ḳayrawān; al-Mahdiyya; Monastir; Nafṭa; Safāḳus; Sūsa

TURQUIE Anadolu; Armīniya; Istanbul; Ḳarā Deniz
voir aussi Libās.IV; *et* → EMPIRE OTTOMAN
architecture → ARCHITECTURE.RÉGIONS
belles-lettres → LITTÉRATURE
dynasties → DYNASTIES.ANATOLIE ET LES TURCS; EMPIRE OTTOMAN
géographie physique
eaux Boghaz-iči; Čanaḳ-ḳalʿe Boghazi̊; Čoruh.I; Djayḥān; Gediz Čayi̊; Göksu; Ḳi̊zi̊l-i̊rmāḳ; Lamas-ṣū; Marmara Deñizi; Menderes; al-Rass; Saḳārya; Sayḥān
montagnes Aghri̊ Dagh; Ala Dagh; Aladja Dagh; Beshparmaḳ; Bingöl Dagh; Deve Boynu; Elma Daghi̊; Erdjiyas Daghi̊; Gāwur Daghlari̊
langue → LANGUES.TURCIQUES
mysticisme → MYSTICISME.MYSTIQUES; SAINT
période moderne (1920-) Baladiyya.I; Demokrat Parti; Djāmiʿa; Djarīda.III; Djümhūriyyet Khalḳ Fi̊rḳasi̊; Dustūr.II; Ḥizb.II; Ishtirākiyya; Khalḳevi; Köy Enstitüleri; Kurdes et Kurdistān.III.C; Madjlis.IV.A.2; Mīthāḳ-i Millī;

Shuyūʿiyya.3; [au Suppl.] Démographie.III
voir aussi Djamʿiyya; Iskandarūn; Iṣlāḥ.III; Ittiḥād we Teraḳḳī Djemʿiyyeti; Karakol Djemʿiyyeti; Ḳawmiyya.IV; Kemāl; Kirkūk; Maʿārif.I.1; Māliyye; Nurculuk; *et* → LITTÉRATURE

chefs religieux Nursī

hommes/femmes d'état Atatürk; Çakmak; Ḥusayn Djāhid; Ileri, Djelāl Nūrī; Kāẓi̊m Karābekir; Khālide Edīb; Köprülü (Meḥmed Fuad); Meḥmed ʿĀkif; Menderes; Okyar; Orbay, Ḥüseyin Raʾūf; Shems al-Dīn Günaltay; Sheref, ʿAbd al-Raḥmān; [au Suppl.] Adi̊var; Aghaoghlu; Atay; Esendal
voir aussi Čerkes Edhem; Gökalp, Ziya; Hi̊sar; *et* → TURQUIE.PÉRIODE OTTOMANE.JEUNES TURCS

période ottomane (1342-1924) Ḥizb.II; Istanbul; Ittiḥād-i Muḥammedī Djemʿiyyeti; Ittiḥād we Teraḳḳī Djemʿiyyeti; Maʿārif.I.1; Madjlis.IV.A.1; Madjlis al-Shūrā; Maṭbakh.II; **ʿOthmānli̊**
voir aussi Aywaz.1; Derebey; Djamʿiyya; Khalīfa.I.E; [au Suppl.] Démographie.II; Djalālī; *et* → EMPIRE OTTOMAN

Jeunes Turcs Djāwīd; Djemāl Pasha; Enwer Pasha; Ḥilmī; Isḥāḳ Sükūtī; Kemāl, Meḥmed Nāmi̊ḳ; Mīzāndji̊ Meḥmed Murād; Niyāzī; Ṣabāḥ al-Dīn; Shükrü Bey
voir aussi Djamʿiyya; Djewdet; Dustūr.II; Fāḍil Pasha; Ḥukūma.I; Ḥurriyya; Ittiḥād we Teraḳḳī Djemʿiyyeti

période pré-ottomane Mengüček
voir aussi Kitābāt.VII; *et* → DYNASTIES.ANATOLIE ET LES TURCS; TURQUIE.TOPONYMES

population [au Suppl.] Démographie.II
voir aussi Muhādjir.2

toponymes

anciens ʿAmmūriya; Ānī; Arzan; ʿAyn Zarba; Baghrās; Bālis; Beshike; Būḳa; al-Djazīra; Duluk; Dunaysir; Ḥarrān, Lādhiḳ.I; Shabakhtān; Sīs; Sulṭān Öñü
voir aussi Diyār Bakr; Shimshāṭ

actuels

districts Shamdīnān

îles Bozdja-ada; Imroz

provinces Aghri̊; Čoruh; Diyār Bakr; Hakkārī; Ičil; Kars; Ḳasṭamūnī; Khanzīt; Ḳodja Eli; Mūsh; Newshehir

régions al-ʿAmḳ; Cilicia; Dersim; Diyār Muḍar; Djānīk; Menteshe-eli

villes Ada Pazari̊; Adana; Adiyaman; Afyūn Ḳara Ḥiṣār; Aḳ Ḥiṣār.I et II; Aḳ Shehr; Akhlāṭ; Ala Shehr; Alanya; Alti̊ntash; Amasya; Anadolu; Anamur; Anḳara; Anṭākiya; Antalya; ʿArabkīr; Ardahān; Artvin; Aya Solūḳ; Āyās; Aydi̊n; ʿAynṭāb; Aywali̊k; Babaeski; Bālā; Bālā Ḥiṣār; Balāṭ; Bālikesrī; Bālṭa Līmānī; Bandirma; Bāyazīd;

Bāybūrd; Baylān; Bergama; Besni; Beyshehir; Bidlīs; Bīgha; Biledjik; Bingöl; Bīredjik; Birge; Bodrum; Bolu; Bolwadin; Bozanti; Burdur; Bursa; Čankiri; Čatāldja; Česhme; Čölemerik; Čorlu; Čorum; Deñizli; Diwrīgī; Diyār Bakr; Edirne; Edremit; Eğin; Eğridir; Elbistan; Elmali; Enos; Ereğli; Ergani; Ermenak; Erzindjan; Erzurum; Eskishehir; Gebze; Gelibolu; Gemlik; Giresun; Göksun; Gördes; Gümüsh-khāne; al-Hārūniyya; Ḥiṣn Kayfā; Iskandarūn; Isparta; Istanbul; Iznīḳ; Ḳarā Ḥiṣār; Ḳaradja Ḥiṣār; Kars; Ḳasṭamūnī; Ḳayṣariyya; Kemākh; Killiz; Ḳirḳ Kilise; Kirmāstī; Ḳirshehir; Ḳoč Ḥiṣār; Konya; Köprü Ḥiṣāri; Ḳoylu Ḥiṣār; Ḳōzān; Ḳūla; Kutāhiya; Lādhiḳ.II et III; Lāranda; Lüleburgaz; Maghnisa; Malaṭya; Malāzgird.I; Malkara; Maʿmūrat al-ʿAzīz; Marʿash; Mārdīn; al-Maṣṣīṣa; Mayyāfāriḳīn; Menemen; Mersin; Merzifūn; Mīlās; Mudanya; Mughla; Mūsh; Naṣībīn; Newshehir; Nīgde; Nīksār; Nizīb; Orāmār; ʿOthmāndjiḳ; Payās; Rize; al-Ruhā; Ṣabandja; Ṣāmsūn; Ṣart; Sarūdj; Siʿird; Silifke; Simaw; Sīnūb; Sīwās; Siwri Ḥiṣār; Sögüd; Sumaysāṭ; al-Suwaydiyya; [au Suppl.] Ghalaṭa
voir aussi Fener; Ḳarasi; (al-)Ḳusṭanṭīniyya

U

UMAYYADES → CALIFAT; DYNASTIES.ESPAGNE ET AFRIQUE DU NORD

(ex-)URSS → ASIE CENTRALE.UNION SOVIÉTIQUE ANCIENNE; CAUCASE; COMMUNISME; EUROPE.EUROPE ORIENTALE; SIBÉRIE

V

VERTUS ʿAdl; Ḍayf; Futuwwa; Ḥasab wa-Nasab; Ḥilm; ʿIrḍ; Murūʾa; Ṣabr
voir aussi Sharaf; Sharīf
vices Bukhl

VÊTEMENTS Banīḳa; Djallāb; Farw; Ḳumāsh; **Libās;** Sirwāl
voir aussi Ghiyār; Iḥrām; Khayyāṭ; Khilʿa; Kurdes et Kurdistān.IV.C.1; *et* → MYSTICISME.COSTUME
accessoires Mandīl; Mirwaḥa
voir aussi Shadd
coiffures Ḳawuḳlu
voir aussi Sharīf.5
voiles Ḥidjāb.I; Lithām

matériaux Farw; Ḥarīr; Kattān; Khaysh; Ḳuṭn; Ṣūf
voir aussi Fanak; Ḳalamkārī; Ḳumāsh; Lubūd; Mukhattam

VIN **Khamr**; Sāḳī
voir aussi Karm
commensaux Ibn Ḥamdūn; al-Ḳāshānī; Khālid b. Yazīd
voir aussi Abū l-Shīṣ; ʿAlī b. al-Djahm
poésie bachique **Khamriyya**
arabe Abū Nuwās; Abū Miḥdjan; Abū l-Shīṣ; ʿAdī b. Zayd; Ḥāritha b. Badr al-Ghudānī; (al-)Ḥusayn b. al-Ḍaḥḥāk; Ibn al-ʿAfīf al-Tilimsānī; Ibn Sayḥān
voir aussi al-Babbaghāʾ; Ibn al-Fāriḍ; Ibn Harma; al-Nawādjī
turque Rewānī; Riyāḍī

VOYAGES **Riḥla**; Safar
et → LITTÉRATURE.VOYAGES, RELATIONS DE
fournitures Mifrāsh
et → NOMADISME

Y

YÉMEN Djarīda.I.A; Dustūr.VIII; Madjlis.IV.A.14 et 15; Maḥkama.IV.8
voir aussi ʿAsīr; Ismaʿīliyya; Mahrī; Makramides, [au Suppl.] Abū Mismār
architecture → ARCHITECTURE.RÉGIONS
avant l'Islam al-Abnāʾ.2; Abraha; Dhū Nuwās; (Djazīrat) al-ʿArab; Ḥabashat; Ḥaḍramawt; Ḳatabān; Ḳayl; Mārib; al-Mathāmina; Sabaʾ; al-Sawdāʾ; [au Suppl.] Ḥaḍramawt
voir aussi [au Suppl.] Bādhām
dynasties Hamdānides; Mahdides; Rasūlides; Ṣulayḥides
voir aussi Rassides; *et* → DYNASTIES.PÉNINSULE ARABIQUE
géographie physique
montagnes Ḥaḍūr; Ḥarāz; Ḥiṣn al-Ghurāb; al-Sarāt; Shahāra; Shibām.4
wadis Barhūt; al-Khārid; al-Saḥūl
historiens al-Djanadī; al-Khazradjī; al-Mawzaʿī; al-Nahrawālī; al-Rāzī, Aḥmad; al-Sharīf Abū Muḥammad Idrīs; al-Shillī
voir aussi Ibn al-Mudjāwir
période ottomane (1517-1635) Maḥmūd Pasha; al-Muṭahhar; Özdemir Pasha; Riḍwān Pasha
voir aussi Baladiyya.II; Khādim Süleymān Pasha
population ʿAbdalī; ʿAḳrabī; Banyar; Hamdān; Ḥāshid wa-Bakīl; Ḥawshabī; Ḥudjriyya; Ḳaḥṭān; Khawlān; Madhḥidj; Mahra

et → TRIBUS.PÉNINSULE ARABIQUE
toponymes
anciens al-ʿĀra; S͟habwa; Ṣirwāḥ
voir aussi Nad͟jrān
actuels
districts Abyan; ʿAlawī; ʿĀmirī; ʿAwd͟halī; Dat͟hīna; Faḍlī; Ḥarāz; Ḥarīb; al-Ḥayma; Ḥud͟jriyya
îles Ḳamarān; Mayyūn; Suḳuṭra
régions ʿAwlaḳī; Ḥaḍramawt; Laḥd͟j; al-S͟hiḥr; [au Suppl.] Ḥaḍramawt.II
villes ʿAdan; ʿAt͟hr; Bayt al-Faḳīh; D͟hamār; G͟halāfiḳa; Ḥabbān; Had͟jarayn; Ḥāmī; Ḥawra; al-Ḥawṭa; al-Ḥudayda; Ibb; ʿIrḳa; Ḳaʿṭaba; Kawkabān; Ḳis͟hn; Laḥd͟j; al-Luḥayya; Mārib; al-Mukallā; al-Muk͟hā; Rayda; Ṣaʿda; al-Saḥūl; Ṣanʿāʾ; Sayʾūn; S͟hahāra; al-S͟hayk͟h Saʿīd; S͟hibām; al-S͟hiḥr; [au Suppl.] ʿĪnāt
voir aussi (D͟jazīrat) al-ʿArab

(ex-)YOUGOSLAVIE Džabić; K͟hosrew Beg; Muslimūn.I.B.6; Pomáks; Riḍwān Begović; [au Suppl.] Handžić
voir aussi ʿÖmer Efendi
toponymes
républiques Bosna; Ḳarā Dāg͟h; Ḳoṣowa; Māḳadūnyā; Ṣirb
voir aussi [au Suppl.] Dalmatie
villes Aḳ Ḥiṣār.III; Alad͟ja Ḥiṣār; Banjaluka; Belgrade; Eszék; Is͟htib; Ḳarlofča; Livno; Manāṣtir; Mostar; Nis͟h; Ok͟hrī; Pasarofča; Pirlepe; Pris͟htina; Prizren; Rag͟hūsa; Sarajevo; Sisak

Z

ZAÏRE Katanga; Kisangani

ZANZIBAR Barg͟has͟h b. Saʿīd b. Sulṭān; Bū Saʿīd; Kizimkazi

ZOOLOGIE **Ḥayawān**.VII
et → ANIMAUX
écrivains sur al-Damīrī; al-Marwazī, S͟haraf al-zamān
voir aussi al-D͟jāḥiẓ

ZOROASTRIENS Gabr; Iran.VI; **Mad͟jūs**; Mōbad͟h
voir aussi Bihʾāfrīd b. Farwardīn; G͟hazal.II; Gud͟jarāt; Pārsīs; Pūr-i Dāwūd; Sarwistān; S͟hīz; al-Ṣug͟hd; Sunbād͟h